1965	1967	1969	1971	1973	1975	1977	1979	1981	1983	1985	1986
492.2	575.4	694.6	751.1	1017.2	1065.2	1328.1	1741.8	2144.7	2114.3	2331.4	2220.9
46.5	47.8	58.1	52.9	81.4	79.9	115.1	154.2	158.6	133.1	137.0	129.3
5.7	5.0	4.8	4.1	4.7	4.6	5.3	5.7	4.7	4.1	3.8	3.7
59.1	62.8	65.3	69.3	73.7	75.1	78.8	79.6	81.1	83.3	87.5	90.0
3.5	2.2	0.5	4.1	3.1	3.5	1.7	−0.1	2.1	3.6	2.3	2.9
20.6	21.9	22.9	21.6	23.4	21.3	23.0	25.0	24.1	22.1	23.6	23.3
40.3	44.0	47.6	49.7	53.5	55.8	59.6	64.9	67.2	68.2	73.9	76.2
399.5	475.1	577.6	658.3	811.3	949.0	1180.4	1498.5	1819.6	2036.0	2412.0	2557.7
41.2	40.6	40.6	39.9	40.7	39.5	40.3	40.2	39.8	40.1	40.5	40.7
2.63	2.85	3.22	3.63	4.14	4.73	5.44	6.34	7.44	8.20	8.74	8.93
101.52	108.02	120.75	133.58	152.77	170.28	195.30	225.70	261.89	286.18	305.03	309.87
1.25	1.40	1.60	1.60	1.60	2.10	2.30	2.90	3.35	3.35	3.35	3.35
4.54	5.61	7.96	5.72	8.03	7.86	6.93	12.67	18.87	10.79	11.55	10.17
4.28	5.07	6.67	6.16	6.85	7.99	7.42	9.43	13.92	11.10	10.62	7.67
12.9	12.3	14.3	15.0	34.4	25.5	19.9	27.4	26.9	14.3	28.5	31.1
—	—	—	—	—	73	73	94	100	98	91	87
—	—	—	—	—	47	53	66	82	86	86	85
33.2	27.8	24.1	25.6	23.0	25.9	24.7	26.1	31.8	35.3	33.1	32.4
17.3	14.2	12.1	12.5	11.1	12.3	11.6	11.7	14.0	15.2	14.0	13.6
26.5	30.7	36.4	43.3	71.4	107.1	120.8	184.4	237.0	201.8	215.9	223.3
21.5	26.9	35.8	45.6	70.5	98.2	151.9	212.0	265.1	288.9	338.1	368.4
194.3	198.7	202.7	207.7	211.9	216.0	220.2	225.1	230.0	234.3	238.5	240.7
297.0	362.0	358.8	370.5	398.5	385.4	458.8	394.2	595.0	550.1	568.1	600.0
13.8	16.0	17.8	17.8	20.7	24.2	28.9	37.1	43.2	63.9	82.4	85.9
2.86	2.92	3.09	3.39	3.89	7.67	8.57	12.64	31.77	26.19	24.09	12.51

(Continued in back of book)

ECONOMICS

STUDENTS...

Want to get **better grades**? *(Who doesn't?)*

Prefer to do your **homework online**? *(After all, you are online anyway...)*

Need **a better way** to **study** before the big test?

(A little peace of mind is a good thing...)

With **McGraw-Hill's** *Connect*™ *Economics*,

YOU GET:

- **Easy online access** to homework, tests, and quizzes assigned by your instructor.

- **Immediate feedback** on how you're doing.

- **Quick access** to lectures, practice materials, an eBook, and more. All the material you need to be successful is right at your fingertips.

- A Self-Quiz and Study tool that **assesses your knowledge** and **recommends** specific readings, supplemental study materials, and additional practice work.

- **LearnSmart**—intelligent flash cards that adapt to your specific needs and provide you with customized learning content based on your strengths and weaknesses.

- **Graphing tools** that enable you to draw graphs from the ground up and perform in-depth analysis of an existing graph.

- **Critical thinking activities** and **logic cases** that explore the key chapter concepts with helpful explanations along the way.

- **Video Cases**—a series of videos that illustrate key economic concepts. Created specifically for the Principles course by leading economic authority Michael Mandel.

- Current **news articles** pulled from live news sources and organized according to your book for easy access.

Want an online, **searchable version** of your textbook?

Wish your textbook could be **available online** while you're doing your assignments?

 ## *Connect™ Plus Economics* eBook

If you choose to use *Connect™ Plus Economics*, you have an affordable and searchable online version of your book integrated with your other online tools.

Connect™ Plus Economics eBook offers features like:

- Topic search
- Direct links from assignments
- Adjustable text size
- Jump to page number
- Print by section

 Want to get more **value** from your textbook purchase?

Think learning economics should be a bit more **interesting**?

 ## Check out the STUDENT RESOURCES section under the *Connect™* Library tab.

Here you'll find a wealth of resources designed to help you achieve your goals in the course. Every student has different needs, so explore the STUDENT RESOURCES to find the materials best suited to you.

Visit **www.mcgraw-hillconnect.com** to learn more.

Microeconomics

Principles, Problems, and Policies

Nineteenth Edition

The McGraw-Hill Series: Economics

ESSENTIALS OF ECONOMICS

Brue, McConnell, and Flynn
Essentials of Economics
Second Edition

Mandel
Economics: The Basics
First Edition

Schiller
Essentials of Economics
Eighth Edition

PRINCIPLES OF ECONOMICS

Colander
Economics, Microeconomics, Macroeconomics
Eighth Edition

Frank and Bernanke
Principles of Economics, Principles of Microeconomics, Principles of Macroeconomics
Fourth Edition

Frank and Bernanke
Brief Editions: Principles of Economics, Principles of Microeconomics, Principles of Macroeconomics
Second Edition

McConnell, Brue, and Flynn
Economics, Microeconomics, Macroeconomics
Nineteenth Edition

McConnell, Brue, and Flynn
Brief Editions: Microeconomics and Macroeconomics
First Edition

Miller
Principles of Microeconomics
First Edition

Samuelson and Nordhaus
Economics, Microeconomics, Macroeconomics
Nineteenth Edition

Schiller
The Economy Today, The Micro Economy Today, The Macro Economy Today
Twelfth Edition

Slavin
Economics, Microeconomics, Macroeconomics
Tenth Edition

ECONOMICS OF SOCIAL ISSUES

Guell
Issues in Economics Today
Fifth Edition

Sharp, Register, and Grimes
Economics of Social Issues
Nineteenth Edition

ECONOMETRICS

Gujarati and Porter
Basic Econometrics
Fifth Edition

Gujarati and Porter
Essentials of Econometrics
Fourth Edition

MANAGERIAL ECONOMICS

Baye
Managerial Economics and Business Strategy
Seventh Edition

Brickley, Smith, and Zimmerman
Managerial Economics and Organizational Architecture
Fifth Edition

Thomas and Maurice
Managerial Economics
Tenth Edition

INTERMEDIATE ECONOMICS

Bernheim and Whinston
Microeconomics
First Edition

Dornbusch, Fischer, and Startz
Macroeconomics
Eleventh Edition

Frank
Microeconomics and Behavior
Eighth Edition

ADVANCED ECONOMICS

Romer
Advanced Macroeconomics
Third Edition

MONEY AND BANKING

Cecchetti and Schoenholtz
Money, Banking, and Financial Markets
Third Edition

URBAN ECONOMICS

O'Sullivan
Urban Economics
Seventh Edition

LABOR ECONOMICS

Borjas
Labor Economics
Fifth Edition

McConnell, Brue, and Macpherson
Contemporary Labor Economics
Ninth Edition

PUBLIC FINANCE

Rosen and Gayer
Public Finance
Ninth Edition

Seidman
Public Finance
First Edition

ENVIRONMENTAL ECONOMICS

Field and Field
Environmental Economics: An Introduction
Fifth Edition

INTERNATIONAL ECONOMICS

Appleyard, Field, and Cobb
International Economics
Seventh Edition

King and King
International Economics, Globalization, and Policy: A Reader
Fifth Edition

Pugel
International Economics
Fourteenth Edition

The Six Versions of McConnell, Brue, Flynn

Chapter	Economics	Microeconomics	Microeconomics: Brief Edition	Macroeconomics	Macroeconomics: Brief Edition	Essentials of Economics
1. Limits, Alternatives, and Choices	x	x	x	x	x	x
2. The Market System and the Circular Flow	x	x	x	x	x	x
3. Demand, Supply, and Market Equilibrium	x	x	x	x	x	x
4. Elasticity	x	x	x	x		x
5. Market Failures: Public Goods and Externalities	x	x	x	x	x	x
6. Consumer Behavior	x	x				
7. Businesses and the Costs of Production	x	x	x			x
8. Pure Competition in the Short Run	x	x	x			x
9. Pure Competition in the Long Run	x	x	x			x
10. Pure Monopoly	x	x	x			x
11. Monopolistic Competition and Oligopoly	x	x	x			x
11W. Technology, R&D, and Efficiency (Web Chapter)	x	x				
12. The Demand for Resources	x	x				
13. Wage Determination	x	x	x			x
14. Rent, Interest, and Profit	x	x				
15. Natural Resource and Energy Economics	x	x				
16. Public Finance: Expenditures and Taxes	x	x	x			
17. Asymmetric Information, Voting, and Public Choice	x	x				
18. Antitrust Policy and Regulation	x	x				
19. Agriculture: Economics and Policy	x	x				
20. Income Inequality, Poverty, and Discrimination	x	x	x			x
21. Health Care	x	x				
22. Immigration	x	x				
23. An Introduction to Macroeconomics	x			x		
24. Measuring Domestic Output and National Income	x			x	x	x
25. Economic Growth	x			x	x	x
26. Business Cycles, Unemployment, and Inflation	x			x	x	x
27. Basic Macroeconomic Relationships	x			x		
28. The Aggregate Expenditures Model	x			x		
29. Aggregate Demand and Aggregate Supply	x			x	x	x
30. Fiscal Policy, Deficits, and Debt	x			x	x	x
31. Money, Banking, and Financial Institutions	x			x	x	x
32. Money Creation	x			x		
33. Interest Rates and Monetary Policy	x			x	x	x
34. Financial Economics	x			x		
35. Extending the Analysis of Aggregate Supply	x			x	x	
36. Current Issues in Macro Theory and Policy	x			x		
37. International Trade	x	x	x	x	x	x
38. The Balance of Payments, Exchange Rates, and Trade Deficits	x	x	x	x	x	x
39W. The Economics of Developing Countries (Web Chapter)	x			x		

*Chapter numbers refer to *Economics: Principles, Problems, and Policies*.

*A Red "X" indicates chapters that combine or consolidate content from two or more *Economics* chapters.

MICROECONOMICS

Special Edition for SOLANO COMMUNITY COLLEGE

with Select Chapters from

ECONOMICS 19/e
PRINCIPLES, PROBLEMS, AND POLICIES

Campbell R. McConnell
University of Nebraska

Stanley L. Brue
Pacific Lutheran University

Sean M. Flynn
Scripps College

 Learning Solutions

Boston   Burr Ridge, IL   Dubuque, IA   New York   San Francisco   St. Louis
Bangkok   Bogotá   Caracas   Lisbon   London   Madrid
Mexico City   Milan   New Delhi   Seoul   Singapore   Sydney   Taipei   Toronto

Microeconomics
Special Edition for Solano Community College

This book is a McGraw-Hill Learning Solutions textbook and contains select material from: *Economics: Principles, Problems
and Policies*, Nineteenth Edition by Campbell R. McConnell, Stanley L. Brue and Sean M. Flynn. Copyright © 2012,
2009, 2008, 2005, 2002, 1999, 1996, 1993, 1990, 1987, 1984, 1981, 1978, 1975, 1972, 1969, 1966, 1963, 1960 by The
McGraw-Hill Companies, Inc. Reprinted with permission of the publisher. Many custom published texts are modified
versions or adaptations of our best-selling textbooks. Some adaptations are printed in black and white to keep prices at a
minimum, while others are in color

1 2 3 4 5 6 7 8 9 0 BRP BRP 13 12 11

ISBN-13: 978-0-07-755836-9
ISBN-10: 0-07-755836-7

Learning Solutions Representative: James Doepke
Production Editor: Nichole Birkenholz
Printer/Binder: BR Printers

To **Mem** and to **Terri** and **Craig**, and to **past instructors**

About the Authors

CAMPBELL R. MCCONNELL earned his Ph.D. from the University of Iowa after receiving degrees from Cornell College and the University of Illinois. He taught at the University of Nebraska–Lincoln from 1953 until his retirement in 1990. He is also coauthor of *Contemporary Labor Economics*, ninth edition; *Essentials of Economics*, second edition; *Macroeconomics: Brief Edition*; and *Microeconomics: Brief Edition* (all The McGraw-Hill Companies), and has edited readers for the principles and labor economics courses. He is a recipient of both the University of Nebraska Distinguished Teaching Award and the James A. Lake Academic Freedom Award and is past president of the Midwest Economics Association. Professor McConnell was awarded an honorary Doctor of Laws degree from Cornell College in 1973 and received its Distinguished Achievement Award in 1994. His primary areas of interest are labor economics and economic education. He has an extensive collection of jazz recordings and enjoys reading jazz history.

STANLEY L. BRUE did his undergraduate work at Augustana College (South Dakota) and received its Distinguished Achievement Award in 1991. He received his Ph.D. from the University of Nebraska–Lincoln. He is retired from a long career at Pacific Lutheran University, where he was honored as a recipient of the Burlington Northern Faculty Achievement Award. Professor Brue has also received the national Leavey Award for excellence in economic education. He has served as national president and chair of the Board of Trustees of Omicron Delta Epsilon International Economics Honorary. He is coauthor of *Economic Scenes*, fifth edition (Prentice-Hall); *Contemporary Labor Economics*, ninth edition; *Essentials of Economics*, second edition; *Macroeconomics: Brief Edition; Microeconomics: Brief Edition* (all The McGraw-Hill Companies); and *The Evolution of Economic Thought*, seventh edition (South-Western). For relaxation, he enjoys international travel, attending sporting events, and skiing with family and friends.

SEAN M. FLYNN did his undergraduate work at the University of Southern California before completing his Ph.D. at U.C. Berkeley, where he served as the Head Graduate Student Instructor for the Department of Economics after receiving the Outstanding Graduate Student Instructor Award. He teaches at Scripps College (of the Claremont Colleges) and is the author of *Economics for Dummies* (Wiley) and coauthor of *Essentials of Economics*, second edition; *Macroeconomics: Brief Edition*; and *Microeconomics: Brief Edition* (all The McGraw-Hill Companies). His research interests include finance and behavioral economics. An accomplished martial artist, he has represented the United States in international aikido tournaments and is the author of *Understanding Shodokan Aikido* (Shodokan Press). Other hobbies include running, traveling, and enjoying ethnic food.

List of Key Graphs

1.2 The Production Possibilities Curve *12*

2.2 The Circular Flow Diagram *40*

3.6 Equilibrium Price and Quantity *57*

6.1 Total and Marginal Utility *118*

7.2 The Law of Diminishing Returns *146*

7.5 The Relationship of the Marginal-Cost Curve to the Average-Total-Cost and Average-Variable-Cost Curves *151*

7.8 The Long-Run Average-Total-Cost Curve: Unlimited Number of Plant Sizes *154*

8.3 Short-Run Profit Maximization for a Purely Competitive Firm *170*

8.6 The $P = MC$ Rule and the Competitive Firm's Short-Run Supply Curve *174*

9.6 Long-Run Equilibrium: A Competitive Firm and Market *187*

10.4 Profit Maximization by a Pure Monopolist *201*

11.1 A Monopolistically Competitive Firm: Short Run and Long Run *220*

11.4 The Kinked-Demand Curve *229*

13.3 Labor Supply and Labor Demand in (a) a Purely Competitive Labor Market and (b) a Single Competitive Firm *270*

23.2 Trading Possibilities Lines and the Gains from Trade *479*

24.1 The Market for Foreign Currency (Pounds) *504*

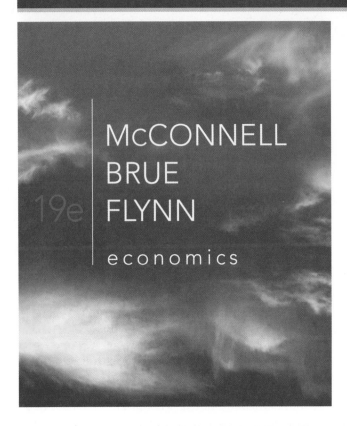

McCONNELL
BRUE
FLYNN
19e | economics

Welcome to the 19th edition of *Economics*, the best-selling economics textbook in the world. An estimated 14 million students have used *Economics* or its companion editions, *Macroeconomics* and *Microeconomics*. *Economics* has been adapted into Australian and Canadian editions and translated into Italian, Russian, Chinese, French, Spanish, Portuguese, and other languages. We are pleased that *Economics* continues to meet the market test: nearly one out of four U.S. students in principles courses used the 18th edition.

Fundamental Objectives

We have three main goals for *Economics:*

- Help the beginning student master the principles essential for understanding the economizing problem, specific economic issues, and policy alternatives.
- Help the student understand and apply the economic perspective and reason accurately and objectively about economic matters.
- Promote a lasting student interest in economics and the economy.

What's New and Improved?

One of the benefits of writing a successful text is the opportunity to revise—to delete the outdated and install the new, to rewrite misleading or ambiguous statements, to introduce more relevant illustrations, to improve the organizational structure, and to enhance the learning aids.

We trust that you will agree that we have used this opportunity wisely and fully. Some of the more significant changes include the following.

Restructured Introductory Chapters

We have divided the five-chapter grouping of introductory chapters common to *Economics*, *Microeconomics*, and *Macroeconomics* into two parts. Part 1 contains Chapter 1 (Limits, Alternatives, and Choices) and Chapter 2 (The Market System and the Circular Flow). The content in Part 2 has changed and now consists of three chapters: Chapter 3 (Demand, Supply, and Market Equilibrium), Chapter 4 (Elasticity), and Chapter 5 (Market Failures: Public Goods and Externalities).

The chapters in Part 2 are much more concept-oriented and analytical and much less general and descriptive than in the previous edition. Our new approach responds to suggestions by reviewers made over the years to:

- Locate the elasticity chapter immediately after the supply and demand chapter.
- Put the elasticity chapter into *Macroeconomics* for those who cover elasticity in their macro course.
- Eliminate the mainly descriptive Chapter 4 on the private and public sectors and move the relevant content to where it fits more closely with related micro and macro materials.
- Provide a single chapter on international trade, rather than two separate chapters that have overlapping coverage (Chapters 5 and 37 in *Economics*, 18th edition).
- Boost the analysis of market failures (public goods and externalities) in the introductory sections to complement and balance the strong but highly stylized introduction to the market system discussed in Chapter 2.

Our new approach embraces these suggestions. For micro instructors, the new ordering provides a clear supply-and-demand path to the subsequent chapters on consumer and producer behavior. For macro instructors, the new ordering provides the option of assigning elasticity or market failures or both. And because this content is both optional and modular, macro instructors can also skip it and move directly to the macroeconomic analysis.

The content on the United States in the global economy that appeared in Chapter 5 of the 18th edition of *Microeconomics* is now integrated into Chapter 23 (International Trade). Because Chapter 23 draws only on production possibilities analysis and supply and demand analysis, it can be assigned at any point after Chapter 3 (Demand, Supply, and Market Equilibrium). Therefore, instructors who want to introduce international economics early in their courses can assign Chapter 23 within the introductory chapters found in Parts 1 and 2.

For instructors who prefer Chapter 5 of the prior edition to Chapter 23 of the new edition, we have fully updated the previous Chapter 5 content and made it freely available for viewing and printing at both the instructor and student portions of our Web site, **www.mcconnell19e. com**. Look for it under the new category called Content Options for Instructors (COI). This substitute for Chapter 23 is fully supported by both the instructor supplement package and the student supplement package.

New "Consider This" and "Last Word" Pieces

Our "Consider This" boxes are used to provide analogies, examples, or stories that help drive home central economic ideas in a student-oriented, real-world manner. For instance, a "Consider This" box titled "McHits and McMisses" illustrates consumer sovereignty through a listing of successful and unsuccessful products. How businesses exploit price discrimination is driven home in a "Consider This" box that explains why ballparks charge different admission prices for adults and children but only one set of prices at their concession stands. These brief vignettes, each accompanied by a photo, illustrate key points in a lively, colorful, and easy-to-remember way. We have added 16 new "Consider This" boxes in this edition of *Economics*.

Our "Last Word" pieces are lengthier applications or case studies that are placed near the end of each chapter. For example, the "Last Word" section for Chapter 1 (Limits, Alternatives, and Choices) examines pitfalls to sound

CONSIDER THIS ...

The Fable of the Bees

Economist Ronald Coase received the Nobel Prize for his so-called **Coase theorem**, which pointed out that under the right conditions, private individuals could often negotiate their own mutually agreeable solutions to externality problems through *private bargaining* without the need for government interventions like pollution taxes.

This is a very important insight because it means that we shouldn't automatically call for government intervention every time we see a potential externality problem. Consider the positive externalities that bees provide by pollinating farmers' crops. Should we assume that beekeeping will be underprovided unless the government intervenes with, for instance, subsidies to encourage more bees to provide for their crops?

As it turns out, no. Research has shown that farmers and beekeepers long ago used private bargaining to develop customs and payment systems that avoid free riding by farmers and encourage beekeepers to keep the optimal number of hives. Free riding is avoided by the custom that all farmers in an area simultaneously hire beekeepers to provide bees to pollinate their crops. And farmers always pay the beekeepers for their pollination services because if they didn't, then no beekeeper would ever work with them in the future—a situation that would lead to massively reduced crop yields due to a lack of pollination.

The "Fable of the Bees" is a good reminder that it is a fallacy to assume that the government must always get involved to remedy externalities. In many cases, the private sector can solve both positive and negative externality problems on its own.

LAST Word Carbon Dioxide Emissions, Cap and Trade, and Carbon Taxes

Cap-and-trade systems and carbon taxes are two approaches to reducing carbon dioxide (CO_2) emissions.

Externality problems are property rights problems. Consider a landfill. Because the owner of the landfill has full rights to his land, people wishing to dump their trash on the landfill have to pay him. This payment implies that there is no externality: He happily accepts their trash in exchange for a dumping fee. By contrast, because nobody owns the atmosphere, all air pollution is an externality, since there is no way for those doing the polluting to work out a payment to compensate those affected by the pollution or for those threatened with pollution to simply refuse to be polluted on.

Conventional property rights therefore cannot fix the externalities associated with air pollution. But that does not mean property rights can't help fight pollution. The trick to making them work is to assign property rights not to the atmosphere itself, but to *polluting* the atmosphere. This is done in "cap-and-trade" systems, under which the government sets an annual limit, or cap, to the number of tons of a pollutant that firms can emit into the atmosphere.

Consider carbon dioxide, or CO_2. It is a colorless, odorless

climate change, specifically global warming. To reduce CO_2 emissions, the U.S. government might set a cap of 5 billion tons of CO_2 emissions per year in the United States (which would be about 10 percent below 2009 emissions levels for that molecule). The government then prints out emissions permits that sum to the limit set in the cap and distributes them to polluting firms. Once they are distributed, the only way a firm can legally emit a ton of CO_2 is if it owns a permit to do so.

Under this policy, the government can obviously adjust the total amount of air pollution by adjusting the cap. This by itself improves efficiency, because the cap imposes scarcity. Because each firm has only a limited number of permits, each firm has a strong incentive to maximize the net benefit that it produces from every ton of pollution that it emits. But the *cap-and-trade* scheme leads to even greater improvements in efficiency, because firms are free to trade (sell) them to each other in what are referred to as *markets for externality rights*.

For instance, suppose Smokestack Toys owns permits for 100 tons of CO_2 emissions and that it could use them to produce toy cars that would generate profits of $100,000. There is a power plant, however, that could make up to $1 million of profits by using those 100 tons of emissions permits to generate electricity. Because firms can trade their permits, Smok

economic reasoning, while the "Last Word" section for Chapter 5 (Market Failures: Public Goods and Externalities) examines cap-and-trade versus carbon taxes as policy responses to excessive carbon dioxide emissions. There are 10 new "Last Word" sections in this edition of *Economics*.

If you are unfamiliar with *Economics* or *Microeconomics*, we encourage you to thumb through the chapters to take a quick look at these highly visible features.

New Content on Behavioral Economics

We have added new material covering the consumer-choice aspects of behavioral economics to the end of our chapter on Consumer Behavior (Chapter 6 of *Economics* and *Microeconomics*). The new material on behavioral economics covers prospect theory, framing effects, loss aversion, anchoring effects, mental accounting, and the endowment effect. The behavioral economics theory and examples are tightly focused on consumer-choice applications so as to flow smoothly from, and build upon, the standard utility-maximization theory and applications developed earlier in the chapter. The new material is intentionally at the end of the chapter, not only to show that behavioral economics extends standard theory (rather than replacing or refuting it) but also so that the new material is modular and thus can be skipped by instructors without loss of continuity. A new "Consider This" box on the "hedonic treadmill" and a new "Last Word" section on "nudges" bolster our overall coverage of behavioral economics.

Divided Pure Competition Chapter

We have divided the very long pure competition chapter (Chapter 9 of the 18th edition) into two logically distinct chapters, one on pure competition in the short run (Chapter 8) and the other on pure competition in the long run (Chapter 9). These more "bite-sized" chapters should improve student retention of the material. Students will first master the logic behind the MC = MR rule for setting output as well as the short-run shutdown condition. Students will then be able to pause to test their understanding of this content through end-of-chapter questions and problems and other supporting materials before moving on to the next chapter's coverage of pure competition in the long run.

We have also combined several table/figure pairs to improve pedagogy in the short-run chapter. In previous editions, the material for this chapter featured three figures that corresponded with the data in three separate tables. We have now combined all three such table/figure pairs, placing each data table directly above its accompanying figure to increase student comprehension. We have also used background highlights on equilibrium numbers in the tables to enable students to more easily move back and forth from references in the body to equilibrium numbers in the tables.

New Public Finance Chapter

By moving the discussion of market failure from Chapter 16 of the 18th edition to Chapter 5 of the 19th edition, we have made room for a new Chapter 16 (Public Finance: Taxation and Expenditures). This traditional public finance chapter adds considerable new content to existing material that previously appeared in Chapter 4 (The U.S. Economy: Private and Public Sectors) and Chapter 17 (Public Choice Theory and the Economics of Taxation). The material adopted from Chapter 4 of the 18th edition includes a circular flow diagram with government; an overview of Federal, state, and local tax revenues and expenditures; and explanations of marginal and average tax rates. The material adopted from Chapter 17 of the 18th edition includes discussions of the benefits-received and ability-to-pay principles of taxation; an explanation of progressive, regressive, and proportional taxes; tax incidence and efficiency losses due to taxation; and the redistributive incidence of the overall tax-spending system in the United States.

This chapter's new material includes a short section on government employment that is built around two pie charts. The first gives a breakdown of what fractions of state and local government employees are dedicated to certain tasks. The second gives a similar accounting for Federal government employees.

Also new to this chapter are "Consider This" boxes on state lotteries and value-added taxes and a "Last Word" section reviewing recent research on the redistributive effects of the *combined* taxation and spending system in the United States.

The new public finance chapter is followed by a restructured chapter covering asymmetric information, voting, and public choice. Reviewers agreed with us that this new two-chapter set covering the microeconomics of government is a major improvement over the prior edition.

Inclusion of Chapter on Exchange Rates

We have returned Chapter 24 (The Balance of Payments, Exchange Rates, and Trade Deficits) to *Microeconomics*. This will provide the option of covering these topics in either the micro principles course or the macro principles course.

Reworked End-of-Chapter Questions and Problems

We have extensively reworked the end-of-chapter Study Questions, splitting them into questions and problems and adding many new problems. The questions are analytic and often ask for free responses, whereas the problems are mainly quantitative. We have aligned the questions and problems with the learning objectives presented at the beginning of the chapters. All of the questions and problems are assignable through McGraw-Hill's *Connect Economics*; all of the problems also contain additional algorithmic variations and can be automatically graded within the system. The new lists of questions and problems were well-received by reviewers, many of them long-time users of the book.

Current Discussions and Examples

The 19th edition of *Microeconomics* refers to and discusses many current topics. Examples include the cost of the war in Iraq; surpluses and shortages of tickets at the Olympics; the myriad impacts of ethanol subsidies; creative destruction; aspects of behavioral economics; applications of game theory; the most rapidly expanding and disappearing U.S. jobs; oil and gasoline prices; cap-and-trade systems and carbon taxes; the value-added tax; state lotteries; the Food, Conservation, and Energy Act of 2008; consumption versus income inequality; the Patient Protection and Affordable Care Act (PPACA) of 2010; immigration issues; U.S. trade deficits; offshoring of American jobs; trade adjustment assistance; the European Union and the Euro Zone; changes in exchange rates; and many other current topics.

Chapter-by-Chapter Changes

Each chapter of *Microeconomics*, 19th edition, contains updated data reflecting the current economy, streamlined Learning Objectives, and reorganized end-of-chapter content.

Chapter-specific updates include:

Chapter 1: Limits, Alternatives, and Choices features a new Learning Objective on consumption possibilities and a revised definition of "entrepreneur" that clarifies why risk taking is socially beneficial and, thus, why entrepreneurial ability is a valuable economic resource.

Chapter 2: The Market System and the Circular Flow includes a revised explanation of property rights, a clarified discussion of firms' motives for choosing the lowest-cost production methods, an updated "McHits and McMisses" "Consider This" box, and a revised discussion of the circular flow model.

Chapter 3: Demand, Supply, and Market Equilibrium contains wording improvements that clarify the main concepts.

Chapter 4: Elasticity is a new chapter that focuses solely on elasticity. This content has been moved forward from Chapter 6 of *Economics*, 18th edition, allowing this topic to be covered directly after supply and demand. This content will be available in both the Macro and Micro splits. The material on consumer and producer surplus has been moved to Chapter 5.

Chapter 5: Market Failures: Public Goods and Externalities is a new chapter that first examines consumer surplus, producer surplus, efficiency, and efficiency losses (all from Chapter 6, *Economics*, 18th edition). It then devotes the remainder of the chapter to market failures, specifically public goods and externalities (both from Chapter 16, *Economics*, 18th edition). The chapter also features a new "Last Word" section that discusses the pros and cons of cap-and-trade emissions-control policies and a new "Consider This" box that concisely discusses the Coase Theorem.

Chapter 6: Consumer Behavior features additional coverage and discussion of the consumer-choice aspects of behavioral economics, including prospect theory, framing effects, loss aversion, anchoring effects, mental accounting, and the endowment effect. A new "Consider This" box discusses the hedonic treadmill and a new "Last Word" section explains how governments and firms may use the insights of behavioral economics to encourage desired outcomes.

Chapter 7: Businesses and the Costs of Production features a revised section on economic costs, explicit costs, implicit costs, accounting profit, normal profit, and economic profit; a new section on the rising price of gasoline that replaces the previous section on the doubling of the price of corn; and a rewritten example on daily newspapers.

Chapter 8: Pure Competition in the Short Run is a new chapter that contains information on pure competition in the short run from Chapter 9 of the 18th edition. This

chapter features improved pedagogy and a new "Last Word" on the short-run shutdown condition.

Chapter 9: Pure Competition in the Long Run is a new chapter that contains information on pure competition in the long run from Chapter 9 of the 18th edition. This chapter features a new overview introductory section, a new figure clarifying decreasing-cost industries, and a revised discussion of why long-run equilibrium in pure competition yields allocative efficiency. This chapter also introduces creative destruction as a long-run competitive force.

Chapter 10: Pure Monopoly features a revised discussion of rate regulation for a natural monopoly and a precise identification of the income transfers of monopoly.

Chapter 11: Monopolistic Competition and Oligopoly features a revised Figure 11.2 with labels at key points, and an updated discussion of OPEC emphasizing the difficulty that it has had with its members complying with its established oil quotas.

Chapter 11 Web: Technology, R&D, and Efficiency contains a revised discussion of creative destruction.

Chapter 12: The Demand for Resources features improved discussions to clarify the main concepts.

Chapter 13: Wage Determination provides an improved introduction to monopsony.

Chapter 14: Rent, Interest, and Profit features a new section on the interest rate on money loans; an expanded explanation of the differences between insurable and noninsurable risks; an additional source of noninsurable risk (new products or production methods pioneered by rivals); and a new "Consider This" piece on Steve Jobs as an entrepreneur.

Chapter 15: Natural Resource and Energy Economics features a new "Consider This" piece that deals with the high risk associated with commercializing alternative fuel sources.

Chapter 16: Public Finance: Expenditures and Taxes is a new chapter on public finance that combines new material with topics from 18th edition Chapters 4, 16, and 17. This chapter features new pie charts on state and local government expenditures and tax revenues, two new "Consider This" boxes on state lotteries and value-added taxes, and a new "Last Word" on recent research that compares the redistributive effects of the tax system by itself with the redistributive effects of the *overall* tax-spending system.

Chapter 17: Asymmetric Information, Voting, and Public Choice adds new material to topics that were located in several other chapters in the 18th edition, including: asymmetric information from Chapter 16, government failures and voting inefficiencies and paradoxes from Chapter 17, and the principal-agent problem from Chapter 4. This chapter has a new "Consider This" box on the collective-action problem, a new discussion of political corruption, and a new "Global Perspective" piece comparing bribery rates in various countries.

Chapter 18: Antitrust Policy and Regulation now emphasizes that monopoly pricing raises significant concerns about income transfers (from consumers to producers) as well as efficiency losses.

Chapter 19: Agriculture: Economics and Policy contains a new update of the historical trends of real agricultural prices and clarifications of some of the main concepts.

Chapter 20: Income Inequality, Poverty, and Discrimination extensively updates the data on the distribution of income, poverty, and family wealth.

Chapter 21: Health Care features a detailed explanation and extensive coverage of the Patient Protection and Affordable Care Act of 2010, a new section that explains the history behind why the United States is uniquely dependent on employer-provided health insurance, an improved discussion of why insurance increases prices by increasing demand, and a new "Last Word" on how the health care system of Singapore uses high out-of-pocket costs to keep medical spending down.

Chapter 22: Immigration provides the latest available data on legal and illegal immigration.

Chapter 23: International Trade contains relevant content from Chapter 5 of the 18th edition. This chapter features additional explanation that clarifies how comparative advantage differs from absolute advantage, a new "Consider This" box on misunderstanding the gains from trade, and a streamlined discussion of multilateral trade agreements and free-trade zones.

Chapter 24: The Balance of Payments, Exchange Rates, and Trade Deficits features a streamlined explanation of why the balance-of-payments statement always balances, a revised discussion of official reserves and balance-of-payments deficits and surpluses, and updated discussions of exchange rates.

Distinguishing Features

Comprehensive Explanations at an Appropriate Level
Economics is comprehensive, analytical, and challenging yet fully accessible to a wide range of students. The thoroughness and accessibility enable instructors to select topics for special classroom emphasis with confidence that students can read and comprehend other independently assigned material in the book. Where needed, an extra sentence of explanation is provided. Brevity at the expense of clarity is false economy.

Fundamentals of the Market System
Many economies throughout the world are still making difficult transitions from planning to markets while a handful of other countries such as Venezuela seem to be trying to reestablish government-controlled, centrally planned economies. Our detailed description of the institutions and operation of the market system in Chapter 2 (The Market System and the Circular Flow) is therefore even more relevant than before. We pay particular attention to property rights, entrepreneurship, freedom of enterprise and choice, competition, and the role of profits because these concepts are often misunderstood by beginning students worldwide.

Extensive Treatment of International Economics
We give the principles and institutions of the global economy extensive treatment. The appendix to Chapter 3 (Demand, Supply, and Market Equilibrium) has an application on exchange rates. Chapter 23 (International Trade) examines key facts of international trade, specialization and comparative advantage, arguments for protectionism, impacts of tariffs and subsidies, and various trade agreements. Chapter 24 (Balance of Payments, Exchange Rates, and Trade Deficits) discusses the balance of payments, fixed and floating exchange rates, and U.S. trade deficits.

As noted previously in this preface, Chapter 23 (International Trade) is constructed such that instructors who want to cover international trade early in the course can assign it immediately after Chapter 3. Chapter 23 requires only a good understanding of production possibilities analysis and supply and demand analysis to comprehend. International competition is integrated throughout the micro. "Global Perspective" boxes add to the international flavor of the text.

Early and Extensive Treatment of Government
The public sector is an integral component of modern capitalism. This book introduces the role of government early. Chapter 5 (Market Failures: Public Goods and Externalities) systematically discusses public goods and government policies toward externalities. Chapter 16 (Public Finance: Expenditures and Taxes) examines taxation and government expenditures in detail, and Chapter 17 (Asymmetric Information, Voting, and Public Choice) looks at salient facets of asymmetric information,

voting, and public choice theory as they relate to market failure and government failure. Part 6 of this volume includes issue- and policy-oriented chapters relating to government.

Stress on the Theory of the Firm

We have given much attention to microeconomics in general and to the theory of the firm in particular, for two reasons. First, the concepts of microeconomics are difficult for most beginning students; abbreviated expositions usually compound these difficulties by raising more questions than they answer. Second, we wanted to couple analysis of the various market structures with a discussion of the impact of each market arrangement on price, output levels, resource allocation, and the rate of technological advance.

Focus on Economic Policy and Issues

For many students, the micro chapters on antitrust, agriculture, income inequality, health care, and immigration are where the action is centered. We guide that action along logical lines through the application of appropriate analytical tools. In the micro, we favor inclusiveness; instructors can effectively choose two or three chapters from Part 6.

Integrated Text and Web Site

Microeconomics and its Web site are highly integrated through in-text Web buttons, Web-based end-of-chapter questions, bonus Web chapters, multiple-choice self-tests at the Web site, math notes, and other features. Our Web site is part and parcel of our student learning package, customized to the book.

The in-text Web buttons (or indicators) merit special mention. Three differing colors of rectangular indicators appear throughout the book, informing readers that complementary content on a subject can be found at our Web site, **www.mcconnell19e.com**. The indicator types are:

Worked Problems Written by Norris Peterson of Pacific Lutheran University (WA), these pieces consist of side-by-

> **WORKED PROBLEMS**
> **W 1.1**
> Budget lines

side computational questions and computational procedures used to derive the answers. In essence, they extend the textbook's explanations of various computations—for example, of per-unit production costs, economic profit, and more. From a student's perspective, they provide "cookbook" help for solving numerical problems.

Interactive Graphs These pieces (developed under the supervision of Norris Peterson) depict 30 major graphs (in

> **INTERACTIVE GRAPHS**
> **G 1.1**
> Production possibilities curve

Economics) and instruct students to shift the curves, observe the outcomes, and derive relevant generalizations. This hands-on graph work will greatly reinforce the graphs and their meaning.

Origin of the Ideas These pieces, written by Randy Grant of Linfield College (OR), are brief histories of 70 major

> **ORIGIN OF THE IDEA**
> **O 1.1**
> Origin of the term "economics"

ideas identified in *Economics*. They identify the particular economists who developed ideas such as opportunity cost, equilibrium price, the multiplier, comparative advantage, and elasticity.

Organizational Alternatives

Although instructors generally agree on the content of principles of economics courses, they sometimes differ on how to arrange the material. *Microeconomics* includes 7 parts, and thus provides considerable organizational flexibility.

Some instructors will prefer to intersperse the microeconomics of Parts 3 and 4 with the problems chapters of Part 6. Chapter 19 on agriculture may follow Chapters 8 and 9 on pure competition; Chapter 18 on antitrust and regulation may follow Chapters 10, 11, and 11Web on imperfect competition models and technological advance. Chapter 22 on immigration may follow Chapter 13 on wages; and Chapter 20 on income inequality may follow Chapters 13 and 14 on distributive shares of national income.

In the opposite direction, Chapter 15 on natural resources and energy economics can be shifted from Part 4 on resource markets to Part 6 on microeconomic issues.

Finally, as noted before, Chapter 23 on international trade can easily be moved up to immediately after Chapter 3 on supply and demand for instructors who want an early discussion of international trade.

Pedagogical Aids

Microeconomics is highly student-oriented. The "To the Student" statement at the beginning of Part 1 details the book's many pedagogical aids. The 19th edition is also accompanied by a variety of high-quality supplements that help students master the subject and help instructors implement customized courses.

Supplements for Students and Instructors

Study Guide One of the world's leading experts on economic education, William Walstad of the University of Nebraska–Lincoln, prepared the *Study Guide*. Many students find either the printed or digital version indispensable. Each chapter contains an introductory statement, a checklist of behavioral objectives, an outline, a list of important terms, fill-in questions, problems and projects, objective questions, and discussion questions.

The *Guide* comprises a superb "portable tutor" for the principles student. Separate *Study Guides* are available for the macro and micro paperback editions of the text.

Instructor's Manual Laura Maghoney of Solano Community College revised and updated the *Instructor's Manual*, and Shawn Knabb of Western Washington University checked and brought the end-of-chapter questions, problems, and solutions to the *Manual*. The revised *Instructor's Manual* includes:

- Chapter summaries.
- Listings of "what's new" in each chapter.
- Teaching tips and suggestions.
- Learning objectives.
- Chapter outlines.
- Extra questions and problems.
- Answers to the end-of-chapter questions and problems, plus correlation guides mapping content to the learning objectives.

The *Instructor's Manual* is available on the instructor's side of the Online Learning Center.

Three Test Banks Test Bank I contains about 6500 multiple-choice and true-false questions, most of which were written by the text authors. Randy Grant revised Test Bank I for the 19th edition. Test Bank II contains around 6000 multiple-choice and true-false questions, updated by Felix Kwan of Maryville University. All Test Bank I and II questions are organized by learning objective, topic, AACSB Assurance of Learning, and Bloom's Taxonomy guidelines. Test Bank III, written by William Walstad, contains more than 600 pages of short-answer questions and problems created in the style of the book's end-of-chapter questions. Test Bank III can be used to construct student assignments or design essay and problem exams. Suggested answers to the essay and problem questions are included. In all, more than 14,000 questions give instructors maximum testing flexibility while ensuring the fullest possible text correlation.

Test Banks I and II are available in *Connect Economics*, through EZ Test Online, and in MS Word. EZ Test Online allows professors to create customized tests that contain both questions that they select from the test banks as well as questions that they craft themselves. Test Bank III is available in MS Word on the password-protected instructor's side of the Online Learning Center, and on the Instructor Resource CD.

PowerPoint Presentations With the assistance of Laura Maghoney, the Web site PowerPoint Presentations for the 19th edition were updated by a dedicated team of instructors: Jill Beccaris-Pescatore of Montgomery County Community College, Stephanie Campbell of Mineral Area College, Amy Chataginer of Mississippi Gulf Coast Community College, and Dorothy Siden of Salem State College. Each chapter is accompanied by a concise yet thorough tour of the key concepts. Instructors can use these Web site presentations in the classroom, and students can use them on their computers.

Digital Image Library Every graph and table in the text is available on the instructor's side of the Web site and on the Instructor's Resource CD-ROM.

McGraw-Hill Connect Economics McGraw-Hill *Connect Economics* is an online assignment and assessment solution that connects students with the tools and resources they'll need to achieve success. McGraw-Hill *Connect Economics* helps prepare students for their future by enabling faster learning, more efficient studying, and higher retention of knowledge.

All of the end-of-chapter questions and problems, the thousands of questions from Test Banks I and II, and additional resources are available in *Connect Economics*. For more information on *Connect Economics* and other technology, please see pages xiv–xxi.

Online Learning Center (www.mcconnell19e. com) The Web site accompanying this book is a central resource for students and instructors alike. The optional Web Chapter (Chapter 11W: Technology, R&D, and Efficiency) plus the two new Content Options for Instructors (The United States in the Global Economy and Previous International Exchange-Rate Systems), are posted as full-color PDF files. The in-text Web buttons alert the students to points in the book where they can springboard to the Web site to get more information.

Students can also review PowerPoint presentations and test their knowledge of a chapter's concepts with a self-graded multiple-choice quiz. The password-protected Instructor Center houses the Instructor's Manual, all three Test Banks, and links to EZ Test Online, PowerPoint presentations, and the Digital Image Library.

Computerized Test Bank Online A comprehensive bank of test questions is provided within McGraw-Hill's flexible electronic testing program EZ Test Online (**www.eztestonline.com**). EZ Test Online allows instructors to simply and quickly create tests or quizzes for their students. Instructors can select questions from multiple McGraw-Hill test banks or author their own, and then either print the finalized test or quiz for paper distribution or publish it online for access via the Internet.

This user-friendly program allows instructors to sort questions by format; select questions by learning objectives or Bloom's taxonomy tags; edit existing questions or add new ones; and scramble questions for multiple versions of the same test. Instructors can export their tests for use in WebCT, Blackboard, and PageOut, making it easy to share assessment materials with colleagues, adjuncts, and TAs. Instant scoring and feedback is provided, and EZ Test Online's record book is designed to easily export to instructor gradebooks.

Assurance-of-Learning Ready Many educational institutions are focused on the notion of assurance of learning, an important element of some accreditation standards. *Microeconomics* is designed to support your assurance-of-learning initiatives with a simple yet powerful solution. Each chapter in the book begins with a list of numbered learning objectives to which each end-of-chapter question and problem is then mapped. In this way, student responses to those questions and problems can be used to assess how well students are mastering each particular learning objective. Each test bank question for *Microeconomics* also maps to a specific learning objective.

You can use our test bank software, EZ Test Online, or *Connect Economics* to easily query for learning outcomes and objectives that directly relate to the learning objectives for your course. You can then use the reporting features to aggregate student results in a similar fashion, making the collection and presentation of assurance-of-learning data simple and easy.

AACSB Statement The McGraw-Hill Companies is a proud corporate member of AACSB International. Understanding the importance and value of AACSB accreditation, *Microeconomics*, 19th edition, has sought to recognize the curricula guidelines detailed in the AACSB standards for business accreditation by connecting end-of-chapter questions in *Microeconomics*, 19th edition, and the accompanying test banks to the general knowledge and skill guidelines found in the AACSB standards.

The AACSB Statement for *Microeconomics*, 19th edition, is provided only as a guide for the users of this text. The AACSB leaves content coverage and assessment within the purview of individual schools, their respective missions, and their respective faculty. While *Microeconomics*, 19th edition, and the teaching package make no claim of any specific AACSB qualification or evaluation, we have, within *Microeconomics*, 19th edition, labeled selected questions according to the six general knowledge and skills areas.

Acknowledgments

We give special thanks to Norris Peterson and Randy Grant, who created the "button" content on our Web site. We again thank James Reese of the University of South Carolina at Spartanburg, who wrote the original Internet exercises. Although many of those questions were replaced or modified in the typical course of revision, several remain virtually unchanged. We also thank Laura Maghoney and the team of instructors who updated the PowerPoint slides for the 19th edition. Shawn Knabb deserves great thanks for accuracy-checking the end-of-chapter questions and problems and their solutions, as well as for creating the variations of all of the problems. Thanks to the dedicated instructors who created and revised our additional study tools, including Steve Price, Shannon Aucoin, Brian Motii, Amy Scott, Emilio Gomez, Amy Stapp, Richard Kramer, and Mark Wilson. Finally, we thank William Walstad and Tom Barbiero (the coauthor of our Canadian edition) for their helpful ideas and insights.

We are greatly indebted to an all-star group of professionals at McGraw-Hill—in particular Douglas Reiner, Noelle Fox Bathurst, Harvey Yep, Lori Koetters, Jen Saxton, Melissa Larmon, and Brent Gordon—for their publishing and marketing expertise.

We thank Keri Johnson for her selection of the "Consider This" and "Last Word" photos and Mary Kazak Sander and Maureen McCutcheon for the design.

The 19th edition has benefited from a number of perceptive formal reviews. The reviewers, listed at the end of the preface, were a rich source of suggestions for this revision. To each of you, and others we may have inadvertently overlooked, thank you for your considerable help in improving *Microeconomics*.

Stanley L. Brue
Sean M. Flynn
Campbell R. McConnell

Reviewers

Richard Agesa, *Marshall University*
Yamin Ahmad, *University of Wisconsin–Whitewater*
Eun Ahn, *University of Hawaii, West Oahu*
Thomas Andrews, *West Chester University of Pennsylvania*
Fatma Antar, *Manchester Community College*
Len Anyanwu, *Union County College*
Emmanuel Asigbee, *Kirkwood Community College*
John Atkins, *Pensacola Junior College*
Moses Ayiku, *Essex County College*
Wendy Bailey, *Troy University*
Dean Baim, *Pepperdine University*
Tyra Barrett, *Pellissippi State Tech*
Jill Beccaris-Pescatore, *Montgomery County Community College*
Kevin Beckwith, *Salem State College*
Christian Beer, *Cape Fear Community College*
Robert Belsterling, *Pennsylvania State University*
Laura Jean Bhadra, *NOVA Community College, Manassas*
Augustine Boakye, *Essex County College*
Stephanie Campbell, *Mineral Area College*
Bruce Carpenter, *Mansfield University*
Thomas Cate, *Northern Kentucky University*
Claude Chang, *Johnson & Wales University*
Amy Chataginer, *Mississippi Gulf Coast Community College–Gautier*
Shuo Chen, *State University College–Geneseo*
Jon Chesbro, *Montana Tech of the University of Montana*
Amod Choudhary, *Lehman College*
Constantinos Christofides, *East Stroudsburg University*
Jane Clary, *College of Charleston*
Jane Cline, *Forsyth Technical Community College*
Anthony Daniele, *St. Petersburg College–Gibbs*
Rosa Lea Danielson, *College of DuPage*
Ribhi Daoud, *Sinclair Community College*
William Davis, *University of Tennessee–Martin*
Richard Dixon, *Thomas Nelson Community College*
Tanya Downing, *Cuesta College*
Scott Dressler, *Villanova University*
Mark Eschenfelder, *Robert Morris University*
Maxwell Eseonu, *Virginia State University*
Tyrone Ferdnance, *Hampton University*
Jeffrey Forrest, *St. Louis Community College–Florissant Valley*
Mark Frascatore, *Clarkson University*
Shelby Frost, *Georgia State University*
Sudip Ghosh, *Penn State University–Berks*
Daniel Giedeman, *Grand Valley State University*
Scott Gilbert, *Southern Illinois University*
James Giordano, *Villanova University*
Susan Glanz, *St. John's University*
Lowell Glenn, *Utah Valley University*
Randy Glover, *Brevard Community College Melbourne*
Terri Gonzales, *Delgado Community College*
Cole Gustafson, *North Dakota State University–Fargo*
Moonsu Han, *North Shore Community College*

Virden Harrison, *Modesto Junior College*
Richard Hawkins, *University of West Florida*
Kim Hawtrey, *Hope College*
Glenn Haynes, *Western Illinois University*
Michael Heslop, *NOVA Community College Annandale*
Jesse Hill, *Tarrant County College SE*
Calvin Hoy, *County College of Morris*
James Hubert, *Seattle Central Community College*
Greg Hunter, *California State Polytechnic University, Pomona*
Christos Ioannou, *University of Minnesota–Minneapolis*
Faridul Islam, *Utah Valley University*
Mahshid Jalilvand, *University of Wisconsin–Stout*
Ricot Jean, *Valencia Community College–Osceola*
Jonatan Jelen, *City College of New York*
Brad Kamp, *University of South Florida–Sarasota*
Kevin Kelley, *Northwest Vista College*
Chris Klein, *Middle Tennessee State University*
Barry Kotlove, *Edmonds Community College*
Richard Kramer, *New England College*
Felix Kwan, *Maryville University*
Ted Labay, *Bishop State Community College*
Tina Lance, *Germanna Community College–Fredericksburg*
Yu-Feng Lee, *New Mexico State University–Las Cruces*
Adam Lei, *Midwestern State University*
Phillip Letting, *Harrisburg Area Community College*
Brian Lynch, *Lake Land College*
Zagros Madjd-Sadjadi, *Winston-Salem State University*
Laura Maghoney, *Solano Community College*
Vincent Mangum, *Grambling State University*
Benjamin Matta, *New Mexico State University–Las Cruces*
Pete Mavrokordatos, *Tarrant County College NE*
Michael McIntyre, *Copiah Lincoln Community College*
Bob McKizzie, *Tarrant County College SE*
Kevin McWoodson, *Moraine Valley Community College*
Edwin Mensah, *University of North Carolina at Pembroke*
Randy Methenitis, *Richland College*
Ida Mirzaie, *Ohio State University*
David Mitch, *University of Maryland–Baltimore City*
Ramesh Mohan, *Bryant University*
Daniel Morvey, *Piedmont Technical College*
Shahriar Mostashari, *Campbell University*
Richard Mount, *Monmouth University*
Ted Muzio, *St. John's University*

Cliff Nowell, *Weber State University*
Albert Okunade, *University of Memphis*
Mary Ellen Overbay, *Seton Hall University*
Tammy Parker, *University of Louisiana at Monroe*
David Peterson, *American River College*
Alberto Perez, *Harford Community College*
Mary Anne Pettit, *Southern Illinois University*
Jeff Phillips, *Morrisville State College*
William Piper, *Piedmont College*
Robert Poulton, *Graceland University*
Dezzie Prewitt, *Rio Hondo College*
Joe Prinzinger, *Lynchburg College*
Jaishankar Raman, *Valparaiso University*
Natalie Reaves, *Rowan University*
Virginia Reilly, *Ocean County College*
Tim Reynolds, *Alvin Community College*
John Romps, *Saint Anselm College*
Tom Scheiding, *Elizabethtown College*
Amy Schmidt, *Saint Anselm College*
Ron Schuelke, *Santa Rosa Junior College*
Alexandra Shiu, *Temple College*
Dorothy Siden, *Salem State College*
Timothy Simpson, *Central New Mexico Community College*
Jonathan Sleeper, *Indian River State College Central*
Camille Soltau-Nelson, *Texas A&M University*
Robert Sonora, *Fort Lewis College*
Nick Spangenberg, *Ozarks Tech Community College*
Dennis Spector, *Naugatuck Valley Community College*
Thomas Stevens, *University of Massachusetts, Amherst*
Tamika Steward, *Tarrant Count College SE*
Robin Sturik, *Cuyahoga Community College Western–Parma*
Travis Taylor, *Christopher Newport University*
Ross Thomas, *Central New Mexico Community College*
Mark Thompson, *Augusta State University*
Deborah Thorsen, *Palm Beach Community College–Lake Worth*
Mike Toma, *Armstrong Atlantic State University*
Dosse Toulaboe, *Fort Hays State University*
Jeff Vance, *Sinclair Community College*
Cheryl Wachenheim, *North Dakota State University–Fargo*
Christine Wathen, *Middlesex County College*
Scott Williams, *County College of Morris*
Wendy Wysocki, *Monroe County Community College*
Edward Zajicek, *Winston-Salem State University*

Brief Contents

Preface   *xvi*

PART TWO

Price, Quantity, and Efficiency

3   Demand, Supply, and Market Equilibrium   *47*
4   Elasticity   *75*

PART THREE

Microeconomics of Product Markets

6   Consumer Behavior   *116*
7   Businesses and the Costs of Production   *140*
8   Pure Competition in the Short Run   *163*
9   Pure Competition in the Long Run   *181*
10   Pure Monopoly   *194*
11   Monopolistic Competition and Oligopoly   *216*

11w   Technology, R&D, and Efficiency
(**WEB CHAPTER,** www.mcconnell19e.com)   *246*

PART SIX

Microeconomic Issues and Policies

18   Antitrust Policy and Regulation   *374*

PART SEVEN

International Economics

23   International Trade   *472*
24   The Balance of Payments, Exchange Rates, and Trade Deficits   *498*

Glossary   *G-1*
Index   *IND-1*

Contents

List of Key Graphs   *xv*
Preface   *xvi*
Reviewers   *xxv*

PART TWO
Price, Quantity, and Efficiency   **46**

Chapter 3
Demand, Supply, and Market Equilibrium   *47*

Markets   *48*
Demand   *48*
Law of Demand / The Demand Curve / Market
Demand / Changes in Demand / Changes in Quantity
Demanded

Supply   *53*
Law of Supply / The Supply Curve / Market Supply /
Determinants of Supply / Changes in Supply /
Changes in Quantity Supplied

Market Equilibrium   *56*
Equilibrium Price and Quantity / Rationing Function of
Prices / Efficient Allocation / Changes in Supply, Demand,
and Equilibrium
Consider This: *Ticket Scalping: A Bum Rap! 58*
Consider This: *Salsa and Coffee Beans 61*

Application: Government-Set Prices   *61*
Price Ceilings on Gasoline / Rent Controls /
Price Floors on Wheat
Last Word: *A Legal Market for Human Organs? 62*

Chapter 3 Appendix: Additional Examples of
Supply and Demand   *69*

Chapter 4
Elasticity   *75*

Price Elasticity of Demand   *76*
The Price-Elasticity Coefficient and Formula /
Interpretations of E_d / The Total-Revenue Test / Price
Elasticity and the Total-Revenue Curve / Determinants of
Price Elasticity of Demand / Applications of Price Elasticity of
Demand
Consider This: *A Bit of a Stretch 78*

Price Elasticity of Supply   *84*
Price Elasticity of Supply: The Market Period / Price
Elasticity of Supply: The Short Run / Price Elasticity of
Supply: The Long Run / Applications of Price Elasticity of
Supply

Cross Elasticity and Income Elasticity of Demand   87
Cross Elasticity of Demand / Income Elasticity of Demand
Last Word: *Elasticity and Pricing Power: Why Different Consumers Pay Different Prices 86*

PART THREE
Microeconomics of Product Markets   115

Chapter 6
Consumer Behavior   116

Law of Diminishing Marginal Utility   117
Terminology / Total Utility and Marginal Utility /
Marginal Utility and Demand
Consider This: *Vending Machines and Marginal Utility 117*

Theory of Consumer Behavior   118
Consumer Choice and the Budget Constraint /
Utility-Maximizing Rule / Numerical Example /
Algebraic Generalization

Utility Maximization and the Demand Curve   122
Deriving the Demand Schedule and Curve / Income and
Substitution Effects

Applications and Extensions   123
iPods / The Diamond-Water Paradox / Opportunity Cost
and the Value of Time / Medical Care Purchases /
Cash and Noncash Gifts

Prospect Theory   125
Losses and Shrinking Packages / Framing Effects and
Advertising / Anchoring and Credit Card Bills /
Mental Accounting and Overpriced Warranties /
The Endowment Effect and Market Transactions
Consider This: *Rising Consumption and the Hedonic Treadmill 126*
Last Word: *Nudging People Toward Better Decisions 128*
Chapter 6 Appendix: Indifference Curve Analysis   133

Chapter 7
Businesses and the Costs of Production   140

Economic Costs   141
Explicit and Implicit Costs / Accounting Profit and Normal
Profit / Economic Profit / Short Run and Long Run

Short-Run Production Relationships   144
Law of Diminishing Returns
Consider This: *Diminishing Returns from Study 144*

Short-Run Production Costs   147
Fixed, Variable, and Total Costs / Per-Unit, or Average,
Costs / Marginal Cost / Shifts of the Cost Curves

Long-Run Production Costs   152
Firm Size and Costs / The Long-Run Cost Curve /
Economies and Diseconomies of Scale / Minimum Efficient
Scale and Industry Structure

Applications and Illustrations   157
Rising Gasoline Prices / Successful Start-Up Firms /
The Verson Stamping Machine / The Daily Newspaper /
Aircraft and Concrete Plants
Last Word: *Don't Cry over Sunk Costs 158*

Chapter 8
Pure Competition in the Short Run   163

Four Market Models   164

Pure Competition: Characteristics and
Occurrence   164

Demand as Seen by a Purely Competitive Seller   165
Perfectly Elastic Demand / Average, Total, and Marginal
Revenue

Profit Maximization in the Short Run: Total-Revenue–
Total-Cost Approach   166

Profit Maximization in the Short Run:
Marginal-Revenue–Marginal-Cost Approach   167
Profit-Maximizing Case / Loss-Minimizing Case /
Shutdown Case
Consider This: *The Still There Motel 173*

Marginal Cost and Short-Run Supply   173
Generalized Depiction / Diminishing Returns, Production
Costs, and Product Supply / Changes in Supply / Firm and
Industry: Equilibrium Price
Last Word: *Fixed Costs: Digging Yourself Out of a Hole 177*

Chapter 9
Pure Competition in the Long Run   181

The Long Run in Pure Competition   182
Profit Maximization in the Long Run / Goal of Our
Analysis / Long-Run Equilibrium / Long-Run Supply for a
Constant-Cost Industry / Long-Run Supply for an Increasing-
Cost Industry / Long-Run Supply for a Decreasing-Cost
Industry

Pure Competition and Efficiency   186
Productive Efficiency: $P = $ Minimum ATC / Allocative
Efficiency: $P = $ MC / Maximum Consumer and Producer
Surplus / Dynamic Adjustments / "Invisible Hand" Revisited

Technological Advance and Competition   189
Creative Destruction
Consider This: *Running a Company Is Hard Business 190*
Last Word: *Efficiency Gains from Entry: The Case of Generic Drugs 191*

Chapter 10

Pure Monopoly   194

An Introduction to Pure Monopoly   195
Examples of Monopoly / Dual Objectives of the
Study of Monopoly

Barriers to Entry   195
Economies of Scale / Legal Barriers to Entry: Patents and
Licenses / Ownership or Control of Essential Resources /
Pricing and Other Strategic Barriers to Entry

Monopoly Demand   197
Marginal Revenue Is Less Than Price / The Monopolist Is a
Price Maker / The Monopolist Sets Prices in the Elastic
Region of Demand

Output and Price Determination   200
Cost Data / MR = MC Rule / No Monopoly Supply
Curve / Misconceptions Concerning Monopoly Pricing /
Possibility of Losses by Monopolist

Economic Effects of Monopoly   203
Price, Output, and Efficiency / Income Transfer / Cost
Complications / Assessment and Policy Options

Price Discrimination   207
Conditions / Examples of Price Discrimination /
Graphical Analysis
Consider This: *Price Discrimination at the Ballpark 208*

Regulated Monopoly   209
Socially Optimal Price: P = MC / Fair-Return Price: P =
ATC / Dilemma of Regulation
Last Word: *De Beers Diamonds: Are Monopolies Forever? 212*

Chapter 11

Monopolistic Competition and Oligopoly   216

Monopolistic Competition   216
Relatively Large Number of Sellers / Differentiated
Products / Easy Entry and Exit / Advertising /
Monopolistically Competitive Industries

Price and Output in Monopolistic Competition   219
The Firm's Demand Curve / The Short Run:
Profit or Loss / The Long Run: Only a Normal Profit

Monopolistic Competition and Efficiency   221
Neither Productive nor Allocative Efficiency / Excess
Capacity

Product Variety   222
Benefits of Product Variety / Further Complexity

Oligopoly   223
A Few Large Producers / Homogeneous or Differentiated
Products / Control over Price, but Mutual Interdependence /
Entry Barriers / Mergers / Oligopolistic Industries
Consider This: *Creative Strategic Behavior 224*

Oligopoly Behavior: A Game Theory Overview   226
Mutual Interdependence Revisited / Collusion /
Incentive to Cheat
Consider This: *The Prisoner's Dilemma 227*

Three Oligopoly Models   228
Kinked-Demand Theory: Noncollusive Oligopoly / Cartels
and Other Collusion / Price Leadership Model

Oligopoly and Advertising   234
Positive Effects of Advertising / Potential Negative
Effects of Advertising

Oligopoly and Efficiency   235
Productive and Allocative Efficiency / Qualifications
Last Word: *Oligopoly in the Beer Industry 236*

Chapter 11 Appendix: Additional
Game Theory Applications   241

WEB Chapter 11   www.mcconnell19e.com

Technology, R&D, and Efficiency   246

Invention, Innovation, and Diffusion   11W-2
Invention / Innovation / Diffusion / R&D
Expenditures / Modern View of Technological Advance

Role of Entrepreneurs and Other Innovators   11W-4
Forming Start-Ups / Innovating within Existing Firms /
Anticipating the Future / Exploiting University and
Government Scientific Research

A Firm's Optimal Amount of R&D   11W-5
Interest-Rate Cost of Funds / Expected Rate
of Return / Optimal R&D Expenditures

Increased Profit via Innovation   11W-8
Increased Revenue via Product Innovation / Reduced Cost
via Process Innovation

Imitation and R&D Incentives   11W-10
Benefits of Being First
Consider This: *Trade Secrets 11W-12*

Role of Market Structure   11W-13
Market Structure and Technological Advance / Inverted-U
Theory of R&D / Market Structure and Technological
Advance: The Evidence

Technological Advance and Efficiency   11W-15
Productive Efficiency / Allocative Efficiency / Creative
Destruction
Last Word: *On the Path to the Personal
Computer and Internet 11W-16*

PART SIX
Microeconomic Issues and Policies 373

Chapter 18
Antitrust Policy and Regulation 374

The Antitrust Laws 375
Historical Background / Sherman Act of 1890 /
Clayton Act of 1914 / Federal Trade Commission
Act of 1914 / Celler-Kefauver Act of 1950

Antitrust Policy: Issues and Impacts 376
Issues of Interpretation / Issues of Enforcement /
Effectiveness of Antitrust Laws
Consider This: *Of Catfish and Art (and Other Things in Common) 381*

Industrial Regulation 381
Natural Monopoly / Problems with Industrial
Regulation / Legal Cartel Theory

Deregulation 383

Social Regulation 384
Distinguishing Features / The Optimal Level of Social
Regulation / Two Reminders
Last Word: *United States v. Microsoft 386*

PART SEVEN
International Economics 471

Chapter 23
International Trade 472

Some Key Trade Facts 473
The Economic Basis for Trade 474
Comparative Advantage 474
Two Isolated Nations / Specializing Based on Comparative
Advantage / Terms of Trade / Gains from Trade /
Trade with Increasing Costs / The Case for Free Trade
Consider This: *A CPA and a House Painter 475*
Consider This: *Misunderstanding the Gains from Trade 480*

Supply and Demand Analysis of Exports
and Imports 482
Supply and Demand in the United States / Supply and
Demand in Canada / Equilibrium World Price, Exports, and
Imports

Trade Barriers and Export Subsidies 485
Economic Impact of Tariffs / Economic Impact of Quotas /
Net Costs of Tariffs and Quotas
Consider This: *Buy American? 485*

The Case for Protection: A Critical Review 488
Military Self-Sufficiency Argument / Diversification-for-
Stability Argument / Infant Industry Argument /
Protection-against-Dumping Argument /
Increased Domestic Employment Argument /
Cheap Foreign Labor Argument

Multilateral Trade Agreements and
Free-Trade Zones 490
General Agreement on Tariffs and Trade / World Trade
Organization / The European Union / North American Free
Trade Agreement

Trade Adjustment Assistance 492

Offshoring of Jobs 492
Last Word: *Petition of the Candlemakers, 1845 493*

Chapter 24
The Balance of Payments, Exchange Rates, and Trade Deficits 498

International Financial Transactions 499

The Balance of Payments 499
Current Account / Capital and Financial Account /
Why the Balance? / Official Reserves, Payments Deficits, and
Payments Surpluses

Flexible Exchange Rates 503
Depreciation and Appreciation / Determinants of Exchange
Rates / Flexible Rates and the Balance of
Payments / Disadvantages of Flexible Exchange Rates

Fixed Exchange Rates 508
Use of Official Reserves / Trade Policies / Exchange
Controls and Rationing / Domestic Macroeconomic
Adjustments

The Current Exchange Rate System:
The Managed Float 510

Recent U.S. Trade Deficits 512
Causes of the Trade Deficits / Implications of
U.S. Trade Deficits
Last Word: *Speculation in Currency Markets 514*

Glossary G-1
Credits C-1
Index IND-1

AFTER READING THIS CHAPTER, YOU SHOULD BE ABLE TO:

1 Describe *demand* and explain how it can change.

2 Describe *supply* and explain how it can change.

3 Relate how supply and demand interact to determine market equilibrium.

4 Explain how changes in supply and demand affect equilibrium prices and quantities.

5 Identify what government-set prices are and how they can cause product surpluses and shortages.

6 (Appendix) Illustrate how supply and demand analysis can provide insights on actual-economy situations.

Demand, Supply, and Market Equilibrium

ORIGIN OF THE IDEA
O 3.1
Demand and supply

The model of supply and demand is the economics profession's greatest contribution to human understanding because it explains the operation of the markets on which we depend for nearly everything that we eat, drink, or consume. The model is so powerful and so widely used that to many people it *is* economics.

This chapter explains how the model works and how it can explain both the *quantities* that are bought and sold in markets as well as the *prices* at which they trade.

Markets

Markets bring together buyers ("demanders") and sellers ("suppliers"). The corner gas station, an e-commerce site, the local music store, a farmer's roadside stand—all are familiar markets. The New York Stock Exchange and the Chicago Board of Trade are markets in which buyers and sellers from all over the world communicate with one another to buy and sell bonds, stocks, and commodities. Auctioneers bring together potential buyers and sellers of art, livestock, used farm equipment, and, sometimes, real estate. In labor markets, new college graduates "sell" and employers "buy" specific labor services.

Some markets are local; others are national or international. Some are highly personal, involving face-to-face contact between demander and supplier; others are faceless, with buyer and seller never seeing or knowing each other.

To keep things simple, we will focus in this chapter on markets in which large numbers of independently acting buyers and sellers come together to buy and sell standardized products. Markets with these characteristics are the economy's most highly competitive. They include the wheat market, the stock market, and the market for foreign currencies. All such markets involve demand, supply, price, and quantity. As you will soon see, the price is "discovered" through the interacting decisions of buyers and sellers.

Demand

Demand is a schedule or a curve that shows the various amounts of a product that consumers are willing and able to purchase at each of a series of possible prices during a specified period of time.[1] Demand shows the quantities of a product that will be purchased at various possible prices, *other things equal.* Demand can easily be shown in table form. The table in Figure 3.1 is a hypothetical **demand schedule** for a *single consumer* purchasing bushels of corn.

The table reveals the relationship between the various prices of corn and the quantity of corn a particular consumer would be willing and able to purchase at each of these prices. We say "willing and able" because willingness alone is not effective in the market. You may be willing to buy a plasma television set, but if that willingness is not backed by the necessary dollars, it will not be effective and, therefore, will not be reflected in the market. In the table in Figure 3.1, if the price of corn were $5 per bushel, our consumer would be willing and able to buy 10 bushels per week; if it were $4, the consumer would be willing and able to buy 20 bushels per week; and so forth.

The table does not tell us which of the five possible prices will actually exist in the corn market. That depends

---

[1]This definition obviously is worded to apply to product markets. To adjust it to apply to resource markets, substitute the word "resource" for "product" and the word "businesses" for "consumers."

FIGURE 3.1 An individual buyer's demand for corn. Because price and quantity demanded are inversely related, an individual's demand schedule graphs as a downsloping curve such as *D*. Other things equal, consumers will buy more of a product as its price declines and less of the product as its price rises. (Here and in later figures, *P* stands for price and *Q* stands for quantity demanded or supplied.)

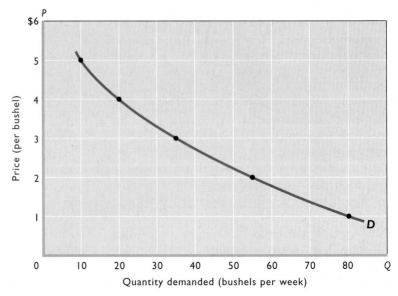

Demand for Corn	
Price per Bushel	Quantity Demanded per Week
$5	10
4	20
3	35
2	55
1	80

on the interaction between demand and supply. Demand is simply a statement of a buyer's plans, or intentions, with respect to the purchase of a product.

To be meaningful, the quantities demanded at each price must relate to a specific period—a day, a week, a month. Saying "A consumer will buy 10 bushels of corn at $5 per bushel" is meaningless. Saying "A consumer will buy 10 bushels of corn *per week* at $5 per bushel" is meaningful. Unless a specific time period is stated, we do not know whether the demand for a product is large or small.

Law of Demand

A fundamental characteristic of demand is this: Other things equal, as price falls, the quantity demanded rises,

> **ORIGIN OF THE IDEA**
> **O 3.2**
> Law of demand

and as price rises, the quantity demanded falls. In short, there is a negative or *inverse* relationship between price and quantity demanded. Economists call this inverse relationship the **law of demand.**

The other-things-equal assumption is critical here. Many factors other than the price of the product being considered affect the amount purchased. For example, the quantity of Nikes purchased will depend not only on the price of Nikes but also on the prices of such substitutes as Reeboks, Adidas, and New Balances. The law of demand in this case says that fewer Nikes will be purchased if the price of Nikes rises and if the prices of Reeboks, Adidas, and New Balances all remain constant. In short, if the *relative price* of Nikes rises, fewer Nikes will be bought. However, if the price of Nikes and the prices of all other competing shoes increase by some amount— say, $5—consumers might buy more, fewer, or the same number of Nikes.

Why the inverse relationship between price and quantity demanded? Let's look at three explanations, beginning with the simplest one:

- The law of demand is consistent with common sense. People ordinarily *do* buy more of a product at a low price than at a high price. Price is an obstacle that deters consumers from buying. The higher that obstacle, the less of a product they will buy; the lower the price obstacle, the more they will buy. The fact that businesses have "sales" to clear out unsold items is evidence of their belief in the law of demand.
- In any specific time period, each buyer of a product will derive less satisfaction (or benefit, or utility) from each successive unit of the product consumed. The second Big Mac will yield less satisfaction to the

> **ORIGIN OF THE IDEA**
> **O 3.3**
> Diminishing marginal utility

consumer than the first, and the third still less than the second. That is, consumption is subject to **diminishing marginal utility.** And because successive units of a particular product yield less and less marginal utility, consumers will buy additional units only if the price of those units is progressively reduced.

- We can also explain the law of demand in terms of income and substitution effects. The **income effect** indicates that a lower price increases the purchasing power of a buyer's money income, enabling the buyer to purchase more of the product than before. A higher price has the opposite effect. The **substitution effect** suggests that at a lower price buyers have the incentive to substitute what is now a less expensive product for other products that are now *relatively* more expensive. The product whose price has fallen is now "a better deal" relative to the other products.

For example, a decline in the price of chicken will increase the purchasing power of consumer incomes, enabling people to buy more chicken (the income effect). At

> **ORIGIN OF THE IDEA**
> **O 3.4**
> Income and substitution effects

a lower price, chicken is relatively more attractive and consumers tend to substitute it for pork, lamb, beef, and fish (the substitution effect). The income and substitution effects combine to make consumers able and willing to buy more of a product at a low price than at a high price.

The Demand Curve

The inverse relationship between price and quantity demanded for any product can be represented on a simple graph, in which, by convention, we measure *quantity demanded* on the horizontal axis and *price* on the vertical axis. In the graph in Figure 3.1 we have plotted the five price-quantity data points listed in the accompanying table and connected the points with a smooth curve, labeled *D*. Such a curve is called a **demand curve.** Its downward slope reflects the law of demand—people buy more of a product, service, or resource as its price falls. The relationship between price and quantity demanded is inverse (or negative).

The table and graph in Figure 3.1 contain exactly the same data and reflect the same relationship between price and quantity demanded. But the graph shows that relationship much more simply and clearly than a table or a description in words.

Market Demand

So far, we have concentrated on just one consumer. But competition requires that more than one buyer be present in each market. By adding the quantities demanded by all consumers at each of the various possible prices, we can get from *individual* demand to *market* demand. If there are just three buyers in the market, as represented in the table in Figure 3.2, it is relatively easy to determine the total quantity demanded at each price. Figure 3.2 shows the graphical summing procedure: At each price we sum horizontally the quantities demanded by Joe, Jen, and Jay to obtain the total quantity demanded at that price; we then plot the price and the total quantity demanded as one point on the market demand curve.

Competition, of course, ordinarily entails many more than three buyers of a product. To avoid hundreds or thousands or millions of additions, we suppose that all the buyers in a market are willing and able to buy the same amounts at each of the possible prices. Then we just multiply those amounts by the number of buyers to obtain the market demand. That is how we arrived at the demand schedule and demand curve D_1 in Figure 3.3 for a market of 200 corn buyers, each with a demand as shown in the table in Figure 3.1.

In constructing a demand curve such as D_1 in Figure 3.3, economists assume that price is the most important influence on the amount of any product purchased. But economists know that other factors can and do affect purchases. These factors, called **determinants of demand,** are assumed to be constant when a demand curve like D_1 is drawn. They are the "other things equal" in the relationship between price and quantity demanded. When any of these determinants changes, the demand curve will shift to the right or left. For this reason, determinants of demand are sometimes referred to as *demand shifters.*

The basic determinants of demand are (1) consumers' tastes (preferences), (2) the number of buyers in the market, (3) consumers' incomes, (4) the prices of related goods, and (5) consumer expectations.

Changes in Demand

A change in one or more of the determinants of demand will change the demand data (the demand schedule) in the table accompanying Figure 3.3 and therefore the location of the demand curve there. A change in the demand schedule or, graphically, a shift in the demand curve is called a *change in demand.*

If consumers desire to buy more corn at each possible price than is reflected in column 2 in the table in Figure 3.3, that *increase in demand* is shown as a shift of the demand curve to the right, say, from D_1 to D_2. Conversely, a *decrease in demand* occurs when consumers buy less corn

FIGURE 3.2 Market demand for corn, three buyers. The market demand curve D is the horizontal summation of the individual demand curves (D_1, D_2, and D_3) of all the consumers in the market. At the price of $3, for example, the three individual curves yield a total quantity demanded of 100 bushels (= 35 + 39 + 26).

Market Demand for Corn, Three Buyers

Price per Bushel	Quantity Demanded						Total Quantity Demanded per Week
	Joe		Jen		Jay		
$5	10	+	12	+	8	=	30
4	20	+	23	+	17	=	60
3	35	+	39	+	26	=	100
2	55	+	60	+	39	=	154
1	80	+	87	+	54	=	221

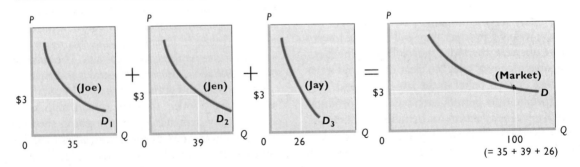

FIGURE 3.3 Changes in the demand for corn. A change in one or more of the determinants of demand causes a change in demand. An increase in demand is shown as a shift of the demand curve to the right, as from D_1 to D_2. A decrease in demand is shown as a shift of the demand curve to the left, as from D_1 to D_3. These changes in demand are to be distinguished from a change in quantity demanded, which is caused by a change in the price of the product, as shown by a movement from, say, point *a* to point *b* on fixed demand curve D_1.

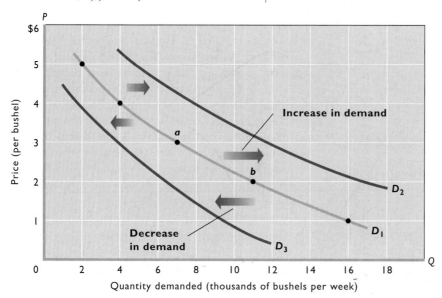

Market Demand for Corn, 200 Buyers, (D_1)	
(1) Price per Bushel	(2) Total Quantity Demanded per Week
$5	2000
4	4000
3	7000
2	11,000
1	16,000

at each possible price than is indicated in column 2. The leftward shift of the demand curve from D_1 to D_3 in Figure 3.3 shows that situation.

Now let's see how changes in each determinant affect demand.

Tastes A favorable change in consumer tastes (preferences) for a product—a change that makes the product more desirable—means that more of it will be demanded at each price. Demand will increase; the demand curve will shift rightward. An unfavorable change in consumer preferences will decrease demand, shifting the demand curve to the left.

New products may affect consumer tastes; for example, the introduction of digital cameras greatly decreased the demand for film cameras. Consumers' concern over the health hazards of cholesterol and obesity have increased the demand for broccoli, low-calorie beverages, and fresh fruit while decreasing the demand for beef, veal, eggs, and whole milk. Over the past several years, the demand for coffee drinks and table wine has greatly increased, driven by a change in tastes. So, too, has the demand for touch-screen mobile phones and fuel-efficient hybrid vehicles.

Number of Buyers An increase in the number of buyers in a market is likely to increase demand; a decrease in the number of buyers will probably decrease demand. For example, the rising number of older persons in the United

States in recent years has increased the demand for motor homes, medical care, and retirement communities. Large-scale immigration from Mexico has greatly increased the demand for a range of goods and services in the Southwest, including Mexican food products in local grocery stores. Improvements in communications have given financial markets international range and have thus increased the demand for stocks and bonds. International trade agreements have reduced foreign trade barriers to American farm commodities, increasing the number of buyers and therefore the demand for those products.

In contrast, emigration (out-migration) from many small rural communities has reduced the population and thus the demand for housing, home appliances, and auto repair in those towns.

Income How changes in income affect demand is a more complex matter. For most products, a rise in income causes an increase in demand. Consumers typically buy more steaks, furniture, and electronic equipment as their incomes increase. Conversely, the demand for such products declines as their incomes fall. Products whose demand varies *directly* with money income are called *superior goods*, or **normal goods.**

Although most products are normal goods, there are some exceptions. As incomes increase beyond some point, the demand for used clothing, retread tires, and third-hand automobiles may decrease, because the higher incomes enable consumers to buy new versions of those products. Rising incomes may also decrease the demand for soy-enhanced hamburger. Similarly, rising incomes may cause the demand for charcoal grills to decline as wealthier consumers switch to gas grills. Goods whose demand varies *inversely* with money income are called **inferior goods.**

Prices of Related Goods

A change in the price of a related good may either increase or decrease the demand for a product, depending on whether the related good is a substitute or a complement:

- A **substitute good** is one that can be used in place of another good.
- A **complementary good** is one that is used together with another good.

Substitutes Häagen-Dazs ice cream and Ben & Jerry's ice cream are substitute goods or, simply, *substitutes*. When two products are substitutes, an increase in the price of one will increase the demand for the other. Conversely, a decrease in the price of one will decrease the demand for the other. For example, when the price of Häagen-Dazs ice cream rises, consumers will buy less of it and increase their demand for Ben & Jerry's ice cream. When the price of Colgate toothpaste declines, the demand for Crest decreases. So it is with other product pairs such as Nikes and Reeboks, Budweiser and Miller beer, or Chevrolets and Fords. They are *substitutes in consumption*.

Complements Because complementary goods (or, simply, *complements*) are used together, they are typically demanded jointly. Examples include computers and software, cell phones and cellular service, and snowboards and lift tickets. If the price of a complement (for example, lettuce) goes up, the demand for the related good (salad dressing) will decline. Conversely, if the price of a complement (for example, tuition) falls, the demand for a related good (textbooks) will increase.

Unrelated Goods The vast majority of goods are not related to one another and are called *independent goods*. Examples are butter and golf balls, potatoes and automobiles, and bananas and wristwatches. A change in the price of one has little or no effect on the demand for the other.

Consumer Expectations

Changes in consumer expectations may shift demand. A newly formed expectation of higher future prices may cause consumers to buy now in order to "beat" the anticipated price rises, thus increasing current demand. That is often what happens in so-called hot real estate markets. Buyers rush in because they think the price of new homes will continue to escalate rapidly. Some buyers fear being "priced out of the market" and therefore not obtaining the home they desire. Other buyers—speculators—believe they will be able to sell the houses later at a higher price. Whichever their motivation, these buyers increase the current demand for houses.

Similarly, a change in expectations concerning future income may prompt consumers to change their current spending. For example, first-round NFL draft choices may splurge on new luxury cars in anticipation of lucrative professional football contracts. Or workers who become fearful of losing their jobs may reduce their demand for, say, vacation travel.

In summary, an *increase* in demand—the decision by consumers to buy larger quantities of a product at each possible price—may be caused by:

- A favorable change in consumer tastes.
- An increase in the number of buyers.
- Rising incomes if the product is a normal good.
- Falling incomes if the product is an inferior good.
- An increase in the price of a substitute good.
- A decrease in the price of a complementary good.
- A new consumer expectation that either prices or income will be higher in the future.

You should "reverse" these generalizations to explain a *decrease* in demand. Table 3.1 provides additional illustrations of the determinants of demand.

TABLE 3.1 Determinants of Demand: Factors That Shift the Demand Curve

Determinant	Examples
Change in buyer tastes	Physical fitness rises in popularity, increasing the demand for jogging shoes and bicycles; cell phone popularity rises, reducing the demand for landline phones.
Change in number of buyers	A decline in the birthrate reduces the demand for children's toys.
Change in income	A rise in incomes increases the demand for normal goods such as restaurant meals, sports tickets, and necklaces while reducing the demand for inferior goods such as cabbage, turnips, and inexpensive wine.
Change in the prices of related goods	A reduction in airfares reduces the demand for bus transportation (substitute goods); a decline in the price of DVD players increases the demand for DVD movies (complementary goods).
Change in consumer expectations	Inclement weather in South America creates an expectation of higher future coffee bean prices, thereby increasing today's demand for coffee beans.

Changes in Quantity Demanded

A *change in demand* must not be confused with a *change in quantity demanded*. A **change in demand** is a shift of the demand curve to the right (an increase in demand) or to the left (a decrease in demand). It occurs because the consumer's state of mind about purchasing the product has been altered in response to a change in one or more of the determinants of demand. Recall that "demand" is a schedule or a curve; therefore, a "change in demand" means a change in the schedule and a shift of the curve.

In contrast, a **change in quantity demanded** is a movement from one point to another point—from one price-quantity combination to another—on a fixed demand curve. The cause of such a change is an increase or decrease in the price of the product under consideration. In the table in Figure 3.3, for example, a decline in the price of corn from $5 to $4 will increase the quantity demanded of corn from 2000 to 4000 bushels.

In Figure 3.3 the shift of the demand curve D_1 to either D_2 or D_3 is a change in demand. But the movement from point *a* to point *b* on curve D_1 represents a change in quantity demanded: Demand has not changed; it is the entire curve, and it remains fixed in place.

QUICK REVIEW 3.1

- Demand is a schedule or a curve showing the amount of a product that buyers are willing and able to purchase, in a particular time period, at each possible price in a series of prices.

- The law of demand states that, other things equal, the quantity of a good purchased varies inversely with its price.

- The demand curve shifts because of changes in (a) consumer tastes, (b) the number of buyers in the market, (c) consumer income, (d) the prices of substitute or complementary goods, and (e) consumer expectations.

- A change in demand is a shift of the demand curve; a change in quantity demanded is a movement from one point to another on a fixed demand curve.

Supply

Supply is a schedule or curve showing the various amounts of a product that producers are willing and able to make available for sale at each of a series of possible prices during a specific period.[2] The table in Figure 3.4 is a hypothetical

supply schedule for a single producer of corn. It shows the quantities of corn that will be supplied at various prices, other things equal.

Law of Supply

The table in Figure 3.4 shows that a positive or direct relationship prevails between price and quantity supplied. As price rises, the quantity supplied rises; as price falls, the quantity supplied falls. This relationship is called the **law of supply.** A supply schedule tells us that, other things equal, firms will produce and offer for sale more of their product at a high price than at a low price. This, again, is basically common sense.

Price is an obstacle from the standpoint of the consumer, who is on the paying end. The higher the price, the less the consumer will buy. But the supplier is on the receiving end of the product's price. To a supplier, price represents *revenue*, which serves as an incentive to produce and sell a product. The higher the price, the greater this incentive and the greater the quantity supplied.

Consider a farmer who is deciding on how much corn to plant. As corn prices rise, as shown in the table in Figure 3.4, the farmer finds it profitable to plant more corn. And the higher corn prices enable the farmer to cover the increased costs associated with more intensive cultivation and the use of more seed, fertilizer, and pesticides. The overall result is more corn.

Now consider a manufacturer. Beyond some quantity of production, manufacturers usually encounter increases in *marginal cost*—the added cost of producing one more unit of output. Certain productive resources—in particular, the firm's plant and machinery—cannot be expanded quickly, so the firm uses more of other resources such as labor to produce more output. But as labor becomes more abundant relative to the fixed plant and equipment, the additional workers have relatively less space and access to equipment. For example, the added workers may have to wait to gain access to machines. As a result, each added worker produces less added output, and the marginal cost of successive units of output rises accordingly. The firm will not produce the more costly units unless it receives a higher price for them. Again, price and quantity supplied are directly related.

The Supply Curve

As with demand, it is convenient to represent individual supply graphically. In Figure 3.4, curve *S* is the **supply curve** that corresponds with the price–quantity supplied data in the accompanying table. The upward slope of the curve reflects the law of supply—producers offer more of

---

[2]This definition is worded to apply to product markets. To adjust it to apply to resource markets, substitute "resource" for "product" and "owners" for "producers."

FIGURE 3.4 An individual producer's supply of corn. Because price and quantity supplied are directly related, the supply curve for an individual producer graphs as an upsloping curve. Other things equal, producers will offer more of a product for sale as its price rises and less of the product for sale as its price falls.

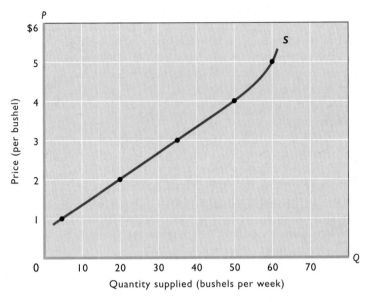

Supply of Corn	
Price per Bushel	Quantity Supplied per Week
$5	60
4	50
3	35
2	20
1	5

a good, service, or resource for sale as its price rises. The relationship between price and quantity supplied is positive, or direct.

Market Supply

Market supply is derived from individual supply in exactly the same way that market demand is derived from individual demand. We sum the quantities supplied by each producer at each price. That is, we obtain the market supply curve by "horizontally adding" the supply curves of the individual producers. The price–quantity supplied data in the table accompanying Figure 3.5 are for an assumed 200 identical producers in the market, each willing to supply corn according to the supply schedule shown in Figure 3.4. Curve S_1 in Figure 3.5 is a graph of the market supply data. Note that the values of the axes in Figure 3.5 are the same as those used in our graph of market demand (Figure 3.3). The only difference is that we change the label on the horizontal axis from "quantity demanded" to "quantity supplied."

Determinants of Supply

In constructing a supply curve, we assume that price is the most significant influence on the quantity supplied of any product. But other factors (the "other things equal") can and do affect supply. The supply curve is drawn on the assumption that these other things are fixed and do not change. If one of them does change, a *change in supply* will occur, meaning that the entire supply curve will shift.

The basic **determinants of supply** are (1) resource prices, (2) technology, (3) taxes and subsidies, (4) prices of other goods, (5) producer expectations, and (6) the number of sellers in the market. A change in any one or more of these determinants of supply, or *supply shifters*, will move the supply curve for a product either right or left. A shift to the *right*, as from S_1 to S_2 in Figure 3.5, signifies an *increase* in supply: Producers supply larger quantities of the product at each possible price. A shift to the *left*, as from S_1 to S_3, indicates a *decrease* in supply: Producers offer less output at each price.

Changes in Supply

Let's consider how changes in each of the determinants affect supply. The key idea is that costs are a major factor underlying supply curves; anything that affects costs (other than changes in output itself) usually shifts the supply curve.

Resource Prices The prices of the resources used in the production process help determine the costs of production incurred by firms. Higher *resource* prices raise production costs and, assuming a particular *product* price, squeeze profits. That reduction in profits reduces the incentive for firms to supply output at each product price. For example, an increase in the price of sand, crushed rock, or Portland cement will increase the cost of producing concrete and reduce its supply.

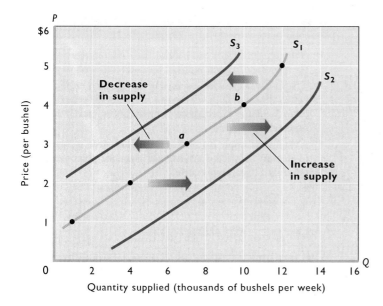

FIGURE 3.5 Changes in the supply of corn. A change in one or more of the determinants of supply causes a change in supply. An increase in supply is shown as a rightward shift of the supply curve, as from S_1 to S_2. A decrease in supply is depicted as a leftward shift of the curve, as from S_1 to S_3. In contrast, a change in the *quantity supplied* is caused by a change in the product's price and is shown by a movement from one point to another, as from b to a on fixed supply curve S_1.

Market Supply of Corn, 200 Producers, (S_1)	
(1) Price per Bushel	(2) Total Quantity Supplied per Week
$5	12,000
4	10,000
3	7000
2	4000
1	1000

In contrast, lower *resource* prices reduce production costs and increase profits. So when resource prices fall, firms supply greater output at each product price. For example, a decrease in the price of iron ore will decrease the price of steel.

Technology
Improvements in technology (techniques of production) enable firms to produce units of output with fewer resources. Because resources are costly, using fewer of them lowers production costs and increases supply. Example: Technological advances in producing flat-panel computer monitors have greatly reduced their cost. Thus, manufacturers will now offer more such monitors than previously at the various prices; the supply of flat-panel monitors has increased.

Taxes and Subsidies
Businesses treat most taxes as costs. An increase in sales or property taxes will increase production costs and reduce supply. In contrast, subsidies are "taxes in reverse." If the government subsidizes the production of a good, it in effect lowers the producers' costs and increases supply.

Prices of Other Goods
Firms that produce a particular product, say, soccer balls, can sometimes use their plant and equipment to produce alternative goods, say, basketballs and volleyballs. The higher prices of these "other goods" may entice soccer ball producers to switch production to those other goods in order to increase profits. This *substitution in production* results in a

decline in the supply of soccer balls. Alternatively, when the prices of basketballs and volleyballs decline relative to the price of soccer balls, producers of those goods may decide to produce more soccer balls instead, increasing their supply.

Producer Expectations
Changes in expectations about the future price of a product may affect the producer's current willingness to supply that product. It is difficult, however, to generalize about how a new expectation of higher prices affects the present supply of a product. Farmers anticipating a higher wheat price in the future might withhold some of their current wheat harvest from the market, thereby causing a decrease in the current supply of wheat. In contrast, in many types of manufacturing industries, newly formed expectations that price will increase may induce firms to add another shift of workers or to expand their production facilities, causing current supply to increase.

Number of Sellers
Other things equal, the larger the number of suppliers, the greater the market supply. As more firms enter an industry, the supply curve shifts to the right. Conversely, the smaller the number of firms in the industry, the less the market supply. This means that as firms leave an industry, the supply curve shifts to the left. Example: The United States and Canada have imposed restrictions on haddock fishing to replenish dwindling stocks. As part of that policy, the Federal government has bought the boats of some of the haddock fishers as a way of putting

TABLE 3.2 Determinants of Supply: Factors That Shift the Supply Curve

Determinant	Examples
Change in resource prices	A decrease in the price of microchips increases the supply of computers; an increase in the price of crude oil reduces the supply of gasoline.
Change in technology	The development of more effective wireless technology increases the supply of cell phones.
Changes in taxes and subsidies	An increase in the excise tax on cigarettes reduces the supply of cigarettes; a decline in subsidies to state universities reduces the supply of higher education.
Change in prices of other goods	An increase in the price of cucumbers decreases the supply of watermelons.
Change in producer expectations	An expectation of a substantial rise in future log prices decreases the supply of logs today.
Change in number of suppliers	An increase in the number of tattoo parlors increases the supply of tattoos; the formation of women's professional basketball leagues increases the supply of women's professional basketball games.

them out of business and decreasing the catch. The result has been a decline in the market supply of haddock.

Table 3.2 is a checklist of the determinants of supply, along with further illustrations.

Changes in Quantity Supplied

The distinction between a *change in supply* and a *change in quantity supplied* parallels the distinction between a change in demand and a change in quantity demanded. Because supply is a schedule or curve, a **change in supply** means a change in the schedule and a shift of the curve. An increase in supply shifts the curve to the right; a decrease in supply shifts it to the left. The cause of a change in supply is a change in one or more of the determinants of supply.

In contrast, a **change in quantity supplied** is a movement from one point to another on a fixed supply curve. The cause of such a movement is a change in the price of the specific product being considered.

Consider supply curve S_1 in Figure 3.5. A decline in the price of corn from $4 to $3 decreases the quantity of corn supplied per week from 10,000 to 7000 bushels. This movement from point b to point a along S_1 is a change in quantity supplied, not a change in supply. Supply is the full schedule of prices and quantities shown, and this schedule does not change when the price of corn changes.

Market Equilibrium

With our understanding of demand and supply, we can now show how the decisions of buyers of corn and sellers of corn interact to determine the equilibrium price and quantity of corn. In the table in Figure 3.6, columns 1 and 2 repeat the market supply of corn (from the table in Figure 3.5), and columns 2 and 3 repeat the market demand for corn (from the table in Figure 3.3). We assume this is a competitive market so that neither buyers nor sellers can set the price.

Equilibrium Price and Quantity

We are looking for the equilibrium price and equilibrium quantity. The **equilibrium price** (or *market-clearing price*) is the price where the intentions of buyers and sellers match. It is the price where quantity demanded equals quantity supplied. The table in Figure 3.6 reveals that at

INTERACTIVE GRAPHS

G 3.1

Supply and demand

$3, *and only at that price*, the number of bushels of corn that sellers wish to sell (7000) is identical to the number consumers want to buy (also 7000). At $3 and 7000 bushels of corn, there is neither a shortage nor a surplus of corn. So 7000 bushels of corn is the **equilibrium quantity:** the quantity at which the intentions of buyers and sellers match, so that the quantity demanded and the quantity supplied are equal.

Graphically, the equilibrium price is indicated by the intersection of the supply curve and the demand curve in **Figure 3.6 (Key Graph).** (The horizontal axis now measures both quantity demanded and quantity supplied.) With neither a shortage nor a surplus at $3, the market is *in equilibrium*, meaning "in balance" or "at rest."

Competition among buyers and among sellers drives the price to the equilibrium price; once there, it will remain there unless it is subsequently disturbed by changes in

FIGURE 3.6 Equilibrium price and quantity. The intersection of the downsloping demand curve *D* and the upsloping supply curve *S* indicates the equilibrium price and quantity, here $3 and 7000 bushels of corn. The shortages of corn at below-equilibrium prices (for example, 7000 bushels at $2) drive up price. The higher prices increase the quantity supplied and reduce the quantity demanded until equilibrium is achieved. The surpluses caused by above-equilibrium prices (for example, 6000 bushels at $4) push price down. As price drops, the quantity demanded rises and the quantity supplied falls until equilibrium is established. At the equilibrium price and quantity, there are neither shortages nor surpluses of corn.

Market Supply of and Demand for Corn			
(1) Total Quantity Supplied per Week	**(2) Price per Bushel**	**(3) Total Quantity Demanded per Week**	**(4) Surplus (+) or Shortage (−)***
12,000	$5	2000	+10,000 ↓
10,000	4	4000	+6000 ↓
7000	**3**	**7000**	**0**
4000	2	11,000	−7000 ↑
1000	1	16,000	−15,000 ↑

*Arrows indicate the effect on price.

QUICK QUIZ FOR FIGURE 3.6

1. Demand curve *D* is downsloping because:
   a. producers offer less of a product for sale as the price of the product falls.
   b. lower prices of a product create income and substitution effects that lead consumers to purchase more of it.
   c. the larger the number of buyers in a market, the lower the product price.
   d. price and quantity demanded are directly (positively) related.

2. Supply curve *S*:
   a. reflects an inverse (negative) relationship between price and quantity supplied.
   b. reflects a direct (positive) relationship between price and quantity supplied.
   c. depicts the collective behavior of buyers in this market.

   d. shows that producers will offer more of a product for sale at a low product price than at a high product price.

3. At the $3 price:
   a. quantity supplied exceeds quantity demanded.
   b. quantity demanded exceeds quantity supplied.
   c. the product is abundant and a surplus exists.
   d. there is no pressure on price to rise or fall.

4. At price $5 in this market:
   a. there will be a shortage of 10,000 units.
   b. there will be a surplus of 10,000 units.
   c. quantity demanded will be 12,000 units.
   d. quantity demanded will equal quantity supplied.

Answers: 1. b; 2. b; 3. d; 4. b

demand or supply (shifts of the curves). To better understand the uniqueness of the equilibrium price, let's consider other prices. At any above-equilibrium price, quantity supplied exceeds quantity demanded. For example, at the $4 price, sellers will offer 10,000 bushels of corn, but buyers will purchase only 4000. The $4 price encourages sellers to offer lots of corn but discourages many consumers from buying it. The result is a **surplus** (or *excess supply*) of 6000 bushels. If corn sellers produced them all, they would find themselves with 6000 unsold bushels of corn.

Surpluses drive prices down. Even if the $4 price existed temporarily, it could not persist. The large surplus would prompt competing sellers to lower the price to encourage buyers to take the surplus off their hands. As the price fell, the incentive to produce corn would decline and the incentive for consumers to buy corn would increase. As shown in Figure 3.6, the market would move to its equilibrium at $3.

Any price below the $3 equilibrium price would create a shortage; quantity demanded would exceed quantity supplied. Consider a $2 price, for example. We see both from column 2 of the table and from the demand curve in Figure 3.6 that quantity demanded exceeds quantity supplied at that price. The result is a **shortage** (or *excess demand*) of 7000 bushels of corn. The $2 price discourages sellers from devoting resources to corn and encourages

consumers to desire more bushels than are available. The $2 price cannot persist as the equilibrium price. Many consumers who want to buy corn at this price will not obtain it. They will express a willingness to pay more than $2 to get corn. Competition among these buyers will drive up the price, eventually to the $3 equilibrium level. Unless disrupted by changes of supply or demand, this $3 price of corn will continue to prevail.

Rationing Function of Prices

The ability of the competitive forces of supply and demand to establish a price at which selling and buying decisions are consistent is called the rationing function of prices. In our case, the equilibrium price of $3 clears the market, leaving no burdensome surplus for sellers and no inconvenient shortage for potential buyers. And it is the combination of freely made individual decisions that sets this market-clearing price. In effect, the market outcome says that all buyers who are willing and able to pay $3 for a bushel of corn will obtain it; all buyers who cannot or will not pay $3 will go without corn. Similarly, all producers who are willing and able to offer corn for sale at $3 a bushel will sell it; all producers who cannot or will not sell for $3 per bushel will not sell their product.

Efficient Allocation

A competitive market such as that we have described not only rations goods to consumers but also allocates society's resources efficiently to the particular product. Competition among corn producers forces them to use the best technology and right mix of productive resources. If they didn't, their costs would be too high relative to the market price, and they would be unprofitable. The result is **productive efficiency:** the production of any particular good in the least costly way. When society produces corn at the lowest achievable per-unit cost, it is expending the least-valued combination of resources to produce that product and therefore is making available more-valued resources to produce other desired goods. Suppose society has only $100 worth of resources available. If it can produce a bushel of corn using $3 of those resources, then it will have available $97 of resources remaining to produce other goods. This is clearly better than producing the corn for $5 and having only $95 of resources available for the alternative uses.

Competitive markets also produce **allocative efficiency:** the *particular mix* of goods and services most highly valued by society (minimum-cost production assumed). For example, society wants land suitable for growing corn used for that purpose, not to grow

CONSIDER THIS . . .

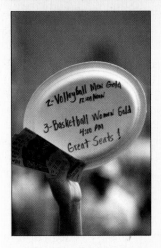

Ticket Scalping: A Bum Rap!

Ticket prices for athletic events and musical concerts are usually set far in advance of the events. Sometimes the original ticket price is too low to be the equilibrium price. Lines form at the ticket window and a severe shortage of tickets occurs at the printed price. What happens next? Buyers who are willing to pay more than the original price bid up the ticket price in resale ticket markets.

Tickets sometimes get resold for much greater amounts than the original price—market transactions known as "scalping." For example, an original buyer may resell a $75 ticket to a concert for $200. Reporters sometimes denounce scalpers for "ripping off" buyers by charging "exorbitant" prices.

But is scalping really a rip-off? We must first recognize that such ticket resales are voluntary transactions. If both buyer and seller did not expect to gain from the exchange, it would not occur! The seller must value the $200 more than seeing the event, and the buyer must value seeing the event at $200 or more. So there are no losers or victims here: Both buyer and seller benefit from the transaction. The scalping market simply redistributes assets (game or concert tickets) from those who would rather have the money (and the other things that the money can buy) to those who would rather have the tickets.

Does scalping impose losses or injury on the sponsors of the event? If the sponsors are injured, it is because they initially priced tickets below the equilibrium level. Perhaps they did this to create a long waiting line and the attendant news media publicity. Alternatively, they may have had a genuine desire to keep tickets affordable for lower-income, ardent fans. In either case, the event sponsors suffer an opportunity cost in the form of less ticket revenue than they might have otherwise received. But such losses are self-inflicted and separate and distinct from the fact that some tickets are later resold at a higher price.

So is ticket scalping undesirable? Not on economic grounds! It is an entirely voluntary activity that benefits both sellers and buyers.

dandelions. It wants diamonds to be used for jewelry, not crushed up and used as an additive to give concrete more sparkle. It wants iPods and MP4 players, not cassette players and tapes. Moreover, society does not want to devote all its resources to corn, diamonds, and portable digital media players. It wants to assign some resources to wheat, gasoline, and cell phones. Competitive markets make those allocatively efficient assignments.

The equilibrium price and quantity in competitive markets usually produce an assignment of resources that is "right" from an economic perspective. Demand essentially reflects the marginal benefit (MB) of the good, based on the utility received. Supply reflects the marginal cost (MC) of producing the good. The market ensures that firms produce all units of goods for which MB exceeds MC and no units for which MC exceeds MB. At the intersection of the demand and supply curves, MB equals MC and allocative efficiency results. As economists say, there is neither an "underallocaton of resources" nor an "overallocation of resources" to the product.

Changes in Supply, Demand, and Equilibrium

We know that demand might change because of fluctuations in consumer tastes or incomes, changes in consumer expectations, or variations in the prices of related goods. Supply might change in response to changes in resource prices, technology, or taxes. What effects will such changes in supply and demand have on equilibrium price and quantity?

Changes in Demand Suppose that the supply of some good (for example, health care) is constant and demand increases, as shown in Figure 3.7a. As a result, the new intersection of the supply and demand curves is at higher values on both the price and the quantity axes. Clearly, an increase in demand raises both equilibrium price and equilibrium quantity. Conversely, a decrease in demand such as that shown in Figure 3.7b reduces both equilibrium price and equilibrium quantity. (The value of graphical analysis is now apparent: We need not fumble with columns of figures to determine the outcomes; we need only compare the new and the old points of intersection on the graph.)

Changes in Supply What happens if the demand for some good (for example, flash drives) is constant but supply increases, as in Figure 3.7c? The new intersection of supply and demand is located at a lower equilibrium price but at a higher equilibrium quantity. An increase in supply

reduces equilibrium price but increases equilibrium quantity. In contrast, if supply decreases, as in Figure 3.7d, equilibrium price rises while equilibrium quantity declines.

Complex Cases When both supply and demand change, the effect is a combination of the individual effects.

Supply Increase; Demand Decrease What effect will a supply increase and a demand decrease for some good (for example, apples) have on equilibrium price? Both changes decrease price, so the net result is a price drop greater than that resulting from either change alone.

What about equilibrium quantity? Here the effects of the changes in supply and demand are opposed: the increase in supply increases equilibrium quantity, but the decrease in demand reduces it. The direction of the change in equilibrium quantity depends on the relative sizes of the changes in supply and demand. If the increase in supply is larger than the decrease in demand, the equilibrium quantity will increase. But if the decrease in demand is greater than the increase in supply, the equilibrium quantity will decrease.

Supply Decrease; Demand Increase A decrease in supply and an increase in demand for some good (for example, gasoline) both increase price. Their combined effect is an increase in equilibrium price greater than that caused by either change separately. But their effect on the equilibrium quantity is again indeterminate, depending on the relative sizes of the changes in supply and demand. If the decrease in supply is larger than the increase in demand, the equilibrium quantity will decrease. In contrast, if the increase in demand is greater than the decrease in supply, the equilibrium quantity will increase.

Supply Increase; Demand Increase What if supply and demand both increase for some good (for example, cell phones)? A supply increase drops equilibrium price, while a demand increase boosts it. If the increase in supply is greater than the increase in demand, the equilibrium price will fall. If the opposite holds, the equilibrium price will rise.

The effect on equilibrium quantity is certain: The increases in supply and demand both raise the equilibrium quantity. Therefore, the equilibrium quantity will increase by an amount greater than that caused by either change alone.

Supply Decrease; Demand Decrease What about decreases in both supply and demand for some good (for example, new homes)? If the decrease in supply is greater

FIGURE 3.7 Changes in demand and supply and the effects on price and quantity. The increase in demand from D_1 to D_2 in (a) increases both equilibrium price and equilibrium quantity. The decrease in demand from D_3 to D_4 in (b) decreases both equilibrium price and equilibrium quantity. The increase in supply from S_1 to S_2 in (c) decreases equilibrium price and increases equilibrium quantity. The decline in supply from S_3 to S_4 in (d) increases equilibrium price and decreases equilibrium quantity. The boxes in the top right corners summarize the respective changes and outcomes. The upward arrows in the boxes signify increases in equilibrium price (P) and equilibrium quantity (Q); the downward arrows signify decreases in these items.

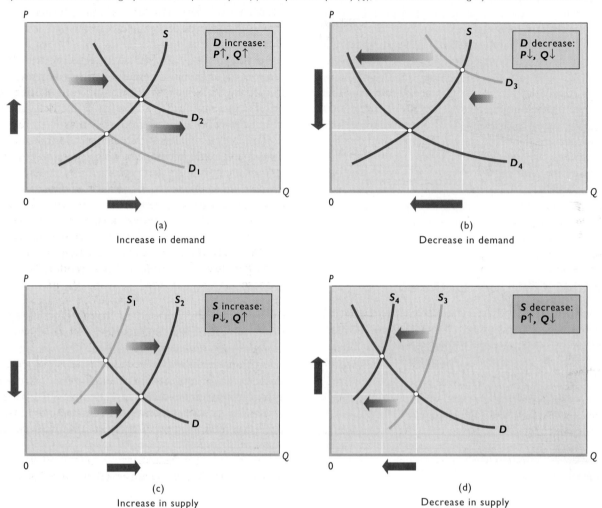

(a) Increase in demand

(b) Decrease in demand

(c) Increase in supply

(d) Decrease in supply

than the decrease in demand, equilibrium price will rise. If the reverse is true, equilibrium price will fall. Because the decreases in supply and demand each reduce equilibrium quantity, we can be sure that equilibrium quantity will fall.

Table 3.3 summarizes these four cases. To understand them fully, you should draw supply and demand diagrams for each case to confirm the effects listed in this table.

Special cases arise when a decrease in demand and a decrease in supply, or an increase in demand and an increase in supply, exactly cancel out. In both cases, the net effect on equilibrium price will be zero; price will not change.

The optional appendix accompanying this chapter provides additional examples of situations in which both supply and demand change at the same time.

TABLE 3.3 Effects of Changes in Both Supply and Demand

Change in Supply	Change in Demand	Effect on Equilibrium Price	Effect on Equilibrium Quantity
1. Increase	Decrease	Decrease	Indeterminate
2. Decrease	Increase	Increase	Indeterminate
3. Increase	Increase	Indeterminate	Increase
4. Decrease	Decrease	Indeterminate	Decrease

CONSIDER THIS . . .

Salsa and Coffee Beans

If you forget the other-things-equal assumption, you can encounter situations that *seem* to be in conflict with the laws of demand and supply. For example, suppose salsa manufacturers sell 1 million bottles of salsa at $4 a bottle in one year; 2 million bottles at $5 in the next year; and 3 million at $6 in the year thereafter. Price and quantity purchased vary directly, and these data seem to be at odds with the law of demand.

But there is no conflict here; the data do not refute the law of demand. The catch is that the law of demand's other-things-equal assumption has been violated over the three years in the example. Specifically, because of changing tastes and rising incomes, the demand for salsa has increased sharply, as in Figure 3.7a. The result is higher prices *and* larger quantities purchased.

Another example: The price of coffee beans occasionally shoots upward at the same time that the quantity of coffee beans harvested declines. These events seemingly contradict the direct relationship between price and quantity denoted by supply. The catch again is that the other-things-equal assumption underlying the upsloping supply curve is violated. Poor coffee harvests decrease supply, as in Figure 3.7d, increasing the equilibrium price of coffee and reducing the equilibrium quantity.

The laws of demand and supply are not refuted by observations of price and quantity made over periods of time in which either demand or supply curves shift.

Application: Government-Set Prices

Prices in most markets are free to rise or fall to their equilibrium levels, no matter how high or low those levels might be. However, government sometimes concludes that supply and demand will produce prices that are unfairly high for buyers or unfairly low for sellers. So government may place legal limits on how high or low a price or prices may go. Is that a good idea?

Price Ceilings on Gasoline

A **price ceiling** sets the maximum legal price a seller may charge for a product or service. A price at or below the ceiling is legal; a price above it is not. The rationale for establishing price ceilings (or ceiling prices) on specific products is that they purportedly enable consumers to obtain some "essential" good or service that they could not afford at the equilibrium price. Examples are rent controls and usury laws, which specify maximum "prices" in the forms of rent and interest that can be charged to borrowers.

Graphical Analysis We can easily show the effects of price ceilings graphically. Suppose that rapidly rising world income boosts the purchase of automobiles and shifts the demand for gasoline to the right so that the market equilibrium price reaches $3.50 per gallon, shown as P_0 in Figure 3.8. The rapidly rising price of gasoline greatly burdens low- and moderate-income households, which pressure government to "do something." To keep gasoline prices down, the government imposes a ceiling price P_c of $3 per gallon. To impact the market, a price ceiling must be below the equilibrium price. A ceiling price of $4, for example, would have had no effect on the price of gasoline in the current situation.

What are the effects of this $3 ceiling price? The rationing ability of the free market is rendered ineffective. Because the ceiling price P_c is below the market-clearing price P_0, there is a lasting shortage of gasoline. The quantity of gasoline demanded at P_c is Q_d and the quantity supplied is only Q_s; a persistent excess demand or shortage of amount $Q_d - Q_s$ occurs.

The price ceiling P_c prevents the usual market adjustment in which competition among buyers bids up price, inducing more production and rationing some buyers out of the market. That process would normally continue until the shortage disappeared at the equilibrium price and quantity, P_0 and Q_0.

By preventing these market adjustments from occurring, the price ceiling poses two related problems.

FIGURE 3.8 A price ceiling. A price ceiling is a maximum legal price such as P_c. When the ceiling price is below the equilibrium price, a persistent product shortage results. Here that shortage is shown by the horizontal distance between Q_d and Q_s.

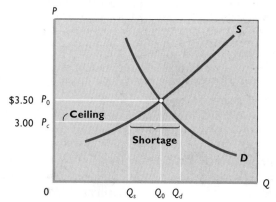

Word A Legal Market for Human Organs?

A Legal Market Might Eliminate the Present Shortage of Human Organs for Transplant. But There Are Many Serious Objections to "Turning Human Body Parts into Commodities" for Purchase and Sale.

It has become increasingly commonplace in medicine to transplant kidneys, lungs, livers, corneas, pancreases, and hearts from deceased individuals to those whose organs have failed or are failing. But surgeons and many of their patients face a growing problem: There are shortages of donated organs available for transplant. Not everyone who needs a transplant can get one. In 2010, there were 105,000 Americans on the waiting list for transplants. Indeed, an inadequate supply of donated organs causes an estimated 6900 deaths in the United States each year.

Why Shortages? Seldom do we hear of shortages of desired goods in market economies. What is different about organs for transplant? One difference is that no legal market exists for human organs. To understand this situation,

observe the demand curve D_1 and supply curve S_1 in the accompanying figure. The downward slope of the demand curve tells us that if there were a market for human organs, the quantity of organs demanded would be greater at lower prices than at higher prices. Vertical supply curve S_1 represents the fixed quantity of human organs now donated via consent before death. Because the price of these donated organs is in effect zero, quantity demanded Q_3 exceeds quantity supplied Q_1. The shortage of $Q_3 - Q_1$ is rationed through a waiting list of those in medical need of transplants. Many people die while still on the waiting list.

Use of a Market A market for human organs would increase the incentive to donate organs. Such a market might work like this: An individual might specify in a legal document that he or she is willing to sell one or more usable human organs upon death or near-death. The person could specify where the money from the sale would go, for example, to family, a church, an educational institution, or a charity. Firms would then emerge to purchase organs and resell them where needed for profit. Under such a

Rationing Problem How will the available supply Q_s be apportioned among buyers who want the greater amount Q_d? Should gasoline be distributed on a first-come, first-served basis, that is, to those willing and able to get in line the soonest or stay in line the longest? Or should gas stations distribute it on the basis of favoritism? Since an unregulated shortage does not lead to an equitable distribution of gasoline, the government must establish some formal system for rationing it to consumers. One option is to issue ration coupons, which authorize bearers to purchase a fixed amount of gasoline per month. The rationing system might entail first the printing of coupons for Q_s gallons of gasoline and then the equal distribution of the coupons among consumers so that the wealthy family of four and the poor family of four both receive the same number of coupons.

Black Markets But ration coupons would not prevent a second problem from arising. The demand curve in Figure 3.8 reveals that many buyers are willing to pay more than

the ceiling price P_c. And, of course, it is more profitable for gasoline stations to sell at prices above the ceiling. Thus, despite a sizable enforcement bureaucracy that would have to accompany the price controls, *black markets* in which gasoline is illegally bought and sold at prices above the legal limits will flourish. Counterfeiting of ration coupons will also be a problem. And since the price of gasoline is now "set by government," government might face political pressure to set the price even lower.

Rent Controls

About 200 cities in the United States, including New York City, Boston, and San Francisco, have at one time or another enacted rent controls: maximum rents established by law (or, more recently, maximum rent increases for existing tenants). Such laws are well intended. Their goals are to protect low-income families from escalating rents caused by perceived housing shortages and to make housing more affordable to the poor.

system, the supply curve of usable organs would take on the normal upward slope of typical supply curves. The higher the expected price of an organ, the greater the number of people who would be willing to have their organs sold at death. Suppose that the supply curve is S_2 in the figure. At the equilibrium price P_1, the number of organs made available for transplant (Q_2) would equal the number purchased for transplant (also Q_2). In this generalized case, the shortage of organs would be eliminated and, of particular importance, the number of organs available for transplanting would rise from Q_1 to Q_2. This means more lives would be saved and enhanced than under the present donor system.

Objections In view of this positive outcome, why is there no such market for human organs? Critics of market-based solutions have two main objections. The first is a moral objection: Critics feel that turning human organs into commodities commercializes human beings and diminishes the special nature of human life. They say there is something unseemly about selling and buying body organs as if they were bushels of wheat or ounces of gold. (There is, however, a market for blood!) Moreover, critics note that the market would

ration the available organs (as represented by Q_2 in the figure) to people who either can afford them (at P_1) or have health insurance for transplants. The poor and uninsured would be left out.

Second, a health-cost objection suggests that a market for body organs would greatly increase the cost of health care. Rather than obtaining freely donated (although "too few") body organs, patients or their insurance companies would have to pay market prices for them, further increasing the cost of medical care.

Rebuttal Supporters of market-based solutions to organ shortages point out that the laws against selling organs are simply driving the market underground. Worldwide, an estimated $1 billion-per-year illegal market in human organs has emerged. As in other illegal markets, the unscrupulous tend to thrive. This fact is dramatized by the accompanying photo, in which four Pakistani villagers show off their scars after they each sold a kidney to pay off debts. Supporters say that legalization of the market for human organs would increase organ supply from legal sources, drive down the price of organs, and reduce the abuses such as those now taking place in illegal markets.

What have been the actual economic effects? On the demand side, the below-equilibrium rents attract a larger number of renters. Some are locals seeking to move into their own places after sharing housing with friends or family. Others are outsiders attracted into the area by the artificially lower rents. But a large problem occurs on the supply side. Price controls make it less attractive for landlords to offer housing on the rental market. In the short run, owners may sell their rental units or convert them to condominiums. In the long run, low rents make it unprofitable for owners to repair or renovate their rental units. (Rent controls are one cause of the many abandoned apartment buildings found in larger cities.) Also, insurance companies, pension funds, and other potential new investors in housing will find it more profitable to invest in office buildings, shopping malls, or motels, where rents are not controlled.

In brief, rent controls distort market signals and thus resources are misallocated: Too few resources are allocated to rental housing and too many to alternative uses.

Ironically, although rent controls are often legislated to lessen the effects of perceived housing shortages, controls in fact are a primary cause of such shortages. For that reason, most American cities either have abandoned or are in the process of dismantling rent controls.

Price Floors on Wheat

A **price floor** is a minimum price fixed by the government. A price at or above the price floor is legal; a price below it is not. Price floors above equilibrium prices are usually invoked when society feels that the free functioning of the market system has not provided a sufficient income for certain groups of resource suppliers or producers. Supported prices for agricultural products and current minimum wages are two examples of price (or wage) floors. Let's look at the former.

Suppose that many farmers have extremely low incomes when the price of wheat is at its equilibrium value of $2 per bushel. The government decides to help out by establishing a legal price floor or price support of $3 per bushel.

FIGURE 3.9 A price floor. A price floor is a minimum legal price such as P_f. When the price floor is above the equilibrium price, a persistent product surplus results. Here that surplus is shown by the horizontal distance between Q_s and Q_d.

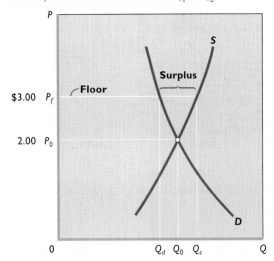

What will be the effects? At any price above the equilibrium price, quantity supplied will exceed quantity demanded—that is, there will be a persistent excess supply or surplus of the product. Farmers will be willing to produce and offer for sale more than private buyers are willing to purchase at the price floor. As we saw with a price ceiling, an imposed legal price disrupts the rationing ability of the free market.

Graphical Analysis Figure 3.9 illustrates the effect of a price floor graphically. Suppose that S and D are the supply and demand curves for wheat. Equilibrium price and quantity are P_0 and Q_0, respectively. If the government imposes a price floor of P_f, farmers will produce Q_s but private buyers will purchase only Q_d. The surplus is the excess of Q_s over Q_d.

The government may cope with the surplus resulting from a price floor in two ways:

- It can restrict supply (for example, by instituting acreage allotments by which farmers agree to take a certain amount of land out of production) or increase demand (for example, by researching new uses for the product involved). These actions may reduce the difference between the equilibrium price and the price floor and that way reduce the size of the resulting surplus.
- If these efforts are not wholly successful, then the government must purchase the surplus output at the $3 price (thereby subsidizing farmers) and store or otherwise dispose of it.

Additional Consequences Price floors such as P_f in Figure 3.9 not only disrupt the rationing ability of prices

but distort resource allocation. Without the price floor, the $2 equilibrium price of wheat would cause financial losses and force high-cost wheat producers to plant other crops or abandon farming altogether. But the $3 price floor allows them to continue to grow wheat and remain farmers. So society devotes too many of its scarce resources to wheat production and too few to producing other, more valuable, goods and services. It fails to achieve allocative efficiency.

That's not all. Consumers of wheat-based products pay higher prices because of the price floor. Taxpayers pay higher taxes to finance the government's purchase of the surplus. Also, the price floor causes potential environmental damage by encouraging wheat farmers to bring hilly, erosion-prone "marginal land" into production. The higher price also prompts imports of wheat. But, since such imports would increase the quantity of wheat supplied and thus undermine the price floor, the government needs to erect tariffs (taxes on imports) to keep the foreign wheat out. Such tariffs usually prompt other countries to retaliate with their own tariffs against U.S. agricultural or manufacturing exports.

So it is easy to see why economists "sound the alarm" when politicians advocate imposing price ceilings or price floors such as price controls, rent controls, interest-rate lids, or agricultural price supports. In all these cases, good intentions lead to bad economic outcomes. Government-controlled prices cause shortages or surpluses, distort resource allocation, and produce negative side effects.

INTERACTIVE GRAPHS

G 3.2

Price floors and ceilings

QUICK REVIEW 3.3

- In competitive markets, prices adjust to the equilibrium level at which quantity demanded equals quantity supplied.
- The equilibrium price and quantity are those indicated by the intersection of the supply and demand curves for any product or resource.
- An increase in demand increases equilibrium price and quantity; a decrease in demand decreases equilibrium price and quantity.
- An increase in supply reduces equilibrium price but increases equilibrium quantity; a decrease in supply increases equilibrium price but reduces equilibrium quantity.
- Over time, equilibrium price and quantity may change in directions that seem at odds with the laws of demand and supply because the other-things-equal assumption is violated.
- Government-controlled prices in the form of ceilings and floors stifle the rationing function of prices, distort resource allocations, and cause negative side effects.

Summary

1. Demand is a schedule or curve representing the willingness of buyers in a specific period to purchase a particular product at each of various prices. The law of demand implies that consumers will buy more of a product at a low price than at a high price. So, other things equal, the relationship between price and quantity demanded is negative or inverse and is graphed as a downsloping curve.

2. Market demand curves are found by adding horizontally the demand curves of the many individual consumers in the market.

3. Changes in one or more of the determinants of demand (consumer tastes, the number of buyers in the market, the money incomes of consumers, the prices of related goods, and consumer expectations) shift the market demand curve. A shift to the right is an increase in demand; a shift to the left is a decrease in demand. A change in demand is different from a change in the quantity demanded, the latter being a movement from one point to another point on a fixed demand curve because of a change in the product's price.

4. Supply is a schedule or curve showing the amounts of a product that producers are willing to offer in the market at each possible price during a specific period. The law of supply states that, other things equal, producers will offer more of a product at a high price than at a low price. Thus, the relationship between price and quantity supplied is positive or direct, and supply is graphed as an upsloping curve.

5. The market supply curve is the horizontal summation of the supply curves of the individual producers of the product.

6. Changes in one or more of the determinants of supply (resource prices, production techniques, taxes or subsidies, the prices of other goods, producer expectations, or the number of sellers in the market) shift the supply curve of a product. A shift to the right is an increase in supply; a shift to the left is a decrease in supply. In contrast, a change in the price of the product being considered causes a change in the quantity supplied, which is shown as a movement from one point to another point on a fixed supply curve.

7. The equilibrium price and quantity are established at the intersection of the supply and demand curves. The interaction of market demand and market supply adjusts the price to the point at which the quantities demanded and supplied are equal. This is the equilibrium price. The corresponding quantity is the equilibrium quantity.

8. The ability of market forces to synchronize selling and buying decisions to eliminate potential surpluses and shortages is known as the rationing function of prices. The equilibrium quantity in competitive markets reflects both productive efficiency (least-cost production) and allocative efficiency (producing the right amount of the product relative to other products).

9. A change in either demand or supply changes the equilibrium price and quantity. Increases in demand raise both equilibrium price and equilibrium quantity; decreases in demand lower both equilibrium price and equilibrium quantity. Increases in supply lower equilibrium price and raise equilibrium quantity; decreases in supply raise equilibrium price and lower equilibrium quantity.

10. Simultaneous changes in demand and supply affect equilibrium price and quantity in various ways, depending on their direction and relative magnitudes (see Table 3.3).

11. A price ceiling is a maximum price set by government and is designed to help consumers. Effective price ceilings produce persistent product shortages, and if an equitable distribution of the product is sought, government must ration the product to consumers.

12. A price floor is a minimum price set by government and is designed to aid producers. Effective price floors lead to persistent product surpluses; the government must either purchase the product or eliminate the surplus by imposing restrictions on production or increasing private demand.

13. Legally fixed prices stifle the rationing function of prices and distort the allocation of resources.

Terms and Concepts

demand	substitute good	change in quantity supplied
demand schedule	complementary good	equilibrium price
law of demand	change in demand	equilibrium quantity
diminishing marginal utility	change in quantity demanded	surplus
income effect	supply	shortage
substitution effect	supply schedule	productive efficiency
demand curve	law of supply	allocative efficiency
determinants of demand	supply curve	price ceiling
normal goods	determinants of supply	price floor
inferior goods	change in supply	

Questions

1. Explain the law of demand. Why does a demand curve slope downward? How is a market demand curve derived from individual demand curves? **LO1**

2. What are the determinants of demand? What happens to the demand curve when any of these determinants change? Distinguish between a change in demand and a movement along a fixed demand curve, noting the cause(s) of each. **LO1**

3. What effect will each of the following have on the demand for small automobiles such as the Mini-Cooper and Smart car? **LO1**
   a. Small automobiles become more fashionable.
   b. The price of large automobiles rises (with the price of small autos remaining the same).
   c. Income declines and small autos are an inferior good.
   d. Consumers anticipate that the price of small autos will greatly come down in the near future.
   e. The price of gasoline substantially drops.

4. Explain the law of supply. Why does the supply curve slope upward? How is the market supply curve derived from the supply curves of individual producers? **LO2**

5. What are the determinants of supply? What happens to the supply curve when any of these determinants changes? Distinguish between a change in supply and a change in the quantity supplied, noting the cause(s) of each. **LO2**

6. What effect will each of the following have on the supply of *auto* tires? **LO2**
   a. A technological advance in the methods of producing tires.
   b. A decline in the number of firms in the tire industry.
   c. An increase in the prices of rubber used in the production of tires.
   d. The expectation that the equilibrium price of auto tires will be lower in the future than currently.
   e. A decline in the price of the large tires used for semi trucks and earth-hauling rigs (with no change in the price of auto tires).
   f. The levying of a per-unit tax on each auto tire sold.
   g. The granting of a 50-cent-per-unit subsidy for each auto tire produced.

7. "In the corn market, demand often exceeds supply and supply sometimes exceeds demand." "The price of corn rises and falls in response to changes in supply and demand." In which of these two statements are the terms "supply" and "demand" used correctly? Explain. **LO2**

8. In 2001 an outbreak of hoof-and-mouth disease in Europe led to the burning of millions of cattle carcasses. What impact do you think this had on the supply of cattle hides, hide prices, the supply of leather goods, and the price of leather goods? **LO4**

9. Critically evaluate: "In comparing the two equilibrium positions in Figure 3.7b, I note that a smaller amount is actually demanded at a lower price. This refutes the law of demand." **LO4**

10. For each stock in the stock market, the number of shares sold daily equals the number of shares purchased. That is, the quantity of each firm's shares demanded equals the quantity supplied. So, if this equality always occurs, why do the prices of stock shares ever change? **LO4**

11. Suppose the total demand for wheat and the total supply of wheat per month in the Kansas City grain market are as shown in the table below. Suppose that the government establishes a price ceiling of $3.70 for wheat. What might prompt the government to establish this price ceiling? Explain carefully the main effects. Demonstrate your answer graphically. Next, suppose that the government establishes a price floor of $4.60 for wheat. What will be the main effects of this price floor? Demonstrate your answer graphically. **LO5**

Thousands of Bushels Demanded	Price per Bushel	Thousands of Bushels Supplied
85	$3.40	72
80	3.70	73
75	4.00	75
70	4.30	77
65	4.60	79
60	4.90	81

12. What do economists mean when they say "price floors and ceilings stifle the rationing function of prices and distort resource allocation"? **LO5**

13. **LAST WORD** In some countries, such as France, every corpse is available for doctors to "harvest" for organs unless the deceased, while still alive, signed a form forbidding the organs to be harvested. In the USA, it is the opposite: No harvesting is allowed unless the deceased had signed, while still alive, an organ donor form authorizing doctors to harvest any needed organs. Use supply and demand figures to show in which country organ shortages are likely to be less severe.

Problems

1. Suppose there are three buyers of candy in a market: Tex, Dex, and Rex. The market demand and the individual demands of Tex, Dex, and Rex are shown on the next page. **LO1**
   a. Fill in the table for the missing values.
   b. Which buyer demands the least at a price of $5? The most at a price of $7?
   c. Which buyer's quantity demanded increases the most when the price is lowered from $7 to $6?

d. Which direction would the market demand curve shift if Tex withdrew from the market? What if Dex doubled his purchases at each possible price?

e. Suppose that at a price of $6, the total quantity demanded increases from 19 to 38. Is this a "change in the quantity demanded" or a "change in demand"?

Price per Candy	Individual Quantities Demanded			Total Quantity Demanded
	Tex	Dex	Rex	
$8	3 +	1 +	0 =	___
7	8 +	2 +	___ =	12
6	___ +	3 +	4 =	19
5	17 +	___ +	6 =	27
4	23 +	5 +	8 =	___

2. The figure below shows the supply curve for tennis balls, S_1, for Drop Volley Tennis, a producer of tennis equipment. Use the figure and the table below to give your answers to the following questions. **LO2**

a. Use the figure to fill in the quantity supplied on supply curve S_1 for each price in the table below.

Price	S_1 Quantity Supplied	S_2 Quantity Supplied	Change in Quantity Supplied
$3	___	4	___
2	___	2	___
1	___	0	___

b. If production costs were to increase, the quantities supplied at each price would be as shown by the third column of the table ("S_2 Quantity Supplied"). Use that data to draw supply curve S_2 on the same graph as supply curve S_1.

c. In the fourth column of the table, enter the amount by which the quantity supplied at each price changes due to the increase in product costs. (Use positive numbers for increases and negative numbers for decreases.)

d. Did the increase in production costs cause a "decrease in supply" or a "decrease in quantity supplied"?

3. Refer to the expanded table below from question 11. **LO3**

a. What is the equilibrium price? At what price is there neither a shortage nor a surplus? Fill in the surplus-shortage column and use it to confirm your answers.

b. Graph the demand for wheat and the supply of wheat. Be sure to label the axes of your graph correctly. Label equilibrium price P and equilibrium quantity Q.

c. How big is the surplus or shortage at $3.40? At $4.90? How big a surplus or shortage results if the price is 60 cents higher than the equilibrium price? 30 cents lower than the equilibrium price?

Thousands of Bushels Demanded	Price per Bushel	Thousands of Bushels Supplied	Surplus (+) or Shortage (−)
85	$3.40	72	___
80	3.70	73	___
75	4.00	75	___
70	4.30	77	___
65	4.60	79	___
60	4.90	81	___

4. How will each of the following changes in demand and/or supply affect equilibrium price and equilibrium quantity in a competitive market; that is, do price and quantity rise, fall, or remain unchanged, or are the answers indeterminate because they depend on the magnitudes of the shifts? Use supply and demand to verify your answers. **LO4**

a. Supply decreases and demand is constant.
b. Demand decreases and supply is constant.
c. Supply increases and demand is constant.
d. Demand increases and supply increases.
e. Demand increases and supply is constant.
f. Supply increases and demand decreases.
g. Demand increases and supply decreases.
h. Demand decreases and supply decreases.

5. Use two market diagrams to explain how an increase in state subsidies to public colleges might affect tuition and enrollments in both public and private colleges. **LO4**

6. **ADVANCED ANALYSIS** Assume that demand for a commodity is represented by the equation $P = 10 - .2Q_d$ and supply by the equation $P = 2 + .2Q_s$, where Q_d and Q_s are quantity demanded and quantity supplied, respectively, and P is price. Using the equilibrium condition $Q_s = Q_d$, solve the equations to determine equilibrium price. Now determine equilibrium quantity. **LO4**

7. Suppose that the demand and supply schedules for rental apartments in the city of Gotham are as given in the table below. LO5

Monthly Rent	Apartments Demanded	Apartments Supplied
$2500	10,000	15,000
2000	12,500	12,500
1500	15,000	10,000
1000	17,500	7500
500	20,000	5000

a. What is the market equilibrium rental price per month and the market equilibrium number of apartments demanded and supplied?

b. If the local government can enforce a rent-control law that sets the maximum monthly rent at $1500, will there be a surplus or a shortage? Of how many units? And how many units will actually be rented each month?

c. Suppose that a new government is elected that wants to keep out the poor. It declares that the minimum rent that can be charged is $2500 per month. If the government can enforce that price floor, will there be a surplus or a shortage? Of how many units? And how many units will actually be rented each month?

d. Suppose that the government wishes to decrease the market equilibrium monthly rent by increasing the supply of housing. Assuming that demand remains unchanged, by how many units of housing would the government have to increase the supply of housing in order to get the market equilibrium rental price to fall to $1500 per month? To $1000 per month? To $500 per month?

FURTHER TEST YOUR KNOWLEDGE AT
www.mcconnell19e.com

At the text's Online Learning Center (OLC), **www.mcconnell19e.com**, you will find one or more Web-based questions that require information from the Internet to answer. We urge you to check them out; they will familiarize you with Web sites that may be helpful in other courses and perhaps even in your career. The OLC also features multiple-choice questions that give instant feedback and provides other helpful ways to further test your knowledge of the chapter.

Additional Examples of Supply and Demand

Our discussion has clearly demonstrated that supply and demand analysis is a powerful tool for understanding equilibrium prices and quantities. The information provided in the main body of this chapter is fully sufficient for moving forward in the book, but you may find that additional examples of supply and demand are helpful. This optional appendix provides several concrete illustrations of changes in supply and demand.

Your instructor may assign all, some, or none of this appendix, depending on time availability and personal preference.

Changes in Supply and Demand

As Figure 3.7 of this chapter demonstrates, changes in supply and demand cause changes in price, quantity, or both. The following applications illustrate this fact in several real-world markets. The simplest situations are those in which either supply changes while demand remains constant or demand changes while supply remains constant. Let's consider two such simple cases first, before looking at more complex applications.

Lettuce

Every now and then we hear on the news that extreme weather has severely reduced the size of some crop. Suppose, for example, that a severe freeze destroys a sizable portion of the lettuce crop. This unfortunate situation implies a significant decline in supply, which we represent as a leftward shift of the supply curve from S_1 to S_2 in Figure 1. At each price, consumers desire as much lettuce as before, so the freeze does not affect the demand for lettuce. That is, demand curve D_1 does not shift.

What are the consequences of the reduced supply of lettuce for equilibrium price and quantity? As shown in Figure 1, the leftward shift of the supply curve disrupts the previous equilibrium in the market for lettuce and drives the equilibrium price upward upward from P_1 to P_2. Consumers respond to that price hike by reducing the quantity of lettuce demanded from Q_1 to Q_2. Equilibrium is restored at P_2 and Q_2.

Consumers who are willing and able to pay price P_2 obtain lettuce; consumers unwilling or unable to pay that

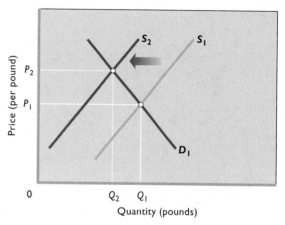

FIGURE 1 **The market for lettuce.** The decrease in the supply of lettuce, shown here by the shift from S_1 to S_2, increases the equilibrium price of lettuce from P_1 to P_2 and reduces the equilibrium quantity from Q_1 to Q_2.

price do not. Some consumers continue to buy as much lettuce as before, even at the higher price. Others buy some lettuce but not as much as before, and still others opt out of the market completely. The latter two groups use the money they would have spent on lettuce to obtain other products, say, carrots. (Because of our other-things-equal assumption, the prices of other products have not changed.)

Exchange Rates

Exchange rates are the prices at which one currency can be traded (exchanged) for another. Exchange rates are normally determined in foreign exchange markets. One of the largest foreign exchange markets is the euro-dollar market in which the currency used in most of Europe, the *euro*, is exchanged for U.S. dollars. In the United States, this market is set up so that euros are priced in dollars—that is, the "product" being traded is euros and the "price" to buy that product is quoted in dollars. Thus, the market equilibrium price one day might be $1.25 to buy 1 euro, while on another day it might be $1.50 to buy 1 euro.

Foreign exchange markets are used by individuals and companies that need to make purchases or payments in a different currency. U.S. companies exporting goods to Germany, for instance, wish to be paid in U.S. dollars.

FIGURE 2 **The market for euros.** The increase in the demand for euros, shown here by the shift from D_1 to D_2, increases the equilibrium price of one euro from $1.25 to $1.50 and increases the equilibrium quantity of euros that are exchanged from Q_1 to Q_2. The dollar has depreciated.

FIGURE 3 **The market for pink salmon.** In the last several decades, the supply of pink salmon has increased and the demand for pink salmon has decreased. As a result, the price of pink salmon has declined, as from P_1 to P_2. Because supply has increased by more than demand has decreased, the equilibrium quantity of pink salmon has increased, as from Q_1 to Q_2.

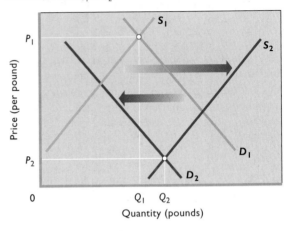

Thus, their German customers will need to convert euros into dollars. The euros that they bring to the euro-dollar market will become part of the overall market supply of euros. Conversely, an American mutual fund may wish to purchase some French real estate outside of Paris. But to purchase that real estate, it will need to pay in euros because the current French owners will only accept payment in euros. Thus, the American mutual fund has a demand to purchase euros that will form part of the overall market demand for euros. The fund will bring dollars to the euro-dollar foreign exchange market in order to purchase the euros it desires.

Sometimes, the demand for euros increases. This might be because a European product surges in popularity in foreign countries. For example, if a new German-made automobile is a big hit in the United States, American car dealers will demand more euros with which to pay for more units of that new model. This will shift the demand curve for euros to the right, as from D_1 to D_2 in Figure 2. Given the fixed euro supply curve S_1, the increase in demand raises the equilibrium exchange rate (the equilibrium number of dollars needed to purchase 1 euro) from $1.25 to $1.50. The equilibrium quantity of euros purchased increases from Q_1 to Q_2. Because a higher dollar amount is now needed to purchase one euro, economists say that the dollar has *depreciated*—gone down in value—relative to the euro. Alternatively, the euro has *appreciated*—gone up in value—relative to the dollar, because one euro now buys $1.50 rather than $1.25.

Pink Salmon

Now let's see what happens when both supply and demand change at the same time. Several decades ago, people who caught salmon earned as much as $1 for each pound of pink salmon—the type of salmon most commonly used for canning. In Figure 3 that price is represented as P_1, at the intersection of supply curve S_1 and demand curve D_1. The corresponding quantity of pink salmon is shown as Q_1 pounds.

As time passed, supply and demand changed in the market for pink salmon. On the supply side, improved technology in the form of larger, more efficient fishing boats greatly increased the catch and lowered the cost of obtaining it. Also, high profits at price P_1 encouraged many new fishers to enter the industry. As a result of these changes, the supply of pink salmon greatly increased and the supply curve shifted to the right, as from S_1 to S_2 in Figure 3.

Over the same years, the demand for pink salmon declined, as represented by the leftward shift from D_1 to D_2 in Figure 3. That decrease was caused by increases in consumer income and reductions of the price of substitute products. As buyers' incomes rose, consumers shifted demand away from canned fish and toward higher-quality fresh or frozen fish, including more-valued Atlantic, chinook, sockeye, and coho salmon. Moreover, the emergence of fish farming, in which salmon are raised in ocean net pens, lowered the prices of these substitute species. That, too, reduced the demand for pink salmon.

The altered supply and demand reduced the price of pink salmon to as low as \$.10 per pound, as represented by the drop in price from P_1 to P_2 in Figure 3. Both the supply increase and the demand decrease helped reduce the equilibrium price. However, in this particular case the equilibrium quantity of pink salmon increased, as represented by the move from Q_1 to Q_2. Both shifts reduced the equilibrium price, but equilibrium quantity increased because the increase in supply exceeded the decrease in demand.

Gasoline

The price of gasoline in the United States has increased rapidly several times during the past several years. For example, the average price of a gallon of gasoline rose from around \$2.25 in January 2007 to about \$4.10 in July 2008. What caused this 80 percent rise in the price of gasoline? How would we diagram this increase?

We begin in Figure 4 with the price of a gallon of gasoline at P_1, representing the \$2.25 price. Simultaneous supply and demand factors disturbed this equilibrium. Supply uncertainties relating to Middle East politics and warfare and expanded demand for oil by fast-growing countries such as China pushed up the price of a barrel of oil from \$50 per barrel in January 2007 to \$145 per barrel in July 2008. Oil is the main input for producing gasoline, so any sustained rise in its price boosts the per-unit cost of producing gasoline. Such cost rises decrease the supply of gasoline, as represented by the leftward shift of the supply curve from

S_1 to S_2 in Figure 4. At times refinery breakdowns in the United States also contributed to this reduced supply.

While the supply of gasoline declined between January 2007 and July 2008, the demand for gasoline increased, as depicted by the rightward shift of the demand curve from D_1 to D_2. Incomes in general were rising over this period because the U.S. economy was rapidly expanding. Rising incomes raise demand for all normal goods, including gasoline. An increased number of low-gas-mileage SUVs and light trucks on the road also contributed to growing gas demand.

The combined decline in gasoline supply and increase in gasoline demand boosted the price of gasoline from \$2.25 to \$4.10, as represented by the rise from P_1 to P_2 in Figure 4. Because the demand increase outweighed the supply decrease, the equilibrium quantity expanded, here from Q_1 to Q_2.

In other periods the price of gasoline has *declined* as the demand for gasoline has increased. Test your understanding of the analysis by explaining how such a price decrease could occur.

Sushi

Sushi bars are springing up like Starbucks in American cities (well, maybe not that fast!). Consumption of sushi, the raw-fish delicacy from Japan, has soared in the United States in recent years. Nevertheless, the price of sushi has remained relatively constant.

Supply and demand analysis helps explain this circumstance of increased quantity and constant price. A change in tastes has increased the U.S. demand for sushi. Many consumers of sushi find it highly tasty when they try it. And, as implied by the growing number of sushi bars in the United States, the supply of sushi has also expanded.

We represent these supply and demand changes in Figure 5 as the rightward shift of the demand curve from D_1 to D_2 and the rightward shift of the supply curve from S_1 to S_2. Observe that the equilibrium quantity of sushi increases from Q_1 to Q_2 and equilibrium price remains constant at P_1. The increase in supply, which taken alone would reduce price, has perfectly offset the increase in demand, which taken alone would raise price. The price of sushi does not change, but the equilibrium quantity greatly increases because both the increase in demand and the increase in supply expand purchases and sales.

Simultaneous increases in demand and supply can cause price to either rise, fall, or remain constant, depending on the relative magnitudes of the supply and demand increases. In this case, price remained constant.

FIGURE 4 The market for gasoline. An increase in the demand for gasoline, as shown by the shift from D_1 to D_2, coupled with a decrease in supply, as shown by the shift from S_1 to S_2, boosts equilibrium price (here from P_1 to P_2). In this case, equilibrium quantity increases from Q_1 to Q_2 because the increase in demand outweighs the decrease in supply.

FIGURE 5 The market for sushi. Equal increases in the demand for sushi, as from D_1 to D_2, and in the supply of sushi, as from S_1 to S_2, expand the equilibrium quantity of sushi (here from Q_1 to Q_2) while leaving the price of sushi unchanged at P_1.

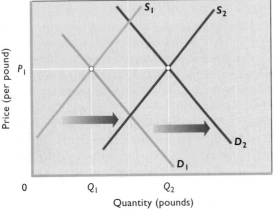

FIGURE 6 The market for tickets to the Olympic women's figure skating finals. The demand curve D and supply curve S for the Olympic women's figure skating finals produce an equilibrium price that is above the P_1 price printed on the ticket. At price P_1 the quantity of tickets demanded, Q_2, greatly exceeds the quantity of tickets available (Q_1). The resulting shortage of ab ($= Q_2Q_1$) gives rise to a legal or illegal secondary market.

Preset Prices

In the body of this chapter, we saw that an effective government-imposed price ceiling (legal maximum price) causes quantity demanded to exceed quantity supplied—a shortage. An effective government-imposed price floor (legal minimum price) causes quantity supplied to exceed quantity demanded—a surplus. Put simply: Shortages result when prices are set below, and surpluses result when prices are set above, equilibrium prices.

We now want to establish that shortages and surpluses can occur in markets other than those in which government imposes price floors and ceilings. Such market imbalances happen when the seller or sellers set prices in advance of sales and the prices selected turn out to be below or above equilibrium prices. Consider the following two examples.

Olympic Figure Skating Finals

Tickets for the women's figure skating championship at the Olympics are among the world's "hottest tickets." The popularity of this event and the high incomes of buyers translate into tremendous ticket demand. The Olympic officials set the price for the tickets in advance. Invariably, the price, although high, is considerably below the equilibrium price that would equate quantity demanded and quantity supplied. A severe shortage of tickets therefore occurs in this *primary market*—the market involving the official ticket office.

The shortage, in turn, creates a *secondary market* in which buyers bid for tickets held by initial purchasers

rather than the original seller. Scalping tickets—selling them above the original ticket price—may be legal or illegal, depending on local laws.

Figure 6 shows how the shortage in the primary ticket market looks in terms of supply and demand analysis. Demand curve D represents the strong demand for tickets and supply curve S represents the supply of tickets. The supply curve is vertical because a fixed number of tickets are printed to match the capacity of the arena. At the printed ticket price of P_1, the quantity of tickets demanded, Q_2, exceeds the quantity supplied, Q_1. The result is a shortage of ab—the horizontal distance between Q_2 and Q_1 in the primary market.

If the printed ticket price had been the higher equilibrium price P_2, no shortage of tickets would have occurred. But at the lower price P_1, a shortage and secondary ticket market will emerge among those buyers willing to pay more than the printed ticket price and those sellers willing to sell their purchased tickets for more than the original price. Wherever there are shortages and secondary markets, it is safe to assume the original price was set below the equilibrium price.

Olympic Curling Preliminaries

Contrast the shortage of tickets for the women's figure skating finals at the Olympics to the surplus of tickets for one of the preliminary curling matches. For the uninitiated, curling is a sport in which participants slide a heavy round object called a "stone" down the ice toward a target while teammates called "sweepers" use brooms to alter the course of the stone when desired.

Curling is a popular spectator sport in a few nations such as Canada, but it does not draw many fans in most countries. So the demand for tickets to most of the preliminary curling events is not very strong. We demonstrate this weak demand as D in Figure 7. As in our previous example, the supply of tickets is fixed by the size of the arena and is shown as vertical line S.

We represent the printed ticket price as P_1 in Figure 7. In this case the printed price is much higher than the equilibrium price of P_2. At the printed ticket price, quantity supplied is Q_1 and quantity demanded is Q_2. So a surplus of tickets of ba ($= Q_1 - Q_2$) occurs. No ticket scalping occurs and there are numerous empty seats. Only if the Olympic officials had priced the tickets at the lower price P_2 would the event have been a sellout. (Actually, the Olympic officials try to adjust to demand realities for curling contests by holding them in smaller arenas and by charging less for tickets. Nevertheless, the stands are rarely full for the preliminary contests, which compete against final events in other winter Olympic sports.)

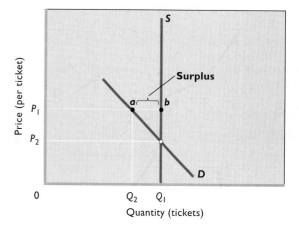

FIGURE 7 The market for tickets to the Olympic curling preliminaries. The demand curve D and supply curve S for the Olympic curling preliminaries produce an equilibrium price below the P_1 price printed on the ticket. At price P_1 the quantity of tickets demanded is less than the quantity of tickets available. The resulting surplus of ba ($= Q_1 - Q_2$) means the event is not sold out.

Appendix Summary

1. A decrease in the supply of a product increases its equilibrium price and reduces its equilibrium quantity. In contrast, an increase in the demand for a product boosts both its equilibrium price and its equilibrium quantity.

2. Simultaneous changes in supply and demand affect equilibrium price and quantity in various ways, depending on the relative magnitudes of the changes in supply and demand. Equal increases in supply and demand, for example, leave equilibrium price unchanged.

3. Sellers set prices of some items such as tickets in advance of the event. These items are sold in the primary market that involves the original seller and buyers. If preset prices turn out to be below the equilibrium prices, shortages occur and scalping in legal or illegal secondary markets arises. The prices in the secondary market then rise above the preset prices. In contrast, surpluses occur when the preset prices happen to exceed the equilibrium prices.

Appendix Questions Mc Graw Hill connect ECONOMICS

1. Why are shortages or surpluses more likely with preset prices, such as those on tickets, than flexible prices, such as those on gasoline? **LO6**

2. Most scalping laws make it illegal to sell—but not to buy—tickets at prices above those printed on the tickets. Assuming that is the case, use supply and demand analysis to explain why the equilibrium ticket price in an illegal secondary market tends to be higher than in a legal secondary market. **LO6**

3. Go to the Web site of the Energy Information Administration, **www.eia.doe.gov**, and follow the links to find the current retail price of gasoline. How does the current price of regular gasoline compare with the price a year ago? What must have happened to either supply, demand, or both to explain the observed price change? **LO6**

4. Suppose the supply of apples sharply increases because of perfect weather conditions throughout the growing season. Assuming no change in demand, explain the effect on the equilibrium price and quantity of apples. Explain why quantity demanded increases even though demand does not change. **LO6**

5. Assume the demand for lumber suddenly rises because of a rapid growth of demand for new housing. Assume no change in supply. Why does the equilibrium price of lumber rise? What would happen if the price did not rise under the demand and supply circumstances described? **LO6**

6. Suppose both the demand for olives and the supply of olives decline by equal amounts over some time period. Use graphical analysis to show the effect on equilibrium price and quantity. **LO6**

7. Assume that both the supply of bottled water and the demand for bottled water rise during the summer but that supply increases more rapidly than demand. What can you conclude about the directions of the impacts on equilibrium price and equilibrium quantity? **LO6**

Appendix Problems

1. Demand and supply often shift in the retail market for gasoline. Here are two demand curves and two supply curves for gallons of gasoline in the month of May in a small town in Maine. Some of the data are missing. **LO6**

	Quantities Demanded		Quantities Supplied	
Price	D_1	D_2	S_1	S_2
$4.00	5000	7500	9000	9500
___	6000	8000	8000	9000
2.00	___	8500	___	8500
___	___	9000	5000	___

  a. Use the following facts to fill in the missing data in the table. If demand is D_1 and supply is S_1, the equilibrium quantity is 7000 gallons per month. When demand is D_2 and supply is S_1, the equilibrium price is $3.00 per gallon. When demand is D_2 and supply is S_1, there is an excess demand of 4000 gallons per month at a price of $1.00 per gallon. If demand is D_1 and supply is S_2, the equilibrium quantity is 8000 gallons per month.
  b. Compare two equilibriums. In the first, demand is D_1 and supply is S_1. In the second, demand is D_1 and supply is S_2. By how much does the equilibrium quantity change? By how much does the equilibrium price change?
  c. If supply falls from S_2 to S_1 while demand declines from D_2 to D_1, does the equilibrium price rise, fall, or stay the same? What if only supply falls? What if only demand falls?
  d. Suppose that supply is fixed at S_1 and that demand starts at D_1. By how many gallons per month would demand have to increase at each price level such that the equilibrium price per gallon would be $3.00? $4.00?

2. The table below shows two demand schedules for a given style of men's shoe—that is, how many pairs per month will be demanded at various prices at a men's clothing store in Seattle called Stromnord.

	D_1	D_2
Price	**Quantity Demanded**	**Quantity Demanded**
$75	53	13
70	60	15
65	68	18
60	77	22
55	87	27

Suppose that Stromnord has exactly 65 pairs of this style of shoe in inventory at the start of the month of July and will not receive any more pairs of this style until at least August 1. **LO6**
  a. If demand is D_1, what is the lowest price that Stromnord can charge so that it will not run out of this model of shoe in the month of July? What if demand is D_2?
  b. If the price of shoes is set at $75 for both July and August and demand will be D_2 in July and D_1 in August, how many pairs of shoes should Stromnord order if it wants to end the month of August with exactly zero pairs of shoes in its inventory? What if the price is set at $55 for both months?

3. Use the table below to answer the questions that follow: **LO6**
  a. If this table reflects the supply of and demand for tickets to a particular World Cup soccer game, what is the stadium capacity?
  b. If the preset ticket price is $45, would we expect to see a secondary market for tickets? Would the price of a ticket in the secondary market be higher than, the same as, or lower than the price in the primary (original) market?
  c. Suppose for some other World Cup game the quantity of tickets demanded is 20,000 lower at each ticket price than shown in the table. If the ticket price remains $45, would the event be a sellout?

Quantity Demanded, Thousands	Price	Quantity Supplied, Thousands
80	$25	60
75	35	60
70	45	60
65	55	60
60	65	60
55	75	60
50	85	60

4

Elasticity

In this chapter we extend Chapter 3's discussion of demand and supply by explaining *elasticity,* an extremely important concept that helps us answer such questions as: Why do buyers of some products (for example, ocean cruises) respond to price increases by substantially reducing their purchases while buyers of other products (say, gasoline) respond by only slightly cutting back their purchases? Why do higher market prices for some products (for example, chicken) cause producers to greatly increase their output while price rises for other products (say, gold) cause only limited increases in output? Why does the demand for some products (for example, books) rise a great deal when household income increases while the demand for other products (say, milk) rises just a little?

Elasticity extends our understanding of markets by letting us know the degree to which changes in prices and incomes affect supply and demand. Sometimes the responses are substantial, other times minimal or even nonexistent. But by knowing what to expect, businesses and the government can do a better job in deciding what to produce, how much to charge, and, surprisingly, what items to tax.

Price Elasticity of Demand

The law of demand tells us that, other things equal, consumers will buy more of a product when its price declines and less when its price increases. But how much more or less will they buy? The amount varies from product to product and over different price ranges for the same product. It also may vary over time. And such variations matter. For example, a firm contemplating a price hike will want to know how consumers will respond. If they remain highly loyal and continue to buy, the firm's revenue will rise. But if consumers defect en masse to other sellers or other products, the firm's revenue will tumble.

The responsiveness (or sensitivity) of consumers to a price change is measured by a product's **price elasticity of demand.** For some products—for example, restaurant meals—consumers are highly responsive to price changes. Modest price changes cause very large changes in the quantity purchased. Economists say that the demand for such products is *relatively elastic* or simply *elastic.*

> **ORIGIN OF THE IDEA**
>
> **O 4.1**
>
> Price elasticity of demand

For other products—for example, toothpaste—consumers pay much less attention to price changes. Substantial price changes cause only small changes in the amount purchased. The demand for such products is *relatively inelastic* or simply *inelastic.*

The Price-Elasticity Coefficient and Formula

Economists measure the degree to which demand is price elastic or inelastic with the coefficient E_d, defined as

$$E_d = \frac{\text{percentage change in quantity demanded of product X}}{\text{percentage change in price of product X}}$$

The percentage changes in the equation are calculated by dividing the *change* in quantity demanded by the original quantity demanded and by dividing the *change* in price by the original price. So we can restate the formula as

$$E_d = \frac{\dfrac{\text{change in quantity demanded of X}}{\text{original quantity demanded of X}}}{\dfrac{\text{change in price of X}}{\text{original price of X}}}$$

Using Averages Unfortunately, an annoying problem arises in computing the price-elasticity coefficient. A price change from, say, $4 to $5 along a demand curve is a 25 percent (= $1/$4) increase, but the opposite price change from $5 to $4 along the same curve is a 20 percent (= $1/$5) decrease. Which percentage change in price should we use in the denominator to compute the price-elasticity coefficient? And when quantity changes, for example, from 10 to 20, it is a 100 percent (=10/10) increase. But when quantity falls from 20 to 10 along the identical demand curve, it is a 50 percent (=10/20) decrease. Should we use 100 percent or 50 percent in the numerator of the elasticity formula? Elasticity should be the same whether price rises or falls!

The simplest solution to the problem is to use the **midpoint formula** for calculating elasticity. This formula simply averages the two prices and the two quantities as the reference points for computing the percentages. That is,

$$E_d = \frac{\text{change in quantity}}{\text{sum of quantities}/2} \div \frac{\text{change in price}}{\text{sum of prices}/2}$$

For the same $5–$4 price range, the price reference is $4.50 [= ($5 + $4)/2], and for the same 10–20 quantity range, the quantity reference is 15 units [= (10 + 20)/2]. The percentage change in price is now $1/$4.50, or about 22 percent, and the percentage change in quantity is $\frac{10}{15}$, or about 67 percent. So E_d is about 3. This solution eliminates the "up versus down" problem. All the price-elasticity coefficients that follow are calculated using this midpoint formula.

> **WORKED PROBLEMS**
>
> **W 4.1**
>
> Elasticity of demand

Using Percentages Why use percentages rather than absolute amounts in measuring consumer responsiveness? There are two reasons.

First, if we use absolute changes, the choice of units will arbitrarily affect our impression of buyer responsiveness. To illustrate: If the price of a bag of popcorn at the local softball game is reduced from $3 to $2 and consumers increase their purchases from 60 to 100 bags, it will seem that consumers are quite sensitive to price changes and therefore that demand is elastic. After all, a price change of 1 unit has caused a change in the amount demanded of 40 units. But by changing the monetary unit from dollars to pennies (why not?), we find that a price change of 100 units (pennies) causes a quantity change of 40 units. This may falsely lead us to believe that demand is inelastic. We avoid this problem by using percentage changes. This particular price decline is the same whether we measure it in dollars or pennies.

Second, by using percentages, we can correctly compare consumer responsiveness to changes in the prices of different products. It makes little sense to compare the effects on quantity demanded of (1) a $1 increase in the price of a $10,000 used car with (2) a $1 increase in the price of a $1 soft drink. Here the price of the used car has increased by .01 percent while the price of the soft drink is up by 100 percent. We can more sensibly compare the consumer responsiveness to price increases by using some common percentage increase in price for both.

Elimination of Minus Sign

We know from the downsloping demand curve that price and quantity demanded are inversely related. Thus, the price-elasticity coefficient of demand E_d will always be a negative number. As an example, if price declines, then quantity demanded will increase. This means that the numerator in our formula will be positive and the denominator negative, yielding a negative E_d. For an increase in price, the numerator will be negative but the denominator positive, again yielding a negative E_d.

Economists usually ignore the minus sign and simply present the absolute value of the elasticity coefficient to avoid an ambiguity that might otherwise arise. It can be confusing to say that an E_d of −4 is greater than one of −2. This possible confusion is avoided when we say an E_d of 4 reveals greater elasticity than one of 2. So, in what follows, we ignore the minus sign in the coefficient of price elasticity of demand and show only the absolute value. Incidentally, the ambiguity does not arise with supply because price and quantity supplied are positively related. All elasticity of supply coefficients therefore are positive numbers.

Interpretations of E_d

We can interpret the coefficient of price elasticity of demand as follows.

Elastic Demand

Demand is **elastic** if a specific percentage change in price results in a larger percentage change in quantity demanded. In such cases, E_d will be greater than 1. Example: Suppose that a 2 percent decline in the price of cut flowers results in a 4 percent increase in quantity demanded. Then demand for cut flowers is elastic and

$$E_d = \frac{.04}{.02} = 2$$

Inelastic Demand

If a specific percentage change in price produces a smaller percentage change in quantity demanded, demand is **inelastic**. In such cases, E_d will be less than 1. Example: Suppose that a 2 percent decline in

the price of coffee leads to only a 1 percent increase in quantity demanded. Then demand is inelastic and

$$E_d = \frac{.01}{.02} = .5$$

Unit Elasticity

The case separating elastic and inelastic demands occurs where a percentage change in price and the resulting percentage change in quantity demanded are the same. Example: Suppose that a 2 percent drop in the price of chocolate causes a 2 percent increase in quantity demanded. This special case is termed **unit elasticity** because E_d is exactly 1, or unity. In this example,

$$E_d = \frac{.02}{.02} = 1$$

Extreme Cases

When we say demand is "inelastic," we do not mean that consumers are completely unresponsive to a price change. In that extreme situation, where a price change results in no change whatsoever in the quantity demanded, economists say that demand is **perfectly inelastic**. The price-elasticity coefficient is zero because there is no response to a change in price. Approximate examples include an acute diabetic's demand for insulin or an addict's demand for heroin. A line parallel to the vertical axis, such as D_1 in Figure 4.1a, shows perfectly inelastic demand graphically.

Conversely, when we say demand is "elastic," we do not mean that consumers are completely responsive to a price change. In that extreme situation, where a small price reduction causes buyers to increase their purchases from zero to all they can obtain, the elasticity coefficient is infinite ($= \infty$) and economists say demand is **perfectly elastic**. A line parallel to the horizontal axis, such as D_2 in Figure 4.1b, shows perfectly elastic demand. You will see in Chapter 8 that such a demand applies to a firm—say, a mining firm—that is selling its output in a purely competitive market.

The Total-Revenue Test

The importance of elasticity for firms relates to the effect of price changes on total revenue and thus on profits (= total revenue minus total costs).

Total revenue (TR) is the total amount the seller receives from the sale of a product in a particular time period; it is calculated by multiplying the product price (P) by the quantity sold (Q). In equation form:

$$TR = P \times Q$$

Graphically, total revenue is represented by the $P \times Q$ rectangle lying below a point on a demand curve. At point

FIGURE 4.1 Perfectly inelastic and elastic demands.
Demand curve D_1 in (a) represents perfectly inelastic demand ($E_d = 0$). A price increase will result in no change in quantity demanded. Demand curve D_2 in (b) represents perfectly elastic demand. A price increase will cause quantity demanded to decline from an infinite amount to zero ($E_d = \infty$).

(a)
Perfectly inelastic demand

(b)
Perfectly elastic demand

CONSIDER THIS . . .

A Bit of a Stretch

The following analogy might help you remember the distinction between "elastic" and "inelastic." Imagine two objects—one an Ace elastic bandage used to wrap injured joints and the other a relatively firm rubber tie-down (rubber strap) used for securing items for transport. The Ace bandage stretches a great deal when pulled with a particular force; the rubber tie-down stretches some, but not a lot.

Similar differences occur for the quantity demanded of various products when their prices change. For some products, a price change causes a substantial "stretch" of quantity demanded. When this stretch in percentage terms exceeds the percentage change in price, demand is elastic. For other products, quantity demanded stretches very little in response to the price change. When this stretch in percentage terms is less than the percentage change in price, demand is inelastic.

In summary:
- Elastic demand displays considerable "quantity stretch" (as with the Ace bandage).
- Inelastic demand displays relatively little "quantity stretch" (as with the rubber tie-down).

And through extension:
- Perfectly elastic demand has infinite quantity stretch.
- Perfectly inelastic demand has zero quantity stretch.

a in Figure 4.2a, for example, price is $2 and quantity demanded is 10 units. So total revenue is $20 (= $2 × 10), shown by the rectangle composed of the yellow and green areas under the demand curve. We know from basic geometry that the area of a rectangle is found by multiplying one side by the other. Here, one side is "price" ($2) and the other is "quantity demanded" (10 units).

Total revenue and the price elasticity of demand are related. In fact, the easiest way to infer whether demand is elastic or inelastic is to employ the **total-revenue test.** Here is the test: Note what happens to total revenue when price changes. If total revenue changes in the opposite direction from price, demand is elastic. If total revenue changes in the same direction as price, demand is inelastic. If total revenue does not change when price changes, demand is unit-elastic.

Elastic Demand

If demand is elastic, a decrease in price will increase total revenue. Even though a lesser price is received per unit, enough additional units are sold to more than make up for the lower price. For an example, look at demand curve D_1 in Figure 4.2a. We have already established that at point *a*, total revenue is $20 (= $2 × 10), shown as the yellow plus green area. If the price

declines from $2 to $1 (point *b*), the quantity demanded becomes 40 units and total revenue is $40 (= $1 × 40). As a result of the price decline, total revenue has increased from $20 to $40. Total revenue has increased in this case because the $1 decline in price applies to 10 units, with a consequent revenue loss of $10 (the yellow area). But 30 more units are sold at $1 each, resulting in a revenue gain of $30 (the blue area). Visually, the gain of the blue area clearly exceeds the loss of the yellow area. As indicated, the overall result is a net increase in total revenue of $20 (= $30 − $10).

The analysis is reversible: If demand is elastic, a price increase will reduce total revenue. The revenue gained on the higher-priced units will be more than offset by the

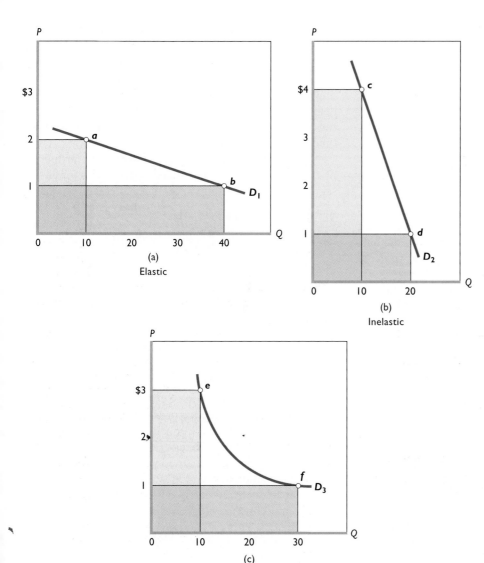

FIGURE 4.2 **The total-revenue test for price elasticity.** (a) Price declines from $2 to $1, and total revenue increases from $20 to $40. So demand is elastic. The gain in revenue (blue area) exceeds the loss of revenue (yellow area). (b) Price declines from $4 to $1, and total revenue falls from $40 to $20. So, demand is inelastic. The gain in revenue (blue area) is less than the loss of revenue (yellow area). (c) Price declines from $3 to $1, and total revenue does not change. Demand is unit-elastic. The gain in revenue (blue area) equals the loss of revenue (yellow area).

revenue lost from the lower quantity sold. Bottom line: Other things equal, when price and total revenue move in opposite directions, demand is elastic. E_d is greater than 1, meaning the percentage change in quantity demanded is greater than the percentage change in price.

Inelastic Demand If demand is inelastic, a price decrease will reduce total revenue. The increase in sales will not fully offset the decline in revenue per unit, and total revenue will decline. To see this, look at demand curve D_2 in Figure 4.2b. At point *c* on the curve, price is $4 and quantity demanded is 10. Thus total revenue is $40, shown by the combined yellow and green rectangle. If the price drops to $1 (point *d*), total revenue declines to $20, which

obviously is less than $40. Total revenue has declined because the loss of revenue (the yellow area) from the lower unit price is larger than the gain in revenue (the blue area) from the accompanying increase in sales. Price has fallen, and total revenue has also declined.

Our analysis is again reversible: If demand is inelastic, a price increase will increase total revenue. So, other things equal, when price and total revenue move in the same direction, demand is inelastic. E_d is less than 1, meaning the percentage change in quantity demanded is less than the percentage change in price.

> **WORKED PROBLEMS**
>
> **W 4.2**
>
> Total-revenue test

Unit Elasticity In the special case of unit elasticity, an increase or a decrease in price leaves total revenue unchanged. The loss in revenue from a lower unit price is exactly offset by the gain in revenue from the accompanying increase in sales. Conversely, the gain in revenue from a higher unit price is exactly offset by the revenue loss associated with the accompanying decline in the amount demanded.

In Figure 4.2c (demand curve D_3) we find that at the price of $3, 10 units will be sold, yielding total revenue of $30. At the lower $1 price, a total of 30 units will be sold, again resulting in $30 of total revenue. The $2 price reduction causes the loss of revenue shown by the yellow area, but this is exactly offset by the revenue gain shown by the blue area. Total revenue does not change. In fact, that would be true for all price changes along this particular curve.

Other things equal, when price changes and total revenue remains constant, demand is unit-elastic (or unitary). E_d is 1, meaning the percentage change in quantity equals the percentage change in price.

Price Elasticity along a Linear Demand Curve

Now a major confession! Although the demand curves depicted in Figure 4.2 nicely illustrate the total-revenue test for elasticity, two of the graphs involve specific movements along linear (straight-line) demand curves. That presents no problem for explaining the total-revenue test. However, you need to know that elasticity typically varies over different price ranges of the same demand curve. (The exception is the curve in Figure 4.2c. Elasticity is 1 along the entire curve.)

Table 4.1 and Figure 4.3 demonstrate that elasticity typically varies over different price ranges of the same demand schedule or curve. Plotting the hypothetical data for movie tickets shown in columns 1 and 2 of Table 4.1 yields demand curve D in Figure 4.3. Observe that the demand curve is linear. But we see from column 3 of the table that the price elasticity coefficient for this demand curve declines as we move from higher to lower prices. For all downsloping straight-line and most other demand curves, demand is more price-elastic toward the upper left (here, the $5–$8 price range of D) than toward the lower right (here, the $4–$1 price range of D).

This is the consequence of the arithmetic properties of the elasticity measure. Specifically, in the upper-left segment of the demand curve, the percentage change in quantity is large because the original reference quantity is small. Similarly, the percentage change in price is small in that segment because the original reference price is large. The relatively large percentage change in quantity divided by the relatively small change in price yields a large E_d—an elastic demand.

> **INTERACTIVE GRAPHS**
>
> G 4.1
>
> Elasticity and revenue

The reverse holds true for the lower-right segment of the demand curve. Here the percentage change in quantity is small because the original reference quantity is large; similarly, the percentage change in price is large because the original reference price is small. The relatively small percentage change in quantity divided by the relatively large percentage change in price results in a small E_d—an inelastic demand.

The demand curve in Figure 4.3a also illustrates that the slope of a demand curve—its flatness or steepness—is not a sound basis for judging elasticity. The catch is that the slope of the curve is computed from *absolute* changes in price and quantity, while elasticity involves *relative* or *percentage* changes in price and quantity. The demand curve

TABLE 4.1 Price Elasticity of Demand for Movie Tickets as Measured by the Elasticity Coefficient and the Total-Revenue Test

(1) Total Quantity of Tickets Demanded per Week, Thousands	(2) Price per Ticket	(3) Elasticity Coefficient (E_d)	(4) Total Revenue, (1) × (2)	(5) Total-Revenue Test
1	$8		$ 8000	
		5.00		Elastic
2	7		14,000	
		2.60		Elastic
3	6		18,000	
		1.57		Elastic
4	5		20,000	
		1.00		Unit-elastic
5	4		20,000	
		0.64		Inelastic
6	3		18,000	
		0.38		Inelastic
7	2		14,000	
		0.20		Inelastic
8	1		8000	

FIGURE 4.3 The relation between price elasticity of demand for movie tickets and total revenue. Demand curve *D* in (a) is based on Table 4.1 and is marked to show that the hypothetical weekly demand for movie tickets is elastic at higher price ranges and inelastic at lower price ranges. The total-revenue curve TR in (b) is derived from demand curve *D*. When price falls and TR increases, demand is elastic; when price falls and TR is unchanged, demand is unit-elastic; and when price falls and TR declines, demand is inelastic.

(a)
Demand curve

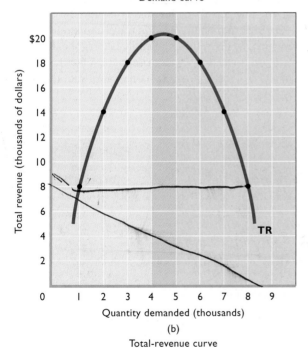

(b)
Total-revenue curve

Price Elasticity and the Total-Revenue Curve

In Figure 4.3b we plot the total revenue per week to the theater owner that corresponds to each price-quantity combination indicated along demand curve *D* in Figure 4.3a. The price–quantity-demanded combination represented by point *a* on the demand curve yields total revenue of $8000 (= $8×1000 tickets). In Figure 4.3b, we plot this $8000 amount vertically at 1 unit (1000 tickets) demanded. Similarly, the price–quantity-demanded combination represented by point *b* in the upper panel yields total revenue of $14,000 (= $7×2000 tickets). This amount is graphed vertically at 2 units (2000 tickets) demanded in the lower panel. The ultimate result of such graphing is total-revenue curve TR, which first slopes upward, then reaches a maximum, and finally turns downward.

Comparison of curves *D* and TR sharply focuses the relationship between elasticity and total revenue. Lowering the ticket price in the elastic range of demand—for example, from $8 to $5—increases total revenue. Conversely, increasing the ticket price in that range reduces total revenue. In both cases, price and total revenue change in opposite directions, confirming that demand is elastic.

The $5–$4 price range of demand curve *D* reflects unit elasticity. When price either decreases from $5 to $4 or increases from $4 to $5, total revenue remains $20,000. In both cases, price has changed and total revenue has remained constant, confirming that demand is unit-elastic when we consider these particular price changes.

In the inelastic range of demand curve *D*, lowering the price—for example, from $4 to $1—decreases total revenue, as shown in Figure 4.3b. Raising the price boosts total revenue. In both cases, price and total revenue move in the same direction, confirming that demand is inelastic.

Table 4.2 summarizes the characteristics of price elasticity of demand. You should review it carefully.

Determinants of Price Elasticity of Demand

We cannot say just what will determine the price elasticity of demand in each individual situation. However, the following generalizations are often helpful.

Substitutability Generally, the larger the number of substitute goods that are available, the greater the price elasticity of demand. Various brands of candy bars are generally substitutable for one another, making the demand for one brand of candy bar, say Snickers, highly elastic. Toward the other extreme, the demand for tooth repair (or

in Figure 4.3a is linear, which by definition means that the slope is constant throughout. But we have demonstrated that such a curve is elastic in its high-price ($8–$5) range and inelastic in its low-price ($4–$1) range.

TABLE 4.2 Price Elasticity of Demand: A Summary

Absolute Value of Elasticity Coefficient	Demand Is:	Description	Impact on Total Revenue of a:	
			Price Increase	**Price Decrease**
Greater than 1 ($E_d > 1$)	Elastic or relatively elastic	Quantity demanded changes by a larger percentage than does price	Total revenue decreases	Total revenue increases
Equal to 1 ($E_d = 1$)	Unit- or unitary elastic	Quantity demanded changes by the same percentage as does price	Total revenue is unchanged	Total revenue is unchanged
Less than 1 ($E_d < 1$)	Inelastic or relatively inelastic	Quantity demanded changes by a smaller percentage than does price	Total revenue increases	Total revenue decreases

tooth pulling) is quite inelastic because there simply are no close substitutes when those procedures are required.

The elasticity of demand for a product depends on how narrowly the product is defined. Demand for Reebok sneakers is more elastic than is the overall demand for shoes. Many other brands are readily substitutable for Reebok sneakers, but there are few, if any, good substitutes for shoes.

Proportion of Income Other things equal, the higher the price of a good relative to consumers' incomes, the greater the price elasticity of demand. A 10 percent increase in the price of low-priced pencils or chewing gum amounts to a few more pennies relative to a consumer's income, and quantity demanded will probably decline only slightly. Thus, price elasticity for such low-priced items tends to be low. But a 10 percent increase in the price of relatively high-priced automobiles or housing means additional expenditures of perhaps $3000 or $20,000, respectively. These price increases are significant fractions of the annual incomes and budgets of most families, and quantities demanded will likely diminish significantly. The price elasticities for such items tend to be high.

Luxuries versus Necessities In general, the more that a good is considered to be a "luxury" rather than a "necessity," the greater is the price elasticity of demand. Electricity is generally regarded as a necessity; it is difficult to get along without it. A price increase will not significantly reduce the amount of lighting and power used in a household. (Note the very low price-elasticity coefficient of this good in Table 4.3.) An extreme case: A person does not decline an operation for acute appendicitis because the physician's fee has just gone up.

On the other hand, vacation travel and jewelry are luxuries, which, by definition, can easily be forgone. If the prices of vacation travel and jewelry rise, a consumer need not buy them and will suffer no great hardship without them.

TABLE 4.3 Selected Price Elasticities of Demand

Product or Service	Coefficient of Price Elasticity of Demand (E_d)	Product or Service	Coefficient of Price Elasticity of Demand (E_d)
Newspapers	.10	Milk	.63
Electricity (household)	.13	Household appliances	.63
Bread	.15	Liquor	.70
Major League Baseball tickets	.23	Movies	.87
Telephone service	.26	Beer	.90
Cigarettes	.25	Shoes	.91
Sugar	.30	Motor vehicles	1.14
Medical care	.31	Beef	1.27
Eggs	.32	China, glassware, tableware	1.54
Legal services	.37	Residential land	1.60
Automobile repair	.40	Restaurant meals	2.27
Clothing	.49	Lamb and mutton	2.65
Gasoline	.60	Fresh peas	2.83

Source: Compiled from numerous studies and sources reporting price elasticity of demand.

What about the demand for a common product like salt? It is highly inelastic on three counts: Few good substitutes are available; salt is a negligible item in the family budget; and it is a "necessity" rather than a luxury.

Time Generally, product demand is more elastic the longer the time period under consideration. Consumers often need time to adjust to changes in prices. For example, when the price of a product rises, time is needed to find and experiment with other products to see if they are acceptable. Consumers may not immediately reduce their purchases very much when the price of beef rises by 10 percent, but in time they may shift to chicken, pork, or fish.

Another consideration is product durability. Studies show that "short-run" demand for gasoline is more inelastic ($E_d = .2$) than is "long-run" demand ($E_d = .7$). In the short run, people are "stuck" with their present cars and trucks, but with rising gasoline prices they eventually replace them with smaller, more fuel-efficient vehicles. They also switch to mass transit where it is available.

Table 4.3 shows estimated price-elasticity coefficients for a number of products. Each reflects some combination of the elasticity determinants just discussed.

Applications of Price Elasticity of Demand

The concept of price elasticity of demand has great practical significance, as the following examples suggest.

Large Crop Yields The demand for most farm products is highly inelastic; E_d is perhaps .20 or .25. As a result, increases in the supply of farm products arising from a good growing season or from increased productivity tend to depress both the prices of farm products and the total revenues (incomes) of farmers. For farmers as a group, the inelastic demand for their products means that large crop yields may be undesirable. For policymakers it means that achieving the goal of higher total farm income requires that farm output be restricted.

Excise Taxes The government pays attention to elasticity of demand when it selects goods and services on which to levy excise taxes. If a $1 tax is levied on a product and 10,000 units are sold, tax revenue will be $10,000 (= $1 × 10,000 units sold). If the government raises the tax to $1.50 but the higher price that results reduces sales to 4000 because of elastic demand, tax revenue will decline to $6000 (= $1.50 × 4000 units sold). Because a higher tax on a product with elastic demand will bring in less tax revenue, legislatures tend to seek out products that have inelastic demand—such as liquor, gasoline, and cigarettes—when levying excises. In fact, the Federal government, in its effort to reduce the budget deficit, increased taxes on those very categories of goods in 1991.

Decriminalization of Illegal Drugs In recent years proposals to legalize drugs have been widely debated. Proponents contend that drugs should be treated like alcohol; they should be made legal for adults and regulated for purity and potency. The current war on drugs, it is argued, has been unsuccessful, and the associated costs—including enlarged police forces, the construction of more prisons, an overburdened court system, and untold human costs—have increased markedly. Legalization would allegedly reduce drug trafficking significantly by taking the profit out of it. Crack cocaine and heroin, for example, are cheap to produce and could be sold at low prices in legal markets. Because the demand of addicts is highly inelastic, the amounts consumed at the lower prices would increase only modestly. Addicts' total expenditures for cocaine and heroin would decline, and so would the street crime that finances those expenditures.

Opponents of legalization say that the overall demand for cocaine and heroin is far more elastic than proponents think. In addition to the inelastic demand of addicts, there is another market segment whose demand is relatively elastic. This segment consists of the occasional users or "dabblers," who use hard drugs when their prices are low but who abstain or substitute, say, alcohol when their prices are high. Thus, the lower prices associated with the legalization of hard drugs would increase consumption by dabblers. Also, removal of the legal prohibitions against using drugs might make drug use more socially acceptable, increasing the demand for cocaine and heroin.

Many economists predict that the legalization of cocaine and heroin would reduce street prices by up to 60 percent, depending on if and how much they were taxed. According to an important study, price declines of that size would increase the number of occasional users of heroin by 54 percent and the number of occasional users of cocaine by 33 percent. The total quantity of heroin demanded would rise by an estimated 100 percent, and the quantity of cocaine demanded would rise by 50 percent.[1] Moreover, many existing and first-time dabblers might in time become addicts. The overall result, say the opponents of legalization, would be higher social costs, possibly including an increase in street crime.

---

[1]Henry Saffer and Frank Chaloupka, "The Demand for Illegal Drugs," *Economic Inquiry,* July 1999, pp. 401–411.

QUICK REVIEW 4.1

- The price elasticity of demand coefficient E_d is the ratio of the percentage change in quantity demanded to the percentage change in price. The *averages* of the two prices and two quantities are used as the base references in calculating the percentage changes.

- When E_d is greater than 1, demand is elastic; when E_d is less than 1, demand is inelastic; when E_d is equal to 1, demand is of unit elasticity.

- When price changes, total revenue will change in the opposite direction if demand is price-elastic, in the same direction if demand is price-inelastic, and not at all if demand is unit-elastic.

- Demand is typically elastic in the high-price (low-quantity) range of the demand curve and inelastic in the low-price (high-quantity) range of the demand curve.

- Price elasticity of demand is greater (a) the larger the number of substitutes available; (b) the higher the price of a product relative to one's budget; (c) the greater the extent to which the product is a luxury; and (d) the longer the time period involved.

Price Elasticity of Supply

ORIGIN OF THE IDEA

O 4.2

Price elasticity of supply

The concept of price elasticity also applies to supply. If the quantity supplied by producers is relatively responsive to price changes, supply is elastic. If it is relatively insensitive to price changes, supply is inelastic.

We measure the degree of price elasticity or inelasticity of supply with the coefficient E_s, defined almost like E_d except that we substitute "percentage change in quantity supplied" for "percentage change in quantity demanded":

$$E_s = \frac{\text{percentage change in quantity supplied of product X}}{\text{percentage change in price of product X}}$$

For reasons explained earlier, the averages, or midpoints, of the before and after quantities supplied and the before and after prices are used as reference points for the percentage changes. Suppose an increase in the price of a good from \$4 to \$6 increases the quantity supplied from 10 units to 14 units. The percentage change in price would be $\frac{2}{5}$, or 40 percent, and the percentage change in quantity would be $\frac{4}{12}$, or 33 percent. Consequently,

$$E_s = \frac{.33}{.40} = .83$$

In this case, supply is inelastic because the price-elasticity coefficient is less than 1. If E_s is greater than 1, supply is elastic. If it is equal to 1, supply is unit-elastic. Also, E_s is never negative, since price and quantity supplied are directly related. Thus, there are no minus signs to drop, as was necessary with elasticity of demand.

The degree of **price elasticity of supply** depends on how easily—and therefore quickly—producers can shift resources between alternative uses. The easier and more rapidly producers can shift resources between alternative uses, the greater the price elasticity of supply. Take the case of Christmas trees. A firm's response to, say, an increase in the price of trees depends on its ability to shift resources from the production of other products (whose prices we assume remain constant) to the production of trees. And shifting resource takes time: The longer the time, the greater the "shiftability." So we can expect a greater response, and therefore greater elasticity of supply, the longer a firm has to adjust to a price change.

In analyzing the impact of time on elasticity, economists distinguish among the immediate market period, the short run, and the long run.

Price Elasticity of Supply: The Market Period

The **market period** is the period that occurs when the time immediately after a change in market price is too short for producers to respond with a change in quantity supplied. Suppose the owner of a small farm brings to market one truckload of tomatoes that is the entire season's output. The supply curve for the tomatoes is perfectly inelastic (vertical); the farmer will sell the truckload whether the price is high or low. Why? Because the farmer can offer only one truckload of tomatoes even if the price of tomatoes is much higher than anticipated. The farmer might like to offer more tomatoes, but tomatoes cannot be produced overnight. Another full growing season is needed to respond to a higher-than-expected price by producing more than one truckload. Similarly, because the product is perishable, the farmer cannot withhold it from the market. If the price is lower than anticipated, the farmer will still sell the entire truckload.

The farmer's costs of production, incidentally, will not enter into this decision to sell. Though the price of tomatoes may fall far short of production costs, the farmer will nevertheless sell everything he brought to market to avoid a total loss through spoilage. In the market period, both the supply of tomatoes and the quantity of tomatoes supplied are fixed. The farmer offers only one truckload no matter how high or low the price.

FIGURE 4.4 Time and the elasticity of supply. The greater the amount of time producers have to adjust to a change in demand, here from D_1 to D_2, the greater will be their output response. In the immediate market period (a) there is insufficient time to change output, and so supply is perfectly inelastic. In the short run (b) plant capacity is fixed, but changing the intensity of its use can alter output; supply is therefore more elastic. In the long run (c) all desired adjustments, including changes in plant capacity, can be made, and supply becomes still more elastic.

(a) Immediate market period

(b) Short run

(c) Long run

Figure 4.4a shows the farmer's vertical supply curve during the market period. Supply is perfectly inelastic because the farmer does not have time to respond to a change in demand, say, from D_1 to D_2. The resulting price increase from P_0 to P_m simply determines which buyers get the fixed quantity supplied; it elicits no increase in output.

However, not all supply curves are perfectly inelastic immediately after a price change. If the product is not perishable and the price rises, producers may choose to increase quantity supplied by drawing down their inventories of unsold, stored goods. This will cause the market supply curve to attain some positive slope. For our tomato farmer, the market period may be a full growing season; for producers of goods that can be inexpensively stored, there may be no market period at all.

Price Elasticity of Supply: The Short Run

The **short run** in microeconomics is a period of time too short to change plant capacity but long enough to use the fixed-sized plant more or less intensively. In the short run, our farmer's plant (land and farm machinery) is fixed. But he does have time in the short run to cultivate tomatoes more intensively by applying more labor and more fertilizer and pesticides to the crop. The result is a somewhat greater output in response to a presumed increase in demand; this greater output is reflected in a more elastic supply of tomatoes, as shown by S_s in Figure 4.4b. Note now that the increase in demand from D_1 to D_2 is met by an increase in quantity (from Q_0 to Q_s), so there is a smaller price adjustment (from P_0 to P_s) than would be the case in the market period. The equilibrium price is therefore lower in the short run than in the market period.

Price Elasticity of Supply: The Long Run

The **long run** in microeconomics is a time period long enough for firms to adjust their plant sizes and for new firms to enter (or existing firms to leave) the industry. In the "tomato industry," for example, our farmer has time to acquire additional land and buy more machinery and equipment. Furthermore, other farmers may, over time, be attracted to tomato farming by the increased demand and higher price. Such adjustments create a larger supply response, as represented by the more elastic supply curve S_L in Figure 4.4c. The outcome is a smaller price rise (P_0 to P_1) and a larger output increase (Q_0 to Q_1) in response to the increase in demand from D_1 to D_2.

There is no total-revenue test for elasticity of supply. Supply shows a positive or direct relationship between price and amount supplied; the supply curve is upsloping. Regardless of the degree of elasticity or inelasticity, price and total revenue always move together.

Applications of Price Elasticity of Supply

The idea of price elasticity of supply has widespread applicability, as suggested by the following examples.

Antiques and Reproductions *Antiques Roadshow* is a popular PBS television program in which people bring antiques to a central location for appraisal by experts. Some people are pleased to learn that their old piece of furniture or funky folk art is worth a large amount, say, $30,000 or more.

The high price of an antique results from strong demand and limited, highly inelastic supply. Because a genuine antique can no longer be reproduced, its quantity

Word Elasticity and Pricing Power:
Why Different Consumers Pay Different Prices

Firms and Nonprofit Institutions Often Recognize and Exploit Differences in Price Elasticity of Demand.

All the buyers of a product traded in a highly competitive market pay the same market price for the product, regardless of their individual price elasticities of demand. If the price rises, Jones may have an elastic demand and greatly reduce her purchases. Green may have a unit-elastic demand and reduce his purchases less than Jones. Lopez may have an inelastic demand and hardly curtail his purchases at all. But all three consumers will pay the single higher price regardless of their respective demand elasticities.

In later chapters we will find that not all sellers must passively accept a "one-for-all" price. Some firms have "market power" or "pricing power" that allows them to set their product prices in their best interests. For some goods and services, firms may find it advantageous to determine differences in price elasticity of demand and then charge different prices to different buyers.

It is extremely difficult to tailor prices for each customer on the basis of price elasticity of demand, but it is relatively easy to observe differences in group elasticities. Consider airline tickets. Business travelers generally have inelastic demand for air travel. Because their time is highly valuable, they do not see slower modes of transportation as realistic substitutes. Also, their employers pay for their tickets as part of their business expenses. In contrast, leisure travelers tend to have elastic demand. They have the option to drive rather than fly or to simply not travel at all. They also pay for their tickets out of their own pockets and thus are more sensitive to price.

Airlines recognize the difference between the groups in terms of price elasticity of demand and charge business travelers more than leisure travelers. To accomplish that, they have to dissuade business travelers from buying the less expensive round-trip tickets aimed at leisure travelers. One way to do this is by placing restrictions on the lower-priced tickets. For instance, airlines have at times made such tickets nonrefundable, required at least a 2-week advance purchase, and required Saturday-night stays. These restrictions chase off most business travelers who engage in last-minute travel and want to be home for the weekend. As a result, a business traveler often pays hundreds of dollars more for a ticket than a leisure traveler on the same plane.

supplied either does not rise or rises only slightly as price goes up. The higher price might prompt the discovery of a few more of the remaining originals and thus add to the quantity available for sale, but this quantity response is usually quite small. So the supply of antiques and other collectibles tends to be inelastic. For one-of-a-kind antiques, the supply is perfectly inelastic.

Factors such as increased population, higher income, and greater enthusiasm for collecting antiques have increased the demand for antiques over time. Because the supply of antiques is limited and inelastic, those increases in demand have greatly boosted the prices of antiques.

Contrast the inelastic supply of original antiques with the elastic supply of modern "made-to-look-old" reproductions. Such faux antiques are quite popular and widely available at furniture stores and knickknack shops. When the demand for reproductions increases, the firms making them simply boost production. Because the supply of reproductions is highly elastic, increased demand raises their prices only slightly.

Volatile Gold Prices The price of gold is quite volatile, sometimes shooting upward one period and plummeting downward the next. The main sources of these fluctuations are shifts in demand interacting with highly inelastic supply. Gold production is a costly and time-consuming process of exploration, mining, and refining. Moreover, the physical availability of gold is highly limited. For both reasons, increases in gold prices do not elicit substantial increases in quantity supplied. Conversely, gold mining is costly to shut down and existing gold bars are expensive to store. Price decreases therefore do not produce large drops in the quantity of gold supplied. In short, the supply of gold is inelastic.

The demand for gold is partly derived from the demand for its uses, such as for jewelry, dental fillings, and coins. But people also demand gold as a speculative financial investment. They increase their demand for gold when they fear general inflation or domestic or international turmoil that might undermine the value of currency and more traditional investments. They reduce

Discounts for children are another example of pricing based on group differences in price elasticity of demand. For many products, children have more elastic demands than adults because children have low budgets, often financed by their parents. Sellers recognize the elasticity difference and price accordingly. The barber spends as much time cutting a child's hair as an adult's but charges the child much less. A child takes up a full seat at the baseball game but pays a lower price than an adult. A child snowboarder occupies the same space on a chairlift as an adult snowboarder but qualifies for a discounted lift ticket.

Finally, consider pricing by colleges and universities. Price elasticity of demand for higher education is greater for prospective students from low-income families than similar students from high-income families. This makes sense because tuition is a much larger proportion of household income for a low-income student or family than for his or her high-income counterpart. Desiring a diverse student body, colleges charge different *net* prices (= tuition *minus* financial aid) to

the two groups on the basis of price elasticity of demand. High-income students pay full tuition, unless they receive merit-based scholarships. Low-income students receive considerable financial aid in addition to merit-based scholarships and, in effect, pay a lower *net* price.

It is common for colleges to announce a large tuition increase and immediately cushion the news by emphasizing that they also are increasing financial aid. In effect, the college is increasing the tuition for students who have inelastic demand by the full amount and raising the *net* tuition of those with elastic demand by some lesser amount or not at all. Through this strategy, colleges boost revenue to cover rising costs while maintaining affordability for a wide range of students.

There are a number of other examples of dual or multiple pricing. All relate directly to price elasticity of demand. We will revisit this topic again in Chapter 10 when we analyze *price discrimination*—charging different prices to different customers for the same product.

their demand when events settle down. Because of the inelastic supply of gold, even relatively small changes in demand produce relatively large changes in price. (This chapter's Web-based question 1 that is posted online provides an Internet source for finding current and past prices of gold.)

Cross Elasticity and Income Elasticity of Demand

Price elasticities measure the responsiveness of the quantity of a product demanded or supplied when its price changes. The consumption of a good also is affected by a change in the price of a related product or by a change in income.

Cross Elasticity of Demand

The **cross elasticity of demand** measures how sensitive consumer purchases of one product (say, X) are to a change in the price of some other product (say, Y). We calculate the coefficient of cross elasticity of demand E_{xy} just as we do the coefficient of simple price elasticity, except that we relate the percentage change in the consumption of X to the percentage change in the price of Y:

$$E_{xy} = \frac{\text{percentage change in quantity demanded of product X}}{\text{percentage change in price of product Y}}$$

This cross-elasticity (or cross-price-elasticity) concept allows us to quantify and more fully understand substitute and complementary goods, introduced in Chapter 3. Unlike price elasticity, we allow the coefficient of cross elasticity of demand to be either positive or negative.

Substitute Goods If cross elasticity of demand is positive, meaning that sales of X move in the same direction as a change in the price of Y, then X and Y are substitute goods. An example is Evian water (X) and Dasani water (Y). An increase in the price of Evian causes consumers to buy more Dasani, resulting in a positive cross elasticity. The larger the positive cross-elasticity coefficient, the greater is the substitutability between the two products.

Complementary Goods When cross elasticity is negative, we know that X and Y "go together"; an increase in the price of one decreases the demand for the other. So the two are complementary goods. For example, a decrease in the price of digital cameras will increase the number of memory sticks purchased. The larger the negative cross-elasticity coefficient, the greater is the complementarity between the two goods.

Independent Goods A zero or near-zero cross elasticity suggests that the two products being considered are unrelated or independent goods. An example is walnuts and plums: We would not expect a change in the price of walnuts to have any effect on purchases of plums, and vice versa.

Application The degree of substitutability of products, measured by the cross-elasticity coefficient, is important to businesses and government. For example, suppose that Coca-Cola is considering whether or not to lower the price of its Sprite brand. Not only will it want to know something about the price elasticity of demand for Sprite (will the price cut increase or decrease total revenue?), but it will also be interested in knowing if the increased sales of Sprite will come at the expense of its Coke brand. How sensitive are the sales of one of its products (Coke) to a change in the price of another of its products (Sprite)? By how much will the increased sales of Sprite "cannibalize" the sales of Coke? A low cross elasticity would indicate that Coke and Sprite are weak substitutes for each other and that a lower price for Sprite would have little effect on Coke sales.

Government also implicitly uses the idea of cross elasticity of demand in assessing whether a proposed merger between two large firms will substantially reduce competition and therefore violate the antitrust laws. For example, the cross elasticity between Coke and Pepsi is high, making them strong substitutes for each other. In addition, Coke and Pepsi together sell about 75 percent of all carbonated cola drinks consumed in the United States. Taken together, the high cross elasticities and the large market shares suggest that the government would likely block a merger between Coke and Pepsi because the merger would substantially lessen competition. In contrast, the cross elasticity between cola and gasoline is low or zero. A merger between Coke and Shell oil company would have a minimal effect on competition. So government would let that merger happen.

Income Elasticity of Demand

Income elasticity of demand measures the degree to which consumers respond to a change in their incomes by buying more or less of a particular good. The coefficient of income elasticity of demand E_i is determined with the formula

$$E_i = \frac{\text{percentage change in quantity demanded}}{\text{percentage change in income}}$$

Normal Goods For most goods, the income-elasticity coefficient E_i is positive, meaning that more of them are demanded as incomes rise. Such goods are called normal or superior goods (and were first described in Chapter 3). But the value of E_i varies greatly among normal goods. For example, income elasticity of demand for automobiles is about +3, while income elasticity for most farm products is only about +.20.

Inferior Goods A negative income-elasticity coefficient designates an inferior good. Retread tires, cabbage, long-distance bus tickets, used clothing, and muscatel wine are likely candidates. Consumers decrease their purchases of inferior goods as incomes rise.

Insights Coefficients of income elasticity of demand provide insights into the economy. For example, when

TABLE 4.4 Cross and Income Elasticities of Demand

Value of Coefficient	Description	Type of Good(s)
Cross elasticity:		
Positive ($E_{wz} > 0$)	Quantity demanded of W changes in same direction as change in price of Z	Substitutes
Negative ($E_{xy} < 0$)	Quantity demanded of X changes in opposite direction from change in price of Y	Complements
Income elasticity:		
Positive ($E_i > 0$)	Quantity demanded of the product changes in same direction as change in income	Normal or superior
Negative ($E_i < 0$)	Quantity demanded of the product changes in opposite direction from change in income	Inferior

recessions (business downturns) occur and incomes fall, income elasticity of demand helps predict which products will decline in demand more rapidly than others.

Products with relatively high income elasticity coefficients, such as automobiles ($E_i = +3$), housing ($E_i = +1.5$), and restaurant meals ($E_i = +1.4$), are generally hit hardest by recessions. Those with low or negative income elasticity coefficients are much less affected. For example, food products prepared at home ($E_i = +.20$) respond relatively little to income fluctuations. When incomes drop, purchases of food (and toothpaste and toilet paper) drop little compared to purchases of movie tickets, luxury vacations, and plasma screen TVs. Products we view as essential tend to have lower income elasticity coefficients than products we view as luxuries. When our incomes fall, we cannot easily eliminate or postpone the purchase of essential products.

In Table 4.4 we provide a convenient synopsis of the cross-elasticity and income-elasticity concepts.

QUICK REVIEW 4.2

- Price elasticity of supply measures the sensitivity of suppliers to changes in the price of a product. The price-elasticity-of-supply coefficient E_s is the ratio of the percentage change in quantity supplied to the percentage change in price. The elasticity of supply varies directly with the amount of time producers have to respond to the price change.

- The cross-elasticity-of-demand coefficient E_{xy} is computed as the percentage change in the quantity demanded of product X divided by the percentage change in the price of product Y. If the cross-elasticity coefficient is positive, the two products are substitutes; if negative, they are complements.

- The income-elasticity coefficient E_i is computed as the percentage change in quantity demanded divided by the percentage change in income. A positive coefficient indicates a normal or superior good. The coefficient is negative for an inferior good.

Summary

1. Price elasticity of demand measures consumer response to price changes. If consumers are relatively sensitive to price changes, demand is elastic. If they are relatively unresponsive to price changes, demand is inelastic.

2. The price-elasticity coefficient E_d measures the degree of elasticity or inelasticity of demand. The coefficient is found by the formula

$$E_d = \frac{\text{percentage change in quantity demanded of X}}{\text{percentage change in price of X}}$$

Economists use the averages of prices and quantities under consideration as reference points in determining percentage changes in price and quantity. If E_d is greater than 1, demand is elastic. If E_d is less than 1, demand is inelastic. Unit elasticity is the special case in which E_d equals 1.

3. Perfectly inelastic demand is graphed as a line parallel to the vertical axis; perfectly elastic demand is shown by a line above and parallel to the horizontal axis.

4. Elasticity varies at different price ranges on a demand curve, tending to be elastic in the upper-left segment and inelastic in the lower-right segment. Elasticity cannot be judged by the steepness or flatness of a demand curve.

5. If total revenue changes in the opposite direction from prices, demand is elastic. If price and total revenue change in the same direction, demand is inelastic. Where demand is of unit elasticity, a change in price leaves total revenue unchanged.

6. The number of available substitutes, the size of an item's price relative to one's budget, whether the product is a luxury or a necessity, and length of time to adjust are all determinants of elasticity of demand.

7. The elasticity concept also applies to supply. The coefficient of price elasticity of supply is found by the formula

$$E_s = \frac{\text{percentage change in quantity supplied of X}}{\text{percentage change in price of X}}$$

The averages of the prices and quantities under consideration are used as reference points for computing percentage changes. Elasticity of supply depends on the ease of shifting resources between alternative uses, which varies directly with the time producers have to adjust to a price change.

8. Cross elasticity of demand indicates how sensitive the purchase of one product is to changes in the price of another product. The coefficient of cross elasticity of demand is found by the formula

$$E_{xy} = \frac{\text{percentage change in quantity demanded of X}}{\text{percentage change in price of Y}}$$

Positive cross elasticity of demand identifies substitute goods; negative cross elasticity identifies complementary goods.

9. Income elasticity of demand indicates the responsiveness of consumer purchases to a change in income. The coefficient of income elasticity of demand is found by the formula

$$E_i = \frac{\text{percentage change in quantity demanded of X}}{\text{percentage change in income}}$$

The coefficient is positive for normal goods and negative for inferior goods.

10. Industries that sell products which have high income elasticity of demand coefficients are particularly hard hit by recessions. Those with products that have low or negative income elasticity of demand coefficients fare much better.

Terms and Concepts

price elasticity of demand	perfectly inelastic demand	market period
midpoint formula	perfectly elastic demand	short run
elastic demand	total revenue (TR)	long run
inelastic demand	total-revenue test	cross elasticity of demand
unit elasticity	price elasticity of supply	income elasticity of demand

Questions

1. Explain why the choice between 1, 2, 3, 4, 5, 6, 7, and 8 "units," or 1000, 2000, 3000, 4000, 5000, 6000, 7000, and 8000 movie tickets, makes no difference in determining elasticity in Table 4.1. **LO1**

2. Graph the accompanying demand data, and then use the midpoint formula for E_d to determine price elasticity of demand for each of the four possible $1 price changes. What can you conclude about the relationship between the slope of a curve and its elasticity? Explain in a nontechnical way why demand is elastic in the northwest segment of the demand curve and inelastic in the southeast segment. **LO1**

Product Price	Quantity Demanded
$5	1
4	2
3	3
2	4
1	5

3. What are the major determinants of price elasticity of demand? Use those determinants and your own reasoning in judging whether demand for each of the following products is probably elastic or inelastic: (a) bottled water; (b) toothpaste, (c) Crest toothpaste, (d) ketchup, (e) diamond bracelets, (f) Microsoft's Windows operating system. **LO1**

4. What effect would a rule stating that university students must live in university dormitories have on the price elasticity of demand for dormitory space? What impact might this in turn have on room rates? **LO1**

5. Calculate total-revenue data from the demand schedule in question 2. Graph total revenue below your demand curve. Generalize about the relationship between price elasticity and total revenue. **LO2**

6. How would the following changes in price affect total revenue? That is, would total revenue increase, decrease, or remain unchanged? **LO2**
   a. Price falls and demand is inelastic.
   b. Price rises and demand is elastic.
   c. Price rises and supply is elastic.
   d. Price rises and supply is inelastic.
   e. Price rises and demand is inelastic.
   f. Price falls and demand is elastic.
   g. Price falls and demand is of unit elasticity.

7. In 2006, Willem de Kooning's abstract painting *Woman III* sold for $137.5 million. Portray this sale in a demand and supply diagram and comment on the elasticity of supply. Comedian George Carlin once mused, "If a painting can be forged well enough to fool some experts, why is the original so valuable?" Provide an answer. **LO3**

8. Suppose the cross elasticity of demand for products A and B is +3.6 and for products C and D is −5.4. What can you conclude about how products A and B are related? Products C and D? **LO4**

9. The income elasticities of demand for movies, dental services, and clothing have been estimated to be +3.4, +1, and +.5, respectively. Interpret these coefficients. What does it mean if an income elasticity coefficient is negative? **LO4**

10. Research has found that an increase in the price of beer would reduce the amount of marijuana consumed. Is cross elasticity of demand between the two products positive or negative? Are these products substitutes or complements? What might be the logic behind this relationship? **LO4**

11. **LAST WORD** What is the purpose of charging different groups of customers different prices? Supplement the three broad examples in the Last Word with two additional examples of your own. Hint: Think of price discounts based on group characteristics or time of purchase.

Problems

1. Look at the demand curve in Figure 4.2a. Use the midpoint formula and points *a* and *b* to calculate the elasticity of demand for that range of the demand curve. Do the same for the demand curves in Figures 4.2b and 4.2c using, respectively, points *c* and *d* for Figure 4.2b and points *e* and *f* for Figure 4.2c. LO1

2. Investigate how demand elastiticities are affected by increases in demand. Shift each of the demand curves in Figures 4.2a, 4.2b, and 4.2c to the right by 10 units. For example, point *a* in Figure 4.2a would shift rightward from location (10 units, $2) to (20 units, $2), while point *b* would shift rightward from location (40 units, $1) to (50 units, $1). After making these shifts, apply the midpoint formula to calculate the demand elasticities for the shifted points. Are they larger or smaller than the elasticities you calculated in Problem 1 for the original points? In terms of the midpoint formula, what explains the change in elasticities? LO1

3. Suppose that the total revenue received by a company selling basketballs is $600 when the price is set at $30 per basketball and $600 when the price is set at $20 per basketball. Without using the midpoint formula, can you tell whether demand is elastic, inelastic, or unit-elastic over this price range? LO2

4. Danny "Dimes" Donahue is a neighborhood's 9-year old entrepreneur. His most recent venture is selling homemade brownies that he bakes himself. At a price of $1.50 each, he sells 100. At a price of $1.00 each, he sells 300. Is demand elastic or inelastic over this price range? *If* demand had the same elasticity for a price decline from $1.00 to $0.50 as it does for the decline from $1.50 to $1.00, would cutting the price from $1.00 to $0.50 increase or decrease Danny's total revenue? LO2

5. What is the formula for measuring the price elasticity of supply? Suppose the price of apples goes up from $20 to $22 a box. In direct response, Goldsboro Farms supplies 1200 boxes of apples instead of 1000 boxes. Compute the coefficient of price elasticity (midpoints approach) for Goldsboro's supply. Is its supply elastic, or is it inelastic? LO3

6. **ADVANCED ANALYSIS** Currently, at a price of $1 each, 100 popsicles are sold per day in the perpetually hot town of Rostin. Consider the elasticity of supply. In the short run, a price increase from $1 to $2 is unit-elastic ($E_s = 1.0$). So how many popsicles will be sold each day in the short run if the price rises to $2 each? In the long run, a price increase from $1 to $2 has an elasticity of supply of 1.50. So how many popsicles will be sold per day in the long run if the price rises to $2 each? (Hint: Apply the midpoints approach to the elasticity of supply.) LO3

7. Lorena likes to play golf. The number of times per year that she plays depends on both the price of playing a round of golf as well as Lorena's income and the cost of other types of entertainment—in particular, how much it costs to go see a movie instead of playing golf. The three demand schedules in the table below show how many rounds of golf per year Lorena will demand at each price under three different scenarios. In scenario D_1, Lorena's income is $50,000 per year and movies cost $9 each. In scenario D_2, Lorena's income is also $50,000 per year, but the price of seeing a movie rises to $11. And in scenario D_3, Lorena's income goes up to $70,000 per year, while movies cost $11. LO4

	Quantity Demanded		
Price	D_1	D_2	D_3
$50	15	10	15
35	25	15	30
20	40	20	50

a. Using the data under D_1 and D_2, calculate the cross elasticity of Lorena's demand for golf at all three prices. (To do this, apply the midpoints approach to the cross elasticity of demand.) Is the cross elasticity the same at all three prices? Are movies and golf substitute goods, complementary goods, or independent goods?

b. Using the data under D_2 and D_3, calculate the income elasticity of Lorena's demand for golf at all three prices. (To do this, apply the midpoints approach to the income elasticity of demand.) Is the income elasticity the same at all three prices? Is golf an inferior good?

FURTHER TEST YOUR KNOWLEDGE AT
www.mcconnell19e.com

At the text's Online Learning Center (OLC), **www.mcconnell19e.com**, you will find one or more Web-based questions that require information from the Internet to answer. We urge you to check them out; they will familiarize you with Web sites that may be helpful in other courses and perhaps even in your career. The OLC also features multiple-choice questions that give instant feedback and provides other helpful ways to further test your knowledge of the chapter.

6

AFTER READING THIS CHAPTER, YOU SHOULD BE ABLE TO:

1 Define and explain the relationship between total utility, marginal utility, and the law of diminishing marginal utility.

2 Describe how rational consumers maximize utility by comparing the marginal utility-to-price ratios of all the products they could possibly purchase.

3 Explain how a demand curve can be derived by observing the outcomes of price changes in the utility-maximization model.

4 Discuss how the utility-maximization model helps highlight the income and substitution effects of a price change.

5 Relate how behavioral economics and prospect theory shed light on many consumer behaviors.

6 (Appendix) Relate how the indifference curve model of consumer behavior derives demand curves from budget lines, indifference curves, and utility maximization.

Consumer Behavior

If you were to compare the shopping carts of almost any two consumers, you would observe striking differences. Why does Paula have potatoes, peaches, and Pepsi in her cart, while Sam has sugar, saltines, and 7-Up in his? Why didn't Paula also buy pasta and plums? Why didn't Sam have soup and spaghetti on his grocery list?

In this chapter, you will see how individual consumers allocate their incomes among the various goods and services available to them. Given a certain budget, how does a consumer decide which goods and services to buy? This chapter will develop a model to answer this question.

This chapter will also survey some of the recent insights about consumer behavior provided by the field of behavioral economics. These insights explain many of the less-rational and oftentimes quirky behaviors exhibited by consumers. Better yet, they also suggest concrete policies that individuals, companies, and governments can use to make consumers better off by working with—rather than against—people's behavioral quirks.

Law of Diminishing Marginal Utility

The simplest theory of consumer behavior rests squarely on the **law of diminishing marginal utility.** This principle, first discussed in Chapter 3, is that added satisfaction declines as a consumer acquires additional units of a given product. Although consumer wants in general may be insatiable, wants for particular items can be satisfied. In a specific span of time over which consumers' tastes remain unchanged, consumers can obtain as much of a particular good or service as they can afford. But the more of that product they obtain, the less they want still more of it.

Consider durable goods, for example. A consumer's desire for an automobile, when he or she has none, may be very strong. But the desire for a second car is less intense; and for a third or fourth, weaker and weaker. Unless they are collectors, even the wealthiest families rarely have more than a half-dozen cars, although their incomes would allow them to purchase a whole fleet of vehicles.

Terminology

Evidence indicates that consumers can fulfill specific wants with succeeding units of a product but that each added unit provides less utility than the last unit purchased. Recall that a consumer derives utility from a product if it can satisfy a want: **Utility** is want-satisfying power. The utility of a good or service is the satisfaction or pleasure one gets from consuming it. Keep in mind three characteristics of this concept:

- "Utility" and "usefulness" are not synonymous. Paintings by Picasso may offer great utility to art connoisseurs but are useless functionally (other than for hiding a crack on a wall).
- Utility is subjective. The utility of a specific product may vary widely from person to person. A lifted pickup truck may have great utility to someone who drives off-road but little utility to someone unable or unwilling to climb into the rig. Eyeglasses have tremendous utility to someone who has poor eyesight but no utility to a person with 20-20 vision.
- Utility is difficult to quantify. But for purposes of illustration we assume that people can measure satisfaction with units called *utils* (units of utility). For example, a particular consumer may get 100 utils of satisfaction from a smoothie, 10 utils of satisfaction from a candy bar, and 1 util of satisfaction from a stick of gum. These imaginary units of satisfaction are convenient for quantifying consumer behavior for explanatory purposes.

Total Utility and Marginal Utility

Total utility and marginal utility are related, but different, ideas. **Total utility** is the total amount of satisfaction or pleasure a person derives from consuming some specific quantity—for example, 10 units—of a good or service. **Marginal utility** is the *extra* satisfaction a consumer realizes from an additional unit of that product—for example, from the eleventh unit. Alternatively, marginal utility is the change in total utility that results from the consumption of 1 more unit of a product.

Figure 6.1 (Key Graph) and the accompanying table demonstrate the relation between total utility and marginal

CONSIDER THIS . . .

Vending Machines and Marginal Utility

Newspaper dispensing devices and soft-drink vending machines are similar in their basic operations. Both enable consumers to buy a product by inserting coins. But there is an important difference in the two devices. The newspaper dispenser opens to the full stack of papers and seemingly "trusts" the customer to take only a single copy, whereas the vending machine displays no such "trust," requiring the consumer to buy one can at a time. Why the difference?

The idea of diminishing marginal utility is key to solving this puzzle. Most consumers take only single copies from the newspaper box because the marginal utility of a second newspaper is nearly zero. They could grab a few extra papers and try to sell them on the street, but the revenue obtained would be small relative to their time and effort. So, in selling their product, newspaper publishers rely on "zero marginal utility of the second unit," not on "consumer honesty." Also, newspapers have little "shelf life"; they are obsolete the next day. In contrast, soft-drink sellers do not allow buyers to make a single payment and then take as many cans as they want. If they did, consumers would clean out the machine because the marginal utility of successive cans of soda diminishes slowly and buyers could take extra sodas and consume them later. Soft-drink firms thus vend their products on a pay-per-can basis.

In summary, newspaper publishers and soft-drink firms use alternative vending techniques because of the highly different rates of decline in marginal utility for their products. The newspaper seller uses inexpensive dispensers that open to the full stack of papers. The soft-drink seller uses expensive vending machines that limit the consumer to a single can at a time. Each vending technique is optimal under the particular economic circumstance.

key graph

FIGURE 6.1 Total and marginal utility. Curves TU and MU are graphed from the data in the table. (a) As more of a product is consumed, total utility increases at a diminishing rate, reaches a maximum, and then declines. (b) Marginal utility, by definition, reflects the changes in total utility. Thus marginal utility diminishes with increased consumption, becomes zero when total utility is at a maximum, and is negative when total utility declines. As shown by the shaded rectangles in (a) and (b), marginal utility is the change in total utility associated with each additional taco. Or, alternatively, each new level of total utility is found by adding marginal utility to the preceding level of total utility.

(a)
Total utility

(b)
Marginal utility

(1) Tacos Consumed per Meal	(2) Total Utility, Utils	(3) Marginal Utility, Utils
0	0	
		10
1	10	
		8
2	18	
		6
3	24	
		4
4	28	
		2
5	30	
		0
6	30	
		−2
7	28	

QUICK QUIZ FOR FIGURE 6.1

1. Marginal utility:
   a. is the extra output a firm obtains when it adds another unit of labor.
   b. explains why product supply curves slope upward.
   c. typically rises as successive units of a good are consumed.
   d. is the extra satisfaction from the consumption of 1 more unit of some good or service.

2. Marginal utility in Figure 6.1b is positive, but declining, when total utility in Figure 6.1a is positive and:
   a. rising at an increasing rate.
   b. falling at an increasing rate.
   c. rising at a decreasing rate.
   d. falling at a decreasing rate.

3. When marginal utility is zero in graph (b), total utility in graph (a) is:
   a. also zero.
   b. neither rising nor falling.
   c. negative.
   d. rising, but at a declining rate.

4. Suppose the person represented by these graphs experienced a diminished taste for tacos. As a result the:
   a. TU curve would get steeper.
   b. MU curve would get flatter.
   c. TU and MU curves would shift downward.
   d. MU curve, but not the TU curve, would collapse to the horizontal axis.

Answers: 1. d; 2. c; 3. b; 4. c

utility. The curves reflect the data in the table. Column 2 shows the total utility associated with each level of consumption of tacos. Column 3 shows the marginal utility—the change in total utility—that results from the consumption of each successive taco. Starting at the origin

in Figure 6.1a, observe that each of the first five units increases total utility (TU), but by a diminishing amount. Total utility reaches a maximum with the addition of the sixth unit and then declines.

So in Figure 6.1b marginal utility (MU) remains positive but diminishes through the first five units (because total utility increases at a declining rate). Marginal utility

is zero for the sixth unit (because that unit doesn't change total utility). Marginal utility then becomes negative with the

seventh unit and beyond (because total utility is falling). Figure 6.1b and table column 3 reveal that each successive taco yields less extra utility, meaning fewer utils, than the preceding taco.[1] That is, the table and graph illustrate the law of diminishing marginal utility.

Marginal Utility and Demand

The law of diminishing marginal utility explains why the demand curve for a given product slopes downward. If successive units of a good yield smaller and smaller amounts of marginal, or extra, utility, then the consumer will buy additional units of a product only if its price falls. The consumer for whom Figure 6.1 is relevant may buy two tacos at a price of $1 each. But because he or she obtains less marginal utility from additional tacos, the consumer will choose not to buy more at that price. The consumer would rather spend additional dollars on products that provide more utility, not less utility. Therefore, additional tacos with less utility are not worth buying unless the price declines. (When marginal utility becomes negative, Taco Bell would have to pay you to consume another taco!) Thus, diminishing marginal utility supports the idea that price must decrease in order for quantity demanded to increase. In other words, consumers behave in ways that make demand curves downsloping.

---

[1]Technical footnote: In Figure 6.1b we graphed marginal utility at half-units. For example, we graphed the marginal utility of 4 utils at $3\frac{1}{2}$ units because "4 utils" refers neither to the third nor the fourth unit per se but to the *addition* or *subtraction* of the fourth unit.

Theory of Consumer Behavior

In addition to explaining the law of demand, the idea of diminishing marginal utility explains how consumers allocate their money incomes among the many goods and services available for purchase.

Consumer Choice and the Budget Constraint

For simplicity, we will assume that the situation for the typical consumer has the following dimensions.

- *Rational behavior* The consumer is a rational person, who tries to use his or her money income to derive the greatest amount of satisfaction, or utility, from it. Consumers want to get "the most for their money" or, technically, to maximize their total utility. They engage in **rational behavior.**
- *Preferences* Each consumer has clear-cut preferences for certain of the goods and services that are available in the market. Buyers also have a good idea of how much marginal utility they will get from successive units of the various products they might purchase.
- *Budget constraint* At any point in time the consumer has a fixed, limited amount of money income. Since each consumer supplies a finite amount of human and property resources to society, he or she earns only limited income. Thus, as noted in Chapter 1, every consumer faces a **budget constraint,** even consumers who earn millions of dollars a year. Of course, this budget limitation is more severe for a consumer with an average income than for a consumer with an extraordinarily high income.
- *Prices* Goods are scarce relative to the demand for them, so every good carries a price tag. We assume that the price of each good is unaffected by the amount of it that is bought by any particular person. After all, each person's purchase is a tiny part of total demand. Also, because the consumer has a limited number of dollars, he or she cannot buy everything wanted. This point drives home the reality of scarcity to each consumer.

So the consumer must compromise; he or she must choose the most personally satisfying mix of goods and services. Different individuals will choose different mixes.

Utility-Maximizing Rule

Of all the different combinations of goods and services a consumer can obtain within his or her budget, which specific combination will yield the maximum utility or satisfaction? *To maximize satisfaction, the consumer should allocate his or her money income so that the last dollar spent on each product yields the same amount of extra (marginal) utility.* We call this the **utility-maximizing rule.** When the consumer has "balanced his margins" using this rule, he has achieved **consumer equilibrium** and has no incentive to alter his expenditure pattern. In fact, any person who has achieved consumer equilibrium would be worse off—total utility would decline—if there were any alteration in the bundle of goods purchased, providing there is no change in taste, income, products, or prices.

Numerical Example

An illustration will help explain the utility-maximizing rule. For simplicity we limit our example to two products, but the analysis also applies if there are more. Suppose consumer Holly is analyzing which combination of two products she should purchase with her fixed daily income of $10. Let's suppose these products are apples and oranges.

Holly's preferences for apples and oranges and their prices are the basic data determining the combination that will maximize her satisfaction. Table 6.1 summarizes those data, with column 2a showing the amounts of marginal utility she will derive from each successive unit of A (apples) and with column 3a showing the same thing for product B (oranges). Both columns reflect the law of diminishing marginal utility, which, in this example, is assumed to begin with the second unit of each product purchased.

Marginal Utility per Dollar To see how the utility-maximizing rule works, we must put the marginal-utility information in columns 2a and 3a on a per-dollar-spent basis. A consumer's choices are influenced not only by the extra utility that successive apples will yield but also by how many dollars (and therefore how many oranges) she must give up to obtain additional apples.

The rational consumer must compare the extra utility from each product with its added cost (that is, its price). Switching examples for a moment, suppose that you prefer a pizza whose marginal utility is, say, 36 utils to a movie whose marginal utility is 24 utils. But if the pizza's price is $12 and the movie costs only $6, you would choose the

TABLE 6.1 The Utility-Maximizing Combination of Apples and Oranges Obtainable with an Income of $10*

(1) Unit of Product	(2) Apple (Product A): Price = $1		(3) Orange (Product B): Price = $2	
	(a) Marginal Utility, Utils	(b) Marginal Utility per Dollar (MU/Price)	(a) Marginal Utility, Utils	(b) Marginal Utility per Dollar (MU/Price)
First	10	10	24	12
Second	8	8	20	10
Third	7	7	18	9
Fourth	6	6	16	8
Fifth	5	5	12	6
Sixth	4	4	6	3
Seventh	3	3	4	2

*It is assumed in this table that the amount of marginal utility received from additional units of each of the two products is independent of the quantity of the other product. For example, the marginal-utility schedule for apples is independent of the number of oranges obtained by the consumer.

movie rather than the pizza! Why? Because the marginal utility per dollar spent would be 4 utils for the movie (= 24 utils/$6) compared to only 3 utils for the pizza (= 36 utils/$12). You could see two movies for $12 and, assuming that the marginal utility of the second movie is, say, 16 utils, your total utility would be 40 utils. Clearly, 40 units of satisfaction (= 24 utils + 16 utils) from two movies are superior to 36 utils from the same $12 expenditure on one pizza.

To make the amounts of extra utility derived from differently priced goods comparable, marginal utilities must be put on a per-dollar-spent basis. We do this in columns 2b and 3b by dividing the marginal-utility data of columns 2a and 3a by the prices of apples and oranges—$1 and $2, respectively.

Decision-Making Process Table 6.1 shows Holly's preferences on a unit basis and a per-dollar basis as well as the price tags of apples and oranges. With $10 to spend, in what order should Holly allocate her dollars on units of apples and oranges to achieve the highest amount of utility within the $10 limit imposed by her income? And what specific combination of the two products will she have obtained at the time she uses up her $10?

Concentrating on columns 2b and 3b in Table 6.1, we find that Holly should first spend $2 on the first orange because its marginal utility per dollar of 12 utils is higher than the first apple's 10 utils. But now Holly finds herself indifferent about whether to buy a second orange or the first apple because the marginal utility per dollar of both is

10 utils per dollar. So she buys both of them. Holly now has 1 apple and 2 oranges. Also, the last dollar she spent on each good yielded the same marginal utility per dollar (10). But this combination of apples and oranges does not represent the maximum amount of utility that Holly can obtain. It cost her only $5 [= (1 × $1) + (2 × $2)], so she has $5 remaining, which she can spend to achieve a still higher level of total utility.

Examining columns 2b and 3b again, we find that Holly should spend the next $2 on a third orange because marginal utility per dollar for the third orange is 9 compared with 8 for the second apple. But now, with 1 apple and 3 oranges, she is again indifferent between a second apple and a fourth orange because both provide 8 utils per dollar. So Holly purchases 1 more of each. Now the last dollar spent on each product provides the same marginal utility per dollar (8), and Holly's money income of $10 is exhausted.

The utility-maximizing combination of goods attainable by Holly is 2 apples and 4 oranges. By summing marginal-utility information from columns 2a and 3a, we find that Holly is obtaining 18 (= 10 + 8) utils of satisfaction from the 2 apples and 78 (= 24 + 20 + 18 + 16) utils of satisfaction from the 4 oranges. Her $10, optimally spent, yields 96 (= 18 + 78) utils of satisfaction.

Table 6.2 summarizes our step-by-step process for maximizing Holly's utility. Note that we have implicitly assumed that Holly spends her entire income. She neither borrows nor saves. However, saving can be regarded as a "commodity" that yields utility and can be incorporated into our analysis. In fact, we treat it that way in problem 4 at the end of this chapter.

Inferior Options Holly can obtain other combinations of apples and oranges with $10, but none will yield as great a total utility as do 2 apples and 4 oranges. As an example, she can obtain 4 apples and 3 oranges for $10. But this combination yields only 93 utils, clearly inferior to the 96 utils

WORKED PROBLEMS
W 6.1
Consumer choice

provided by 2 apples and 4 oranges. True, there are other combinations apples and oranges (such as 4 apples and 5 oranges or 1 apple and 2 oranges) in which the marginal utility of the last dollar spent is the same for both goods. But all such combinations either are unobtainable with Holly's limited money income (as 4 apples and 5 oranges) or do not exhaust her money income (as 1 apple and 2 oranges) and therefore do not yield the maximum utility attainable.

Algebraic Generalization

Economists generalize the utility-maximizing rule by saying that a consumer will maximize her satisfaction when she allocates her money income so that the last dollar spent on product A, the last on product B, and so forth, yield equal amounts of additional, or marginal, utility. The marginal utility per dollar spent on A is indicated by the MU of product A divided by the price of A (column 2b in Table 6.1), and the marginal utility per dollar spent on B by the MU of product B divided by the price of B (column 3b in Table 6.1). Our utility-maximizing rule merely requires that these ratios be equal for the last dollar spent on A and the last dollar spent on B. Algebraically,

$$\frac{\text{MU of product A}}{\text{Price of A}} = \frac{\text{MU of product B}}{\text{Price of B}}$$

And, of course, the consumer must exhaust her available income. Table 6.1 shows us that the combination of 2 units of A (apples) and 4 of B (oranges) fulfills these conditions in that

$$\frac{8 \text{ utils}}{\$1} = \frac{16 \text{ utils}}{\$2}$$

and the consumer's $10 income is all spent.

TABLE 6.2 Sequence of Purchases to Achieve Consumer Equilibrium, Given the Data in Table 6.1

Choice Number	Potential Choices	Marginal Utility per Dollar	Purchase Decision	Income Remaining
1	First apple	10	First orange for $2	$8 = $10 − $2
	First orange	12		
2	First apple	10	First apple for $1 and second orange for $2	$5 = $8 − $3
	Second orange	10		
3	Second apple	8	Third orange for $2	$3 = $5 − $2
	Third orange	9		
4	Second apple	8	Second apple for $1 and fourth orange for $2	$0 = $3 − $3
	Fourth orange	8		

If the equation is not fulfilled, then some reallocation of the consumer's expenditures between A and B (from the low to the high marginal-utility-per-dollar product) will increase the consumer's total utility. For example, if the consumer spent $10 on 4 of A (apples) and 3 of B (oranges), we would find that

$$\frac{\text{MU of A of 6 utils}}{\text{Price of A of \$1}} < \frac{\text{MU of B of 18 utils}}{\text{Price of B of \$2}}$$

Here the last dollar spent on A provides only 6 utils of satisfaction, while the last dollar spent on B provides 9 (= 18/$2). So the consumer can increase total satisfaction by purchasing more of B and less of A. As dollars are reallocated from A to B, the marginal utility per dollar of A will increase while the marginal utility per dollar of B will decrease. At some new combination of A and B the two will be equal and consumer equilibrium will be achieved. Here that combination is 2 of A (apples) and 4 of B (oranges).

Utility Maximization and the Demand Curve

Once you understand the utility-maximizing rule, you can easily see why product price and quantity demanded are inversely related. Recall that the basic determinants of an individual's demand for a specific product are (1) preferences or tastes, (2) money income, and (3) the prices of other goods. The utility data in Table 6.1 reflect our consumer's preferences. We continue to suppose that her money income is $10. And, concentrating on the construction of an individual demand curve for oranges, we assume that the price of apples, now representing all "other goods," is still $1.

Deriving the Demand Schedule and Curve

We can derive a single consumer's demand schedule for oranges by considering alternative prices at which oranges might be sold and then determining the quantity the consumer will purchase. We already know one such price-quantity combination in the utility-maximizing example: Given tastes, income, and the prices of other goods, Holly will purchase 4 oranges at $2.

Now let's assume the price of oranges falls to $1. The marginal-utility-per-dollar data of column 3b in Table 6.1 will double because the price of oranges has been halved; the new data for column 3b are (by coincidence) identical to the data in column 3a. The doubling of the MU per dollar for each successive orange means that the purchase of 2

FIGURE 6.2 Deriving an individual demand curve. The consumer represented by the data in the table maximizes utility by purchasing 4 oranges at a price of $2. The decline in the price of oranges to $1 disrupts the consumer's initial utility-maximizing equilibrium. The consumer restores equilibrium by purchasing 6 rather than 4 oranges. Thus, a simple price-quantity schedule emerges, which locates two points on a downsloping demand curve.

Price per Orange	Quantity Demanded
$2	4
1	6

apples and 4 oranges is no longer an equilibrium combination. By applying the same reasoning we used previously, we now find that Holly's utility-maximizing combination is 4 apples and 6 oranges. As summarized in the table in Figure 6.2, Holly will purchase 6 oranges when the price of oranges is $1. Using the data in this table, we can sketch the downward-sloping demand curve for oranges, D_o, shown in Figure 6.2. This exercise, then, clearly links the utility-maximizing behavior of a consumer and that person's downsloping demand curve for a particular product.

Income and Substitution Effects

Recall from Chapter 3 that the **income effect** is the impact that a change in the price of a product has on a consumer's real income and consequently on the quantity demanded of that good. In contrast, the **substitution effect** is the impact that a change in a product's price has on its relative expensiveness and consequently on the quantity demanded. Both effects help explain why a demand curve such as that in Figure 6.2 is downsloping.

Let's first look at the substitution effect. Recall that before the price of oranges declined, Holly was in equilibrium when purchasing 2 apples and 4 oranges because

$$\frac{\text{MU of apples of 8}}{\text{Price of apples of \$1}} = \frac{\text{MU of oranges of 16}}{\text{Price of oranges of \$2}}$$

But after the price of oranges declines from $2 to $1,

$$\frac{\text{MU of apples of 8}}{\text{Price of apples of \$1}} < \frac{\text{MU of oranges of 16}}{\text{Price of oranges of \$1}}$$

Clearly, the last dollar spent on oranges now yields greater utility (16 utils) than does the last dollar spent on apples (8 utils). This will lead Holly to switch, or substitute, purchases away from apples and towards oranges so as to restore consumer equilibrium. This substitution effect contributes to the inverse relationship between price and quantity that is found along her demand curve for oranges: When the price of oranges declines, the substitution effect causes Holly to buy more oranges.

What about the income effect? The decline in the price of oranges from $2 to $1 increases Holly's real income. Before the price decline, she maximized her utility and achieved consumer equilibrium by selecting 2 apples and 4 oranges. But at the lower $1 price for oranges, Holly would have to spend only $6 rather than $10 to buy that particular combination of goods. That means that the lower price of oranges has freed up $4 that can be spent on buying more apples, more oranges, or more of both. How many more of each fruit she ends up buying will be determined by applying the utility-maximizing rule to the new situation. But it is quite likely that the increase in real income caused by the reduction in the price of oranges will cause Holly to end up buying more oranges than before the price reduction. Any such increase in orange purchases is referred to as the income effect of the reduction in the price of oranges and it, too, helps to explain why demand curves are downward sloping: When the price of oranges falls, the income effect causes Holly to buy more oranges.

> ### ORIGIN OF THE IDEA
> **O 6.2**
> Income and substitution effects

QUICK REVIEW 6.2

- The theory of consumer behavior assumes that, with limited income and a set of product prices, consumers make rational choices on the basis of well-defined preferences.
- A consumer maximizes utility by allocating income so that the marginal utility per dollar spent is the same for every good purchased.
- A downsloping demand curve can be derived by changing the price of one product in the consumer-behavior model and noting the change in the utility-maximizing quantity of that product demanded.
- By providing insights on the income effect and substitution effects of a price decline, the utility-maximization model helps explain why demand curves are downsloping.

Applications and Extensions

Many real-world phenomena can be explained by applying the theory of consumer behavior.

iPods

Every so often a new product totally captures consumers' imaginations. One such product is Apple's iPod, which debuted in November 2001. Less than six years later, Apple sold its 100 millionth unit. Furthermore, those units enabled Apple to sell more than 2.5 billion songs through its online iTunes Store.

The swift ascendancy of the iPod resulted mainly from a leapfrog in technology. Not only is the iPod much more compact than the portable digital CD player that it replaced, it can store and play back several thousand songs—whereas a single CD only has a 74-minute recording capacity. The improved portability and storage—and enhanced consumer satisfaction—caused a major shift in consumer demand away from the portable CD player and toward the iPod.

In the language of our analysis, Apple's introduction of the iPod severely disrupted consumer equilibrium. Consumers en masse concluded that iPods had a higher marginal-utility-to-price ratio (= MU/P) than the ratios for alternative products. They therefore shifted spending away from those other products and toward iPods as a way to increase total utility. Of course, for most people the marginal utility of a second or third iPod relative to price is quite low, so most consumers purchased only a single iPod. But Apple continued to enhance the iPod, enticing some of the buyers of older models to buy new models.

This example demonstrates a simple but important point: New products succeed by enhancing consumers' total utility. This "delivery of value" generates a revenue stream. If revenues exceed production costs, substantial profits can result—as they have for Apple.

The Diamond-Water Paradox

Early economists such as Adam Smith were puzzled by the fact that some "essential" goods had much lower prices than some "unimportant" goods. Why would water, essential to life, be priced below diamonds, which have much less usefulness? The paradox is resolved when we acknowledge that water is in great supply relative to demand and thus has a very low price per gallon. Diamonds, in contrast, are rare. Their supply is small relative to demand and, as a result, they have a very high price per carat.

Moreover, the marginal utility of the last unit of water consumed is very low. The reason follows from our utility-maximizing rule. Consumers (and producers) respond to the very low price of water by using a great deal of it—for generating electricity, irrigating crops, heating buildings, watering lawns, quenching thirst, and so on. Consumption is expanded until marginal utility, which declines as more water is consumed, equals its low price. On the other hand, relatively few diamonds are purchased because of their prohibitively high price, meaning that their marginal utility remains high. In equilibrium:

$$\frac{\text{MU of water (low)}}{\text{Price of water (low)}} = \frac{\text{MU of diamonds (high)}}{\text{Price of diamonds (high)}}$$

Although the marginal utility of the last unit of water consumed is low and the marginal utility of the last diamond purchased is high, the total utility of water is very high and the total utility of diamonds quite low. The total utility derived from the consumption of water is large because of the enormous amounts of water consumed. Total utility is the sum of the marginal utilities of all the gallons of water consumed, including the trillions of gallons that have far higher marginal utilities than the last unit consumed. In contrast, the total utility derived from diamonds is low since their high price means that relatively few of them are bought. Thus the water-diamond "paradox" is solved: Water has much more total utility (roughly, usefulness) than diamonds even though the price of diamonds greatly exceeds the price of water. These relative prices relate to marginal utility, not total utility.

ORIGIN OF THE IDEA

O 6.3

Diamond-water paradox

Opportunity Cost and the Value of Time

The theory of consumer behavior has been generalized to account for the economic value of *time*. Both consumption and production take time. Time is a valuable economic commodity; by using an hour in productive work a person can earn $6, $10, $50, or more, depending on her or his education and skills. By using that hour for leisure or in consumption activities, the individual incurs the opportunity cost of forgone income; she or he sacrifices the $6, $10, or $50 that could have been earned by working.

Imagine a self-employed consumer named Linden who is considering buying a round of golf, on the one hand, and a concert, on the other. The market price of the golf game is $30 and that of the concert is $40. But the golf game takes more time than the concert. Suppose Linden spends 4 hours on the golf course but only 2 hours at the concert. If her time is worth $10 per hour, as evidenced by the $10 wage she can obtain by working, then the "full price" of the golf game is $70 (the $30 market price plus $40 worth of time). Similarly, the full price of the concert is $60 (the $40 market price plus $20 worth of time). We find that, contrary to what market prices alone indicate, the full price of the concert is really less than the full price of the golf game.

If we now assume that the marginal utilities derived from successive golf games and concerts are identical, traditional theory would indicate that Linden should consume more golf games than concerts because the market price of the former ($30) is lower than that of the latter ($40). But when time is taken into account, the situation is reversed and golf games ($70) are more expensive than concerts ($60). So it is rational for Linden to consume more concerts than golf games.

By accounting for the opportunity cost of a consumer's time, we can explain certain phenomena that are otherwise quite puzzling. It may be rational for the unskilled worker or retiree whose time has little market value to ride a bus from Chicago to Pittsburgh. But the corporate executive, whose time is very valuable, will find it cheaper to fly, even though bus fare is only a fraction of plane fare. It is sensible for the retiree, living on a modest company pension and a Social Security check, to spend many hours shopping for bargains at the mall or taking long trips in a motor home. It is equally intelligent for the highly paid physician, working 55 hours per week, to buy a new personal computer over the Internet and take short vacations at expensive resorts.

People in other nations often feel affluent Americans are "wasteful" of food and other material goods but "overly economical" in their use of time. Americans who visit developing countries find that time is used casually or "squandered," while material goods are very highly prized and carefully used. These differences are not a paradox or a case of radically different temperaments. The differences are primarily a rational reflection of the fact that the high productivity of labor in an industrially advanced society gives time a high market value, whereas the opposite is true in a low-income, developing country.

Medical Care Purchases

The method of payment for certain goods and services affects their prices at the time we buy them and significantly changes the amount purchased. Let's go back to Table 6.1. Suppose the $1 price for apples is its "true" value or opportunity cost. But now, for some reason, its price is only, say, $.20. A rational consumer clearly would buy more apples at the $.20 price than at the $1 price.

That is what happens with medical care. People in the United States who have health insurance pay a fixed premium once a month that covers, say, 80 percent of all incurred health care costs. This means that when they actually need health care, its price to them will be only 20 percent of the actual market price. How would you act in such a situation? When you are ill, you would likely purchase a great deal more medical care than you would if you were confronted with the full price. As a result, financing health care through insurance is an important factor in explaining today's high expenditures on health care and the historical growth of such spending as a percentage of domestic output.

Similar reasoning applies to purchases of buffet meals. If you buy a meal at an all-you-can-eat buffet, you will tend to eat more than if you purchased it item by item. Why not eat that second dessert? Its marginal utility is positive and its "price" is zero!

Cash and Noncash Gifts

Marginal-utility analysis also helps us understand why people generally prefer cash gifts to noncash gifts costing the same amount. The reason is simply that the noncash gifts may not match the recipient's preferences and thus may not add as much as cash to total utility. Thought of differently, consumers know their own preferences better than the gift giver does, and the $100 cash gift provides more choices.

Look back at Table 6.1. Suppose Holly has zero earned income but is given the choice of a $2 cash gift or a noncash gift of 2 apples. Because 2 apples can be bought with $2, these two gifts are of equal monetary value. But by spending the $2 cash gift on the first orange, Holly could obtain 24 utils. The noncash gift of the first 2 apples would yield only 18 (= 10 + 8) units of utility. Conclusion: The noncash gift yields less utility to the beneficiary than does the cash gift.

Since giving noncash gifts is common, a considerable value of those gifts is potentially lost because they do not match their recipients' tastes. For example, Uncle Fred may have paid $15 for the Frank Sinatra CD he gave you for the holidays, but you would pay only $7.50 for it. Thus, a $7.50, or 50 percent, value loss is involved. Multiplied by billions of gifts a year, the total potential loss of value is huge.

But some of that loss is avoided by the creative ways individuals handle the problem. For example, newlyweds set up gift registries for their weddings to help match up their wants to the noncash gifts received. Also, people obtain cash refunds or exchanges for gifts so they can buy goods that provide more utility. And people have even been known to "recycle gifts" by giving them to someone else at a later time. All three actions support the proposition that individuals take actions to maximize their total utility.

Prospect Theory

Up to this point, we have restricted ourselves to dealing with consumer-choice situations in which people only have to deal with "goods" as opposed to "bads." When deciding on how to spend a budget, people only consider items that can bring them positive marginal utility—that is "good" things. They then use the utility-maximizing rule to select how much of each of those good things they should consume to get as much utility as possible from their limited budgets.

Unfortunately, life often forces us to deal with bad things, too. Our houses may burn down. A potential investment may go bad. The money we lend out may not be repaid.

How people deal with these negative possibilities is a central focus of **behavioral economics**—the branch of economics that combines insights from economics, psychology, and neuroscience to better understand those situations in which actual choice behavior deviates from the predictions made by earlier theories, which incorrectly concluded that people were *always* rational, deliberate, and unswayed by emotions. By studying how people actually deal with the prospect of bad things as well as good things, behavioral economists discovered three very interesting facts about how people react to goods and bads:

- People judge good things and bad things in relative terms, as gains and losses relative to their current situation, or **status quo.**
- People experience both diminishing marginal utility for gains (as you have already seen) as well as diminishing marginal disutility for losses (meaning that each successive unit of loss hurts, but less painfully than the previous unit).

- People are **loss averse,** meaning that for losses and gains near the status quo, losses are felt *much* more intensely than gains—in fact, about 2.5 times more intensely. Thus, for instance, the pain experienced by an investor who loses one dollar from his current status quo level of wealth will be about 2.5 times more intense than the pleasure he would have felt if he had gained one dollar relative to his current level of wealth.

These three facts about how people deal with goods and bads form the basis of **prospect theory,** which sheds important light on how consumers plan for and deal with

ORIGIN OF THE IDEA

O 6.4

Prospect theory

life's ups and downs as well as why they often appear narrow-minded and fail to "see the big picture." To give you an idea of how powerful prospect theory is—and why its pioneer, Daniel Kahneman, was awarded the Nobel Prize in Economics—let's go through some examples of consumer behavior that would be hard to explain without the insights provided by prospect theory.

Losses and Shrinking Packages

Because people see the world in terms of gains and losses relative to the status quo situations that they are used to, businesses have to be very careful about increasing the prices they charge for their products. This is because once consumers become used to a given price, they will view any increase in the price as a loss relative to the status quo price they were used to.

The fact that consumers may view a price increase as a loss explains the otherwise curious fact that many food producers react to rising input costs by shrinking the sizes of their products. The company most famous for doing this was Hershey's chocolates, which during its first decades of operation about 100 years ago would always charge exactly 5 cents for one of its Hershey's chocolate bars. But the size of the bars would increase or decrease depending on the cost of the company's inputs. When the cost of raw materials rose, the company would keep the price fixed at 5 cents but decrease the size of the bar. When the cost of raw materials fell, it would again keep the price fixed at 5 cents but increase the size of the bar.

This seems rather bizarre when you consider that consumers were not in any way *actually* being shielded from the changes in input prices. That is because what should rationally matter to consumers is the price per ounce that they are paying for Hershey's Bars. And that *does* go up and down when the price remains fixed but the size of the bars changes.

But people aren't being fully rational here. They mentally fixate on the product's price because that is the characteristic that they are used to focusing on when making their purchasing decisions. And because the 5-cent price had become the status quo that they were used to, Hershey's understood that any price increase would be mentally categorized as a loss. Thus, Hershey's wisely chose to keep the price of its product fixed at 5 cents even when input prices were rising.

Other companies employ the same strategy today. In 2008, the prices of many raw materials, including sugar,

Rising Consumption and the Hedonic Treadmill

For many sensations, people's brains are wired to notice changes rather than states. For example, your brain can sense acceleration—your change in speed—but not speed itself. As a result, standing still feels the same as moving at a constant 50 miles per hour. And if you accelerate from one constant speed to another—say, from 50 miles per hour to 70 miles per hour—you will feel the acceleration only while it's happening. Once you settle down at the new higher speed, it will feel like you are standing still again.

Consumption appears to work in much the same way. If you are used to a given level of consumption—say, $50,000 per year—then you will get a lot of enjoyment for a while if your consumption accelerates to $100,000 per year. But, as time passes, you will get used to that higher level of consumption, so that $100,000 per year seems ordinary and doesn't bring you any more pleasure than $50,000 per year used to bring you when it was your status quo.

Economist Richard Easterlin coined the term *hedonic treadmill* (pleasure treadmill) to describe this phenomenon. Just as a person walking on a real treadmill gets nowhere, people trying to make themselves permanently happier by consuming more also get nowhere, because they end up getting used to any higher level of consumption. Indeed, except for the extremely poor, people across the income spectrum report similar levels of happiness and satisfaction with their lives. This has led several economists, including Robert Frank, to argue that we should all stop trying to consume more, because doing so doesn't make us any happier in the long run. What do you think? Should we all step off of the hedonic treadmill?

wheat, and corn, rose substantially. Many major manufacturers reacted by reducing product sizes while keeping prices fixed. Kellogg's reduced the size of its Frosted Flakes and Rice Krispies cereal boxes from 19 to 18 ounces. Frito-Lay reduced Doritos bags from 12 to 10 ounces. Dial Soap bars shrank from 4.5 to 4 ounces. And Procter and Gamble reduced the size of Bounty paper towel rolls from 60 to 52 sheets.

Framing Effects and Advertising

Because people evaluate situations in terms of gains and losses, their decision-making can be very sensitive to the *mental frame* that they use to evaluate whether a possible outcome should be viewed as a gain or a loss. Here are a couple of examples in which differences in the context or "frame" change the perception of whether a situation should be treated as a gain or loss. See how you react to them.

- Would you be happy with a salary of $100,000 per year? You might say yes. But what if your salary last year had been $140,000? Are you still going to say yes? Now that you know you are taking a $40,000 pay cut, does that $100,000 salary seem as good as it did before?

- Similarly, suppose you have a part-time job. One day, your boss Joe walks in and says that he is going to give you a 10 percent raise. Would that please you? Now, what if he also mentioned that *everyone else* at your firm would be getting a 15 percent raise. Are you still going to be just as pleased? Or does your raise now seem like a loss compared to what everyone else will be getting?

Changes in people's preferences that are caused by new information that alters the frame used to define whether situations are gains or losses are referred to as **framing effects.** These are important to recognize because they can be manipulated by advertisers, lawyers, and politicians to try to alter people's decisions. For instance, would an advertising company be better off marketing a particular brand of hamburger as "20% fat" or as "80% lean"? Both phrases describe the same meat, but one frames the situation as a loss (20 percent fat) while the other frames it as a gain (80 percent lean).

And would you be more willing to take a particular medicine if you were told that 99.9 percent of the people who take it live or if you were told that 0.1 percent of the people who take it die? Continuing to live is a gain, whereas dying is clearly a loss. Which frame sounds better to you?

Finally, note that framing effects have important consequences for the utility-maximizing rule that we studied earlier in this chapter. If a frame alters people's valuations of marginal utility, it *will* affect their consumption decisions!

Anchoring and Credit Card Bills

Before people can calculate their gains and losses, they must first define the status quo from which to measure those changes. But it turns out that irrelevant information can unconsciously influence people's feelings about the status quo. Here's a striking example. Find a group of people and ask each person to write down the last two digits of his or her Social Security number. Then ask each person to write down his or her best estimate of the value of some object that you display to them—say, a nice cordless keyboard. What you will find is that the people whose Social Security numbers end in higher numbers—say, 67 or 89—will give higher estimates for the value of the keyboard than people whose Social Security numbers end in smaller numbers like 18 or 37. The effect can be huge. Among students in one MBA class at MIT, those with Social Security numbers ending between 80 and 99 gave average estimates of $56 for a cordless keyboard, while their classmates whose Social Security numbers ended in numbers from 00 to 20 gave average estimates of just $16.

Psychologists and behavioral economists refer to this phenomenon as **anchoring** because people's estimates about the value of the keyboard are influenced, or "anchored," by the recently considered information about the last two digits of their Social Security numbers. Why irrelevant information can anchor subsequent valuations is not fully understood. But the anchoring effect is real and can lead people to unconsciously alter how they evaluate different options.

Unfortunately, credit card companies have figured this out. They use anchoring to increase their profits by showing very small minimum-payment amounts on borrowers' monthly credit card statements. The companies could require larger minimum payments, but the minimum-payment numbers that they present are only typically about 2% of what a customer owes. Why such a small amount? Because it acts as an anchor that causes people to unconsciously make smaller payments each month. This can make a huge difference in how long it takes to pay off their bill and how much in total interest they will end up paying. For a customer who owes $1000 on a credit card that charges the typical interest rate of 19 percent per year, it will take 22 years and $3398.12 in total payments (including accumulated interest) to pay off the debt if he only makes 2 percent monthly payments. By showing such small minimum-payment amounts, credit card companies anchor many customers into the expensive habit of paying off their debts slowly rather than quickly.

<u>Word</u> Nudging People Toward Better Decisions

Behavioral Economists Have Recently Found Success in Using People's Behavioral Quirks to "Nudge" Them Toward Making Better Decisions.*

Behavioral economics began as a descriptive science, meaning that its first goal was to develop theories that accurately described human economic behavior. In particular, it sought to explain a number of behaviors that at first glance seemed irrational. Now that behavioral economics has made significant headway in explaining many of those behaviors, some economists are suggesting that its insights be used to nudge people toward choices that are better for themselves and others.

A key feature of "nudges" is that they are subtle. This subtlety means that nudges can cause large changes in behavior without making people feel bullied or coerced—and also without imposing stringent new rules or having to offer people big monetary incentives or disincentives to get them to do what you want.

Take retirement savings. As you may know, people tend to consume too much in the present and therefore undersave for

---

*The term "nudge" was popularized by Richard Thaler and Cass Sunstein in their book *Nudge: Improving Decisions about Health, Wealth, and Happiness*, Yale University Press, 2008.

retirement. But as it turns out, this unfortunate behavioral tendency can be easily offset by another behavioral tendency: the tendency people have to stick with default options. In terms of retirement savings, this comes down to designing corporate retirement programs in which each worker is "defaulted into" her company's retirement savings program.

Under those savings programs, money is automatically deducted each month from a worker's paycheck and deposited in her retirement savings account. It used to be the case that the default for such programs was for workers to start out *not* enrolled in them. To get enrolled, they would have to request to join the program. That is, they would have to choose to go against the default option of not being enrolled.

And because people have the behavioral tendency of sticking with whatever option is presented to them as the default, relatively few workers would make the change and enroll in their company's savings program. That was disappointing. But instead of being deterred, behavioral economists saw an opportunity. Why not change the default? Why not make automatic enrollment the default option? By making that change, people's tendency to stick with default options would work in their own favor—they would stay enrolled and save money for retirement.

When this strategy of switching the default was actually implemented, the number of workers participating in retirement

Mental Accounting and Overpriced Warranties

The utility-maximizing rule assumes that people will look at all of their potential consumption options simultaneously when trying to maximize the total utility that they can get from spending their limited incomes. But economist Richard Thaler famously noted that people sometimes look at consumption options in isolation, thereby irrationally failing to look at all their options simultaneously. Thaler coined the term **mental accounting** to describe this behavior, because it was as if people arbitrarily put certain options into totally separate "mental accounts" that they dealt with without any thought to options outside of those accounts.

An example of where this suboptimal tendency leads is the warranties that patrons of big electronic stores are offered when they purchase an expensive product, such as a plasma TV that costs $1000. These

warranties are very much overpriced given that the products they insure hardly ever break down. Personal financial experts universally tell people not to buy them. Yet many people do buy them because they engage in mental accounting.

They do this by mentally labeling their purchase of the TV as an isolated, individual transaction, sticking it into a separate mental account in their brain that might have a title like, "Purchase of New TV." Viewing the purchase in isolation exaggerates the size of the potential loss that would come from a broken TV. Customers who view the transaction in isolation see the possibility of a $1000 loss on their $1000 purchase as a potential total loss— "Holy cow! I could lose $1000 on a $1000 TV!" By contrast, people who see the big picture compare the potential loss with their entire future income stream—thereby seeing it correctly as a relatively minor loss. Because of this difference, mental accounting inclines people to pay for overpriced warranties.

savings programs skyrocketed—jumping from 60 percent to 98 percent. Those workers can now look forward to much more pleasant retirements thanks to this simple change that works *with* people's preference to stick with default options.

People's tendency to look around them for social cues as to what constitutes good behavior can also be exploited to modify their consumption behavior. But you have to be careful about how you do it, as was discovered by a California power company that wanted to encourage its customers to conserve electricity. Its first attempt to use social cues involved sending each customer a bill that showed not only his or her own usage of electricity in kilowatt-hours, but also the average usage of nearby houses. The company hoped that by showing the average usage of neighbors, customers would receive a subtle hint about their own usage. In particular, it was hoped that customers who used more than their neighbors would feel that they were being wasteful and would thus cut back on their usage.

And that did indeed happen. *But,* their reduction in electricity usage ended up being completely swamped by an increase in electricity usage on the part of the customers who had previously been below-average users. Those customers interpreted the new information that they were below-average electricity users to mean that they should feel free to consume more. After all, why should they use so little when their neighbors were using so much more?

The power company finally hit upon a solution that worked. Smilies. Yes, symbols like ☺ and ☹. In addition to printing people's own usage and the average usage of their neighbors, the company also started printing a ☺ on a customer's bill if his usage was below average and a ☹ on his bill if his usage was above average. The unhappy smilies embarrassed the heavy users into reducing their consumption even more, while the happy smilies gave a pat on the back to the light users—a pat on the back that kept their usage low.

Bear in mind that both the electricity customers and the workers saving for retirement were being *manipulated* by the people who designed the nudges. This fact is perhaps even more disturbing when you consider that the changes in behavior that were caused by the nudges were most likely *unconscious* on the part of those being manipulated. Keep this in mind as you consider for yourself when and if it is morally or ethically acceptable to use nudges to guide people's behavior.

The Endowment Effect and Market Transactions

Prospect theory also offers an explanation for the **endowment effect,** which is the tendency that people have to put a higher valuation on anything that they currently possess (are endowed with) than on identical items that they do not own but might purchase. For instance, if we show a person a new coffee mug and ask him what the maximum amount is that he would pay to buy it, he might say $10. But if we then give the mug to him so that he now owns it, and we then ask how much we would have to pay him to buy it back, he will very likely report a much higher value—say, $15.

The interesting thing is that he is not just bluffing or driving a hard bargain. Human brains appear wired to do this, to put a higher value on things we own than on things we don't. Economist John List has shown that this tendency can moderate if people are used to buying things for resale—that is, buying them with the intention of getting rid of them—but without such experience the endowment effect can be quite strong. If it is, it can make market transactions between buyers and sellers harder because sellers will be demanding higher prices for the items they are selling ("Hey, *my* mug is worth $15 to me!") than the values put on those items by potential buyers ("Dude, *your* mug is only worth $10 to me").

Several researchers have pointed to the fact that human beings are loss averse as providing an explanation for the endowment effect. Once a person possesses something, the thought of parting with it seems like a potential loss. And because potential losses are felt so intensely (2.5 times more intensely than potential gains), the owners of items end up demanding a lot of money as compensation when asked to sell their property. The potential purchasers, on the other hand, do not own the property and thus do not feel any potential sense of loss. So they put lower valuations on the items in question than do the sellers.

Summary

1. The law of diminishing marginal utility states that beyond a certain quantity, additional units of a specific good will yield declining amounts of extra satisfaction to a consumer.

2. The utility-maximization model assumes that the typical consumer is rational and acts on the basis of well-defined preferences. Because income is limited and goods have prices, the consumer cannot purchase all the goods and services he or she might want. The consumer therefore selects the attainable combination of goods that maximizes his or her utility or satisfaction.

3. A consumer's utility is maximized when income is allocated so that the last dollar spent on each product purchased yields the same amount of extra satisfaction. Algebraically, the utility-maximizing rule is fulfilled when

$$\frac{\text{MU of product A}}{\text{Price of A}} = \frac{\text{MU of product B}}{\text{Price of B}}$$

and the consumer's total income is spent.

4. The utility-maximizing rule and the demand curve are logically consistent. Because marginal utility declines, a lower price is needed to induce the consumer to buy more of a particular product.

5. The utility-maximization model illuminates the income and substitution effects of a price change. The income effect implies that a decline in the price of a product increases the consumer's real income and enables the consumer to buy more of that product with a fixed money income. The substitution effect implies that a lower price makes a product relatively more attractive and therefore increases the consumer's willingness to substitute it for other products.

6. Behavioral economics explains many consumption behaviors, including why irrelevant information can anchor valuations, how people value possibilities in terms of gains and losses relative to a status quo, and how framing effects can change people's decisions by affecting whether particular consumption possibilities seem like gains or losses.

Terms and Concepts

law of diminishing marginal utility

utility

total utility

marginal utility

rational behavior

budget constraint

utility-maximizing rule

consumer equilibrium

income effect

substitution effect

behavioral economics

status quo

loss averse

prospect theory

framing effects

anchoring

mental accounting

endowment effect

Questions

1. Complete the following table and answer the questions below: **LO1**

Units Consumed	Total Utility	Marginal Utility
0	0	
1	10	10
2	—	8
3	25	—
4	30	—
5	—	3
6	34	—

   a. At which rate is total utility increasing: a constant rate, a decreasing rate, or an increasing rate? How do you know?

   b. "A rational consumer will purchase only 1 unit of the product represented by these data, since that amount maximizes marginal utility." Do you agree? Explain why or why not.

   c. "It is possible that a rational consumer will not purchase any units of the product represented by these data." Do you agree? Explain why or why not.

2. Mrs. Simpson buys loaves of bread and quarts of milk each week at prices of $1 and 80 cents, respectively. At present she is buying these products in amounts such that the marginal utilities from the last units purchased of the two products are 80 and 70 utils, respectively. Is she buying the utility-maximizing combination of bread and milk? If not, how should she reallocate her expenditures between the two goods? **LO2**

3. How can time be incorporated into the theory of consumer behavior? Explain the following comment: "Want to make

millions of dollars? Devise a product that saves Americans lots of time." LO2

4. Explain: LO2
   a. Before economic growth, there were too few goods; after growth, there is too little time.
   b. It is irrational for an individual to take the time to be completely rational in economic decision making.
   c. Telling your spouse where you would like to go out to eat for your birthday makes sense in terms of utility maximization.

5. In the last decade or so, there has been a dramatic expansion of small retail convenience stores (such as 7-Eleven, Kwik Shop, and Circle K), although their prices are generally much higher than prices in large supermarkets. What explains the success of the convenience stores? LO2

6. Many apartment-complex owners are installing water meters for each apartment and billing the occupants according to the amount of water they use. This is in contrast to the former procedure of having a central meter for the entire complex and dividing up the collective water expense as part of the rent. Where individual meters have been installed, water usage has declined 10 to 40 percent. Explain that drop, referring to price and marginal utility. LO3

7. Using the utility-maximization rule as your point of reference, explain the income and substitution effects of an increase in the price of product B, with no change in the price of product A. LO4

8. **ADVANCED ANALYSIS** A "mathematically fair bet" is one in which the amount won will on average equal the amount bet,

for example, when a gambler bets, say, $100 for a 10 percent chance to win $1000 ($100 = .10 × $1000). Assuming diminishing marginal utility of dollars, explain why this is *not* a fair bet in terms of utility. Why is it even a less fair bet when the "house" takes a cut of each dollar bet? So is gambling irrational? LO4

9. Suppose that Ike is loss averse. In the morning, Ike's stockbroker calls to tell him that he has gained $1000 on his stock portfolio. In the evening, his accountant calls to tell him that he owes an extra $1000 in taxes. At the end of the day, does Ike feel emotionally neutral since the dollar value of the gain in his stock portfolio exactly offsets the amount of extra taxes he has to pay? Explain. LO5

10. You just accepted a campus job helping to raise money for your school's athletic program. You are told to draft a fundraising letter. The bottom of the letter asks recipients to write down a donation amount. If you want to raise as much money as possible, would it be better if the text of that section mentioned that your school is #3 in the nation in sports or that you are better than 99% of other schools at sports? Explain. LO5

11. **LAST WORD** What do you think of the ethics of using unconscious nudges to alter people's behavior? Before you answer, consider the following argument made by economists Richard Thaler and Cass Sunstein, who favor the use of nudges. They argue that in most situations, we couldn't avoid nudging even if we wanted to, because whatever policy we choose will contain some set of unconscious nudges and incentives that will influence people. Thus, they say, we might as well choose the wisest set of nudges.

Problems

1. Mylie's total utility from singing the same song over and over is 50 utils after one repetition, 90 utils after two repetitions, 70 utils after three repetitions, 20 utils after four repetitions, −50 utils after five repetitions, and −200 utils after six repetitions. Write down her marginal utility for each repetition. Once Mylie's total utility begins to decrease, does each additional singing of the song hurt more than the previous one or less than the previous one? LO1

2. John likes Coca-Cola. After consuming one Coke, John has a total utility of 10 utils. After two Cokes, he has a total utility of 25 utils. After three Cokes, he has a total utility of 50 utils. Does John show diminishing marginal utility for Coke, or does he show increasing marginal utility for Coke? Suppose that John has $3 in his pocket. If Cokes cost $1 each and John is willing to spend one of his dollars on purchasing a first can of Coke, would he spend his second dollar on a Coke, too? What about the third dollar? If John's marginal utility for Coke keeps on increasing no matter

how many Cokes he drinks, would it be fair to say that he is addicted to Coke? LO1

3. Suppose that Omar's marginal utility for cups of coffee is constant at 1.5 utils per cup no matter how many cups he drinks. On the other hand, his marginal utility per doughnut is 10 for the first doughnut he eats, 9 for the second he eats, 8 for the third he eats, and so on (that is, declining by 1 util per additional doughnut). In addition, suppose that coffee costs $1 per cup, doughnuts cost $1 each, and Omar has a budget that he can spend only on doughnuts, coffee, or both. How big would that budget have to be before he would spend a dollar buying a first cup of coffee? LO2

4. Columns 1 through 4 in the table at the top of the next page show the marginal utility, measured in utils, that Ricardo would get by purchasing various amounts of products A, B, C, and D. Column 5 shows the marginal utility Ricardo gets from saving. Assume that the prices of A, B, C, and D are, respectively, $18, $6, $4, and $24 and that Ricardo has an income of $106. LO2

Column 1		Column 2		Column 3		Column 4		Column 5	
Units of A	MU	Units of B	MU	Units of C	MU	Units of D	MU	Number of Dollars Saved	MU
1	72	1	24	1	15	1	36	1	5
2	54	2	15	2	12	2	30	2	4
3	45	3	12	3	8	3	24	3	3
4	36	4	9	4	7	4	18	4	2
5	27	5	7	5	5	5	13	5	1
6	18	6	5	6	4	6	7	6	$\frac{1}{2}$
7	15	7	2	7	$3\frac{1}{2}$	7	4	7	$\frac{1}{4}$
8	12	8	1	8	3	8	2	8	$\frac{1}{8}$

a. What quantities of A, B, C, and D will Ricardo purchase in maximizing his utility?

b. How many dollars will Ricardo choose to save?

c. Check your answers by substituting them into the algebraic statement of the utility-maximizing rule.

5. You are choosing between two goods, X and Y, and your marginal utility from each is as shown in the table below. If your income is $9 and the prices of X and Y are $2 and $1, respectively, what quantities of each will you purchase to maximize utility? What total utility will you realize? Assume that, other things remaining unchanged, the price of X falls to $1. What quantities of X and Y will you now purchase? Using the two prices and quantities for X, derive a demand schedule (a table showing prices and quantities demanded) for X. LO3

Units of X	MU_x	Units of Y	MU_y
1	10	1	8
2	8	2	7
3	6	3	6
4	4	4	5
5	3	5	4
6	2	6	3

6. **ADVANCED ANALYSIS** Let $MU_A = z = 10 - x$ and $MU_B = z = 21 - 2y$, where z is marginal utility per dollar measured in utils, x is the amount spent on product A, and y is the amount spent on product B. Assume that the consumer has $10 to spend on A and B—that is, $x + y = 10$. How is the $10 best allocated between A and B? How much utility will the marginal dollar yield? LO3

7. Suppose that with a budget of $100, Deborah spends $60 on sushi and $40 on bagels when sushi costs $2 per piece and bagels cost $2 per bagel. But then, after the price of bagels falls to $1 per bagel, she spends $50 on sushi and $50 on bagels. How many pieces of sushi and how many bagels did Deborah consume before the price change? At the new prices, how much money would it have cost Deborah to buy those same quantities (the ones that she consumed before the price change)? Given that it used to take Deborah's entire $100 to buy those quantities, how big is the income effect caused by the reduction in the price of bagels? LO4

FURTHER TEST YOUR KNOWLEDGE AT
www.mcconnell19e.com

At the text's Online Learning Center (OLC), **www.mcconnell19e.com**, you will find one or more Web-based questions that require information from the Internet to answer. We urge you to check them out; they will familiarize you with Web sites that may be helpful in other courses and perhaps even in your career. The OLC also features multiple-choice questions that give instant feedback and provides other helpful ways to further test your knowledge of the chapter.

Indifference Curve Analysis

The utility-maximization rule previously discussed requires individuals to measure and compare utility, much as a business would measure and compare costs or revenues. Such *cardinal utility* is measured in units such as 1, 2, 3, and 4 and can be added, subtracted, multiplied, and divided, just like the cardinal numbers in mathematics. More importantly, cardinal utility allows precise quantification of the marginal utilities upon which the utility-maximizing rule depends. In fact, the marginal-utility theory of consumer demand that we explained in the body of this chapter rests squarely on the assumption that economists be able to measure cardinal utility. The reality, however, is that measuring cardinal utility is highly difficult, at best. (Can you, for instance, state exactly how many utils you are getting from reading this book right now or how many utils you would get from watching a sunset?)

To avoid this measurement problem, economists have developed an alternative explanation of consumer behavior and equilibrium in which cardinal measurement is not required. In this more-advanced analysis, the consumer must simply *rank* various combinations of goods in terms of preference. For instance, Sally can simply report that she *prefers* 4 units of A to 6 units of B without having to put number values on how much she likes either option. The model of consumer behavior that is based upon such *ordinal utility* rankings is called indifference curve analysis. It has two main elements: budget lines and indifference curves.

The Budget Line: What Is Attainable

We know from Chapter 1 that a **budget line** (or, more technically, a *budget constraint*) is a schedule or curve showing various combinations of two products a consumer can purchase with a specific money income. If the price of product A is $1.50 and the price of product B is $1, a consumer could purchase all the combinations of A and B shown in the table in Figure 1 with $12 of money income. At one extreme, the consumer might spend all of his or her income on 8 units of A and have nothing left to spend on B. Or, by giving up 2 units of A and thereby "freeing" $3, the consumer could have 6 units of A and 3 of B. And so on to the other extreme, at which the consumer could buy 12 units of B at $1 each, spending his or her entire money income on B with nothing left to spend on A.

Figure 1 also shows the budget line graphically. Note that the graph is not restricted to whole units of A and B as is the table. Every point on the graph represents a possible combination of A and B, including fractional quantities. The slope of the graphed budget line measures the ratio of the price of B to the price of A; more precisely, the absolute value of the slope is $P_B/P_A = \$1.00/\$1.50 = \frac{2}{3}$. This is the mathematical way of saying that the consumer must forgo 2 units of A (measured on the vertical axis) to buy

---

FIGURE 1 A consumer's budget line. The budget line shows all the combinations of any two products that someone can purchase, given the prices of the products and the person's money income.

Units of A (Price = $1.50)	Units of B (Price = $1)	Total Expenditure
8	0	$12 (= $12 + $0)
6	3	$12 (= $9 + $3)
4	6	$12 (= $6 + $6)
2	9	$12 (= $3 + $9)
0	12	$12 (= $0 + $12)

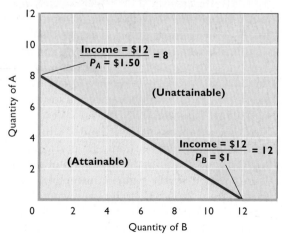

FIGURE 2 A consumer's indifference curve. Every point on indifference curve *I* represents some combination of products A and B, and all those combinations are equally satisfactory to the consumer. That is, each combination of A and B on the curve yields the same total utility.

Combination	Units of A	Units of B
j	12	2
k	6	4
l	4	6
m	3	8

3 units of B (measured on the horizontal axis). In moving down the budget or price line, 2 units of A (at $1.50 each) must be given up to obtain 3 more units of B (at $1 each). This yields a slope of $\frac{2}{3}$.

The budget line has two other significant characteristics:

- **Income changes** The location of the budget line varies with money income. An increase in money income shifts the budget line to the right; a decrease in money income shifts it to the left. To verify this, recalculate the table in Figure 1, assuming that money income is (a) $24 and (b) $6, and plot the new budget lines in Figure 1.
- **Price changes** A change in product prices also shifts the budget line. A decline in the prices of both products—the equivalent of an increase in real income—shifts the curve to the right. (You can verify this by recalculating the table in Figure 1 and replotting Figure 1 assuming that $P_A = \$.75$ and $P_B = \$.50$.) Conversely, an increase in the prices of A and B shifts the curve to the left. (Assume $P_A = \$3$ and $P_B = \$2$, and rework the table and Figure 1 to substantiate this statement.)

Note what happens if P_B changes while P_A and money income remain constant. In particular, if P_B drops, say, from $1 to $.50, the lower end of the budget line fans outward to the right. Conversely, if P_B increases, say, from $1 to $1.50, the lower end of the line fans inward to the left. In both instances the line remains "anchored" at 8 units on the vertical axis because P_A has not changed.

Indifference Curves: What Is Preferred

Budget lines reflect "objective" market data, specifically income and prices. They reveal combinations of products A and B that can be purchased, given current money income and prices.

Indifference curves, on the other hand, reflect "subjective" information about consumer preferences for A and B. An **indifference curve** shows all the combinations of two products A and B that will yield the same total satisfaction or total utility to a consumer. The table and graph in Figure 2 present a hypothetical indifference curve for products A and B. The consumer's subjective preferences are such that he or she will realize the same total utility from each combination of A and B shown in the table or on the curve. So the consumer will be indifferent (will not care) as to which combination is actually obtained.

Indifference curves have several important characteristics.

ORIGIN OF THE IDEA

O 6.5

Indifference curves

Indifference Curves Are Downsloping

An indifference curve slopes downward because more of one product means less of the other if total utility is to remain unchanged. Suppose the consumer moves from one combination of A and B to another, say, from *j* to *k* in Figure 2. In so doing, the consumer obtains more of product B, increasing his or her total utility. But because total utility is the same everywhere on the curve, the consumer must give up some of the other product, A, to reduce total utility by a precisely offsetting amount. Thus "more of B" necessitates "less of A," and the quantities of A and B are inversely related. A curve that reflects inversely related variables is downsloping.

Indifference Curves Are Convex to the Origin

Recall from the appendix to Chapter 1 that the slope of a curve at a particular point is measured by drawing a straight line that is tangent to that point and then measuring the "rise over run" of the straight line. If you drew such straight lines for several points on the curve in Figure 2, you would find that their slopes decline (in absolute terms) as you move down the curve. An indifference curve is therefore convex (bowed inward) to the origin of the graph. Its slope diminishes or becomes flatter as we move down the curve from *j* to *k* to *l*, and so on. Technically, the slope of an indifference curve at each point measures the **marginal rate of substitution (MRS)** of the combination of two goods represented by that point. The slope or MRS shows the rate at which the consumer who possesses the combination must substitute one good for the other (say, B for A) to remain equally satisfied. The diminishing slope of the indifference curve means that the willingness to substitute B for A diminishes as more of B is obtained.

The rationale for this convexity—that is, for a diminishing MRS—is that a consumer's subjective willingness to substitute B for A (or A for B) will depend on the amounts of B and A he or she has to begin with. Consider the table and graph in Figure 2 again, beginning at point *j*. Here, in relative terms, the consumer has a substantial amount of A and very little of B. Within this combination, a unit of B is very valuable (that is, its marginal utility is high), while a unit of A is less valuable (its marginal utility is low). The consumer will then be willing to give up a substantial amount of A to get, say, 2 more units of B. In this case, the consumer is willing to forgo 6 units of A to get 2 more units of B; the MRS is $\frac{6}{2}$, or 3, for the *jk* segment of the curve.

But at point *k* the consumer has less A and more B. Here A is somewhat more valuable, and B less valuable, "at the margin." In a move from point *k* to point *l*, the consumer is willing to give up only 2 units of A to get 2 more units of B, so the MRS is only $\frac{2}{2}$, or 1. Having still less of A and more of B at point *l*, the consumer is willing to give up only 1 unit of A in return for 2 more units of B and the MRS falls to $\frac{1}{2}$ between *l* and *m*.[1]

---
[1] MRS declines continuously between *j* and *k*, *k* and *l*, and *l* and *m*. Our numerical values for MRS relate to the curve segments between points and are not the actual values of the MRS at each point. For example, the MRS *at* point *l* is $\frac{2}{3}$.

In general, as the amount of B *increases*, the marginal utility of additional units of B *decreases*. Similarly, as the quantity of A *decreases*, its marginal utility *increases*. In Figure 2 we see that in moving down the curve, the consumer will be willing to give up smaller and smaller amounts of A to offset acquiring each additional unit of B. The result is a curve with a diminishing slope, a curve that is convex to the origin. The MRS declines as one moves southeast along the indifference curve.

The Indifference Map

The single indifference curve of Figure 2 reflects some constant (but unspecified) level of total utility or satisfaction. It is possible and useful to sketch a whole series of indifference curves or an **indifference map,** as shown in Figure 3. Each curve reflects a different level of total utility and therefore never crosses another indifference curve. Specifically, each curve to the right of our original curve (labeled I_3 in Figure 3) reflects combinations of A and B that yield more utility than I_3. Each curve to the left of I_3 reflects less total utility than I_3. As we move out from the origin, each successive indifference curve represents a higher level of utility. To demonstrate this fact, draw a line in a northeasterly direction from the origin; note that its points of intersection with successive curves entail larger

Higher the curve the more income it takes to get

FIGURE 3 An indifference map. An indifference map is a set of indifference curves. Curves farther from the origin indicate higher levels of total utility. Thus any combination of products A and B represented by a point on I_4 has greater total utility than any combination of A and B represented by a point on I_3, I_2, or I_1.

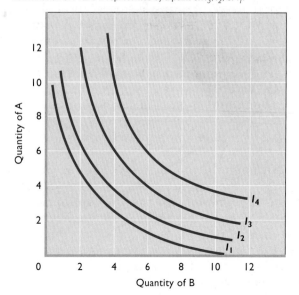

amounts of both A and B and therefore higher levels of total utility.

Equilibrium at Tangency

Since the axes in Figures 1 and 3 are identical, we can superimpose a budget line on the consumer's indifference map, as shown in Figure 4. By definition, the budget line indicates all the combinations of A and B that the consumer can attain with his or her money income, given the prices of A and B. Of these attainable combinations, the consumer will prefer the combination that yields the greatest satisfaction or utility. Specifically, the utility-maximizing combination will be the combination lying on the highest attainable indifference curve. It is called the consumer's **equilibrium position.**

In Figure 4 the consumer's equilibrium position is at point X, where the budget line is *tangent* to I_3. Why not point Y? Because Y is on a lower indifference curve, I_2. By moving "down" the budget line—by shifting dollars from purchases of A to purchases of B—the consumer can attain an indifference curve farther from the origin and thereby increase the total utility derived from the same income. Why not point Z? For the same reason: Point Z is on a lower indifference curve, I_1. By moving "up" the budget line—by reallocating dollars from B to A—the consumer can get on higher indifference curve I_3 and increase total utility.

How about point W on indifference curve I_4? While it is true that W would yield a greater total utility than X,

point W is beyond (outside) the budget line and hence is *not* attainable by the consumer. Point X represents the optimal *attainable* combination of products A and B. Note that at the equilibrium position, X, the definition of tangency implies that the slope of the highest attainable indifference curve equals the slope of the budget line. Because the slope of the indifference curve reflects the MRS (marginal rate of substitution) and the slope of the budget line is P_B/P_A, the consumer's optimal or equilibrium position is the point where

$$\text{MRS} = \frac{P_B}{P_A}$$

(You may benefit by trying Appendix Question 3 at this time.)

Equivalency at Equilibrium

As indicated at the beginning of this appendix, an important difference exists between the marginal-utility theory of consumer demand and the indifference curve theory. The marginal-utility theory assumes that utility is *numerically* measurable, that is, that the consumer can say how much extra utility he or she derives from each extra unit of A or B. The consumer needs that information to determine the utility-maximizing (equilibrium) position, which is defined by

$$\frac{\text{Marginal utility of A}}{\text{Price of A}} = \frac{\text{Marginal utility of B}}{\text{Price of B}}$$

The indifference curve approach imposes a less stringent requirement on the consumer. He or she need only specify whether a particular combination of A and B will yield more than, less than, or the same amount of utility as some other combination of A and B will yield. The consumer need only say, for example, that 6 of A and 7 of B will yield more (or less) satisfaction than will 4 of A and 9 of B. Indifference curve theory does not require that the consumer specify *how much* more (or less) satisfaction will be realized.

That being said, it is a remarkable mathematical fact that both models of consumer behavior will, in any given situation, point to exactly the same consumer equilibrium and, consequently, exactly the same demand behavior. This fact allows us to combine the separate pieces of information that each theory gives us about equilibrium in order to deduce an interesting property about marginal utilities that must also hold true in equilibrium. To see this, note that when we compare the equilibrium situations in the two theories, we find that in the indifference curve analysis the MRS equals P_B/P_A at equilibrium; however, in the marginal-utility approach the ratio of marginal

FIGURE 4 **The consumer's equilibrium position.** The consumer's equilibrium position is represented by point X, where the black budget line is tangent to indifference curve I_3. The consumer buys 4 units of A at \$1.50 per unit and 6 of B at \$1 per unit with a \$12 money income. Points Z and Y represent attainable combinations of A and B but yield less total utility, as is evidenced by the fact that they are on lower indifference curves. Point W would entail more utility than X, but it requires a greater income than the \$12 represented by the budget line.

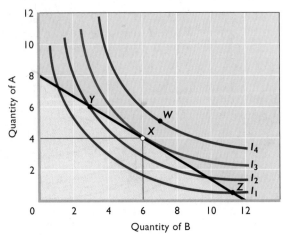

CONSIDER THIS . . .

Indifference Maps and Topographical Maps

The familiar topographical map may help you understand the idea of indifference curves and indifference maps. Each line on a topographical map represents a particular elevation above sea level, say, 500 feet. Similarly, an indifference curve represents a particular level of total utility. When you move from one point on a specific elevation line to another, the elevation remains the same. So it is with an indifference curve. A move from one position to another on the curve leaves total utility unchanged. Neither elevation lines nor indifference curves can intersect. If they did, the meaning of each line or curve would be violated. An elevation line is "an equal-elevation line"; an indifference curve is "an equal-total-utility curve."

Like the topographical map, an indifference map contains not just one line but a series of lines. That is, the topographical map may have elevation lines representing successively higher elevations of 100, 200, 300, 400, and 500 feet. Similarly, the indifference curves on the indifference map represent successively higher levels of total utility. The climber whose goal is to maximize elevation wants to get to the highest attainable elevation line; the consumer desiring to maximize total utility wants to get to the highest attainable indifference curve.

Finally, both topographical maps and indifference maps show only a few of the many such lines that could be drawn. The topographical map, for example, leaves out the elevation lines for 501 feet, 502, 503, and so on. The indifference map leaves out all the indifference curves that could be drawn between those that are displayed.

utilities equals P_B/P_A. We therefore deduce that at equilibrium the MRS is equivalent in the marginal-utility approach to the ratio of the marginal utilities of the last purchased units of the two products.[2]

---

[2]Technical footnote: If we begin with the utility-maximizing rule, $MU_A/P_A = MU_B/P_B$, and then multiply through by P_B and divide through by MU_A, we obtain $P_B/P_A = MU_B/MU_A$. In indifference curve analysis we know that at the equilibrium position MRS $= P_B/P_A$. Hence, at equilibrium, MRS also equals MU_B/MU_A.

The Derivation of the Demand Curve

We noted earlier that with a fixed price for A, an increase in the price of B will cause the bottom of the budget line to fan inward to the left. We can use that fact to derive a demand curve for product B. In Figure 5a we reproduce the part of Figure 4 that shows our initial consumer equilibrium at point X. The budget line determining this

FIGURE 5 Deriving the demand curve. (a) When the price of product B is increased from $1 to $1.50, the equilibrium position moves from X to X', decreasing the quantity demanded of product B from 6 to 3 units. (b) The demand curve for product B is determined by plotting the $1–6-unit and the $1.50–3-unit price-quantity combinations for product B.

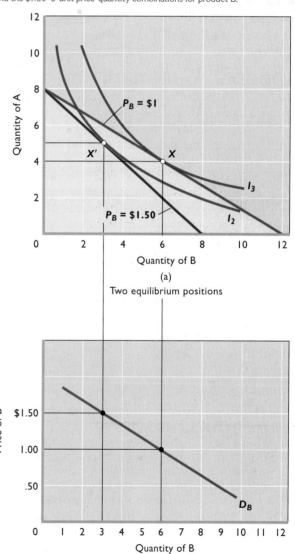

(a)
Two equilibrium positions

(b)
The demand curve for product B

equilibrium position assumes that money income is $12 and that $P_A = \$1.50$ and $P_B = \$1$. Let's see what happens to the equilibrium position when we increase P_B to $1.50 and hold both money income and the price of A constant. The result is shown in Figure 5a. The budget line fans to the left, yielding a new equilibrium point X' where it is tangent to lower indifference curve I_2. At X' the consumer buys 3 units of B and 5 of A, compared with 4 of A and 6 of B at X. Our interest is in B, and we now have sufficient information to locate two points on the demand curve for product B. We know that at equilibrium point X the price of B is $1 and 6 units are purchased; at equilibrium point X' the price of B is $1.50 and 3 units are purchased.

These data are shown graphically in Figure 5b as points on the consumer's demand curve for B. Note that the horizontal axes of Figures 5a and 5b are identical; both measure the quantity demanded of B. We can therefore drop vertical reference lines from Figure 5a down to the horizontal axis of Figure 5b. On the vertical axis of Figure 5b we locate the two chosen prices of B. Knowing that these prices yield the relevant quantities demanded, we locate two points on the demand curve for B. By simple manipulation of the price of B in an indifference curve–budget line context, we have obtained a downward-sloping demand curve for B. We have thus again derived the law of demand assuming "other things equal," since only the price of B was changed (the price of A and the consumer's money income and tastes remained constant). But, in this case, we have derived the demand curve without resorting to the questionable assumption that consumers can measure utility in units called "utils." In this indifference curve approach, consumers simply compare combinations of products A and B and determine which combination they prefer, given their incomes and the prices of the two products.

Appendix Summary

1. The indifference curve approach to consumer behavior is based on the consumer's budget line and indifference curves.

2. The budget line shows all combinations of two products that the consumer can purchase, given product prices and his or her money income.

3. A change in either product prices or money income moves the budget line.

4. An indifference curve shows all combinations of two products that will yield the same total utility to a consumer. Indifference curves are downsloping and convex to the origin.

5. An indifference map consists of a number of indifference curves; the farther from the origin, the higher the total utility associated with a curve.

6. The consumer is in equilibrium (utility is maximized) at the point on the budget line that lies on the highest attainable indifference curve. At that point the budget line and indifference curve are tangent.

7. Changing the price of one product shifts the budget line and determines a new equilibrium point. A downsloping demand curve can be determined by plotting the price-quantity combinations associated with two or more equilibrium points.

Appendix Terms and Concepts

budget line

indifference curve

marginal rate of
substitution (MRS)

indifference map

equilibrium position

Appendix Questions

1. What information is embodied in a budget line? What shifts occur in the budget line when money income (*a*) increases and (*b*) decreases? What shifts occur in the budget line when the price of the product shown on the vertical axis (*c*) increases and (*d*) decreases? **LO6**

2. What information is contained in an indifference curve? Why are such curves (*a*) downsloping and (*b*) convex to the origin? Why does total utility increase as the consumer moves to indifference curves farther from the origin? Why can't indifference curves intersect? **LO6**

3. Using Figure 4, explain why the point of tangency of the budget line with an indifference curve is the consumer's equilibrium position. Explain why any point where the budget line intersects an indifference curve is not equilibrium. Explain: "The consumer is in equilibrium where $MRS = P_B/P_A$." **LO6**

Appendix Problems

1. Assume that the data in the accompanying table give an indifference curve for Mr. Chen. Graph this curve, putting A on the vertical axis and B on the horizontal axis. Assuming that the prices of A and B are $1.50 and $1, respectively, and that Mr. Chen has $24 to spend, add his budget line to your graph. What combination of A and B will Mr. Chen purchase? Does your answer meet the MRS = P_B/P_A rule for equilibrium? LO6

Units of A	Units of B
16	6
12	8
8	12
4	24

2. Explain graphically how indifference analysis can be used to derive a demand curve. LO6

3. **ADVANCED ANALYSIS** First, graphically illustrate a doubling of income without price changes in the indifference curve model. Next, on the same graph, show a situation in which the person whose indifference curves you are drawing buys considerably more of good B than good A after the income increase. What can you conclude about the relative coefficients of the income elasticity of demand for goods A and B (Chapter 4)? LO6

7

Businesses and the Costs of Production

Our attention now turns from the behavior of consumers to the behavior of producers. In market economies, a wide variety of businesses produce an even wider variety of goods and services. Each of those businesses requires economic resources in order to produce its products. In obtaining and using resources, a firm makes monetary payments to resource owners (for example, workers) and incurs opportunity costs when using resources it already owns (for example, entrepreneurial talent). Those payments and opportunity costs together make up the firm's *costs of production,* which we discuss in this chapter.

Then, in the next several chapters, we bring product demand, product prices, and revenue back into the analysis and explain how firms compare revenues and costs in determining how much to produce. Our ultimate purpose is to show how those comparisons relate to economic efficiency.

Economic Costs

Firms face costs because the resources they need to produce their products are scarce and have alternative uses. Because of scarcity, firms wanting a particular resource have to bid it away from other firms. That process is costly for firms because it requires a payment to the resource owner. This reality causes economists to define **economic cost** as the payment that must be made to obtain and retain the services of a resource. It is the income the firm must provide to resource suppliers to attract resources away from alternative uses.

This section explains how firms incorporate opportunity costs to calculate economic costs. If you need a refresher on opportunity costs, a brief review of the section on opportunity costs in Chapter 1 might be useful before continuing on with the rest of this section.

Explicit and Implicit Costs

To properly calculate a firm's economic costs, you must remember that *all* of the resources used by the firm have an opportunity cost. This is true both for the resources that a firm purchases from outsiders as well as for the resources that it already owns.

As an example, consider a table-making firm that starts this month with $5000 in cash as well as ownership of a small oak forest from which it gets the oak that it turns into tables.

Suppose that during the month the firm uses the entire $5000 of cash to pay its workers. Clearly, the $5000 it spends purchasing their labor comes at the opportunity cost of forgoing the best alternatives that could have been bought with that money.

Less obvious, however, is the opportunity cost of the oak that the firm grows itself and which it uses to make tables. Suppose that the oak has a market value of $1500, meaning that our table-making firm could sell it to outsiders for $1500. This implies that using the oak to make tables has an opportunity cost of $1500. Choosing to convert the oak into tables means giving up the best alternatives that the firm could have purchased with the $1500.

As a result, keep in mind that *all* of the resources that a firm uses—whether purchased from outside or already owned—have opportunity costs and thus economic costs. Economists refer to these two types of economic costs as *explicit costs* and *implicit costs*:

- A firm's **explicit costs** are the monetary payments it makes to those from whom it must purchase resources that it does not own. Because these costs involve an obvious cash transaction, they are

referred to as explicit costs. Be sure to remember that explicit costs are opportunity costs because every monetary payment used to purchase outside resources necessarily involves forgoing the best alternatives that could have been purchased with the money.

- A firm's **implicit costs** are the opportunity costs of using the resources that it already owns to make the firm's own product rather than selling those resources to outsiders for cash. Because these costs are present but not obvious, they are referred to as implicit costs.

A firm's economic costs are the sum of its explicit costs and its implicit costs:

$$\frac{\text{Economic}}{\text{costs}} = \frac{\text{explicit}}{\text{costs}} + \frac{\text{implicit}}{\text{costs}}$$

The following example makes clear how both explicit costs and implicit costs affect firm profits and firm behavior.

Accounting Profit and Normal Profit

Suppose that after many years working as a sales representative for a large T-shirt manufacturer, you decided to strike out on your own. After considering many potential business ventures, you decide to open a retail T-shirt shop. As we explain in Chapter 2, you will be providing two different economic resources to your new enterprise: labor and entrepreneurial ability. The part of your job that involves providing labor includes any of the routine tasks that are needed to help run the business—things like answering customer e-mails, taking inventory, and sweeping the floor. The part of your job that involves providing entrepreneurial ability includes any of the nonroutine tasks involved with organizing the business and directing its strategy—things like deciding on whether to use Internet ads or in-person events to promote your business, whether to include children's clothing in your product mix, and how to decorate your store to maximize its appeal to potential customers.

You begin providing entrepreneurial ability to your new firm by making some initial organizational decisions. You decide to work full time at your new business, so you quit your old job that paid you $22,000 per year. You invest $20,000 of savings that has been earning $1000 per year. You decide that your new firm will occupy a small retail space that you own and had been previously renting out for $5000 per year. Finally, you decide to hire one clerk to help you in the store. She agrees to work for you for $18,000 per year.

After a year in business, you total up your accounts and find the following:

Total sales revenue	$120,000
Cost of T-shirts	$40,000
Clerk's salary	18,000
Utilities	5000
Total (explicit) costs	63,000
Accounting profit	57,000

These numbers look very good. In particular, you are happy with your $57,000 **accounting profit,** the profit number that accountants calculate by subtracting total explicit costs from total sales revenue. This is the profit (or net income) that would appear on your accounting statement and that you would report to the government for tax purposes.

But don't celebrate yet! Your $57,000 accounting profit overstates the economic success of your business because it ignores your implicit costs. Success is not defined as "having a total sales revenue that exceeds total explicit costs." Rather, the true measure of success is doing as well as you possibly can—that is, making more money in your new venture selling T-shirts than you could pursuing any other business venture.

To figure out whether you are achieving that goal, you must take into account all of your opportunity costs—both your implicit costs as well as your explicit costs. Doing so will indicate whether your new business venture is earning more money than what you could have earned in any other business venture.

To see how these calculations are made, let's continue with our example.

By providing your own financial capital, retail space, and labor, you incurred three different implicit costs during the year: $1000 of forgone interest, $5000 of forgone rent, and $22,000 of forgone wages. But don't forget that there is another implicit cost that you must also take account of—how much income you chose to forgo by applying your entrepreneurial abilities to your current retail T-shirt venture rather than applying them to other potential business ventures.

But what dollar value should we place on the size of the profits that you might have made if you had provided your entrepreneurial ability to one of those other ventures?

The answer is given by estimating a **normal profit,** the typical (or "normal") amount of accounting profit that you would most likely have earned in one of these other ventures. For the sake of argument, let us assume that with your particular set of skills and talents your entrepreneurial abilities would have on average yielded a normal profit of

$5000 in one of the other potential ventures. Knowing that value, we can take all of your implicit costs properly into account by subtracting them from your accounting profit:

Accounting profit	$57,000
Forgone interest	$ 1000
Forgone rent	5000
Forgone wages	22,000
Forgone entrepreneurial income	5000
Total implicit costs	33,000
Economic profit	24,000

Economic Profit

After subtracting your $33,000 of implicit costs from your accounting profit of $57,000, we are left with an *economic profit* of $24,000.

Please distinguish clearly between accounting profit and economic profit. Accounting profit is the result of subtracting only explicit costs from revenue: *Accounting Profit = Revenue − Explicit Costs*. By contrast, **economic profit** is the result of subtracting all of your economic costs—both explicit costs and implicit costs—from revenue: *Economic Profit = Revenue − Explicit Costs − Implicit Costs*.

WORKED PROBLEMS

W 7.1

Economic profit

By subtracting all of your economic costs from your revenue, you determine how your current business venture compares with your best alternative business venture. In our example, the fact that you are generating an economic profit of $24,000 means that you are making $24,000 more than you could expect to make in your best alternative business venture.

By contrast, suppose that you had instead done poorly in business, so that this year your firm generated an economic loss (a negative economic profit) of $8000. This would mean that you were doing worse in your current venture than you could have done in your best alternative venture. You would, as a result, wish to switch to that alternative.

Generalizing this point, we see that there is an important behavioral threshold at $0 of economic profit. If a firm is breaking even (that is, earning exactly $0 of economic profit), then its entrepreneurs know that they are doing exactly as well as they could expect to do in their best alternative business venture. They are earning enough to cover all their explicit and implicit costs, including the normal profit that they could expect to earn in other business ventures. Thus, they have no incentive to change. By

FIGURE 7.1 Economic profit versus accounting

profit. Economic profit is equal to total revenue less economic costs. Economic costs are the sum of explicit and implicit costs and include a normal profit to the entrepreneur. Accounting profit is equal to total revenue less accounting (explicit) costs.

contrast, anyone running a positive economic profit knows they are doing better than they could in alternative ventures and will want to continue doing what they are doing or maybe even expand their business. And anyone running an economic loss (a negative economic profit) knows that they could do better by switching to something else.

It is for this reason that economists focus on economic profits rather than accounting profits. Simply put, economic profits direct how resources are allocated in the economy. Entrepreneurs running economic losses close their current businesses, thereby freeing up the land, labor, capital, and entrepreneurial ability that they had been using. These resources are freed up to be used by firms that are generating positive economic profits or which are at least breaking even. Resources thus flow from producing goods and services with lower net benefits toward producing goods and services with higher net benefits. Allocative efficiency increases as firms are led by their profit signals to produce more of what consumers want the most.

Figure 7.1 shows the relationship among the various cost and profit concepts that we have just discussed. To test yourself, you might want to enter cost data from our example in the appropriate blocks.

Short Run and Long Run

When the demand for a firm's product changes, the firm's profitability may depend on how quickly it can adjust the amounts of the various resources it employs. It can easily and quickly adjust the quantities employed of many resources such as hourly labor, raw materials, fuel, and power. It needs much more time, however, to adjust its *plant capacity*—the size of the factory building, the amount of machinery and equipment, and other capital resources. In some heavy industries such as aircraft manufacturing, a firm may need several years to alter plant capacity. Because

of these differences in adjustment time, economists find it useful to distinguish between two conceptual periods: the short run and the long run. We will discover that costs differ in these two time periods.

Short Run: Fixed Plant In microeconomics, the **short run** is a period too brief for a firm to alter its plant capacity, yet long enough to permit a change in the degree to which the plant's current capacity is used. The firm's plant capacity is fixed in the short run. However, the firm can vary its output by applying larger or smaller amounts of labor, materials, and other resources to that plant. It can use its existing plant capacity more or less intensively in the short run.

Long Run: Variable Plant In microeconomics, the **long run** is a period long enough for it to adjust the quantities of all the resources that it employs, including plant capacity. From the industry's viewpoint, the long run also includes enough time for existing firms to dissolve and leave the industry or for new firms to be created and enter the industry. While the short run is a "fixed-plant" period, the long run is a "variable-plant" period.

Illustrations If Boeing hires 100 extra workers for one of its commercial airline plants or adds an entire shift of workers, we are speaking of the short run. If it adds a new production facility and installs more equipment, we are referring to the long run. The first situation is a *short-run adjustment;* the second is a *long-run adjustment.*

The short run and the long run are conceptual periods rather than calendar time periods. In light-manufacturing industries, changes in plant capacity may be accomplished almost overnight. A small T-shirt manufacturer can increase its plant capacity in a matter of days by ordering and installing two or three new cutting tables and several extra sewing machines. But for heavy industry the long run is a different matter. Shell Oil may require several years to construct a new gasoline refinery.

QUICK REVIEW 7.1

- Explicit costs are money payments a firm makes to outside suppliers of resources; implicit costs are the opportunity costs associated with a firm's use of resources it owns.
- Normal profit is the implicit cost of entrepreneurship. Economic profit is total revenue less all explicit and implicit costs, including normal profit.
- In the short run, a firm's plant capacity is fixed; in the long run, a firm can vary its plant size and firms can enter or leave the industry.

Short-Run Production Relationships

A firm's costs of producing a specific output depend on the prices of the needed resources and the quantities of resources (inputs) needed to produce that output. Resource supply and demand determine resource prices. The technological aspects of production, specifically the relationships between inputs and output, determine the quantities of resources needed. Our focus will be on the *labor*-output relationship, given a fixed plant capacity. But before examining that relationship, we need to define three terms:

- **Total product (TP)** is the total quantity, or total output, of a particular good or service produced.
- **Marginal product (MP)** is the extra output or added product associated with adding a unit of a variable resource, in this case labor, to the production process. Thus,

$$\text{Marginal product} = \frac{\text{change in total product}}{\text{change in labor input}}$$

- **Average product (AP),** also called labor productivity, is output per unit of labor input:

$$\text{Average product} = \frac{\text{total product}}{\text{units of labor}}$$

In the short run, a firm can for a time increase its output by adding units of labor to its fixed plant. But by how much will output rise when it adds more labor? Why do we say "for a time"?

Law of Diminishing Returns

The answers are provided in general terms by the **law of diminishing returns.** This law assumes that technology is

ORIGIN OF THE IDEA

O 7.1

Law of diminishing returns

fixed and thus the techniques of production do not change. It states that as successive units of a variable resource (say, labor) are added to a fixed resource (say, capital or land), beyond some point the extra, or marginal, product that can be attributed to each additional unit of the variable resource will decline. For example, if additional workers are hired to work with a constant amount of capital equipment, output will eventually rise by smaller and smaller amounts as more workers are hired.

Rationale Suppose a farmer has a fixed resource—80 acres of land—planted in corn. If the farmer does not cultivate the cornfields (clear the weeds) at all, the yield will be

CONSIDER THIS . . .

Diminishing Returns from Study

Here is a noneconomic example of a relationship between "inputs" and "output" that may help you better understand the idea of diminishing returns. Suppose for an individual that

Total course learning = f (intelligence, quality of course materials, instructor effectiveness, class time, and study time)

where f means "function of" or "depends on." So this relationship supposes that total course learning depends on intelligence (however defined), quality of course materials such as the textbook, the effectiveness of the instructor, the amount of class time, and the amount of personal study time outside the class.

For analytical purposes, let's assume that one's intelligence, the quality of course materials, the effectiveness of the instructor, and the amount of class time are *fixed*—meaning they do not change over the length of the course. Now let's add units of study time per day over the length of the course to "produce" greater course learning. The first hour of study time per day increases total course learning. Will the second hour enhance course learning by as much as the first? By how much will the third, fourth, fifth, . . . fifteenth hour of study per day contribute to total course learning relative to the *immediate previous hour*?

We think you will agree that eventually diminishing returns to course learning will set in as successive hours of study are added each day. At some point the marginal product of an extra hour of study time will decline and, at some further point, become zero.

This is also true of production relationships within firms. As successive units of a variable input (say, labor) are added to a fixed input (say, capital), the marginal product of the variable input eventually declines. In short, diminishing returns will occur sooner or later. Total product eventually will rise at a diminishing rate, reach a maximum, and then decline.

40 bushels per acre. If he cultivates the land once, output may rise to 50 bushels per acre. A second cultivation may increase output to 57 bushels per acre, a third to 61, and a fourth to 63. Succeeding cultivations will add less and less to the land's yield. If this were not so, the world's needs for corn could be fulfilled by extremely intense cultivation of this single 80-acre plot of land. Indeed, if diminishing returns did not occur, the world could be fed out of a flowerpot. Why not? Just keep adding more seed, fertilizer, and harvesters!

TABLE 7.1 Total, Marginal, and Average Product: The Law of Diminishing Returns

(1) Units of the Variable Resource (Labor)	(2) Total Product (TP)	(3) Marginal Product (MP), Change in (2)/ Change in (1)		(4) Average Product (AP), (2)/(1)
0	0			—
1	10	10	Increasing	10.00
2	25	15	marginal	12.50
3	45	20	returns	15.00
4	60	15	Diminishing	15.00
5	70	10	marginal	14.00
6	75	5	returns	12.50
7	75	0	Negative	10.71
8	70	−5	marginal returns	8.75

The law of diminishing returns also holds true in non-agricultural industries. Assume a wood shop is manufacturing furniture frames. It has a specific amount of equipment such as lathes, planes, saws, and sanders. If this shop hired just one or two workers, total output and productivity (output per worker) would be very low. The workers would have to perform many different jobs, and the advantages of specialization would not be realized. Time would be lost in switching from one job to another, and machines would stand idle much of the time. In short, the plant would be understaffed, and production would be inefficient because there would be too much capital relative to the amount of labor.

The shop could eliminate those difficulties by hiring more workers. Then the equipment would be more fully used, and workers could specialize on doing a single job. Time would no longer be lost switching from job to job. As more workers were added, production would become more efficient and the marginal product of each succeeding worker would rise.

But the rise could not go on indefinitely. Beyond a certain point, adding more workers would cause overcrowding. Since workers would then have to wait in line to use the machinery, they would be underused. Total output would increase at a diminishing rate because, given the fixed size of the plant, each worker would have less capital equipment to work with as more and more labor was hired. The marginal product of additional workers would decline because there would be more labor in proportion to the fixed amount of capital. Eventually, adding still more workers would cause so much congestion that marginal product would become negative and total product would decline. At the extreme, the addition of more and more labor would exhaust all the standing room, and total product would fall to zero.

Note that the law of diminishing returns assumes that all units of labor are of equal quality. Each successive worker is presumed to have the same innate ability, motor coordination, education, training, and work experience. Marginal product ultimately diminishes, but not because successive workers are less skilled or less energetic. It declines because the firm is using more workers relative to the amount of plant and equipment available.

Tabular Example Table 7.1 is a numerical illustration of the law of diminishing returns. Column 2 shows the total product, or total output, resulting from combining each level of a variable input (labor) in column 1 with a fixed amount of capital.

Column 3 shows the marginal product (MP), the change in total product associated with each additional unit of labor. Note that with no labor input, total product is zero; a plant with no workers will produce no output. The first three units of labor reflect increasing marginal returns, with marginal products of 10, 15, and 20 units, respectively. But beginning with the fourth unit of labor, marginal product diminishes continuously, becoming zero with the seventh unit of labor and negative with the eighth.

Average product, or output per labor unit, is shown in column 4. It is calculated by dividing total product (column 2) by the number of labor units needed to produce it (column 1). At 5 units of labor, for example, AP is 14 (= 70/5).

Graphical Portrayal **Figure 7.2 (Key Graph)** shows the diminishing-returns data in Table 7.1 graphically and further clarifies the relationships between total, marginal,

WORKED PROBLEMS

W 7.2

Total, marginal, and average product

key graph

(a)
Total product

FIGURE 7.2 **The law of diminishing returns.** (a) As a variable resource (labor) is added to fixed amounts of other resources (land or capital), the total product that results will eventually increase by diminishing amounts, reach a maximum, and then decline. (b) Marginal product is the change in total product associated with each new unit of labor. Average product is simply output per labor unit. Note that marginal product intersects average product at the maximum average product.

(b)
Marginal and average product

QUICK QUIZ FOR FIGURE 7.2

1. Which of the following is an assumption underlying these figures?
   a. Firms first hire "better" workers and then hire "poorer" workers.
   b. Capital and labor are both variable, but labor increases more rapidly than capital.
   c. Consumers will buy all the output (total product) produced.
   d. Workers are of equal quality.

2. Marginal product is:
   a. the change in total product divided by the change in the quantity of labor.
   b. total product divided by the quantity of labor.
   c. always positive.
   d. unrelated to total product.

3. Marginal product in graph (b) is zero when:
   a. average product in graph (b) stops rising.
   b. the slope of the marginal-product curve in graph (b) is zero.
   c. total product in graph (a) begins to rise at a diminishing rate.
   d. the slope of the total-product curve in graph (a) is zero.

4. Average product in graph (b):
   a. rises when it is less than marginal product.
   b. is the change in total product divided by the change in the quantity of labor.
   c. can never exceed marginal product.
   d. falls whenever total product in graph (a) rises at a diminishing rate.

Answers: 1. d; 2. a; 3. d; 4. a

and average products. (Marginal product in Figure 7.2b is plotted halfway between the units of labor since it applies to the addition of each labor unit.)

Note first in Figure 7.2a that total product, TP, goes through three phases: It rises initially at an increasing rate; then it increases, but at a diminishing rate; finally, after reaching a maximum, it declines.

Geometrically, marginal product—shown by the MP curve in Figure 7.2b—is the slope of the total-product curve. Marginal product measures the change in total product associated with each succeeding unit of labor. Thus, the three phases of total product are also reflected in marginal product. Where total product is increasing at an increasing rate, marginal product is rising. Here, extra units of labor are adding larger and larger amounts to total product. Similarly, where total product is increasing but at a decreasing rate, marginal product is positive but falling. Each additional unit of labor adds less to total product than did the previous unit. When total product is at a maximum, marginal product is zero. When total product declines, marginal product becomes negative.

Average product, AP (Figure 7.2b), displays the same tendencies as marginal product. It increases, reaches a maximum, and then decreases as more and more units of labor are added to the fixed plant. But note the relationship between marginal product and average product: Where marginal product exceeds average product, average product rises. And where marginal product is less than average product, average product declines. It follows that marginal product intersects average product where average product is at a maximum.

This relationship is a mathematical necessity. If you add a larger number to a total than the current average of that total, the average must rise. And if you add a smaller number to a total than the current average of that total, the average must fall. You raise your average examination grade only when your score on an additional (marginal) examination is greater than the average of all your past scores. You lower your average when your grade on an additional exam is below your current average. In our production example, when the amount an extra worker adds to total product exceeds the average product of all workers currently employed, average product will rise. Conversely, when the amount an extra worker adds to total product is less than the current average product, average product will decrease.

ORIGIN OF THE IDEA

O 7.2

Production relationship

The law of diminishing returns is embodied in the shapes of all three curves. But, as our definition of the law

of diminishing returns indicates, economists are most concerned with its effects on marginal product. The regions of increasing, diminishing, and negative marginal product (returns) are shown in Figure 7.2b.

Short-Run Production Costs

Production information such as that provided in Table 7.1 and Figures 7.2a and 7.2b must be coupled with resource prices to determine the total and per-unit costs of producing various levels of output. We know that in the short run, resources associated with the firm's plant are fixed. Other resources, however, are variable in the short run. As a result, short-run costs can be either fixed or variable.

Fixed, Variable, and Total Costs

Let's see what distinguishes fixed costs, variable costs, and total costs from one another.

Fixed Costs **Fixed costs** are those costs that do not vary with changes in output. Fixed costs are associated with the very existence of a firm's plant and therefore must be paid even if its output is zero. Such costs as rental payments, interest on a firm's debts, a portion of depreciation on equipment and buildings, and insurance premiums are generally fixed costs; they are fixed and do not change even if a firm produces more. In column 2 of Table 7.2 we assume that the firm's total fixed cost is $100. By definition, this fixed cost is incurred at all levels of output, including zero. The firm cannot avoid paying fixed costs in the short run.

Variable Costs **Variable costs** are those costs that change with the level of output. They include payments for materials, fuel, power, transportation services, most labor, and similar variable resources. In column 3 of Table 7.2 we find that the total of variable costs changes directly with output. But note that the increases in variable cost associated with succeeding one-unit increases in output are not equal. As production begins, variable cost will for a time increase by a decreasing amount; this is true through the fourth unit of output in Table 7.2. Beyond the fourth unit, however, variable cost rises by increasing amounts for succeeding units of output.

The reason lies in the shape of the marginal-product curve. At first, as in Figure 7.2b, marginal product is increasing, so smaller and smaller increases in the amounts of variable resources are needed to produce successive units of output. Hence the variable cost of successive units of output decreases. But when, as diminishing returns are encountered, marginal product begins to decline, larger and larger additional amounts of variable resources are

TABLE 7.2 Total-, Average-, and Marginal-Cost Schedules for an Individual Firm in the Short Run

	Total-Cost Data			Average-Cost Data			Marginal Cost
(1) Total Product (Q)	(2) Total Fixed Cost (TFC)	(3) Total Variable Cost (TVC)	(4) Total Cost (TC) TC = TFC + TVC	(5) Average Fixed Cost (AFC) $AFC = \dfrac{TFC}{Q}$	(6) Average Variable Cost (AVC) $AVC = \dfrac{TVC}{Q}$	(7) Average Total Cost (ATC) $ATC = \dfrac{TC}{Q}$	(8) Marginal Cost (MC) $MC = \dfrac{\text{change in TC}}{\text{change in Q}}$
0	$100	$ 0	$ 100				
1	100	90	190	$100.00	$90.00	$190.00	$ 90
2	100	170	270	50.00	85.00	135.00	80
3	100	240	340	33.33	80.00	113.33	70
4	100	300	400	25.00	75.00	100.00	60
5	100	370	470	20.00	74.00	94.00	70
6	100	450	550	16.67	75.00	91.67	80
7	100	540	640	14.29	77.14	91.43	90
8	100	650	750	12.50	81.25	93.75	110
9	100	780	880	11.11	86.67	97.78	130
10	100	930	1030	10.00	93.00	103.00	150

needed to produce successive units of output. Total variable cost therefore increases by increasing amounts.

Total Cost

Total cost is the sum of fixed cost and variable cost at each level of output:

$$TC = TFC + TVC$$

TC is shown in column 4 of Table 7.2. At zero units of output, total cost is equal to the firm's fixed cost. Then for each unit of the 10 units of production, total cost increases by the same amount as variable cost.

Figure 7.3 shows graphically the fixed-, variable-, and total-cost data given in Table 7.2. Observe that total variable cost, TVC, is measured vertically from the horizontal axis at each level of output. The amount of fixed cost, shown as TFC, is added vertically to the total-variable-cost curve to obtain the points on the total-cost curve TC.

The distinction between fixed and variable costs is significant to the business manager. Variable costs can be controlled or altered in the short run by changing production levels. Fixed costs are beyond the business manager's current control; they are incurred in the short run and must be paid regardless of output level.

Per-Unit, or Average, Costs

Producers are certainly interested in their total costs, but they are equally concerned with per-unit, or average, costs. In particular, average-cost data are more meaningful for making comparisons with product price, which is always stated on a per-unit basis. Average fixed cost, average variable

cost, and average total cost are shown in columns 5 to 7, Table 7.2.

AFC

Average fixed cost (AFC) for any output level is found by dividing total fixed cost (TFC) by that amount of output (Q). That is,

$$AFC = \frac{TFC}{Q}$$

FIGURE 7.3 Total cost is the sum of fixed cost and variable cost. Total variable cost (TVC) changes with output. Total fixed cost (TFC) is independent of the level of output. The total cost (TC) at any output is the vertical sum of the fixed cost and variable cost at that output.

FIGURE 7.4 The average-cost curves. AFC falls as a given amount of fixed costs is apportioned over a larger and larger output. AVC initially falls because of increasing marginal returns but then rises because of diminishing marginal returns. Average total cost (ATC) is the vertical sum of average variable cost (AVC) and average fixed cost (AFC).

Rephrased, production is relatively inefficient—and therefore costly—at low levels of output. Because the firm's fixed plant is understaffed, average variable cost is relatively high. As output expands, however, greater specialization and better use of the firm's capital equipment yield more efficiency, and variable cost per unit of output declines. As still more variable resources are added, a point is reached where crowding causes diminishing returns to set in. Once diminishing returns start, each additional unit of input does not increase output by as much as preceding units did. This means that AVC eventually increases.

You can verify the U or saucer shape of the AVC curve by returning to Table 7.1. Assume the price of labor is $10 per unit. Labor cost per unit of output is then $10 (the price per labor unit in this example) divided by average product (output per labor unit). Because we have assumed labor to be the only variable input, the labor cost per unit of output is the variable cost per unit of output, or AVC. When average product is initially low, AVC is high. As workers are added, average product rises and AVC falls. When average product is at its maximum, AVC is at its minimum. Then, as still more workers are added and average product declines, AVC rises. The "hump" of the average-product curve is reflected in the saucer or U shape of the AVC curve. As you will soon see, the two are mirror images of each other.

Because the total fixed cost is, by definition, the same regardless of output, AFC must decline as output increases. As output rises, the total fixed cost is spread over a larger and larger output. When output is just 1 unit in Table 7.2, TFC and AFC are the same at $100. But at 2 units of output, the total fixed cost of $100 becomes $50 of AFC or fixed cost per unit; then it becomes $33.33 per unit as $100 is spread over 3 units, and $25 per unit when spread over 4 units. This process is sometimes referred to as "spreading the overhead." Figure 7.4 shows that AFC graphs as a continuously declining curve as total output is increased.

AVC **Average variable cost (AVC)** for any output level is calculated by dividing total variable cost (TVC) by that amount of output (Q):

$$AVC = \frac{TVC}{Q}$$

Due to increasing and then diminishing returns, AVC declines initially, reaches a minimum, and then increases again. A graph of AVC is a U-shaped or saucer-shaped curve, as shown in Figure 7.4.

Because total variable cost reflects the law of diminishing returns, so must AVC, which is derived from total variable cost. Because marginal returns increase initially, fewer and fewer additional variable resources are needed to produce each of the first four units of output. As a result, variable cost per unit declines. AVC hits a minimum with the fifth unit of output, and beyond that point AVC rises as diminishing returns require more and more variable resources to produce each additional unit of output.

ATC **Average total cost (ATC)** for any output level is found by dividing total cost (TC) by that output (Q) or by adding AFC and AVC at that output:

$$ATC = \frac{TC}{Q} = \frac{TFC}{Q} + \frac{TVC}{Q} = AFC + AVC$$

Graphically, ATC can be found by adding vertically the AFC and AVC curves, as in Figure 7.4. Thus the vertical distance between the ATC and AVC curves measures AFC at any level of output.

Marginal Cost

One final and very crucial cost concept remains: **Marginal cost (MC)** is the extra, or additional, cost of producing one more unit of output. MC can be determined for each added unit of output by noting the change in total cost that unit's production entails:

$$MC = \frac{\text{change in TC}}{\text{change in } Q}$$

Calculations In column 4, Table 7.2, production of the first unit of output increases total cost from $100 to $190. Therefore, the additional, or marginal, cost of that first unit is $90 (column 8). The marginal cost of the second unit is $80 (= $270 − $190); the MC of the third is $70 (= $340 − $270); and so forth. The MC for each of the 10 units of output is shown in column 8.

MC can also be calculated from the total-variable-cost column because the only difference between total cost and total variable cost is the constant amount of fixed costs ($100). Thus, the change in total cost and the change in total variable cost associated with each additional unit of output are always the same.

Marginal Decisions Marginal costs are costs the firm can control directly and immediately. Specifically, MC

designates all the cost incurred in producing the last unit of output. Thus, it also designates the cost that can be "saved" by not producing that last unit. Average-cost figures do not provide this information. For example, suppose the firm is undecided whether to produce 3 or 4 units of output. At 4 units Table 7.2 indicates that ATC is $100. But the firm does not increase its total costs by $100 by producing the fourth unit, nor does it save $100 by not producing that unit. Rather, the change in costs involved here is only $60, as the MC column in Table 7.2 reveals.

A firm's decisions as to what output level to produce are typically marginal decisions, that is, decisions to produce a few more or a few less units. Marginal cost is the change in costs when one more or one less unit of output is produced. When coupled with marginal revenue (which, as you will see in Chapter 8, indicates the change in revenue from one more or one less unit of output), marginal cost allows a firm to determine if it is profitable to expand or contract its production. The analysis in the next four chapters focuses on those marginal calculations.

Graphical Portrayal Marginal cost is shown graphically in **Figure 7.5 (Key Graph)**. Marginal cost at first

declines sharply, reaches a minimum, and then rises rather abruptly. This reflects the fact that variable cost, and therefore total cost, increase at first by decreasing amounts and then by increasing amounts (see columns 3 and 4, Table 7.2).

MC and Marginal Product The marginal-cost curve's shape is a consequence of the law of diminishing returns. Looking back at Table 7.1, we can see the relationship between marginal product and marginal cost. If

all units of a variable resource (here labor) are hired at the same price, the marginal cost of each extra unit of output will fall as long as the marginal product of each additional worker is rising. This is true because marginal cost is the (constant) cost of an extra worker divided by his or her marginal product. Therefore, in Table 7.1, suppose that each worker can be hired for $10. Because the first worker's marginal product is 10 units of output, and hiring this worker increases the firm's costs by $10, the marginal cost of each of these 10 extra units of output is $1 (= $10/10 units). The second worker also increases costs by $10, but the marginal product is 15, so the marginal cost of each of these 15 extra units of output is $.67 (= $10/15 units). Similarly, the MC of each of the 20 extra units of output contributed by the third worker is $.50 (= $10/20 units). To generalize, as long as marginal product is rising, marginal cost will fall.

But with the fourth worker diminishing returns set in and marginal cost begins to rise. For the fourth worker, marginal cost is $.67 (= $10/15 units); for the fifth worker, MC is $1 ($10/10 units); for the sixth, MC is $2 (= $10/5 units); and so on. If the price (cost) of the variable resource remains constant, increasing marginal returns will be reflected in a declining marginal cost, and diminishing marginal returns in a rising marginal cost. The MC curve is a mirror reflection of the marginal-product curve. As you can see in Figure 7.6, when marginal product is rising, marginal cost is necessarily falling. When marginal product is at its maximum, marginal cost is at its minimum. And when marginal product is falling, marginal cost is rising.

Relation of MC to AVC and ATC Figure 7.5 shows that the marginal-cost curve MC intersects both the AVC and the ATC curves at their respective minimum points. As noted earlier, this marginal-average relationship is a mathematical necessity, which a simple illustration will reveal. Suppose an NBA basketball player has scored an average of 20 points a game over the first three games of the season. Now, whether his average rises or falls as a result of playing a fourth (marginal) game will depend on whether the additional points he scores in that game are fewer or more than his current 20-point average. If in the fourth game he scores fewer than 20 points, his average will fall. For example, if he scores 16 points in the fourth game, his total points will rise from 60 to 76 and his average will fall from 20 to 19 (= 76/4). Conversely, if in the fourth (marginal) game he scores more than 20 points, say, 24, his total will increase from 60 to 84 and his average will rise from 20 to 21 (= 84/4).

So it is with costs. When the amount (the marginal cost) added to total cost is less than the current average

key graph

FIGURE 7.5 The relationship of the marginal-cost curve to the average-total-cost and average-variable-cost curves. The marginal-cost (MC) curve cuts through the average-total-cost (ATC) curve and the average-variable-cost (AVC) curve at their minimum points. When MC is below average total cost, ATC falls; when MC is above average total cost, ATC rises. Similarly, when MC is below average variable cost, AVC falls; when MC is above average variable cost, AVC rises.

QUICK QUIZ FOR FIGURE 7.5

1. The marginal-cost curve first declines and then increases because of:
   a. increasing, then diminishing, marginal utility.
   b. the decline in the gap between ATC and AVC as output expands.
   c. increasing, then diminishing, marginal returns.
   d. constant marginal revenue.

2. The vertical distance between ATC and AVC measures:
   a. marginal cost.
   b. total fixed cost.
   c. average fixed cost.
   d. economic profit per unit.

3. ATC is:
   a. AVC − AFC.
   b. MC + AVC.
   c. AFC + AVC.
   d. (AFC + AVC) × Q.

4. When the marginal-cost curve lies:
   a. above the ATC curve, ATC rises.
   b. above the AVC curve, ATC rises.
   c. below the AVC curve, total fixed cost increases.
   d. below the ATC curve, total fixed cost falls.

Answers: 1. c; 2. c; 3. c; 4. a

---

total cost, ATC will fall. Conversely, when the marginal cost exceeds ATC, ATC will rise. This means in Figure 7.5 that as long as MC lies below ATC, ATC will fall, and whenever MC lies above ATC, ATC will rise. Therefore, at the point of intersection where MC equals ATC, ATC has just ceased to fall but has not yet begun to rise. This, by definition, is the minimum point on the ATC curve. The marginal-cost curve intersects the average-total-cost curve at the ATC curve's minimum point.

Marginal cost can be defined as the addition either to total cost or to total variable cost resulting from one more unit of output; thus this same rationale explains why the MC curve also crosses the AVC curve at the AVC curve's minimum point. No such relationship exists between the MC curve and the average-fixed-cost curve because the two are not related; marginal cost includes only those costs that change with output, and fixed costs by definition are those that are independent of output.

Shifts of the Cost Curves

Changes in either resource prices or technology will cause costs to change and cost curves to shift. If fixed costs double from $100 to $200, the AFC curve in Figure 7.5 would be shifted upward. At each level of output, fixed costs are higher. The ATC curve would also move upward because AFC is a component of ATC. But the positions of the AVC and MC curves would be unaltered because their locations are based on the prices of variable rather than fixed resources. However, if the price (wage) of labor or some other variable input rose, AVC, ATC, and MC would rise and those cost curves would all shift upward. The AFC curve would remain in place because fixed costs have not changed. And, of course, reductions in the prices of fixed or variable resources would reduce costs and produce shifts of the cost curves exactly opposite to those just described.

The discovery of a more efficient technology would increase the productivity of all inputs. The cost figures in Table 7.2 would all be lower. To illustrate, if labor is the only variable input, if wages are $10 per hour, and if average product is 10 units, then AVC would be $1. But if a technological improvement increases the average product of labor to 20 units, then AVC will decline to $.50. More generally, an upward shift in the productivity curves shown in Figure 7.6a means a downward shift in the cost curves portrayed in Figure 7.6b.

QUICK REVIEW 7.2

- The law of diminishing returns indicates that, beyond some point, output will increase by diminishing amounts as more units of a variable resource (labor) are added to a fixed resource (capital).
- In the short run, the total cost of any level of output is the sum of fixed and variable costs (TC = TFC + TVC).
- Average fixed, average variable, and average total costs are fixed, variable, and total costs per unit of output; marginal cost is the extra cost of producing one more unit of output.
- Average fixed cost declines continuously as output increases; the average-variable-cost and average-total-cost curves are U-shaped, reflecting increasing and then diminishing returns; the marginal-cost curve falls but then rises, intersecting both the average-variable-cost curve and the average-total-cost curve at their minimum points.

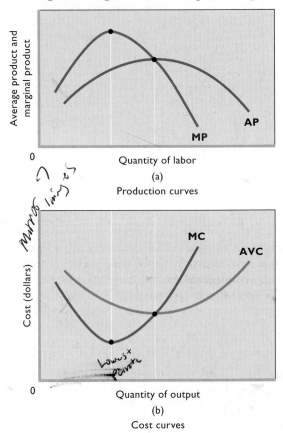

FIGURE 7.6 The relationship between productivity curves and cost curves. The marginal-cost (MC) curve and the average-variable-cost (AVC) curve in (b) are mirror images of the marginal-product (MP) and average-product (AP) curves in (a). Assuming that labor is the only variable input and that its price (the wage rate) is constant, then when MP is rising, MC is falling, and when MP is falling, MC is rising. Under the same assumptions, when AP is rising, AVC is falling, and when AP is falling, AVC is rising.

Long-Run Production Costs

In the long run an industry and its individual firms can undertake all desired resource adjustments. That is, they can change the amount of all inputs used. The firm can alter its plant capacity; it can build a larger plant or revert to a smaller plant than that assumed in Table 7.2. The industry also can change its overall capacity; the long run allows sufficient time for new firms to enter or for existing firms to leave an industry. We will discuss the impact of the entry and exit of firms to and from an industry in the next chapter; here we are concerned only with changes in plant capacity made by a single firm. Let's couch our analysis in terms of average total cost (ATC), making no distinction between fixed and variable costs because all resources, and therefore all costs, are variable in the long run.

Firm Size and Costs

Suppose a manufacturer with a single plant begins on a small scale and, as the result of successful operations, expands to successively larger plant sizes with larger output capacities. What happens to average total cost as this occurs? For a time, successively larger plants will reduce average total cost. However, eventually the building of a still larger plant will cause ATC to rise.

Figure 7.7 illustrates this situation for five possible plant sizes. ATC-1 is the short-run average-total-cost curve for the smallest of the five plants, and ATC-5, the curve for the largest. Constructing larger plants will lower the minimum average total costs through plant size 3. But then larger plants will mean higher minimum average total costs.

FIGURE 7.7 The long-run average-total-cost curve: five possible plant sizes. The long-run-average-total-cost curve is made up of segments of the short-run cost curves (ATC-1, ATC-2, etc.) of the various-size plants from which the firm might choose. Each point on the bumpy planning curve shows the lowest unit cost attainable for any output when the firm has had time to make all desired changes in its plant size.

The Long-Run Cost Curve

The vertical lines perpendicular to the output axis in Figure 7.7 indicate the outputs at which the firm should change plant size to realize the lowest attainable average total costs of production. These are the outputs at which the per-unit costs for a larger plant drop below those for the current, smaller plant. For all outputs up to 20 units, the lowest average total costs are attainable with plant size 1. However, if the firm's volume of sales expands beyond 20 units but less than 30, it can achieve lower per-unit costs by constructing a larger plant, size 2. Although total cost will be higher at the expanded levels of production, the cost per unit of output will be less. For any output between 30 and 50 units, plant size 3 will yield the lowest average total costs. From 50 to 60 units of output, the firm must build the size-4 plant to achieve the lowest unit costs. Lowest average total costs for any output over 60 units require construction of the still larger plant, size 5.

Tracing these adjustments, we find that the long-run ATC curve for the enterprise is made up of segments of the short-run ATC curves for the various plant sizes that can be constructed. The long-run ATC curve shows the lowest average total cost at which *any output level* can be produced after the firm has had time to make all appropriate adjustments in its plant size. In Figure 7.7 the blue, bumpy curve is the firm's long-run ATC curve or, as it is often called, the firm's *planning curve*.

In most lines of production the choice of plant size is much wider than in our illustration. In many industries the number of possible plant sizes is virtually unlimited, and in time quite small changes in the volume of output will lead to changes in plant size. Graphically, this implies an unlimited number of short-run ATC curves, one for each output level, as suggested by **Figure 7.8 (Key Graph)**. Then, rather than being made up of segments of short-run ATC curves as in Figure 7.7, the long-run ATC curve is made up of all the points of tangency of the unlimited number of short-run ATC curves from which the long-run ATC curve is derived. Therefore, the planning curve is smooth rather than bumpy. Each point on it tells us the minimum ATC of producing the corresponding level of output.

Economies and Diseconomies of Scale

We have assumed that, for a time, larger and larger plant sizes will lead to lower unit costs but that, beyond some point, successively larger plants will mean higher average total costs. That is, we have assumed the long-run ATC curve is U-shaped. But why should this be? It turns out that the U shape is caused by economies and diseconomies of large-scale production, as we explain in a moment. But before we do, please understand that the U shape of the long-run average-total-cost curve *cannot* be the result of rising resource prices or the law of diminishing returns. First, our discussion assumes that resource prices are constant. Second, the law of diminishing returns does not apply to production in the long run. This is true because the law of diminishing returns only deals with situations in which a productive resource or input is held constant. Under our definition of "long run," all resources and inputs are variable.

Economies of Scale **Economies of scale,** or economies of mass production, explain the downsloping part of

key graph

FIGURE 7.8 The long-run average-total-cost curve: unlimited number of plant sizes. If the number of possible plant sizes is very large, the long-run average-total-cost curve approximates a smooth curve. Economies of scale, followed by diseconomies of scale, cause the curve to be U-shaped.

QUICK QUIZ FOR FIGURE 7.8

1. The unlabeled red curves in this figure illustrate the:
   a. long-run average-total-cost curves of various firms constituting the industry.
   b. short-run average-total-cost curves of various firms constituting the industry.
   c. short-run average-total-cost curves of various plant sizes available to a particular firm.
   d. short-run marginal-cost curves of various plant sizes available to a particular firm.

2. The unlabeled red curves in this figure derive their shapes from:
   a. decreasing, then increasing, short-run returns.
   b. increasing, then decreasing, short-run returns.
   c. economies, then diseconomies, of scale.
   d. diseconomies, then economies, of scale.

3. The long-run ATC curve in this figure derives its shape from:
   a. decreasing, then increasing, short-run returns.
   b. increasing, then decreasing, short-run returns.
   c. economies, then diseconomies, of scale.
   d. diseconomies, then economies, of scale.

4. The long-run ATC curve is often called the firm's:
   a. planning curve.
   b. capital-expansion path.
   c. total-product curve.
   d. production possibilities curve.

Answers: 1. c; 2. b; 3. c; 4. a

---

the long-run ATC curve, as indicated in Figure 7.9, graphs (a), (b), and (c). As plant size increases, a number of factors will for a time lead to lower average costs of production.

Labor Specialization Increased specialization in the use of labor becomes more achievable as a plant increases in size. Hiring more workers means jobs can be divided and subdivided. Each worker may now have just one task to perform instead of five or six. Workers can work full-time on the tasks for which they have special skills. By contrast, skilled machinists in a small plant may spend half their time performing unskilled tasks, leading to higher production costs.

Further, by working at fewer tasks, workers become even more proficient at those tasks. The jack-of-all-trades doing five or six jobs is not likely to be efficient in any of them. Concentrating on one task, the same worker may become highly efficient.

Finally, greater labor specialization eliminates the loss of time that occurs whenever a worker shifts from one task to another.

Managerial Specialization Large-scale production also means better use of, and greater specialization in, management. A supervisor who can handle 20 workers is underused in a small plant that employs only 10 people. The production staff could be doubled with no increase in supervisory costs.

Small firms cannot use management specialists to best advantage. For example, a marketing specialist working in

154

FIGURE 7.9 **Various possible long-run average-total-cost curves.** In (a), economies of scale are rather rapidly obtained as plant size rises, and diseconomies of scale are not encountered until a considerably large scale of output has been achieved. Thus, long-run average total cost is constant over a wide range of output. In (b), economies of scale are extensive, and diseconomies of scale occur only at very large outputs. Average total cost therefore declines over a broad range of output. In (c), economies of scale are exhausted quickly, followed immediately by diseconomies of scale. Minimum ATC thus occurs at a relatively low output.

a small plant may have to spend some of her time on functions outside of her area of expertise—for example, accounting, personnel, and finance. A larger scale of operations would allow her to supervise marketing full-time, while other specialists perform other managerial functions. Greater productivity and efficiency, along with lower unit costs, would be the net result.

Efficient Capital Small firms often cannot afford the most efficient equipment. In many lines of production such machinery is available only in very large and extremely expensive units. Furthermore, effective use of

the equipment demands a high volume of production, and that again requires large-scale producers.

In the automobile industry the most efficient fabrication method employs robotics and elaborate assembly-line equipment. Effective use of this equipment demands an annual output of several hundred thousand automobiles. Only very large-scale producers can afford to purchase and use this equipment efficiently. The small-scale producer is faced with a dilemma. To fabricate automobiles using other equipment is inefficient and therefore more costly per unit. But so, too, is buying and underutilizing the equipment used by the large manufacturers. Because it cannot spread the high equipment cost over very many units of output, the small-scale producer will be stuck with high costs per unit of output.

Other Factors Many products entail design and development costs, as well as other "start-up" costs, which must be incurred regardless of projected sales. These costs decline per unit as output is increased. Similarly, advertising costs decline per auto, per computer, per stereo system, and per box of detergent as more units are produced and sold. Also, the firm's production and marketing expertise usually rises as it produces and sells more output. This *learning by doing* is a further source of economies of scale.

All these factors contribute to lower average total costs for the firm that is able to expand its scale of operations. Where economies of scale are possible, an increase in all resources of, say, 10 percent will cause a more-than-proportionate increase in output of, say, 20 percent. The result will be a decline in ATC.

In many U.S. manufacturing industries, economies of scale have been of great significance. Firms that have expanded their scale of operations to obtain economies of mass production have survived and flourished. Those unable to expand have become relatively high-cost producers, doomed to struggle to survive.

Diseconomies of Scale In time the expansion of a firm may lead to diseconomies and therefore higher average total costs.

The main factor causing **diseconomies of scale** is the difficulty of efficiently controlling and coordinating a firm's operations as it becomes a large-scale producer. In a small plant a single key executive may make all the basic decisions for the plant's operation. Because of the firm's small size, the executive is close to the production line, understands the firm's operations, and can make efficient decisions because the small plant size requires only a relatively small amount of information to be examined and understood in optimizing production.

This neat picture changes as a firm grows. One person cannot assemble, digest, and understand all the information essential to decision making on a large scale. Authority must be delegated to many vice presidents, second vice presidents, and so forth. This expansion of the management hierarchy leads to problems of communication and cooperation, bureaucratic red tape, and the possibility that decisions will not be coordinated. At the same time, each new manager must be paid a salary. Thus, declining efficiency in making and executing decisions goes hand-in-hand with rising average total costs as bureaucracy expands beyond a certain point.

Also, in massive production facilities workers may feel alienated from their employers and care little about working efficiently. Opportunities to shirk, by avoiding work in favor of on-the-job leisure, may be greater in large plants than in small ones. Countering worker alienation and shirking may require additional worker supervision, which increases costs.

Where diseconomies of scale are operative, an increase in all inputs of, say, 10 percent will cause a less-than-proportionate increase in output of, say, 5 percent. As a consequence, ATC will increase. The rising portion of the long-run cost curves in Figure 7.9 illustrates diseconomies of scale.

Constant Returns to Scale In some industries a rather wide range of output may exist between the output at which economies of scale end and the output at which diseconomies of scale begin. That is, there may be a range of **constant returns to scale** over which long-run average cost does not change. The q_1q_2 output range of Figure 7.9a is an example. Here a given percentage increase in all inputs of, say, 10 percent will cause a proportionate 10 percent increase in output. Thus, in this range ATC is constant.

Minimum Efficient Scale and Industry Structure

Economies and diseconomies of scale are an important determinant of an industry's structure. Here we introduce the concept of **minimum efficient scale (MES),** which is the lowest level of output at which a firm can minimize long-run average costs. In Figure 7.9a that level occurs at q_1 units of output. Because of the extended range of constant returns to scale, firms producing substantially greater outputs could also realize the minimum attainable long-run average costs. Specifically, firms within the q_1 to q_2 range would be equally efficient. So we would not be surprised to find an industry with such cost conditions to be populated by firms of quite different sizes. The apparel, food processing, furniture, wood products, snowboard, banking, and small-appliance industries are examples. With an extended range of constant returns to scale, relatively large and relatively small firms can coexist in an industry and be equally successful.

Compare this with Figure 7.9b, where economies of scale continue over a wide range of outputs and diseconomies of scale appear only at very high levels of output. This pattern of declining long-run average total cost occurs in the automobile, aluminum, steel, and other heavy industries. The same pattern holds in several of the new industries related to information technology, for example, computer microchips, operating system software, and Internet service provision.

Given consumer demand, efficient production will be achieved with a few large-scale producers. Small firms cannot realize the minimum efficient scale and will not be able to compete. In the extreme, economies of scale might extend beyond the market's size, resulting in what is termed **natural monopoly,** a relatively rare market situation in which average total cost is minimized when only one firm produces the particular good or service.

Where economies of scale are few and diseconomies come into play quickly, the minimum efficient size occurs at a low level of output, as shown in Figure 7.9c. In such industries a particular level of consumer demand will support a large number of relatively small producers. Many retail trades and some types of farming fall into this category. So do certain kinds of light manufacturing such as the baking, clothing, and shoe industries. Fairly small firms are more efficient than larger-scale producers in such industries.

Our point here is that the shape of the long-run average-total-cost curve is determined by technology and

the economies and diseconomies of scale that result. The shape of the long-run ATC curve, in turn, can be significant in determining whether an industry is populated by a relatively large number of small firms or is dominated by a few large producers, or lies somewhere in between.

But we must be cautious in our assessment because industry structure does not depend on cost conditions alone. Government policies, the geographic size of markets, managerial strategy and skill, and other factors must be considered in explaining the structure of a particular industry.

Applications and Illustrations

The business world offers many examples relating to short-run costs, economies of scale, and minimum efficient scale (MES). Here are just a few.

Rising Gasoline Prices

As we discuss in the appendix to Chapter 3, changes in supply and demand often lead to rapid increases in the price of gasoline. Because gasoline is used to power nearly all motor vehicles, including those used by businesses, increases in the price of gasoline lead to increases in firms' short-run variable costs, marginal costs, and average total costs. In terms of our analysis, their AVC, MC, and ATC curves all shift upward when an increase in the price of gasoline increases their production costs.

The extent of these upward shifts depends upon the relative importance of gasoline as a variable input in the various firms' individual production processes. Package-delivery companies like FedEx that use a lot of gasoline-powered vehicles will see substantial upward shifts while software companies like Symantec (Norton) that mainly deliver their products through Internet downloads may see only small upward shifts.

Successful Start-Up Firms

The U.S. economy has greatly benefited over the past several decades from the explosive growth of scores of highly successful start-up firms. These firms typically reduce their costs by moving from higher to lower points on their short-run cost curves and by downward and to-the-right shifts of their short-run cost curves via economies of scale. That has certainly been the case for such former start-up firms as Intel (microchips), Starbucks (coffee), Microsoft (software), Dell (personal computers), Google (Internet searches), and Cisco Systems (Internet switching).

A major source of lower average total cost for rapidly growing firms is the ability to spread huge product development and advertising costs over a larger number of units of output. These firms also achieve economies of scale from learning by doing and through increased specialization of labor, management, and equipment. After starting up, such firms experience declining average total costs over the years or even decades it takes them to eventually reach their respective MESs.

The Verson Stamping Machine

In 1996 Verson (a U.S. firm located in Chicago) introduced a 49-foot-tall metal-stamping machine that is the size of a house and weighs as much as 12 locomotives.

LAST

<u>Word</u> Don't Cry over Sunk Costs

Sunk Costs Are Irrelevant in Decision Making.

There is an old saying: Don't cry over spilt milk. The message is that once you have spilled a glass of milk, there is nothing you can do to recover it, so you should forget about it and "move on from there." This saying has great relevance to what economists call sunk costs. Once these costs are incurred, they cannot be recovered.

Let's gain an understanding of this idea by applying it first to consumers and then to businesses. Suppose you buy an expensive ticket to an upcoming football game, but the morning of the game you wake up with a bad case of the flu. Feeling miserable, you step outside to find that the windchill is about −10 degrees. You absolutely do not want to go to the game, but you remind yourself that you paid a steep price for the ticket. You call several people to try to sell the ticket, but you soon discover that no one is interested in it, even at a discounted price. You conclude that everyone who wants a ticket has one.

Should you go to the game? Economic analysis says that you should not take actions for which marginal cost exceeds marginal benefit. In this case, if the marginal cost of going to the game is greater than the marginal benefit, the best decision is to go back to bed. In correctly applying this rule, however, it is crucial that you recognize that the price you paid for the ticket is *not* a marginal cost. Even if the ticket was hideously expensive, it was purchased previously. Thus, its cost is not a marginal, extra cost that depends on whether or not you go to the game. The cost has already been incurred and must therefore be dealt with even if you decide not to attend!

With the cost of the ticket out of the picture, your cost-benefit analysis is going to be settled by your opinion that "you absolutely do not want to go." With such a strongly negative opinion, the marginal cost obviously exceeds the marginal benefit, and you should not go.

Here is a second consumer example: Suppose a family is on vacation and stops at a roadside stand to buy some apples. The kids get back into the car and bite into their apples, immediately pronouncing them "totally mushy" and unworthy of another bite. Both parents agree that the apples are "terrible," but the father continues to eat his because, as he says, "We paid a premium price for them." One of the older children replies, "Dad, that is irrelevant."

This $30 million machine, which cuts and sculpts raw sheets of steel into automobile hoods and fenders, enables automakers to make new parts in just 5 minutes, compared with 8 hours for older stamping presses. A single machine is designed to make 5 million auto parts per year. So, to achieve the cost saving from the machine, an auto manufacturer must have sufficient auto production to use all these parts. By allowing the use of this cost-saving piece of equipment, large firm size achieves economies of scale.

The Daily Newspaper

Daily newspapers have been going bankrupt in rapid succession over the past several years as both advertising dollars and news readership have shifted to the Internet. The falling circulation numbers have caused average fixed costs to rise significantly as newspapers are forced to spread their substantial fixed costs over fewer and fewer papers. The spike in average fixed costs has, in turn, forced newspapers to sharply increase their prices. Between July 2007 and July 2009, for instance, the *New York Times* had to raise its cover price three times as advertising revenues plunged and fixed costs had to be spread over fewer and fewer papers. Starting at $1 per copy, the cover price had to be raised to $1.25, then $1.50, and then $2.00.

With readership continuing to fall, newspapers face an average-fixed-cost death spiral. The more they raise their prices, the less they will sell. But the less their sales, the higher their average fixed costs and thus the more they must raise their prices. As a result, printed newspapers could ultimately be a thing of the past, with both advertising and news delivery shifting mainly to the Internet.

Aircraft and Concrete Plants

Why are there only two plants in the United States (both operated by Boeing) that produce large commercial aircraft and thousands of plants (owned by hundreds of firms) that produce ready-mixed concrete? The simple answer is that MES is radically different in the two industries. Why is that? First, while economies of scale are extensive in assembling large commercial aircraft, they are only very modest in mixing concrete. Manufacturing airplanes is a complex process that requires huge facilities, thousands of workers, and very expensive, specialized machinery. Economies of scale extend to huge plant sizes.

Although not stated very diplomatically, the child is exactly right. In making a new decision, you should ignore all costs that are not affected by the decision. The prior bad decision (in retrospect) to buy the apples should not dictate a second decision for which marginal benefit is less than marginal cost.

Now let's apply the idea of sunk costs to firms. Some of a firm's costs are not only fixed (recurring, but unrelated to the level of output) but sunk (unrecoverable). For example, a nonrefundable annual lease payment for the use of a store cannot be recouped once it has been paid. A firm's decision about whether to move from the store to a more profitable location does not depend on the amount of time remaining on the lease. If moving means greater profit, it makes sense to move whether there are 300 days, 30 days, or 3 days left on the lease.

Or, as another example, suppose a firm spends $1 million on R&D to bring out a new product, only to discover that

the product sells very poorly. Should the firm continue to produce the product at a loss even when there is no realistic hope for future success? Obviously, it should not. In making this decision, the firm realizes that the amount it has spent in developing the product is irrelevant; it should stop production of the product and cut its losses. In fact, many firms have dropped products after spending millions of dollars on their development.

A recent example is Pfizer's decision in 2007 to shelve its novel insulin inhaler because of poor sales and concerns about long-term side effects. The product withdrawal forced Pfizer to take a $2.8 billion pretax loss on this highly touted product.

In short, if a cost has been incurred and cannot be partly or fully recouped by some other choice, a rational consumer or firm should ignore it. Sunk costs are irrelevant. Don't cry over sunk costs.

But mixing portland cement, sand, gravel, and water to produce concrete requires only a handful of workers and relatively inexpensive equipment. Economies of scale are exhausted at relatively small size.

The differing MESs also derive from the vastly different sizes of the geographic markets. The market for commercial airplanes is global, and aircraft manufacturers can deliver new airplanes anywhere in the world by flying them there. In contrast, the geographic market for a concrete plant is roughly the 50-mile radius within which the concrete can be delivered before it "sets up." So thousands of small concrete plants locate close to their customers in hundreds of small and large cities in the United States.

Summary

1. The economic cost of using a resource to produce a good or service is the value or worth that the resource would have had in its best alternative use. Economic costs include explicit costs, which flow to resources owned and supplied by others, and implicit costs, which are payments for the use of self-owned and self-employed resources. One implicit cost is a normal profit to the entrepreneur. Economic profit occurs when total revenue exceeds total cost (= explicit costs + implicit costs, including a normal profit).

2. In the short run a firm's plant capacity is fixed. The firm can use its plant more or less intensively by adding or subtracting units of variable resources, but it does not have sufficient time in the short run to alter plant size.

3. The law of diminishing returns describes what happens to output as a fixed plant is used more intensively. As successive units of a variable resource such as labor are added to a fixed plant, beyond some point the marginal product associated with each additional unit of a resource declines.

4. Because some resources are variable and others are fixed, costs can be classified as variable or fixed in the short run. Fixed costs are independent of the level of output; variable costs vary with output. The total cost of any output is the sum of fixed and variable costs at that output.

5. Average fixed, average variable, and average total costs are fixed, variable, and total costs per unit of output. Average fixed cost declines continuously as output increases because a fixed sum is being spread over a larger and larger number of units of production. A graph of average variable cost is U-shaped, reflecting increasing returns followed by diminishing returns. Average total cost is the sum of average fixed and average variable costs; its graph is also U-shaped.

6. Marginal cost is the extra, or additional, cost of producing one more unit of output. It is the amount by which total cost and total variable cost change when one more or one less unit of output is produced. Graphically, the marginal-cost curve intersects the ATC and AVC curves at their minimum points.

7. Lower resource prices shift cost curves downward, as does technological progress. Higher input prices shift cost curves upward.

8. The long run is a period of time sufficiently long for a firm to vary the amounts of all resources used, including plant size. In the long run all costs are variable. The long-run ATC, or planning, curve is composed of segments of the short-run ATC curves, and it represents the various plant sizes a firm can construct in the long run.

9. The long-run ATC curve is generally U-shaped. Economies of scale are first encountered as a small firm expands. Greater specialization in the use of labor and management, the ability to use the most efficient equipment, and the spreading of start-up costs among more units of output all contribute to economies of scale. As the firm continues to grow, it will encounter diseconomies of scale stemming from the managerial complexities that accompany large-scale production. The output ranges over which economies and diseconomies of scale occur in an industry are often an important determinant of the structure of that industry.

10. A firm's minimum efficient scale (MES) is the lowest level of output at which it can minimize its long-run average cost. In some industries, MES occurs at such low levels of output that numerous firms can populate the industry. In other industries, MES occurs at such high output levels that only a few firms can exist in the long run.

Terms and Concepts

economic cost	total product (TP)	average variable cost (AVC)
explicit costs	marginal product (MP)	average total cost (ATC)
implicit costs	average product (AP)	marginal cost (MC)
accounting profit	law of diminishing returns	economies of scale
normal profit	fixed costs	diseconomies of scale
economic profit	variable costs	constant returns to scale
short run	total cost	minimum efficient scale (MES)
long run	average fixed cost (AFC)	natural monopoly

Questions

1. Distinguish between explicit and implicit costs, giving examples of each. What are some explicit and implicit costs of attending college? **LO1**

2. Distinguish between accounting profit, economic profit, and normal profit. Does accounting profit or economic profit determine how entrepreneurs allocate resources between different business ventures? Explain. **LO1**

3. Which of the following are short-run and which are long-run adjustments? **LO1**
   a. Wendy's builds a new restaurant.
   b. Harley-Davidson Corporation hires 200 more production workers.
   c. A farmer increases the amount of fertilizer used on his corn crop.
   d. An Alcoa aluminum plant adds a third shift of workers.

4. Complete the table directly below by calculating marginal product and average product.

Inputs of Labor	Total Product	Marginal Product	Average Product
0	0	_____	_____
1	15	_____	_____
2	34	_____	_____
3	51	_____	_____
4	65	_____	_____
5	74	_____	_____
6	80	_____	_____
7	83	_____	_____
8	82	_____	_____

Plot the total, marginal, and average products and explain in detail the relationship between each pair of curves. Explain why marginal product first rises, then declines, and ultimately becomes negative. What bearing does the law of diminishing returns have on short-run costs? Be specific. "When marginal product is rising, marginal cost is falling. And when marginal-product is diminishing, marginal cost is rising." Illustrate and explain graphically. LO2

5. Why can the distinction between fixed costs and variable costs be made in the short run? Classify the following as fixed or variable costs: advertising expenditures, fuel, interest on company-issued bonds, shipping charges, payments for raw materials, real estate taxes, executive salaries, insurance premiums, wage payments, depreciation and obsolescence charges, sales taxes, and rental payments on leased office machinery. "There are no fixed costs in the long run; all costs are variable." Explain. LO3

6. List several fixed and variable costs associated with owning and operating an automobile. Suppose you are considering whether to drive your car or fly 1000 miles to Florida for spring break. Which costs—fixed, variable, or both—would you take into account in making your decision? Would any implicit costs be relevant? Explain. LO3

7. A firm has fixed costs of $60 and variable costs as indicated in the table at the bottom of this page. Complete the table and check your calculations by referring to question 4 at the end of Chapter 8. LO3
   a. Graph total fixed cost, total variable cost, and total cost. Explain how the law of diminishing returns influences the shapes of the variable-cost and total-cost curves.
   b. Graph AFC, AVC, ATC, and MC. Explain the derivation and shape of each of these four curves and their relationships to one another. Specifically, explain in nontechnical terms why the MC curve intersects both the AVC and the ATC curves at their minimum points.
   c. Explain how the location of each curve graphed in question 7b would be altered if (1) total fixed cost had been $100 rather than $60 and (2) total variable cost had been $10 less at each level of output.

8. Indicate how each of the following would shift the (1) marginal-cost curve, (2) average-variable-cost curve, (3) average-fixed-cost curve, and (4) average-total-cost curve of a manufacturing firm. In each case specify the direction of the shift. LO3
   a. A reduction in business property taxes.
   b. An increase in the nominal wages of production workers.
   c. A decrease in the price of electricity.
   d. An increase in insurance rates on plant and equipment.
   e. An increase in transportation costs.

9. Suppose a firm has only three possible plant-size options, represented by the ATC curves shown in the accompanying figure. What plant size will the firm choose in producing (a) 50, (b) 130, (c) 160, and (d) 250 units of output? Draw the firm's long-run average-cost curve on the diagram and describe this curve. LO4

10. Use the concepts of economies and diseconomies of scale to explain the shape of a firm's long-run ATC curve. What is the concept of minimum efficient scale? What bearing can the shape of the long-run ATC curve have on the structure of an industry? LO4

11. **LAST WORD** What is a sunk cost? Provide an example of a sunk cost other than one from this book. Why are such costs irrelevant in making decisions about future actions?

Total Product	Total Fixed Cost	Total Variable Cost	Total Cost	Average Fixed Cost	Average Variable Cost	Average Total Cost	Marginal Cost
0	$____	$ 0	$____			$____	$____
1	____	45	____	$____	$____	____	____
2	____	85	____	____	____	____	____
3	____	120	____	____	____	____	____
4	____	150	____	____	____	____	____
5	____	185	____	____	____	____	____
6	____	225	____	____	____	____	____
7	____	270	____	____	____	____	____
8	____	325	____	____	____	____	____
9	____	390	____	____	____	____	____
10	____	465	____	____	____	____	____

Problems

1. Gomez runs a small pottery firm. He hires one helper at $12,000 per year, pays annual rent of $5000 for his shop, and spends $20,000 per year on materials. He has $40,000 of his own funds invested in equipment (pottery wheels, kilns, and so forth) that could earn him $4000 per year if alternatively invested. He has been offered $15,000 per year to work as a potter for a competitor. He estimates his entrepreneurial talents are worth $3000 per year. Total annual revenue from pottery sales is $72,000. Calculate the accounting profit and the economic profit for Gomez's pottery firm. **LO1**

2. Imagine you have some workers and some handheld computers that you can use to take inventory at a warehouse. There are diminishing returns to taking inventory. If one worker uses one computer, he can inventory 100 items per hour. Two workers sharing a computer can together inventory 150 items per hour. Three workers sharing a computer can together inventory 160 items per hour. And four or more workers sharing a computer can together inventory fewer than 160 items per hour. Computers cost $100 each and you must pay each worker $25 per hour. If you assign one worker per computer, what is the cost of inventorying a single item? What if you assign two workers per computer? Three? How many workers per computer

should you assign if you wish to minimize the cost of inventorying a single item? **LO2**

3. You are a newspaper publisher. You are in the middle of a one-year rental contract for your factory that requires you to pay $500,000 per month, and you have contractual labor obligations of $1 million per month that you can't get out of. You also have a marginal printing cost of $.25 per paper as well as a marginal delivery cost of $.10 per paper. If sales fall by 20 percent from 1 million papers per month to 800,000 papers per month, what happens to the AFC per paper, the MC per paper, and the minimum amount that you must charge to break even on these costs? **LO3**

4. There are economies of scale in ranching, especially with regard to fencing land. Suppose that barbed-wire fencing costs $10,000 per mile to set up. How much would it cost to fence a single property whose area is one square mile if that property also happens to be perfectly square, with sides that are each one mile long? How much would it cost to fence exactly four such properties, which together would contain four square miles of area? Now, consider how much it would cost to fence in four square miles of ranch land if, instead, it comes as a single large square that is two miles long on each side. Which is more costly—fencing in the four, one-square-mile properties or the single four-square-mile property? **LO4**

FURTHER TEST YOUR KNOWLEDGE AT
www.mcconnell19e.com

At the text's Online Learning Center (OLC), **www.mcconnell19e.com**, you will find one or more Web-based questions that require information from the Internet to answer. We urge you to check them out; they will familiarize you with Web sites that may be helpful in other courses and perhaps even in your career. The OLC also features multiple-choice questions that give instant feedback and provides other helpful ways to further test your knowledge of the chapter.

8

1 **Give the names and summarize the main
characteristics of the four basic market models.**

2 **List the conditions required for purely competitive
markets.**

3 **Convey how purely competitive firms maximize
profits or minimize losses in the short run.**

4 **Explain why a competitive firm's marginal cost
curve is the same as its supply curve.**

Pure Competition in the Short Run

In Chapter 4 we examined the relationship between product demand and total revenue, and in Chapter 7 we discussed production costs. Now we want to connect revenues and costs to see how a business decides what price to charge and how much output to produce. A firm's decisions concerning price and production depend greatly on the character of the industry in which it is operating. There is no "average" or "typical" industry. At one extreme is an industry in which a single producer dominates the market; at the other extreme are industries in which thousands of firms each produce a tiny fraction of market supply. Between these extremes are many other types of industries.

Since we cannot examine each industry individually, we will focus on four basic *models* of market structure. Together, these models will help you understand how price and output are determined in the many product markets in the economy. They also will help you evaluate the efficiency or inefficiency of those markets. Finally, these four models will provide a crucial background for assessing public policies (such as antitrust policy) relating to certain firms and industries.

TABLE 8.1 Characteristics of the Four Basic Market Models

Characteristic	Market Model			
	Pure Competition	Monopolistic Competition	Oligopoly	Pure Monopoly
Number of firms	A very large number	Many	Few	One
Type of product	Standardized	Differentiated	Standardized or differentiated	Unique; no close substitutes
Control over price	None	Some, but within rather narrow limits	Limited by mutual interdependence; considerable with collusion	Considerable
Conditions of entry	Very easy, no obstacles	Relatively easy	Significant obstacles	Blocked
Nonprice competition	None	Considerable emphasis on advertising, brand names, trademarks	Typically a great deal, particularly with product differentiation	Mostly public relations advertising
Examples	Agriculture	Retail trade, dresses, shoes	Steel, automobiles, farm implements, many household appliances	Local utilities

Four Market Models

Economists group industries into four distinct market structures: pure competition, pure monopoly, monopolistic competition, and oligopoly. These four market models differ in several respects: the number of firms in the industry, whether those firms produce a standardized product or try to differentiate their products from those of other firms, and how easy or how difficult it is for firms to enter the industry.

Very briefly the four models are as follows:

- **Pure competition** involves a very large number of firms producing a standardized product (that is, a product like cotton, for which each producer's output is virtually identical to that of every other producer.) New firms can enter or exit the industry very easily.
- **Pure monopoly** is a market structure in which one firm is the sole seller of a product or service (for example, a local electric utility). Since the entry of additional firms is blocked, one firm constitutes the entire industry. The pure monopolist produces a single unique product, so product differentiation is not an issue.
- **Monopolistic competition** is characterized by a relatively large number of sellers producing differentiated products (clothing, furniture, books). Present in this model is widespread *nonprice competition*, a selling strategy in which a firm does not try to distinguish its product on the basis of price but instead on attributes like design and workmanship (an approach called *product differentiation*). Either entry to or exit from monopolistically competitive industries is quite easy.
- **Oligopoly** involves only a few sellers of a standardized or differentiated product, so each firm is affected by the decisions of its rivals and must take those decisions into account in determining its own price and output.

Table 8.1 summarizes the characteristics of the four models for easy comparison and later reference. In discussing these market models, we will occasionally distinguish the characteristics of *pure competition* from those of the three other basic market structures, which together we will designate as **imperfect competition.**

Pure Competition: Characteristics and Occurrence

Although pure competition is relatively rare in the real world, this market model is highly relevant to several industries. In particular, we can learn much about markets for agricultural goods, fish products, foreign exchange, basic metals, and stock shares by studying the pure-competition model. Also, pure competition is a meaningful starting point for any discussion of price and output determination. Moreover, the operation of a purely competitive economy provides a standard, or norm, for evaluating the efficiency of the real-world economy.

Let's take a fuller look at pure competition, the focus of the remainder of this chapter:

- *Very large numbers* A basic feature of a purely competitive market is the presence of a large number of independently acting sellers, often offering their products in large national or international markets. Examples: markets for farm commodities, the stock market, and the foreign exchange market.
- *Standardized product* Purely competitive firms produce a standardized (identical or homogeneous) product. As long as the price is the same, consumers

will be indifferent about which seller to buy the product from. Buyers view the products of firms B, C, D, and E as perfect substitutes for the product of firm A. Because purely competitive firms sell standardized products, they make no attempt to differentiate their products and do not engage in other forms of nonprice competition.

- *"Price takers"* In a purely competitive market, individual firms do not exert control over product price. Each firm produces such a small fraction of total output that increasing or decreasing its output will not perceptibly influence total supply or, therefore, product price. In short, the competitive firm is a **price taker:** It cannot change market price; it can only adjust to it. That means that the individual competitive producer is at the mercy of the market. Asking a price higher than the market price would be futile. Consumers will not buy from firm A at $2.05 when its 9999 competitors are selling an identical product, and therefore a perfect substitute, at $2 per unit. Conversely, because firm A can sell as much as it chooses at $2 per unit, it has no reason to charge a lower price, say, $1.95. Doing that would shrink its profit.

- *Free entry and exit* New firms can freely enter and existing firms can freely leave purely competitive industries. No significant legal, technological, financial, or other obstacles prohibit new firms from selling their output in any competitive market.

Demand as Seen by a Purely Competitive Seller

We begin by examining demand from a purely competitive seller's viewpoint to see how it affects revenue. This seller might be a wheat farmer, a strawberry grower, a sheep rancher, a foreign-currency broker, or some other pure competitor. Because each purely competitive firm offers only a negligible fraction of total market supply, it must accept the price determined by the market; it is a price taker, not a price maker.

Perfectly Elastic Demand

The demand schedule faced by the *individual firm* in a purely competitive industry is perfectly elastic at the market price, as demonstrated in Figure 8.1. As shown in column 1 of the table in Figure 8.1, the market price is $131. The firm represented cannot obtain a higher price by restricting its output, nor does it need to lower its price to increase its sales volume. Columns 1 and 2 show that the firm can produce and sell as many or as few units as it likes at the market price of $131.

We are *not* saying that *market* demand is perfectly elastic in a competitive market. Rather, market demand graphs as a downsloping curve. An entire industry (all firms producing a particular product) can affect price by changing industry output. For example, all firms, acting independently but simultaneously, can increase price by reducing output. But the individual competitive firm cannot do that because its output represents such a small fraction of its industry's total output. For the individual competitive firm, the market price is therefore a fixed value at which it can sell as many or as few units as it cares to. Graphically, this implies that the individual competitive firm's demand curve will plot as a straight, horizontal line such as *D* in Figure 8.1

Average, Total, and Marginal Revenue

The firm's demand schedule is also its average-revenue schedule. Price per unit to the purchaser is also revenue per unit, or average revenue, to the seller. To say that all buyers must pay $131 per unit is to say that the revenue per unit, or **average revenue** received by the seller, is $131. Price and average revenue are the same thing.

The **total revenue** for each sales level is found by multiplying price by the corresponding quantity the firm can sell. (Column 1 multiplied by column 2 in the table in Figure 8.1 yields column 3.) In this case, total revenue increases by a constant amount, $131, for each additional unit of sales. Each unit sold adds exactly its constant price—no more or no less—to total revenue.

When a firm is pondering a change in its output, it will consider how its total revenue will change as a result. **Marginal revenue** is the change in total revenue (or the extra revenue) that results from selling one more unit of output. In column 3 of the table in Figure 8.1, total revenue is zero when zero units are sold. The first unit of output sold increases total revenue from zero to $131, so marginal revenue for that unit is $131. The second unit sold increases total revenue from $131 to $262, and marginal revenue is again $131. Note in column 4 that marginal revenue is a constant $131, as is price. *In pure competition, marginal revenue and price are equal.*

Figure 8.1 shows the purely competitive firm's total-revenue, demand, marginal-revenue, and average-revenue curves. Total revenue (TR) is a straight line that slopes upward to the right. Its slope is constant because each extra unit of sales increases TR by $131. The demand curve (*D*) is horizontal, indicating perfect price elasticity. The marginal-revenue (MR) curve coincides with the demand curve because the product price (and hence MR) is constant. The average revenue (AR) curve equals price and therefore also coincides with the demand curve.

FIGURE 8.1 A purely competitive firm's demand and revenue curves. The demand curve (*D*) of a purely competitive firm is a horizontal line (perfectly elastic) because the firm can sell as much output as it wants at the market price (here, $131). Because each additional unit sold increases total revenue by the amount of the price, the firm's total-revenue (TR) curve is a straight upsloping line and its marginal-revenue (MR) curve coincides with the firm's demand curve. The average-revenue (AR) curve also coincides with the demand curve.

Firm's Demand Schedule		Firm's Revenue Data	
(1) **Product Price (P)** **(Average Revenue)**	**(2)** **Quantity** **Demanded (Q)**	**(3)** **Total Revenue** **(TR), (1) × (2)**	**(4)** **Marginal** **Revenue (MR)**
$131	0	$ 0	$131
131	1	131	131
131	2	262	131
131	3	393	131
131	4	524	131
131	5	655	131
131	6	786	131
131	7	917	131
131	8	1048	131
131	9	1179	131
131	10	1310	131

- In a purely competitive industry a large number of firms produce a standardized product and there are no significant barriers to entry.
- The demand seen by a purely competitive firm is perfectly elastic—horizontal on a graph—at the market price.
- Marginal revenue and average revenue for a purely competitive firm coincide with the firm's demand curve; total revenue rises by the product price for each additional unit sold.

Profit Maximization in the Short Run: Total-Revenue–Total-Cost Approach

Because the purely competitive firm is a price taker, it cannot attempt to maximize its profit by raising or lowering the price it charges. With its price set by supply and demand in the overall market, the only variable that the firm can control is its output. As a result, the purely competitive firm attempts to maximize its economic profit (or minimize its economic loss) by adjusting its *output*. And, in the short run, the firm has a fixed plant. Thus it can adjust its output only through changes in the amount of variable resources (materials, labor) it uses. It adjusts its variable resources to achieve the output level that maximizes its profit.

There are two ways to determine the level of output at which a competitive firm will realize maximum profit or minimum loss. One method is to compare total revenue and total cost; the other is to compare marginal revenue and marginal cost. Both approaches apply to all firms, whether they are pure competitors, pure monopolists, monopolistic competitors, or oligopolists.[1]

We begin by examining profit maximization using the total-revenue–total-cost approach. Confronted with the market price of its product, the competitive producer will ask three questions: (1) Should we produce this product? (2) If so, in what amount? (3) What economic profit (or loss) will we realize?

Let's demonstrate how a pure competitor answers these questions, given a particular set of cost data and a

| **WORKED PROBLEMS** |
| W 8.1 |
| Profit maximization: TR–TC approach |

specific market price. Our cost data are already familiar because they are the fixed-cost, variable-cost, and total-cost data in Table 7.2, repeated in columns 1 to 4 of the table in Figure 8.2. (Recall that these data reflect explicit and implicit costs, including a normal profit.) Assuming that the market price is $131, the total revenue for each output level is found by multiplying output (total product) by price. Total-revenue data are in column 5. Then in column 6 we find the profit or loss at each output level by subtracting total cost, TC (column 4), from total revenue, TR (column 5).

Should the firm produce? Definitely. It can obtain a profit by doing so. How much should it produce? Nine units. Column 6 tells us that this is the output at which total economic profit is at a maximum. What economic profit (or loss) will it realize? A $299 economic profit—the difference between total revenue ($1179) and total cost ($880).

Figure 8.2a compares total revenue and total cost graphically for this profit-maximizing case. Observe again that the total-revenue curve for a purely competitive firm

is a straight line (Figure 8.1). Total cost increases with output because more production requires more resources. But the *rate* of increase in total cost varies with the efficiency of the firm, which in turn varies with the amount of variable inputs that are being combined with the firm's current amount of capital (which is fixed in the short run). Stated slightly differently, the cost data reflect Chapter 7's law of diminishing returns. From zero to four units of output, total cost increases at a decreasing rate as the firm temporarily experiences increasing returns. At higher levels of output, however, efficiency falls as crowding causes diminishing returns to set in. Once that happens, the firm's total cost increases at an increasing rate because each additional unit of input yields less output than the previous unit.

Total revenue and total cost are equal where the two curves in Figure 8.2a intersect (at roughly 2 units of output). Total revenue covers all costs (including a normal profit, which is included in the cost curve), but there is no economic profit. For this reason economists call this output a **break-even point:** an output at which a firm makes a *normal profit* but not an economic profit. If we extended the data beyond 10 units of output, another break-even point would occur where total cost catches up with total revenue, somewhere between 13 and 14 units of output in Figure 8.2a. Any output within the two break-even points identified in the figure will yield an economic profit. The firm achieves maximum profit, however, where the vertical distance between the total-revenue and total-cost curves is greatest. For our particular data, this is at 9 units of output, where maximum profit is $299.

The profit-maximizing output is easier to see in Figure 8.2b, where total profit is graphed for each level of output. Where the total-revenue and total-cost curves intersect in Figure 8.2a, economic profit is zero, as shown by the total-profit line in Figure 8.2b. Where the vertical distance between TR and TC is greatest in the upper graph, economic profit is at its peak ($299), as shown in the lower graph. This firm will choose to produce 9 units since that output maximizes its profit.

Profit Maximization in the Short Run: Marginal-Revenue–Marginal-Cost Approach

In the second approach, the firm compares the amounts that each *additional* unit of output would add to total revenue and to total cost. In other words, the firm compares the *marginal revenue* (MR) and the *marginal cost* (MC) of each successive unit of output. Assuming that producing

---

[1]To make sure you understand these two approaches, we will apply both of them to output determination under pure competition. But since we want to emphasize the marginal approach, we will limit our graphical application of the total-revenue approach to a situation where the firm maximizes profits. We will then use the marginal approach to examine three cases: profit maximization, loss minimization, and shutdown.

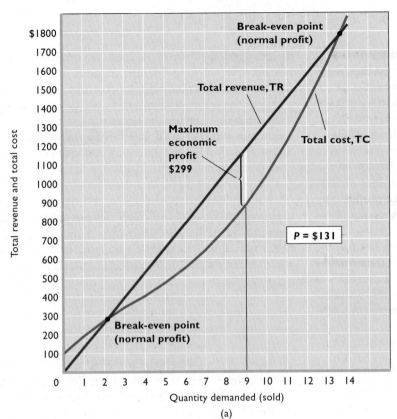

FIGURE 8.2 Total-revenue–total-cost approach to profit maximization for a purely competitive firm. (a) The firm's profit is maximized at that output (9 units) where total revenue, TR, exceeds total cost, TC, by the maximum amount. (b) The vertical distance between TR and TC in (a) is plotted as a total-economic-profit curve. Maximum economic profit is $299 at 9 units of output.

(a) Profit-maximizing case

(b) Total economic profit

(1) Total Product (Output) (Q)	(2) Total Fixed Cost (TFC)	(3) Total Variable Cost (TVC)	(4) Total Cost (TC)	PRICE: $131 (5) Total Revenue (TR)	(6) Profit (+) or Loss (−)
0	$100	$ 0	$ 100	$ 0	$−100
1	100	90	190	131	−59
2	100	170	270	262	−8
3	100	240	340	393	+53
4	100	300	400	524	+124
5	100	370	470	655	+185
6	100	450	550	786	+236
7	100	540	640	917	+277
8	100	650	750	1048	+298
9	100	780	880	1179	+299
10	100	930	1030	1310	+280

is preferable to shutting down, the firm should produce any unit of output whose marginal revenue exceeds its marginal cost because the firm would gain more in revenue from selling that unit than it would add to its costs by producing it. Conversely, if the marginal cost of a unit of output exceeds its marginal revenue, the firm should not produce that unit. Producing it would add more to costs than to revenue, and profit would decline or loss would increase.

In the initial stages of production, where output is relatively low, marginal revenue will usually (but not always) exceed marginal cost. So it is profitable to produce through this range of output. But at later stages of production, where output is relatively high, rising marginal costs will exceed marginal revenue. Obviously, a profit-maximizing firm will want to avoid output levels in that range. Separating these two production ranges is a unique point at which marginal revenue equals marginal cost. This point is the key to the output-determining rule: *In the short run, the firm will maximize profit or minimize loss by producing the output at which marginal revenue equals marginal cost (as long as producing is preferable to shutting down).* This profit-maximizing guide is known as the **MR = MC rule.**

Keep in mind these features of the MR = MC rule:

- For most sets of MR and MC data, MR and MC will be precisely equal at a fractional level of output. In such instances the firm should produce the last complete unit of output for which MR exceeds MC.
- As noted, the rule applies only if producing is preferable to shutting down. We will show shortly that if marginal revenue does not equal or exceed average variable cost, the firm will shut down rather than produce the amount of output at which MR = MC.
- The rule is an accurate guide to profit maximization for all firms whether they are purely competitive, monopolistic, monopolistically competitive, or oligopolistic.
- The rule can be restated as $P = MC$ when applied to a purely competitive firm. Because the demand schedule faced by a competitive seller is perfectly elastic at the going market price, product price and marginal revenue are equal. So under pure competition (and only under pure competition) we may substitute P for MR in the rule: When producing is preferable to shutting down, the competitive firm that wants to maximize its profit or minimize its loss should produce at that point where price equals marginal cost ($P = MC$).

Now let's apply the MR = MC rule or, because we are considering pure competition, the $P = MC$ rule, first using the same price as used in our total-revenue–total-cost approach to profit maximization. Then, by considering other prices, we will demonstrate two additional cases: loss minimization and shutdown. It is crucial that you understand the MR = MC analysis that follows since it reappears in Chapters 10, 11, and 12.

Profit-Maximizing Case

The first five columns of the table in **Figure 8.3 (Key Graph)** reproduce the AFC, AVC, ATC, and MC data derived for our product in Table 7.2. It is the marginal-cost data of column 5 that we will compare with price (equals marginal revenue) for each unit of output. Suppose first that the market price, and therefore marginal revenue, is $131, as shown in column 6.

What is the profit-maximizing output? Every unit of output up to and including the ninth unit represents greater marginal revenue than marginal cost of output. Each of the first 9 units therefore adds to the firm's profit and should be produced. The tenth unit, however, should not be produced. It would add more to cost ($150) than to revenue ($131). So 9 units is the profit-maximizing output.

The economic profit realized by producing 9 units can be calculated by subtracting total cost from total revenue. Multiplying price ($131) by output (9), we find that total revenue is $1179. From the average-total-cost data in column 4, we see that ATC is $97.78 at 9 units of output. Multiplying $97.78 by 9 gives us total cost of $880.[2] The difference of $299 (= $1179 − $880) is the economic profit. Clearly, this firm will prefer to operate rather than shut down.

Perhaps an easier way to calculate the economic profit is to use this simple equation, in which A is average total cost:

$$\text{Profit} = (P - A) \times Q$$

So by subtracting the average total cost ($97.78) from the product price ($131), we obtain a per-unit profit of $33.22. Multiplying that amount by 9 units of output, we determine that the profit is $299. Take some time now to verify the num-

WORKED PROBLEMS

W 8.2

Profit maximization: MR = MC approach

---

[2]Most of the unit-cost data are rounded figures. Therefore, economic profits calculated from them will typically vary by a few cents from the profits determined in the total-revenue–total-cost approach. Here we simply ignore the few-cents differentials to make our answers consistent with the results of the total-revenue–total-cost approach.

FIGURE 8.3 **Short-run profit maximization for a purely competitive firm.** The MR = MC output enables the purely competitive firm to maximize profits or to minimize losses. In this case MR (= P in pure competition) and MC are equal at an output Q of 9 units. There, P exceeds the average total cost A = $97.78, so the firm realizes an economic profit of P − A per unit. The total economic profit is represented by the green rectangle and is 9 × (P − A).

(1) Total Product (Output)	(2) Average Fixed Cost (AFC)	(3) Average Variable Cost (AVC)	(4) Average Total Cost (ATC)	(5) Marginal Cost (MC)	(6) Price = Marginal Revenue (MR)	(7) Total Economic Profit (+) or Loss (−)
0						$−100
1	$100.00	$90.00	$190.00	$ 90	$131	−59
2	50.00	85.00	135.00	80	131	−8
3	33.33	80.00	113.33	70	131	+53
4	25.00	75.00	100.00	60	131	+124
5	20.00	74.00	94.00	70	131	+185
6	16.67	75.00	91.67	80	131	+236
7	14.29	77.14	91.43	90	131	+277
8	12.50	81.25	93.75	110	131	+298
9	11.11	86.67	97.78	130	131	+299
10	10.00	93.00	103.00	150	131	+280

QUICK QUIZ FOR FIGURE 8.3

1. Curve MR is horizontal because:
   a. product price falls as output increases.
   b. the law of diminishing marginal utility is at work.
   c. the market demand for this product is perfectly elastic.
   d. the firm is a price taker.

2. At a price of $131 and 7 units of output:
   a. MR exceeds MC, and the firm should expand its output.
   b. total revenue is less than total cost.
   c. AVC exceeds ATC.
   d. the firm would earn only a normal profit.

3. In maximizing profits at 9 units of output, this firm is adhering to which of the following decision rules?

a. Produce where MR exceeds MC by the greatest amount.
b. Produce where P exceeds ATC by the greatest amount.
c. Produce where total revenue exceeds total cost by the greatest amount.
d. Produce where average fixed costs are zero.

4. Suppose price declined from $131 to $100. This firm's:
a. marginal-cost curve would shift downward.
b. economic profit would fall to zero.
c. profit-maximizing output would decline.
d. total cost would fall by more than its total revenue.

Answers: 1. d; 2. a; 3. c; 4. c

bers in column 7. You will find that any output other than that which adheres to the MR = MC rule will mean either profits below $299 or losses.

The graph in Figure 8.3 shows price (= MR) and marginal cost graphically. Price equals marginal cost at the profit-maximizing output of 9 units. There the per-unit economic profit is $P - A$, where P is the market price and A is the average total cost for an output of 9 units. The total economic profit is $9 \times (P - A)$, shown by the green rectangular area.

Note that the firm wants to maximize its total profit, not its per-unit profit. Per-unit profit is greatest at 7 units of output, where price exceeds average total cost by $39.57

INTERACTIVE GRAPHS
G 8.1
Short-run profit maximization

(= $131 − $91.43). But by producing only 7 units, the firm would be forgoing the production of 2 additional units of output that would clearly contribute to total profit. The firm is happy to accept lower per-unit profits for additional units of output because they nonetheless add to total profit.

Loss-Minimizing Case

Now let's assume that the market price is $81 rather than $131. Should the firm still produce? If so, how much? And what will be the resulting profit or loss? The answers, respectively, are "Yes," "Six units," and "A loss of $64."

The first five columns of the table in Figure 8.4 are the same as the first five columns of the table in Figure 8.3. But column 6 of the table in Figure 8.4 shows the new price (equal to MR), $81. Comparing columns 5 and 6, we find that the first unit of output adds $90 to total cost but only $81 to total revenue. One might conclude: "Don't produce—close down!" But that would be hasty. Remember that in the very early stages of production, marginal product is low, making marginal cost unusually high. The price–marginal cost relationship improves with increased production. For units 2 through 6, price exceeds marginal cost. Each of these 5 units adds more to revenue than to cost, and as shown in column 7, they decrease the total loss. Together they more than compensate for the "loss" taken on the first unit. Beyond 6 units, however, MC exceeds MR (= P). The firm should therefore produce 6 units. In general, the profit-seeking producer should always compare marginal revenue (or price under pure competition) with the rising portion of the marginal-cost schedule or curve.

Will production be profitable? No, because at 6 units of output the average total cost of $91.67 exceeds the price

of $81 by $10.67 per unit. If we multiply that by the 6 units of output, we find the firm's total loss is $64. Alternatively, comparing the total revenue of $486 (= 6 × $81) with the total cost of $550 (= 6 × $91.67), we see again that the firm's loss is $64.

Then why produce? Because this loss is less than the firm's $100 of fixed costs, which is the $100 loss the firm would incur in the short run by closing down. The firm receives enough revenue per unit ($81) to cover its average variable costs of $75 and also provide $6 per unit, or a total of $36, to apply against fixed costs. Therefore, the firm's loss is only $64 (= $100 − $36), not $100.

This loss-minimizing case is illustrated in the graph in Figure 8.4. Wherever price P exceeds average variable cost AVC but is less than ATC, the firm can pay part, but not all, of its fixed costs by producing. The loss is minimized by producing the output at which MC = MR (here, 6 units). At that output, each unit contributes $P - V$ to covering fixed cost, where V is the AVC at 6 units of output. The per-unit loss is $A - P = $10.67, and the total loss is $6 \times (A - P)$, or $64, as shown by the red area.

Shutdown Case

Suppose now that the market yields a price of only $71. Should the firm produce? No, because at every output level the firm's average variable cost is greater than the price (compare columns 3 and 8 of the table in Figure 8.4). The smallest loss it can incur by producing is greater than the $100 fixed cost it will lose by shutting down (as shown by column 9). The best action is to shut down.

You can see this shutdown situation in Figure 8.5. Price comes closest to covering average variable costs at the MR (= P) = MC output of 5 units. But even here, price or revenue per unit would fall short of average variable cost by $3 (= $74 − $71). By producing at the MR (= P) = MC output, the firm would lose its $100 worth of fixed cost plus $15 ($3 of variable cost on each of the 5 units), for a total loss of $115. This compares unfavorably with the $100 fixed-cost loss the firm would incur by shutting down and producing no output. So it will make sense for the firm to shut down rather than produce at a $71 price—or at any price less than the minimum average variable cost of $74.

The shutdown case reminds us of the qualifier to our MR (= P) = MC rule. A competitive firm will maximize profit or minimize loss in the short run by producing that output at which MR (= P) = MC, *provided that market price exceeds minimum average variable cost.*

FIGURE 8.4 Short-run loss minimization for a purely competitive firm. If price P exceeds the minimum AVC (here, $74 at $Q = 5$) but is less than ATC, the MR = MC output (here, 6 units) will permit the firm to minimize its losses. In this instance the loss is $A - P$ per unit, where A is the average total cost at 6 units of output. The total loss is shown by the red area and is equal to $6 \times (A - P)$.

					Loss-Minimizing Case		Shutdown Case	
(1) Total Product (Output)	(2) Average Fixed Cost (AFC)	(3) Average Variable Cost (AVC)	(4) Average Total Cost (ATC)	(5) Marginal Cost (MC)	(6) $81 Price = Marginal Revenue (MR)	(7) Profit (+) or Loss (−), $81 Price	(8) $71 Price = Marginal Revenue (MR)	(9) Profit (+) or Loss (−), $71 Price
0				$90	$81	$−100	$71	$−100
1	$100.00	$90.00	$190.00	80	81	−109	71	−119
2	50.00	85.00	135.00	70	81	−108	71	−128
3	33.33	80.00	113.33	60	81	−97	71	−127
4	25.00	75.00	100.00	70	81	−76	71	−116
5	20.00	74.00	94.00	80	81	−65	71	−115
6	**16.67**	**75.00**	**91.67**	90	**81**	**−64**	71	−124
7	14.29	77.14	91.43	110	81	−73	71	−143
8	12.50	81.25	93.75	130	81	−102	71	−182
9	11.11	86.67	97.78	150	81	−151	71	−241
10	10.00	93.00	103.00		81	−220	71	−320

FIGURE 8.5 The short-run shutdown case for a purely competitive firm. If price P falls below the minimum AVC (here, $74 at $Q = 5$), the competitive firm will minimize its losses in the short run by shutting down. There is no level of output at which the firm can produce and incur a loss smaller than its total fixed cost.

Marginal Cost and Short-Run Supply

In the preceding section we simply selected three different prices and asked what quantity the profit-seeking competitive firm, faced with certain costs, would choose to offer in the market at each price. This set of product prices and corresponding quantities supplied constitutes part of the supply schedule for the competitive firm.

Table 8.2 summarizes the supply schedule data for those three prices ($131, $81, and $71) and four others. This table confirms the direct relationship between product price and quantity supplied that we identified in Chapter 3. Note first that the firm will not produce at price $61 or $71 because both are less than the $74 minimum AVC. Then note that quantity supplied increases as price increases. Observe finally that economic profit is higher at higher prices.

Generalized Depiction

Figure 8.6 (Key Graph) generalizes the MR = MC rule and the relationship between short-run production costs and the firm's supply behavior. The ATC, AVC, and MC curves are shown, along with several marginal-revenue lines drawn at possible market prices. Let's observe quantity supplied at each of these prices:

- Price P_1 is below the firm's minimum average variable cost, so at this price the firm won't operate at all.

TABLE 8.2 The Supply Schedule of a Competitive Firm Confronted with the Cost Data in the table in Figure 8.3

Price	Quantity Supplied	Maximum Profit (+) or Minimum Loss (−)
$151	10	$+480
131	9	+299
111	8	+138
91	7	−3
81	6	−64
71	0	−100
61	0	−100

The Still There Motel

Have you ever driven by a poorly maintained business facility and wondered why the owner does not either fix up the property or go out of business? The somewhat surprising reason is that it may be unprofitable to improve the facility yet profitable to continue to operate the business as it deteriorates. Seeing why will aid your understanding of the "stay open or shut down" decision facing firms experiencing declining demand.

Consider the story of the Still There Motel on Old Highway North, Anytown, USA. The owner built the motel on the basis of traffic patterns and competition existing several decades ago. But as interstate highways were built, the motel found itself located on a relatively untraveled stretch of road. Also, it faced severe competition from "chain" motels located much closer to the interstate highway.

As demand and revenue fell, Still There moved from profitability to loss (P < ATC). But at first its room rates and annual revenue were sufficient to cover its total variable costs and contribute some to the payment of fixed costs such as insurance and property taxes (P > AVC). By staying open, Still There lost less than it would have if it shut down. But since its total revenue did not cover its total costs (or P < ATC), the owner realized that something must be done in the long run. The owner decided to lower total costs by reducing annual maintenance. In effect, the owner opted to allow the motel to deteriorate as a way of regaining temporary profitability.

This renewed profitability of Still There cannot last because in time no further reduction of maintenance costs will be possible. The deterioration of the motel structure will produce even lower room rates, and therefore even less total revenue. The owner of Still There knows that sooner or later total revenue will again fall below total cost (or P will again fall below ATC), even with an annual maintenance expense of zero. When that occurs, the owner will close down the business, tear down the structure, and sell the vacant property. But, in the meantime, the motel is still there—open, deteriorating, and profitable.

Quantity supplied will be zero, as it will be at all other prices below P_2.

- Price P_2 is just equal to the minimum average variable cost. The firm will supply Q_2 units of output (where $MR_2 = MC$) and just cover its total variable cost. Its loss will equal its total fixed cost. (Actually, the firm would be indifferent as to shutting down

key graph

FIGURE 8.6 The P = MC rule and the competitive firm's short-run supply curve. Application of the P = MC rule, as modified by the shutdown case, reveals that the (solid) segment of the firm's MC curve that lies above AVC is the firm's short-run supply curve. More specifically, at price P_1, P = MC at point a, but the firm will produce no output because P_1 is less than minimum AVC. At price P_2 the firm will operate at point b, where it produces Q_2 units and incurs a loss equal to its total fixed cost. At P_3 it operates at point c, where output is Q_3 and the loss is less than total fixed cost. With the price of P_4, the firm operates at point d; in this case the firm earns a normal profit because at output Q_4 price equals ATC. At price P_5 the firm operates at point e and maximizes its economic profit by producing Q_5 units.

QUICK QUIZ FOR FIGURE 8.6

1. Which of the following might increase product price from P_3 to P_5?
   a. An improvement in production technology.
   b. A decline in the price of a substitute good.
   c. An increase in the price of a complementary good.
   d. Rising incomes if the product is a normal good.

2. An increase in price from P_3 to P_5 would:
   a. shift this firm's MC curve to the right.
   b. mean that MR_5 exceeds MC at Q_3 units, inducing the firm to expand output to Q_5.
   c. decrease this firm's average variable costs.
   d. enable this firm to obtain a normal, but not an economic, profit.

3. At P_4:
   a. this firm has no economic profit.
   b. this firm will earn only a normal profit and thus will shut down.
   c. MR_4 will be less than MC at the profit-maximizing output.
   d. the profit-maximizing output will be Q_5.

4. Suppose P_4 is $10, P_5 is $15, Q_4 is 8 units, and Q_5 is 10 units. This firm's:
   a. supply curve is elastic over the Q_4–Q_5 range of output.
   b. supply curve is inelastic over the Q_4–Q_5 range of output.
   c. total revenue will decline if price rises from P_4 to P_5.
   d. marginal-cost curve will shift downward if price falls from P_5 to P_4.

Answers: 1. d; 2. b; 3. a; 4. b

or supplying Q_2 units of output, but we assume it produces.)
- At price P_3 the firm will supply Q_3 units of output to minimize its short-run losses. At any of the other prices between P_2 and P_4 the firm will also minimize its losses by producing and supplying the quantity at which MR (= P) = MC.
- The firm will just break even at price P_4. There it will supply Q_4 units of output (where MR_4 = MC), earning a normal profit but not an economic profit. Total revenue will just cover total cost, including a

normal profit, because the revenue per unit (MR_4 = P_4) and the total cost per unit (ATC) are the same.
- At price P_5 the firm will realize an economic profit by producing and supplying Q_5 units of output. In fact, at any price above P_4 the firm will obtain economic profit by producing to the point where MR (= P) = MC.

Note that each of the MR (= P) = MC intersection points labeled b, c, d and e in Figure 8.6 indicates a possible product price (on the vertical axis) and the corresponding quantity that the firm would supply at that price (on the

TABLE 8.3 Output Determination in Pure Competition in the Short Run

Question	Answer
Should this firm produce?	Yes, if price is equal to, or greater than, minimum average variable cost. This means that the firm is profitable or that its losses are less than its fixed cost.
What quantity should this firm produce?	Produce where MR (= P) = MC; there, profit is maximized (TR exceeds TC by a maximum amount) or loss is minimized.
Will production result in economic profit?	Yes, if price exceeds average total cost (so that TR exceeds TC). No, if average total cost exceeds price (so that TC exceeds TR).

horizontal axis). Thus, points such as these are on the upsloping supply curve of the competitive firm. Note, too, that quantity supplied would be zero at any price below the minimum average variable cost (AVC). *We can conclude that the portion of the firm's marginal-cost curve lying above its average-variable-cost curve is its short-run supply curve.* In Figure 8.6, the solid segment of the marginal-cost curve MC is this firm's **short-run supply curve.** It tells us the amount of output the firm will supply at each price in a series of prices.

Table 8.3 summarizes the MR = MC approach to determining the competitive firm's profit-maximizing output level. It also shows the equivalent analysis in terms of total revenue and total cost.

Diminishing Returns, Production Costs, and Product Supply

We have now identified the links between the law of diminishing returns (Chapter 7), production costs, and product supply in the short run. Because of the law of diminishing returns, marginal costs eventually rise as more units of output are produced. And because marginal costs rise with output, a purely competitive firm must get successively higher prices to motivate it to produce additional units of output.

Viewed alternatively, higher product prices and marginal revenue encourage a purely competitive firm to expand output. As its output increases, the firm's marginal costs rise as a result of the law of diminishing returns. At some now greater output, the higher MC equals the new product price and MR. Profit once again is maximized, but at a greater total amount. Quantity supplied has increased in direct response to an increase in product price and the desire to maximize profit.

Changes in Supply

In Chapter 7 we saw that changes in such factors as the prices of variable inputs or in technology will alter costs and shift the marginal-cost or short-run supply curve to a new location. All else equal, for example, a wage increase would increase marginal cost and shift the supply curve in Figure 8.6 upward as viewed from the horizontal axis (leftward as viewed from the vertical axis). That is, supply would decrease. Similarly, technological progress that increases the productivity of labor would reduce marginal cost and shift the marginal-cost or supply curve downward as viewed from the horizontal axis (rightward as viewed from the vertical axis). This represents an increase in supply.

Firm and Industry: Equilibrium Price

In the preceding section we established the competitive firm's short-run supply curve by applying the MR (= P) = MC rule. But which of the various possible prices will actually be the market equilibrium price?

From Chapter 3 we know that the market equilibrium price will be the price at which the total quantity supplied of the product equals the total quantity demanded. So to determine the equilibrium price, we first need to obtain a total supply schedule and a total demand schedule. We find the total supply schedule by assuming a particular number of firms in the industry and supposing that each firm has the same individual supply schedule as the firm represented in Figure 8.6. Then we sum the quantities supplied at each price level to obtain the total (or market) supply schedule. Columns 1 and 3 in Table 8.4 repeat the supply schedule for the individual competitive firm, as derived in Table 8.2.

TABLE 8.4 Firm and Market Supply and Market Demand

(1) Quantity Supplied, Single Firm	(2) Total Quantity Supplied, 1000 Firms	(3) Product Price	(4) Total Quantity Demanded
10	10,000	$151	4000
9	9000	131	6000
8	8000	111	8000
7	7000	91	9000
6	6000	81	11,000
0	0	71	13,000
0	0	61	16,000

Suppose 1000 firms compete in this industry, all having the same total and unit costs as the single firm we discussed. This lets us calculate the market supply schedule (columns 2 and 3) by multiplying the quantity-supplied figures of the single firm (column 1) by 1000.

Market Price and Profits To determine the equilibrium price and output, these total-supply data must be compared with total-demand data. Let's assume that total demand is as shown in columns 3 and 4 in Table 8.4. By comparing the total quantity supplied and the total quantity demanded at the seven possible prices, we determine that the equilibrium price is $111 and the equilibrium quantity is 8000 units for the industry—8 units for each of the 1000 identical firms.

Will these conditions of market supply and demand make this a profitable or unprofitable industry? Multiplying product price ($111) by output (8 units), we find that the total revenue of each firm is $888. The total cost is $750, found by looking at column 4 of the table in Figure 8.2. The $138 difference is the economic profit of each firm. For the industry, total economic profit is $138,000. This, then, is a profitable industry.

Another way of calculating economic profit is to determine per-unit profit by subtracting average total cost ($93.75) from product price ($111) and multiplying the difference (per-unit profit of $17.25) by the firm's equilibrium level of output (8). Again we obtain an economic profit of $138 per firm and $138,000 for the industry.

Figure 8.7 shows this analysis graphically. The individual supply curves of each of the 1000 identical firms—one of which is shown as $s = MC$ in Figure 8.7a—are summed horizontally to get the total-supply curve $S =$ ΣMC of Figure 8.7b. With total-demand curve D, it yields the equilibrium price $111 and equilibrium quantity (for the industry) 8000 units. This equilibrium price is given and unalterable to the individual firm; that is, each firm's demand curve is perfectly elastic at the equilibrium price, as indicated by d in Figure 8.7a. Because the individual firm is a price taker, the marginal-revenue curve coincides with the firm's demand curve d. This $111 price exceeds the average total cost at the firm's equilibrium MR = MC output of 8 units, so the firm earns an economic profit represented by the green area in Figure 8.7a.

Assuming no changes in costs or market demand, these diagrams reveal a genuine equilibrium in the short run. No shortages or surpluses occur in the market to cause price or total quantity to change. Nor can any firm in the industry increase its profit by altering its output. Note, too, that higher unit and marginal costs, on the one hand, or weaker market demand, on the other, could change the situation so that Figure 8.7a resembles Figure 8.4 or Figure 8.5.

Firm versus Industry Figure 8.7 underscores a point made earlier: Product price is a given fact to the *individual* competitive firm, but the supply plans of all competitive producers *as a group* are a basic determinant of product price. If we recall the fallacy of composition (Last Word, Chapter 1), we find there is no inconsistency here. Although one firm, supplying a negligible fraction of total supply, cannot affect price, the sum of the supply curves of all the firms in the industry constitutes the industry supply curve, and that curve does have an important bearing on price.

> **WORKED PROBLEMS**
>
> **W 8.3**
>
> Short-run competitive equilibrium

(a)
Single firm

(b)
Industry

FIGURE 8.7 Short-run competitive equilibrium for (a) a firm and (b) the industry. The horizontal sum of the 1000 firms' individual supply curves (s) determines the industry supply curve (S). Given industry demand (D), the short-run equilibrium price and output for the industry are $111 and 8000 units. Taking the equilibrium price as given, the individual firm establishes its profit-maximizing output at 8 units and, in this case, realizes the economic profit represented by the green area.

For Firms Facing Losses Due to Fixed Costs, Shutting Down in the Short Run Does Not Mean Shutting Down Forever.

A firm with fixed costs starts each month standing at the bottom of a deep financial hole. The depth of that "money pit" is equal to the dollar value of all the payments that the firm is legally obligated to make even if it is producing nothing. These fixed costs include contractually guaranteed salaries, interest payments on loans, and equipment rental fees that are locked-in by long-term contracts. As the firm stands at the bottom of this fixed-cost financial hole and stares upward looking for a way out, it has to ask itself the following question: Will producing output make the hole even deeper?

Naturally, the firm hopes that producing output will generate positive cash flows that will offset its fixed costs and start filling in the hole. If those positive flows are large enough, they may completely offset the firm's fixed costs and fill up the hole, thereby allowing the firm to break even. And if they are just a bit larger, they will not only fill up the hole but also accumulate a nice little pile of profits above ground.

But those are just the firm's hopes. The firm's reality may be quite unpleasant. In particular, the firm may be facing a situation in which producing output would make its financial situation worse rather than better. As explained in this chapter, if the price of the firm's output falls too low, then producing output will yield cash flows that are negative rather than positive because revenues will be less than variable costs. If that happens, producing output will lose money for the firm so that the firm would be better off shutting down production rather than producing output. By shutting down, it will lose only its fixed costs. By shutting down, its financial hole won't get even deeper.

A crucial thing to understand, however, is that the low prices that cause firms to shut down production are often temporary—so that shutdowns are also often temporary. Just because a firm shuts down at a given moment to prevent its financial hole from getting any deeper does not mean that the firm will go out of business forever. To the contrary, many industries are characterized by firms that regularly switch production on and off depending upon the market price they can get for their output and,

consequently, whether producing output will generate positive or negative cash flows.

Oil production is a good example. Different wells have different variable production costs. If the price of oil drops below a given well's variable costs, then it would be better to halt production on that well and just lose the value of its fixed costs rather than pumping oil whose variable costs exceed the revenue that it generates when sold.

Seasonal resorts are another good example of turning production on and off depending on the price. The demand for hotel rooms near ski resorts in New Hampshire, for instance, is much higher during the winter ski season than it is during the summer. As a result, the market price of hotel rooms falls so low during the summer that many inns and resorts close during the warmer months. They have all sorts of fixed costs, but it makes more sense for them to shut down rather than remain open, because operating in the summer would cost more in variable costs than it would generate in revenues. Better to lose only their fixed costs.

Numerous other examples of temporary shutdowns occur during recessions, the occasional economy-wide economic slowdowns during which demand declines for nearly all goods and services. The 2007–2009 recession in the United States, for instance, saw many manufacturing companies temporarily shut down and mothball their production facilities. The recession witnessed the mothballing of electric generating plants, factories that make fiber optic cable, automobile factories, chemical plants, textile mills, and even the plant in McIntosh, Alabama, that makes the artificial sweetener Splenda. Many other firms also shut down production to wait out the recession—so many, in fact, that there was a mini-boom for consulting firms that specialized in helping firms mothball their factories (the main problem being how to properly store idle machinery so that it will work again when it is eventually brought back into service).

Firms that mothball factories or equipment during a recession do so expecting to eventually turn them back on. But the lengths of recessions vary, as do the specific circumstances of individual firms. So while many firms shut down in the short run with the expectation of reopening as soon as their particular business conditions improve, sometimes their business conditions do not improve. Sometimes the only way to terminate fixed costs is to terminate the firm.

Summary

1. Economists group industries into four models based on their market structures: (a) pure competition, (b) pure monopoly, (c) monopolistic competition, and (d) oligopoly.

2. A purely competitive industry consists of a large number of independent firms producing a standardized product. Pure competition assumes that firms and resources are mobile among different industries.

3. In a competitive industry, no single firm can influence market price. This means that the firm's demand curve is perfectly elastic and price equals marginal revenue.

4. We can analyze short-run profit maximization by a competitive firm by comparing total revenue and total cost or by applying marginal analysis. A firm maximizes its short-run profit by producing the output at which total revenue exceeds total cost by the greatest amount.

5. Provided price exceeds minimum average variable cost, a competitive firm maximizes profit or minimizes loss in the short run by producing the output at which price or marginal revenue equals marginal cost. •

6. If price is less than minimum average variable cost, a competitive firm minimizes its loss by shutting down. If price is greater than average variable cost but is less than average total cost, a competitive firm minimizes its loss by producing the $P = MC$ amount of output. If price also exceeds average total cost, the firm maximizes its economic profit at the $P = MC$ amount of output.

7. Applying the MR ($= P$) $= MC$ rule at various possible market prices leads to the conclusion that the segment of the firm's short-run marginal-cost curve that lies above the firm's average-variable-cost curve is its short-run supply curve.

8. A competitive firm shuts down production at least temporarily if price is less than minimum average variable cost, because in those situations, producing any amount of output will always result in variable costs exceeding revenues. Shutting down therefore results in a smaller loss, because the firm will lose only its fixed cost, whereas, if it operated, it would lose its fixed cost plus whatever money is lost due to variable costs exceeding revenues.

9. Competitive firms choose to operate rather than shut down whenever price is greater than average variable cost but less than average total cost, because in those situations, revenues will always exceed variable costs. The amount by which revenues exceed variable costs can be used to help pay down some of the firms fixed costs. Thus, the firm loses less money by operating (and paying down some of its fixed costs) than it would if it shut down (in which case it would suffer a loss equal to the full amount of its fixed costs).

Terms and Concepts

pure competition

pure monopoly

monopolistic competition

oligopoly

imperfect competition

price taker

average revenue

total revenue

marginal revenue

break-even point

MR = MC rule

short-run supply curve

Questions

1. Briefly state the basic characteristics of pure competition, pure monopoly, monopolistic competition, and oligopoly. Under which of these market classifications does each of the following most accurately fit? (a) a supermarket in your hometown; (b) the steel industry; (c) a Kansas wheat farm; (d) the commercial bank in which you or your family has an account; (e) the automobile industry. In each case, justify your classification. LO1

2. Strictly speaking, pure competition is relatively rare. Then why study it? LO2

3. Use the demand schedule to the right to determine total revenue and marginal revenue for each possible level of sales: LO2
   a. What can you conclude about the structure of the industry in which this firm is operating? Explain.

Product Price	Quantity Demanded	Total Revenue	Marginal Revenue
$2	0	$____	
2	1	____	$____
2	2	____	____
2	3	____	____
2	4	____	____
2	5	____	____

b. Graph the demand, total-revenue, and marginal-revenue curves for this firm.

c. Why do the demand and marginal-revenue curves coincide?

d. "Marginal revenue is the change in total revenue associ-ated with additional units of output." Explain verbally and graphically, using the data in the table.

4. "Even if a firm is losing money, it may be better to stay in business in the short run." Is this statement ever true? Under what condition(s)? LO3

5. Consider a firm that has no fixed costs and which is currently losing money. Are there any situations in which it would want to stay open for business in the short run? If a firm has no fixed costs, is it sensible to speak of the firm distinguishing between the short run and the long run? LO3

6. Why is the equality of marginal revenue and marginal cost essential for profit maximization in all market structures? Explain why price can be substituted for marginal revenue in the MR = MC rule when an industry is purely competitive. LO3

7. "That segment of a competitive firm's marginal-cost curve that lies above its average-variable-cost curve constitutes the short-run supply curve for the firm." Explain using a graph and words. LO4

8. **LAST WORD** If a firm's current revenues are less than its current variable costs, when should it shut down? If the firm decides to shut down, should we expect that decision to be final? Explain using an example that is not in the book.

Problems

1. A purely competitive firm finds that the market price for its product is $20. It has a fixed cost of $100 and a variable cost of $10 per unit for the first 50 units and then $25 per unit for all successive units. Does price exceed average variable cost for the first 50 units? What about for the first 100 units? What is the marginal cost per unit for the first 50 units? What about for units 51 and higher? For each of the first 50 units, does MR exceed MC? What about for units 51 and higher? What output level will yield the largest possible profit for this purely competitive firm? (Hint: Draw a graph similar to Figure 8.2 using data for this firm.) LO3

2. A purely competitive wheat farmer can sell any wheat he grows for $10 per bushel. His five acres of land show diminishing returns, because some are better suited for wheat production than others. The first acre can produce 1000 bushels of wheat, the second acre 900, the third 800, and so on. Draw a table with multiple columns to help you answer the following questions. How many bushels will each of the farmer's five acres produce? How much revenue will each acre generate? What are the TR and MR for each acre? If the marginal cost of planting and harvesting an acre is $7000 per acre for each of the five acres, how many acres should the farmer plant and harvest? LO3

3. Karen runs a print shop that makes posters for large companies. It is a very competitive business. The market price is currently $1 per poster. She has fixed costs of $250. Her variable costs are $1000 for the first thousand posters, $800 for the second thousand, and then $750 for each additional thousand posters. What is her AFC per poster (not per thousand!) if she prints 1000 posters? 2000? 10,000? What is her ATC per poster if she prints 1000? 2000? 10,000? If the market price fell to 70 cents per poster, would there be *any* output level at which Karen would *not* shut down production immediately? LO3

4. Assume that the cost data in the top table of the next column are for a purely competitive producer: LO3

Total Product	Average Fixed Cost	Average Variable Cost	Average Total Cost	Marginal Cost
0				
1	$60.00	$45.00	$105.00	$45
2	30.00	42.50	72.50	40
3	20.00	40.00	60.00	35
4	15.00	37.50	52.50	30
5	12.00	37.00	49.00	35
6	10.00	37.50	47.50	40
7	8.57	38.57	47.14	45
8	7.50	40.63	48.13	55
9	6.67	43.33	50.00	65
10	6.00	46.50	52.50	75

a. At a product price of $56, will this firm produce in the short run? If it is preferable to produce, what will be the profit-maximizing or loss-minimizing output? What economic profit or loss will the firm realize per unit of output?

b. Answer the questions of 4a assuming product price is $41.

c. Answer the questions of 4a assuming product price is $32.

d. In the table below, complete the short-run supply schedule for the firm (columns 1 and 2) and indicate the profit or loss incurred at each output (column 3).

(1) Price	(2) Quantity Supplied, Single Firm	(3) Profit (+) or Loss (−)	(4) Quantity Supplied 1500 Firms
$26	_____	$_____	_____
32	_____	_____	_____
38	_____	_____	_____
41	_____	_____	_____
46	_____	_____	_____
56	_____	_____	_____
66	_____	_____	_____

e. Now assume that there are 1500 identical firms in this competitive industry; that is, there are 1500 firms, each of which has the cost data shown in the table. Complete the industry supply schedule (column 4).

f. Suppose the market demand data for the product are as follows:

Price	Total Quantity Demanded
$26	17,000
32	15,000
38	13,500
41	12,000
46	10,500
56	9500
66	8000

What will be the equilibrium price? What will be the equilibrium output for the industry? For each firm? What will profit or loss be per unit? Per firm? Will this industry expand or contract in the long run?

FURTHER TEST YOUR KNOWLEDGE AT
www.mcconnell19e.com

At the text's Online Learning Center (OLC), **www.mcconnell19e.com**, you will find one or more Web-based questions that require information from the Internet to answer. We urge you to check them out; they will familiarize you with Web sites that may be helpful in other courses and perhaps even in your career. The OLC also features multiple-choice questions that give instant feedback and provides other helpful ways to further test your knowledge of the chapter.

AFTER READING THIS CHAPTER, YOU SHOULD BE ABLE TO:

1 Explain how the long run differs from the short run in pure competition.

2 Describe why profits encourage entry into a purely competitive industry and losses result in firms exiting the industry.

3 Explain how the entry and exit of firms affects resource flows and long-run profits and losses.

4 Explain the differences between constant-cost, increasing-cost, and decreasing-cost industries.

5 Show how long-run equilibrium in pure competition produces an efficient allocation of resources.

6 Discuss creative destruction and the profit incentives for innovation.

Pure Competition in the Long Run

The previous chapter discussed how pure competition operates in the short run, the time period during which the individual firms in an industry are stuck with their current plant sizes and fixed-cost commitments. As you know, pure competitors shut down their operation if prices are too low or, if prices are high enough, produce where MR = MC to minimize their losses or maximize their profits. Whether they make a profit or a loss depends on how high the market price is relative to their costs.

That being said, profits and losses cannot be the end of the pure competition story because one of the key characteristics of pure competition is the freedom of firms to enter or exit the industry. We know from Chapter 2 that profits attract entry and losses prompt exit.

In this chapter, we are keenly interested in how entry and exit relate to allocative and productive efficiency. We are also interested in how continuing competition leads to new products and new business methods replacing older products and older business methods through a process aptly referred to as *creative destruction*.

The Long Run in Pure Competition

The entry and exit of firms in our market models can only take place in the long run. In the short run, the industry is composed of a specific number of firms, each with a plant size that is fixed and unalterable in the short run. Firms may shut down in the sense that they can produce zero units of output in the short run, but they do not have sufficient time to liquidate their assets and go out of business.

In the long run, by contrast, the firms already in an industry have sufficient time to either expand or contract their capacities. More important, the number of firms in the industry may either increase or decrease as new firms enter or existing firms leave.

The length of time constituting the long run varies substantially by industry, however, so that you should not fix in your mind any specific number of years, months, or days. Instead, focus your attention on the incentives provided by profits and losses for the entry and exit of firms into any purely competitive industry and, later in the chapter, on how those incentives lead to productive and allocative efficiency. The time horizons are far less important than the process by which profits and losses guide business managers toward the efficient use of society's resources.

Profit Maximization in the Long Run

The first part of the pure competition story (Chapter 8) was about profit, loss, and shutdown in the short run. The rest of the story (this chapter) is about entry and exit and their effects on industry size and allocative and productive efficiency in the long run.

To tell the rest of story well, we need to return to our graphical analysis and examine profit maximization by pure competitors in the long run. Several assumptions, none of which affect our conclusions, will keep things simple:

- **Entry and exit only** The only long-run adjustment in our graphical analysis is caused by the entry or exit of firms. Moreover, we ignore all short-run adjustments in order to concentrate on the effects of the long-run adjustments.
- **Identical costs** All firms in the industry have identical cost curves. This assumption lets us discuss an "average," or "representative," firm, knowing that all other firms in the industry are similarly affected by any long-run adjustments that occur.
- **Constant-cost industry** The industry is a constant-cost industry. This means that the entry and exit of firms does not affect resource prices or, consequently, the locations of the average-total-cost curves of individual firms.

Goal of Our Analysis

The basic conclusion we seek to explain is this: After all long-run adjustments are completed in a purely competitive industry, product price will be exactly equal to, and production will occur at, each firm's minimum average total cost.

This conclusion follows from two basic facts: (1) Firms seek profits and shun losses, and (2) under pure competition, firms are free to enter and leave an industry. If market price initially exceeds minimum average total costs, the resulting economic profits will attract new firms to the industry. But this industry expansion will increase supply until price is brought back down to equality with minimum average total cost. Conversely, if price is initially less than minimum average total cost, the resulting losses will cause firms to leave the industry. As they leave, total supply will decline, bringing the price back up to equality with minimum average total cost.

Long-Run Equilibrium

Consider the average firm in a purely competitive industry that is initially in long-run equilibrium. This firm is represented in Figure 9.1a, where MR = MC and price and minimum average total cost are equal at $50. Economic profit here is zero; the industry is in equilibrium or "at rest" because there is no tendency for firms to enter or to leave. The existing firms are earning normal profits, which means that their accounting profits are equal to those that the owners of these firms could expect to receive on average in other industries. It is because their current profits are the same as they could expect to earn elsewhere that there is no tendency for firms to enter or leave the industry. The $50 market price is determined in Figure 9.1b by market or industry demand D_1 and supply S_1. (S_1 is a short-run supply curve; we will develop the long-run industry supply curve in our discussion.) And remember that normal profits earned by these firms are considered an opportunity cost and, therefore, are included in the firms' cost curves.

As shown on the quantity axes of the two graphs, equilibrium output in the industry is 100,000 while equilibrium output for the single firm is 100. If all firms in the industry are identical, there must be 1000 firms (= 100,000/100).

Entry Eliminates Economic Profits

Let's upset the long-run equilibrium in Figure 9.1 and see what happens. Suppose a change in consumer tastes increases product demand from D_1 to D_2. Price will rise to $60, as determined at the intersection of D_2 and S_1, and the firm's

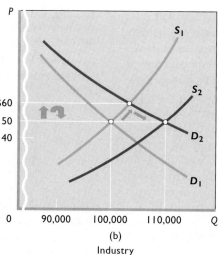

(a)
Single firm

(b)
Industry

FIGURE 9.1 Temporary profits and the reestablishment of long-run equilibrium in (a) a representative firm and (b) the industry. A favorable shift in demand (D_1 to D_2) will upset the original industry equilibrium and produce economic profits. But those profits will entice new firms to enter the industry, increasing supply (S_1 to S_2) and lowering product price until economic profits are once again zero.

marginal-revenue curve will shift upward to $60. This $60 price exceeds the firm's average total cost of $50 at output 100, creating an economic profit of $10 per unit. This economic profit will lure new firms into the industry. Some entrants will be newly created firms; others will shift from less prosperous industries.

As firms enter, the market supply of the product increases, pushing the product price below $60. Economic profits persist, and entry continues until short-run supply increases to S_2. Market price falls to $50, as does marginal revenue for the firm. Price and minimum average total cost are again equal at $50. The economic profits caused by the boost in demand have been eliminated, and, as a result, the previous incentive for more firms to enter the industry has disappeared because the firms that remain are earning only a normal profit (zero economic

profit). Entry ceases and a new long-run equilibrium is reached.

Observe in Figure 9.1a and 9.1b that total quantity supplied is now 110,000 units and each firm is producing 100 units. Now 1100 firms rather than the original 1000 populate the industry. Economic profits have attracted 100 more firms.

Exit Eliminates Losses Now let's consider a shift in the opposite direction. We begin in Figure 9.2b with curves S_1 and D_1 setting the same initial long-run equilibrium situation as in our previous analysis, including the $50 price.

Suppose consumer demand declines from D_1 to D_3. This forces the market price and marginal revenue down to $40, making production unprofitable at the minimum ATC of $50. In time the resulting economic losses will

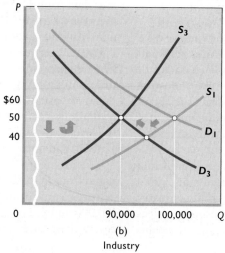

(a)
Single firm

(b)
Industry

FIGURE 9.2 Temporary losses and the reestablishment of long-run equilibrium in (a) a representative firm and (b) the industry. An unfavorable shift in demand (D_1 to D_3) will upset the original industry equilibrium and produce losses. But those losses will cause firms to leave the industry, decreasing supply (S_1 to S_3) and increasing product price until all losses have disappeared.

induce firms to leave the industry. Their owners will seek a normal profit elsewhere rather than accept the below-normal profits (losses) now confronting them. As this exodus of firms proceeds, however, industry supply decreases, pushing the price up from $40 toward $50. Losses continue and more firms leave the industry until the supply curve shifts to S_3. Once this happens, price is again $50, just equal to the minimum average total cost. Losses have been eliminated so that the firms that remain are earning only a normal profit (zero economic profit). Since this is no better or worse than entrepreneurs could expect to earn in other business ventures, there is no longer any incentive to exit the industry. Long-run equilibrium is restored.

In Figure 9.2a and 9.2b, total quantity supplied is now 90,000 units and each firm is producing 100 units. Only 900 firms, not the original 1000, populate the industry. Losses have forced 100 firms out.

You may have noted that we have sidestepped the question of which firms will leave the industry when losses occur by assuming that all firms have identical cost curves. In the real world, of course, managerial talents differ. Even if resource prices and technology are the same for all firms, less skillfully managed firms tend to incur higher costs and therefore are the first to leave an industry when demand declines. Similarly, firms with less productive labor forces or higher transportation costs will be higher-cost producers and likely candidates to quit an industry when demand decreases.

We have now reached an intermediate goal: Our analysis verifies that competition, reflected in the entry and exit of firms, eliminates economic profits or losses by adjusting price to equal minimum long-run average total cost. In addition, this competition forces firms to select output levels at which average total cost is minimized.

Long-Run Supply for a Constant-Cost Industry

Although our analysis has dealt with the long run, we have noted that the market supply curves in Figures 9.1b and 9.2b are short-run curves. What then is the character of the **long-run supply curve** of a competitive industry? Our analysis points us toward an answer. The crucial factor here is the effect, if any, that changes in the number of firms in the industry will have on costs of the individual firms in the industry.

In our analysis of long-run competitive equilibrium we assumed that the industry under discussion was a **constant-cost industry.** This means that industry expansion or contraction will not affect resource prices and therefore production costs. Graphically, it means

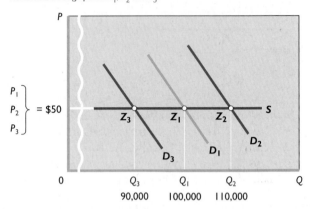

FIGURE 9.3 The long-run supply curve for a constant-cost industry is horizontal. In a constant-cost industry, the entry and exit of firms does not affect resource prices, or, therefore, unit costs. So an increase in demand (D_1 to D_2) raises industry output (Q_1 to Q_2) but not price ($50). Similarly, a decrease in demand (D_1 to D_3) reduces output (Q_1 to Q_3) but not price. Thus the long-run industry supply curve (S) is horizontal through points Z_1, Z_2 and Z_3.

that the entry or exit of firms does not shift the long-run ATC curves of individual firms. This is the case when the industry's demand for resources is small in relation to the total demand for those resources. Then the industry can expand or contract without significantly affecting resource prices and costs.

What does the long-run supply curve of a constant-cost industry look like? The answer is contained in our previous analysis. There we saw that the entry and exit of firms changes industry output but always brings the product price back to its original level, where it is just equal to the constant minimum ATC. Specifically, we discovered that the industry would supply 90,000, 100,000, or 110,000 units of output, all at a price of $50 per unit. In other words, the long-run supply curve of a constant-cost industry is perfectly elastic.

This is demonstrated graphically in Figure 9.3, which uses data from Figures 9.1 and 9.2. Suppose industry demand is originally D_1, industry output is Q_1 (100,000 units), and product price is P_1 ($50). This situation, from Figure 9.1, is one of long-run equilibrium. We saw that when demand increases to D_2, upsetting this equilibrium, the resulting economic profits attract new firms. Because this is a constant-cost industry, entry continues and industry output expands until the price is driven back down to the level of the unchanged minimum ATC. This is at price P_2 ($50) and output Q_2 (110,000).

From Figure 9.2, we saw that a decline in market demand from D_1 to D_3 causes an exit of firms and ultimately restores equilibrium at price P_3 ($50) and output Q_3 (90,000 units). The points Z_1, Z_2, and Z_3 in Figure 9.3 represent these three price-quantity combinations. A line or curve connecting all such points shows the various price-quantity combinations that firms would produce if they had enough time to make all desired adjustments to changes in demand. This line or curve is the industry's long-run supply curve. In a constant-cost industry this curve (straight line) is horizontal, as in Figure 9.3, thus representing perfectly elastic supply.

Long-Run Supply for an Increasing-Cost Industry

Constant-cost industries are a special case. Most industries are **increasing-cost industries,** in which firms' ATC curves shift upward as the industry expands and downward as the industry contracts. Usually, the entry of new firms will increase resource prices, particularly in industries using specialized resources whose long-run supplies do not readily increase in response to increases in resource demand. Higher resource prices result in higher long-run average total costs for all firms in the industry. These higher costs cause upward shifts in each firm's long-run ATC curve.

Thus, when an increase in product demand results in economic profits and attracts new firms to an increasing-cost industry, a two-way squeeze works to eliminate those profits. As before, the entry of new firms increases market supply and lowers the market price. But now each firm's entire ATC curve also shifts upward. The overall result is a higher-than-original equilibrium price. The industry produces a larger output at a higher product price because the industry expansion has increased resource prices and the minimum average total cost.

Since greater output will be supplied at a higher price, the long-run industry supply curve is upsloping. Instead of supplying 90,000, 100,000, or 110,000 units at the same price of $50, an increasing-cost industry might supply 90,000 units at $45, 100,000 units at $50, and 110,000 units at $55. A higher price is required to induce more production, because costs per unit of output increase as production rises.

Figure 9.4 nicely illustrates the situation. Original market demand is D_1 and industry price and output are P_1 ($50) and Q_1 (100,000 units), respectively, at equilibrium point Y_1. An increase in demand to D_2 upsets this equilibrium and leads to economic profits. New firms enter the industry, increasing both market supply and the production costs of individual firms. A new price is established at point Y_2, where P_2 is $55 and Q_2 is 110,000 units.

Conversely, a decline in demand from D_1 to D_3 makes production unprofitable and causes firms to leave the industry. The resulting decline in resource prices reduces

FIGURE 9.4 The long-run supply curve for an increasing-cost industry is upsloping. In an increasing-cost industry, the entry of new firms in response to an increase in demand (D_3 to D_1 to D_2) will bid up resource prices and thereby increase unit costs. As a result, an increased industry output (Q_3 to Q_1 to Q_2) will be forthcoming only at higher prices ($55 > $50 > $45). The long-run industry supply curve (S) therefore slopes upward through points Y_3, Y_1, and Y_2.

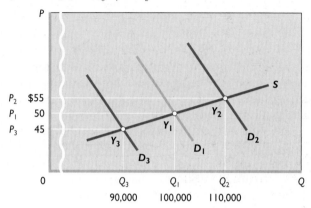

the minimum average total cost of production for firms that stay. A new equilibrium price is established at some level below the original price, say, at point Y_3, where P_3 is $45 and Q_3 is 90,000 units. Connecting these three equilibrium positions, we derive the upsloping long-run supply curve S in Figure 9.4.

Long-Run Supply for a Decreasing-Cost Industry

In **decreasing-cost industries,** firms experience lower costs as their industry expands. The personal computer industry is an example. As demand for personal computers increased, new manufacturers of computers entered the industry and greatly increased the resource demand for the components used to build them (for example, memory chips, hard drives, monitors, and operating software). The expanded production of the components enabled the producers of those items to achieve substantial economies of scale. The decreased production costs of the components reduced their prices, which greatly lowered the computer manufacturers' average costs of production. The supply of personal computers increased by more than demand, and the price of personal computers declined.

Unfortunately, however, the industries that show decreasing costs when output expands also show increasing costs if output contracts. A good example is the American shoe-manufacturing industry as it contracted due to

INTERACTIVE GRAPHS
G 9.1
Long-run competitive supply

FIGURE 9.5 The long-run supply curve for a decreasing-cost industry is downsloping. In a decreasing-cost industry, the entry of new firms in response to an increase in demand (D_3 to D_1 to D_2) will lead to decreased input prices and, consequently, decreased unit costs. As a result, an increase in industry output (Q_3 to Q_1 to Q_2) will be accompanied by lower prices ($55 > $50 > $45). The long-run industry supply curve (S) therefore slopes downward through points X_3, X_1, and X_2.

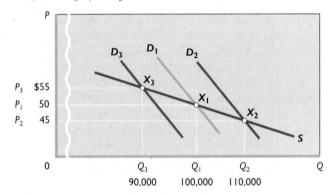

- In pure competition, entrepreneurs remove resources from industries and firms that are generating economic losses in order to transfer them to industries and firms that are generating economic profits.

- In the long run, the entry of firms into an industry will compete away any economic profits, and the exit of firms will eliminate economic losses, so price and minimum average total cost are equal. Entry and exit cease when the firms in the industry return to making a normal profit (zero economic profit).

- The long-run supply curves of constant-, increasing-, and decreasing-cost industries are horizontal, upsloping, and downsloping, respectively.

foreign competition. Back when the industry was doing well and there were many shoemaking firms, the cost of specialized technicians who repair shoemaking machinery could be spread across many firms. This was because the repairmen worked as independent contractors going from one firm's factory to another firm's factory on a daily basis as various pieces of equipment at different factories needed repairs. But as the demand for American footwear fell over time, there were fewer and fewer factories, so the cost of a repair technician had to be spread over fewer and fewer firms. Thus, costs per firm and per unit of output increased.

Figure 9.5 illustrates the situation. The original market demand is D_1 and industry price and output are P_1($50) and Q_1(100,000 units), respectively, at equilibrium point X_1. An increase in demand to D_2 upsets this equilibrium and leads to economic profits. New firms enter the industry, increasing market supply but decreasing the production costs of individual firms. A new price is established at point X_2, where P_2 is $45 and Q_2 is 110,000 units.

Conversely, a decline in demand from D_1 to D_3 makes production unprofitable and causes firms to leave the industry. The resulting increase in input prices increases the minimum average total cost of production for the firms that remain. A new equilibrium price is established at some level above the original price, say at point X_3, where P_3 is $55 and Q_3 is 90,000 units. Connecting these three equilibrium positions in Figure 9.5, we derive the downsloping long-run supply curve S for this decreasing-cost industry.

Pure Competition and Efficiency

Figure 9.6 (Key Graph) demonstrates the efficiency characteristics of the individual firms (Figure 9.6a) and the market (Figure 9.6b) after long-run adjustments in pure competition. Assuming a constant- or increasing-cost industry, the final long-run equilibrium positions of all firms have the same basic efficiency characteristics. As shown in Figure 9.6a, price (and marginal revenue) will settle where it is equal to minimum average total cost: P (and MR) = minimum ATC. Moreover, since the marginal-cost curve intersects the average-total-cost curve at its minimum point, marginal cost and average total cost are equal: MC = minimum ATC. So in long-run equilibrium a triple equality occurs: P (and MR) = MC = minimum ATC. Thus, in long-run equilibrium, each firm produces at the output level Q_f that is associated with this triple equality.[1]

The triple equality tells us two very important things about long-run equilibrium. First, it tells us that although a competitive firm may realize economic profit or loss in the short run, it will earn only a normal profit by producing in accordance with the MR (= P) = MC rule in the long run. Second, the triple equality tells us that in long-run equilibrium, the profit-maximizing decision rule that leads each firm to produce the quantity at which P = MR also implies that each firm will produce at the output level Q_f that is associated with the minimum point on each identical firm's ATC curve.

This is very important because it suggests that pure competition leads to the most efficient possible use of society's resources. Indeed, subject only to Chapter 5's

---

[1] This triple equality does not always hold for decreasing-cost industries in which individual firms produce a large fraction of the total market output. In such cases, MC may remain below ATC if average costs are decreasing. We will discuss this situation of "natural monopoly" in Chapter 10.

FIGURE 9.6 Long-run equilibrium: a competitive firm and market. (a) The equality of price (P), marginal cost (MC), and minimum average total cost (ATC) at output Q_f indicates that the firm is achieving productive efficiency and allocative efficiency. It is using the most efficient technology, charging the lowest price, and producing the greatest output consistent with its costs. It is receiving only a normal profit, which is incorporated into the ATC curve. The equality of price and marginal cost indicates that society allocated its scarce resources in accordance with consumer preferences. (b) In the purely competitive market, allocative efficiency occurs at the market equilibrium output Q_e. The sum of consumer surplus (green area) and producer surplus (blue area) is maximized.

(a) Single firm

(b) Market

QUICK QUIZ FOR FIGURE 9.6

1. We know the firm is a price taker because:
   a. its MC curve slopes upward.
   b. its ATC curve is U-shaped.
   c. its MR curve is horizontal.
   d. MC and ATC are equal at the profit-maximizing output.

2. At this firm's profit-maximizing output:
   a. total revenue equals total cost.
   b. it is earning an economic profit.
   c. allocative, but not necessarily productive, efficiency is achieved.
   d. productive, but not necessarily allocative, efficiency is achieved.

3. The equality of P, MC, and minimum ATC:
   a. occurs only in constant-cost industries.
   b. encourages entry of new firms.
   c. means that the "right goods" are being produced in the "right ways."
   d. results in a zero accounting profit.

4. When $P = $ MC $=$ lowest ATC for individual firms, in the market:
   a. consumer surplus necessarily exceeds producer surplus.
   b. consumer surplus plus producer surplus is at a maximum.
   c. producer surplus necessarily exceeds consumer surplus.
   d. supply and demand are identical.

Answers: 1. c; 2. a; 3. c; 4. b

---

qualifications relating to public goods and externalities, an idealized purely competitive market economy composed of constant- or increasing-cost industries will generate both productive efficiency and allocative efficiency.

Productive Efficiency: $P = $ Minimum ATC

Productive efficiency requires that goods be produced in the least costly way. In the long run, pure competition forces firms to produce at the minimum average total cost of production and to charge a price that is just consistent with that cost. This is true because firms that do not use the best available (least-cost) production methods and combinations of inputs will not survive.

To see why that is true, let's suppose that Figure 9.6 has to do with pure competition in the cucumber industry. In the final equilibrium position shown in Figure 9.6a, suppose each firm in the cucumber industry is producing 100 units (say, truckloads) of cucumbers by using $5000 (equal to average total cost of $50 × 100 units) worth of resources. If any firm produced that same amount of output at any higher total cost, say $7000, it would be wasting resources because all of the other firms in the industry are able to produce that same amount of output using only $5000 of resources. Society would be faced with a net loss of $2000 worth of alternative products. But this cannot happen in pure competition; this firm would incur a loss of $2000, requiring it either to reduce its costs or to go out of business.

Note, too, that consumers benefit from productive efficiency by paying the lowest product price possible under the prevailing technology and cost conditions. And the firm receives only a normal profit, which is part of its economic costs and thus incorporated in its ATC curve.

Allocative Efficiency: $P = MC$

Long-run equilibrium in pure competition guarantees productive efficiency, such that output will be produced in the least-cost way. But productive efficiency by itself does not guarantee that anyone will want to buy the items that are being produced in the least-cost manner. For all we know, consumers might prefer that the resources used to produce those items be redirected toward producing other products instead.

ORIGIN OF THE IDEA

O 9.1

Allocative efficiency

Fortunately, long-run equilibrium in pure competition also guarantees **allocative efficiency,** so we can be certain that society's scarce resources are directed toward producing the goods and services that people most want to consume. Stated formally, allocative efficiency occurs when it is impossible to produce any net gains for society by altering the combination of goods and services that are produced from society's limited supply of resources.

To understand how pure competition leads to allocative efficiency, recall the concept of opportunity cost while looking at Figure 9.6b, where Q_e total units are being produced in equilibrium by the firms in a purely competitive industry. For every unit up to Q_e, market demand curve D lies above market supply curve S. Recall from Chapter 5 what this means in terms of marginal benefits and marginal costs.

- For each unit of output on the horizontal axis, the point directly above it on demand curve D shows how many dollars' worth of other goods and services consumers are willing to give up to obtain that unit of output. Consequently, the demand curve shows the dollar value of the marginal benefit that consumers place on each unit.
- For each unit of output on the horizontal axis, the point directly above it on supply curve S shows how many dollars' worth of other products have to be sacrificed in order to direct the underlying resources toward producing each unit of this product. Consequently, the supply curve shows the dollar value of the marginal opportunity cost of each unit.

Keeping these definitions in mind, the fact that the demand curve lies above the supply curve for every unit up to Q_e means that marginal benefit exceeds marginal cost for every one of these units. Stated slightly differently,

producing and consuming these units brings net benefits, because consumers are willing to give up more of other goods to obtain these units than must actually be forgone to produce them. Furthermore, because the supply curve includes the opportunity cost of the other goods that must be given up when resources are directed to producing these units, we can be certain that consumers prefer to have the necessary resources directed toward producing these units rather than anything else. In other words, allocative efficiency has been achieved because redirecting the necessary resources toward producing anything else would make people less happy.

The fact that pure competition yields allocative efficiency can also be understood by looking at the situation facing each individual firm in long-run equilibrium. To see this, take the market equilibrium price P that is determined in Figure 9.6b and see how it affects the behavior of the individual firm shown in Figure 9.6a. This profit-maximizing firm takes P as fixed and produces Q_f units, the output level at which $P = MC$.

By comparing the horizontal line at P with the upsloping MC curve, it is clear that for every unit up to Q_f, the price at which each unit can be sold exceeds the marginal cost of producing it. That is equivalent to saying that these units are worth more to consumers than they cost to make. Why? Because consumers are willing to forgo P dollars' worth of other goods and services when they pay P dollars for these units, but at the same time the firm only has to use less than P dollars' worth of resources to produce them. Thus, if these units are produced and consumed, there are net benefits and society comes out ahead. And, as with our previous analysis, allocative efficiency also obtains because by spending their P dollars per unit on these units rather than anything else, consumers are indicating that they would rather have the necessary resources directed toward producing these units rather than anything else.

Maximum Consumer and Producer Surplus

We confirm the existence of allocative efficiency in Figure 9.6b, where we see that pure competition maximizes the sum of the "benefit surpluses" to consumers and producers. Recall from Chapter 5 that **consumer surplus** is the difference between the maximum prices that consumers are willing to pay for a product (as shown by the demand curve) and the market price of that product. In Figure 9.6b, consumer surplus is the green triangle, which is the sum of the vertical distances between the demand curve and equilibrium price. In contrast, **producer surplus** is the difference between the minimum prices that producers are willing to accept for a product (as shown by the supply curve) and the market price of the product. Producer surplus is the sum of the vertical distances between the equilibrium price and the supply curve. Here producer surplus is the blue area.

At the equilibrium quantity Q_e, the combined amount of consumer surplus and producer surplus is maximized. Allocative efficiency occurs because, at Q_e, marginal benefit, reflected by points on the demand curve, equals marginal cost, reflected by the points on the supply curve. Alternatively, the maximum willingness of consumers to pay for unit Q_e equals the minimum acceptable price of that unit to producers. At any output less than Q_e, the sum of consumer and producer surplus—the combined size of the green and blue area—would be less than that shown. At any output greater than Q_e, an efficiency loss (deadweight loss) would subtract from the combined consumer and producer surplus shown by the green and blue area.

After long-run adjustments, pure competition produces both productive and allocative efficiency. It yields a level of output at which $P = MC = $ lowest ATC, marginal benefit = marginal cost, maximum willingness to pay for the last unit = minimum acceptable price for that unit, and combined consumer and producer surplus are maximized.

Dynamic Adjustments

A further attribute of purely competitive markets is their ability to restore the efficiency just described when disrupted by changes in the economy. A change in consumer tastes, resource supplies, or technology will automatically set in motion the appropriate realignments of resources. For example, suppose that cucumbers and pickles become dramatically more popular. First, the demand for cucumbers will increase in the market, increasing the price of cucumbers. So, at current output, the price of cucumbers will exceed their marginal cost. At this point efficiency will be lost, but the higher price will create economic profits in the cucumber industry and stimulate its expansion. The profitability of cucumbers will permit the industry to bid resources away from now less pressing uses, say, watermelons. Expansion of the industry will end only when the supply of cucumbers has expanded such that the price of cucumbers and their marginal cost are equal—that is, when allocative efficiency has been restored.

Similarly, a change in the supply of a particular resource—for example, the field laborers who pick cucumbers—or in a production technique will upset an existing price–marginal-cost equality by either raising or lowering marginal cost. The resulting inequality of MC and P will cause producers, in either pursuing profit or avoiding loss, to reallocate resources until product supply is such that price once again equals marginal cost. In so doing, they

will correct any inefficiency in the allocation of resources that the original change may have temporarily imposed on the economy.

"Invisible Hand" Revisited

The highly efficient allocation of resources that a purely competitive economy promotes comes about because businesses and resource suppliers seek to further their self-interest. For private goods with no externalities (Chapter 5), the "invisible hand" (Chapter 2) is at work. The competitive system not only maximizes profits for individual producers but also, at the same time, creates a pattern of resource allocation that maximizes consumer satisfaction. The invisible hand thus organizes the private interests of producers in a way that is fully in sync with society's interest in using scarce resources efficiently. Striving to obtain a profit produces highly desirable economic outcomes.

Technological Advance and Competition

In explaining the model of pure competition, we assumed for simplicity that all the firms in an industry had the same cost curves. Competition, as a result, only involved entrepreneurs entering and exiting industries in response to changes in profits caused by changes in the market price. This form of competition is important, but it is just a game of copycat, because firms entering an industry simply duplicate the production methods and cost curves of existing firms in order to duplicate their above-normal profits. In this type of competition, there is no dynamism and no innovation, just more of the same.

By contrast, the most dynamic and interesting parts of competition are the fights between firms over the creation of new production technologies and new products. As we explain in detail in Web Chapter 11, firms have a strong profit incentive to develop both improved ways of making existing products as well as totally new products. To put that incentive in context, recall what you just learned about long-run equilibrium in perfect competition. When each firm in a purely competitive industry has the same productive technology and therefore the same cost structure for producing output, entry and exit assure that in the long run every firm will make the exact same normal profit.

Entrepreneurs, of course, would like to earn more than a normal profit. As a result, they are constantly attempting two different strategies for increasing their profits. The first involves attempting to lower the production costs of existing products through better technology or improved business organization. Because pure competition implies that individual firms cannot affect the market price, anything that lowers an innovating firm's production costs will result in higher profits, since the innovating firm's revenues per unit (which are equal to the market price per unit) will stay the same while its costs per unit fall due to its improved production technology.

The second strategy for earning a rate of return greater than a normal profit is to try to develop a totally new product that is popular with consumers. If a firm is first-to-market with a popular new product, it will face no competition, as it is the only producer. As long as the product remains popular and the firm remains the only producer, it will be able to charge prices that are higher than production costs, thereby allowing it to earn above-normal profits. (We say much more about this in the next chapter, which covers pure monopoly).

Notably, however, any advantages that innovative firms gain either by lowering the production costs of existing products or by introducing entirely new products will not normally persist. An innovative entrepreneur may put some of her current rivals out of business, but there are always other entrepreneurs with new ideas so that soon it may be *her* firm that is going out of business due to innovations made by others. The Consider This box below shows just how rapid the destruction and creation of new firms is.

CONSIDER THIS . . .

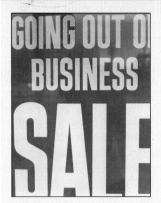

Running a Company Is Hard Business

The life expectancy of a U.S. business is just 10.2 years. About 9.5 percent of U.S. firms go out of business each year. In addition, 22 percent of new start-up firms go bankrupt within 2 years, 53 percent within 5 years, and nearly 65 percent within 10 years.

These numbers testify to the ability of competition to quickly dispose of firms that have high production costs or unpopular products. In a competitive environment, such firms quickly prove unprofitable and are shut down by their owners.

Balancing out the bankrupt firms are start-ups that hope to use the resources freed up by the closed firms to deliver better products or lower costs. In a typical year, more than 650,000 new businesses are started in the United States. Most of these new firms will themselves eventually fall victim to creative destruction and the pressures of competition, but one of them may just be the next Google, Starbucks, or Walmart.

Creative Destruction

The innovations that firms achieve thanks to competition are considered by many economists to be the driving force behind economic growth and rising living standards. The

> **ORIGIN OF THE IDEA**
> **O 9.2**
> Creative destruction

transformative effects of competition are often referred to as **creative destruction** to capture the idea that the creation of new products and new production methods destroys the market positions of firms committed to existing products and old ways of doing business. In addition, just the *threat* that a rival may soon come out with a new technology or product can cause other firms to innovate and thereby replace or destroy their old ways of doing business. As argued decades ago by Harvard economist Joseph Schumpeter, the most important type of competition is

> competition from the new commodity, the new technology, the new source of supply, the new type of business organization—competition which commands a decisive cost or quality advantage and which strikes not at the margins of profits of the existing firms but at their foundation and their very lives. This kind of competition is . . . so . . . important that it becomes a matter of comparative indifference whether competition in the ordinary [short-run or long-run] sense functions more or less promptly. . . .
>
> . . . competition of the kind we now have in mind acts not only when in being but also when it is merely an ever-present threat. It disciplines before it attacks. The businessman feels himself to be in a competitive situation even if he is alone in his field.[2]

There are many examples of creative destruction. In the 1800s wagons, ships, and barges were the only means of transporting freight until the railroads broke up their monopoly; the dominant market position of the railroads was, in turn, undermined by trucks and, later, by airplanes. Movies brought new competition to live theater, at one time the "only show in town." But movies were later challenged by broadcast television, which was then challenged by cable TV. Both are now challenged by Hulu, YouTube, and other online video-on-demand services. Cassettes replaced records before compact discs undermined cassettes. Now iPods, MP3 players, and Internet music downloads will soon make the compact disc obsolete. Electronic communications—including faxes and e-mails—have greatly affected the United States Postal Service. And online retailers like Amazon.com have stolen substantial business away from brick-and-mortar retailers.

---

[2]Joseph A. Schumpeter, *Capitalism, Socialism, and Democracy*, 3d ed. (New York: Harper & Row, 1950), pp. 84–85.

Word Efficiency Gains from Entry: The Case of Generic Drugs

When a Generic Drug Becomes Available, the Price of the Drug Falls, Consumer Surplus Rises, and Society Experiences an Efficiency Gain.

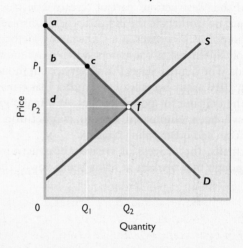

The competitive model predicts that entry will lower price, expand output, and increase efficiency. A good actual-economy test of this prediction occurs where entry of new producers occurs in a formerly monopolized market. Such a situation occurs when prescription drugs lose their patent protection. A patent on a prescription drug gives the pharmaceutical company that developed it an exclusive right to produce and sell the medication for 20 years from the time of patent application. Because the FDA approval process averages 8 years, the exclusive right may last for as few as 12 years. The purpose of drug patents is to encourage research and development (R&D) leading to new medications and the increased well-being they enable. With patent protection, a firm can charge prices that exceed marginal cost and average total cost and thus earn economic profits on its popular brand-name medicines. Those economic profits provide a return on past development costs and help fund more R&D.

Although competitors can and often do develop similar drugs, they cannot copy and sell the patented medication. Such drugs as Lipitor (for high cholesterol), Singulair (for allergies), and Nexium (for gastrointestinal disorders) are examples of best-selling brand-name, patented drugs.

When a patent expires, any pharmaceutical company can produce and sell the drug under the generic name for the medication. An example of a generic is metoprolol (a substitute for

the brand-name drug Lopressor), a beta-blocker used to treat high blood pressure. Because such generic drugs have the same chemical composition as the branded drug, they directly compete against it. The generic price is lower than the branded price, so the price of the drug (at least on average) drops as generics claim a share of the market. Studies indicate that price drop is typically 30–40 percent. Medical insurance plans either mandate that patients buy generics or provide financial incentives to encourage them do so when generics become available. Today, generics make up about 63 percent of all prescription drugs dispensed in the United States.

Seeing how patent expiration and the competition from generic drugs relate to consumer surplus and efficiency gains is useful. Consider the accompanying figure, which is similar to Figure 9.6b. The patent gives the firm monopoly power that allows it to charge a higher-than-competitive price. Suppose that the sole seller's profit-maximizing price is P_1. (In Chapter 10 we explain how a monopolist chooses this price.)

The expiration of the patent creates competition from generics, which reduces the price of the medication from P_1 to, say, P_2. If you compare the consumer surplus triangles above the price lines, you can see that consumer surplus rises from *bac* to *daf* when the price falls. As the price of the medication drops from P_1 to P_2, output increases from Q_1 to Q_2. In this case, the efficiency gain from competition is shown by the addition of the gray triangle. At price P_2 and quantity Q_2, the combined amounts of consumer surplus and producer surplus are at a maximum. (In reality, the price might not drop all the way to P_2 because of continued loyalty to the branded drug by prescribing physicians.)

Patents aid consumers and society by encouraging the development of new medicines that might otherwise not be available. Entry of the generics at the time of patent expiration further helps consumers by lowering prices, increasing consumer surplus, and enhancing efficiency—just like the competitive model predicts.

191

The "creative" part of "creative destruction" leads to new products and lower-cost production methods that are of great benefit to society because they allow for a more efficient use of society's scarce resources. Keep in mind, however, that the "destruction" part of "creative destruction" can be hard on workers in the industries being displaced by new technologies. A worker at a CD-making factory may see her job eliminated as consumers switch to online music downloads. The United States Postal Service cut thousands of jobs in 2010 partly because of the impact that e-mail has had on the demand for postal services. And many jobs in retail have been eliminated due to competition with Amazon.com and other online retailers.

Normally, the process of creative destruction goes slowly enough that workers at firms being downsized can transition smoothly to jobs in firms that are expanding. But sometimes the change is too swift for all of them to find new jobs easily. And in other instances, such as a town with only one major employer—like a rural coal-mining town or a small town with a large auto factory—the loss of that one major employer can be devastating because there are not enough other firms in the local area to employ the workers laid off by the major employer.

While the net effects of creative destruction are indisputably positive—including ongoing economic growth and rising living standards—creative destruction involves costs as well as benefits. And while the benefits are widespread, the costs tend to be borne almost entirely by the relatively few workers in declining industries who are not positioned to make easy transitions to new jobs.

Summary

1. In the short run, when plant and equipment are fixed, the firms in a purely competitive industry may earn profits or suffer losses. In the long run, when plant and equipment are adjustable, profits will attract new entrants, while losses will cause existing firms to leave the industry.

2. The entry or exit of firms will change industry supply. Entry or exit will continue until the market price determined by industry supply interacting with market demand generates a normal profit for firms in the industry. With firms earning a normal profit, there will be no incentive to either enter or exit the industry. This situation constitutes long-run equilibrium in a purely competitive industry.

3. Entry and exit help to improve resource allocation. Firms that exit an industry due to low profits release their resources to be used more profitably in other industries. Firms that enter an industry chasing higher profits bring with them resources that were less profitably used in other industries. Both processes increase allocative efficiency.

4. In the long run, the market price of a product will equal the minimum average total cost of production. At a higher price, economic profits would cause firms to enter the industry until those profits had been competed away. At a lower price, losses would force the exit of firms from the industry until the product price rose to equal average total cost.

5. The long-run supply curve is horizontal for a constant-cost industry, upsloping for an increasing-cost industry, and downsloping for a decreasing-cost industry.

6. The long-run equality of price and minimum average total cost means that competitive firms will use the most efficient known technology and charge the lowest price consistent with their production costs. That is, the purely competitive firms will achieve productive efficiency.

7. The long-run equality of price and marginal cost implies that resources will be allocated in accordance with consumer tastes. Allocative efficiency will occur. In the market, the combined amount of consumer surplus and producer surplus will be at a maximum.

8. The competitive price system will reallocate resources in response to a change in consumer tastes, in technology, or in resource supplies and will thereby maintain allocative efficiency over time.

9. Competition involves the never-ending attempts by entrepreneurs and managers to earn above-normal profits by either creating new products or developing lower-cost production methods for existing products. These efforts cause creative destruction, the financial undoing of the market positions of firms committed to existing products and old ways of doing business by new firms with new products and innovative ways of doing business.

Terms and Concepts

long-run supply curve	decreasing-cost industry	consumer surplus
constant-cost industry	productive efficiency	producer surplus
increasing-cost industry	allocative efficiency	creative destruction

Questions

1. Explain how the long run differs from the short run in pure competition. **LO1**
2. Relate opportunity costs to why profits encourage entry into purely competitive industries and how losses encourage exit from purely competitive industries. **LO2**
3. How do the entry and exit of firms in a purely competitive industry affect resource flows and long-run profits and losses? **LO3**
4. Using diagrams for both the industry and a representative firm, illustrate competitive long-run equilibrium. Assuming constant costs, employ these diagrams to show how (a) an increase and (b) a decrease in market demand will upset that long-run equilibrium. Trace graphically and describe verbally the adjustment processes by which long-run equilibrium is restored. Now rework your analysis for increasing- and decreasing-cost industries and compare the three long-run supply curves. **LO4**
5. In long-run equilibrium, P = minimum ATC = MC. Of what significance for economic efficiency is the equality of P and minimum ATC? The equality of P and MC? Distinguish between productive efficiency and allocative efficiency in your answer. **LO5**
6. Suppose that purely competitive firms producing cashews discover that P exceeds MC. Will their combined output of cashews be too little, too much, or just right to achieve allocative efficiency? In the long run, what will happen to the supply of cashews and the price of cashews? Use a supply and demand diagram to show how that response will change the combined amount of consumer surplus and producer surplus in the market for cashews. **LO5**
7. The basic model of pure competition reviewed in this chapter finds that in the long run all firms in a purely competitive industry will earn normal profits. If all firms will only earn a normal profit in the long run, why would any firms bother to develop new products or lower-cost production methods? Explain. **LO6**
8. "Ninety percent of new products fail within two years—so you shouldn't be so eager to innovate." Do you agree? Explain why or why not. **LO6**
9. **LAST WORD** How does a generic drug differ from its brand-name, previously patented equivalent? Explain why the price of a brand-name drug typically declines when an equivalent generic drug becomes available. Explain how that drop in price affects allocative efficiency.

Problems

1. A firm in a purely competitive industry has a typical cost structure. The normal rate of profit in the economy is 5 percent. This firm is earning $5.50 on every $50 invested by its founders. What is its percentage rate of return? Is the firm earning an economic profit? If so, how large? Will this industry see entry or exit? What will be the rate of return earned by firms in this industry once the industry reaches long-run equilibrium? **LO3**
2. A firm in a purely competitive industry is currently producing 1000 units per day at a total cost of $450. If the firm produced 800 units per day, its total cost would be $300, and if it produced 500 units per day, its total cost would be $275. What are the firm's ATC per unit at these three levels of production? If every firm in this industry has the same cost structure, is the industry in long-run competitive equilibrium? From what you know about these firms' cost structures, what is the highest possible price per unit that could exist as the market price in long-run equilibrium? If that price ends up being the market price and if the normal rate of profit is 10 percent, then how big will each firm's accounting profit per unit be? **LO5**
3. There are 300 purely competitive farms in the local dairy market. Of the 300 dairy farms, 298 have a cost structure that generates profits of $24 for every $300 invested. What is their percentage rate of return? The other two dairies have a cost structure that generates profits of $22 for every $200 invested. What is their percentage rate of return? Assuming that the normal rate of profit in the economy is 10 percent, will there be entry or exit? Will the change in the number of firms affect the two that earn $22 for every $200 invested? What will be the rate of return earned by most firms in the industry in long-run equilibrium? If firms can copy each other's technology, what will be the rate of return eventually earned by all firms? **LO5**

FURTHER TEST YOUR KNOWLEDGE AT
www.mcconnell19e.com

At the text's Online Learning Center (OLC), **www.mcconnell19e.com**, you will find one or more Web-based questions that require information from the Internet to answer. We urge you to check them out; they will familiarize you with Web sites that may be helpful in other courses and perhaps even in your career. The OLC also features multiple-choice questions that give instant feedback and provides other helpful ways to further test your knowledge of the chapter.

10

AFTER READING THIS CHAPTER, YOU SHOULD BE ABLE TO:

1 List the characteristics of pure monopoly.

2 Explain how a pure monopoly sets its profit-maximizing output and price.

3 Discuss the economic effects of monopoly.

4 Describe why a monopolist might prefer to charge different prices in different markets.

5 Distinguish between the monopoly price, the socially optimal price, and the fair-return price of a government-regulated monopoly.

Pure Monopoly

We turn now from pure competition to pure monopoly, which is at the opposite end of the spectrum of industry structures listed in Table 8.1. You deal with monopolies more often than you might think. If you see the logo for Microsoft's Windows on your computer, you are dealing with a monopoly (or, at least, a near-monopoly). When you purchase certain prescription drugs, you are buying monopolized products. When you make a local telephone call, turn on your lights, or subscribe to cable TV, you may be patronizing a monopoly, depending on your location.

What precisely do we mean by pure monopoly, and what conditions enable it to arise and survive? How does a pure monopolist determine its profit-maximizing price and output? Does a pure monopolist achieve the efficiency associated with pure competition? If not, what, if anything, should the government do about it? A simplified model of pure monopoly will help us answer these questions. It will be the first of three models of imperfect competition.

An Introduction to Pure Monopoly

Pure monopoly exists when a single firm is the sole producer of a product for which there are no close substitutes. Here are the main characteristics of pure monopoly:

- *Single seller* A pure, or absolute, monopoly is an industry in which a single firm is the sole producer of a specific good or the sole supplier of a service; the firm and the industry are synonymous.

- *No close substitutes* A pure monopoly's product is unique in that there are no close substitutes. The consumer who chooses not to buy the monopolized product must do without it.

- *Price maker* The pure monopolist controls the total quantity supplied and thus has considerable control over price; it is a *price maker* (unlike a pure competitor, which has no such control and therefore is a *price taker*). The pure monopolist confronts the usual downsloping product demand curve. It can change its product price by changing the quantity of the product it produces. The monopolist will use this power whenever it is advantageous to do so.

- *Blocked entry* A pure monopolist has no immediate competitors because certain barriers keep potential competitors from entering the industry. Those barriers may be economic, technological, legal, or of some other type. But entry is totally blocked in pure monopoly.

- *Nonprice competition* The product produced by a pure monopolist may be either standardized (as with natural gas and electricity) or differentiated (as with Windows or Frisbees). Monopolists that have standardized products engage mainly in public relations advertising, whereas those with differentiated products sometimes advertise their products' attributes.

> **ORIGIN OF THE IDEA**
>
> **O 10.1**
>
> Monopoly

Examples of Monopoly

Examples of *pure* monopoly are relatively rare, but there are many examples of less pure forms. In most cities, government-owned or government-regulated public utilities—natural gas and electric companies, the water company, the cable TV company, and the local telephone company—are all monopolies or virtually so.

There are also many "near-monopolies" in which a single firm has the bulk of sales in a specific market. Intel, for example, produces 80 percent of the central microprocessors used in personal computers. First Data Corporation, via its Western Union subsidiary, accounts for 80 percent of the market for money order transfers. Brannock Device Company has an 80 percent market share of the shoe sizing devices found in shoe stores. Wham-O, through its Frisbee brand, sells 90 percent of plastic throwing disks. The De Beers diamond syndicate effectively controls 55 percent of the world's supply of rough-cut diamonds (see this chapter's Last Word).

Professional sports teams are, in a sense, monopolies because they are the sole suppliers of specific services in large geographic areas. With a few exceptions, a single major-league team in each sport serves each large American city. If you want to see a live Major League Baseball game in St. Louis or Seattle, you must patronize the Cardinals or the Mariners, respectively. Other geographic monopolies exist. For example, a small town may be served by only one airline or railroad. In a small, isolated community, the local barber shop, dry cleaner, or grocery store may approximate a monopoly.

Of course, there is almost always some competition. Satellite television is a substitute for cable, and amateur softball is a substitute for professional baseball. The Linux operating system can substitute for Windows, and so on. But such substitutes are typically either more costly or in some way less appealing.

Dual Objectives of the Study of Monopoly

Monopoly is worth studying both for its own sake and because it provides insights about the more common market structures of monopolistic competition and oligopoly (Chapter 11). These two market structures combine, in differing degrees, characteristics of pure competition and pure monopoly.

Barriers to Entry

The factors that prohibit firms from entering an industry are called **barriers to entry.** In pure monopoly, strong barriers to entry effectively block all potential competition. Somewhat weaker barriers may permit oligopoly, a market structure dominated by a few firms. Still weaker barriers may permit the entry of a fairly large number of competing firms giving rise to monopolistic competition. And the absence of any effective entry barriers permits the entry of a very large number of firms, which provide the basis of pure competition. So barriers to entry are pertinent not only to the extreme case of pure monopoly but also to other market structures in which there are monopoly-like characteristics or monopoly-like behaviors.

FIGURE 10.1 Economies of scale: the natural monopoly case. A declining long-run average-total-cost curve over a wide range of output quantities indicates extensive economies of scale. A single monopoly firm can produce, say, 200 units of output at lower cost ($10 each) than could two or more firms that had a combined output of 200 units.

We now discuss the four most prominent barriers to entry.

Economies of Scale

Modern technology in some industries is such that economies of scale—declining average total cost with added firm size—are extensive. In such cases, a firm's long-run average-cost schedule will decline over a wide range of output. Given market demand, only a few large firms or, in the extreme, only a single large firm can achieve low average total costs.

Figure 10.1 indicates economies of scale over a wide range of outputs. If total consumer demand is within that output range, then only a single producer can satisfy demand at least cost. Note, for example, that a monopolist can produce 200 units at a per-unit cost of $10 and a total cost of $2000. If the industry has two firms and each produces 100 units, the unit cost is $15 and total cost rises to $3000 (= 200 units × $15). A still more competitive situation with four firms each producing 50 units would boost unit and total cost to $20 and $4000, respectively. Conclusion: When long-run ATC is declining, only a single producer, a monopolist, can produce any particular output at minimum total cost.

If a pure monopoly exists in such an industry, economies of scale will serve as an entry barrier and will protect the monopolist from competition. New firms that try to enter the industry as small-scale producers cannot realize the cost economies of the monopolist. They therefore will be undercut and forced out of business by the monopolist, which can sell at a much lower price and still make a profit because of its lower per-unit cost associated with its economies of scale. A new firm might try to start out big, that is, to enter the industry as a large-scale producer so as to achieve the necessary economies of scale. But the massive plant facilities required would necessitate huge amounts of financing, which a new and untried enterprise would find difficult to secure. In most cases the financial obstacles and risks to "starting big" are prohibitive. This explains why efforts to enter such industries as computer operating software, commercial aircraft, and basic steel are so rare.

A monopoly firm is referred to as a *natural monopoly* if the market demand curve intersects the long-run ATC curve at any point where average total costs are declining. If a natural monopoly were to set its price where market demand intersects long-run ATC, its price would be lower than if the industry were more competitive. But it will probably set a higher price. As with any monopolist, a natural monopolist may, instead, set its price far above ATC and obtain substantial economic profit. In that event, the lowest-unit-cost advantage of a natural monopolist would accrue to the monopolist as profit and not as lower prices to consumers. That is why the government regulates some natural monopolies, specifying the price they may charge. We will say more about that later.

> **ORIGIN OF THE IDEA**
> **O 10.2**
> Natural monopoly

Legal Barriers to Entry: Patents and Licenses

Government also creates legal barriers to entry by awarding patents and licenses.

Patents A *patent* is the exclusive right of an inventor to use, or to allow another to use, her or his invention. Patents and patent laws aim to protect the inventor from rivals who would use the invention without having shared in the effort and expense of developing it. At the same time, patents provide the inventor with a monopoly position for the life of the patent. The world's nations have agreed on a uniform patent length of 20 years from the time of application. Patents have figured prominently in the growth of modern-day giants such as IBM, Pfizer, Intel, Xerox, General Electric, and DuPont.

Research and development (R&D) is what leads to most patentable inventions and products. Firms that gain monopoly power through their own research or by purchasing the patents of others can use patents to strengthen their market position. The profit from one patent can finance the research required to develop new patentable products. In the pharmaceutical industry, patents on prescription drugs have produced large monopoly profits that have helped finance the discovery of new patentable medicines. So monopoly power achieved through patents may well be self-sustaining, even though patents eventually expire and generic drugs then compete with the original brand.

Licenses Government may also limit entry into an industry or occupation through *licensing*. At the national level, the Federal Communications Commission licenses only so many radio and television stations in each geographic area. In many large cities one of a limited number of municipal licenses is required to drive a taxicab. The consequent restriction of the supply of cabs creates economic profit for cab owners and drivers. New cabs cannot enter the industry to drive down prices and profits. In a few instances the government might "license" itself to provide some product and thereby create a public monopoly. For example, in some states only state-owned retail outlets can sell liquor. Similarly, many states have "licensed" themselves to run lotteries.

Ownership or Control of Essential Resources

A monopolist can use private property as an obstacle to potential rivals. For example, a firm that owns or controls a resource essential to the production process can prohibit the entry of rival firms. At one time the International Nickel Company of Canada (now called Inco) controlled 90 percent of the world's known nickel reserves. A local firm may own all the nearby deposits of sand and gravel. And it is very difficult for new sports leagues to be created because existing professional sports leagues have contracts with the best players and have long-term leases on the major stadiums and arenas.

Pricing and Other Strategic Barriers to Entry

Even if a firm is not protected from entry by, say, extensive economies of scale or ownership of essential resources, entry may effectively be blocked by the way the monopolist responds to attempts by rivals to enter the industry. Confronted with a new entrant, the monopolist may "create an entry barrier" by slashing its price, stepping up its advertising, or taking other strategic actions to make it difficult for the entrant to succeed.

Examples of entry deterrence: In 2005 Dentsply, the dominant American maker of false teeth (70 percent market share) was found to have unlawfully precluded independent distributors of false teeth from carrying competing brands. The lack of access to the distributors deterred potential foreign competitors from entering the U.S. market. As another example, in 2001 a U.S. court of appeals upheld a lower court's finding that Microsoft used a series of illegal actions to maintain its monopoly in Intel-compatible PC operating systems (95 percent market share). One such action was charging higher prices for its Windows operating system to computer manufacturers that featured Netscape's Navigator rather than Microsoft's Internet Explorer.

Monopoly Demand

Now that we have explained the sources of monopoly, we want to build a model of pure monopoly so that we can analyze its price and output decisions. Let's start by making three assumptions:

- Patents, economies of scale, or resource ownership secure the firm's monopoly.
- No unit of government regulates the firm.
- The firm is a single-price monopolist; it charges the same price for all units of output.

The crucial difference between a pure monopolist and a purely competitive seller lies on the demand side of the market. The purely competitive seller faces a perfectly elastic demand at the price determined by market supply and demand. It is a price taker that can sell as much or as little as it wants at the going market price. Each additional unit sold will add the amount of the constant product price to the firm's total revenue. That means that marginal revenue for the competitive seller is constant and equal to product price. (Refer to the table and graph in Figure 8.1 for price, marginal-revenue, and total-revenue relationships for the purely competitive firm.)

The demand curve for the monopolist (and for any imperfectly competitive seller) is quite different from that of the pure competitor. Because the pure monopolist *is* the industry, its demand curve *is* the market demand curve. And because market demand is not perfectly elastic, the monopolist's demand curve is downsloping. Columns 1 and 2 in Table 10.1 illustrate this concept. Note that quantity demanded increases as price decreases.

TABLE 10.1 Revenue and Cost Data of a Pure Monopolist

Revenue Data				Cost Data			
(1) Quantity of Output	(2) Price (Average Revenue)	(3) Total Revenue, (1) × (2)	(4) Marginal Revenue	(5) Average Total Cost	(6) Total Cost, (1) × (5)	(7) Marginal Cost	(8) Profit [+] or Loss [−]
0	$172	$ 0			$ 100		$−100
1	162	162	$162	$190.00	190	$ 90	−28
2	152	304	142	135.00	270	80	+34
3	142	426	122	113.33	340	70	+86
4	132	528	102	100.00	400	60	+128
5	122	610	82	94.00	470	70	+140
6	112	672	62	91.67	550	80	+122
7	102	714	42	91.43	640	90	+74
8	92	736	22	93.75	750	110	−14
9	82	738	2	97.78	880	130	−142
10	72	720	−18	103.00	1030	150	−310

In Figure 8.7 we drew separate demand curves for the purely competitive industry and for a single firm in such an industry. But only a single demand curve is needed in pure monopoly because the firm and the industry are one and the same. We have graphed part of the demand data in Table 10.1 as demand curve *D* in Figure 10.2. This is the monopolist's demand curve *and* the market demand curve. The downsloping demand curve has three implications that are essential to understanding the monopoly model.

FIGURE 10.2 Price and marginal revenue in pure monopoly. A pure monopolist, or any other imperfect competitor with a downsloping demand curve such as *D*, must set a lower price in order to sell more output. Here, by charging $132 rather than $142, the monopolist sells an extra unit (the fourth unit) and gains $132 from that sale. But from this gain must be subtracted $30, which reflects the $10 less the monopolist charged for each of the first 3 units. Thus, the marginal revenue of the fourth unit is $102 (= $132 − $30), considerably less than its $132 price.

Marginal Revenue Is Less Than Price

With a fixed downsloping demand curve, the pure monopolist can increase sales only by charging a lower price. Consequently, marginal revenue—the change in total revenue associated with a one unit change in output—is less than price (average revenue) for every unit of output except the first. Why so? The reason is that the lower price of the extra unit of output also applies to all prior units of output. The monopolist could have sold these prior units at a higher price if it had not produced and sold the extra output. Each additional unit of output sold increases total revenue by an amount equal to its own price less the sum of the price cuts that apply to all prior units of output.

Figure 10.2 confirms this point. There, we have highlighted two price-quantity combinations from the monopolist's demand curve. The monopolist can sell 1 more unit at $132 than it can at $142 and that way obtain $132 (the blue area) of extra revenue. But to sell that fourth unit for $132, the monopolist must also sell the first 3 units at $132 rather than $142. The $10 reduction in revenue on 3 units results in a $30 revenue loss (the red area). Thus, the net difference in total revenue from selling a fourth unit is $102: the $132 gain from the fourth unit minus the $30 forgone on the first 3 units. This net gain (marginal revenue) of $102 from the fourth unit is clearly less than the $132 price of the fourth unit.

Column 4 in Table 10.1 shows that marginal revenue is always less than the corresponding product price in column 2, except for the first unit of output. Because marginal revenue is the change in total revenue associated with each additional unit of output, the declining amounts of marginal revenue in column 4 mean that total revenue increases at a diminishing rate (as shown in column 3).

We show the relationship between the monopolist's marginal-revenue curve and total-revenue curve in Figure 10.3. For this figure, we extended the demand and revenue data of columns 1 through 4 in Table 10.1, assuming that successive $10 price cuts each elicit 1 additional unit of sales. That is, the monopolist can sell 11 units at $62, 12 units at $52, and so on.

Note that the monopolist's MR curve lies below the demand curve, indicating that marginal revenue is less than price at every output quantity but the very first unit. Observe also the special relationship between total revenue (shown in the lower graph) and marginal revenue (shown in the top graph). Because marginal revenue is the change in total revenue, marginal revenue is positive while total revenue is increasing. When total revenue reaches its maximum, marginal revenue is zero. When total revenue is diminishing, marginal revenue is negative.

The Monopolist Is a Price Maker

All imperfect competitors, whether pure monopolists, oligopolists, or monopolistic competitors, face downsloping demand curves. As a result, any change in quantity produced causes a movement along their respective demand curves and a change in the price they can charge for their respective products. Economists summarize this fact by saying that firms with downsloping demand curves are *price makers*.

This is most evident in pure monopoly, where an industry consists of a single monopoly firm so that total industry output is exactly equal to whatever the single monopoly firm chooses to produce. As we just mentioned, the monopolist faces a downsloping demand curve in

(a)
Demand and marginal-revenue curves

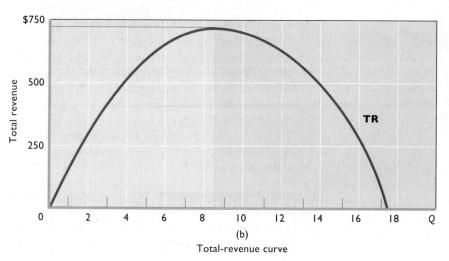

(b)
Total-revenue curve

FIGURE 10.3 Demand, marginal revenue, and total revenue for a pure monopolist. (a) Because it must lower price on all units sold in order to increase its sales, an imperfectly competitive firm's marginal-revenue curve (MR) lies below its downsloping demand curve (D). The elastic and inelastic regions of demand are highlighted. (b) Total revenue (TR) increases at a decreasing rate, reaches a maximum, and then declines. Note that in the elastic region, TR is increasing and hence MR is positive. When TR reaches its maximum, MR is zero. In the inelastic region of demand, TR is declining, so MR is negative.

which each amount of output is associated with some unique price. Thus, in deciding on the quantity of output to produce, the monopolist is also determining the price it will charge. Through control of output, it can "make the price." From columns 1 and 2 in Table 10.1 we find that the monopolist can charge a price of $72 if it produces and offers for sale 10 units, a price of $82 if it produces and offers for sale 9 units, and so forth.

The Monopolist Sets Prices in the Elastic Region of Demand

The total-revenue test for price elasticity of demand is the basis for our third implication. Recall from Chapter 4 that the total-revenue test reveals that when demand is elastic, a decline in price will increase total revenue. Similarly, when demand is inelastic, a decline in price will reduce total revenue. Beginning at the top of demand curve D in Figure 10.3a, observe that as the price declines from $172 to approximately $82, total revenue increases (and marginal revenue therefore is positive). This means that demand is elastic in this price range. Conversely, for price declines below $82, total revenue decreases (marginal revenue is negative), indicating that demand is inelastic there.

The implication is that a monopolist will never choose a price-quantity combination where price reductions cause total revenue to decrease (marginal revenue to be negative). The profit-maximizing monopolist will always want to avoid the inelastic segment of its demand curve in favor of some price-quantity combination in the elastic region. Here's why: To get into the inelastic region, the monopolist must lower price and increase output. In the inelastic region a lower price means less total revenue. And increased output always means increased total cost. Less total revenue and higher total cost yield lower profit.

QUICK REVIEW 10.1

- A pure monopolist is the sole supplier of a product or service for which there are no close substitutes.
- A monopoly survives because of entry barriers such as economies of scale, patents and licenses, the ownership of essential resources, and strategic actions to exclude rivals.
- The monopolist's demand curve is downsloping and its marginal-revenue curve lies below its demand curve.
- The downsloping demand curve means that the monopolist is a price maker.
- The monopolist will operate in the elastic region of demand since in the inelastic region it can increase total revenue and reduce total cost by reducing output.

Output and Price Determination

At what specific price-quantity combination will a profit-maximizing monopolist choose to operate? To answer this question, we must add production costs to our analysis.

Cost Data

On the cost side, we will assume that although the firm is a monopolist in the product market, it hires resources competitively and employs the same technology and, therefore, has the same cost structure as the purely competitive firm that we studied in Chapters 9 and 10. By using the same cost data that we developed in Chapter 7 and applied to the competitive firm in Chapters 9 and 10, we will be able to directly compare the price and output decisions of a pure monopoly with those of a pure competitor. This will help us demonstrate that the price and output differences between a pure monopolist and a pure competitor are not the result of two different sets of costs. Columns 5 through 7 in Table 10.1 restate the pertinent cost data from Table 7.2.

MR = MC Rule

A monopolist seeking to maximize total profit will employ the same rationale as a profit-seeking firm in a competitive industry. If producing is preferable to shutting down, it will produce up to the output at which marginal revenue equals marginal cost (MR = MC).

A comparison of columns 4 and 7 in Table 10.1 indicates that the profit-maximizing output is 5 units because the fifth unit is the last unit of output whose marginal revenue exceeds its marginal cost. What price will the monopolist charge? The demand schedule shown as columns 1 and 2 in Table 10.1 indicates there is only one price at which 5 units can be sold: $122.

This analysis is shown in **Figure 10.4 (Key Graph)**, where we have graphed the demand, marginal-revenue, average-total-cost, and marginal-cost data of Table 10.1. The profit-maximizing output occurs at 5 units of output (Q_m), where the marginal-revenue (MR) and marginal-cost (MC) curves intersect. There, MR = MC.

To find the price the monopolist will charge, we extend a vertical line from Q_m up to the demand curve D. The unique price P_m at which Q_m units can be sold is $122. In this case, $122 is the profit-maximizing price. So the monopolist sets the quantity at Q_m to charge its profit-maximizing price of $122.

INTERACTIVE GRAPHS

G 10.1

Monopoly

Columns 2 and 5 in Table 10.1 show that at 5 units of output, the product price ($122) exceeds the average total

QUICK QUIZ FOR FIGURE 10.4

1. The MR curve lies below the demand curve in this figure because the:
   a. demand curve is linear (a straight line).
   b. demand curve is highly inelastic throughout its full length.
   c. demand curve is highly elastic throughout its full length.
   d. gain in revenue from an extra unit of output is less than the price charged for that unit of output.

2. The area labeled "Economic profit" can be found by multiplying the difference between P and ATC by quantity. It also can be found by:
   a. dividing profit per unit by quantity.
   b. subtracting total cost from total revenue.
   c. multiplying the coefficient of demand elasticity by quantity.
   d. multiplying the difference between P and MC by quantity.

3. This pure monopolist:
   a. charges the highest price that it could achieve.
   b. earns only a normal profit in the long run.
   c. restricts output to create an insurmountable entry barrier.
   d. restricts output to increase its price and total economic profit.

4. At this monopolist's profit-maximizing output:
   a. price equals marginal revenue.
   b. price equals marginal cost.
   c. price exceeds marginal cost.
   d. profit per unit is maximized.

Answers: 1. d; 2. b; 3. d; 4. c

---

cost ($94). The monopolist thus obtains an economic profit of $28 per unit, and the total economic profit is $140 (= 5 units × $28). In Figure 10.4, per-unit profit is $P_m - A$, where A is the average total cost of producing Q_m units. Total economic profit—the green rectangle—is found by multiplying this per-unit profit by the profit-maximizing output Q_m.

Another way to determine the profit-maximizing output is by comparing total revenue and total cost at each possible level of production and choosing the output with the greatest positive difference. Use columns 3 and 6 in Table 10.1 to

verify that 5 units is the profit-maximizing output. An accurate graphing of total revenue and total cost against output would also show the greatest difference (the maximum profit) at 5 units of output. Table 10.2 summarizes the process for determining the profit-maximizing output, profit-maximizing price, and economic profit in pure monopoly.

No Monopoly Supply Curve

Recall that MR equals P in pure competition and that the supply curve of a purely competitive firm is determined by applying the MR (= P) = MC profit-maximizing rule. At

TABLE 10.2 Steps for Graphically Determining the Profit-Maximizing Output, Profit-Maximizing Price, and Economic Profit (if Any) in Pure Monopoly

Step 1.	Determine the profit-maximizing output by finding where MR = MC.
Step 2.	Determine the profit-maximizing price by extending a vertical line upward from the output determined in step 1 to the pure monopolist's demand curve.
Step 3.	Determine the pure monopolist's economic profit using one of two methods:
Method 1.	Find profit per unit by subtracting the average total cost of the profit-maximizing output from the profit-maximizing price. Then multiply the difference by the profit-maximizing output to determine economic profit (if any).
Method 2.	Find total cost by multiplying the average total cost of the profit-maximizing output by that output. Find total revenue by multiplying the profit-maximizing output by the profit-maximizing price. Then subtract total cost from total revenue to determine economic profit (if any).

any specific market-determined price, the purely competitive seller will maximize profit by supplying the quantity at which MC is equal to that price. When the market price increases or decreases, the competitive firm produces more or less output. Each market price is thus associated with a specific output, and all such price-output pairs define the supply curve. This supply curve turns out to be the portion of the firm's MC curve that lies above the average-variable-cost curve (see Figure 8.6).

At first glance we would suspect that the pure monopolist's marginal-cost curve would also be its supply curve. But that is *not* the case. *The pure monopolist has no supply curve.* There is no unique relationship between price and quantity supplied for a monopolist. Like the competitive firm, the monopolist equates marginal revenue and marginal cost to determine output, but for the monopolist marginal revenue is less than price. Because the monopolist does not equate marginal cost to price, it is possible for different demand conditions to bring about different prices for the same output. To understand this point, refer to Figure 10.4 and pencil in a new, steeper marginal-revenue curve that intersects the marginal-cost curve at the same point as does the present marginal-revenue curve. Then draw in a new demand curve that is roughly consistent with your new marginal-revenue curve. With the new curves, the same MR = MC output of 5 units now means a higher profit-maximizing price. Conclusion: There is no single, unique price associated with each output level Q_m, and so there is no supply curve for the pure monopolist.

Misconceptions Concerning Monopoly Pricing

Our analysis exposes two fallacies concerning monopoly behavior.

Not Highest Price Because a monopolist can manipulate output and price, people often believe it "will charge the highest price possible." That is incorrect. There are many prices above P_m in Figure 10.4, but the monopolist shuns them because they yield a smaller-than-maximum total profit. The monopolist seeks maximum total profit, not maximum price. Some high prices that could be charged would reduce sales and total revenue too severely to offset any decrease in total cost.

Total, Not Unit, Profit The monopolist seeks maximum *total* profit, not maximum *unit* profit. In Figure 10.4 a careful comparison of the vertical distance between average total cost and price at various possible outputs indicates that per-unit profit is greater at a point slightly to the left of the profit-maximizing output Q_m. This is seen in Table 10.1, where the per-unit profit at 4 units of output is $32 (= $132 − $100) compared with $28 (= $122 − $94) at the profit-maximizing output of 5 units. Here the monopolist accepts a lower-than-maximum per-unit profit because additional sales more than compensate for the lower unit profit. A monopolist would rather sell 5 units at a profit of $28 per unit (for a total profit of $140) than 4 units at a profit of $32 per unit (for a total profit of only $128).

Possibility of Losses by Monopolist

The likelihood of economic profit is greater for a pure monopolist than for a pure competitor. In the long run the pure competitor is destined to have only a normal profit, whereas barriers to entry mean that any economic profit realized by the monopolist can persist. In pure monopoly there are no new entrants to increase supply, drive down price, and eliminate economic profit.

But pure monopoly does not guarantee profit. The monopolist is not immune from changes in tastes that reduce the demand for its product. Nor is it immune from upward-shifting cost curves caused by escalating resource prices. If the demand and cost situation faced by the monopolist is far less favorable than that in Figure 10.4, the

FIGURE 10.5 The loss-minimizing position of a pure monopolist. If demand D is weak and costs are high, the pure monopolist may be unable to make a profit. Because P_m exceeds V, the average variable cost at the MR = MC output Q_m, the monopolist will minimize losses in the short run by producing at that output. The loss per unit is $A - P_m$, and the total loss is indicated by the red rectangle.

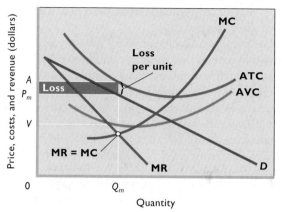

Like the pure competitor, the monopolist will not persist in operating at a loss. Faced with continuing losses, in the long run the firm's owners will move their resources to alternative industries that offer better profit opportunities. A monopolist such as the one depicted in Figure 10.5 must obtain a minimum of a normal profit in the long run or it will go out of business.

Economic Effects of Monopoly

Let's now evaluate pure monopoly from the standpoint of society as a whole. Our reference for this evaluation will be the outcome of long-run efficiency in a purely competitive market, identified by the triple equality $P =$ MC = minimum ATC.

Price, Output, and Efficiency

Figure 10.6 graphically contrasts the price, output, and efficiency outcomes of pure monopoly and a purely competitive *industry*. The S = MC curve in Figure 10.6a reminds us that the market supply curve S for a purely competitive industry is the horizontal sum of the marginal-cost curves of all the firms in the industry. Suppose there are 1000 such firms. Comparing their combined supply curves S with market demand D, we see that the purely competitive price and output are P_c and Q_c.

Recall that this price-output combination results in both productive efficiency and allocative efficiency.

monopolist will incur losses in the short run. Despite its dominance in the market (as, say, a seller of home sewing machines), the monopoly enterprise in Figure 10.5 suffers a loss, as shown, because of weak demand and relatively high costs. Yet it continues to operate for the time being because its total loss is less than its fixed cost. More precisely, at output Q_m the monopolist's price P_m exceeds its average variable cost V. Its loss per unit is $A - P_m$, and the total loss is shown by the red rectangle.

FIGURE 10.6 Inefficiency of pure monopoly relative to a purely competitive industry. (a) In a purely competitive industry, entry and exit of firms ensure that price (P_c) equals marginal cost (MC) and that the minimum average-total-cost output (Q_c) is produced. Both productive efficiency (P = minimum ATC) and allocative efficiency (P = MC) are obtained. (b) In pure monopoly, the MR curve lies below the demand curve. The monopolist maximizes profit at output Q_m, where MR = MC, and charges price P_m. Thus, output is lower (Q_m rather than Q_c) and price is higher (P_m rather than P_c) than they would be in a purely competitive industry. Monopoly is inefficient, since output is less than that required for achieving minimum ATC (here, at Q_c) and because the monopolist's price exceeds MC. Monopoly creates an efficiency loss (here, of triangle *abc*). There is also a transfer of income from consumers to the monopoly (here, of rectangle P_cP_mbd).

(a)
Purely competitive industry

(b)
Pure monopoly

Productive efficiency is achieved because free entry and exit force firms to operate where average total cost is at a minimum. The sum of the minimum-ATC outputs of the 1000 pure competitors is the industry output, here, Q_c. Product price is at the lowest level consistent with minimum average total cost. The *allocative efficiency* of pure competition results because production occurs up to that output at which price (the measure of a product's value or marginal benefit to society) equals marginal cost (the worth of the alternative products forgone by society in producing any given commodity). In short: $P = MC = $ minimum ATC.

Now let's suppose that this industry becomes a pure monopoly (Figure 10.6b) as a result of one firm acquiring all its competitors. We also assume that no changes in costs or market demand result from this dramatic change in the industry structure. What formerly were 1000 competing firms is now a single pure monopolist consisting of 1000 noncompeting branches.

The competitive market supply curve S has become the marginal-cost curve (MC) of the monopolist, the summation of the individual marginal-cost curves of its many branch plants. (Since the monopolist does not have a supply curve, as such, we have removed the S label.) The important change, however, is on the demand side. From the viewpoint of each of the 1000 individual competitive firms, demand was perfectly elastic, and marginal revenue was therefore equal to the market equilibrium price P_c. So each firm equated its marginal revenue of P_c dollars per unit with its individual marginal cost curve to maximize profits. But market demand and individual demand are the same to the pure monopolist. The firm *is* the industry, and thus the monopolist sees the downsloping demand curve D shown in Figure 10.6b.

This means that marginal revenue is less than price, that graphically the MR curve lies below demand curve D. In using the MR = MC rule, the monopolist selects output Q_m and price P_m. A comparison of both graphs in Figure 10.6 reveals that the monopolist finds it profitable to sell a smaller output at a higher price than do the competitive producers.

Monopoly yields neither productive nor allocative efficiency. The lack of productive efficiency can be understood most directly by noting that the monopolist's output Q_m is less than Q_c, the output at which average total cost is lowest. In addition, the monopoly price P_m is higher than the competitive price P_c that we know in long-run equilibrium in pure competition equals minimum average total cost. Thus, the monopoly price exceeds minimum average total cost, thereby demonstrating in another way that the monopoly will not be productively efficient.

The monopolist's underproduction also implies allocative inefficiency. One way to see this is to note that at the monopoly output level Q_m, the monopoly price P_m that consumers are willing to pay exceeds the marginal cost of production. This means that consumers value additional units of this product more highly than they do the alternative products that could be produced from the resources that would be necessary to make more units of the monopolist's product.

The monopolist's allocative inefficiency can also be understood by noting that for every unit between Q_m and Q_c, marginal benefit exceeds marginal cost because the demand curve lies above the supply curve. By choosing not to produce these units, the monopolist reduces allocative efficiency because the resources that should have been used to make these units will be redirected instead toward producing items that bring lower net benefits to society. The total dollar value of this efficiency loss (or *deadweight loss*) is equal to the area of the gray triangle labeled *abc* in Figure 10.6b.

Income Transfer

In general, a monopoly transfers income from consumers to the owners of the monopoly. The income is received by the owners as revenue. Because a monopoly has market power, it can charge a higher price than would a purely competitive firm with the same costs. So the monopoly in effect levies a "private tax" on consumers. This private tax can often generate substantial economic profits that can persist because entry to the industry is blocked.

The transfer from consumers to the monopolist is evident in Figure 10.6b. For the Q_m units of output demanded, consumers pay price P_m rather than the price P_c that they would pay to a pure competitor. The total amount of income transferred from consumers to the monopolist is $P_m - P_c$ multiplied by the number of units sold, Q_m. So the total transfer is the dollar amount of rectangle $P_c P_m bd$. What the consumer loses, the monopolist gains. In contrast, the efficiency loss *abc* is a *deadweight* loss—society totally loses the net benefits of the Q_c minus Q_m units that are not produced.

Cost Complications

Our evaluation of pure monopoly has led us to conclude that, given identical costs, a purely monopolistic industry will charge a higher price, produce a smaller output, and allocate economic resources less efficiently than a purely competitive industry. These inferior results are rooted in the entry barriers characterizing monopoly.

Now we must recognize that costs may not be the same for purely competitive and monopolistic producers. The unit cost incurred by a monopolist may be either larger or smaller than that incurred by a purely competitive firm. There are four reasons why costs may differ: (1) economies of scale, (2) a factor called "X-inefficiency," (3) the need for monopoly-preserving expenditures, and (4) the "very long run" perspective, which allows for technological advance.

Economies of Scale Once Again

Where economies of scale are extensive, market demand may not be sufficient to support a large number of competing firms, each producing at minimum efficient scale. In such cases, an industry of one or two firms would have a lower average total cost than would the same industry made up of numerous competitive firms. At the extreme, only a single firm—a natural monopoly—might be able to achieve the lowest long-run average total cost.

Some firms relating to new information technologies—for example, computer software, Internet service, and wireless communications—have displayed extensive economies of scale. As these firms have grown, their long-run average total costs have declined because of greater use of specialized inputs, the spreading of product development costs, and learning by doing. Also, *simultaneous consumption* and *network effects* have reduced costs.

A product's ability to satisfy a large number of consumers at the same time is called **simultaneous consumption** (or *nonrivalrous consumption*). Dell Computers needs to produce a personal computer for each customer, but Microsoft needs to produce its Windows program only once. Then, at very low marginal cost, Microsoft delivers its program by disk or Internet to millions of consumers. Similar low cost of delivering product to additional customers is true for Internet service providers, music producers, and wireless communication firms. Because marginal costs are so low, the average total cost of output declines as more customers are added.

Network effects are present if the value of a product to each user, including existing users, increases as the total number of users rises. Good examples are computer software, cell phones, and Web sites like Facebook where the content is provided by users. When other people have Internet service and devices to access it, a person can conveniently send e-mail messages to them. And when they have similar software, various documents, spreadsheets, and photos can be attached to the e-mail messages. The greater the number of persons connected to the system, the more the benefits of the product to each person are magnified.

Such network effects may drive a market toward monopoly because consumers tend to choose standard products that everyone else is using. The focused demand for these products permits their producers to grow rapidly and thus achieve economies of scale. Smaller firms, which either have higher-cost "right" products or "wrong" products, get acquired or go out of business.

Economists generally agree that some new information firms have not yet exhausted their economies of scale. But most economists question whether such firms are truly natural monopolies. Most firms eventually achieve their minimum efficient scale at less than the full size of the market. That means competition among firms is possible.

But even if natural monopoly develops, the monopolist is unlikely to pass cost reductions along to consumers as price reductions. So, with perhaps a handful of exceptions, economies of scale do not change the general conclusion that monopoly industries are inefficient relative to competitive industries.

X-Inefficiency

In constructing all the average-total-cost curves used in this book, we have assumed that the firm uses the most efficient existing technology. This assumption is only natural, because firms cannot maximize profits

> **ORIGIN OF THE IDEA**
>
> **O 10.3**
>
> X-inefficiency

unless they are minimizing costs. **X-inefficiency** occurs when a firm produces output at a higher cost than is necessary to produce it. In Figure 10.7 X-inefficiency is represented by operation at points X and X' above the lowest-cost ATC curve. At these points, per-unit costs are ATC_X (as opposed to ATC_1) for output Q_1 and $ATC_{X'}$ (as opposed to ATC_2) for output Q_2. Producing at any point above the average-total-cost curve in Figure 10.7 reflects inefficiency or "bad management" by the firm.

Why is X-inefficiency allowed to occur if it reduces profits? The answer is that managers may have goals, such as expanding power, an easier work life, avoiding business risk, or giving jobs to incompetent relatives, that conflict with cost minimization. Or X-inefficiency may arise because a firm's workers are poorly motivated or ineffectively supervised. Or a firm may simply become lethargic and inert, relying on rules of thumb in decision making as opposed to careful calculations of costs and revenues.

For our purposes the relevant question is whether monopolistic firms tend more toward X-inefficiency than competitive producers do. Presumably they do. Firms in competitive industries are continually under pressure from rivals, forcing them to be internally efficient to survive. But monopolists are sheltered from such competitive forces by entry barriers. That lack of pressure may lead to X-inefficiency.

Rent-Seeking Expenditures

Rent-seeking behavior is any activity designed to transfer income or wealth to a particular firm or resource supplier at someone else's, or

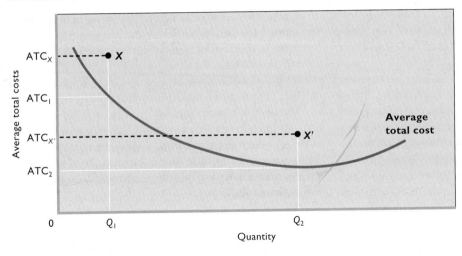

FIGURE 10.7 X-inefficiency. The average-total-cost curve (ATC) is assumed to reflect the minimum cost of producing each particular level of output. Any point above this "lowest-cost" ATC curve, such as X or X', implies X-inefficiency: operation at greater than lowest cost for a particular level of output.

even society's, expense. We have seen that a monopolist can obtain an economic profit even in the long run. Therefore, it is no surprise that a firm may go to great expense to acquire or maintain a monopoly granted by government through legislation or an exclusive license. Such rent-seeking expenditures add nothing to the firm's output, but they clearly increase its costs. Taken alone, rent-seeking implies that monopoly involves higher costs and less efficiency than suggested in Figure 10.6b.

Technological Advance In the very long run, firms can reduce their costs through the discovery and implementation of new technology. If monopolists are more likely than competitive producers to develop more efficient production techniques over time, then the inefficiency of monopoly might be overstated. Because research and development (R&D) is the topic of optional Web Chapter 11, we will provide only a brief assessment here.

The general view of economists is that a pure monopolist will not be technologically progressive. Although its economic profit provides ample means to finance research and development, it has little incentive to implement new techniques (or products). The absence of competitors means that there is no external pressure for technological advance in a monopolized market. Because of its sheltered market position, the pure monopolist can afford to be complacent and lethargic. There simply is no major penalty for not being innovative.

One caveat: Research and technological advance may be one of the monopolist's barriers to entry. Thus, the monopolist may continue to seek technological advance to avoid falling prey to new rivals. In this case technological advance is essential to the maintenance of monopoly. But then it is *potential* competition, not the monopoly market structure, that is driving the technological advance. By

assumption, no such competition exists in the pure monopoly model; entry is completely blocked.

Assessment and Policy Options

Monopoly is a legitimate concern. Monopolists can charge higher-than-competitive prices that result in an underallocation of resources to the monopolized product. They can stifle innovation, engage in rent-seeking behavior, and foster X-inefficiency. Even when their costs are low because of economies of scale, there is no guarantee that the price they charge will reflect those low costs. The cost savings may simply accrue to the monopoly as greater economic profit.

Fortunately, however, monopoly is not widespread in the United States. Barriers to entry are seldom completely successful. Although research and technological advance may strengthen the market position of a monopoly, technology may also undermine monopoly power. Over time, the creation of new technologies may work to destroy monopoly positions. For example, the development of courier delivery, fax machines, and e-mail has eroded the monopoly power of the U.S. Postal Service. Similarly, cable television monopolies are now challenged by satellite TV and by technologies that permit the transmission of audio and video over the Internet.

Patents eventually expire; and even before they do, the development of new and distinct substitutable products often circumvents existing patent advantages. New sources of monopolized resources sometimes are found and competition from foreign firms may emerge. (See Global Perspective 10.1.) Finally, if a monopoly is sufficiently fearful of future competition from new products, it may keep its prices relatively low so as to discourage rivals from developing such products. If so, consumers may pay nearly competitive prices even though competition is currently lacking.

So what should government do about monopoly when it arises in the real world? Economists agree that government needs to look carefully at monopoly on a case-by-case basis. Three general policy options are available:

- If the monopoly is achieved and sustained through anticompetitive actions, creates substantial economic inefficiency, and appears to be long-lasting, the government can file charges against the monopoly under the antitrust laws. If found guilty of monopoly abuse, the firm can either be expressly prohibited from engaging in certain business activities or be broken into two or more competing firms. An example of the breakup approach was the dissolution of Standard Oil into several competing firms in 1911. In contrast, in 2001 an appeals court overruled a lower-court decision to divide Microsoft into two firms. Instead, Microsoft was prohibited from engaging in a number of specific anticompetitive business activities. (We discuss the antitrust laws and the Microsoft case in Chapter 18.)

- If the monopoly is a natural monopoly, society can allow it to continue to expand. If no competition

emerges from new products, government may then decide to regulate its prices and operations. (We discuss this option later in this chapter and also in Chapter 18.)

- If the monopoly appears to be unsustainable because of emerging new technology, society can simply choose to ignore it. In such cases, society simply lets the process of creative destruction (discussed in Chapter 9) do its work. In Web Chapter 11, we discuss in detail the likelihood that real-world monopolies will collapse due to creative destruction and competition brought on by new technologies.

QUICK REVIEW 10.2

- The monopolist maximizes profit (or minimizes loss) at the output where MR = MC and charges the price that corresponds to that output on its demand curve.
- The monopolist has no supply curve, since any of several prices can be associated with a specific quantity of output supplied.
- Assuming identical costs, a monopolist will be less efficient than a purely competitive industry because it will fail to produce units of output for which marginal benefits exceed marginal costs.
- The inefficiencies of monopoly may be offset or lessened by economies of scale and, less likely, by technological progress, but they may be intensified by the presence of X-inefficiency and rent-seeking expenditures.

Price Discrimination

We have assumed in this chapter that the monopolist charges a single price to all buyers. But under certain conditions the monopolist can increase its profit by charging different prices to different buyers. In so doing, the monopolist is engaging in **price discrimination,** the practice of selling a specific product at more than one price when the price differences are not justified by cost differences. Price discrimination can take three forms:

ORIGIN OF THE IDEA
O 10.4
Price discrimination

- Charging each customer in a single market the maximum price she or he is willing to pay.
- Charging each customer one price for the first set of units purchased and a lower price for subsequent units purchased.
- Charging some customers one price and other customers another price.

Conditions

The opportunity to engage in price discrimination is not readily available to all sellers. Price discrimination is possible when the following conditions are met:

- *Monopoly power* The seller must be a monopolist or, at least, must possess some degree of monopoly power, that is, some ability to control output and price.
- *Market segregation* At relatively low cost to itself, the seller must be able to segregate buyers into distinct classes, each of which has a different willingness or ability to pay for the product. This separation of buyers is usually based on different price elasticities of demand, as the examples below will make clear.
- *No resale* The original purchaser cannot resell the product or service. If buyers in the low-price segment of the market could easily resell in the high-price segment, the monopolist's price-discrimination strategy would create competition in the high-price segment. This competition would reduce the price in the high-price segment and undermine the monopolist's price-discrimination policy. This condition suggests that service industries such as the transportation industry or legal and medical services, where resale is impossible, are good candidates for price discrimination.

Examples of Price Discrimination

Price discrimination is widely practiced in the U.S. economy. For example, we noted in Chapter 4's Last Word that airlines charge high fares to business travelers, whose demand for travel is inelastic, and offer lower, highly restricted, nonrefundable fares to attract vacationers and others whose demands are more elastic.

Electric utilities frequently segment their markets by end uses, such as lighting and heating. The absence of reasonable lighting substitutes means that the demand for electricity for illumination is inelastic and that the price per kilowatt-hour for such use is high. But the availability of natural gas and petroleum for heating makes the demand for electricity for this purpose less inelastic and the price lower.

Movie theaters and golf courses vary their charges on the basis of time (for example, higher evening and weekend rates) and age (for example, lower rates for children, senior discounts). Railroads vary the rate charged per ton-mile of freight according to the market value of the product being shipped. The shipper of 10 tons of television sets or refrigerators is charged more than the shipper of 10 tons of gravel or coal.

The issuance of discount coupons, redeemable at purchase, is a form of price discrimination. It enables firms to give price discounts to their most price-sensitive

CONSIDER THIS . . .

Price Discrimination at the Ballpark

Take me out to the ball game . . .

Buy me some peanuts and Cracker Jack . . .

Professional baseball teams earn substantial revenues through ticket sales. To maximize profit, they offer significantly lower ticket prices for children (whose demand is elastic) than for adults (whose demand is inelastic). This discount may be as much as 50 percent.

If this type of price discrimination increases revenue and profit, why don't teams also price discriminate at the concession stands? Why don't they offer half-price hot dogs, soft drinks, peanuts, and Cracker Jack to children?

The answer involves the three requirements for successful price discrimination. All three requirements are met for game tickets: (1) The team has monopoly power; (2) it can segregate ticket buyers by age group, each group having a different elasticity of demand; and (3) children cannot resell their discounted tickets to adults.

It's a different situation at the concession stands. Specifically, the third condition is *not* met. If the team had dual prices, it could not prevent the exchange or "resale" of the concession goods from children to adults. Many adults would send children to buy food and soft drinks for them: "Here's some money, Billy. Go buy *six* hot dogs." In this case, price discrimination would reduce, not increase, team profit. Thus, children and adults are charged the same high prices at the concession stands. (These prices are high relative to those for the same goods at the local convenience store because the stadium sellers have a captive audience and thus considerable monopoly power.)

customers who have elastic demand. Less price-sensitive consumers who have less elastic demand are not as likely to take the time to clip and redeem coupons. The firm thus makes a larger profit than if it had used a single-price, no-coupon strategy.

Finally, price discrimination often occurs in international trade. A Russian aluminum producer, for example, might sell aluminum for less in the United States than in Russia. In the United States, this seller faces an elastic demand because several substitute suppliers are available. But in Russia, where the manufacturer dominates the market and trade barriers impede imports, consumers have fewer choices and thus demand is less elastic.

FIGURE 10.8 Price discrimination to different groups of buyers. The price-discriminating monopolist represented here maximizes its total profit by dividing the market into two segments based on differences in elasticity of demand. It then produces and sells the MR = MC output in each market segment. (For visual clarity, average total cost (ATC) is assumed to be constant. Therefore MC equals ATC at all output levels.) (a) The firm charges a higher price (here, P_b) to customers who have a less elastic demand curve and (b) a lower price (here, P_s) to customers with a more elastic demand. The price discriminator's total profit is larger than it would be with no discrimination and therefore a single price.

(a) Small businesses

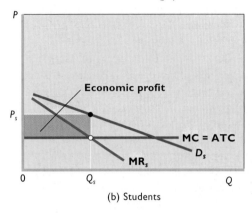

(b) Students

Graphical Analysis

Figure 10.8 demonstrates graphically the most frequently seen form or price discrimination—charging different prices to different classes of buyers. The two side-to-side graphs are for a single pure monopolist selling its product, say, software, in two segregated parts of the market. Figure 10.8a illustrates demand for software by small-business customers; Figure 10.8b, the demand for software by students. Student versions of the software are identical to the versions sold to businesses but are available (1 per person) only to customers with a student ID. Presumably, students have lower ability to pay for the software and are charged a discounted price.

The demand curve D_b in the graph to the left indicates a relatively inelastic demand for the product on the part of business customers. The demand curve D_s in the righthand graph reflects the more elastic demand of students. The marginal revenue curves (MR$_b$ and MR$_s$) lie below their respective demand curves, reflecting the demand–marginal revenue relationship previously described.

For visual clarity we have assumed that average total cost (ATC) is constant. Therefore marginal cost (MC) equals average total cost (ATC) at all quantities of output. These costs are the same for both versions of the software and therefore appear as the identical straight lines labeled "MC = ATC."

What price will the pure monopolist charge to each set of customers? Using the MR = MC rule for profit maximization, the firm will offer Q_b units of the software for sale to small businesses. It can sell that profit-maximizing

WORKED PROBLEMS

W 10.2

Price discrimination

output by charging price P_b. Again using the MR = MC rule, the monopolist will offer Q_s units of software to students. To sell those Q_s units, the firm will charge students the lower price P_s.

Firms engage in price discrimination because it enhances their profit. The numbers (not shown) behind the curves in Figure 10.8 would clearly reveal that the sum of the two profit rectangles shown in green exceeds the single profit rectangle the firm would obtain from a single monopoly price. How do consumers fare? In this case, students clearly benefit by paying a lower price than they would if the firm charged a single monopoly price; in contrast, the price discrimination results in a higher price for business customers. Therefore, compared to the single-price situation, students buy more of the software and small businesses buy less.

Such price discrimination is widespread in the economy and is illegal only when it is part of a firm's strategy to lessen or eliminate competition. We will discuss illegal price discrimination in Chapter 18, which covers antitrust policy.

Regulated Monopoly

Natural monopolies traditionally have been subject to *rate regulation* (price regulation), although the recent trend has been to deregulate wherever competition seems possible. For example, long-distance telephone calls, natural gas distribution, wireless communications, cable television, and long-distance electricity transmission have been, to one degree or another, deregulated over the past several decades. And regulators in some states are beginning to allow new entrants to compete with existing local telephone and electricity providers. Nevertheless, state and local regulatory commissions still regulate the prices that most local natural

FIGURE 10.9 Regulated monopoly. The socially optimal price P_r, found where D and MC intersect, will result in an efficient allocation of resources but may entail losses to the monopoly. The fair-return price P_f will allow the monopolist to break even but will not fully correct the underallocation of resources.

gas distributors, regional telephone companies, and local electricity suppliers can charge. These locally regulated monopolies are commonly called "public utilities."

Let's consider the regulation of a local natural monopoly. Our example will be a single firm that is the only seller of natural gas in the town of Springfield. Figure 10.9 shows the demand and the long-run cost curves facing our firm. Because of extensive economies of scale, the demand curve cuts the natural monopolist's long-run average-total-cost curve at a point where that curve is still falling. It would be inefficient to have several firms in this industry because each would produce a much smaller output, operating well to the left on the long-run average-total-cost curve. In short, each firm's lowest average total cost would be substantially higher than that of a single firm. So efficient, lowest-cost production requires a single seller.

We know by application of the MR = MC rule that Q_m and P_m are the profit-maximizing output and price that an unregulated monopolist would choose. Because price exceeds average total cost at output Q_m, the monopolist enjoys a substantial economic profit. Furthermore, price exceeds marginal cost, indicating an underallocation of resources to this product or service. Can government regulation bring about better results from society's point of view?

Socially Optimal Price: $P = MC$

One sensible goal for regulators would be to get the monopoly to produce the allocatively efficient output level. For our monopolist in Figure 10.9, this is output level Q_r, determined by where the demand curve D intersects the MC curve. Q_r is the allocatively efficient output level,

because for each unit of output up to Q_r, the demand curve lies above the MC curve, indicating that for all of these units marginal benefits exceed marginal costs.

But how can the regulatory commission actually motivate the monopoly to produce this output level? The trick is to set the regulated price P_r at a level such that the monopoly will be led by its profit-maximizing rule to voluntarily produce the allocatively efficiently level of output. To see how this works, note that because the monopoly will receive the regulated price P_r for all units that it sells, P_r becomes the monopoly's marginal revenue per unit. Thus, the monopoly's MR curve becomes the horizontal white line moving rightward from price P_r on the vertical axis.

The monopoly will at this point follow its usual rule for maximizing profits or minimizing losses: It will produce where marginal revenue equals marginal cost. As a result, the monopoly will produce where the horizontal white MR (= P_r) line intersects the MC curve at point r. That is, the monopoly will end up producing the socially optimal output Q_r not because it is socially minded but because Q_r happens to be the output that either maximizes profits or minimizes losses when the firm is forced by the regulators to sell all units at the regulated price P_r.

The regulated price P_r that achieves allocative efficiency is called the **socially optimal price.** Because it is determined by where the MC curve intersects the demand curve, this type of regulation is often summarized by the equation $P = MC$.

Fair-Return Price: $P = ATC$

The socially optimal price suffers from a potentially fatal problem. P_r may be so low that average total costs are not covered, as is the case in Figure 10.9. In such situations, forcing the socially optimal price on the regulated monopoly would result in short-run losses and long-run exit. In our example, Springfield would be left without a gas company and its citizens without gas.

What can be done to rectify this problem? One option is to provide a public subsidy to cover the loss that the socially optimal price would entail. Another possibility is to condone price discrimination, allow the monopoly to charge some customers prices above P_r, and hope that the additional revenue that the monopoly gains from price discrimination will be enough to permit it to break even.

In practice, regulatory commissions in the United States have often pursued a third option that abandons the goal of producing every unit for which marginal benefits exceed marginal costs but which guarantees that regulated monopolies will be able to break even and continue in operation. Under this third option, regulators set a regulated price that is high enough for monopolists to break even and continue in operation. This price has come to be referred to as a **fair-return price** because of a ruling in which the Supreme Court held that regulatory agencies must permit regulated utility owners to enjoy a "fair return" on their investments.

In practice, a fair return is equal to a normal profit. That is, a fair return is an accounting profit equal in size to what the owners of the monopoly would on average receive if they entered another type of business.

The regulator determines the fair-return price P_f by where the average total cost curve intersects the demand curve at point f. As we will explain, setting the regulated price at this level will cause the monopoly to produce Q_f units while guaranteeing that it will break even and not wish to exit the industry. To see why the monopoly will voluntarily produce Q_f units, note that because the monopoly will receive P_f dollars for each unit it sells, its marginal revenue per unit becomes P_f dollars so that the horizontal line moving rightward from P_f on the vertical axis becomes the regulated monopoly's MR curve. Because this horizontal MR curve is always higher than the monopoly's MC curve, it is obvious that marginal revenues will exceed marginal costs for every possible level of output shown in Figure 10.9. Thus, the monopoly should be willing to supply whatever quantity of output is demanded by consumers at the regulated price P_f. That quantity is, of course, given by the demand curve. At price P_f consumers will demand exactly Q_f units. Thus, by setting the regulated price at P_f, the regulator gets the monopoly to voluntarily supply exactly Q_f units.

Even better, the regulator also guarantees that the monopoly firm will earn exactly a normal profit. This can be seen in Figure 10.9 by noting that the rectangle $0afb$ is equal to both the monopoly's total cost and its total revenue. Its economic profit is therefore equal to zero, implying that it must be earning a normal accounting profit for its owners.

One final point about allocative efficiency: By choosing the fair-return price P_f, the regulator leads the monopoly to produce Q_f units. This is less than the socially optimal quantity Q_r, but still more than the Q_m units that the monopolist would produce if left unregulated. So while fair-return pricing does not lead to full allocative efficiency, it is still an improvement on what the monopoly would do if left to its own devices.

Dilemma of Regulation

Comparing results of the socially optimal price ($P = MC$) and the fair-return price ($P = ATC$) suggests a policy dilemma, sometimes termed the *dilemma of regulation*. When its price is set to achieve the most efficient allocation of resources ($P = MC$), the regulated monopoly is likely to suffer losses. Survival of the firm would presumably depend on permanent public subsidies out of tax revenues. On the other hand, although a fair-return price ($P = ATC$) allows the monopolist to cover costs, it only partially resolves the underallocation of resources that the unregulated monopoly price would foster. Despite this dilemma, regulation can improve on the results of monopoly from the social point of view. Price regulation (even at the fair-return price) can simultaneously reduce price, increase output, and reduce the economic profits of monopolies.

That said, we need to provide an important caution: "Fair-price" regulation of monopoly looks rather simple in theory but is amazingly complex in practice. In the actual economy, rate regulation is accompanied by large, expensive rate-setting bureaucracies and maze-like sets of procedures. Also, rate decisions require extensive public input via letters and through public hearings. Rate decisions are subject to lengthy legal challenges. Further, because regulatory commissions must set prices sufficiently above costs to create fair returns, regulated monopolists have little incentive to minimize average total costs. When these costs creep up, the regulatory commissions must set higher prices.

Regulated firms therefore are noted for higher-than-competitive wages, more managers and staff than necessary, nicer-than-typical office buildings, and other forms of X-inefficiency. These inefficiencies help explain the trend of Federal, state, and local governments abandoning price regulation where the possibility of competition looks promising.

> ### QUICK REVIEW 10.3
>
> - Price discrimination occurs when a firm sells a product at different prices that are not based on cost differences.
> - The conditions necessary for price discrimination are (a) monopoly power, (b) the ability to segregate buyers on the basis of demand elasticities, and (c) the inability of buyers to resell the product.
> - Compared with single pricing by a monopolist, perfect price discrimination results in greater profit and greater output. Many consumers pay higher prices, but other buyers pay prices below the single price.
> - Monopoly price can be reduced and output increased through government regulation.
> - The socially optimal price ($P = MC$) achieves allocative efficiency but may result in losses; the fair-return price ($P = ATC$) yields a normal profit but fails to achieve allocative efficiency.

Word De Beers Diamonds: Are Monopolies Forever?

De Beers Was One of the World's Strongest and Most Enduring Monopolies. But in Mid-2000 It Announced That It Could No Longer Control the Supply of Diamonds and Thus Would Abandon Its 66-Year Policy of Monopolizing the Diamond Trade.

De Beers, a Swiss-based company controlled by a South African corporation, produces about 45 percent of the world's rough-cut diamonds and purchases for resale a sizable number of the rough-cut diamonds produced by other mines worldwide. As a result, De Beers markets about 55 percent of the world's diamonds to a select group of diamond cutters and dealers. But that percentage has declined from 80 percent in the mid-1980s. Therein lies the company's problem.

Classic Monopoly Behavior

De Beers's past monopoly behavior is a classic example of the unregulated monopoly model illustrated in Figure 10.4. No matter how many diamonds it mined or purchased, it sold only the quantity of diamonds that would yield an "appropriate" (monopoly) price. That price was well above production costs, and De Beers and its partners earned monopoly profits.

When demand fell, De Beers reduced its sales to maintain price. The excess of production over sales was then reflected in growing diamond stockpiles held by De Beers. It also attempted to bolster demand through advertising ("Diamonds are forever"). When demand was strong, it increased sales by reducing its diamond inventories.

De Beers used several methods to control the production of many mines it did not own. First, it convinced a number of independent producers that "single-channel" or monopoly marketing through De Beers would maximize their profit. Second, mines that circumvented De Beers often found their market suddenly flooded with similar diamonds from De Beers's vast stockpiles. The resulting price decline and loss of profit often would encourage a "rogue" mine into the De Beers fold. Finally, De Beers simply purchased and stockpiled diamonds produced by independent mines so that their added supplies would not "undercut" the market.

An End of an Era? Several factors have come together to unravel the De Beers monopoly. New diamond discoveries resulted in a growing leakage of diamonds into world markets outside De Beers's control. For example, significant prospecting and trading in Angola occurred. Recent diamond discoveries in Canada's Northwest Territories pose another threat. Although De Beers is a participant in that region, a large uncontrolled supply of diamonds is expected to emerge. Another challenge has been technological improvements that now allow chemical firms to manufacture flawless artificial diamonds. To prevent consumers from switching to synthetic diamonds, De Beers had to launch a costly campaign to promote "mined diamonds" over synthetics.

If that was not enough, Australian diamond producer Argyle opted to withdraw from the De Beers monopoly. Its annual production of mostly low-grade industrial diamonds accounts for about 6 percent of the global $8 billion diamond market. Moreover, the international media began to focus heavily on the role that diamonds play in financing bloody civil wars in Africa. Fearing a consumer boycott of diamonds, De Beers pledged not to buy these "conflict" diamonds or do business with any firm that did. These diamonds, however, continue to find their way into the marketplace, eluding De Beers's control.

In mid-2000 De Beers abandoned its attempt to control the supply of diamonds. It announced that it planned to transform itself from a diamond cartel to a modern firm selling "premium" diamonds and other luxury goods under the De Beers label. It therefore would gradually reduce its $4 billion stockpile of diamonds and turn its efforts to increasing the overall demand for diamonds through advertising. De Beers proclaimed that it was changing its strategy to being "the diamond supplier of choice."

Diamonds may be forever, but the DeBeers diamond monopoly was not. Nevertheless, with its high market share and ability to control its own production levels, De Beers will continue to wield considerable influence over the price of rough-cut diamonds.

Summary

1. A pure monopolist is the sole producer of a commodity for which there are no close substitutes.

2. The existence of pure monopoly and other imperfectly competitive market structures is explained by barriers to entry in the form of (a) economies of scale, (b) patent ownership and research, (c) ownership or control of essential resources, and (d) pricing and other strategic behavior.

3. The pure monopolist's market situation differs from that of a competitive firm in that the monopolist's demand curve is downsloping, causing the marginal-revenue curve to lie below the demand curve. Like the competitive seller, the pure monopolist will maximize profit by equating marginal revenue and marginal cost. Barriers to entry may permit a monopolist to acquire economic profit even in the long run. However, (a) the monopolist does not charge "the highest price possible"; (b) the price that yields maximum total profit to the monopolist rarely coincides with the price that yields maximum unit profit; (c) high costs and a weak demand may prevent the monopolist from realizing any profit at all; and (d) the monopolist avoids the inelastic region of its demand curve.

4. With the same costs, the pure monopolist will find it profitable to restrict output and charge a higher price than would sellers in a purely competitive industry. This restriction of output causes resources to be misallocated, as is evidenced by the fact that price exceeds marginal cost in monopolized markets. Monopoly creates an efficiency loss (or deadweight loss) for society.

5. Monopoly transfers income from consumers to monopolists because a monopolist can charge a higher price than would

a purely competitive firm with the same costs. So monopolists in effect levy a "private tax" on consumers and, if demand is strong enough, obtain substantial economic profits.

6. The costs monopolists and competitive producers face may not be the same. On the one hand, economies of scale may make lower unit costs available to monopolists but not to competitors. Also, pure monopoly may be more likely than pure competition to reduce costs via technological advance because of the monopolist's ability to realize economic profit, which can be used to finance research. On the other hand, X-inefficiency—the failure to produce with the least costly combination of inputs—is more common among monopolists than among competitive firms. Also, monopolists may make costly expenditures to maintain monopoly privileges that are conferred by government. Finally, the blocked entry of rival firms weakens the monopolist's incentive to be technologically progressive.

7. A monopolist can increase its profit by practicing price discrimination, provided (a) it can segregate buyers on the basis of elasticities of demand and (b) its product or service cannot be readily transferred between the segregated markets.

8. Price regulation can be invoked to eliminate wholly or partially the tendency of monopolists to underallocate resources and to earn economic profits. The socially optimal price is determined where the demand and marginal-cost curves intersect; the fair-return price is determined where the demand and average-total-cost curves intersect.

Terms and Concepts

pure monopoly	network effects	price discrimination
barriers to entry	X-inefficiency	socially optimal price
simultaneous consumption	rent-seeking behavior	fair-return price

Questions

1. "No firm is completely sheltered from rivals; all firms compete for consumer dollars. If that is so, then pure monopoly does not exist." Do you agree? Explain. How might you use Chapter 4's concept of cross elasticity of demand to judge whether monopoly exists? **LO1**

2. Discuss the major barriers to entry into an industry. Explain how each barrier can foster either monopoly or oligopoly. Which barriers, if any, do you feel give rise to monopoly that is socially justifiable? **LO1**

3. How does the demand curve faced by a purely monopolistic seller differ from that confronting a purely competitive firm? Why does it differ? Of what significance is the differ-

ence? Why is the pure monopolist's demand curve not perfectly inelastic? **LO1**

4. Use the demand schedule at the top of the next page to calculate total revenue and marginal revenue at each quantity. Plot the demand, total-revenue, and marginal-revenue curves, and explain the relationships between them. Explain why the marginal revenue of the fourth unit of output is $3.50, even though its price is $5. Use Chapter 4's total-revenue test for price elasticity to designate the elastic and inelastic segments of your graphed demand curve. What generalization can you make as to the relationship between marginal revenue and elasticity of demand? Suppose the

marginal cost of successive units of output was zero. What output would the profit-seeking firm produce? Finally, use your analysis to explain why a monopolist would never produce in the inelastic region of demand. LO1

Price (P)	Quantity Demanded (Q)	Price (P)	Quantity Demanded (Q)
$7.00	0	$4.50	5
6.50	1	4.00	6
6.00	2	3.50	7
5.50	3	3.00	8
5.00	4	2.50	9

5. Assume that a pure monopolist and a purely competitive firm have the same unit costs. Contrast the two with respect to (a) price, (b) output, (c) profits, (d) allocation of resources, and (e) impact on income transfers. Since both monopolists and competitive firms follow the MC = MR rule in maximizing profits, how do you account for the different results? Why might the costs of a purely competitive firm and those of a monopolist be different? What are the implications of such a cost difference? LO3

6. Critically evaluate and explain each statement: LO3
   a. Because they can control product price, monopolists are always assured of profitable production by simply charging the highest price consumers will pay.
   b. The pure monopolist seeks the output that will yield the greatest per-unit profit.
   c. An excess of price over marginal cost is the market's way of signaling the need for more production of a good.
   d. The more profitable a firm, the greater its monopoly power.

e. The monopolist has a pricing policy; the competitive producer does not.
f. With respect to resource allocation, the interests of the seller and of society coincide in a purely competitive market but conflict in a monopolized market.

7. Assume a monopolistic publisher has agreed to pay an author 10 percent of the total revenue from the sales of a text. Will the author and the publisher want to charge the same price for the text? Explain. LO3

8. U.S. pharmaceutical companies charge different prices for prescription drugs to buyers in different nations, depending on elasticity of demand and government-imposed price ceilings. Explain why these companies, for profit reasons, oppose laws allowing reimportation of drugs to the United States. LO4

9. Explain verbally and graphically how price (rate) regulation may improve the performance of monopolies. In your answer distinguish between (a) socially optimal (marginal-cost) pricing and (b) fair-return (average-total-cost) pricing. What is the "dilemma of regulation"? LO5

10. It has been proposed that natural monopolists should be allowed to determine their profit-maximizing outputs and prices and then government should tax their profits away and distribute them to consumers in proportion to their purchases from the monopoly. Is this proposal as socially desirable as requiring monopolists to equate price with marginal cost or average total cost? LO5

11. **LAST WORD** How was De Beers able to control the world price of diamonds even though it produced only 45 percent of the diamonds? What factors ended its monopoly? What is its new strategy for earning economic profit, rather than just normal profit?

Problems

1. Suppose a pure monopolist is faced with the demand schedule shown below and the same cost data as the competitive producer discussed in problem 4 at the end of Chapter 8. Calculate the missing total-revenue and marginal-revenue amounts, and determine the profit-maximizing price and profit-maximizing output for this monopolist. What is the monopolist's profit? Verify your answer graphically and by comparing total revenue and total cost. LO2

Price	Quantity Demanded	Total Revenue	Marginal Revenue
$115	0	$_____	
100	1	_____	$_____
83	2	_____	_____
71	3	_____	_____
63	4	_____	_____
55	5	_____	_____
48	6	_____	_____
42	7	_____	_____
37	8	_____	_____
33	9	_____	_____
29	10	_____	_____

2. Suppose that a price-discriminating monopolist has segregated its market into two groups of buyers. The first group is described by the demand and revenue data that you developed for problem 1. The demand and revenue data for the second group of buyers is shown in the table at the top-left corner of the next page. Assume that MC is $13 in both markets and MC = ATC at all output levels. What price will the firm charge in each market? Based solely on these two prices, which market has the higher price elasticity of demand? What will be this monopolist's total economic profit? LO4

Price	Quantity Demanded	Total Revenue	Marginal Revenue
$71	0	$ 0	
			$63
63	1	63	
			47
55	2	110	
			34
48	3	144	
			24
42	4	168	
			17
37	5	185	
			13
33	6	198	
			5
29	7	203	

Output	TC
25,000	$50,000
50,000	70,000
75,000	75,000
100,000	80,000

3. Assume that the most efficient production technology available for making vitamin pills has the cost structure given in the following table. Note that output is measured as the number of bottles of vitamins produced per day and that costs include a normal profit. **LO4**

Output	TC	MC
25,000	$100,000	$0.50
50,000	150,000	1.00
75,000	187,500	2.50
100,000	275,500	3.00

a. What is ATC per unit for each level of output listed in the table?

b. Is this a decreasing-cost industry? (Answer yes or no).

c. Suppose that the market price for a bottle of vitamins is $2.50 and that at that price the total market quantity demanded is 75,000,000 bottles. How many firms will there be in this industry?

d. Suppose that, instead, the market quantity demanded at a price of $2.50 is only 75,000. How many firms do you expect there to be in this industry?

e. Review your answers to parts b, c, and d. Does the level of demand determine this industry's market structure?

4. A new production technology for making vitamins is invented by a college professor who decides not to patent it. Thus, it is available for anybody to copy and put into use. The TC per bottle for production up to 100,000 bottles per day is given in the following table. **LO4**

a. What is ATC for each level of output listed in the table?

b. Suppose that for each 25,000-bottle-per-day increase in production above 100,000 bottles per day, TC increases

by $5000 (so that, for instance, 125,000 bottles per day would generate total costs of $85,000 and 150,000 bottles per day would generate total costs of $90,000). Is this a decreasing-cost industry?

c. Suppose that the price of a bottle of vitamins is $1.33 and that at that price the total quantity demanded by consumers is 75,000,000 bottles. How many firms will there be in this industry?

d. Suppose that, instead, the market quantity demanded at a price of $1.33 is only 75,000. How many firms do you expect there to be in this industry?

e. Review your answers to parts b, c, and d. Does the level of demand determine this industry's market structure?

f. Compare your answer to part d of this problem with your answer to part d of problem 3. Do both production technologies show constant returns to scale?

5. Suppose you have been tasked with regulating a single monopoly firm that sells 50-pound bags of concrete. The firm has fixed costs of $10 million per year and a variable cost of $1 per bag no matter how many bags are produced. **LO5**

a. If this firm kept on increasing its output level, would ATC per bag ever increase? Is this a decreasing-cost industry?

b. If you wished to regulate this monopoly by charging the socially optimal price, what price would you charge? At that price, what would be the size of the firm's profit or loss? Would the firm want to exit the industry?

c. You find out that if you set the price at $2 per bag, consumers will demand 10 million bags. How big will the firm's profit or loss be at that price?

d. If consumers instead demanded 20 million bags at a price of $2 per bag, how big would the firm's profit or loss be?

e. Suppose that demand is perfectly inelastic at 20 million bags, so that consumers demand 20 million bags no matter what the price is. What price should you charge if you want the firm to earn only a fair rate of return? Assume as always that TC includes a normal profit.

FURTHER TEST YOUR KNOWLEDGE AT
www.mcconnell19e.com

At the text's Online Learning Center (OLC), **www.mcconnell19e.com**, you will find one or more Web-based questions that require information from the Internet to answer. We urge you to check them out; they will familiarize you with Web sites that may be helpful in other courses and perhaps even in your career. The OLC also features multiple-choice questions that give instant feedback and provides other helpful ways to further test your knowledge of the chapter.

Monopolistic Competition and Oligopoly

In the United States, most industries have a market structure that falls somewhere between the two poles of pure competition and pure monopoly. To begin with, most real-world industries have fewer than the large number of producers required for pure competition but more than the single producer that defines pure monopoly. In addition, most firms in most industries have both distinguishable rather than standardized products as well as some discretion over the prices they charge. As a result, competition often occurs on the basis of price, quality, location, service, and advertising. Finally, entry to most real-world industries ranges from easy to very difficult but is rarely completely blocked.

This chapter examines two models that more closely approximate these widespread industry structures. You will discover that *monopolistic competition* mixes a small amount of monopoly power with a large amount of competition. *Oligopoly*, in contrast, blends a large amount of monopoly power with both considerable rivalry among existing firms and the threat of increased future competition due to foreign firms and new technologies. (You should quickly review Table 8.1, page 164, at this point.)

Monopolistic Competition

Let's begin by examining **monopolistic competition,** which is characterized by (1) a relatively large number of

ORIGIN OF THE IDEA

O 11.1

Monopolistic competition

sellers, (2) differentiated products (often promoted by heavy advertising), and (3) easy entry to, and exit from, the industry. The first and third characteristics provide the "competitive" aspect of monopolistic competition; the second characteristic provides the "monopolistic" aspect. In general, however, monopolistically competitive industries are much more competitive than they are monopolistic.

Relatively Large Number of Sellers

Monopolistic competition is characterized by a fairly large number of firms, say, 25, 35, 60, or 70, not by the hundreds or thousands of firms in pure competition. Consequently, monopolistic competition involves:

- *Small market shares* Each firm has a comparatively small percentage of the total market and consequently has limited control over market price.
- *No collusion* The presence of a relatively large number of firms ensures that collusion by a group of firms to restrict output and set prices is unlikely.
- *Independent action* With numerous firms in an industry, there is no feeling of interdependence among them; each firm can determine its own pricing policy without considering the possible reactions of rival firms. A single firm may realize a modest increase in sales by cutting its price, but the effect of that action on competitors' sales will be nearly imperceptible and will probably trigger no response.

Differentiated Products

In contrast to pure competition, in which there is a standardized product, monopolistic competition is distinguished by **product differentiation.** Monopolistically competitive firms turn out variations of a particular product. They produce products with slightly different physical characteristics, offer varying degrees of customer service, provide varying amounts of locational convenience, or proclaim special qualities, real or imagined, for their products.

Let's examine these aspects of product differentiation in more detail.

Product Attributes Product differentiation may entail physical or qualitative differences in the products themselves. Real differences in functional features, materials, design, and workmanship are vital aspects of product differentiation. Personal computers, for example, differ in terms of storage capacity, speed, graphic displays, and included software. There are dozens of competing principles of economics textbooks that differ in content, organization, presentation and readability, pedagogical aids, and graphics and design. Most cities have a variety of retail stores selling men's and women's clothes that differ greatly in styling, materials, and quality of work. Similarly, one pizza place may feature thin-crust Neapolitan style pizza, while another may tout its thick-crust Chicago-style pizza.

Service Service and the conditions surrounding the sale of a product are forms of product differentiation too. One shoe store may stress the fashion knowledge and helpfulness of its clerks. A competitor may leave trying on shoes and carrying them to the register to its customers but feature lower prices. Customers may prefer one-day over three-day dry cleaning of equal quality. The prestige appeal of a store, the courteousness and helpfulness of clerks, the firm's reputation for servicing or exchanging its products, and the credit it makes available are all service aspects of product differentiation.

Location Products may also be differentiated through the location and accessibility of the stores that sell them. Small convenience stores manage to compete with large supermarkets, even though these minimarts have a more limited range of products and charge higher prices. They compete mainly on the basis of location—being close to customers and situated on busy streets. A motel's proximity to an interstate highway gives it a locational advantage that may enable it to charge a higher room rate than nearby motels in less convenient locations.

Brand Names and Packaging Product differentiation may also be created through the use of brand names and trademarks, packaging, and celebrity connections. Most aspirin tablets are very much alike, but many headache sufferers believe that one brand—for example, Bayer, Anacin, or Bufferin—is superior and worth a higher price than a generic substitute. A celebrity's name associated with watches, perfume, or athletic shoes may enhance the appeal of those products for some buyers. Many customers prefer one style of ballpoint pen to another. Packaging that touts "natural spring" bottled water may attract additional customers.

Some Control over Price Despite the relatively large number of firms, monopolistic competitors do have some control over their product prices because of product differentiation. If consumers prefer the products of specific sellers, then within limits they will pay more to satisfy their preferences. Sellers and buyers are not linked randomly, as in a purely competitive market. But the monopolistic competitor's control over price is quite limited since there are numerous potential substitutes for its product.

Easy Entry and Exit

Entry into monopolistically competitive industries is relatively easy compared to oligopoly or pure monopoly. Because monopolistic competitors are typically small firms, both absolutely and relatively, economies of scale are few and capital requirements are low. On the other hand, compared with pure competition, financial barriers may result from the need to develop and advertise a product that differs from rivals' products. Some firms have trade secrets relating to their products or hold trademarks on their brand names, making it difficult and costly for other firms to imitate them.

Exit from monopolistically competitive industries is relatively easy. Nothing prevents an unprofitable monopolistic competitor from holding a going-out-of-business sale and shutting down.

Advertising

The expense and effort involved in product differentiation would be wasted if consumers were not made aware of product differences. Thus, monopolistic competitors advertise their products, often heavily. The goal of product differentiation and advertising—so-called **nonprice competition**—is to make price less of a factor in consumer purchases and make product differences a greater factor. If successful, the firm's demand curve will shift to the right and will become less elastic.

Monopolistically Competitive Industries

Table 11.1 lists several manufacturing industries that approximate monopolistic competition. Economists measure the degree of industry concentration—the extent to which the largest firms account for the bulk of the industry's output—to identify monopolistically competitive (versus oligopolistic) industries. Two such measures are the four-firm concentration ratio and the Herfindahl index. They are listed in columns 2 and 3 of the table.

A **four-firm concentration ratio,** expressed as a percentage, is the ratio of the output (sales) of the four largest firms in an industry relative to total industry sales.

$$\text{Four-firm concentration ratio} = \frac{\text{Output of four largest firms}}{\text{Total output in the industry}}$$

Four-firm concentration ratios are very low in purely competitive industries in which there are hundreds or even

TABLE 11.1 Percentage of Output Produced by Firms in Selected Low-Concentration U.S. Manufacturing Industries

(1) Industry	(2) Percentage of Industry Output* Produced by the Four Largest Firms	(3) Herfindahl Index for the Top 50 Firms	(1) Industry	(2) Percentage of Industry Output* Produced by the Four Largest Firms	(3) Herfindahl Index for the Top 50 Firms
Asphalt paving	25	207	Metal windows and doors	14	114
Plastic pipe	24	262	Women's dresses	13	84
Textile bags	24	263	Ready-mix concrete	11	63
Bolts, nuts, and rivets	24	205	Wood trusses	10	50
Plastic bags	23	240	Stone products	10	59
Quick printing	22	319	Metal stamping	8	31
Textile machinery	20	206	Wood pallets	7	24
Sawmills	18	117	Sheet metal work	6	25
Jewelry	16	117	Signs	5	19
Curtains and draperies	16	111	Retail bakeries	4	7

*As measured by value of shipments. Data are for 2002. See **www.census.gov/epcd/www/concentration.html**.

Source: Bureau of Census, *Census of Manufacturers, 2002.*

thousands of firms, each with a tiny market share. In contrast, four-firm ratios are high in oligopoly and pure monopoly. Industries in which the largest four firms account for 40 percent or more of the market are generally considered to be oligopolies. If the largest four firms account for less than 40 percent, they are likely to be monopolistically competitive. Observe that the four-firm concentration ratios in Table 11.1 range from 4 percent to 25 percent.

Published concentration ratios such as those in Table 11.1 are helpful in categorizing industries but must be used cautiously because the market shares (percentage of total sales) that they list are national in scope, whereas competition in many industries is often local in scope. As a result, some industries with low national concentration ratios are in fact substantially concentrated if one focuses on local markets.

As an example, the national four-firm concentration ratio for ready-mix concrete shown in Table 11.1 is only 11 percent. This suggests that ready-mix concrete is a monopolistically competitive industry. But the sheer bulk of ready-mix concrete and the fact that it "sets up" as it dries limits the relevant market to a specific town, city, or metropolitan area. In most of these local markets, only a few firms compete, not the numerous firms needed for monopolistic competition.

Column 3 of Table 11.1 lists a second measure of concentration: the **Herfindahl index.** This index is the sum of the squared percentage market shares of all firms in the industry. In equation form:

$$\text{Herfindahl index} = (\%S_1)^2 + (\%S_2)^2 + (\%S_3)^2 + \cdots + (\%S_n)^2$$

where $\%S_1$ is the percentage market share of firm 1, $\%S_2$ is the percentage market share of firm 2, and so on for each of the n total firms in the industry. By squaring the percentage market shares of all firms in the industry, the Herfindahl index purposely gives much greater weight to larger, and thus more powerful, firms than to smaller ones. For a purely competitive industry, the index would approach zero since each firm's market share—$\%S$ in the equation—is extremely small. In the case of a single-firm industry, the index would be at its maximum of $10,000 \ (= 100^2)$, indicating an industry with complete monopoly power.

We will discover later in this chapter that the Herfindahl index is important for assessing oligopolistic industries. But for now, the relevant generalization is that the lower the Herfindahl index, the greater is the likelihood that an industry is monopolistically competitive rather than oligopolistic. Column 3 of Table 11.1 lists the Herfindahl index (computed for the top 50 firms, not all the industry firms) for several industries. Note that the index

values are decidedly closer to the bottom limit of the Herfindahl index—0—than to its top limit—10,000.

The numbers in Table 11.1 are for manufacturing industries. In addition, many retail establishments in metropolitan areas are monopolistically competitive, including grocery stores, gasoline stations, hair salons, dry cleaners, clothing stores, and restaurants. Also, many providers of professional services such as medical care, legal assistance, real estate sales, and basic bookkeeping are monopolistic competitors.

Price and Output in Monopolistic Competition

How does a monopolistic competitor decide on its price and output? To explain, we initially assume that each firm in the industry is producing a specific differentiated product and engaging in a particular amount of advertising. Later we will see how changes in the product and in the amount of advertising modify our conclusions.

The Firm's Demand Curve

Our explanation is based on **Figure 11.1 (Key Graph),** which shows that the demand curve faced by a monopolistically competitive seller is highly, but not perfectly, elastic. It is precisely this feature that distinguishes monopolistic competition from both pure monopoly and pure competition. The monopolistic competitor's demand is more elastic than the demand faced by a pure monopolist because the monopolistically competitive seller has many competitors producing closely substitutable goods. The pure monopolist has no rivals at all. Yet, for two reasons, the monopolistic competitor's demand is not perfectly elastic like that of the pure competitor. First, the monopolistic competitor has fewer rivals; second, its products are differentiated, so they are not perfect substitutes.

The price elasticity of demand faced by the monopolistically competitive firm depends on the number of rivals and the degree of product differentiation. The larger the number of rivals and the weaker the product differentiation, the greater the price elasticity of each seller's demand, that is, the closer monopolistic competition will be to pure competition.

The Short Run: Profit or Loss

In the short run, monopolistically competitive firms maximize profit or minimize loss using exactly the same strategy as pure competitors and monopolists: They produce the level of output at which marginal revenue equals marginal cost (MR = MC). Thus, the monopolistically

key graph

(a)
Short-run profits

FIGURE 11.1 A monopolistically competitive firm: short run and long run. The monopolistic competitor maximizes profit or minimizes loss by producing the output at which MR = MC. The economic profit shown in (a) will induce new firms to enter, eventually eliminating economic profit. The loss shown in (b) will cause an exit of firms until normal profit is restored. After such entry and exit, the price will settle in (c) to where it just equals average total cost at the MR = MC output. At this price P_3 and output Q_3, the monopolistic competitor earns only a normal profit, and the industry is in long-run equilibrium.

(b)
Short-run losses

(c)
Long-run equilibrium

QUICK QUIZ FOR FIGURE 11.1

1. Price exceeds MC in:
   a. graph (a) only.
   b. graph (b) only.
   c. graphs (a) and (b) only.
   d. graphs (a), (b), and (c).
2. Price exceeds ATC in:
   a. graph (a) only.
   b. graph (b) only.
   c. graphs (a) and (b) only.
   d. graphs (a), (b), and (c).
3. The firm represented by Figure 11.1c is:
   a. making a normal profit.
   b. incurring a loss.

   c. producing at the same level of output as a purely competitive firm.
   d. producing a standardized product.

4. Which of the following pairs are both "competitionlike elements" in monopolistic competition?
   a. Price exceeds MR; standardized product.
   b. Entry is relatively easy; only a normal profit in the long run.
   c. Price equals MC at the profit-maximizing output; economic profits are likely in the long run.
   d. The firms' demand curve is downsloping; differentiated products.

Answers: 1. d; 2. a; 3. a; 4. b

competitive firm in Figure 11.1a produces output Q_1, where MR = MC. As shown by demand curve D_1, it then can charge price P_1. It realizes an economic profit, shown by the green area [= $(P_1 - A_1) \times Q_1$].

But with less favorable demand or costs, the firm may incur a loss in the short run. We show this possibility in Figure 11.1b, where the firm's best strategy is to minimize its loss. It does so by producing output Q_2 (where MR =

MC) and, as determined by demand curve D_2, by charging price P_2. Because price P_2 is less than average total cost A_2, the firm incurs a per-unit loss of $A_2 - P_2$ and a total loss represented as the red area $[= (A_2 - P_2) \times Q_2]$.

The Long Run: Only a Normal Profit

In the long run, firms will enter a profitable monopolistically competitive industry and leave an unprofitable one. So a monopolistic competitor will earn only a normal profit in the long run or, in other words, will only break even. (Remember that the cost curves include both explicit and implicit costs, including a normal profit.)

Profits: Firms Enter In the case of short-run profit (Figure 11.1a), economic profits attract new rivals because entry to the industry is relatively easy. As new firms enter, the demand curve faced by the typical firm shifts to the left (falls). Why? Because each firm has a smaller share of total demand and now faces a larger number of close-substitute products. This decline in the firm's demand reduces its economic profit. When entry of new firms has reduced demand to the extent that the demand curve is tangent to the average-total-cost curve at the profit-maximizing output, the firm is just making a normal profit. This situation is shown in Figure 11.1c, where demand is D_3 and the firm's long-run equilibrium output is Q_3. As Figure 11.1c indicates, any greater or lesser output will entail an average total cost that exceeds product price P_3, meaning a loss for the firm. At the tangency point between the demand curve and ATC, total revenue equals total costs. With the economic profit gone, there is no further incentive for additional firms to enter.

Losses: Firms Leave When the industry suffers short-run losses, as in Figure 11.1b, some firms will exit in the long run. Faced with fewer substitute products and blessed with an expanded share of total demand, the surviving firms will see their demand curves shift to the right (rise), as to D_3. Their losses will disappear and give way to normal profits (Figure 11.1c). (For simplicity we have assumed constant costs; shifts in the cost curves as firms enter or leave would complicate our discussion slightly but would not alter our conclusions.)

Complications The representative firm in the monopolistic competition model earns only a normal profit in the long run. That outcome may not always occur, however, in the real world of small firms as opposed to the theoretical model.

- Some firms may achieve sufficient product differentiation such that other firms cannot duplicate them, even over time. One hotel in a major city may have the best location relative to business and tourist activities. Or a firm may have developed a well-known brand name that gives it a slight but very long-lasting advantage over imitators. Such firms may have sufficient monopoly power to realize modest economic profits even in the long run.

- Entry to some industries populated by small firms is not as free in reality as it is in theory. Because of product differentiation, financial barriers to entry are likely to be greater than they would be if the product were standardized. This suggests some monopoly power, with small economic profits continuing even in the long run.

> **INTERACTIVE GRAPHS**
> **G 11.1**
> Monopolistic competition

With all things considered, however, the outcome that yields only a normal profit—the long-run equilibrium shown in Figure 11.1c—is a reasonable approximation of reality.

Monopolistic Competition and Efficiency

We know from Chapter 9 that economic efficiency requires each firm to produce the amount of output at which $P = MC = $ minimum ATC. The equality of price and minimum average total cost yields *productive efficiency*. The good is being produced in the least costly way, and the price is just sufficient to cover average total cost, including a normal profit. The equality of price and marginal cost yields *allocative efficiency*. The right amount of output is being produced, and thus the right amount of society's scarce resources is being devoted to this specific use.

How efficient is monopolistic competition, as measured against this triple equality? In particular, do monopolistically competitive firms produce the efficient output level associated with $P = MC = $ minimum ATC?

Neither Productive nor Allocative Efficiency

In monopolistic competition, neither productive nor allocative efficiency occurs in long-run equilibrium. Figure 11.2 includes an enlargement of part of Figure 11.1c and clearly shows this. First note that the profit-maximizing price P_3 slightly exceeds the lowest average total cost, A_4. In producing the profit-maximizing output Q_3, the firm's average total cost therefore is slightly higher than optimal from society's perspective—productive efficiency is not

FIGURE 11.2 The inefficiency of monopolistic competition. In long-run equilibrium a monopolistic competitor achieves neither productive nor allocative efficiency. Productive efficiency is not realized because production occurs where the average total cost A_3 exceeds the minimum average total cost A_4. Allocative efficiency is not achieved because the product price P_3 exceeds the marginal cost M_3. The results are an underallocation of resources as well as an efficiency loss and excess production capacity at every firm in the industry. This firm's efficiency loss is area acd and its excess production capacity is $Q_4 - Q_3$.

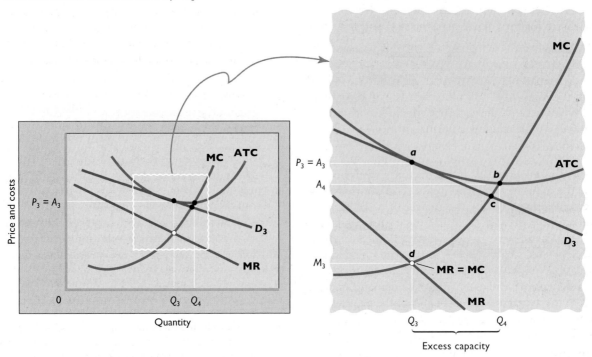

achieved. Also note that the profit-maximizing price P_3 exceeds marginal cost (here M_3), meaning that monopolistic competition causes an underallocation of resources. To measure the size of this inefficiency, note that the allocatively optimal amount of output is determined by point c, where demand curve D intersects the MC curve. So for all units between Q_3 and the level of output associated with point c, marginal benefits exceed marginal costs. Consequently, by producing only Q_3 units, this monopolistic competitor creates an efficiency loss (deadweight loss) equal in size to area acd. The total efficiency loss for the industry as a whole will be the sum of the individual efficiency losses generated by each of the firms in the industry.

Excess Capacity

In monopolistic competition, the gap between the minimum-ATC output and the profit-maximizing output identifies **excess capacity:** plant and equipment that are underused because firms are producing less than the minimum-ATC output. This gap is shown as the distance between Q_4 and Q_3 in Figure 11.2. Note in the figure that the minimum ATC is at point b. If each monopolistic competitor could profitably produce at this point on its ATC curve,

the lower average total cost would enable a lower price than P_3. More importantly, if each firm produced at b rather than at a, fewer firms would be needed to produce the industry output. But because monopolistically competitive firms produce at a in long-run equilibrium, monopolistically competitive industries are overpopulated with firms, each operating below its optimal capacity. This situation is typified by many kinds of retail establishments. For example, in most cities there is an abundance of small motels and restaurants that operate well below half capacity.

Product Variety

The situation portrayed in Figures 11.1c and 11.2 is not very satisfying to monopolistic competitors, since it foretells only a normal profit. But the profit-realizing firm of Figure 11.1a need not stand by and watch new competitors eliminate its profit by imitating its product, matching its customer service, and copying its advertising. Each firm has a product that is distinguishable in some way from those of the other producers. So the firm can attempt to stay ahead of competitors and sustain its profit through further product differentiation and better advertising. By developing or improving its product, it may be able to postpone, at least for a while, the outcome of Figure 11.1c.

Although product differentiation and advertising will add to the firm's costs, they can also increase the demand for its product. If demand increases by more than enough to compensate for the added costs, the firm will have improved its profit position. As Figure 11.2 suggests, the firm has little or no prospect of increasing profit by price cutting. So why not engage in nonprice competition?

Benefits of Product Variety

The product variety and product improvement that accompany the drive to maintain economic profit in monopolistic competition are a benefit for society—one that may offset the cost of the inefficiency associated with monopolistic competition. Consumers have a wide diversity of tastes: Some like regular fries, others like curly fries; some like contemporary furniture, others like traditional furniture. If a product is differentiated, then at any time the consumer will be offered a wide range of types, styles, brands, and quality gradations of that product. Compared with pure competition, this provides an advantage to the consumer. The range of choice is widened, and producers more fully meet the wide variation in consumer tastes.

The product improvement promoted by monopolistic competition further differentiates products and expands choices. And a successful product improvement by one firm obligates rivals to imitate or improve on that firm's temporary market advantage or else lose business. So society benefits from better products.

In fact, product differentiation creates a trade-off between consumer choice and productive efficiency. The stronger the product differentiation, the greater is the excess capacity and, therefore, the greater is the productive inefficiency. But the greater the product differentiation, the more likely it is that the firms will satisfy the great diversity of consumer tastes. The greater the excess-capacity problem, the wider the range of consumer choice.

Further Complexity

Finally, the ability to engage in nonprice competition makes the market situation of a monopolistic competitor more complex than Figure 11.1 indicates. That figure assumes a given (unchanging) product and a given level of advertising expenditures. But we know that, in practice, product attributes and advertising are not fixed. The monopolistically competitive firm juggles three factors—price, product, and advertising—in seeking maximum profit. It must determine what variety of product, selling at what price, and supplemented by what level of advertising will

result in the greatest profit. This complex situation is not easily expressed in a simple, meaningful economic model. At best, we can say that each possible combination of price, product, and advertising poses a different demand and cost (production cost plus advertising cost) situation for the firm and that one combination yields the maximum profit. In practice, this optimal combination cannot be readily forecast but must be found by trial and error.

QUICK REVIEW 11.1

- Monopolistic competition involves a relatively large number of firms operating in a noncollusive way and producing differentiated products with easy industry entry and exit.

- In the short run, a monopolistic competitor will maximize profit or minimize loss by producing that output at which marginal revenue equals marginal cost.

- In the long run, easy entry and exit of firms cause monopolistic competitors to earn only a normal profit.

- A monopolistic competitor's long-run equilibrium output is such that price exceeds the minimum average total cost (implying that consumers do not get the product at the lowest price attainable) and price exceeds marginal cost (indicating that resources are underallocated to the product).

- The efficiency loss (or deadweight loss) associated with monopolistic competition is greatly muted by the benefits consumers receive from product variety.

Oligopoly

In terms of competitiveness, the spectrum of market structures reaches from pure competition, to monopolistic competition, to oligopoly, to pure monopoly (review Table 8.1). We now direct our attention to **oligopoly,** a market dominated by a few large producers of a homogeneous or differentiated product. Because of their "fewness," oligopolists have considerable control over their prices, but each must consider the possible reaction of rivals to its own pricing, output, and advertising decisions.

A Few Large Producers

The phrase "a few large producers" is necessarily vague because the market model of oligopoly covers much ground, ranging between pure monopoly, on the one hand, and monopolistic competition, on the other. Oligopoly encompasses the U.S. aluminum industry, in which three huge firms dominate an entire national market, and the situation in which four or five much smaller auto-parts stores enjoy roughly equal shares of the market in a medium-size town. Generally, however, when you hear a term such as "Big

Three," "Big Four," or "Big Six," you can be sure it refers to an oligopolistic industry.

Homogeneous or Differentiated Products

An oligopoly may be either a **homogeneous oligopoly** or a **differentiated oligopoly,** depending on whether the firms in the oligopoly produce standardized (homogeneous) or differentiated products. Many industrial products (steel, zinc, copper, aluminum, lead, cement, industrial alcohol) are virtually standardized products that are produced in oligopolies. Alternatively, many consumer goods industries (automobiles, tires, household appliances, electronics equipment, breakfast cereals, cigarettes, and many sporting goods) are differentiated oligopolies. These differentiated oligopolies typically engage in considerable nonprice competition supported by heavy advertising.

Control over Price, but Mutual Interdependence

Because firms are few in oligopolistic industries, each firm is a "price maker"; like the monopolist, it can set its price and output levels to maximize its profit. But unlike the monopolist, which has no rivals, the oligopolist must consider how its rivals will react to any change in its price, output, product characteristics, or advertising. Oligopoly is thus characterized by *strategic behavior* and *mutual interdependence.* By **strategic behavior,** we simply mean self-interested behavior that takes into account the reactions of others. Firms develop and implement price, quality, location, service, and advertising strategies to "grow their business" and expand their profits. But because rivals are few, there is **mutual interdependence:** a situation in which each firm's profit depends not just on its own price and sales strategies but also on those of the other firms in its highly concentrated industry. So oligopolistic firms base their decisions on how they think their rivals will react. Example: In deciding whether to increase the price of its cosmetics, L'Oreal will try to predict the response of the other major producers, such as Clinique. Second example: In deciding on its advertising strategy, Burger King will take into consideration how McDonald's might react.

Entry Barriers

The same barriers to entry that create pure monopoly also contribute to the creation of oligopoly. Economies of scale are important entry barriers in a number of oligopolistic industries, such as the aircraft, rubber, and copper industries. In those industries, three or four firms might each

CONSIDER THIS . . .

Creative Strategic Behavior

The following story, offered with tongue in cheek, illustrates a localized market that exhibits some characteristics of oligopoly, including strategic behavior.

Tracy Martinez's Native American Arts and Crafts store is located in the center of a small tourist town that borders on a national park. In its early days, Tracy had a minimonopoly. Business was brisk, and prices and profits were high.

To Tracy's annoyance, two "copycat" shops opened adjacent to her store, one on either side of her shop. Worse yet, the competitors named their shops to take advantage of Tracy's advertising. One was "Native Arts and Crafts"; the other, "Indian Arts and Crafts." These new sellers drew business away from Tracy's store, forcing her to lower her prices. The three side-by-side stores in the small, isolated town constituted a localized oligopoly for Native American arts and crafts.

Tracy began to think strategically about ways to boost profit. She decided to distinguish her shop from those on either side by offering a greater mix of high-quality, expensive products and a lesser mix of inexpensive souvenir items. The tactic worked for a while, but the other stores eventually imitated her product mix.

Then, one of the competitors next door escalated the rivalry by hanging up a large sign proclaiming: "We Sell for Less!" Shortly thereafter, the other shop put up a large sign stating: "We Won't Be Undersold!"

Not to be outdone, Tracy painted a colorful sign of her own and hung it above her door. It read: "Main Entrance."

have sufficient sales to achieve economies of scale, but new firms would have such a small market share that they could not do so. They would then be high-cost producers, and as such they could not survive. A closely related barrier is the large expenditure for capital—the cost of obtaining necessary plant and equipment—required for entering certain industries. The jet engine, automobile, commercial aircraft, and petroleum-refining industries, for example, are all characterized by very high capital requirements.

The ownership and control of raw materials help explain why oligopoly exists in many mining industries, including gold, silver, and copper. In the computer, chemicals, consumer electronics, and pharmaceutical industries, patents have served as entry barriers. Moreover, oligopolists can preclude the entry of new competitors through preemptive and retaliatory pricing and advertising strategies.

Mergers

Some oligopolies have emerged mainly through the growth of the dominant firms in a given industry (examples: breakfast cereals, chewing gum, candy bars). But for other industries the route to oligopoly has been through mergers (examples: steel, in its early history, and, more recently, airlines, banking, and entertainment). The merging, or combining, of two or more competing firms may substantially increase their market share, and this in turn may allow the new firm to achieve greater economies of scale.

Another motive underlying the "urge to merge" is the desire for monopoly power. The larger firm that results from a merger has greater control over market supply and thus the price of its product. Also, since it is a larger buyer of inputs, it may be able to demand and obtain lower prices (costs) on its production inputs.

Oligopolistic Industries

Previously, we listed the four-firm concentration ratio—the percentage of total industry sales accounted for by the four largest firms—for a number of monopolistically competitive industries (see Table 11.1). Column 2 of Table 11.2 shows the four-firm concentration ratios for 21 oligopolistic industries. For example, the four largest U.S. producers of breakfast cereals make 78 percent of all breakfast cereals produced in the United States.

When the largest four firms in an industry control 40 percent or more of the market (as in Table 11.2), that industry is considered oligopolistic. Using this benchmark, about one-half of all U.S. manufacturing industries are oligopolies.

Although concentration ratios help identify oligopoly, they have four shortcomings.

Localized Markets We have already noted that concentration ratios apply to the nation as a whole, whereas the markets for some products are highly localized because of high transportation costs. Local oligopolies can exist even though national concentration ratios are low.

Interindustry Competition Concentration ratios are based on somewhat arbitrary definitions of industries. In some cases, they disguise significant **interindustry competition**—competition between two products associated with different industries. The high concentration ratio for the copper industry shown in Table 11.2 understates the competition in that industry because aluminum competes with copper in many applications (for example, in the market for long-distance power lines).

World Trade The data in Table 11.2 are only for products produced in the United States and may overstate concentration because they do not account for the **import competition** of foreign suppliers. The truck and auto tire industry is a good example. Although Table 11.2 shows that four U.S. firms produce 77 percent of the domestic output of tires, it ignores the fact that a very large portion

TABLE 11.2 Percentage of Output Produced by Firms in Selected High-Concentration U.S. Manufacturing Industries

(1) Industry	(2) Percentage of Industry Output* Produced by the Four Largest Firms	(3) Herfindahl Index for the Top 50 Firms	(1) Industry	(2) Percentage of Industry Output* Produced by the Four Largest Firms	(3) Herfindahl Index for the Top 50 Firms
Primary copper	99	ND†	Petrochemicals	85	2662
Cane sugar refining	99	ND	Small-arms ammunition	83	1901
Cigarettes	95	ND	Motor vehicles	81	2321
Household laundry			Men's slacks and jeans	80	2515
equipment	93	ND	Aircraft	81	ND
Beer	91	ND	Breakfast cereals	78	2521
Electric light bulbs	89	2582	Household vacuum		
Glass containers	88	2582	cleaners	78	2096
Turbines and generators	88	ND	Phosphate fertilizers	78	1853
Household refrigerators			Tires	77	1807
and freezers	85	1986	Electronic computers	76	2662
Primary aluminum	85	ND	Alcohol distilleries	71	1609

*As measured by value of shipments. Data are for 2002. See **www.census.gov/epcd/www/concentration.html**.
†ND = not disclosed.

Source: Bureau of Census, *Census of Manufacturers, 2002.*

Dominant Firms

The four-firm concentration ratio does not reveal the extent to which one or two firms dominate an industry. Suppose that in industry X one firm produces the entire industry output. In a second industry, Y, four firms compete, each with 25 percent of the market. The concentration ratio is 100 percent for both these industries. But industry X is a pure monopoly, while industry Y is an oligopoly that may be experiencing significant economic rivalry. Most economists would agree that monopoly power (or market power) is substantially greater in industry X than in industry Y, a fact disguised by their identical 100 percent concentration ratios.

The Herfindahl index addresses this problem. Recall that this index is the sum of the squared percentage market shares of all firms in the industry. In equation form:

$$\text{Herfindahl index} = (\%S_1)^2 + (\%S_2)^2 + (\%S_3)^2 + \cdots + (\%S_n)^2$$

where $\%S_1$ is the percentage market share of firm 1, $\%S_2$ is the percentage market share of firm 2, and so on for each firm in the industry. Also remember that by squaring the percentage market shares of all firms in the industry, the Herfindahl index gives much greater weight to larger, and thus more powerful, firms than to smaller ones. In the case of the single-firm industry X, the index would be at its maximum of 100^2, or 10,000, indicating an industry with complete monopoly power. For our supposed four-firm industry Y, the index would be $25^2 + 25^2 + 25^2 + 25^2$, or 2500, indicating much less market power.

The larger the Herfindahl index, the greater the market power within an industry. Note in Table 11.2 that the four-firm concentration ratios for the electronic computer industry and the tire industry are similar: 76 and 77 percent. But the Herfindahl index of 2662 for the electronic computer industry suggests greater market power than the 1807 index for the tire industry. Also, contrast the much larger Herfindahl indexes in Table 11.2 with those for the low-concentration industries in Table 11.1.

WORKED PROBLEMS

W 11.1

Measures of industry competition

Oligopoly Behavior: A Game-Theory Overview

Oligopoly pricing behavior has the characteristics of certain games of strategy such as poker, chess, and bridge. The best way to play such a game depends on the way

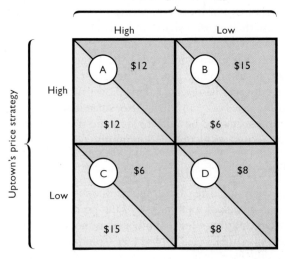

FIGURE 11.3 Profit payoff (in millions) for a two-firm oligopoly. Each firm has two possible pricing strategies. RareAir's strategies are shown in the top margin, and Uptown's in the left margin. Each lettered cell of this four-cell payoff matrix represents one combination of a RareAir strategy and an Uptown strategy and shows the profit that combination would earn for each. Assuming no collusion, the outcome of this game is Cell D, with both parties using low price strategies and earning $8 million of profits.

one's opponent plays. Players (and oligopolists) must pattern their actions according to the actions and expected reactions of rivals. The study of how people behave in strategic situations is called **game theory.** A classic example of game theory is called the prisoner's dilemma, in which each of two prisoners confess to a crime even though they might go free if neither confesses. The logic of this outcome is explained in the nearby Consider This box, which you should read now.

ORIGIN OF THE IDEA

O 11.2

Game theory

The "confess-confess" outcome of the prisoner's dilemma is conceptually identical to the "low price–low price" outcome in the game shown in Figure 11.3. In Figure 11.3 we assume that a duopoly, or two-firm oligopoly, is producing athletic shoes. Each of the two firms—let's call them RareAir and Uptown—has a choice of two pricing strategies: price high or price low. The profit each firm earns will depend on the strategy it chooses *and* the strategy its rival chooses.

There are four possible combinations of strategies for the two firms, and a lettered cell in Figure 11.3 represents each combination. For example, cell C represents a low-price strategy for Uptown along with a high-price strategy for RareAir. Figure 11.3 is called a *payoff matrix* because each cell shows the payoff (profit) to each firm that would result

CONSIDER THIS . . .

The Prisoner's Dilemma

One of the classic illustrations of game theory is the prisoner's dilemma game in which two people—let's call them Betty and Al—have committed a diamond heist and are being detained by the police as prime suspects. Unbeknownst to the two, the evidence against them is weak, so the best hope the police have for getting a conviction is if one or both of the thieves confess to the crime. The police place Betty and Al in separate holding cells and offer each the same deal: Confess to the crime and receive a lighter prison sentence.

Each detainee therefore faces a dilemma. If Betty remains silent and Al confesses, Betty will end up with a long prison sentence. If Betty confesses and Al says nothing, Al will receive a long prison sentence. What happens? Fearful that the other person will confess, both confess, even though they each would be better off saying nothing.

from each combination of strategies. Cell C shows that if Uptown adopts a low-price strategy and RareAir a high-price strategy, then Uptown will earn $15 million (yellow portion) and RareAir will earn $6 million (blue portion).

Mutual Interdependence Revisited

The data in Figure 11.3 are hypothetical, but their relationships are typical of real situations. Recall that oligopolistic firms can increase their profits, and influence their rivals' profits, by changing their pricing strategies. Each firm's profit depends on its own pricing strategy and that of its rivals. This mutual interdependence of oligopolists is the most obvious point demonstrated by Figure 11.3. If Uptown adopts a high-price strategy, its profit will be $12 million provided that RareAir also employs a high-price strategy (cell A). But if RareAir uses a low-price strategy against Uptown's high-price strategy (cell B), RareAir will increase its market share and boost its profit from $12 to $15 million. RareAir's higher profit will come at the expense of Uptown, whose profit will fall from $12 million to $6 million. Uptown's high-price strategy is a good strategy only if RareAir also employs a high-price strategy.

Collusion

Figure 11.3 also suggests that oligopolists often can benefit from **collusion**—that is, cooperation with rivals. To see the benefits of collusion, first suppose that both firms in

Figure 11.3 are acting independently and following high-price strategies. Each realizes a $12 million profit (cell A).

Note that either RareAir or Uptown could increase its profit by switching to a low-price strategy (cell B or C). The low-price firm would increase its profit to $15 million and the high-price firm's profit would fall to $6 million. The high-price firm would be better off if it, too, adopted a low-price policy. Doing so would increase its profit from $6 million to $8 million (cell D). The effect of all this independent strategy shifting would be the reduction of both firms' profits from $12 million (cell A) to $8 million (cell D).

In real situations, too, independent action by oligopolists may lead to mutually "competitive" low-price strategies: Independent oligopolists compete with respect to price, and this leads to lower prices and lower profits. This outcome is clearly beneficial to consumers but not to the oligopolists, whose profits decrease.

How could oligopolists avoid the low-profit outcome of cell D? The answer is that they could collude, rather than establish prices competitively or independently. In our example, the two firms could agree to establish and maintain a high-price policy. So each firm will increase its profit from $8 million (cell D) to $12 million (cell A).

Incentive to Cheat

The payoff matrix also explains why an oligopolist might be strongly tempted to cheat on a collusive agreement.

INTERACTIVE GRAPHS
G 11.2
Game theory

Suppose Uptown and RareAir agree to maintain high-price policies, with each earning $12 million in profit (cell A). Both are tempted to cheat on this collusive pricing agreement because either firm can increase its profit to $15 million by lowering its price. For instance, if Uptown secretly cheats and sells at the low price while RareAir keeps on charging the high price, the payoff would move from cell A to cell C so that Uptown's profit would rise to $15 million while RareAir's profit would fall to $6 million. On the other hand, if RareAir cheats and sets a low price while Uptown keeps the agreement and charges the high price, the payoff matrix would move from cell A to cell B so that RareAir would get $15 million while Uptown would get only $6 million. As you can see, cheating is both very lucrative to the cheater as well as very costly to the firm that gets cheated on. As a result, both firms will probably cheat so that the game will settle back to cell D, with each firm using its low-price strategy. (The Consider This box on the prisoner's dilemma is highly relevant and we urge you to read it now. Also, the appendix to this chapter provides several additional applications of game theory.)

Three Oligopoly Models

To gain further insight into oligopolistic pricing and output behavior, we will examine three distinct pricing models: (1) the kinked-demand curve, (2) collusive pricing, and (3) price leadership.

Why not a single model, as in our discussions of the other market structures? There are two reasons:

- *Diversity of oligopolies* Oligopoly encompasses a greater range and diversity of market situations than do other market structures. It includes the *tight* oligopoly, in which two or three firms dominate an entire market, and the *loose* oligopoly, in which six or seven firms share, say, 70 or 80 percent of a market while a "competitive fringe" of firms shares the remainder. It includes both differentiated and standardized products. It includes cases in which firms act in collusion and those in which they act independently. It embodies situations in which barriers to entry are very strong and situations in which they are not quite so strong. In short, the diversity of oligopoly does not allow us to explain all oligopolistic behaviors with a single market model.

- *Complications of interdependence* The mutual interdependence of oligopolistic firms complicates matters significantly. Because firms cannot predict the reactions of their rivals with certainty, they cannot estimate their own demand and marginal-revenue data. Without such data, firms cannot determine their profit-maximizing price and output, even in theory, as we will see.

Despite these analytical difficulties, two interrelated characteristics of oligopolistic pricing have been observed. First, if the macroeconomy is generally stable, oligopolistic prices are typically inflexible (or "rigid" or "sticky"). Prices change less frequently under oligopoly than under pure competition, monopolistic competition, and, in some instances, pure monopoly. Second, when oligopolistic prices do change, firms are likely to change their prices together, suggesting that there is a tendency to act in concert, or collusively, in setting and changing prices (as we mentioned in the preceding section). The diversity of oligopolies and the presence of mutual interdependence are reflected in the models that follow.

Kinked-Demand Theory: Noncollusive Oligopoly

Imagine an oligopolistic industry made up of three hypothetical firms (Arch, King, and Dave's), each having about one-third of the total market for a differentiated product. Assume that the firms are "independent," meaning that they do not engage in collusive price practices. Assume, too, that the going price for Arch's product is P_0 and its current sales are Q_0, as shown in **Figure 11.4a (Key Graph)**.

Now the question is, "What does the firm's demand curve look like?" Mutual interdependence and the uncertainty about rivals' reactions make this question hard to answer. The location and shape of an oligopolist's demand curve depend on how the firm's rivals will react to a price change introduced by Arch. There are two plausible assumptions about the reactions of Arch's rivals:

- *Match price changes* One possibility is that King and Dave's will exactly match any price change initiated by Arch. In this case, Arch's demand and marginal-revenue curves will look like the straight lines labeled D_1 and MR_1 in Figure 11.4a. Why are they so steep? Reason: If Arch cuts its price, its sales will increase only modestly because its two rivals will also cut their prices to prevent Arch from gaining an advantage over them. The small increase in sales that Arch (and its two rivals) will realize is at the expense of other industries; Arch will gain no sales from King and Dave's. If Arch raises its price, its sales will fall only modestly because King and Dave's will match its price increase. The industry will lose sales to other industries, but Arch will lose no customers to King and Dave's.

- *Ignore price changes* The other possibility is that King and Dave's will ignore any price change by Arch. In this case, the demand and marginal-revenue curves faced by Arch will resemble the straight lines D_2 and MR_2 in Figure 11.4a. Demand in this case is considerably more

FIGURE 11.4 The kinked-demand curve. (a) The slope of a noncollusive oligopolist's demand and marginal-revenue curves depends on whether its rivals match (straight lines D_1 and MR_1) or ignore (straight lines D_2 and MR_2) any price changes that it may initiate from the current price P_0. (b) In all likelihood an oligopolist's rivals will ignore a price increase but follow a price cut. This causes the oligopolist's demand curve to be kinked (D_2eD_1) and the marginal-revenue curve to have a vertical break, or gap (fg). Because any shift in marginal costs between MC_1 and MC_2 will cut the vertical (dashed) segment of the marginal-revenue curve, no change in either price P_0 or output Q_0 will result from such a shift.

QUICK QUIZ FOR FIGURE 11.4

1. Suppose Q_0 in this figure represents annual sales of 5 million units for this firm. The other two firms in this three-firm industry sell 3 million and 2 million units, respectively. The Herfindahl index for this industry is:
   a. 100 percent.
   b. 400.
   c. 10.
   d. 3800.

2. The D_2e segment of the demand curve D_2eD_1 in graph (b) implies that:
   a. this firm's total revenue will fall if it increases its price above P_0.
   b. other firms will match a price increase above P_0.
   c. the firm's relevant marginal-revenue curve will be MR_1 for price increases above P_0.
   d. the product in this industry is necessarily standardized.

3. By matching a price cut, this firm's rivals can:
   a. increase their market shares.
   b. increase their marginal revenues.
   c. maintain their market shares.
   d. lower their total costs.

4. A shift of the marginal-cost curve from MC_2 to MC_1 in graph (b) would:
   a. increase the "going price" above P_0.
   b. leave price at P_0 but reduce this firm's total profit.
   c. leave price at P_0 but reduce this firm's total revenue.
   d. make this firm's demand curve more elastic.

Answers: 1. d; 2. a; 3. c; 4. b

elastic than it was under the previous assumption. The reasons are clear: If Arch lowers its price and its rivals do not, Arch will gain sales significantly at the expense of its two rivals because it will be underselling them. Conversely, if Arch raises its price and its rivals do not, Arch will lose many customers to King and Dave's, which will be underselling it. Because of product differentiation, however, Arch's sales will not fall to zero when it raises its price; some of Arch's customers will pay the higher price because they have a strong preference for Arch's product. Nevertheless, Arch's demand curve will be much more elastic when its rivals ignore price changes than when they match them.

A Combined Strategy Now, which is the most logical assumption for Arch to make about how its rivals will react to any price change it might initiate? The answer is, "It depends on the direction of the price change." Common sense and observation of oligopolistic industries suggest that a firm's rivals will match price declines below P_0 as they act to prevent the price cutter from taking their customers. But they will ignore price increases above P_0 because the rivals of the price-increasing firm stand to gain the business lost by the price booster. In other words, the dark-green left-hand segment of the "rivals ignore" demand curve D_2 in Figure 11.4a seems relevant for price increases, and the dark-green right-hand segment of the "rivals match" demand curve D_1 seems relevant for price cuts. It is therefore reasonable to assume that the noncollusive oligopolist faces the **kinked-demand curve** D_2eD_1, as shown in Figure 11.4b. Demand is highly elastic above the going price P_0 but much less elastic or even inelastic below that price.

Note also that if rivals match a price cut but ignore an increase, the marginal-revenue curve of the oligopolist will also have an odd shape. It, too, will be made up of two segments: the dark gray left-hand part of marginal-revenue curve MR_2 in Figure 11.4a and the dark gray right-hand part of marginal-revenue curve MR_1. Because of the sharp difference in elasticity of demand above and below the going price, there is a gap, or what we can simply treat as a vertical segment, in the marginal-revenue curve. We show this gap as the dashed segment in the combined marginal-revenue curve MR_2fgMR_1 in Figure 11.4b.

Price Inflexibility This analysis helps explain why prices are generally stable in noncollusive oligopolistic industries. There are both demand and cost reasons.

On the demand side, the kinked-demand curve gives each oligopolist reason to believe that any change in price will be for the worse. If it raises its price, many of its customers will desert it. If it lowers its price, its sales at best will increase very modestly since rivals will match the lower price. Even if a price cut increases the oligopolist's total revenue somewhat, its costs may increase by a greater amount, depending on demand elasticity. For instance, if its demand is inelastic to the right of Q_0, as it may well be, then the firm's profit will surely fall. A price decrease in the inelastic region lowers the firm's total revenue, and the production of a larger output increases its total costs.

On the cost side, the broken marginal-revenue curve suggests that even if an oligopolist's costs change substantially, the firm may have no reason to change its price. In particular, all positions of the marginal-cost curve between MC_1 and MC_2 in Figure 11.4b will result in the firm's deciding on exactly the same price and output. For all those positions, MR equals MC at output Q_0; at that output, it will charge price P_0.

Criticisms of the Model The kinked-demand analysis has two shortcomings. First, it does not explain how the going price gets to be at P_0 in Figure 11.4 in the first place. It only helps explain why oligopolists tend to stick with an existing price. The kinked-demand curve explains price inflexibility but not price itself.

Second, when the macroeconomy is unstable, oligopoly prices are not as rigid as the kinked-demand theory implies. During inflationary periods, many oligopolists have raised their prices often and substantially. And during downturns (recessions), some oligopolists have cut prices. In some instances these price reductions have set off a **price war:** successive and continuous rounds of price cuts by rivals as they attempt to maintain their market shares.

Cartels and Other Collusion

Our game-theory model demonstrated that oligopolists might benefit from collusion. We can say that collusion occurs whenever firms in an industry reach an agreement to fix prices, divide up the market, or otherwise restrict competition among themselves. The disadvantages and uncertainties of noncollusive, kinked-demand oligopolies are obvious. There is always the danger of a price war breaking out, especially during a general business recession. Then each firm finds that, because of unsold goods and excess capacity, it can reduce per-unit costs by increasing market share. Then, too, a new firm may surmount entry barriers and initiate aggressive price cutting to gain a foothold in the market. In addition, the kinked-demand curve's tendency toward rigid prices may adversely affect profits if general inflationary pressures increase costs. However, by controlling price through collusion, oligopolists may be able to reduce uncertainty, increase profits, and perhaps even prohibit the entry of new rivals.

Price and Output Assume once again that there are three hypothetical oligopolistic firms (Gypsum, Sheetrock, and GSR) producing, in this instance, gypsum drywall panels for finishing interior walls. All three firms produce a homogeneous product and have identical cost curves. Each firm's demand curve is indeterminate unless we know how its rivals will react to any price change. Therefore, we suppose each firm assumes that its two rivals will match either a price cut or a price increase. In other words, each firm has a demand curve like the straight line D_1 in Figure 11.4a. And since they have identical cost data, and the same demand and thus marginal-revenue data, we can say that Figure 11.5 represents the position of each of our three oligopolistic firms.

What price and output combination should, say, Gypsum select? If Gypsum were a pure monopolist, the answer

FIGURE 11.5 Collusion and the tendency toward joint-profit maximization. If oligopolistic firms face identical or highly similar demand and cost conditions, they may collude to limit their joint output and to set a single, common price. Thus each firm acts as if it were a pure monopolist, setting output at Q_0 and charging price P_0. This price and output combination maximizes each oligopolist's profit (green area) and thus the combined or joint profit of the colluding firms.

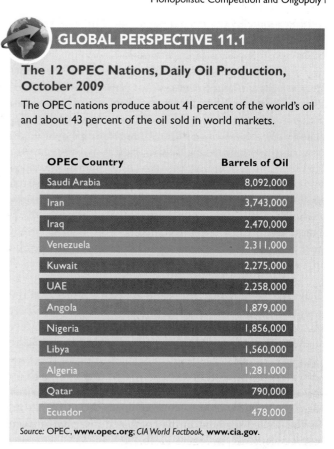

The 12 OPEC Nations, Daily Oil Production, October 2009

The OPEC nations produce about 41 percent of the world's oil and about 43 percent of the oil sold in world markets.

OPEC Country	Barrels of Oil
Saudi Arabia	8,092,000
Iran	3,743,000
Iraq	2,470,000
Venezuela	2,311,000
Kuwait	2,275,000
UAE	2,258,000
Angola	1,879,000
Nigeria	1,856,000
Libya	1,560,000
Algeria	1,281,000
Qatar	790,000
Ecuador	478,000

Source: OPEC, **www.opec.org**; *CIA World Factbook*, **www.cia.gov**.

would be clear: Establish output at Q_0, where marginal revenue equals marginal cost, charge the corresponding price P_0, and enjoy the maximum profit attainable. However, Gypsum does have two rivals selling identical products, and if Gypsum's assumption that its rivals will match its price of P_0 proves to be incorrect, the consequences could be disastrous for Gypsum. Specifically, if Sheetrock and GSR actually charge prices below P_0, then Gypsum's demand curve D will shift sharply to the left as its potential customers turn to its rivals, which are now selling the same product at a lower price. Of course, Gypsum can retaliate by cutting its price too, but this will move all three firms down their demand curves, lowering their profits. It may even drive them to a point where average total cost exceeds price and losses are incurred.

So the question becomes, "Will Sheetrock and GSR want to charge a price below P_0?" Under our assumptions, and recognizing that Gypsum has little choice except to match any price they may set below P_0, the answer is no. Faced with the same demand and cost circumstances, Sheetrock and GSR will find it in their interest to produce Q_0 and charge P_0. This is a curious situation; each firm finds it most profitable to charge the same price, P_0, but only if its rivals actually do so! How can the three firms ensure the price P_0 and quantity Q_0 solution in which each is keenly interested? How can they avoid the less profitable outcomes associated with either higher or lower prices?

The answer is evident: They can collude. They can get together, talk it over, and agree to charge the same price, P_0.

In addition to reducing the possibility of price wars, this will give each firm the maximum profit. (But it will also subject them to antitrust prosecution if they are caught!) For society, the result will be the same as would occur if the industry were a pure monopoly composed of three identical plants.

Overt Collusion: The OPEC Cartel Collusion may assume a variety of forms. The most comprehensive form of collusion is the **cartel**, a group of producers that typically creates a formal written agreement specifying how much each member will produce and charge. Output must be controlled—the market must be divided up—in order to maintain the agreed-upon price. The collusion is overt, or open to view.

Undoubtedly the most significant international cartel is the Organization of Petroleum Exporting Countries (OPEC), comprising 12 oil-producing nations (see Global Perspective 11.1). OPEC produces 41 percent of the world's oil and supplies 43 percent of all oil traded internationally.

OPEC has in some cases been able to drastically alter oil prices by increasing or decreasing supply. In 1973 for instance, it caused the price of oil to more than triple by getting its members to restrict output. And again, in the late 1990s it caused oil prices to rise from $11 per barrel to $34 per barrel over a 15-month period.

That being said, it should be kept in mind that most increases in the price of oil are not caused by OPEC. Between 2005 and 2008, for example, oil prices went from $40 per barrel to $140 per barrel due to rapidly rising demand from China and supply uncertainties related to armed conflict in the Middle East. But as the recession that began in December 2007 took hold, demand slumped and oil prices collapsed back down to about $40 per barrel. OPEC was largely a nonfactor in this rise and fall in the price of oil. But in those cases where OPEC can effectively enforce its production agreements, there is little doubt that it can hold the price of oil substantially above the marginal cost of production.

Covert Collusion: Examples

Cartels are illegal in the United States, and hence any collusion that exists is covert or secret. Yet there are numerous examples, as shown by evidence from antitrust (antimonopoly) cases. In 1993 the Borden, Pet, and Dean food companies, among others, either pleaded guilty to or were convicted of rigging bids on the prices of milk products sold to schools and military bases. By phone or at luncheons, company executives agreed in advance on which firm would submit the low bid for each school district or military base. In 1996 American agribusiness Archer Daniels Midland and three Japanese and South Korean firms were found to have conspired to fix the worldwide price and sales volume of a livestock feed additive. Executives for the firms secretly met in Hong Kong, Paris, Mexico City, Vancouver, and Zurich to discuss their plans.

In many other instances collusion is much subtler. Unwritten, informal understandings (historically called "gentlemen's agreements") are frequently made at cocktail parties, on golf courses, through phone calls, or at trade association meetings. In such agreements, executives reach verbal or even tacit (unspoken) understandings on product price, leaving market shares to be decided by nonprice competition. Although these agreements, too, violate antitrust laws—and can result in severe personal and corporate penalties—the elusive character of informal understandings makes them more difficult to detect.

Obstacles to Collusion

Normally, cartels and similar collusive arrangements are difficult to establish and maintain. Here are several barriers to collusion:

Demand and Cost Differences

When oligopolists face different costs and demand curves, it is difficult for them to agree on a price. This is particularly the case in industries where products are differentiated and change frequently. Even with highly standardized products, firms usually have somewhat different market shares and operate with differing degrees of productive efficiency. Thus it is unlikely that even homogeneous oligopolists would have the same demand and cost curves.

In either case, differences in costs and demand mean that the profit-maximizing price will differ among firms; no single price will be readily acceptable to all, as we assumed was true in Figure 11.5. So price collusion depends on compromises and concessions that are not always easy to obtain and hence act as an obstacle to collusion.

Number of Firms

Other things equal, the larger the number of firms, the more difficult it is to create a cartel or some other form of price collusion. Agreement on price by three or four producers that control an entire market may be relatively easy to accomplish. But such agreement is more difficult to achieve where there are, say, 10 firms, each with roughly 10 percent of the market, or where the Big Three have 70 percent of the market while a competitive fringe of 8 or 10 smaller firms battles for the remainder.

Cheating

As the game-theory model makes clear, collusive oligopolists are tempted to engage in secret price cutting to increase sales and profit. The difficulty with such cheating is that buyers who are paying a high price for a product may become aware of the lower-priced sales and demand similar treatment. Or buyers receiving a price concession from one producer may use the concession as a wedge to get even larger price concessions from a rival producer. Buyers' attempts to play producers against one another may precipitate price wars among the producers. Although secret price concessions are potentially profitable, they threaten collusive oligopolies over time. Collusion is more likely to succeed when cheating is easy to detect and punish. Then the conspirators are less likely to cheat on the price agreement.

Recession

Long-lasting recession usually serves as an enemy of collusion because slumping markets increase average total cost. In technical terms, as the oligopolists' demand and marginal-revenue curves shift to the left in Figure 11.5 in response to a recession, each firm moves leftward and upward to a higher operating point on its average-total-cost curve. Firms find they have substantial excess production capacity, sales are down, unit costs are up, and profits are being squeezed. Under such conditions, businesses may feel they can avoid serious profit reductions (or even losses) by cutting price and thus gaining sales at the expense of rivals.

Potential Entry

The greater prices and profits that result from collusion may attract new entrants, including foreign firms. Since that would increase market supply and reduce prices and profits, successful collusion requires that colluding oligopolists block the entry of new producers.

Legal Obstacles: Antitrust Law U.S. antitrust laws prohibit cartels and price-fixing collusion. So less obvious means of price control have evolved in this country.

Price Leadership Model

Price leadership entails a type of implicit understanding by which oligopolists can coordinate prices without engaging in outright collusion based on formal agreements and secret meetings. Rather, a practice evolves whereby the "dominant firm"—usually the largest or most efficient in the industry—initiates price changes and all other firms more or less automatically follow the leader. Many industries, including farm machinery, cement, copper, newsprint, glass containers, steel, beer, fertilizer, cigarettes, and tin, are practicing, or have in the recent past practiced, price leadership.

Leadership Tactics An examination of price leadership in a variety of industries suggests that the price leader is likely to observe the following tactics.

Infrequent Price Changes Because price changes always carry the risk that rivals will not follow the lead, price adjustments are made only infrequently. The price leader does not respond to minuscule day-to-day changes in costs and demand. Price is changed only when cost and demand conditions have been altered significantly and on an industrywide basis as the result of, for example, industrywide wage increases, an increase in excise taxes, or an increase in the price of some basic input such as energy. In the automobile industry, price adjustments traditionally have been made when new models are introduced each fall.

Communications The price leader often communicates impending price adjustments to the industry through speeches by major executives, trade publication interviews, or press releases. By publicizing "the need to raise prices," the price leader seeks agreement among its competitors regarding the actual increase.

Limit Pricing The price leader does not always choose the price that maximizes short-run profits for the industry because the industry may want to discourage new firms from entering. If the cost advantages (economies of scale) of existing firms are a major barrier to entry, new entrants could surmount that barrier if the price leader and the other firms set product price high enough. New firms that are relatively inefficient because of their small size might survive and grow if the industry sets price very high. So, in

order to discourage new competitors and to maintain the current oligopolistic structure of the industry, the price leader may keep price below the short-run profit-maximizing level. The strategy of establishing a price that blocks the entry of new firms is called *limit pricing*.

Breakdowns in Price Leadership: Price Wars Price leadership in oligopoly occasionally breaks down, at least temporarily, and sometimes results in a price war. An example of price leadership temporarily breaking down occurred in the breakfast cereal industry, in which Kellogg traditionally had been the price leader. General Mills countered Kellogg's leadership in 1995 by reducing the prices of its cereals by 11 percent. In 1996 Post responded with a 20 percent price cut, which Kellogg then followed. Not to be outdone, Post reduced its prices by another 11 percent.

As another example, in October 2009 with the Christmas shopping season just getting underway, Walmart cut its price on 10 highly anticipated new books to just $10 each. Within hours, Amazon.com matched the price cut. Walmart then retaliated by cutting its price for the books to just $9 each. Amazon.com matched that reduction—at which point Walmart went to $8.99! Then, out of nowhere, Target jumped in at $8.98, a price that Amazon.com and Walmart immediately matched. And that is where the price finally came to rest—at a level so low that each company was losing money on each book it sold.

Most price wars eventually run their course. After a period of low or negative profits, they again yield price leadership to one of the industry's leading firms. That firm then begins to raise prices, and the other firms willingly follow suit.

QUICK REVIEW 11.3

- In the kinked-demand theory of oligopoly, price is relatively inflexible because a firm contemplating a price change assumes that its rivals will follow a price cut and ignore a price increase.
- Cartels agree on production limits and set a common price to maximize the joint profit of their members as if each were a unit of a single pure monopoly.
- Collusion among oligopolists is difficult because of (a) demand and cost differences among sellers, (b) the complexity of output coordination among producers, (c) the potential for cheating, (d) a tendency for agreements to break down during recessions, (e) the potential entry of new firms, and (f) antitrust laws.
- Price leadership involves an informal understanding among oligopolists to match any price change initiated by a designated firm (often the industry's dominant firm).

Oligopoly and Advertising

We have noted that oligopolists would rather not compete on the basis of price and may become involved in price collusion. Nonetheless, each firm's share of the total market is typically determined through product development and advertising, for two reasons:

- Product development and advertising campaigns are less easily duplicated than price cuts. Price cuts can be quickly and easily matched by a firm's rivals to cancel any potential gain in sales derived from that strategy. Product improvements and successful advertising, however, can produce more permanent gains in market share because they cannot be duplicated as quickly and completely as price reductions.
- Oligopolists have sufficient financial resources to engage in product development and advertising. For most oligopolists, the economic profits earned in the past can help finance current advertising and product development.

Product development (or, more broadly, "research and development") is the subject of Web Chapter 11, so we will confine our present discussion to advertising. In 2008, firms spent an estimated $137 billion on advertising in the United States and $490 billion worldwide. Advertising is prevalent in both monopolistic competition and oligopoly. Table 11.3 lists the 10 leading U.S. advertisers in 2008.

Advertising may affect prices, competition, and efficiency both positively and negatively, depending on the circumstances. While our focus here is on advertising by oligopolists, the analysis is equally applicable to advertising by monopolistic competitors.

Positive Effects of Advertising

In order to make rational (efficient) decisions, consumers need information about product characteristics and prices. Media advertising may be a low-cost means for consumers to obtain that information. Suppose you are in the market for a high-quality camera that is not advertised or promoted in newspapers, in magazines, or on the Internet. To make a rational choice, you may have to spend several days visiting stores to determine the availability, prices, and features of various brands. This search entails both direct costs (gasoline, parking fees) and indirect costs (the value of your time). By providing information about the available options, advertising and Internet promotion reduce your search time and minimize these direct and indirect costs.

By providing information about the various competing goods that are available, advertising diminishes monopoly power. In fact, advertising is frequently associated with the introduction of new products designed to compete with existing brands. Could Toyota and Honda have so strongly

TABLE 11.3 The Largest U.S. Advertisers, 2008

Company	Advertising Spending Millions of $
Procter & Gamble	$4831
Verizon	3700
AT&T	3073
General Motors	2901
Johnson & Johnson	2529
Unilever	2423
Walt Disney	2218
Time Warner	2208
General Electric	2019
Sears	1865

Source: Advertising Age, **www.adage.com**. Copyright 2010, Crain Communications. 69284-36mpf.

challenged U.S. auto producers without advertising? Could FedEx have sliced market share away from UPS and the U.S. Postal Service without advertising?

Viewed this way, advertising is an efficiency-enhancing activity. It is a relatively inexpensive means of providing useful information to consumers and thus lowering their search costs. By enhancing competition, advertising results in greater economic efficiency. By facilitating the introduction of new products, advertising speeds up technological progress. By increasing sales and output, advertising can reduce long-run average total cost by enabling firms to obtain economies of scale.

Potential Negative Effects of Advertising

Not all the effects of advertising are positive, of course. Much advertising is designed simply to manipulate or persuade consumers—that is, to alter their preferences in favor of the advertiser's product. A television commercial that indicates that a popular personality drinks a particular brand of soft drink—and therefore that you should too—conveys little or no information to consumers about price or quality. In addition, advertising is sometimes based on misleading and extravagant claims that confuse consumers rather than enlighten them. Indeed, in some cases advertising may well persuade consumers to pay high prices for much-acclaimed but inferior products, forgoing better but unadvertised products selling at lower prices. Example: *Consumer Reports* has found that heavily advertised premium motor oils provide no better engine performance and longevity than do cheaper brands.

Firms often establish substantial brand-name loyalty and thus achieve monopoly power via their advertising (see Global Perspective 11.2). As a consequence, they are able to increase their sales, expand their market shares, and enjoy greater profits. Larger profits permit still more advertising and further enlargement of the firm's market share and profit. In time, consumers may lose the advantages of competitive markets and face the disadvantages of monopolized markets. Moreover, new entrants to the industry need to incur large advertising costs in order to establish their products in the marketplace; thus, advertising costs may be a barrier to entry.

Advertising can also be self-canceling. The advertising campaign of one fast-food hamburger chain may be offset by equally costly campaigns waged by rivals, so each firm's demand actually remains unchanged. Few, if any, extra burgers will be purchased and each firm's market share will stay the same. But because of the advertising, all firms will experience higher costs and either their profits will fall or, through successful price leadership, their product prices will rise.

When advertising either leads to increased monopoly power or is self-canceling, economic inefficiency results.

Oligopoly and Efficiency

Is oligopoly, then, an efficient market structure from society's standpoint? How do the price and output decisions of the oligopolist measure up to the triple equality $P = MC =$ minimum ATC that occurs in pure competition?

Productive and Allocative Efficiency

Many economists believe that the outcome of some oligopolistic markets is approximately as shown in Figure 11.5. This view is bolstered by evidence that many oligopolists sustain sizable economic profits year after year. In that case, the oligopolist's production occurs where price exceeds marginal cost and average total cost. Moreover, production is below the output at which average total cost is minimized. In this view, neither productive efficiency ($P =$ minimum ATC) nor allocative efficiency ($P = MC$) is likely to occur under oligopoly.

A few observers assert that oligopoly is actually less desirable than pure monopoly because government usually regulates pure monopoly in the United States to guard against abuses of monopoly power. Informal collusion among oligopolists may yield price and output results similar to those under pure monopoly yet give the outward appearance of competition involving independent firms.

Qualifications

We should note, however, three qualifications to this view:

- **Increased foreign competition** In recent decades foreign competition has increased rivalry in a number of oligopolistic industries—steel, automobiles, video games, electric shavers, outboard motors, and copy machines, for example. This has helped to break down such cozy arrangements as price leadership and to stimulate much more competitive pricing.

- **Limit pricing** Recall that some oligopolists may purposely keep prices below the short-run profit-maximizing level in order to bolster entry barriers. In essence, consumers and society may get some of the benefits of competition—prices closer to marginal cost and minimum average total cost—even without the competition that free entry would provide.

- **Technological advance** Over time, oligopolistic industries may foster more rapid product development and greater improvement of production techniques than would be possible if they were purely competitive. Oligopolists have large economic profits from which they can fund expensive research and development (R&D). Moreover, the existence of barriers to entry may give the oligopolist some assurance that it will reap the rewards of successful R&D. Thus, the short-run economic inefficiencies of oligopolists may be partly or wholly offset by the oligopolists' contributions to better products, lower prices, and lower costs over time. We say more about these dynamic aspects of rivalry in optional Web Chapter 11.

LAST

Word Oligopoly in the Beer Industry

The Beer Industry Was Once Populated by Hundreds of Firms and an Even Larger Number of Brands. But It Now Is an Oligopoly Dominated by a Handful of Producers.

Since the Second World War, profound changes have increased the level of concentration in the U.S. beer industry. In 1947 more than 400 independent brewing companies operated in the United States. By 1967, the number had declined to 124 and by 1980 it had dropped to just 33. In 1947 the largest five brewers sold only 19 percent of the nation's beer. In 2007, the Big Three brewers (Anheuser-Busch, SABMiller, and Molson Coors) sold 76 percent. In 2007, Anheuser-Busch (48 percent) and SABMiller (18 percent) alone combined for 66 percent of industry sales. And, in late 2007, SABMiller acquired the U.S. operations of Molson Coors, thus creating MillerCoors and turning the Big Three into the Big Two. In 2008, Belgian brewer InBev purchased Anheuser-Busch, thereby forming international brewing giant A-B. The U.S. beer industry clearly meets all the criteria of oligopoly.

Changes on the demand side of the market have contributed to the "shakeout" of small brewers from the industry. First, consumer tastes in the mass market have generally shifted from the stronger-flavored beers of the small brewers to the light products of the larger brewers. Second, there has been a shift from the consumption of beer in taverns to consumption of it in the home. The beer consumed in taverns was mainly "draft" or "tap" beer from kegs, supplied by local and regional brewers that could deliver the kegs in a timely fashion at relatively low transportation cost. But the large increase in the demand for beer consumed at home opened the door for large brewers that sold their beer in bottles and aluminum cans. The large brewers could ship their beer by truck or rail over long distances and compete directly with the local brewers.

Developments on the supply side of the market have been even more profound. Technological advances speeded up the bottling and canning lines. Today, large brewers can fill and close 2000 cans per line per minute. Large plants are also able to reduce labor costs through the automating of brewing and warehousing. Furthermore, plant construction costs per barrel of production capacity are about one-third less for a 4.5-million-barrel plant than for a 1.5-million-barrel plant. As a consequence of these and other factors, the minimum efficient scale in brewing is a plant size of about 4.5 million barrels. Additionally, studies indicate that further cost savings are available to brewing firms that have two or more separate large breweries in different regions of the country. Between the economies of scale from plant size and these cost savings from multiple plants, cost considerations deter entry to the mainline beer industry.

"Blindfold" taste tests confirm that most mass-produced American beers taste alike. Undaunted, brewers spend large amounts of money touting the supposed differences between their brands in order to build brand loyalty. And here Anheuser-Busch and MillerCoors, which sell national brands, enjoy major cost advantages over producers such as Pabst that have many regional brands (for example, Lone Star, Rainier, Schaefer, and Schmidt). The reason is that national television advertising is less costly per viewer than local TV advertising.

Up until the recent combination of Molson Coors and SABMiller, mergers had not been the dominant factor in explaining the industry consolidation. Rather, that was largely caused by failing smaller breweries (such as Heileman's) selling their assets and brands to competitors. Dominant firms have

Summary

1. The distinguishing features of monopolistic competition are (a) there are enough firms in the industry to ensure that each firm has only limited control over price, mutual interdependence is absent, and collusion is nearly impossible; (b) products are characterized by real or perceived differences so that economic rivalry entails both price and non-price competition; and (c) entry to the industry is relatively easy. Many aspects of retailing, and some manufacturing industries in which economies of scale are few, approximate monopolistic competition.

2. The four-firm concentration ratio measures the percentage of total industry output accounted for by the largest four firms. The Herfindahl index sums the squares of the percent market shares of all firms in the industry.

expanded by heavily advertising their main brands and by creating new brands such as Lite, Bud Light, Genuine Draft, Keystone Light, and Icehouse rather than acquiring other brewers. This has sustained significant product differentiation, despite the declining number of major brewers.

The rise of the Miller Brewing Company from the seventh- to the second-largest producer in the 1970s was due in large measure to advertising and product differentiation. When the Philip Morris Company acquired Miller in 1970, the new management made two big changes. First, it "repositioned" Miller High Life beer into that segment of the market where potential sales were the greatest. Sold previously as the "champagne of beers," High Life had appealed heavily to upper-income consumers and to occasional women beer drinkers. Miller's new television ads featured young blue-collar workers, who were known to be larger consumers of beer. Second, Miller then developed its low-calorie Lite beer, which was extensively promoted with Philip Morris advertising dollars. Lite proved to be the most popular new product in the history of the beer industry. Miller later introduced its Genuine Draft beer, which found its place within the top 10 brands.

But the story of the last three decades has been Anheuser-Busch InBev, (A-B), which has greatly expanded its market share. A-B now makes the nation's top two brands: Bud Light and Budweiser account for nearly half the beer sold in the United States. Part of A-B's success owes to the demise of regional competitors. But part also is the result of A-B's competitive prowess. It has constructed state-of-the-art breweries, created effective advertising campaigns, and forged strong relationships with regional distributors. Meanwhile, Miller's market share has declined slightly in recent years. In 2002 Philip Morris sold Miller to London-based SAB. SABMiller, as the combined firm was called, significantly redesigned Miller's labeling and marketing to enhance its appeal both domestically and overseas. Perhaps of greater importance, SABMiller's acquisition of Coors to form MillerCoors immediately expanded its U.S. market share from 18 percent to 29 percent. MillerCoors thus became the number two brewer in the United States after A-B, which controls 49 percent of the market.

Imported beers such as Heineken, Corona, and Guinness constitute about 15 percent of the market, with individual brands seeming to wax and wane in popularity. Some local or regional microbreweries such as Samuel Adams and Pyramid, which brew "craft" or specialty beers and charge super-premium prices, have whittled into the sales of the major brewers. Craft and specialty beers account for only 6 percent of beer consumed in the United States, but they are the fastest-growing segment of the U.S. industry. A-B, Miller, and Coors have taken notice, responding with specialty brands of their own (for example, Red Wolf, Red Dog, Killarney's Red Lager, Icehouse, and Blue Moon) and by buying stakes in microbrewers Redhook Ale and Celis.

Sources: Based on Kenneth G. Elzinga, "Beer," in Walter Adams and James Brock (eds.), *The Structure of American Industry*, 10th ed. (Upper Saddle River, N.J.: Prentice Hall, 2001), pp. 85–113; and Douglas F. Greer, "Beer: Causes of Structural Change," in Larry Duetsch (ed.), *Industry Studies*, 2d ed. (New York: M. E. Sharpe, 1998), pp. 28–64. Updated data and information are mainly from *Beer Marketer's Insights*, **www.beerinsights.com**, and the Association of Brewers, **www.beertown.com**.

3. Monopolistically competitive firms may earn economic profits or incur losses in the short run. The easy entry and exit of firms results in only normal profits in the long run.

4. The long-run equilibrium position of the monopolistically competitive producer is less efficient than that of the pure competitor. Under monopolistic competition, price exceeds marginal cost, indicating an underallocation of resources to the product, and price exceeds minimum average total cost, indicating that consumers do not get the product at the lowest price that cost conditions might allow.

5. Nonprice competition provides a way that monopolistically competitive firms can offset the long-run tendency for economic profit to fall to zero. Through product differentiation, product development, and advertising, a firm may

strive to increase the demand for its product more than enough to cover the added cost of such nonprice competition. Consumers benefit from the wide diversity of product choice that monopolistic competition provides.

6. In practice, the monopolistic competitor seeks the specific combination of price, product, and advertising that will maximize profit.

7. Oligopolistic industries are characterized by the presence of few firms, each having a significant fraction of the market. Firms thus situated engage in strategic behavior and are mutually interdependent: The behavior of any one firm directly affects, and is affected by, the actions of rivals. Products may be either virtually uniform or significantly differentiated. Various barriers to entry, including economies of scale, underlie and maintain oligopoly.

8. High concentration ratios are an indication of oligopoly (monopoly) power. By giving more weight to larger firms, the Herfindahl index is designed to measure market dominance in an industry.

9. Game theory (a) shows the interdependence of oligopolists' pricing policies, (b) reveals the tendency of oligopolists to collude, and (c) explains the temptation of oligopolists to cheat on collusive arrangements.

10. Noncollusive oligopolists may face a kinked-demand curve. This curve and the accompanying marginal-revenue curve help explain the price rigidity that often characterizes oligopolies; they do not, however, explain how the actual prices of products were first established.

11. The uncertainties inherent in oligopoly promote collusion. Collusive oligopolists such as cartels maximize joint profits—

that is, they behave like pure monopolists. Demand and cost differences, a "large" number of firms, cheating through secret price concessions, recessions, and the antitrust laws are all obstacles to collusive oligopoly.

12. Price leadership is an informal means of collusion whereby one firm, usually the largest or most efficient, initiates price changes and the other firms in the industry follow the leader.

13. Market shares in oligopolistic industries are usually determined on the basis of product development and advertising. Oligopolists emphasize nonprice competition because (a) advertising and product variations are less easy for rivals to match and (b) oligopolists frequently have ample resources to finance nonprice competition.

14. Advertising may affect prices, competition, and efficiency either positively or negatively. Positive: It can provide consumers with low-cost information about competing products, help introduce new competing products into concentrated industries, and generally reduce monopoly power and its attendant inefficiencies. Negative: It can promote monopoly power via persuasion and the creation of entry barriers. Moreover, it can be self-canceling when engaged in by rivals; then it boosts costs and creates inefficiency while accomplishing little else.

15. Neither productive nor allocative efficiency is realized in oligopolistic markets, but oligopoly may be superior to pure competition in promoting research and development and technological progress.

16. Table 8.1, page 164, provides a concise review of the characteristics of monopolistic competition and oligopoly as they compare to those of pure competition and pure monopoly.

Terms and Concepts

monopolistic competition	homogeneous oligopoly	collusion
product differentiation	differentiated oligopoly	kinked-demand curve
nonprice competition	strategic behavior	price war
four-firm concentration ratio	mutual interdependence	cartel
Herfindahl index	interindustry competition	price leadership
excess capacity	import competition	
oligopoly	game theory	

Questions

1. How does monopolistic competition differ from pure competition in its basic characteristics? From pure monopoly? Explain fully what product differentiation may involve. Explain how the entry of firms into its industry affects the demand curve facing a monopolistic competitor and how that, in turn, affects its economic profit. LO1

2. Compare the elasticity of a monopolistic competitor's demand with that of a pure competitor and a pure monopolist. Assuming identical long-run costs, compare graphically the prices and outputs that would result in the long run under pure competition and under monopolistic competition. Contrast the two market structures in terms of productive

and allocative efficiency. Explain: "Monopolistically competitive industries are populated by too many firms, each of which produces too little." **LO2**

3. "Monopolistic competition is monopolistic up to the point at which consumers become willing to buy close-substitute products and competitive beyond that point." Explain. **LO2**

4. "Competition in quality and service may be just as effective as price competition in giving buyers more for their money." Do you agree? Why? Explain why monopolistically competitive firms frequently prefer nonprice competition to price competition. **LO2**

5. Critically evaluate and explain: **LO2**
   a. In monopolistically competitive industries, economic profits are competed away in the long run; hence, there is no valid reason to criticize the performance and efficiency of such industries.
   b. In the long run, monopolistic competition leads to a monopolistic price but not to monopolistic profits.

6. Why do oligopolies exist? List five or six oligopolists whose products you own or regularly purchase. What distinguishes oligopoly from monopolistic competition? **LO3**

7. Answer the following questions, which relate to measures of concentration: **LO3**
   a. What is the meaning of a four-firm concentration ratio of 60 percent? 90 percent? What are the shortcomings of concentration ratios as measures of monopoly power?
   b. Suppose that the five firms in industry A have annual sales of 30, 30, 20, 10, and 10 percent of total industry sales. For the five firms in industry B, the figures are 60, 25, 5, 5, and 5 percent. Calculate the Herfindahl index for each industry and compare their likely competitiveness.

8. Explain the general meaning of the profit payoff matrix at the top of the next column for oligopolists X and Y. All profit figures are in thousands. **LO4**
   a. Use the payoff matrix to explain the mutual interdependence that characterizes oligopolistic industries.
   b. Assuming no collusion between X and Y, what is the likely pricing outcome?
   c. In view of your answer to 8b, explain why price collusion is mutually profitable. Why might there be a temptation to cheat on the collusive agreement?

X's Possible prices

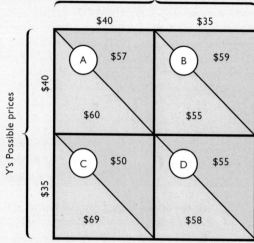

9. What assumptions about a rival's response to price changes underlie the kinked-demand curve for oligopolists? Why is there a gap in the oligopolists' marginal-revenue curve? How does the kinked-demand curve explain price rigidity in oligopoly? What are the shortcomings of the kinked-demand model? **LO5**

10. Why might price collusion occur in oligopolistic industries? Assess the economic desirability of collusive pricing. What are the main obstacles to collusion? Speculate as to why price leadership is legal in the United States, whereas price-fixing is not. **LO6**

11. Why is there so much advertising in monopolistic competition and oligopoly? How does such advertising help consumers and promote efficiency? Why might it be excessive at times? **LO7**

12. **ADVANCED ANALYSIS** Construct a game-theory matrix involving two firms and their decisions on high versus low advertising budgets and the effects of each on profits. Show a circumstance in which both firms select high advertising budgets even though both would be more profitable with low advertising budgets. Why won't they unilaterally cut their advertising budgets? **LO7**

13. **LAST WORD** What firm dominates the U.S. beer industry? What demand and supply factors have contributed to "fewness" in this industry?

Problems

1. Suppose that a small town has seven burger shops whose respective shares of the local hamburger market are (as percentages of all hamburgers sold): 23%, 22%, 18%, 12%, 11%, 8%, and 6%. What is the four-firm concentration ratio of the hamburger industry in this town? What is the Herfindahl index for the hamburger industry in this town?

If the top three sellers combined to form a single firm, what would happen to the four-firm concentration ratio and to the Herfindahl index? **LO3**

2. Suppose that the most popular car dealer in your area sells 10 percent of all vehicles. If all other car dealers sell either the same number of vehicles or fewer, what is the largest

value that the Herfindahl index could possibly take for car dealers in your area? In that same situation, what would the four-firm concentration ratio be? **LO3**

3. Suppose that an oligopolistically competitive restaurant is currently serving 230 meals per day (the output where MR = MC). At that output level, ATC per meal is $10 and consumers are willing to pay $12 per meal. What is the size of this firm's profit or loss? Will there be entry or exit? Will this restaurant's demand curve shift left or right? In long-run equilibrium, suppose that this restaurant charges $11 per meal for 180 meals and that the marginal cost of the 180th meal is $8. What is the size of the firm's profit? Suppose that the allocatively efficient output level in long-run equilibrium is 200 meals. Is the deadweight loss for this firm greater than or less than $60? **LO3**

FURTHER TEST YOUR KNOWLEDGE AT
www.mcconnell19e.com

At the text's Online Learning Center (OLC), **www.mcconnell19e.com**, you will find one or more Web-based questions that require information from the Internet to answer. We urge you to check them out; they will familiarize you with Web sites that may be helpful in other courses and perhaps even in your career. The OLC also features multiple-choice questions that give instant feedback and provides other helpful ways to further test your knowledge of the chapter.

Additional Game Theory Applications

We have seen that game theory is helpful in explaining mutual interdependence and strategic behavior by oligopolists. This appendix provides additional oligopoly-based applications of game theory.

A One-Time Game: Strategies and Equilibrium

Consider Figure 1, which lists strategies and outcomes for two fictitious producers of the computer memory chips referred to as DRAMs (Dynamic Random Access Memory circuits). Chipco is the single producer of these chips in the United States and Dramco is the only producer in China. Each firm has two alternative strategies: an international strategy, in which it competes directly against the other firm in both countries; and a national strategy, in which it sells only in its home country.

The game and payoff matrix shown in Figure 1 is a **one-time game** because the firms select their optimal strategies in a single time period without regard to possible interactions in subsequent time periods. The game is also a **simultaneous game** because the firms choose their

strategies at the same time; and a **positive-sum game**, a game in which the sum of the two firms' outcomes (here, profits) is positive. In contrast, the net gain in a **zero-sum game** is zero because one firm's gain must equal the other firm's loss, and the net gain in a **negative-sum game** is negative. In some positive-sum games, both firms may have positive outcomes. That is the case in Figure 1.

To determine optimal strategies, Chipco looks across the two rows in the payoff matrix (yellow portion of cells in millions of dollars) and Dramco looks down the two columns (blue portion of cells). These payoffs indicate that both firms have a **dominant strategy**—an option that is better than any alternative option *regardless of what the other firm does*. To see this, notice that Chipco's international strategy will give it a higher profit than its national strategy—regardless of whether Dramco chooses to utilize an international or a national strategy. An international strategy will produce an $11 million profit for Chipco (yellow portion of cell A) if Dramco also uses an international strategy while a national strategy will result in a $20 million profit for Chipco (yellow portion of cell B) if Dramco uses a national strategy. Chipco's possible $11 million and $20 million outcomes are clearly better than the $5 million (cell C) and $17 million (cell D) outcomes it could receive if it chose to pursue a national strategy. Chipco's international strategy is, consequently, its dominant strategy. Using similar logic, Dramco also concludes that its international strategy is its dominant strategy.

In this particular case, the outcome (cell A) of the two dominant strategies is the game's **Nash equilibrium**—an outcome from which neither rival wants to deviate.[1] At the Nash equilibrium, both rivals see their current strategy as optimal *given the other firm's strategic choice*. The Nash equilibrium is the only outcome in the payoff matrix in Figure 1 that, once achieved, is stable and therefore will persist.[2]

Credible and Empty Threats

In looking for optimal strategies, Chipco and Dramco both note that they could increase their profit from $11 million to $17 million if they could agree to jointly pursue national strategies (cell D) instead of independently

FIGURE 1 A One-Time Game In this single-period, positive-sum game, Chipco's international strategy is its dominant strategy—the alternative that is superior to any other strategy regardless of whatever Dramco does. Similarly, Dramco's international strategy is also its dominant strategy. With both firms choosing international strategies, the outcome of the game is Cell A, where each firm receives an $11 million profit. Cell A is a Nash equilibrium because neither firm will independently want to move away from it given the other firm's strategy.

Dramco's strategies

	International	National
Chipco's strategies — International	A $11 / $11	B $5 / $20
Chipco's strategies — National	C $20 / $5	D $17 / $17

[1]The Nash equilibrium is named for its discoverer, John F. Nash. Nash's life and Nobel Prize are the subject of the motion picture *A Beautiful Mind*, directed by Ron Howard and starring Russell Crowe.

[2]Nash equilibriums can exist even in games that lack dominant strategies.

pursuing international strategies (cell A). Presumably the national strategies would leave the firms as pure monopolists in their domestic economies, with each able to set higher prices and obtain greater profits as a result. But if this territorial agreement were put in place, both firms would have an incentive to cheat on the agreement by secretly selling DRAMs in the other's country. That would temporarily move the game to either cell B or cell C. Once discovered, however, such cheating would undermine the territorial agreement and return the game to the Nash equilibrium (cell A).

Now let's add a new twist—a credible threat—to the game shown in Figure 1. A **credible threat** is a statement of coercion (a threat!) that is believable by the other firm. Suppose that Chipco is the lower-cost producer of DRAMs because of its superior technology. Also, suppose that Chipco approaches Dramco saying that Chipco intends to use its national strategy and expects Dramco to do the same. If Dramco decides against the national strategy or agrees to the strategy and then later cheats on the agreement, Chipco will immediately drop its price to an ultra-low level equal to its average total cost (ATC). Both firms know that Chipco's ATC price is below Dramco's ATC. Although Chipco will see its economic profit fall to zero, Dramco will suffer an economic loss and possibly go out of business.

If Chipco's threat is credible, the two firms represented in Figure 1 will abandon the Nash equilibrium (cell A) to deploy their national strategies and achieve highly profitable cell D. In game theory, credible threats such as this can help establish and maintain collusive agreements. A strong "enforcer" can help prevent cheating and maintain the group discipline needed for cartels, price-fixing conspiracies, and territorial understandings to successfully generate high profits.

But credible threats are difficult to achieve in the actual economy. For example, Dramco might rightly wonder why Chipco had not previously driven it out of business through an ultra-low price strategy. Is Chipco fearful of the U.S. antitrust authorities?

If Dramco does not wish to participate in the proposed scheme, it might counter Chipco's threat with its own: Forget that you ever talked to us and we will not take this illegal "offer" to the U.S. Justice Department. Dramco can make this threat because strict laws are in place against attempts to restrain trade through price-fixing and territorial agreements.

So Dramco may view Chipco's threat as simply an **empty threat**—a statement of coercion that is not believable by the threatened firm. If so, the Nash equilibrium will prevail, with both firms pursuing an international strategy.

Repeated Games and Reciprocity Strategies

The Chipco-Dramco game was a one-time game, but many strategic situations are repeated by the same oligopolists over and over again. For example, Coca Cola and Pepsi are mutually interdependent on pricing, advertising, and product development year after year, decade after decade. The same is true for Boeing and Airbus, Walmart and Target, Toyota and General Motors, Budweiser and Miller, Nike and Adidas, and numerous other dominant pairs.

In a **repeated game**—a game that recurs more than once—the optimal strategy may be to cooperate and restrain oneself from competing as hard as possible so long as the other firm reciprocates by also not competing as hard as possible.[3] To see how this works, consider two hypothetical producers of soft drinks: 2Cool and ThirstQ. If ThirstQ competes hard with 2Cool in today's situation in which 2Cool would like ThirstQ to take things easy, 2Cool will most likely retaliate against ThirstQ in any subsequent situation where the circumstances are reversed. In contrast, if ThirstQ cooperates with 2Cool in game 1, ThirstQ can expect 2Cool to reciprocate in game 2 of their repeated interaction. Both firms know full well the negative long-run consequences of ever refusing to cooperate. So the cooperation continues, not only in game 2, but in games 3, 4, 5, and beyond.

Figure 2 shows two side-by-side payoff matrixes for the two games. In Figure 2a, 2Cool and ThirstQ face a situation in which 2Cool is introducing a new cola called Cool Cola and has two advertising options: a high promotional budget to introduce the new product and a normal advertising budget. ThirstQ has the same two options: a high promotional budget to try to counter 2Cool's product introduction and a normal advertising budget.

The analysis is now familiar to you. The dominant strategies for both firms in game 1 (Figure 2a) are their large promotional advertising budgets and the Nash equilibrium is cell A. Both firms could do better at cell D if each agreed to use normal advertising budgets. But 2Cool could do better still. It could achieve the $16 million of profit in cell B, but only if ThirstQ holds its advertising budget to its normal level during the introduction of Cool Cola.

ThirstQ might voluntarily do just that! It knows that game 2 (Figure 2b) is forthcoming in which it will be introducing its new product, Quench It. By leaving its

---

[3]We are assuming either an infinitely repeated game or a game of unknown time-horizon. Games with a known ending date undermine reciprocity strategies.

FIGURE 2 A Repeated Game with Reciprocity (a) in the payoff matrix to the left, 2Cool introduces its new Cool Cola with a large promotional advertising budget, but its rival ThirstQ maintains its normal advertising budget even though it could counter 2Cool with a large advertising budget of its own and drive the outcome from Cell B to Cell A. ThirstQ forgoes this $2 million of extra profit because it knows that it will soon be introducing its own new product (Quench It). (b) In the payoff matrix to the right, ThirstQ introduces Quench It with a large promotional advertising budget. Cool2 reciprocates ThirstQ's earlier accommodation by not matching ThirstQ's promotional advertising budget and instead allowing the outcome of the repeated game to be Cell C. The profit of both 2Cool and ThirstQ therefore is larger over the two periods than if each firm had aggressively countered each other's single-period strategy.

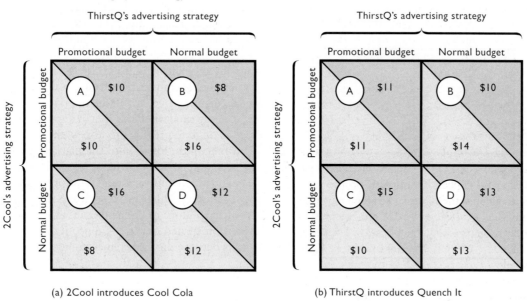

(a) 2Cool introduces Cool Cola

(b) ThirstQ introduces Quench It

advertising budget at its normal level during 2Cool's introduction of Cool Cola, and thereby sacrificing profit of $2 million (= $10 million in cell A − $8 million in cell B), ThirstQ can expect 2Cool to reciprocate in the subsequent game in which ThirstQ introduces Quench It. Without formally colluding—and risking antitrust penalties—game 1 ends at cell B and repeated game 2 ends at cell C. With reciprocity, 2Cool's total profit of $26 million (= $16 million in game 1 + $10 million in game 2) exceeds the $21 million (= $10 million + $11 million) it would have earned without the reciprocity. ThirstQ similarly benefits. To check your understanding, confirm this fact using the numbers in the two matrixes.

First-Mover Advantages and Preemption of Entry

The games we have highlighted thus far have been games in which the two firms simultaneously select their optimal strategies. But in some actual economic circumstances, firms apply strategies sequentially: One firm moves first and commits to a strategy to which a rival firm must subsequently respond. In such a **sequential game,** the final outcome may depend critically upon which firm

moves first since the first mover may have the opportunity to establish a Nash equilibrium that works in its favor.

Consider Figure 3, which identifies a game in which two large retailers—let's call them Big Box and Huge Box—are each considering building a large retail store in a small rural city. As indicated in the figure, each firm has two strategies: build or don't build. The payoff matrix reflects the fact that the city is not large enough to support two big box retailers profitably. If both retailers simultaneously build, the outcome will be cell A and each firm will lose $5 million. If neither firm builds, the outcome will be cell D with both firms securing zero profit. If only Big Box builds, the outcome will be cell C and Big Box will profit handsomely at $12 million. If Huge Box builds, but Big Box stays out, the outcome will be cell B and Huge Box will secure the $12 million profit. Either cell B or cell C is the possible Nash equilibrium. At either cell, both firms will have selected their best option in view of the strategy taken by the other firm.

The payoff matrix in Figure 3 clearly reveals that whoever builds first will preempt the other retailer from entering the market. An extremely large **first-mover advantage** exists in this particular game. Suppose that a well-thought-out strategy and adequate financing leave Big Box better prepared than Huge Box to move quickly to

FIGURE 3 **A First-Mover Advantage and the Preemption of Entry** In this game in which strategies are pursued sequentially, the firm that moves first can take advantage of the particular situation represented in which only a single firm can exist profitably in some geographical market. Here, we suppose that Big Box moves first with its "Build" strategy to achieve the $12 million profit outcome in Cell C. Huge Box then will find that it will lose money if it also builds because that will result in a $5 million loss, as shown in Cell A.

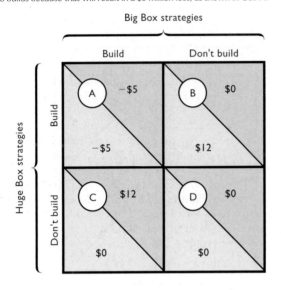

build a large retail store in this city. By exploiting its first-mover advantage, Big Box drives the outcome to Cell C and preempts Huge Box's entry into this market.

Many firms in the actual economy have used variations of this first-mover strategy to a greater or lesser extent to preempt major rivals, or at least greatly slow their entry. Examples are Walmart, Home Depot, Costco, Walgreens, Starbucks, and many more. The strategy, however, is highly risky because it requires the commitment of huge amounts of investment funds to saturate the market and preclude entry by other firms. Also, to be the first-mover in places that are being transformed from rural land into urban areas, firms may need to build their stores many months prior to the time when the area in question becomes developed enough to provide the store with significant business. That may mean losses until the market grows sufficiently for profitability. Some firms such as Walmart have become huge, profitable international enterprises by using a first-mover strategy. Other firms, such as Krispy Kreme Donuts, have lost millions of dollars because their extremely rapid expansion turned out to be unprofitable in many of their outlets because the expected customers never materialized.

Appendix Summary

1. Positive-sum games are games in which the payoffs to the firms sum to a positive number; zero-sum games are games in which the payoffs sum to zero; and negative-sum games are games in which the payoffs sum to less than zero. Positive-sum games allow for "win-win" opportunities, whereas zero-sum games always feature "I win-you lose" outcomes. Games can be either one-time games or repeated games. Decisions in games may be made either simultaneously or sequentially.

2. When two firms are playing a strategic game, a firm is said to have a dominant strategy if there is an option that leads to better outcomes than all other options regardless of what the other firm does. Not all games have dominant strategies. The Nash equilibrium is an outcome from which neither firm wants to deviate because both firms see their current strategy as optimal given the other firm's chosen strategy. The Nash equilibrium is stable and persistent. Attempts by the firms to rig games to achieve some other outcome are difficult to accomplish and maintain, although

credible threats can sometimes work. In contrast, empty threats accomplish nothing and leave the outcome at the Nash equilibrium.

3. Reciprocity can improve outcomes for firms participating in repeated games. In such games, one firm avoids taking advantage of the other firm because it knows that the other firm can take advantage of it in subsequent games. This reciprocity increases firm profits relative to what they would have been without reciprocity.

4. Two possible Nash equilibriums can exist in sequential games with first-mover advantages. Which one occurs depends on which firm moves first since that firm can preempt the other firm, making it unprofitable for the other firm to match the move. Several real-world firms, including Walmart, have successfully used first-mover advantages to saturate markets and preempt entry by rivals.

Appendix Terms and Concepts

one-time game

simultaneous game

positive-sum game

zero-sum game

negative-sum game

dominant strategy

Nash equilibrium

credible threat

empty threat

repeated game

sequential game

first-mover advantage

Appendix Questions ![Mc Graw Hill] connect™ | ECONOMICS

1. Is the game shown by Figure 11.3 in the chapter (not this appendix) a zero-sum game or is it a positive-sum game? How can you tell? Are there dominant strategies in this game? If so, what are they? What cell represents a Nash equilibrium and why? Explain why it is so difficult for Uptown and RareAir to achieve and maintain a more favorable cell than the Nash equilibrium in this single-period pricing game. **LO8**

2. Refer to the payoff matrix in question 8 at the end of this chapter. First, assume this is a one-time game. Explain how the $60/$57 outcome might be achieved through a credible threat. Next, assume this is a repeated game (rather than a one-time game) and that the interaction between the two firms occurs indefinitely. Why might collusion with a credible threat not be necessary to achieve the $60/$57 outcome? **LO8**

3. Refer to the payoff matrix below. **LO8**

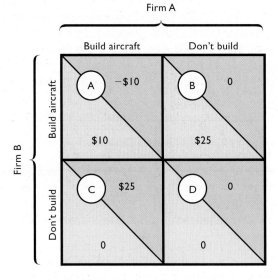

Firm A

Assuming this is a sequential game with no collusion, what is the outcome if Firm A moves first to build a new type of commercial aircraft? Explain why first-mover strategies in the real world are only as good as the profit projections on which they are based. How could a supposed "win" from moving first turn out to be a big loss, whereas the "loss" of being preempted turn out to be a blessing in disguise?

4. **ADVANCED** Suppose you are playing a game in which you and one other person each pick a number between 1 and 100, with the person closest to some randomly selected number between 1 and 100 winning the jackpot. (Ask your instructor to fund the jackpot.) Your opponent picks first. What number do you expect her to choose? Why? What number would you then pick? Why are the two numbers so close? How might this example relate to why Home Depot and Lowes, Walgreens and Rite-Aid, McDonald's and Burger King, Borders and Barnes & Noble, and other major pairs of rivals locate so close to each other in many well-defined geographical markets that are large enough for both firms to be profitable? **LO8**

Appendix Problems

1. Consider a "punishment" variation of the two-firm oligopoly situation shown in Figure 11.3 in the chapter (not in this appendix). Suppose that if one firm sets a low price while the other sets a high price, then the firm setting the high price can fine the firm setting the low price. Suppose that whenever a fine is imposed, X dollars is taken from the low-price firm and given to the high-price firm. What is the smallest amount that the fine X can be such that both firms will want to always set the high price? **LO8**

2. Consider whether the promises and threats made toward each other by duopolists and oligopolists are always credible (believable). Look back at Figure 11.3 in the chapter (not in this appendix). Imagine that the two firms will play this game twice in sequence and that each firm claims the following policy. Each says that if both it and the other firm choose the high price in the first game, then it will also choose the high price in the second game (as a reward to the other firm for cooperating in the first game). **LO8**

   a. As a first step toward thinking about whether this policy is credible, consider the situation facing both firms in the second game. If each firm bases its decision on what to do in the second game entirely on the payouts facing the firms in the second game, which strategy will each firm choose in the second game?

   b. Now move backward in time one step. Imagine that it is the start of the first game and each firm must decide what to do during the first game. Given your answer to 2a, is the publicly stated policy credible? (Hint: No matter what happens in the first game, what will both firms do in the second game?)

   c. Given your answers to 2a and 2b, what strategy will each firm choose in the first game?

AFTER READING THIS CHAPTER, YOU SHOULD BE ABLE TO:

1 Differentiate between an invention, an innovation, and technological diffusion.

2 Explain how entrepreneurs and other innovators further technological advance.

3 Summarize how a firm determines its optimal amount of research and development (R&D).

4 Relate why firms can benefit from their innovation even though rivals have an incentive to imitate it.

5 Discuss the role of market structure in promoting technological advance.

6 Show how technological advance enhances productive efficiency and allocative efficiency.

Technology, R&D, and Efficiency

Web Chapter 11 is a bonus chapter found at the book's Web site, **www.mcconnell19e.com**. It extends the analysis of Part 3, "Microeconomics of Product Markets," by examining such topics as invention, innovation, R&D decision making, and creative destruction. Your instructor may (or may not) assign all or part of this chapter.

PART SIX

18 ANTITRUST POLICY AND REGULATION

19 AGRICULTURE: ECONOMICS AND POLICY

20 INCOME INEQUALITY, POVERTY, AND
    DISCRIMINATION

21 HEALTH CARE

22 IMMIGRATION

MICROECONOMIC ISSUES AND POLICIES

18

1 **List and explain the core elements of the major antitrust (antimonopoly) laws in the United States.**

2 **Describe some of the key issues relating to the interpretation and application of antitrust laws.**

3 **Identify and explain the economic principles and difficulties relating to the setting of prices (rates) charged by so-called natural monopolies.**

4 **Discuss the nature of "social regulation," its benefits and costs, and its optimal level.**

Antitrust Policy and Regulation

We now can apply the economics of product markets (Part 3), resource markets (Part 4), and government (Part 5) to selected microeconomic issues and policies.

In this chapter we look at three sets of government policies toward business: antitrust policy, industrial regulation, and social regulation. **Antitrust policy** consists of laws and government actions designed to prevent monopoly and promote competition. **Industrial regulation** pertains to government regulation of firms' prices (or "rates") within selected industries. **Social regulation** is government regulation of the conditions under which goods are produced, the physical characteristics of goods, and the impact of the production and consumption of goods on society.

Then, in the remaining four chapters of Part 6, we discuss issues and policies relating to agriculture, income inequality, health care, and immigration.

The Antitrust Laws

The underlying purpose of antitrust policy (antimonopoly policy) is to prevent monopolization, promote competition, and achieve allocative efficiency. Although all economists would agree that these are meritorious goals, there is sharp conflict of opinion about the appropriateness and effectiveness of U.S. antitrust policy. As we will see, antitrust policy over the years has been neither clear-cut nor consistent.

Historical Background

Just after the U.S. Civil War (1861–1865), local markets widened into national markets because of improved transportation facilities, mechanized production methods, and sophisticated corporate structures. In the 1870s and 1880s, dominant firms formed in several industries, including petroleum, meatpacking, railroads, sugar, lead, coal, whiskey, and tobacco. Some of these oligopolists, near-monopolists, or monopolists were known as *trusts*—business combinations that assign control to a single decision group ("trustees"). Because these trusts "monopolized" industries, the word "trust" became synonymous with "monopoly" in common usage. The public, government, and historians began to define a business monopoly as a large-scale dominant seller, even though that seller was not always "a sole seller" as specified in the model of pure monopoly.

These dominant firms often used questionable tactics in consolidating their industries and then charged high prices to customers and extracted price concessions from resource suppliers. Farmers and owners of small businesses were particularly vulnerable to the power of large corporate monopolies and were among the first to oppose them. Consumers, labor unions, and economists were not far behind in their opposition.

The main economic case against monopoly is familiar to you from Chapter 10. Monopolists tend to produce less output and charge higher prices than would be the case if their industries were competitive. With pure competition, each competitive firm maximizes profit by producing the output level at which $P = MC$. That output level generates allocative efficiency because price P measures the marginal benefit to society of an extra unit of output while marginal cost MC reflects the cost of an extra unit. When $P = MC$, society cannot gain by producing 1 more or 1 less unit of the product. In contrast, a monopolist maximizes profit by producing the lower output level at which marginal revenue (rather than price) equals marginal cost. At this MR = MC point, price exceeds marginal cost, meaning that society would obtain more benefit than it would incur cost by producing extra units. An underallocation of resources to the monopolized product occurs, and the economy suffers an efficiency loss. So society's economic well-being is less than it would be with greater competition.

But an efficiency loss isn't the only consequence of the monopolist's higher-than-competitive price. The higher price also transfers income from consumers to the monopolist. This transfer causes significant resentment because it results purely from the monopolist's ability to restrict output and cannot be justified on the basis of increased production costs. Consumers consequently express their ire to elected officials to "do something about the situation."

Responding to that pressure, government officials concluded in the late 1800s and early 1900s that monopolized industries lacked enough of the beneficial market forces that in competitive industries help to protect consumers, achieve fair competition, and achieve allocative efficiency. So the government instituted two alternative means of control as substitutes for, or supplements to, market forces:

- ***Regulatory agencies*** In the few markets where the nature of the product or technology creates a *natural monopoly*, the government established public regulatory agencies to control economic behavior.
- ***Antitrust laws*** In most other markets, social control took the form of antitrust (antimonopoly) legislation designed to inhibit or prevent the growth of monopoly.

Four particular pieces of Federal legislation, as refined and extended by various amendments, constitute the basic law relating to monopoly structure and conduct.

Sherman Act of 1890

The public resentment of trusts that emerged in the 1870s and 1880s culminated in the **Sherman Act** of 1890. This cornerstone of antitrust legislation is surprisingly brief and, at first glance, directly to the point. The core of the act resides in two provisions:

- ***Section 1*** "Every contract, combination in the form of a trust or otherwise, or conspiracy, in restraint of trade or commerce among the several States, or with foreign nations is declared to be illegal."
- ***Section 2*** "Every person who shall monopolize, or attempt to monopolize, or combine or conspire with any person or persons, to monopolize any part of the trade or commerce among the several states, or with foreign nations, shall be deemed guilty of a felony" (as later amended from "misdemeanor").

The Sherman Act thus outlawed *restraints of trade* (for example, collusive price-fixing and dividing up markets) as well as *monopolization*. Today, the U.S. Department of Justice, the Federal Trade Commission, injured private parties, or state attorney generals can file antitrust suits against alleged violators of the act. The courts can issue injunctions to prohibit anticompetitive practices or, if necessary, break up monopolists into competing firms. Courts can also fine and imprison violators. Further, parties injured by illegal combinations and conspiracies can sue the perpetrators for *treble damages*—awards of three times the amount of the monetary injury done to them.

The Sherman Act seemed to provide a sound foundation for positive government action against business monopolies. However, early court interpretations limited the scope of the act and created ambiguities of law. It became clear that a more explicit statement of the government's antitrust sentiments was needed. The business community itself sought a clearer statement of what was legal and what was illegal.

Clayton Act of 1914

The **Clayton Act** of 1914 contained the desired elaboration of the Sherman Act. Four sections of the act, in particular, were designed to strengthen and make explicit the intent of the Sherman Act:

- Section 2 outlaws *price discrimination* when such discrimination is not justified on the basis of cost differences and when it reduces competition.
- Section 3 prohibits **tying contracts,** in which a producer requires that a buyer purchase another (or others) of its products as a condition for obtaining a desired product.
- Section 7 prohibits the acquisition of stocks of competing corporations when the outcome would be less competition.
- Section 8 prohibits the formation of **interlocking directorates**—situations where a director of one firm is also a board member of a competing firm—in large corporations where the effect would be reduced competition.

The Clayton Act simply sharpened and clarified the general provisions of the Sherman Act. It also sought to outlaw the techniques that firms might use to develop monopoly power and, in that sense, was a preventive measure. Section 2 of the Sherman Act, by contrast, was aimed more at breaking up existing monopolies.

Federal Trade Commission Act of 1914

The **Federal Trade Commission Act** created the five-member Federal Trade Commission (FTC), which has joint Federal responsibility with the U.S. Justice Department for enforcing the antitrust laws. The act gave the FTC the power to investigate unfair competitive practices on its own initiative or at the request of injured firms. It can hold public hearings on such complaints and, if necessary, issue **cease-and-desist orders** in cases where it discovers "unfair methods of competition in commerce."

The **Wheeler-Lea Act** of 1938 amended the Federal Trade Commission Act to give the FTC the additional responsibility of policing "deceptive acts or practices in commerce." In so doing, the FTC tries to protect the public against false or misleading advertising and the misrepresentation of products. So the Federal Trade Commission Act, as modified by the Wheeler-Lea Act, (1) established the FTC as an independent antitrust agency and (2) made unfair and deceptive sales practices illegal.

The FTC is highly active in enforcing the deceptive advertising statues. As one recent example, in 2007 the FTC fined four makers of over-the-counter diet pills a collective $25 million for claiming their products produced fast and permanent weight loss.

Celler-Kefauver Act of 1950

The **Celler-Kefauver Act** amended the Clayton Act, Section 7, which prohibits a firm from merging with a competing firm (and thereby lessening competition) by acquiring its stock. Firms could evade Section 7, however, by instead acquiring the physical assets (plant and equipment) of competing firms. The Celler-Kefauver Act closed that loophole by prohibiting one firm from obtaining the physical assets of another firm when the effect would be reduced competition. Section 7 of the Clayton Act now prohibits anticompetitive mergers no matter how they are undertaken.

Antitrust Policy: Issues and Impacts

The effectiveness of any law depends on how the courts interpret it and on the vigor of government enforcement. The courts have been inconsistent in interpreting the antitrust laws. At times, they have applied them vigorously, adhering closely to their spirit and objectives. At other times, their interpretations have rendered certain laws nearly powerless. The Federal government itself has varied considerably in its aggressiveness in enforcing the antitrust laws. Some administrations have made tough antitrust enforcement a high priority. Other administrations have taken a more laissez-faire approach, initiating few antitrust actions or even scaling back the budgets of the enforcement agencies.

Issues of Interpretation

Differences in judicial interpretations have led to vastly different applications of the antitrust laws. Two questions, in particular, have arisen: (1) Should the focus of antitrust policy be on monopoly behavior or on monopoly structure? (2) How broadly should markets be defined in antitrust cases?

Monopoly Behavior versus Monopoly Structure

A comparison of three landmark Supreme Court decisions reveals two distinct interpretations of Section 2 of the Sherman Act as it relates to monopoly behavior and structure.

In the 1911 **Standard Oil case,** the Supreme Court found Standard Oil guilty of monopolizing the petroleum industry through a series of abusive and anticompetitive actions. The Court's remedy was to divide Standard Oil into several competing firms. But the Standard Oil case left open an important question: Is every monopoly in violation of Section 2 of the Sherman Act or just those created or maintained by anticompetitive actions?

In the 1920 **U.S. Steel case,** the courts established the so-called **rule of reason,** under which not every monopoly is illegal. Only monopolies that "unreasonably" restrain trade violate Section 2 of the Sherman Act and are subject to antitrust action. Size alone is not an offense. Under the rule of reason, U.S. Steel was innocent of "monopolizing" because it had not resorted to illegal acts against competitors in obtaining and then maintaining its monopoly power. Unlike Standard Oil, which was a so-called bad trust, U.S. Steel was a "good trust" and therefore not in violation of the law.

In the **Alcoa case** of 1945 the courts touched off a 20-year turnabout. The Supreme Court sent the case to the U.S. court of appeals in New York because four of the Supreme Court justices had been involved with litigation of the case before their appointments. Led by Judge Learned Hand, the court of appeals held that, even though a firm's behavior might be legal, the mere possession of monopoly power (Alcoa held 90 percent of the aluminum ingot market) violated the antitrust laws. So Alcoa was found guilty of violating the Sherman Act.

These two cases point to a controversy in antitrust policy. Should a firm be judged by its behavior (as in the U.S. Steel case) or by its structure or market share (as in the Alcoa case)?

- "Structuralists" assume that any firm with a very high market share will behave like a monopoly. As a result, they assert that any firm with a very high market share is a legitimate target for antitrust action. Structuralists argue that changes in the structure of an industry, say, by splitting the monopolist into several smaller firms, will improve behavior and performance.

- "Behavioralists" assert that the relationship among structure, behavior, and performance is tenuous and unclear. They feel a monopolized or highly concentrated industry may be technologically progressive and have a good record of providing products of increasing quality at reasonable prices. If a firm has served society well and has engaged in no anticompetitive practices, it should not be accused of antitrust violation just because it has an extraordinarily large market share. That share may be the product of superior technology, superior products, and economies of scale. "Why use antitrust laws to penalize efficient, technologically progressive, well-managed firms?" they ask.

Over the past 25 years, the courts have returned to the rule of reason first established in the 1920 U.S. Steel case, and most contemporary economists and antitrust enforcers reject strict structuralism. For instance, in 1982 the government dropped its 13-year-long monopolization case against IBM on the grounds that IBM had not unreasonably restrained trade, despite having possessed extremely high market share in the market for mainframe computers. More recently, the government has made no attempt to break up Intel's near monopoly in the sale of microprocessors for personal computers. And in prosecuting the Microsoft case (the subject of this chapter's Last Word), the Federal government made it clear that the behavior used by Microsoft to maintain and extend its monopoly, not the presence of its large market share, violated the Sherman Act. In essence, the government declared Microsoft to be "a bad monopoly" that could become a good monopoly if it stopped doing bad things.

The Relevant Market

Courts often decide whether or not market power exists by considering the share of the market held by the dominant firm. They have roughly adhered to a "90-60-30 rule" in defining monopoly: If a firm has a 90 percent market share, it is definitely a monopolist; if it has a 60 percent market share, it probably is a monopolist; if it has a 30 percent market share, it clearly is not a monopolist. The market share will depend on how the market is defined. If the market is defined broadly to include a wide range of somewhat similar products, the firm's market share will appear small. If the market is defined narrowly to exclude such products, the market share will seem large. The Supreme Court has the final say on how broadly to define relevant markets, but the Supreme Court has not always been consistent.

In the Alcoa case, the Court used a narrow definition of the relevant market: the aluminum ingot market. But in the **DuPont cellophane case** of 1956 the Court defined the market very broadly. The government contended that DuPont, along with a licensee, controlled 100 percent of the cellophane market. But the Court accepted DuPont's contention that the relevant market included all "flexible packaging materials"—waxed paper, aluminum foil, and so forth, in addition to cellophane. Despite DuPont's monopoly in the "cellophane market," it controlled only 20 percent of the market for "flexible wrapping materials." The Court ruled that this did not constitute a monopoly.

Issues of Enforcement

Some U.S. presidential administrations have enforced the antitrust laws more strictly than others. The degree of Federal antitrust enforcement makes a difference in the overall degree of antitrust action in the economy. It is true that individual firms can sue other firms under the antitrust laws. For example, in 2005 AMD—a maker of microprocessors—filed an antitrust suit against Intel, claiming that Intel was a monopolist that used anticompetitive business practices to thwart the growth of AMD's market share. But major antitrust suits often last years and are highly expensive. Injured parties therefore often look to the Federal government to initiate and litigate such cases. Once the Federal government gains a conviction, the injured parties no longer need to prove guilt and can simply sue the violator to obtain treble damages. In many cases, lack of Federal antitrust action therefore means diminished legal action by firms.

Why might one administration enforce the antitrust laws more or less strictly than another? The main reason is differences in political philosophies about the market economy and the wisdom of intervention by government. There are two contrasting general perspectives on antitrust policy.

The *active antitrust perspective* is that competition is insufficient in some circumstances to achieve allocative efficiency and ensure fairness to consumers and competing firms. Firms occasionally use illegal tactics against competitors to dominate markets. In other instances, competitors collude to fix prices or merge to enhance their monopoly power. Active, strict enforcement of the antitrust laws is needed to stop illegal business practices, prevent anticompetitive mergers, and remedy monopoly. This type of government intervention maintains the viability and vibrancy of the market system and thus allows society to reap its full benefits. In this view, the antitrust authorities need to act much like the officials in a football game. They must observe the players, spot infractions, and enforce the rules.

In contrast, the *laissez-faire perspective* holds that antitrust intervention is largely unnecessary, particularly as it relates to monopoly. Economists holding this position view competition as a long-run dynamic process in which firms battle against each other for dominance of markets. In some markets, a firm successfully monopolizes the market, usually because of its superior innovativeness or business skill. But in exploiting its monopoly power to raise prices, these firms inadvertently create profit incentives and profit opportunities for other entrepreneurs and firms to develop alternative technologies and new products to better serve consumers. As discussed in Chapter 2 and expanded upon in Chapter 9, a process of *creative destruction* occurs in which today's monopolies are eroded and eventually destroyed by tomorrow's technologies and products. The government therefore should not try to break up a monopoly. It should stand aside and allow the long-run competitive process to work.

ORIGIN OF THE IDEA
O 18.1
Creative destruction

The extent to which a particular administration adheres to—or leans toward—one of these contrasting antitrust perspectives usually gets reflected in the appointments to the agencies overseeing antitrust policy. Those appointees help determine how strictly the laws are enforced.

Effectiveness of Antitrust Laws

Have the antitrust laws been effective? Although this question is difficult to answer, we can at least observe how the laws have been applied to monopoly, mergers, price-fixing, price discrimination, and tying contracts.

Monopoly On the basis of the rule of reason, the government has generally been lenient in applying antitrust laws to monopolies that have developed naturally. Generally, a firm will be sued by the Federal government only if it has a very high market share and there is evidence of abusive conduct in achieving, maintaining, or extending its market dominance.

But even if the Federal government wins the antitrust lawsuit, there is still the matter of *remedy:* What actions should the court order to correct for the anticompetitive practices of the monopoly that lost the lawsuit?

The issue of remedy arose in two particularly noteworthy monopoly cases. The first was the AT&T (American Telephone and Telegraph) case in which the government charged AT&T with violating the Sherman Act by engaging in anticompetitive practices designed to maintain its domestic telephone monopoly. As part of an out-of-court settlement between the government and AT&T, in 1982 AT&T agreed to divest itself of its 22 regional telephone-operating companies.

A second significant monopoly case was the **Microsoft case.** In 2000 Microsoft was found guilty of violating the Sherman Act by taking several unlawful actions designed to maintain its monopoly of operating systems for

FIGURE 18.1 Types of mergers. Horizontal mergers (T + U) bring together firms selling the same product in the same geographic market; vertical mergers (F + Z) connect firms having a buyer-seller relationship; and conglomerate mergers (C + D) join firms in different industries or firms operating in different geographic areas.

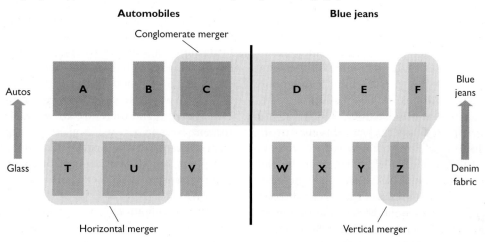

personal computers. A lower court ordered that Microsoft be split into two competing firms. A court of appeals upheld the lower-court finding of abusive monopoly but rescinded the breakup of Microsoft. Instead of the structural remedy, the eventual outcome was a behavioral remedy in which Microsoft was prohibited from engaging in a set of specific anticompetitive business practices.

The antitrust agency for the European Union (EU) has generally been more aggressive than the United States in prosecuting monopolists. For example, in 2004 the EU fined Microsoft $600 million for monopolization and required it to share its computer code with other firms that supplied Windows applications (such as media players). The purpose of the code-sharing requirement was to enable competitors to compete on an equal footing against Microsoft's own application software. Microsoft was fined a further $1.3 billion by the EU in 2008 for failing to quickly and fully comply with the 2004 remedy ordering Microsoft to share its computer code.

Mergers   The treatment of mergers, or combinations of existing firms, varies with the type of merger and its effect on competition.

Merger Types

There are three basic types of mergers, as represented in Figure 18.1. This figure shows two stages of production (the input stage and the output, or final-product, stage) for two distinct final-goods industries (autos and blue jeans). Each rectangle (A, B, C, . . . X, Y, Z) represents a particular firm.

A **horizontal merger** is a merger between two competitors that sell similar products in the same geographic market. In Figure 18.1 this type of merger is shown as a combination of glass producers T and U. Actual examples of such mergers include Chase Manhattan's merger with Chemical Bank, Boeing's merger with McDonnell Douglas, and Exxon's merger with Mobil.

A **vertical merger** is a merger between firms at different stages of the production process. In Figure 18.1, the merger between firm Z, a producer of denim fabric, and firm F, a producer of blue jeans, is a vertical merger. Vertical mergers are mergers between firms that have buyer-seller relationships. Actual examples of such mergers are PepsiCo's mergers with Pizza Hut, Taco Bell, and Kentucky Fried Chicken. PepsiCo supplies soft drinks to each of these fast-food outlets. (In 1997, PepsiCo spun off these entities into a separate company now called Yum! Brands.)

A **conglomerate merger** is officially defined as any merger that is not horizontal or vertical; in general, it is the combination of firms in different industries or firms operating in different geographic areas. Conglomerate mergers can extend the line of products sold, extend the territory in which products are sold, or combine totally unrelated companies. In Figure 18.1, the merger between firm C, an auto manufacturer, and firm D, a blue jeans producer, is a conglomerate merger. Real-world examples of conglomerate mergers include the merger between Walt Disney Company (movies) and the American Broadcasting Company (radio and television) and the merger between America Online (Internet service provider) and Time Warner (communications).

Merger Guidelines: The Herfindahl Index

The Federal government has established very loose merger

guidelines based on the Herfindahl index. Recall from Chapter 11 that this measure of concentration is the sum of the squared percentage market shares of the firms within an industry. An industry of only four firms, each with a 25 percent market share, has a Herfindahl index of $2500 \ (= 25^2 + 25^2 + 25^2 + 25^2)$. In pure competition, where each firm's market share is minuscule, the index approaches $0 \ (= 0^2 + 0^2 + \ldots + 0^2)$. In pure monopoly, the index for that single firm is $10,000 \ (= 100^2)$.

The U.S. government uses Section 7 of the Clayton Act to block horizontal mergers that will substantially lessen competition. It is likely to challenge a horizontal merger if the postmerger Herfindahl index would be high (above 1800) and if the merger has substantially increased the index (added 100 or more points). However, other factors, such as economies of scale, the degree of foreign competition, and the ease of entry of new firms, are also considered. Furthermore, horizontal mergers are usually allowed if one of the merging firms is suffering major and continuing losses. (This is one reason Boeing was allowed to acquire McDonnell Douglas in 1996: MD was losing money in producing its commercial airplanes.)

During the past several decades, the Federal government has blocked several proposed horizontal mergers. For example, it blocked mergers between Staples and Office Depot, two major office-supply retailers; WorldCom and Sprint, two competing telecommunications firms; and Hughes (DirecTV) and Echostar (DISH Network), providers of direct-broadcast satellite television.

More recently, the Federal government successfully challenged mergers between Snyder's of Hanover and Utz Quality Foods, makers of pretzels; Polypore and Microporous, battery-parts makers; and Blue Cross Blue Shield of Michigan and Physician's Health Plan of Michigan, health insurance providers.

Most *vertical mergers* escape antitrust prosecution because they do not substantially lessen competition in either of the two markets. (In Figure 18.1 neither the Herfindahl index in the industry producing denim fabric nor the index in the blue jeans industry changes when firms Z and F merge vertically.) However, a vertical merger between large firms in highly concentrated industries may be challenged. For example, in 1999 the threat of FTC action spurred Barnes & Noble to abandon its merger with Ingram Book Company, the nation's largest book wholesaler. The merger would have enabled Barnes & Noble to set the wholesale price of books charged to its direct retail competitors such as Borders and Amazon.com.

Conglomerate mergers are generally permitted. If an auto manufacturer acquires a blue jeans producer, no antitrust action is likely since neither firm has increased its own market share as a result. That means the Herfindahl index remains unchanged in each industry.

Price-Fixing Price-fixing among competitors is treated strictly. Evidence of price-fixing, even by small firms, will bring antitrust action, as will other collusive activities such as scheming to rig bids on government contracts or dividing up sales in a market. In antitrust law, these activities are known as **per se violations;** they are "in and of themselves" illegal, and therefore are *not* subject to the rule of reason. To gain a conviction, the government or other party making the charge need show only that there was a conspiracy to fix prices, rig bids, or divide up markets, not that the conspiracy succeeded or caused serious damage to other parties.

Price-fixing investigations and court actions are common. (See the Consider This box to the right).

Price Discrimination Price discrimination is a common business practice that rarely reduces competition and therefore is rarely challenged by government. The exception occurs when a firm engages in price discrimination as part of a strategy to block entry or drive out competitors.

Tying Contracts The Federal government strictly enforces the prohibition of tying contracts, particularly when practiced by dominant firms. For example, it stopped movie distributors from forcing theaters to buy the projection rights to a full package of films as a condition of showing a blockbuster movie. Also, it prevented Kodak—the dominant maker of photographic film—from requiring that consumers process their film only through Kodak.

What then can we conclude about the overall effectiveness of antitrust laws? Antitrust policy has not been very effective in restricting the rise of or in breaking up monopolies or oligopolies resulting from legally undertaken internal expansions of firms. But most economists do not deem that to be a flaw. The antitrust laws have been used more effectively against predatory or abusive monopoly, but that effectiveness has been diminished by the slow legal process and consequently long time between the filing of charges and the implementation of remedies. In contrast, antitrust policy *has* been effective in blocking blatantly anticompetitive mergers and in identifying and prosecuting price-fixing and tying contracts.

Most economists conclude that, overall, U.S. antitrust policy has been moderately effective in achieving its goal of promoting competition and efficiency. Much of the success of antitrust policy arises from its deterrent effect on price-fixing and anticompetitive mergers. Some

CONSIDER THIS . . .

Of Catfish and Art (and Other Things in Common)

Examples of price-fixing are numerous. Here are just a few:

- In 1996 ConAgra and Hormel agreed to pay more than $21 million to settle their roles in a nationwide price-fixing case involving catfish.
- In 1996 Archer Daniels Midland (ADM) and other agribusinesses admitted fixing the prices of citric acid and an additive to livestock feed. In the early 2000s ADM, Cargill, and Corn Products admitted fixing the price of high-fructose syrup, a sweetener made from corn. In 2004 ADM paid $430 million to resolve the government's antitrust action.
- The U.S. Justice Department fined UCAR International $110 million in 1998 for scheming with competitors to fix prices and divide up the world market for graphite electrodes used in steel mills.
- In 2001 a court found the auction houses Sotheby's and Christie's guilty of conspiring over a 6-year period to set the same commission rates for sellers at auctions.
- In the early 2000s Samsung (South Korea), Hynix Semiconductor (South Korea), Infineon (Germany), and Micron (United States) were found to have fixed the price of dynamic random access memory chips (DRAMs), which are used in personal computers, printers, cell phones, and other electronic devices. In 2004 and 2005, the companies paid fines totaling $645 million.
- In 2007 British Airlines and Korean Air agreed to pay fines of $300 million each for conspiring to fix fuel surcharges on passenger tickets and cargo.
- Between 2008 and 2010, five manufacturers of liquid crystal displays—LG, Sharp, Hitachi, Chi Mei Optoelectronics, and Chunghwa Picture Tubes—were fined a total of over $860 million by the U.S. Justice Department for fixing the prices of the displays they sold to computer maker Dell Inc.
- In 2009, three international cargo airlines—Cargolux of Luxembourg, Nippon Cargo of Japan, and Asiana Airlines of South Korea—were fined $214 million by the U.S. Justice Department for conspiring to fix international airline cargo rates.

economists, however, think that enforcement of antitrust laws has been too weak. Others believe that parts of U.S. antitrust policy are anachronistic in an era of rapidly changing technology that continuously undermines existing monopoly power.

QUICK REVIEW 18.1

- The Sherman Act of 1890 outlaws restraints of trade and monopolization; the Clayton Act of 1914 as amended by the Celler-Kefauver Act of 1950 outlaws price discrimination (when anticompetitive), tying contracts, anticompetitive mergers, and interlocking directorates.
- The Federal Trade Commission Act of 1914 as bolstered by the Wheeler-Lea Act of 1938 created the Federal Trade Commission (FTC) and gave it authority to investigate unfair methods of competition and deceptive acts or practices in commerce.
- Currently, the courts judge monopoly using a "rule of reason," first established in the U.S. Steel case of 1920. Under this rule, only monopolists that achieve or maintain their status abusively are in violation of the Sherman Act.
- "Structuralists" say highly concentrated industries will behave like monopolists; "behaviorists" hold that the relationship between industry structure and firm behavior is uncertain.
- The degree of strictness of enforcement of antitrust laws depends on the general antitrust philosophy of each U.S. administration and its appointees.
- Government treats existing monopoly relatively leniently, as long as it is not abusive; blocks most horizontal mergers between dominant, profitable firms in highly concentrated industries; and vigorously prosecutes price-fixing and tying contracts.

Industrial Regulation

Antitrust policy assumes that society will benefit if a monopoly is prevented from evolving or if it is dissolved where it already exists. We now return to a special situation in which there is an economic reason for an industry to be organized monopolistically.

Natural Monopoly

A **natural monopoly** exists when economies of scale are so extensive that a single firm can supply the entire market at a lower average total cost than could a number of competing firms. Clear-cut circumstances of natural monopoly are relatively rare, but such conditions exist for many *public utilities*, such as local electricity, water, and natural gas providers. As discussed in Chapter 10, large-scale operations in some cases are necessary to obtain low unit costs and a low product price. Where natural monopoly occurs, competition is uneconomical. If the market were divided among many producers, economies of scale would not be achieved and unit costs and prices would be higher than necessary.

There are two possible alternatives for promoting better economic outcomes where natural monopoly exists. One is public ownership, and the other is public regulation.

TABLE 18.1 The Main Regulatory Commissions Providing Industrial Regulation

Commission (Year Established)	Jurisdiction
Federal Energy Regulatory Commission (1930)*	Electricity, gas, gas pipelines, oil pipelines, water-power sites
Federal Communications Commission (1934)	Telephones, television, cable television, radio, telegraph, CB radios, ham operators
State public utility commissions (various years)	Electricity, gas, telephones

*Originally called the Federal Power Commission; renamed in 1977.

Public ownership or some approximation of it has been established in a few instances. Examples: the Postal Service, the Tennessee Valley Authority, and Amtrak at the national level and mass transit, water supply systems, and garbage collection at the local level.

But *public regulation,* or what economists call *industrial regulation,* has been the preferred option in the United States. In this type of regulation, government commissions regulate the prices (or "rates") charged by natural monopolists. Table 18.1 lists the two major Federal regulatory commissions and their jurisdictions. It also notes that all 50 states have commissions that regulate the intrastate activities and "utility rates" of local natural monopolies.

The economic objective of industrial regulation is embodied in the **public interest theory of regulation.** In that theory, industrial regulation is necessary to keep a natural monopoly from charging monopoly prices and thus harming consumers and society. The goal of such regulation is to garner for society at least part of the cost reductions associated with natural monopoly while avoiding the restrictions of output and high prices associated with unregulated monopoly. If competition is inappropriate or impractical, society should allow or even encourage a monopoly but regulate its prices. Regulation should then be structured so that ratepayers benefit from the economies of scale—the lower per-unit costs—that natural monopolists are able to achieve.

In practice, regulators seek to establish rates that will cover production costs and yield a "fair" return to the enterprise. The goal is to set price equal to average total cost so that the regulated firm receives a normal profit, as described in the "Regulated Monopoly" section of Chapter 10. In particular, you should carefully review Figure 10.9.

Problems with Industrial Regulation

There is considerable disagreement on the effectiveness of industrial regulation. Let's examine two criticisms.

Costs and Inefficiency An unregulated firm has a strong incentive to reduce its costs at each level of output because that will increase its profit. The regulatory commission, however, confines the regulated firm to a normal profit or a "fair return" on the value of its assets. If a regulated firm lowers its operating costs, the rising profit eventually will lead the regulatory commission to require that the firm lower its rates in order to return its profits to normal. The regulated firm therefore has little or no incentive to reduce its operating costs.

Worse yet, higher costs do not result in lower profit. Because the regulatory commission must allow the public utility a fair return, the regulated monopolist can simply pass through higher production costs to consumers by charging higher rates. A regulated firm may reason that it might as well have high salaries for its workers, opulent working conditions for management, and the like, since the "return" is the same in percentage terms whether costs are minimized or not. So, although a natural monopoly reduces costs through economies of scale, industrial regulation fosters considerable X-inefficiency (Figure 10.7). Due to the absence of competition, the potential cost savings from natural monopoly may never actually materialize.

Perpetuating Monopoly A second general problem with industrial regulation is that it sometimes perpetuates monopoly long after the conditions of natural monopoly have ended.

Technological change often creates the potential for competition in some or even all portions of the regulated industry. Examples: Trucks began competing with railroads; transmission of voice and data by microwave and satellites began competing with transmission over telephone wires; satellite television began competing with cable television; and cell phones began competing with landline phones.

But spurred by the firms they regulate, commissions often protect the regulated firms from new competition by either blocking entry or extending regulation to competitors. Industrial regulation therefore may perpetuate a monopoly that is no longer a natural monopoly and would otherwise erode. Ordinary monopoly, protected by government, may supplant natural monopoly. If so, the regulated prices may exceed those that would occur with competition. The beneficiaries of outdated regulation are the regulated firms and their employees. The losers are consumers and the potential entrants.

Example: Regulation of the railroads by the Interstate Commerce Commission (ICC) was justified in the late 1800s and early 1900s. But by the 1930s, with the emergence of a network of highways, the trucking industry had seriously undermined the monopoly power of the railroads.

That is, for the transport of many goods over many routes, railroad service was no longer a natural monopoly. At that time it would have been desirable to dismantle the ICC and let railroads and truckers, along with barges and airlines, compete with one another. Instead, in the 1930s the ICC extended regulation of rates to interstate truckers. The ICC remained in place until its elimination in 1996. It was eliminated because the deregulation of railroads and trucking in the late 1970s and early 1980s had made its work irrelevant.

Second example: Until recently, both long-distance telephone companies such as AT&T as well as cable-television providers such as Time Warner were prohibited from offering local telephone services in competition with regulated local and regional telephone companies. But the very fact that AT&T, Time Warner, and other firms wanted to compete with regulated monopolies calls into question whether those local providers are in fact natural monopolies or government-protected monopolies.

Legal Cartel Theory

The regulation of potentially competitive industries has produced the **legal cartel theory of regulation.** In place of having socially minded officials forcing regulation on natural monopolies to protect consumers, holders of this view see practical politicians "supplying" regulation to local, regional, and national firms that fear the impact of competition on their profits or even on their long-term survival. These firms desire regulation because it yields a legal monopoly that can virtually guarantee a profit. Specifically, the regulatory commission performs such functions as blocking entry (for example, in local telephone service). Or, where there are several firms, the commission divides up the market much like an illegal cartel (for example, prior to airline deregulation, the Civil Aeronautics Board assigned routes to specific airlines). The commission may also restrict potential competition by enlarging the "cartel" (for example, the ICC's addition of trucking to its regulatory domain).

While private cartels are illegal and unstable and often break down, the special attraction of a government-sponsored cartel under the guise of regulation is that it endures. The legal cartel theory of regulation suggests that regulation results from the rent-seeking activities of private firms and the desire of politicians to be responsive in order to win reelection (Chapter 17).

Proponents of the legal cartel theory of regulation note that the Interstate Commerce Commission was welcomed by the railroads and that the trucking and airline industries both supported the extension of ICC regulation to their industries, arguing that unregulated competition was severe and destructive.

Occupational licensing is a labor market application of the legal cartel theory. Certain occupational groups—barbers, dentists, hairstylists, interior designers, dietitians, lawyers—demand stringent licensing on the grounds that it protects the public from charlatans and quacks. But skeptics say the real reason may be to limit entry into the occupational group so that practitioners can receive monopoly incomes.

Deregulation

Beginning in the 1970s, evidence of inefficiency in regulated industries and the contention that the government was regulating potentially competitive industries contributed to a wave of deregulation. Since then, Congress and many state legislatures have passed legislation that has deregulated in varying degrees the airline, trucking, banking, railroad, natural gas, television, and electricity industries. Deregulation has also occurred in the telecommunications industry, where antitrust authorities dismantled the regulated monopoly known as the Bell System (AT&T). Deregulation in the 1970s and 1980s was one of the most extensive experiments in economic policy to take place during the last 50 years.

The overwhelming consensus among economists is that deregulation has produced large net benefits for consumers and society. Most of the gains from deregulation have occurred in three industries: airlines, railroads, and trucking. Airfares (adjusted for inflation) declined by about one-third, and airline safety has continued to improve. Trucking and railroad freight rates (again, adjusted for inflation) dropped by about one-half.

Significant efficiency gains were also realized in long-distance telecommunications, and there have been slight efficiency gains in cable television, stock brokerage services, and the natural gas industry. Moreover, deregulation has unleashed a wave of technological advances that have resulted in such new and improved products and services as fax machines, cellular phones, fiber-optic cable, microwave communication systems, and the Internet.

The most recent and perhaps controversial industry to be deregulated is electricity. Deregulation is relatively advanced at the wholesale level, where firms can buy and sell electricity at market prices. They are also free to build generating facilities and sell electricity to local electricity providers at unregulated prices. In addition, several states have deregulated retail prices and encouraged households and businesses to choose among available electricity suppliers. This competition has generally lowered electricity rates for consumers and enhanced allocative efficiency.

But deregulation suffered a severe setback in California, where wholesale electricity prices, but not retail rates, were deregulated. Wholesale electricity prices surged in 2001 when California experienced electricity shortages. Because they could not pass on wholesale price increases to consumers, California electric utilities suffered large financial losses. California then filed lawsuits against several energy-trading companies that allegedly manipulated electricity supplies to boost the wholesale price of electricity during the California energy crisis. One multibillion-dollar energy trader—Enron—collapsed in 2002 when Federal investigators uncovered a pattern of questionable and fraudulent business and accounting practices.

The California deregulation debacle and the Enron collapse have muddied the overall assessment of electricity deregulation in the United States. It is simply much too soon to declare that deregulation of electricity is either a success or a failure.

QUICK REVIEW 18.2

- Natural monopoly occurs where economies of scale are so extensive that only a single firm can produce the product at minimum average total cost.

- The public interest theory of regulation says that government must regulate natural monopolies to prevent abuses arising from monopoly power. Regulated firms, however, have less incentive than competitive firms to reduce costs. That is, regulated firms tend to be X-inefficient.

- The legal cartel theory of regulation suggests that some firms seek government regulation to reduce price competition and ensure stable profits.

- Deregulation initiated by government in the past several decades has yielded large annual efficiency gains for society.

Social Regulation

The industrial regulation discussed in the preceding section has focused on the regulation of prices (or rates) in natural monopolies. But in the early 1960s a new type of regulation began to emerge. This *social regulation* is concerned with the conditions under which goods and services are produced, the impact of production on society, and the physical qualities of the goods themselves.

The Federal government carries out most of the social regulation, although states also play a role. In Table 18.2 we list the main Federal regulatory commissions engaged in social regulation.

Distinguishing Features

Social regulation differs from industrial regulation in several ways.

First, social regulation applies to far more firms than does industrial regulation. Social regulation is often

TABLE 18.2 The Main Federal Regulatory Commissions Providing Social Regulation

Commission (Year Established)	Jurisdiction
Food and Drug Administration (1906)	Safety and effectiveness of food, drugs, and cosmetics
Equal Employment Opportunity Commission (1964)	Hiring, promotion, and discharge of workers
Occupational Safety and Health Administration (1971)	Industrial health and safety
Environmental Protection Agency (1972)	Air, water, and noise pollution
Consumer Product Safety Commission (1972)	Safety of consumer products

applied "across the board" to all industries and directly affects more producers than does industrial regulation. For instance, while the industrial regulation of the Federal Energy Regulatory Commission (FERC) applies to a relatively small number of firms, the rules and regulations issued by the Occupational Safety and Health Administration (OSHA) apply to firms in all industries.

Second, social regulation intrudes into the day-to-day production process to a greater extent than industrial regulation. While industrial regulation focuses on rates, costs, and profits, social regulation often dictates the design of products, the conditions of employment, and the nature of the production process. As examples, the Consumer Product Safety Commission (CPSC) regulates the design of potentially unsafe products, and the Environmental Protection Agency (EPA) regulates the amount of pollution allowed during production.

Finally, social regulation has expanded rapidly during the same period in which industrial regulation has waned. Between 1970 and 1980, the U.S. government created 20 new social regulatory agencies. More recently, Congress has established new social regulations to be enforced by existing regulatory agencies. For example, the Equal Employment Opportunity Commission, which is responsible for enforcing laws against workplace discrimination on the basis of race, gender, age, or religion, has been given the added duty of enforcing the Americans with Disabilities Act of 1990. Under this social regulation, firms must provide reasonable accommodations for qualified workers and job applicants with disabilities. Also, sellers must provide reasonable access for customers with disabilities.

The names of the regulatory agencies in Table 18.2 suggest the reasons for their creation and growth: As much of our society had achieved a fairly affluent standard of living by the 1960s, attention shifted to improvement in the nonmaterial quality of life. The new focus called for safer products, less pollution, improved working conditions, and greater equality of economic opportunity.

The Optimal Level of Social Regulation

While economists agree on the need for social regulation, they disagree on whether or not the current level of such regulation is optimal. Recall that an activity should be expanded as long as its marginal benefit (MB) exceeds its marginal cost (MC). If the MB of social regulation exceeds its MC, then there is too little social regulation. But if MC exceeds MB, there is too much (review Figure 5.9). Unfortunately, the marginal costs and benefits of social regulation are not always easy to measure. So ideology about the proper size and role of government often drives the debate over social regulation as much as, or perhaps more than, economic cost-benefit analysis.

In Support of Social Regulation
Defenders of social regulation say that it has achieved notable successes and, overall, has greatly enhanced society's well-being. They point out that the problems that social regulation confronts are serious and substantial. According to the National Safety Council, about 5000 workers die annually in job-related accidents and 3.7 million workers suffer injuries that force them to miss a day or more of work. Air pollution continues to cloud major U.S. cities, imposing large costs in terms of reduced property values and increased health care expense. Numerous children and adults die each year because of poorly designed or manufactured products (for example, car tires) or tainted food (for example, *E. coli* in beef). Discrimination against some ethnic and racial minorities, persons with disabilities, and older workers reduces their earnings and imposes heavy costs on society.

Proponents of social regulation acknowledge that social regulation is costly. But they correctly point out that a high "price" for something does not necessarily mean that it should not be purchased. They say that the appropriate economic test should be not whether the costs of social regulation are high or low but, rather, whether the benefits of social regulation exceed the costs. After decades of neglect, they further assert, society cannot expect to cleanse the environment, enhance the safety of the workplace, and promote economic opportunity for all without incurring substantial costs. So statements about the huge costs of social regulation are irrelevant, say defenders, since the benefits are even greater. The public often underestimates those benefits since they are more difficult to measure than costs and often become apparent only after

some time has passed (for example, the benefits of reducing global warming).

Proponents of social regulation point to its many specific benefits. Here are just a few examples: It is estimated that highway fatalities would be 40 percent greater annually in the absence of auto safety features mandated through regulation. Compliance with child safety-seat and seat belt laws has significantly reduced the auto fatality rate for small children. The national air quality standards set by law have been reached in nearly all parts of the nation for sulfur dioxide, nitrogen dioxide, and lead. Moreover, recent studies clearly link cleaner air, other things equal, with increases in the values of homes. Affirmative action regulations have increased the labor demand for racial and ethnic minorities and females. The use of child-proof lids has resulted in a 90 percent decline in child deaths caused by accidental swallowing of poisonous substances.

Some defenders of social regulation say there are many remaining areas in which greater regulation would generate net benefits to society. For instance, some call for greater regulation of the meat, poultry, and seafood industries to improve food safety. Others favor greater regulation of health care organizations and insurance companies to ensure "patients' rights" for consumers of health care services. Still others say that more regulation is needed to ensure that violent movies, CDs, and video games are not marketed to children.

Advocates of social regulation say that the benefits of such regulation are well worth the considerable costs. The costs are simply the price we must pay to create a hospitable, sustainable, and just society.

Criticisms of Social Regulation
Critics of social regulation contend that, in many instances, it has been expanded to the point where the marginal costs exceed the marginal benefits. In this view, society would achieve net benefits by cutting back on irritating social regulation. Critics say that many social regulation laws are poorly written, making regulatory objectives and standards difficult to understand. As a result, regulators pursue goals well beyond the original intent of the legislation. Businesses complain that regulators often press for additional increments of improvement, unmindful of costs.

Also, decisions must often be made and rules formed on the basis of inadequate information. Examples: Consumer Product Safety Commission (CPSC) officials may make decisions about certain ingredients in products on the basis of limited laboratory experiments that suggest that those ingredients might cause cancer. Or government agencies may establish costly pollution standards to attack

The Microsoft Antitrust Case Is the Most Significant Monopoly Case since the Breakup of AT&T in the Early 1980s.

The Charges In May 1998 the U.S. Justice Department (under President Clinton), 19 individual states, and the District of Columbia (hereafter, "the government") filed antitrust charges against Microsoft under the Sherman Antitrust Act. The government charged that Microsoft had violated Section 2 of the act through a series of unlawful actions designed to maintain its "Windows" monopoly. It also charged that some of that conduct violated Section 1 of the Sherman Act.

Microsoft denied the charges, arguing it had achieved its success through product innovation and lawful business practices. Microsoft contended it should not be penalized for its superior foresight, business acumen, and technological prowess. It also pointed out that its monopoly was highly transitory because of rapid technological advance.

The District Court Findings In June 2000 the district court ruled that the relevant market was software used to operate Intel-compatible personal computers (PCs). Microsoft's 95 percent share of that market clearly gave it monopoly power. The court pointed out, however, that being a monopoly is not illegal. The violation of

the Sherman Act occurred because Microsoft used anticompetitive means to maintain its monopoly power.

According to the court, Microsoft feared that the success of Netscape's Navigator, which allowed people to browse the Internet, might allow Netscape to expand its software to include a competitive PC operating system—software that would threaten the Windows monopoly. It also feared that Sun's Internet applications of its Java programming language might eventually threaten Microsoft's Windows monopoly.

To counter these and similar threats, Microsoft illegally signed contracts with PC makers that required them to feature Internet Explorer on the PC desktop and penalized companies that promoted software products that competed with Microsoft products. Moreover, it gave friendly companies coding that linked Windows to software applications and withheld such coding from companies featuring Netscape. Finally, under license from Sun, Microsoft developed Windows-related Java software that made Sun's own software incompatible with Windows.

The District Court Remedy The district court ordered Microsoft to split into two competing companies, one initially selling the Windows operating system and the other initially selling Microsoft applications (such as Word, Hotmail, MSN, PowerPoint, and Internet Explorer). Both companies would be free to develop new products that compete with each other, and both could derive

the global-warming problem without knowing for certain whether pollution is the main cause of the problem. These efforts, say critics, lead to excessive regulation of business.

Moreover, critics argue that social regulations produce many unintended and costly side effects. For instance, the Federal gas mileage standard for automobiles has been blamed for an estimated 2000 to 3900 traffic deaths a year because auto manufacturers have reduced the weight of vehicles to meet the higher miles-per-gallon standards. Other things equal, drivers of lighter cars have a higher fatality rate than drivers of heavier vehicles.

Finally, opponents of social regulation say that the regulatory agencies may attract overzealous workers who are hostile toward the market system and "believe" too fervently in regulation. For example, some staff members of government agencies may see large corporations as "bad guys" who regularly cause pollution, provide inadequate safety for workers, deceive their customers, and

generally abuse their power in the community. Such biases can lead to seemingly never-ending calls for still more regulation, rather than objective assessments of the costs and benefits of added regulation.

Two Reminders

The debate over the proper amount of social regulation will surely continue. By helping determine costs and benefits, economic analysis can lead to more informed discussions and to better decisions. In this regard, economic analysis provides pertinent reminders for both ardent supporters and ardent opponents of social regulation.

There Is No Free Lunch Fervent supporters of social regulation need to remember that "there is no free lunch." Social regulation can produce higher prices, stifle innovation, and reduce competition.

those products from the intellectual property embodied in the common products existing at the time of divestiture.

The Appeals Court Ruling In late 2000 Microsoft appealed the district court decision to a U.S. court of appeals. In 2001 the higher court affirmed that Microsoft illegally maintained its monopoly but tossed out the district court's decision to break up Microsoft. It agreed with Microsoft that the company was denied due process during the penalty phase of the trial and concluded that the district court judge had displayed an appearance of bias by holding extensive interviews with the press. The appeals court sent the remedial phase of the case to a new district court judge to determine appropriate remedies. The appeals court also raised issues relating to the wisdom of a structural remedy.

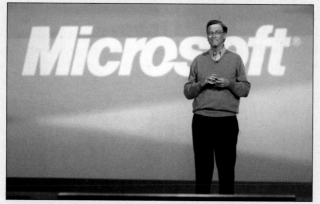

The Final Settlement At the urging of the new district court judge, the Federal government (then under President George W. Bush) and Microsoft negotiated a proposed settlement. With minor modification, the settlement became the final court order in 2002. The breakup was rescinded and replaced with a behavioral remedy. It (1) prevents Microsoft from retaliating against any firm that is developing, selling, or using software that competes with Microsoft Windows or Internet Explorer or is shipping a personal computer that includes both Windows and a non-Microsoft operating system; (2) requires Microsoft to establish uniform royalty and licensing terms for computer manufacturers wanting to include Windows on their PCs; (3) requires that manufacturers be allowed to remove Microsoft icons and replace them with other icons on the Windows desktop; and (4) calls for Microsoft to provide technical information to other companies so that they can develop programs that work as well with Windows as Microsoft's own products.

The Microsoft actions and conviction have indirectly resulted in billions of dollars of fines and payouts by Microsoft. Main examples: To AOL Time Warner (Netscape), $750 million; to the European Commission, $1.9 billion; to Sun Microsystems, $1.6 billion; to Novell, $536 million; to Burst.com, $60 million; to Gateway, $150 million; to InterTrust, $440 million; to RealNetworks, $761 million; and to IBM, $850 million.

Source: United States v. Microsoft (District Court Conclusions of Law), April 2000; *United States v. Microsoft* (Court of Appeals), June 2001; *U.S. v. Microsoft* (Final Judgment), November 2002; and Reuters and Associated Press News Services.

Social regulation raises product prices in two ways. It does so directly because compliance costs normally get passed on to consumers, and it does so indirectly by reducing labor productivity. Resources invested in making workplaces accessible to disabled workers, for example, are not available for investment in new machinery designed to increase output per worker. Where the wage rate is fixed, a drop in labor productivity increases the marginal and average total costs of production. In effect, the supply curve for the product shifts leftward, causing the price of the product to rise.

Social regulation may have a negative impact on the rate of innovation. Technological advance may be stifled by, say, the fear that a new plant will not meet EPA guidelines or that a new medicine will require years of testing before being approved by the Food and Drug Administration (FDA).

Social regulation may weaken competition since it usually places a relatively greater burden on small firms than on large ones. The costs of complying with social regulation are, in effect, fixed costs. Because smaller firms produce less output over which to distribute those costs, their compliance costs per unit of output put them at a competitive disadvantage with their larger rivals. Social regulation is more likely to force smaller firms out of business, thus contributing to the increased concentration of industry.

Finally, social regulation may prompt some U.S. firms to move their operations to countries in which the rules are not as burdensome and therefore production costs are lower.

Less Government Is Not Always Better Than More On the opposite side of the issue, opponents of social regulation need to remember that less government is not always better than more government. While the market system is a powerful engine for producing goods and services and generating income, it has certain flaws and can camouflage certain abuses. Through appropriate amounts of social regulation government can clearly increase economic efficiency and thus society's well-being. Ironically, by "taking the rough edges off of capitalism," social regulation may be a strong pro-capitalism force. Properly conceived and executed, social regulation helps maintain political support for the market system. Such support could quickly wane should there be a steady drumbeat of reports of unsafe workplaces, unsafe products, discriminatory hiring, choking pollution, deceived loan customers, and the like. Social regulation helps the market system deliver not only goods and services but also a "good society."

> ## QUICK REVIEW 18.3
>
> - Social regulation is concerned with the conditions under which goods and services are produced, the effects of production on society, and the physical characteristics of the goods themselves.
> - Defenders of social regulation point to the benefits arising from policies that keep dangerous products from the marketplace, reduce workplace injuries and deaths, contribute to clean air and water, and reduce employment discrimination.
> - Critics of social regulation say uneconomical policy goals, inadequate information, unintended side effects, and overzealous personnel create excessive regulation, for which regulatory costs exceed regulatory benefits.

Summary

1. The cornerstones of antitrust policy are the Sherman Act of 1890 and the Clayton Act of 1914. The Sherman Act specifies that "every contract, combination . . . or conspiracy in the restraint of interstate trade . . . is . . . illegal" and that any person who monopolizes or attempts to monopolize interstate trade is guilty of a felony.

2. If a company is found guilty of violating the antimonopoly provisions of the Sherman Act, the government can either break up the monopoly into competing firms (a structural remedy) or prohibit it from engaging in specific anticompetitive business practices (a behavioral remedy).

3. The Clayton Act was designed to bolster and make more explicit the provisions of the Sherman Act. It declares that price discrimination, tying contracts, intercorporate stock acquisitions, and interlocking directorates are illegal when their effect is to reduce competition.

4. The Federal Trade Commission Act of 1914 created the Federal Trade Commission to investigate antitrust violations and to prevent the use of "unfair methods of competition." The FTC Act was amended by the Wheeler-Lea Act of 1938 to outlaw false and deceptive representation of products to consumers. Empowered by cease-and-desist orders, the FTC serves as a watchdog agency over unfair, deceptive, or false claims made by firms about their own products or the products of their competitors.

5. The Celler-Kefauver Act of 1950 amended the Clayton Act of 1914 to prohibit one firm from acquiring the assets of another firm when doing so would substantially reduce competition.

6. Issues in applying antitrust laws include (a) determining whether an industry should be judged by its structure or by its behavior; (b) defining the scope and size of the dominant firm's market; and (c) deciding how strictly to enforce the antitrust laws.

7. The courts treat price-fixing among competitors as a *per se violation*, meaning that the conduct is illegal independently of whether the conspiracy causes harm. In contrast, a *rule of reason* is used to assess monopoly. Only monopolies that unreasonably (abusively) achieve or maintain their status violate the law. Antitrust officials are more likely to challenge price-fixing, tying contracts, and horizontal mergers than to try to break up existing monopolies. Nevertheless, antitrust suits by the Federal government led to the breakup of the AT&T monopoly in the early 1980s.

8. The objective of industrial regulation is to protect the public from the market power of natural monopolies by regulating prices and quality of service.

9. Critics of industrial regulation contend that it can lead to inefficiency and rising costs and that in many instances it constitutes a legal cartel for the regulated firms. Legislation passed in the late 1970s and the 1980s has brought about varying degrees of deregulation in the airline, trucking, banking, railroad, and television broadcasting industries.

10. Studies indicate that deregulation of airlines, railroads, trucking, and telecommunications is producing sizable annual gains to society through lower prices, lower costs, and increased output. Less certain is the effect of the more recent deregulation of the electricity industry.

11. Social regulation is concerned with product safety, working conditions, and the effects of production on society. Whereas industrial regulation is on the wane, social regulation continues to expand. The optimal amount of social regulation occurs where $MB = MC$.

12. People who support social regulation point to its numerous specific successes and assert that it has greatly enhanced society's well-being. Critics of social regulation contend that businesses are excessively regulated to the point where marginal costs exceed marginal benefits. They also say that social regulation often produces unintended and costly side effects.

Terms and Concepts

antitrust policy	cease-and-desist order	Microsoft case
industrial regulation	Wheeler-Lea Act	horizontal merger
social regulation	Celler-Kefauver Act	vertical merger
Sherman Act	Standard Oil case	conglomerate merger
Clayton Act	U.S. Steel case	per se violations
tying contracts	rule of reason	natural monopoly
interlocking directorates	Alcoa case	public interest theory of regulation
Federal Trade Commission Act	DuPont cellophane case	legal cartel theory of regulation

Questions

1. Both antitrust policy and industrial regulation deal with monopoly. What distinguishes the two approaches? How does government decide to use one form of remedy rather than the other? **LO1, LO3**

2. Describe the major provisions of the Sherman and Clayton acts. What government entities are responsible for enforcing those laws? Are firms permitted to initiate antitrust suits on their own against other firms? **LO1**

3. Contrast the outcomes of the Standard Oil and U.S. Steel cases. What was the main antitrust issue in the DuPont cellophane case? In what major way do the Microsoft and Standard Oil cases differ? **LO2**

4. Why might one administration interpret and enforce the antitrust laws more strictly than another? How might a change of administrations affect a major monopoly case in progress? **LO2**

5. How would you expect antitrust authorities to react to: **LO2**
   a. A proposed merger of Ford and General Motors.
   b. Evidence of secret meetings by contractors to rig bids for highway construction projects.
   c. A proposed merger of a large shoe manufacturer and a chain of retail shoe stores.
   d. A proposed merger of a small life-insurance company and a regional candy manufacturer.
   e. An automobile rental firm that charges higher rates for last-minute rentals than for rentals reserved weeks in advance.

6. Suppose a proposed merger of firms would simultaneously lessen competition and reduce unit costs through economies of scale. Do you think such a merger should be allowed? **LO2**

7. In the 1980s, PepsiCo Inc., which then had 28 percent of the soft-drink market, proposed to acquire the Seven-Up Company. Shortly thereafter, the Coca-Cola Company, with 39 percent of the market, indicated it wanted to acquire the Dr Pepper Company. Seven-Up and Dr Pepper each controlled about 7 percent of the market. In your judgment, was the government's decision to block these mergers appropriate? **LO2**

8. Why might a firm charged with violating the Clayton Act, Section 7, try arguing that the products sold by the merged firms are in separate markets? Why might a firm charged with violating Section 2 of the Sherman Act try convincing the court that none of its behavior in achieving and maintaining its monopoly was illegal? **LO2**

9. "The social desirability of any particular firm should be judged not on the basis of its market share but on the basis of its conduct and performance." Make a counterargument, referring to the monopoly model in your statement. **LO2**

10. What types of industries, if any, should be subjected to industrial regulation? What specific problems does industrial regulation entail? **LO3**

11. In view of the problems involved in regulating natural monopolies, compare socially optimal (marginal-cost) pricing and fair-return pricing by referring again to Figure 10.9. Assuming that a government subsidy might be used to cover any loss resulting from marginal-cost pricing, which pricing policy would you favor? Why? What problems might such a subsidy entail? **LO3**

12. How does social regulation differ from industrial regulation? What types of benefits and costs are associated with social regulation? **LO4**

13. Use economic analysis to explain why the optimal amount of product safety may be less than the amount that would totally eliminate risks of accidents and deaths. Use automobiles as an example. **LO4**

14. **LAST WORD** Under what law and on what basis did the Federal district court find Microsoft guilty of violating the antitrust laws? What was the initial district court's remedy? How did Microsoft fare with its appeal to the court of appeals? Was the final remedy in the case a structural remedy or a behavioral remedy?

Problems

1. Suppose that there are only three types of fruit sold in the United States. Annual sales are 1 million tons of blueberries, 5 million tons of strawberries, and 10 million tons of bananas. Suppose that of those total amounts, the Sunny Valley Fruit Company sells 900,000 tons of blueberries, 900,000 tons of strawberries, and 7.9 million tons of bananas. **LO2**
   a. What is Sunny Valley's market share if the relevant market is blueberries? If a court applies the "90-60-30 rule" when considering just the blueberry market, would it rule that Sunny Valley is a monopoly?
   b. What is Sunny Valley's market share if the relevant market is all types of berries? Would the court rule Sunny Valley to be a monopolist in that market?
   c. What if the relevant market is all types of fruit? What is Sunny Valley's market share, and would the court consider Sunny Valley to be a monopolist?

2. Carrot Computers and its competitors purchase touch screens for their handheld computers from several suppliers. The six makers of touch screens have market shares of, respectively, 19 percent, 18 percent, 14 percent, 16 percent, 20 percent, and 13 percent. **LO2**
   a. What is the Herfindahl index for the touch screen manufacturing industry?
   b. By how much would a proposed merger between the two smallest touch screen makers increase the Herfindahl index? Would the government be likely to challenge that proposed merger?
   c. If Carrot Computers horizontally merges with its competitor Blueberry Handhelds, by how much would the Herfindahl index change for the touch screen industry?

FURTHER TEST YOUR KNOWLEDGE AT
www.mcconnell19e.com

At the text's Online Learning Center (OLC), **www.mcconnell19e.com**, you will find one or more Web-based questions that require information from the Internet to answer. We urge you to check them out; they will familiarize you with Web sites that may be helpful in other courses and perhaps even in your career. The OLC also features multiple-choice questions that give instant feedback and provides other helpful ways to further test your knowledge of the chapter.

PART SEVEN

23   INTERNATIONAL TRADE

24   THE BALANCE OF PAYMENTS,
      EXCHANGE RATES, AND TRADE
      DEFICITS

INTERNATIONAL ECONOMICS

23

AFTER READING THIS CHAPTER, YOU SHOULD BE ABLE TO:

1 List and discuss several key facts about international trade.

2 Define comparative advantage, and demonstrate how specialization and trade add to a nation's output.

3 Describe how differences between world prices and domestic prices prompt exports and imports.

4 Analyze the economic effects of tariffs and quotas.

5 Analyze the validity of the most frequently presented arguments for protectionism.

6 Identify and explain the objectives of GATT, WTO, EU, Euro Zone, and NAFTA, and discuss offshoring and trade adjustment assistance.

International Trade*

Backpackers in the wilderness like to think they are "leaving the world behind," but, like Atlas, they carry the world on their shoulders. Much of their equipment is imported—knives from Switzerland, rain gear from South Korea, cameras from Japan, aluminum pots from England, sleeping bags from China, and compasses from Finland. Moreover, they may have driven to the trailheads in Japanese-made Toyotas or German-made BMWs, sipping coffee from Brazil or snacking on bananas from Honduras.

International trade and the global economy affect all of us daily, whether we are hiking in the wilderness, driving our cars, buying groceries, or working at our jobs. We cannot "leave the world behind." We are enmeshed in a global web of economic relationships, such as trading of goods and

---

*Note to Instructors: This chapter is a consolidation of Chapters 5 and 37 of *Economics* 18e. If you prefer to cover international trade early in your course, you can assign this chapter at the end of either Part 1 or Part 2. This chapter builds on the introductory ideas of opportunity costs, supply and demand analysis, and economic efficiency but does not require an understanding of either elasticity or market failures.

services, multinational corporations, cooperative ventures among the world's firms, and ties among the world's financial markets.

The focus of this chapter is the trading of goods and services. Then in Chapter 24, we examine the U.S. balance of payments, exchange rates, and U.S. trade deficits.

Some Key Trade Facts

The following are several important facts relating to international trade.

- U.S. exports and imports have more than doubled as percentages of GDP since 1980.
- A *trade deficit* occurs when imports exceed exports. The United States has a trade deficit in goods. In 2009 U.S. imports of goods exceeded U.S. exports of goods by $517 billion.
- A *trade surplus* occurs when exports exceed imports. The United States has a trade surplus in services (such as air transportation services and financial services). In 2009 U.S. exports of services exceeded U.S. imports of services by $138 billion.
- Principal U.S. exports include chemicals, agricultural products, consumer durables, semiconductors, and aircraft; principal imports include petroleum, automobiles, metals, household appliances, and computers.
- As with other advanced industrial nations, the United States imports many goods that are in some of the same categories as the goods that it exports. Examples: automobiles, computers, chemicals, semiconductors, and telecommunications equipment.
- Canada is the United States' most important trading partner quantitatively. In 2009 about 20 percent of U.S. exported goods were sold to Canadians, who in turn provided 15 percent of imported U.S. goods.
- The United States has a sizable trade deficit with China. In 2009 it was $220 billion.
- The U.S. dependence on foreign oil is reflected in its trade with members of OPEC. In 2009 the United States imported $112 billion of goods (mainly oil) from OPEC members, while exporting $48 billion of goods to those countries.
- The United States leads the world in the combined volume of exports and imports, as measured in dollars. China, Germany, the United States, Japan, and the Netherlands were the top five exporters by dollar in 2009.
- Currently, the United States provides about 8.5 percent of the world's exports. (See Global Perspective 23.1.)
- Exports of goods and services (on a national income account basis) make up about 13 percent of total U.S.

GLOBAL PERSPECTIVE 23.1

Shares of World Exports, Selected Nations

China has the largest share of world exports, followed by Germany and the United States. The eight largest export nations account for about 46 percent of world exports.

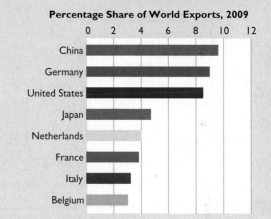

Percentage Share of World Exports, 2009

Source: International Trade Statistics, WTO Publications. Used with permission of the World Trade Organization, www.wto.org.

output. That percentage is much lower than the percentage in many other nations, including Canada, France, Germany, the Netherlands, and South Korea. (See Global Perspective 23.2.)

- China has become a major international trader, with an estimated $1.2 trillion of exports in 2009. Other Asian economies—including South Korea, Taiwan, and Singapore—are also active in international trade. Their combined exports exceed those of France, Britain, or Italy.
- International trade links world economies. Through trade, changes in economic conditions in one place on the globe can quickly affect other places.
- International trade is often at the center of debates over economic policy, both within the United States and internationally.

With this information in mind, let's turn to the economics of international trade.

Exports of Goods and Services as a Percentage of GDP, Selected Countries

Although the United States is one of the world's largest exporters, as a percentage of GDP, its exports are quite low relative to many other countries.

Exports as Percentage of GDP, 2008

Country	
Belgium	
Netherlands	
South Korea	
Germany	
Canada	
New Zealand	
Italy	
United Kingdom	
France	
Spain	
Japan	
United States	

Source: Derived by authors from *IMF International Financial Statistics,* 2009.

The Economic Basis for Trade

Sovereign nations, like individuals and the regions of a nation, can gain by specializing in the products they can produce with the greatest relative efficiency and by trading for the goods they cannot produce as efficiently. The simple answer to the question "Why do nations trade?" is "They trade because it is beneficial." The benefits that emerge relate to three underlying facts:

- The distribution of natural, human, and capital resources among nations is uneven; nations differ in their endowments of economic resources.

- Efficient production of various goods requires different technologies, and not all nations have the same level of technological expertise.

- Products are differentiated as to quality and other attributes, and some people may prefer certain goods imported from abroad rather than similar goods produced domestically.

To recognize the character and interaction of these three facts, think of China, which has abundant and inexpensive labor. As a result, China can produce efficiently (at low cost of other goods forgone) a variety of **labor-intensive goods,** such as textiles, electronics, apparel, toys, and sporting goods.

In contrast, Australia has vast amounts of land and can inexpensively produce such **land-intensive goods** as beef, wool, and meat. Mexico has the soil, tropical climate, rainfall, and ready supply of unskilled labor that allow for the efficient, low-cost production of vegetables. Industrially advanced economies such as the United States and Germany that have relatively large amounts of capital can inexpensively produce goods whose production requires much capital, including such **capital-intensive goods** as airplanes, automobiles, agricultural equipment, machinery, and chemicals.

Also, regardless of their resource intensities, nations can develop individual products that are in demand worldwide because of their special qualities. Examples: fashions from Italy, chocolates from Belgium, software from the United States, and watches from Switzerland.

The distribution of resources, technology, and product distinctiveness among nations is relatively stable in short time periods but certainly can change over time. When that distribution changes, the relative efficiency and success that nations have in producing and selling goods also changes. For example, in the past several decades, South Korea has greatly expanded its stock of capital. Although South Korea was primarily an exporter of agricultural products and raw materials a half-century ago, it now exports large quantities of manufactured goods. Similarly, the new technologies that gave us synthetic fibers and synthetic rubber drastically altered the resource mix needed to produce fibers and rubber and changed the relative efficiency of nations in manufacturing them.

As national economies evolve, the size and quality of their labor forces may change, the volume and composition of their capital stocks may shift, new technologies may develop, and even the quality of land and the quantity of natural resources may be altered. As such changes take place, the relative efficiency with which a nation can produce specific goods will also change. As economists would say, comparative advantage can and does sometimes change.

Comparative Advantage

In an open economy (one with an international sector), a country produces more of certain goods (exports) and fewer of other goods (imports) than it would otherwise. Thus, the country shifts the use of labor and other productive resources toward export industries and away from import industries. For example, in the presence of international trade, the United States uses more resources to make commercial aircraft and to grow wheat and fewer resources to make television sets and sew clothes. So we ask: Do such shifts of resources make economic sense? Do they enhance U.S. total output and thus the U.S. standard of living?

The answers are affirmative. Specialization and international trade increase the productivity of U.S. resources and allow the United States to obtain greater total output than otherwise would be possible. These benefits are the result of exploiting both *absolute advantages* and *comparative advantages*. A country is said to have an *absolute advantage* over other producers of a product if it is the most efficient producer of that product (by which we mean that it can produce more output of that product from any given amount of resource inputs than can any other producer). A country is said to have a *comparative advantage* over other producers of a product if it can produce the product at a lower opportunity cost (by which we mean that it must forgo less output of alternative products when allocating productive resources to producing the product in question).

In 1776 Adam Smith used the concept of absolute advantage to argue for international specialization and trade. His point was that nations would be better off if they each specialized in the production of those products in which they had an absolute advantage and were therefore the most efficient producers:

> It is the maxim of every prudent master of a family, never to attempt to make at home what it will cost him more to make than to buy. The taylor does not attempt to make his own shoes, but buys them of the shoemaker. The shoemaker does not attempt to make his own clothes, but employs a taylor. The farmer attempts to make neither the one nor the other, but employs those different artificers. . . .
>
> What is prudence in the conduct of every private family, can scarce be folly in that of a great kingdom. If a foreign country can supply us with a commodity cheaper than we can make it, better buy it of them with some part of the produce of our own industry, employed in a way in which we have some advantage.[1]

In the early 1800s, David Ricardo extended Smith's idea by demonstrating that it is advantageous for a country to specialize and trade with another country even if it is more productive in all economic activities than that other country. Stated more formally, a nation does not need Smith's absolute advantage—total superiority in the efficiency with which it produces products—to benefit from specialization and trade. It needs only a comparative advantage.

The nearby Consider This box provides a simple, two-person illustration of Ricardo's principle of comparative

---

[1]Adam Smith, *The Wealth of Nations* (originally published, 1776; New York: Modern Library, 1937), p. 424.

CONSIDER THIS . . .

A CPA and a House Painter

Suppose that Madison, a certified public accountant (CPA), is a swifter painter than Mason, the professional painter she is thinking of hiring. Also assume that Madison can earn $50 per hour as an accountant but would have to pay Mason $15 per hour. And suppose that Madison would need 30 hours to paint her house but Mason would need 40 hours.

Should Madison take time from her accounting to paint her own house, or should she hire the painter? Madison's opportunity cost of painting her house is $1500 (= 30 hours of sacrificed CPA time × $50 per CPA hour). The cost of hiring Mason is only $600 (= 40 hours of painting × $15 per hour of painting). Although Madison is better at both accounting and painting, she will get her house painted at lower cost by specializing in accounting and using some of her earnings from accounting to hire a house painter.

Similarly, Mason can reduce his cost of obtaining accounting services by specializing in painting and using some of his income to hire Madison to prepare his income tax forms. Suppose Mason would need 10 hours to prepare his tax return, while Madison could handle the task in 2 hours. Mason would sacrifice $150 of income (= 10 hours of painting time × $15 per hour) to do something he could hire Madison to do for $100 (= 2 hours of CPA time × $50 per CPA hour). By specializing in painting and hiring Madison to prepare his tax return, Mason lowers the cost of getting his tax return prepared.

We will see that what is true for our CPA and house painter is also true for nations. Specializing on the basis of comparative advantage enables nations to reduce the cost of obtaining the goods and services they desire.

---

advantage. Be sure to read it now, because it will greatly help you understand the graphical analysis that follows.

Two Isolated Nations

Our goal is to place the idea of comparative advantage into the context of trading nations. Our method is to build a simple model that relies on the familiar concepts of production possibilities curves. Suppose the world consists of just two nations, the United States and Mexico. Also for simplicity, suppose that the labor forces in the United States and Mexico are of equal size. Each nation can

(a)
United States

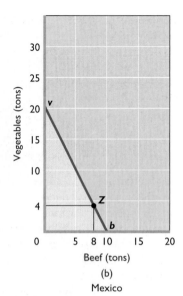

(b)
Mexico

FIGURE 23.1 Production possibilities for the United States and Mexico. The two production possibilities curves show the combinations of vegetables and beef that (a) the United States and (b) Mexico can produce domestically. The curves for both countries are straight lines because we are assuming constant opportunity costs. The different cost ratios, 1 vegetables ≡ 1 beef for the United States, and 2 vegetables ≡ 1 beef for Mexico, are reflected in the different slopes of the two lines.

produce both beef and raw (unprocessed) vegetables but at different levels of economic efficiency. Suppose the U.S. and Mexican domestic production possibilities curves for beef and vegetables are those shown in Figure 23.1a and Figure 23.1b. Note three realities relating to the production possibilities curves in the two graphs:

- **Constant costs** The curves derive from the tables and are drawn as straight lines, in contrast to the bowed-outward production possibilities frontiers we examined in Chapter 1. This means that we have replaced the law of increasing opportunity costs with the assumption of constant costs. This substitution simplifies our discussion but does not impair the validity of our analysis and conclusions. Later we will consider the effects of increasing opportunity costs.

- **Different costs** The production possibilities curves of the United States and Mexico reflect different resource mixes and differing levels of technology. Specifically, the differing slopes of the two curves reflect the numbers in the figures and reveal that the opportunity costs of producing beef and vegetables differ between the two nations.

- **U.S. absolute advantage in both** A producer (an individual, firm, or country) has an *absolute advantage* over another producer if it can produce more of a product than the other producer using the same amount of resources. Because of our convenient assumption that the U.S. and Mexican labor forces are the same size, the two production possibilities curves show that the United States has an absolute advantage in producing both products. If the United States and Mexico use

their entire (equal-size) labor forces to produce either vegetables or beef, the United States can produce more of either than Mexico. The United States, using the same number of workers as Mexico, has greater production possibilities. So output per worker—labor productivity—in the United States exceeds that in Mexico in producing both products.

Opportunity-Cost Ratio in the United States In Figure 23.1a, with full employment, the United States will operate at some point on its production possibilities curve. On that curve, it can increase its output of beef from 0 tons to 30 tons by forgoing 30 tons of vegetables output. So the slope of the production possibilities curve is 1 (= 30 vegetables/30 beef), meaning that 1 ton of vegetables must be sacrificed for each extra ton of beef. In the United States the **opportunity-cost ratio** (domestic exchange ratio) for the two products is 1 ton of vegetables (V) for 1 ton of beef (B), or

United States: $1V \equiv 1B$ (The "≡" sign simply means "equivalent to.")

Within its borders, the United States can "exchange" a ton of vegetables from itself for a ton of beef from itself. Our constant-cost assumption means that this exchange or opportunity-cost relationship prevails for all possible moves from one point to another along the U.S. production possibilities curve.

Opportunity-Cost Ratio in Mexico Mexico's production possibilities curve in Figure 23.1b represents a

TABLE 23.1 International Specialization According to Comparative Advantage and the Gains from Trade

Country	(1) Outputs before Specialization	(2) Outputs after Specialization	(3) Amounts Exported (−) and Imported (+)	(4) Outputs Available after Trade	(5) Gains from Specialization and Trade (4) − (1)
United States	18 beef 12 vegetables	30 beef 0 vegetables	−10 beef +15 vegetables	20 beef 15 vegetables	2 beef 3 vegetables
Mexico	8 beef 4 vegetables	0 beef 20 vegetables	+10 beef −15 vegetables	10 beef 5 vegetables	2 beef 1 vegetables

different full-employment opportunity-cost ratio. In Mexico, 20 tons of vegetables must be given up to obtain 10 tons of beef. The slope of the production possibilities curve is 2 (= 20 vegetables/10 beef). This means that in Mexico the opportunity-cost ratio for the two goods is 2 tons of vegetables for 1 ton of beef, or

$$\text{Mexico: } 2V \equiv 1B$$

Self-Sufficiency Output Mix

If the United States and Mexico are isolated and self-sufficient, then each country must choose some output mix on its production possibilities curve. It will select the mix that provides the greatest total utility or satisfaction. Let's assume that combination point A in Figure 23.1a is the optimal mix in the United States. That is, society deems the combination of 18 tons of beef and 12 tons of vegetables preferable to any other combination of the goods available along the production possibilities curve. Suppose Mexico's optimal product mix is 8 tons of beef and 4 tons of vegetables, indicated by point Z in Figure 23.1b. These choices by the two countries are reflected in column 1 of Table 23.1.

Specializing Based on Comparative Advantage

A producer (an individual, firm, or nation) has a **comparative advantage** in producing a particular product if it can produce that product at a lower opportunity cost than other producers. Comparative advantage is the key determinant in whether or not nations can gain from specialization and trade. In fact, absolute advantage turns out to be irrelevant.

In our example, for instance, the United States has an absolute advantage over Mexico in producing both vegetables and beef. But it is still the case that the United States can gain from specialization and trade with Mexico. That is because what actually matters is whether the opportunity costs of producing the two products (beef and vegetables) differ in the two countries. If they do, then each nation will enjoy a comparative advantage in one of the products,

meaning that it can produce that product at a lower opportunity cost than the other country. As a result, total output can increase if each country specializes in the production of the good in which it has the lower opportunity cost.

This idea is summarized in the **principle of comparative advantage,** which says that total output will be greatest when each good is produced by the nation that has the lowest domestic opportunity cost for producing that good. In our two-nation illustration, the United States has the lower domestic opportunity cost for beef; the United States must forgo only 1 ton of vegetables to produce 1 ton of beef, whereas Mexico must forgo 2 tons of vegetables for 1 ton of beef. The United States has a comparative (cost) advantage in beef and should specialize in beef production. The "world" (that is, the United States and Mexico) in our example would clearly not be economizing in the use of its resources if a high-cost producer (Mexico) produced a specific product (beef) when a low-cost producer (the United States) could have produced it. Having Mexico produce beef would mean that the world economy would have to give up more vegetables than is necessary to obtain a ton of beef.

Mexico has the lower domestic opportunity cost for vegetables. It must sacrifice only $\frac{1}{2}$ ton of beef to produce 1 ton of vegetables, while the United States must forgo 1 ton of beef to produce 1 ton of vegetables. Mexico has a comparative advantage in vegetables and should specialize in vegetable production. Again, the world would not be employing its resources economically if vegetables were produced by a high-cost producer (the United States) rather than by a low-cost producer (Mexico). If the United States produced vegetables, the world would be giving up more beef than necessary to obtain each ton of vegetables. Economizing requires that any particular good be produced by the nation having the lowest domestic opportunity cost or the nation having the comparative advantage for that good. The United States should produce beef, and Mexico should produce vegetables. The situation is summarized in Table 23.2.

TABLE 23.2 Comparative-Advantage Example: A Summary

Beef	Vegetables
Mexico: Must give up 2 tons of vegetables to get 1 ton of beef.	**Mexico:** Must give up $\frac{1}{2}$ ton of beef to get 1 ton of vegetables.
United States: Must give up 1 ton of vegetables to get 1 ton of beef.	**United States:** Must give up 1 ton of beef to get 1 ton of vegetables.
Comparative advantage: United States	**Comparative advantage:** Mexico

A comparison of columns 1 and 2 in Table 23.1 verifies that specialized production enables the world to obtain more output from its fixed amount of resources. By specializing completely in beef, the United States can produce 30 tons of beef and no vegetables. Mexico, by specializing completely in vegetables, can produce 20 tons of vegetables and no beef. These figures exceed the yields generated without specialization: 26 tons of beef (= 18 in the United States + 8 in Mexico) and 16 tons of vegetables (= 12 in the United States + 4 in Mexico). As a result, the world ends up with 4 more tons of beef (= 30 tons − 26 tons) and 4 more tons of vegetables (= 20 tons − 16 tons) than it would if there were self-sufficiency and unspecialized production.

ORIGIN OF THE IDEA

O 23.1

Absolute and comparative advantage

Terms of Trade

We have just seen that specialization in production will allow for the largest possible amounts of both beef and vegetables to be produced. But with each country specializing in the production of only one item, how will the vegetables that are all produced by Mexico and the beef that is all produced by the United States be divided between consumers in the two countries? The key turns out to be the **terms of trade,** the exchange ratio at which the United States and Mexico trade beef and vegetables.

Crucially, the terms of trade also establish whether each country will find it in its own better interest to bother specializing at all. This is because the terms of trade determine whether each country can "get a better deal" by specializing and trading than it could if it opted instead for self sufficiency. To see how this works, note that because $1B \equiv 1V$ (= $1V \equiv 1B$) in the United States, it must get more than 1 ton of vegetables for each 1 ton of beef exported; otherwise, it will not benefit from exporting beef in exchange for Mexican vegetables. The United States must get a better "price" (more vegetables) for its beef through international trade than it can get domestically; otherwise, no gain from trade exists and such trade will not occur.

Similarly, because $1B \equiv 2V$ (= $2V \equiv 1B$) in Mexico, Mexico must obtain 1 ton of beef by exporting less than 2 tons of vegetables to get it. Mexico must be able to pay a lower "price" for beef in the world market than it must pay domestically, or else it will not want to trade. The international exchange ratio or terms of trade must therefore lie somewhere between

$$1B \equiv 1V \text{ (United States' cost conditions)}$$

and

$$1B \equiv 2V \text{ (Mexico's cost conditions)}$$

Where between these limits will the world exchange ratio fall? The United States will prefer a rate close to $1B \equiv 2V$, say, $1B \equiv 1\frac{3}{4}V$. The United States wants to obtain as many vegetables as possible for each 1 ton of beef it exports. By contrast, Mexico wants a rate near $1B \equiv 1V$, say, $1B \equiv 1\frac{1}{4}V$. This is true because Mexico wants to export as few vegetables as possible for each 1 ton of beef it receives in exchange.

The actual exchange ratio depends on world supply and demand for the two products. If overall world demand for vegetables is weak relative to its supply and if the demand for beef is strong relative to its supply, the price of vegetables will be lower and the price of beef will be higher. The exchange ratio will settle nearer the $1B \equiv 2V$ figure the United States prefers. If overall world demand for vegetables is great relative to its supply and if the demand for beef is weak relative to its supply, the ratio will settle nearer the $1B \equiv 1V$ level favorable to Mexico. In this manner, the actual exchange ratio that is set by world supply and demand determines how the gains from international specialization and trade are divided between the two nations and, consequently, how the beef that is all produced in the United States and the vegetables that are all produced in Mexico get divided among consumers in the two countries. (We discuss equilibrium world prices later in this chapter.)

Gains from Trade

Suppose the international terms of trade are $1B \equiv 1\frac{1}{2}V$. The possibility of trading on these terms permits each nation to supplant its domestic production possibilities curve with a trading possibilities line (or curve), as shown in **Figure 23.2 (Key Graph).** Just as a production possibilities curve shows the amounts of these products that a full-employment economy can obtain by shifting resources from one to the other, a **trading possibilities line** shows

(a)
United States

(b)
Mexico

FIGURE 23.2 Trading possi ... **the gains from trade.** As a result ... and trade, both the United States an ... have higher levels of output than the ... attainable on their domestic production possibilities curves. (a) The United States can move from point A on its domestic production possibilities curve to, say, A' on its trading possibilities line. (b) Mexico can move from Z to Z'.

QUICK QUIZ FOR FIGURE 23.2

1. The production possibilities curves in graphs (a) and (b) imply:
   a. increasing domestic opportunity costs.
   b. decreasing domestic opportunity costs.
   c. constant domestic opportunity costs.
   d. first decreasing, then increasing, domestic opportunity costs.

2. Before specialization, the domestic opportunity cost of producing 1 unit of beef is:
   a. 1 unit of vegetables in both the United States and Mexico.
   b. 1 unit of vegetables in the United States and 2 units of vegetables in Mexico.
   c. 2 units of vegetables in the United States and 1 unit of vegetables in Mexico.
   d. 1 unit of vegetables in the United States and $\frac{1}{2}$ unit of vegetables in Mexico.

3. After specialization and international trade, the world output of beef and vegetables is:
   a. 20 tons of beef and 20 tons of vegetables.
   b. 45 tons of beef and 15 tons of vegetables.
   c. 30 tons of beef and 20 tons of vegetables.
   d. 10 tons of beef and 30 tons of vegetables.

4. After specialization and international trade:
   a. the United States can obtain units of vegetables at less cost than it could before trade.
   b. Mexico can obtain more than 20 tons of vegetables, if it so chooses.
   c. the United States no longer has a comparative advantage in producing beef.
   d. Mexico can benefit by prohibiting vegetables imports from the United States.

Answers: 1. c; 2. b; 3. c; 4. a

the amounts of the two products that a nation can obtain by specializing in one product and trading for the other. The trading possibilities lines in Figure 23.2 reflect the assumption that both nations specialize on the basis of comparative advantage: The United States specializes completely in beef (at point B in Figure 23.2a), and Mexico specializes completely in vegetables (at point v in Figure 23.2b).

Improved Alternatives With specialization and trade, the United States is no longer constrained by its domestic production possibilities line, which requires it to give up 1 ton of beef for every 1 ton of vegetables it wants as it moves up its domestic production possibilities line from, say, point B. Instead, the United States, through trade with Mexico, can get $1\frac{1}{2}$ tons of vegetables for every ton of beef that it exports to Mexico, as long as Mexico has vegetables o export. Trading possibilities line BV' thus represents the $1B \equiv 1\frac{1}{2}V$ trading ratio.

Similarly, Mexico, starting at, say, point v, no longer has to move down its domestic production possibilities curve, giving up 2 tons of vegetables for each ton of beef it wants. It can now export just $1\frac{1}{2}$ tons of vegetables for each 1 ton of beef that it wants by moving down its trading possibilities line vb'.

Specialization and trade create a new exchange ratio between beef and vegetables, and that ratio is reflected in each nation's trading possibilities line. For both nations, this exchange ratio is superior to the unspecialized exchange ratio embodied in their respective production possibilities curves. By specializing in beef and trading for Mexico's vegetables, the United States can obtain more than 1 ton of vegetables for 1 ton of beef. By specializing in vegetables and trading for U.S. beef, Mexico can obtain 1 ton of beef for less than 2 tons of vegetables. In both cases, self-sufficiency is inefficient and therefore undesirable.

Greater Output By specializing on the basis of comparative advantage and by trading for goods that are produced in the nation with greater domestic efficiency, the United States and Mexico can achieve combinations of beef and vegetables beyond their own individual production possibilities curves. Specialization according to comparative advantage results in a more efficient allocation of world resources, and larger outputs of both products are therefore available to both nations.

Suppose that at the $1B \equiv 1\frac{1}{2}V$ terms of trade, the United States exports 10 tons of beef to Mexico and in return Mexico exports 15 tons of vegetables to the United States. How do the new quantities of beef and vegetables available to the two nations compare with the optimal product mixes that existed before specialization and trade? Point A in Figure 23.2a reminds us that the United States chose 18 tons of beef and 12 tons of vegetables originally. But by producing 30 tons of beef and no vegetables and by trading 10 tons of beef for 15 tons of vegetables, the United States can obtain 20 tons of beef and 15 tons of vegetables. This new, superior combination of beef and vegetables is indicated by point A' in Figure 23.2a. Compared with the no-trade amounts of 18 tons of beef and 12 tons of vegetables, the United States' **gains from trade** are 2 tons of beef and 3 tons of vegetables.

INTERACTIVE GRAPHS

G 23.1

Comparative advantage

WORKED PROBLEMS

W 23.1

Gains from trade

Similarly, recall that Mexico's optimal product mix was 4 tons of vegetables and 8 tons of beef (point Z) before specialization and trade. Now, after specializing in vegetables and trading for beef, Mexico can have 5 tons of vegetables and 10 tons of beef. It accomplishes that by producing 20 tons of vegetables and no beef and exporting 15 tons of its vegetables in exchange for 10 tons of American beef. This new position is indicated by point Z' in Figure 23.2b. Mexico's gains from trade are 1 ton of vegetables and 2 tons of beef.

Points A' and Z' in Figure 23.2 are superior economic positions to points A and Z. This fact is enormously important! We know that a nation can expand its production possibilities boundary by (1) expanding the quantity and improving the quality of its resources or (2) realizing technological progress. We have now established that international trade can enable a nation to circumvent the output constraint illustrated by its production possibilities curve. An economy can grow by expanding international trade. The outcome of international specialization and trade is equivalent to having more and better resources or discovering and implementing improved production techniques.

Table 23.1 summarizes the transactions and outcomes in our analysis. Please give it one final careful review.

CONSIDER THIS . . .

Misunderstanding the Gains from Trade

It is a common myth that the greatest benefit to be derived from international trade is greater domestic employment in the export sector. This suggests that exports are "good" because they increase domestic employment, whereas imports are "bad" because they deprive people of jobs at home. As we have demonstrated, the true benefit created by international trade is the overall increase in output available through specialization and exchange.

A nation does not need international trade to operate *on* its production possibilities curve. It can fully employ its resources, including labor, with or without international trade. International trade, however, enables a country to reach a point of consumption beyond its domestic production possibilities curve. The gain from trade to a nation is the extra output obtained from abroad—the imports obtained for less sacrifice of other goods than if they were produced at home.

Trade with Increasing Costs

To explain the basic principles underlying international trade, we simplified our analysis in several ways. For example, we limited discussion to two products and two nations. But multiproduct and multinational analysis yield the same conclusions. We also assumed constant opportunity costs (linear production possibilities curves), which is a more substantive simplification. Let's consider the effect of allowing increasing opportunity costs (concave-to-the-origin production possibilities curves) to enter the picture.

Suppose that the United States and Mexico initially are at positions on their concave production possibilities curves where their domestic cost ratios are $1B \equiv 1V$ and $1B \equiv 2V$, as they were in our constant-cost analysis. As before, comparative advantage indicates that the United States should specialize in beef and Mexico in vegetables. But now, as the United States begins to expand beef production, its cost of beef will rise; it will have to sacrifice more than 1 ton of vegetables to get 1 additional ton of beef. Resources are no longer perfectly substitutable between alternative uses, as the constant-cost assumption implied. Resources less and less suitable to beef production must be allocated to the U.S. beef industry in expanding beef output, and that means increasing costs—the sacrifice of larger and larger amounts of vegetables for each additional ton of beef.

Similarly, suppose that Mexico expands vegetable production starting from its $1B \equiv 2V$ cost ratio position. As production increases, it will find that its $1B \equiv 2V$ cost ratio begins to rise. Sacrificing 1 ton of beef will free resources that are capable of producing only something less than 2 tons of vegetables, because those transferred resources are less suitable to vegetable production.

As the U.S. cost ratio falls from $1B \equiv 1V$ and the Mexican ratio rises from $1B \equiv 2V$, a point will be reached where the cost ratios are equal in the two nations, perhaps at $1B \equiv 1\frac{3}{4}V$. At this point the underlying basis for further specialization and trade—differing cost ratios—has disappeared, and further specialization is therefore uneconomical. And, most important, this point of equal cost ratios may be reached while the United States is still producing some vegetables along with its beef and Mexico is producing some beef along with its vegetables. The primary effect of increasing opportunity costs is less-than-complete specialization. For this reason, we often find domestically produced products competing directly against identical or similar imported products within a particular economy.

The Case for Free Trade

The case for free trade reduces to one compelling argument: Through free trade based on the principle of comparative advantage, the world economy can achieve a more efficient allocation of resources and a higher level of material well-being than it can without free trade.

Since the resource mixes and technological knowledge of the world's nations are all somewhat different, each nation can produce particular commodities at different real costs. Each nation should produce goods for which its domestic opportunity costs are lower than the domestic opportunity costs of other nations and exchange those goods for products for which its domestic opportunity costs are high relative to those of other nations. If each nation does this, the world will realize the advantages of geographic and human specialization. The world and each free-trading nation can obtain a larger real income from the fixed supplies of resources available to it.

Government trade barriers lessen or eliminate gains from specialization. If nations cannot trade freely, they must shift resources from efficient (low-cost) to inefficient (high-cost) uses to satisfy their diverse wants. A recent study suggests that the elimination of trade barriers since the Second World War has increased the income of the average U.S. household by at least $7000 and perhaps by as much as $13,000. These income gains are recurring; they happen year after year.[2]

One side benefit of free trade is that it promotes competition and deters monopoly. The increased competition from foreign firms forces domestic firms to find and use the lowest-cost production techniques. It also compels them to be innovative with respect to both product quality and production methods, thereby contributing to economic growth. And free trade gives consumers a wider range of product choices. The reasons to favor free trade are the same as the reasons to endorse competition.

A second side benefit of free trade is that it links national interests and breaks down national animosities. Confronted with political disagreements, trading partners tend to negotiate rather than make war.

QUICK REVIEW 23.1

- International trade enables nations to specialize, increase productivity, and increase output available for consumption.
- Comparative advantage means total world output will be greatest when each good is produced by the nation that has the lowest domestic opportunity cost.
- Specialization is less than complete among nations because opportunity costs normally rise as any specific nation produces more of a particular good.

---

[2]Scott C. Bradford, Paul L. E. Grieco, and Gary C. Hufbauer, "The Payoff to America from Globalization," *The World Economy*, July 2006, pp. 893–916.

Supply and Demand Analysis of Exports and Imports

Supply and demand analysis reveals how equilibrium prices and quantities of exports and imports are determined. The amount of a good or a service a nation will export or import depends on differences between the equilibrium world price and the equilibrium domestic price. The interaction of *world* supply and demand determines the equilibrium **world price**—the price that equates the quantities supplied and demanded globally. *Domestic* supply and demand determine the equilibrium **domestic price**—the price that would prevail in a closed economy that does not engage in international trade. The domestic price equates quantity supplied and quantity demanded domestically.

In the absence of trade, the domestic prices in a closed economy may or may not equal the world equilibrium prices. When economies are opened for international trade, differences between world and domestic prices encourage exports or imports. To see how, consider the international effects of such price differences in a simple two-nation world, consisting of the United States and

Canada, that are both producing aluminum. We assume there are no trade barriers, such as tariffs and quotas, and no international transportation costs.

Supply and Demand in the United States

Figure 23.3a shows the domestic supply curve S_d and the domestic demand curve D_d for aluminum in the United States, which for now is a closed economy. The intersection of S_d and D_d determines the equilibrium domestic price of $1 per pound and the equilibrium domestic quantity of 100 million pounds. Domestic suppliers produce 100 million pounds and sell them all at $1 a pound. So there are no domestic surpluses or shortages of aluminum.

But what if the U.S. economy were opened to trade and the world price of aluminum were above or below this $1 domestic price?

U.S. Export Supply If the aluminum price in the rest of the world (that is, Canada) exceeds $1, U.S. firms will produce more than 100 million pounds and will export the excess domestic output. First, consider a world price of

FIGURE 23.3 U.S. export supply and import demand. (a) Domestic supply S_d and demand D_d set the domestic equilibrium price of aluminum at $1 per pound. At world prices above $1 there are domestic surpluses of aluminum. At prices below $1 there are domestic shortages. (b) Surpluses are exported (top curve), and shortages are met by importing aluminum (lower curve). The export supply curve shows the direct relationship between world prices and U.S. exports; the import demand curve portrays the inverse relationship between world prices and U.S. imports.

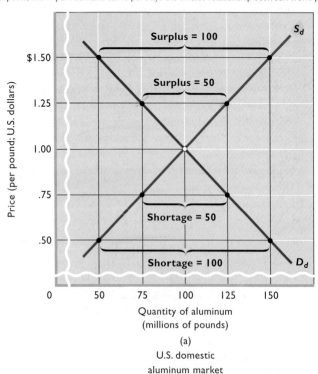

(a)
U.S. domestic
aluminum market

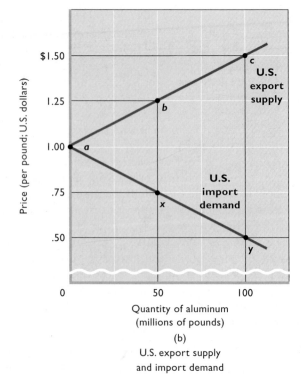

(b)
U.S. export supply
and import demand

$1.25. We see from the supply curve S_d that U.S. aluminum firms will produce 125 million pounds of aluminum at that price. The demand curve D_d tells us that the United States will purchase only 75 million pounds at $1.25. The outcome is a domestic surplus of 50 million pounds of aluminum. U.S. producers will export those 50 million pounds at the $1.25 world price.

What if the world price were $1.50? The supply curve shows that U.S. firms will produce 150 million pounds of aluminum, while the demand curve tells us that U.S. consumers will buy only 50 million pounds. So U.S. producers will export the domestic surplus of 100 million pounds.

Toward the top of Figure 23.3b we plot the domestic surpluses—the U.S. exports—that occur at world prices above the $1 domestic equilibrium price. When the world and domestic prices are equal (= $1), the quantity of exports supplied is zero (point *a*). There is no surplus of domestic output to export. But when the world price is $1.25, U.S. firms export 50 million pounds of surplus aluminum (point *b*). At a $1.50 world price, the domestic surplus of 100 million pounds is exported (point *c*).

The U.S. **export supply curve,** found by connecting points *a*, *b*, and *c*, shows the amount of aluminum U.S. producers will export at each world price above $1. This curve *slopes upward*, indicating a direct or positive relationship between the world price and the amount of U.S. exports. As world prices increase relative to domestic prices, U.S. exports rise.

U.S. Import Demand If the world price is below the domestic $1 price, the United States will import aluminum. Consider a $.75 world price. The supply curve in Figure 23.3a reveals that at that price U.S. firms produce only 75 million pounds of aluminum. But the demand curve shows that the United States wants to buy 125 million pounds at that price. The result is a domestic shortage of 50 million pounds. To satisfy that shortage, the United States will import 50 million pounds of aluminum.

At an even lower world price, $.50, U.S. producers will supply only 50 million pounds. Because U.S. consumers want to buy 150 million pounds at that price, there is a domestic shortage of 100 million pounds. Imports will flow to the United States to make up the difference. That is, at a $.50 world price U.S. firms will supply 50 million pounds and 100 million pounds will be imported.

In Figure 23.3b we plot the U.S. **import demand curve** from these data. This *downsloping curve* shows the amounts of aluminum that will be imported at world prices below the $1 U.S. domestic price. The relationship between world prices and imported amounts is inverse or negative. At a world price of $1, domestic output will satisfy U.S. demand; imports will be zero (point *a*). But at $.75 the United States will import 50 million pounds of aluminum (point *x*); at $.50, the United States will import 100 million pounds (point *y*). Connecting points *a*, *x*, and *y* yields the *downsloping* U.S. import demand curve. It reveals that as world prices fall relative to U.S. domestic prices, U.S. imports increase.

Supply and Demand in Canada

We repeat our analysis in Figure 23.4, this time from the viewpoint of Canada. (We have converted Canadian dollar prices to U.S. dollar prices via the exchange rate.) Note that the domestic supply curve S_d and the domestic demand curve D_d for aluminum in Canada yield a domestic price of $.75, which is $.25 lower than the $1 U.S. domestic price.

The analysis proceeds exactly as above except that the domestic price is now the Canadian price. If the world price is $.75, Canadians will neither export nor import aluminum (giving us point *q* in Figure 23.4b). At world prices above $.75, Canadian firms will produce more aluminum than Canadian consumers will buy. Canadian firms will export the surplus. At a $1 world price, Figure 23.4b tells us that Canada will have and export a domestic surplus of 50 million pounds (yielding point *r*). At $1.25, it will have and will export a domestic surplus of 100 million pounds (point *s*). Connecting these points yields the upsloping Canadian export supply curve, which reflects the domestic surpluses (and hence the exports) that occur when the world price exceeds the $.75 Canadian domestic price.

At world prices below $.75, domestic shortages occur in Canada. At a $.50 world price, Figure 23.4a shows that Canadian consumers want to buy 125 million pounds of aluminum but Canadian firms will produce only 75 million pounds. The shortage will bring 50 million pounds of imports to Canada (point *t* in Figure 23.4b). The Canadian import demand curve in that figure shows the Canadian imports that will occur at all world aluminum prices below the $.75 Canadian domestic price.

Equilibrium World Price, Exports, and Imports

We now have the tools for determining the **equilibrium world price** of aluminum and the equilibrium world levels of exports and imports when the world is opened to trade. Figure 23.5 combines the U.S. export supply curve and import demand curve in Figure 23.3b and the Canadian export supply curve and import demand curve in Figure 23.4b. The two U.S. curves proceed rightward from the $1 U.S. domestic price; the two Canadian curves proceed rightward from the $.75 Canadian domestic price.

FIGURE 23.4 Canadian export supply and import demand. (a) At world prices above the $.75 domestic price, production in Canada exceeds domestic consumption. At world prices below $.75, domestic shortages occur. (b) Surpluses result in exports, and shortages result in imports. The Canadian export supply curve and import demand curve depict the relationships between world prices and exports or imports.

(a)

Canada's domestic
aluminum market

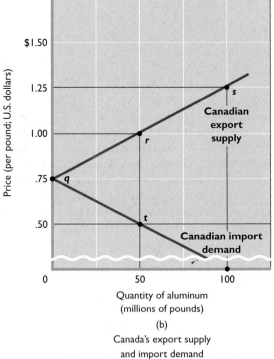

(b)

Canada's export supply
and import demand

FIGURE 23.5 Equilibrium world price and quantity of exports and imports. In a two-nation world, the equilibrium world price (= $.88) is determined by the intersection of one nation's export supply curve and the other nation's import demand curve. This intersection also decides the equilibrium volume of exports and imports. Here, Canada exports 25 million pounds of aluminum to the United States.

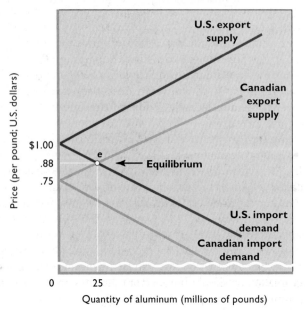

Quantity of aluminum (millions of pounds)

International equilibrium occurs in this two-nation model where one nation's import demand curve intersects another nation's export supply curve. In this case the U.S. import demand curve intersects Canada's export supply curve at *e*. There, the world price of aluminum is $.88. The Canadian export supply curve indicates that Canada will export 25 million pounds of aluminum at this price. Also at this price the United States will import 25 million pounds from Canada, indicated by the U.S. import demand curve. The $.88 world price equates the quantity of imports demanded and the quantity of exports supplied (25 million pounds). Thus, there will be world trade of 25 million pounds of aluminum at $.88 per pound.

Note that after trade, the single $.88 world price will prevail in both Canada and the United States. Only one price for a standardized commodity can persist in a highly competitive world market. With trade, all consumers can buy a pound of aluminum for $.88, and all producers can sell it for that price. This world price means that Canadians will pay more for aluminum with trade ($.88) than without it ($.75). The increased Canadian output caused

> **WORKED PROBLEMS**
>
> **W 23.2**
> ────────
> Equilibrium world price, exports,
> and imports

by trade raises Canadian per-unit production costs and therefore raises the price of aluminum in Canada. The United States, however, pays less for aluminum with trade ($.88) than without it ($1). The U.S. gain comes from Canada's comparative cost advantage in producing aluminum.

Why would Canada willingly send 25 million pounds of its aluminum output to the United States for U.S. consumption? After all, producing this output uses up scarce Canadian resources and drives up the price of aluminum for Canadians. Canadians are willing to export aluminum to the United States because Canadians gain the means— the U.S. dollars—to import other goods, say, computer software, from the United States. Canadian exports enable Canadians to acquire imports that have greater value to Canadians than the exported aluminum. Canadian exports to the United States finance Canadian imports from the United States.

QUICK REVIEW 23.2

- A nation will export a particular product if the world price exceeds the domestic price; it will import the product if the world price is less than the domestic price.
- In a two-country world model, equilibrium world prices and equilibrium quantities of exports and imports occur where one nation's export supply curve intersects the other nation's import demand curve.

Trade Barriers and Export Subsidies

While a nation as a whole gains from trade, trade may harm particular domestic industries and their workers. Those industries might seek to preserve their economic positions by persuading their respective governments to protect them from imports—perhaps through tariffs, import quotas, or other trade barriers.

Indeed, the public may be won over by the apparent plausibility ("Cut imports and prevent domestic unemployment") and the patriotic ring ("Buy American!") of the arguments. The alleged benefits of tariffs are immediate and clear-cut to the public, but the adverse effects cited by economists are obscure and dispersed over the entire economy. When political deal-making is added in—"You back tariffs for the apparel industry in my state, and I'll back tariffs for the auto industry in your state"—the outcome can be a politically robust network of trade barriers. These impediments to free international trade can take several forms.

CONSIDER THIS . . .

Buy American?

Will "buying American" make Americans better off? No, says Dallas Federal Reserve economist W. Michael Cox:

A common myth is that it is better for Americans to spend their money at home than abroad. The best way to expose the fallacy of this argument is to take it to its logical extreme. If it is better for me to spend my money here than abroad, then it is even better yet to buy in Texas than in New York, better yet to buy in Dallas than in Houston . . . in my own neighborhood . . . within my own family . . . to consume only what I can produce. Alone and poor.*

*"The Fruits of Free Trade," 2002 Annual Report, by W. Michael Cox and Richard Alm, p. 16, Federal Reserve Bank of Dallas. Used with permission.

Tariffs are excise taxes or "duties" on the dollar values or physical quantities of imported goods. They may be imposed to obtain revenue or to protect domestic firms. A **revenue tariff** is usually applied to a product that is not being produced domestically, for example, tin, coffee, or bananas in the case of the United States. Rates on revenue tariffs tend to be modest and are designed to provide the Federal government with revenue. A **protective tariff** is implemented to shield domestic producers from foreign competition. These tariffs impede free trade by increasing the prices of imported goods and therefore shifting sales toward domestic producers. Although protective tariffs are usually not high enough to stop the importation of foreign goods, they put foreign producers at a competitive disadvantage. A tariff on imported auto tires, for example, would make domestically produced tires more attractive to consumers.

An **import quota** is a limit on the quantities or total values of specific items that are imported in some period. Once a quota is filled, further imports of that product are choked off. Import quotas are more effective than tariffs in impeding international trade. With a tariff, a product can go on being imported in large quantities. But with an import quota, all imports are prohibited once the quota is filled.

A **nontariff barrier (NTB)** includes onerous licensing requirements, unreasonable standards pertaining to product quality, or simply bureaucratic hurdles and delays in customs procedures. Some nations require that importers of foreign goods obtain licenses and then restrict the number of licenses issued. Although many nations carefully inspect imported agricultural products to prevent the introduction of potentially harmful insects, some countries use lengthy inspections to impede imports. Japan and the European countries frequently require that their domestic importers of foreign goods obtain licenses. By restricting the issuance of licenses, governments can limit imports.

A **voluntary export restriction (VER)** is a trade barrier by which foreign firms "voluntarily" limit the amount of their exports to a particular country. VERs have the same effect as import quotas and are agreed to by exporters to avoid more stringent tariffs or quotas. In the late 1990s, for example, Canadian producers of softwood lumber (fir, spruce, cedar, pine) agreed to a VER on exports to the United States under the threat of a permanently higher U.S. tariff.

ORIGIN OF THE IDEA

O 23.2

Trade protectionism

An **export subsidy** consists of a government payment to a domestic producer of export goods and is designed to aid that producer. By reducing production costs, the subsidies enable the domestic firm to charge a lower price and thus to sell more exports in world markets. Two examples: Some European governments have heavily subsidized Airbus Industries, a European firm that produces commercial aircraft. The subsidies help Airbus compete against the American firm Boeing. The United States and other nations have subsidized domestic farmers to boost the domestic food supply. Such subsidies have artificially lowered export prices on agricultural produce.

Later in this chapter we will discuss some of the specific arguments and appeals that are made to justify protection.

Economic Impact of Tariffs

We will confine our in-depth analysis of the effects of trade barriers to the two most common forms: tariffs and quotas. Once again, we turn to supply and demand analysis for help. Curves D_d and S_d in Figure 23.6 show domestic demand and supply for a product in which a nation, say, the United States, does *not* have a comparative advantage—for example, DVD players. (Disregard curve $S_d + Q$ for now.) Without world trade, the domestic price and output would be P_d and q, respectively.

Assume now that the domestic economy is opened to world trade and that Japan, which *does* have a comparative advantage in DVD players, begins to sell its players in the United States. We assume that with free trade the domestic price cannot differ from the world price, which here is P_w. At P_w domestic consumption is d and domestic production is a.

FIGURE 23.6 The economic effects of a protective tariff or an import quota. A tariff that increases the price of a good from P_w to P_t will reduce domestic consumption from d to c. Domestic producers will be able to sell more output (b rather than a) at a higher price (P_t rather than P_w). Foreign exporters are injured because they sell less output (bc rather than ad). The yellow area indicates the amount of tariff paid by domestic consumers. An import quota of bc units has the same effect as the tariff, with one exception: The amount represented by the yellow area will go to foreign producers rather than to the domestic government.

The horizontal distance between the domestic supply and demand curves at P_w represents imports of ad. Thus far, our analysis is similar to the analysis of world prices in Figure 23.3.

Direct Effects   Suppose now that the United States imposes a tariff on each imported DVD player. The tariff, which raises the price of imported players from P_w to P_t, has four effects:

- *Decline in consumption* Consumption of DVD players in the United States declines from d to c as the higher price moves buyers up and to the left along their demand curve. The tariff prompts consumers to buy fewer players, and reallocate a portion of their expenditures to less desired substitute products. U.S. consumers are clearly injured by the tariff, since they pay $P_t - P_w$ more for each of the c units they buy at price P_t.
- *Increased domestic production* U.S. producers—who are not subject to the tariff—receive the higher price P_t per unit. Because this new price is higher than the pretariff world price P_w, the domestic DVD-player industry moves up and to the right along its supply curve S_d, increasing domestic output from a to b. Domestic producers thus enjoy both a higher price and expanded sales; this explains why domestic producers lobby for protective tariffs. But from a social point of

view, the increase in domestic production from *a* to *b* means that the tariff permits domestic producers of players to bid resources away from other, more efficient, U.S. industries.

- **Decline in imports** Japanese producers are hurt. Although the sales price of each player is higher by $P_t - P_w$, that amount accrues to the U.S. government, not to Japanese producers. The after-tariff world price, or the per-unit revenue to Japanese producers, remains at P_w, but the volume of U.S. imports (Japanese exports) falls from *ad* to *bc*.

- **Tariff revenue** The yellow rectangle represents the amount of revenue the tariff yields. Total revenue from the tariff is determined by multiplying the tariff, $P_t - P_w$ per unit, by the number of players imported, *bc*. This tariff revenue is a transfer of income from consumers to government and does not represent any net change in the nation's economic well-being. The result is that government gains this portion of what consumers lose by paying more for DVD players.

Indirect Effect Tariffs have a subtle effect beyond what our supply and demand diagram can show. Because Japan sells fewer DVD players in the United States, it earns fewer dollars and so must buy fewer U.S. exports. U.S. export industries must then cut production and release resources. These are highly efficient industries, as we know from their comparative advantage and their ability to sell goods in world markets.

Tariffs directly promote the expansion of inefficient industries that do not have a comparative advantage; they also indirectly cause the contraction of relatively efficient industries that do have a comparative advantage. Put bluntly, tariffs cause resources to be shifted in the wrong direction—and that is not surprising. We know that specialization and world trade lead to more efficient use of world resources and greater world output. But protective tariffs reduce world trade. Therefore, tariffs also reduce efficiency and the world's real output.

Economic Impact of Quotas

We noted earlier that an import quota is a legal limit placed on the amount of some product that can be imported in a given year. Quotas have the same economic impact as a tariff, with one big difference: While tariffs generate revenue for the domestic government, a quota transfers that revenue to foreign producers.

Suppose in Figure 23.6 that, instead of imposing a tariff, the United States prohibits any imports of Japanese DVD players in excess of *bc* units. In other words, an import quota

of *bc* players is imposed on Japan. We deliberately chose the size of this quota to be the same amount as imports would be under a $P_t - P_w$ tariff so that we can compare "equivalent" situations. As a consequence of the quota, the supply of players is $S_d + Q$ in the United States. This supply consists of the domestic supply plus the fixed amount *bc* (= Q) that importers will provide at each domestic price. The supply curve $S_w + Q$ does not extend below price P_w because Japanese producers would not export players to the United States at any price below P_w; instead, they would sell them to other countries at the world market price of P_w.

Most of the economic results are the same as those with a tariff. Prices of DVD players are higher (P_t instead of P_w) because imports have been reduced from *ad* to *bc*. Domestic consumption of DVD players is down from *d* to *c*. U.S. producers enjoy both a higher price (P_t rather than P_w) and increased sales (*b* rather than *a*).

The difference is that the price increase of $P_t - P_w$ paid by U.S. consumers on imports of *bc*—the yellow area—no longer goes to the U.S. Treasury as tariff (tax) revenue but flows to the Japanese firms that have acquired the quota rights to sell DVD players in the United States. For consumers in the United States, a tariff produces a better economic outcome than a quota, other things being the same. A tariff generates government revenue that can be used to cut other taxes or to finance public goods and services that benefit the United States. In contrast, the higher price created by quotas results in additional revenue for foreign producers.

Net Costs of Tariffs and Quotas

Figure 23.6 shows that tariffs and quotas impose costs on domestic consumers but provide gains to domestic producers and, in the case of tariffs, revenue to the Federal government. The consumer costs of trade restrictions are calculated by determining the effect the restrictions have on consumer prices. Protection raises the price of a product in three ways: (1) The price of the imported product goes up; (2) the higher price of imports causes some consumers to shift their purchases to higher-priced domestically produced goods; and (3) the prices of domestically produced goods rise because import competition has declined.

Study after study finds that the costs to consumers substantially exceed the gains to producers and government. A sizable net cost or efficiency loss to society arises from trade protection. Furthermore, industries employ large amounts of economic resources to influence Congress to pass and retain protectionist laws. Because these rent-seeking efforts divert resources away from more socially desirable purposes, trade restrictions impose these additional costs on society as well.

Conclusion: The gains that U.S. trade barriers create for protected industries and their workers come at the expense of much greater losses for the entire economy. The result is economic inefficiency, reduced consumption, and lower standards of living.

The Case for Protection: A Critical Review

Despite the logic of specialization and trade, there are still protectionists in some union halls, corporate boardrooms, and congressional conference rooms. What arguments do protectionists make to justify trade barriers? How valid are those arguments?

Military Self-Sufficiency Argument

The argument here is not economic but political-military: Protective tariffs are needed to preserve or strengthen industries that produce the materials essential for national defense. In an uncertain world, the political-military objectives (self-sufficiency) sometimes must take precedence over economic goals (efficiency in the use of world resources).

Unfortunately, it is difficult to measure and compare the benefit of increased national security against the cost of economic inefficiency when protective tariffs are imposed. The economist can only point out that when a nation levies tariffs to increase military self-sufficiency it incurs economic costs.

All people in the United States would agree that relying on hostile nations for necessary military equipment is not a good idea, yet the self-sufficiency argument is open to serious abuse. Nearly every industry can claim that it makes direct or indirect contributions to national security and hence deserves protection from imports.

Diversification-for-Stability Argument

Highly specialized economies such as Saudi Arabia (based on oil) and Cuba (based on sugar) are dependent on international markets for their income. In these economies, wars, international political developments, recessions abroad, and random fluctuations in world supply and demand for one or two particular goods can cause deep declines in export revenues and therefore in domestic income. Tariff and quota protection are allegedly needed in such nations to enable greater industrial diversification. That way, these economies will not be so dependent on exporting one or two products to obtain the other goods they need. Such goods will be available domestically, thereby providing greater domestic stability.

There is some truth in this diversification-for-stability argument. But the argument has little or no relevance to the United States and other advanced economies. Also, the economic costs of diversification may be great; for example, one-crop economies may be highly inefficient at manufacturing.

Infant Industry Argument

The infant industry argument contends that protective tariffs are needed to allow new domestic industries to establish themselves. Temporarily shielding young domestic firms from the severe competition of more mature and more efficient foreign firms will give infant industries a chance to develop and become efficient producers.

This argument for protection rests on an alleged exception to the case for free trade. The exception is that young industries have not had, and if they face mature foreign competition will never have, the chance to make the long-run adjustments needed for larger scale and greater efficiency in production. In this view, tariff protection for such infant industries will correct a misallocation of world resources perpetuated by historically different levels of economic development between domestic and foreign industries.

There are some logical problems with the infant industry argument. In the developing nations it is difficult to determine which industries are the infants that are capable of achieving economic maturity and therefore deserving protection. Also, protective tariffs may persist even after industrial maturity has been realized.

Most economists feel that if infant industries are to be subsidized, there are better means than tariffs for doing so. Direct subsidies, for example, have the advantage of making explicit which industries are being aided and to what degree.

Protection-against-Dumping Argument

The protection-against-dumping argument contends that tariffs are needed to protect domestic firms from "dumping" by foreign producers. **Dumping** is the sale of a product in a foreign country at prices either below cost or below the prices commonly charged at home.

Economists cite two plausible reasons for this behavior. First, with regard to below-cost dumping, firms in country A may dump goods at below cost into country B in an attempt to drive their competitors in country B out of business. If the firms in country A succeed in driving their competitors in country B out of business, they will enjoy monopoly power and monopoly prices and profits on the goods they subsequently sell in country B. Their hope is that the longer-term monopoly profits will more than offset the losses from below-cost sales that must take place while they are attempting to drive their competitors in country B out of business.

Second, dumping that involves selling abroad at a price that is below the price commonly charged in the home country (but that is still at or above production costs) may be a form of price discrimination, which is charging different prices to different customers. As an example, a foreign seller that has a monopoly in its home market may find that it can maximize its overall profit by charging a high price in its monopolized domestic market while charging a lower price in the United States, where it must compete with U.S. producers. Curiously, it may pursue this strategy even if it makes no profit at all from its sales in the United States, where it must charge the competitive price. So why bother selling in the United States? Because the increase in overall production that comes about by exporting to the United States may allow the firm to obtain the per-unit cost savings often associated with large-scale production. These cost savings imply even higher profits in the monopolized domestic market.

Because dumping is an "unfair trade practice," most nations prohibit it. For example, where dumping is shown to injure U.S. firms, the Federal government imposes tariffs called *antidumping duties* on the goods in question. But relatively few documented cases of dumping occur each year, and specific instances of unfair trade do not justify widespread, permanent tariffs. Moreover, antidumping duties can be abused. Often, what appears to be dumping is simply comparative advantage at work.

Increased Domestic Employment Argument

Arguing for a tariff to "save U.S. jobs" becomes fashionable when the economy encounters a recession (such as the severe recession of 2007–2009 in the United States). In an economy that engages in international trade, exports involve spending on domestic output and imports reflect spending to obtain part of another nation's output. So, in this argument, reducing imports will divert spending on another nation's output to spending on domestic output. Thus, domestic output and employment will rise. But this argument has several shortcomings.

While imports may eliminate some U.S. jobs, they create others. Imports may have eliminated the jobs of some U.S. steel and textile workers in recent years, but other workers have gained jobs unloading ships, flying imported aircraft, and selling imported electronic equipment. Import restrictions alter the composition of employment, but they may have little or no effect on the volume of employment.

The *fallacy of composition*—the false idea that what is true for the part is necessarily true for the whole—is also present in this rationale for tariffs. All nations cannot simultaneously succeed in restricting imports while maintaining their exports; what is true for one nation is not true for all nations. The exports of one nation must be the imports of another nation. To the extent that one country is able to expand its economy through an excess of exports over imports, the resulting excess of imports over exports worsens another economy's unemployment problem. It is no wonder that tariffs and import quotas meant to achieve domestic full employment are called "beggar my neighbor" policies: They achieve short-run domestic goals by making trading partners poorer.

Moreover, nations adversely affected by tariffs and quotas are likely to retaliate, causing a "trade war" (more precisely, a *trade barrier war*) that will choke off trade and make all nations worse off. The **Smoot-Hawley Tariff Act** of 1930 is a classic example. Although that act was meant to reduce imports and stimulate U.S. production, the high tariffs it authorized prompted adversely affected nations to retaliate with tariffs equally high. International trade fell, lowering the output and income of all nations. Economic historians generally agree that the Smoot-Hawley Tariff Act was a contributing cause of the Great Depression.

Finally, forcing an excess of exports over imports cannot succeed in raising domestic employment over the long run. It is through U.S. imports that foreign nations earn dollars for buying U.S. exports. In the long run, a nation must import in order to export. The long-run impact of tariffs is not an increase in domestic employment but, at best, a reallocation of workers away from export industries and to protected domestic industries. This shift implies a less efficient allocation of resources.

Cheap Foreign Labor Argument

The cheap foreign labor argument says that domestic firms and workers must be shielded from the ruinous competition of countries where wages are low. If protection is not provided, cheap imports will flood U.S. markets and the prices of U.S. goods—along with the wages of U.S. workers—will be pulled down. That is, domestic living standards in the United States will be reduced.

This argument can be rebutted at several levels. The logic of the argument suggests that it is not mutually beneficial for rich and poor persons to trade with one another. However, that is not the case. A low-income farmworker may pick lettuce or tomatoes for a rich landowner, and both may benefit from the transaction. And both U.S. consumers and Chinese workers gain when they "trade" a pair of athletic shoes priced at $30 as opposed to U.S. consumers being restricted to buying a similar shoe made in the United States for $60.

Also, recall that gains from trade are based on comparative advantage, not on absolute advantage. Look back at Figure 23.1, where we supposed that the United States and Mexico had labor forces of exactly the same size. Noting the positions of the production possibilities curves, observe that U.S. labor can produce more of either good. Thus, it is more productive. Because of this greater productivity, we can expect wages and living standards to be higher for U.S. labor. Mexico's less productive labor will receive lower wages.

The cheap foreign labor argument suggests that, to maintain its standard of living, the United States should not trade with low-wage Mexico. What if it does not trade with Mexico? Will wages and living standards rise in the United States as a result? No. To obtain vegetables, the United States will have to reallocate a portion of its labor from its relatively more-efficient beef industry to its relatively less-efficient vegetables industry. As a result, the average productivity of U.S. labor will fall, as will real wages and living standards. The labor forces of both countries will have diminished standards of living because without specialization and trade they will have less output available to them. Compare column 4 with column 1 in Table 23.1 or points A' and Z' with A and Z in Figure 23.2 to confirm this point.

Another problem with the cheap foreign labor argument is that its proponents incorrectly focus on labor costs per hour when what really matters is labor costs per unit of output. As an example, suppose that a U.S. factory pays its workers $20 per hour while a factory in a developing country pays its workers $4 per hour. The proponents of the cheap foreign labor argument look at these numbers and conclude—incorrectly—that it is impossible for the U.S. factory to compete with the factory in the developing country. But this conclusion fails to take into account two crucial facts:

- What actually matters is labor costs per *unit of output*, not labor costs per *hour of work*.
- Differences in productivity typically mean that labor costs per unit of output are often nearly identical despite huge differences in hourly labor costs.

To see why these points matter so much, let's take into account how productive the two factories are. Because the U.S. factory uses much more sophisticated technology, better trained workers, and a lot more capital per worker, one worker in one hour can produce 20 units of output. Since the U.S. workers get paid $20 per hour, this means the U.S. factory's labor cost *per unit of output* is $1. The factory in the developing country is much less productive

since it uses less efficient technology and its relatively untrained workers have a lot less machinery and equipment to work with. A worker there produces only 4 units per hour. Given the foreign wage of $4 per hour, this means that the labor cost per unit of output at the factory in the developing country is also $1.

As you can see, the lower wage rate per hour at the factory in the developing country does not translate into lower labor costs per unit—meaning that it won't be able to undersell its U.S. competitor just because its workers get paid lower wages per hour.

Proponents of the cheap foreign labor argument tend to focus exclusively on the large international differences that exist in labor costs per hour. They typically fail to mention that these differences in labor costs per hour are mostly the result of tremendously large differences in productivity and that these large differences in productivity serve to equalize labor costs per unit of output. As a result, firms in developing countries only *sometimes* have an advantage in terms of labor costs per unit of output. Whether they do in any specific situation will vary by industry and firm and will depend on differences in productivity as well as differences in labor costs per hour. For many goods, labor productivity in high-wage countries like the United States is so much higher than labor productivity in low-wage countries that it is actually cheaper *per unit of output* to manufacture those goods in high-wage countries. That is why, for instance, Intel still makes microchips in the United States and why most automobiles are still produced in the United States, Japan, and Europe rather than in low-wage countries.

QUICK REVIEW 23.3

- A tariff on a product increases its price, reduces its consumption, increases its domestic production, reduces its imports, and generates tariff revenue for government; an import quota does the same, except a quota generates revenue for foreign producers rather than for the government imposing the quota.
- Most rationales for trade protections are special-interest requests that, if followed, would create gains for protected industries and their workers at the expense of greater losses for the economy.

Multilateral Trade Agreements and Free-Trade Zones

Aware of the detrimental effects of trade wars and the general weaknesses of arguments for trade protections, nations have worked to lower tariffs worldwide. Their pursuit of freer trade has been aided by recently emerged special-interest groups that have offset the more-established special-interest groups that have traditionally supported tariffs and quotas. Specifically, lower tariffs are now supported by exporters of goods and services, importers of foreign components used in "domestic" products, and domestic sellers of imported products.

General Agreement on Tariffs and Trade

In 1947, 23 nations, including the United States, signed the **General Agreement on Tariffs and Trade (GATT)**. GATT was based on three principles: (1) equal, nondiscriminatory trade treatment for all member nations; (2) the reduction of tariffs by multilateral negotiation; and (3) the elimination of import quotas. Basically, GATT provided a forum for the multilateral negotiation of reduced trade barriers.

Since the Second World War, member nations have completed eight "rounds" of GATT negotiations to reduce trade barriers. The eighth round of negotiations began in Uruguay in 1986. After seven years of complex discussions, in 1993 a new agreement was reached by the 128 nations that were by that time members of GATT. The Uruguay Round agreement took effect on January 1, 1995, and its provisions were phased in through 2005.

Under this agreement, tariffs on thousands of products were eliminated or reduced, with overall tariffs dropping by 33 percent. The agreement also liberalized government rules that in the past impeded the global market for such services as advertising, legal services, tourist services, and financial services. Quotas on imported textiles and apparel were phased out and replaced with tariffs. Other provisions reduced agricultural subsidies paid to farmers and protected intellectual property (patents, trademarks, and copyrights) against piracy.

World Trade Organization

The Uruguay Round agreement established the **World Trade Organization (WTO)** as GATT's successor. Some 153 nations belonged to the WTO in 2010. The WTO oversees trade agreements reached by the member nations, and rules on trade disputes among them. It also provides forums for further rounds of trade negotiations. The ninth and latest round of negotiations—the **Doha Development Agenda**—was launched in Doha, Qatar, in late 2001. (The trade rounds occur over several years in several venues but are named after the city or country of origination.) The negotiations are aimed at further reducing tariffs and quotas, as well as agricultural subsidies that distort trade. You can get an update on the status of the complex negotiations at **www.wto.org**.

GATT and the WTO have been positive forces in the trend toward liberalized world trade. The trade rules agreed upon by the member nations provide a strong and necessary bulwark against the protectionism called for by the special-interest groups in the various nations.

For that reason and others, the WTO is quite controversial. Critics are concerned that rules crafted to expand international trade and investment enable firms to circumvent national laws that protect workers and the environment. Critics ask: What good are minimum-wage laws, worker-safety laws, collective-bargaining rights, and environmental laws if firms can easily shift their production to nations that have weaker laws or if consumers can buy goods produced in those countries?

Proponents of the WTO respond that labor and environmental protections should be pursued directly in nations that have low standards and via international organizations other than the WTO. These issues should not be linked to the process of trade liberalization, which confers widespread economic benefits across nations. Moreover, say proponents of the WTO, many environmental and labor concerns are greatly overblown. Most world trade is among advanced industrial countries, not between them and countries that have lower environmental and labor standards. Moreover, the free flow of goods and resources raises output and income in the developing nations. Historically, such increases in living standards have eventually resulted in stronger, not weaker, protections for the environment and for workers.

The European Union

Countries have also sought to reduce tariffs by creating regional free-trade zones. The most dramatic example is the **European Union (EU)**. Initiated in 1958 as the Common Market, in 2003 the EU comprised 15 European nations—Austria, Belgium, Denmark, Finland, France, Germany, Greece, Ireland, Italy, Luxembourg, the Netherlands, Portugal, Spain, Sweden, and the United Kingdom. In 2004, the EU expanded by 10 additional European countries—Cyprus, the Czech Republic, Estonia, Hungary, Latvia, Lithuania, Malta, Poland, Slovakia, and Slovenia. In 2007, the addition of Bulgaria and Romania expanded the EU to its present size of 27 nations.

The EU has abolished tariffs and import quotas on nearly all products traded among the participating nations and established a common system of tariffs applicable to all goods received from nations outside the EU. It has also liberalized the movement of capital and labor within the EU and has created common policies in other economic matters of joint concern, such as agriculture, transportation, and business practices.

EU integration has achieved for Europe what the U.S. constitutional prohibition on tariffs by individual states has achieved for the United States: increased regional specialization, greater productivity, greater output, and faster economic growth. The free flow of goods and services has created large markets for EU industries. The resulting economies of large-scale production have enabled these industries to achieve much lower costs than they could have achieved in their small, single-nation markets.

One of the most significant accomplishments of the EU was the establishment of the so-called **Euro Zone** in the early 2000s. As of 2010, 16 members of the EU (Austria, Belgium, Cyprus, Germany, Greece, Ireland, Finland, France, Italy, Luxembourg, Malta, the Netherlands, Portugal, Slovenia, Slovakia, and Spain) use the euro as a common currency. Notably, the United Kingdom, Denmark, and Sweden have opted not to use the common currency, at least for now. But gone are French francs, German marks, Italian liras, and other national currencies that were once used by Euro Zone countries.

Economists expect the adoption of the euro to raise the standard of living in the Euro Zone nations over time. By ending the inconvenience and expense of exchanging currencies, the euro has enhanced the free flow of goods, services, and resources among the Euro Zone members. Companies that previously sold products in only one or two European nations have found it easier to price and sell their products in all 16 Euro Zone countries. The euro has also allowed consumers and businesses to comparison shop for outputs and inputs, and this capability has increased competition, reduced prices, and lowered costs.

North American Free Trade Agreement

In 1993 Canada, Mexico, and the United States created a major free-trade zone. The **North American Free Trade Agreement (NAFTA)** established a free-trade area that has about the same combined output as the EU but encompasses a much larger geographic area. NAFTA has eliminated tariffs and other trade barriers between Canada, Mexico, and the United States for most goods and services.

Critics of NAFTA feared that it would cause a massive loss of U.S. jobs as firms moved to Mexico to take advantage of lower wages and weaker regulations on pollution and workplace safety. Also, they were concerned that Japan and South Korea would build plants in Mexico and transport goods tariff-free to the United States, further hurting U.S. firms and workers.

In retrospect, critics were much too pessimistic. Since the passage of NAFTA in 1993, employment in the United States has increased by more than 20 million workers. NAFTA has increased trade among Canada, Mexico, and the United States and has enhanced the standard of living in all three countries.

Trade Adjustment Assistance

Shifts in patterns of comparative advantage and removal of long-standing trade protection can hurt specific groups of workers. For example, the erosion of the United States' once strong comparative advantage in steel has caused production plant shutdowns and layoffs in the U.S. steel industry. The textile and apparel industries in the United States face similar difficulties. Clearly, not everyone wins from free trade (or freer trade). Some workers lose.

The **Trade Adjustment Assistance Act** of 2002 introduced some innovative policies to help those hurt by shifts in international trade patterns. The law provides cash assistance (beyond unemployment insurance) for up to 78 weeks for workers displaced by imports or plant relocations abroad. To obtain the assistance, workers must participate in job searches, training programs, or remedial education. Also provided are relocation allowances to help displaced workers move geographically to new jobs within the United States. Refundable tax credits for health insurance serve as payments to help workers maintain their insurance coverage during the retraining and job-search period. Workers who are 50 years of age or older are eligible for "wage insurance," which replaces some of the difference in pay (if any) between their old and new jobs. Many economists support trade adjustment assistance because it not only helps workers hurt by international trade but also helps create the political support necessary to reduce trade barriers and export subsidies.

But not all economists favor trade adjustment assistance. Loss of jobs from imports, sending some work abroad, and plant relocations to other countries are only a small fraction (about 4 percent in recent years) of total job losses in the economy each year. Many workers also lose their jobs because of changing patterns of demand, changing technology, bad management, and other dynamic aspects of a market economy. Some critics ask, "What makes losing one's job to international trade worthy of such special treatment, compared to losing one's job to, say, technological change or domestic competition?" Economists can find no totally satisfying answer.

Offshoring of Jobs

Not only are some U.S. jobs lost because of international trade, but some are lost because of globalization of resource markets. In recent years U.S. firms have found the

Word Petition of the Candlemakers, 1845

French Economist Frédéric Bastiat (1801–1850) Devastated the Proponents of Protectionism by Satirically Extending Their Reasoning to Its Logical and Absurd Conclusions.

Petition of the Manufacturers of Candles, Waxlights, Lamps, Candlesticks, Street Lamps, Snuffers, Extinguishers, and of the Producers of Oil Tallow, Rosin, Alcohol, and, Generally, of Everything Connected with Lighting.

TO MESSIEURS THE MEMBERS OF THE CHAMBER OF DEPUTIES.

Gentlemen—You are on the right road. You reject abstract theories, and have little consideration for cheapness and plenty. Your chief care is the interest of the producer. You desire to emancipate him from external competition, and reserve the national market for national industry.

We are about to offer you an admirable opportunity of applying your—what shall we call it? your theory? No; nothing is more deceptive than theory; your doctrine? your system? your principle? but you dislike doctrines, you abhor systems, and as for principles, you deny that there are any in social economy: we shall say, then, your practice, your practice without theory and without principle.

We are suffering from the intolerable competition of a foreign rival, placed, it would seem, in a condition so far superior to ours for the production of light, that he absolutely inundates our national market with it at a price fabulously reduced. The moment he shows himself, our trade leaves us—all consumers apply to him; and a branch of native industry, having countless ramifications, is all at once rendered completely stagnant. This rival . . . is no other than the Sun.

What we pray for is, that it may please you to pass a law ordering the shutting up of all windows, skylights, dormer windows, outside and inside shutters, curtains, blinds, bull's-eyes; in a word, of all openings, holes, chinks, clefts, and fissures, by or through which the light of the sun has been in use to enter houses, to the prejudice of the meritorious manufacturers with which we flatter ourselves we have accommodated our country,— a country which, in gratitude, ought not to abandon us now to a strife so unequal.

If you shut up as much as possible all access to natural light, and create a demand for artificial light, which of our French manufacturers will not be encouraged by it? If more tallow is consumed, then there must be more oxen and sheep; and, consequently, we shall behold the multiplication of artificial meadows, meat, wool, hides, and, above all, manure, which is the basis and foundation of all agricultural wealth.

The same remark applies to navigation. Thousands of vessels will proceed to the whale fishery; and, in a short time, we shall possess a navy capable of maintaining the honor of France, and gratifying the patriotic aspirations of your petitioners, the undersigned candlemakers and others.

Only have the goodness to reflect, Gentlemen, and you will be convinced that there is, perhaps, no Frenchman, from the wealthy coalmaster to the humblest vender of lucifer matches, whose lot will not be ameliorated by the success of this our petition.

Source: Frédéric Bastiat, *Economic Sophisms* (Irvington-on-Hudson, NY: The Foundation for Economic Education, Inc., 1996), abridged. Used with permission of Foundation for Economic Education, **www.FEE.org**.

---

outsourcing of work abroad to be increasingly profitable. Economists call this business activity **offshoring**—shifting work previously done by American workers to workers located in other nations. Offshoring is not a new practice but traditionally has involved components for U.S. manufacturing goods. For example, Boeing has long offshored the production of major airplane parts for its "American" aircraft.

Recent advances in computer and communications technology have enabled U.S. firms to offshore service jobs such as data entry, book composition, software coding, call-center operations, medical transcription, and claims processing to countries such as India. Where off-shoring occurs, some of the value added in the production process accrues to foreign countries rather than the United States. So part of the income generated from the production of U.S. goods is paid to foreigners, not to American workers.

Offshoring is a wrenching experience for many Americans who lose their jobs, but it is not necessarily bad for the overall economy. Offshoring simply reflects growing specialization and international trade in services, or, more descriptively, "tasks." That growth has been made possible by recent trade agreements and new information and communication technologies. As with trade in goods, trade in services reflects comparative advantage and is beneficial to both trading parties. Moreover, the United States has a sizable trade surplus with other nations in services. The United States gains by specializing in high-valued services such as transportation services, accounting services, legal services, and advertising services, where it still has a comparative advantage. It then "trades" to obtain lower-valued services such as call-center and data-entry work, for which comparative advantage has gone abroad.

Offshoring also increases the demand for complementary jobs in the United States. Jobs that are close substitutes for existing U.S. jobs are lost, but complementary jobs in the United States are expanded. For example, the lower price of writing software code in India may mean a lower cost of software sold in the United States and abroad. That, in turn, may create more jobs for U.S.-based workers such as software designers, marketers, and distributors. Moreover, offshoring may encourage domestic investment and the expansion of firms in the United States by reducing their production costs and keeping them competitive worldwide. In some instances, "offshoring jobs" may equate to "importing competitiveness." Entire firms that might otherwise disappear abroad may remain profitable in the United States only because they can offshore some of their work.

QUICK REVIEW 23.4

- The General Agreement on Tariffs and Trade (GATT) of 1947 reduced tariffs and quotas and established a process for numerous subsequent rounds of multinational trade negotiations that have liberalized international trade.
- The World Trade Organization (WTO)—GATT's successor—rules on trade disputes and provides forums for negotiations on further rounds of trade liberalization. The current round of negotiations is called the Doha Development Agenda.
- The European Union (EU) and the North American Free Trade Agreement (NAFTA) have reduced internal trade barriers among their member nations by establishing multination free-trade zones.
- Increased international trade and offshoring of jobs have harmed some specific U.S. workers and have led to policies such as trade adjustment assistance to try to help them with their transitions to new lines of work.

Summary

1. The United States leads the world in the combined volume of exports and imports. Other major trading nations are Germany, Japan, the western European nations, and the Asian economies of China, South Korea, Taiwan, and Singapore. The United States' principal exports include chemicals, agricultural products, consumer durables, semiconductors, and aircraft; principal imports include petroleum, automobiles, metals, household appliances, and computers.

2. World trade is based on three considerations: the uneven distribution of economic resources among nations, the fact that efficient production of various goods requires particular techniques or combinations of resources, and the differentiated products produced among nations.

3. Mutually advantageous specialization and trade are possible between any two nations if they have different domestic opportunity-cost ratios for any two products. By specializing on the basis of comparative advantage, nations can obtain larger real incomes with fixed amounts of resources. The terms of trade determine how this increase in world output is shared by the trading nations. Increasing (rather than constant) opportunity costs limit specialization and trade.

4. A nation's export supply curve shows the quantities of a product the nation will export at world prices that exceed the domestic price (the price in a closed, no-international-trade economy). A nation's import demand curve reveals the quantities of a product it will import at world prices below the domestic price.

5. In a two-nation model, the equilibrium world price and the equilibrium quantities of exports and imports occur where one nation's export supply curve intersects the other nation's import demand curve. A nation will export a particular product if the world price exceeds the domestic price; it will import the product if the world price is less than the domestic price. The country with the lower costs of production will be the exporter and the country with the higher costs of production will be the importer.

6. Trade barriers take the form of protective tariffs, quotas, nontariff barriers, and "voluntary" export restrictions. Export subsidies also distort international trade. Supply and demand analysis demonstrates that protective tariffs and quotas increase the prices and reduce the quantities demanded of the affected goods. Sales by foreign exporters diminish; domestic producers, however, gain higher prices and enlarged sales. Consumer losses from trade restrictions greatly exceed producer and government gains, creating an efficiency loss to society.

7. The strongest arguments for protection are the infant industry and military self-sufficiency arguments. Most other arguments for protection are interest-group appeals or reasoning fallacies that emphasize producer interests over consumer interests or stress the immediate effects of trade barriers while ignoring long-run consequences.

8. The cheap foreign labor argument for protection fails because it focuses on labor costs per hour rather than on what really matters, labor costs per unit of output. Due to higher productivity, firms in high-wage countries like the United States can have lower wage costs per unit of output than competitors in low-wage countries. Whether they do will depend on how their particular wage and productivity levels compare with those of their competitors in low-wage countries.

9. In 1947 the General Agreement on Tariffs and Trade (GATT) was formed to encourage nondiscriminatory treatment for all member nations, to reduce tariffs, and to eliminate import quotas. The Uruguay Round of GATT negotiations (1993) reduced tariffs and quotas, liberalized trade in services, reduced agricultural subsidies, reduced pirating of intellectual property, and phased out quotas on textiles.

10. GATT's successor, the World Trade Organization (WTO), had 153 member nations in 2010. It implements WTO agreements, rules on trade disputes between members, and provides forums for continued discussions on trade liberalization. The latest round of trade negotiations—the Doha Development Agenda—began in late 2001 and as of 2010 was still in progress.

11. Free-trade zones liberalize trade within regions. Two examples of free-trade arrangements are the 27-member European Union (EU) and the North American Free Trade Agreement (NAFTA), comprising Canada, Mexico, and the United States. Sixteen EU nations have abandoned their national currencies for a common currency called the euro.

12. The Trade Adjustment Assistance Act of 2002 recognizes that trade liberalization and increased international trade can create job loss for many workers. The Act therefore provides cash assistance, education and training benefits, health care subsidies, and wage subsidies (for persons aged 50 or older) to qualified workers displaced by imports or relocations of plants from the United States to abroad.

13. Offshoring is the practice of shifting work previously done by Americans in the United States to workers located in other nations. Although offshoring reduces some U.S. jobs, it lowers production costs, expands sales, and therefore may create other U.S. jobs. Less than 4 percent of all job losses in the United States each year are caused by imports, offshoring, and plant relocation abroad.

Terms and Concepts

labor-intensive goods

land-intensive goods

capital-intensive goods

opportunity-cost ratio

comparative advantage

principle of comparative advantage

terms of trade

trading possibilities line

gains from trade

world price

domestic price

export supply curve

import demand curve

equilibrium world price

tariffs

revenue tariff

protective tariff

import quota

nontariff barrier (NTB)

voluntary export restriction (VER)

export subsidy

dumping

Smoot-Hawley Tariff Act

General Agreement on Tariffs and Trade (GATT)

World Trade Organization (WTO)

Doha Development Agenda

European Union (EU)

Euro Zone

North American Free Trade Agreement (NAFTA)

Trade Adjustment Assistance Act

offshoring

Questions

1. Quantitatively, how important is international trade to the United States relative to the importance of trade to other nations? What country is the United States' most important trading partner, quantitatively? With what country does the United States have the largest trade deficit? **LO1**

2. Distinguish among land-, labor-, and capital-intensive goods, citing an example of each without resorting to book examples. How do these distinctions relate to international trade? How do distinctive products, unrelated to resource intensity, relate to international trade? **LO1, LO2**

3. Explain: "The United States can make certain toys with greater productive efficiency than can China. Yet we import those toys from China." Relate your answer to the ideas of Adam Smith and David Ricardo. **LO2**

4. Suppose Big Country can produce 80 units of X by using all its resources to produce X or 60 units of Y by devoting all its resources to Y. Comparable figures for Small Nation are 60 units of X and 60 units of Y. Assuming constant costs, in which product should each nation specialize? Explain why. What are the limits of the terms of trade between these two countries? How would rising costs (rather than constant costs) affect the extent of specialization and trade between these two countries? **LO2**

5. What is an export demand curve? What is an import supply curve? How do such curves relate to the determination of the equilibrium world price of a tradable good? **LO3**

6. Why is a quota more detrimental to an economy than a tariff that results in the same level of imports as the quota? What is the net outcome of either tariffs or quotas for the world economy? **LO4**

7. Draw a domestic supply-and-demand diagram for a product in which the United States does not have a comparative advantage. What impact do foreign imports have on domestic price and quantity? On your diagram show a protective tariff that eliminates approximately one-half of the assumed imports. What are the price-quantity effects of this tariff on (a) domestic consumers, (b) domestic producers, and (c) foreign exporters? How would the effects of a quota that creates the same amount of imports differ? **LO4**

8. "The potentially valid arguments for tariff protection—military self-sufficiency, infant industry protection, and diversification for stability—are also the most easily abused." Why are these arguments susceptible to abuse? **LO4**

9. Evaluate the effectiveness of artificial trade barriers, such as tariffs and import quotas, as a way to achieve and maintain full employment throughout the U.S. economy. How might such policies reduce unemployment in one U.S. industry but increase it in another U.S. industry? **LO4**

10. In 2007, manufacturing workers in the United States earned average compensation of $30.56 per hour. That same year, manufacturing workers in Mexico earned average compensation of $3.91 per hour. How can U.S. manufacturers possibly compete? Why isn't all manufacturing done in Mexico and other low-wage countries? **LO4**

11. How might protective tariffs reduce both the imports and the exports of the nation that levies tariffs? In what way do foreign firms that "dump" their products onto the U.S. market in effect provide bargains to American consumers? How might the import competition lead to quality improvements and cost reductions by American firms? **LO4**

12. Identify and state the significance of each of the following trade-related entities: (a) the WTO; (b) the EU; (c) the Euro Zone; and (d) NAFTA. **LO5**

13. What form does trade adjustment assistance take in the United States? How does such assistance promote political support for free-trade agreements? Do you think workers who lose their jobs because of changes in trade laws deserve special treatment relative to workers who lose their jobs because of other changes in the economy, say, changes in patterns of government spending? **LO6**

14. What is offshoring of white-collar service jobs and how does that practice relate to international trade? Why has offshoring increased over the past few decades? Give an example (other than that in the textbook) of how offshoring can eliminate some American jobs while creating other American jobs. **LO6**

15. **LAST WORD** What was the central point that Bastiat was trying to make in his imaginary petition of the candlemakers?

Problems

1. Assume that the comparative-cost ratios of two products—baby formula and tuna fish—are as follows in the nations of Canswicki and Tunata:

    Canswicki: 1 can baby formula ≡ 2 cans tuna fish
    Tunata: 1 can baby formula ≡ 4 cans tuna fish

    In what product should each nation specialize? Which of the following terms of trade would be acceptable to both nations: (a) 1 can baby formula ≡ $2\frac{1}{2}$ cans tuna fish; (b) 1 can baby formula ≡ 1 can tuna fish; (c) 1 can baby formula ≡ 5 cans tuna fish? **LO2**

2. The accompanying hypothetical production possibilities tables are for New Zealand and Spain. Each country can produce apples and plums. Plot the production possibilities data for each of the two countries separately. Referring to your graphs, answer the following: **LO2**

New Zealand's Production Possibilities Table (Millions of Bushels)

Product	Production Alternatives			
	A	B	C	D
Apples	0	20	40	60
Plums	15	10	5	0

Spain's Production Possibilities Table (Millions of Bushels)

Product	Production Alternatives			
	R	S	T	U
Apples	0	20	40	60
Plums	60	40	20	0

a. What is each country's cost ratio of producing plums and apples?

b. Which nation should specialize in which product?

c. Show the trading possibilities lines for each nation if the actual terms of trade are 1 plum for 2 apples. (Plot these lines on your graph.)

d. Suppose the optimum product mixes before specialization and trade were alternative B in New Zealand and alternative S in Spain. What would be the gains from specialization and trade?

3. The following hypothetical production possibilities tables are for China and the United States. Assume that before specialization and trade the optimal product mix for China is alternative B and for the United States is alternative U. **LO2**

a. Are comparative-cost conditions such that the two areas should specialize? If so, what product should each produce?

b. What is the total gain in apparel and chemical output that would result from such specialization?

c. What are the limits of the terms of trade? Suppose that the actual terms of trade are 1 unit of apparel for $1\frac{1}{2}$ units of chemicals and that 4 units of apparel are exchanged for 6 units of chemicals. What are the gains from specialization and trade for each nation?

| | China Production Possibilities | | | | | |
Product	A	B	C	D	E	F
Apparel (in thousands)	30	24	18	12	6	0
Chemicals (in tons)	0	6	12	18	24	30

| | U.S. Production Possibilities | | | | | |
Product	R	S	T	U	V	W
Apparel (in thousands)	10	8	6	4	2	0
Chemicals (in tons)	0	4	8	12	16	20

4. Refer to Figure 3.6, page 57. Assume that the graph depicts the U.S. domestic market for corn. How many bushels of corn, if any, will the United States export or import at a world price of $1, $2, $3, $4, and $5? Use this information to construct the U.S. export supply curve and import demand curve for corn. Suppose that the only other corn-producing nation is France, where the domestic price is $4. Which country will export corn; which county will import it? **LO3**

FURTHER TEST YOUR KNOWLEDGE AT
www.mcconnell19e.com

At the text's Online Learning Center (OLC), **www.mcconnell19e.com**, you will find one or more Web-based questions that require information from the Internet to answer. We urge you to check them out; they will familiarize you with Web sites that may be helpful in other courses and perhaps even in your career. The OLC also features multiple-choice questions that give instant feedback and provides other helpful ways to further test your knowledge of the chapter.

24

AFTER READING THIS CHAPTER, YOU SHOULD BE ABLE TO:

1 Explain how currencies of different nations are exchanged when international transactions take place.

2 Analyze the balance sheet the United States uses to account for the international payments it makes and receives.

3 Discuss how exchange rates are determined in currency markets.

4 Describe the difference between flexible exchange rates and fixed exchange rates.

5 Identify the causes and consequences of recent U.S. trade deficits.

The Balance of Payments, Exchange Rates, and Trade Deficits

If you take a U.S. dollar to the bank and ask to exchange it for U.S. currency, you will get a puzzled look. If you persist, you may get a dollar's worth of change: One U.S. dollar can buy exactly one U.S. dollar. But on April 4, 2010, for example, 1 U.S. dollar could buy 1922 Colombian pesos, 1.09 Australian dollars, .66 British pound, 1.01 Canadian dollars, .74 European euro, 94.61 Japanese yen, or 12.30 Mexican pesos. What explains this seemingly haphazard array of exchange rates?

In Chapter 23 we examined comparative advantage as the underlying economic basis of world trade and discussed the effects of barriers to free trade. Now we introduce the highly important monetary and financial aspects of international trade.

International Financial Transactions

This chapter focuses on international financial transactions, the vast majority of which fall into two broad categories: international trade and international asset transactions. International trade involves either purchasing or selling currently produced goods or services across an international border. Examples include an Egyptian firm exporting cotton to the United States and an American company hiring an Indian call center to answer its phones. International asset transactions involve the transfer of the property rights to either real or financial assets between the citizens of one country and the citizens of another country. It includes activities like buying foreign stocks or selling your house to a foreigner.

These two categories of international financial transactions reflect the fact that whether they are from different countries or the same country, individuals and firms can only exchange two things with each other: currently produced goods and services or preexisting assets. With regard to assets, however, money is by far the most commonly exchanged asset. Only rarely would you ever find a barter situation in which people directly exchanged other assets—such as trading a car for 500 shares of Microsoft stock or a cow for 30 chickens and a tank of diesel fuel.

As a result, there are two basic types of transactions:

- People trading either goods or services for money.
- People trading assets for money.

In either case, money flows from the buyers of the goods, services, or assets to the sellers of the goods, services, or assets.

When the people engaged in any such transactions are both from places that use the same currency, what type of money to use is not an issue. Americans from California and Wisconsin will use their common currency, the dollar. People from France and Germany will use their common currency, the euro. However, when the people involved in an exchange are from places that use different currencies, intermediate asset transactions have to take place: the buyers must convert their own currencies into the currencies that the sellers use and accept.

As an example, consider the case of an English software design company that wants to buy a supercomputer made by an American company. The American company sells these high-powered machines for $300,000. To pay for the machine, the English company has to convert some of the money it has (British pounds sterling) into the money that the American company will accept (U.S. dollars). This process is not difficult. As we will soon explain in detail, there are many easy-to-use foreign exchange markets in which those who wish to sell pounds and buy dollars can interact with others who wish to sell dollars and buy pounds. The demand and supply created by these two groups determine the equilibrium exchange rate, which, in turn, determines how many pounds our English company will have to convert to pay for the supercomputer. If, for instance, the exchange rate is $2 = £1, then the English company will have to convert £150,000 to obtain the $300,000 necessary to purchase the computer.

The Balance of Payments

A nation's **balance of payments** is the sum of all the financial transactions that take place between its residents and the residents of foreign nations. Most of these transactions fall into the two main categories that we have just discussed: international trade and international asset transactions. As a result, nearly all the items included in the balance of payments are things such as exports and imports of goods, exports and imports of services, and international purchases and sales of financial and real assets. But the balance of payments also includes international transactions that fall outside of these main categories—things such as tourist expenditures, interest and dividends received or paid abroad, debt forgiveness, and remittances made by immigrants to their relatives back home.

The U.S. Commerce Department's Bureau of Economic Analysis compiles a balance-of-payments statement each year. This statement summarizes all of the millions of payments that individuals and firms in the United States receive from foreigners as well as all of the millions of payments that individuals and firms in the United States make to foreigners. It shows "flows" of inpayments of money *to* the United States and outpayments of money *from* the United States. For convenience, all of these money payments are given in terms of dollars. This is true despite the fact that some of them actually may have been made using foreign currencies—as when, for instance, an American company converts dollars into euros to buy something from an Italian company. When including this outpayment of money from the United States, the accountants who compile the balance-of-payments statement use the number of dollars the American company converted—rather than the number of euros that were actually used to make the purchase.

Table 24.1 is a simplified balance-of-payments statement for the United States in 2009. Because most international financial transactions fall into only two categories—international trade and international asset exchanges—the balance-of-payments statement is organized into two broad

TABLE 24.1 **The U.S. Balance of Payments, 2009 (in Billions)**

CURRENT ACCOUNT			
(1) U.S. goods exports	$+1046		
(2) U.S. goods imports	−1563		
(3) *Balance on goods*		$−517	
(4) U.S. exports of services	+509		
(5) U.S. imports of services	−371		
(6) *Balance on services*		+138	
(7) *Balance on goods and services*		−379	
(8) Net investment income	+89*		
(9) Net transfers	−130		
(10) **Balance on current account**		**−420**	
CAPITAL AND FINANCIAL ACCOUNT			
Capital account			
(11) *Balance on capital account*		−3	
Financial account			
(12) Foreign purchases of assets in the United States	+548†		
(13) U.S. purchases of assets abroad	−125†		
(14) *Balance on financial account*		+423	
(15) **Balance on capital and financial account**		**+420**	
		$ 0	

*Includes other, less significant, categories of income.
†Includes one-half of a $225 billion statistical discrepancy that is listed in the capital account.

Source: U.S. Department of Commerce, Bureau of Economic Analysis, **www.bea.gov**. Preliminary 2009 data. The export and import data are on a "balance-of-payment basis," and usually vary from the data on exports and imports reported in the National Income and Product Accounts.

categories. *The current account* located at the top of the table primarily treats international trade. *The capital and financial account* at the bottom of the table primarily treats international asset exchanges.

Current Account

The top portion of Table 24.1 that mainly summarizes U.S. trade in currently produced goods and services is called the **current account.** Items 1 and 2 show U.S. exports and imports of goods (merchandise) in 2009. U.S. exports have a *plus* (+) sign because they are a *credit*; they generate flows of money toward the United States. U.S. imports have a *minus* (−) sign because they are a *debit*; they cause flows of money out of the United States.

Balance on Goods Items 1 and 2 in Table 24.1 reveal that in 2009 U.S. goods exports of $1046 billion were less than U.S. goods imports of $1563 billion. A country's *balance of trade on goods* is the difference between its exports and its imports of goods. If exports exceed imports, the result is a surplus on the balance of goods. If imports exceed exports, there is a trade deficit on the balance of goods.

We note in item 3 that in 2009 the United States incurred a trade deficit on goods of $517 billion.

Balance on Services The United States exports not only goods, such as airplanes and computer software, but also services, such as insurance, consulting, travel, and investment advice, to residents of foreign nations. Item 4 in Table 24.1 shows that these service "exports" totaled $509 billion in 2009. Since they generate flows of money toward the United States, they are a credit (thus the + sign). Item 5 indicates that the United States "imports" similar services from foreigners. Those service imports were $371 billion in 2009, and since they generate flows of money out of the United States, they are a debit (thus the − sign). Summed together, items 4 and 5 indicate that the balance on services (item 6) in 2009 was $138 billion. The **balance on goods and services** shown as item 7 is the difference between U.S. exports of goods and services (items 1 and 4) and U.S. imports of goods and services (items 2 and 5). In 2009, U.S. imports of goods and services exceeded U.S. exports of goods and services by $379 billion. So a **trade deficit** of that amount occurred. In contrast, a **trade surplus** occurs

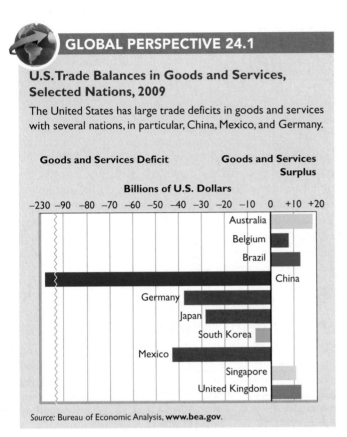

GLOBAL PERSPECTIVE 24.1

U.S. Trade Balances in Goods and Services, Selected Nations, 2009

The United States has large trade deficits in goods and services with several nations, in particular, China, Mexico, and Germany.

Source: Bureau of Economic Analysis, **www.bea.gov**.

when exports of goods and services exceed imports of goods and services. (Global Perspective 24.1 shows U.S. trade deficits and surpluses with selected nations.)

Balance on Current Account Items 8 and 9 are not items relating directly to international trade in goods and services. But they are listed as part of the current account (which is mostly about international trade in goods and services) because they are international financial flows that in some sense compensate for things that can be conceptualized as being *like* international trade in either goods or services. For instance, item 8, *net investment income*, represents the difference between (1) the interest and dividend payments foreigners paid U.S. citizens and companies for the services provided by U.S. capital invested abroad ("exported" capital) and (2) the interest and dividends the U.S. citizens and companies paid for the services provided by foreign capital invested here ("imported" capital). Observe that in 2009 U.S. net investment income was a positive $89 billion.

Item 9 shows net transfers, both public and private, between the United States and the rest of the world. Included here is foreign aid, pensions paid to U.S. citizens

living abroad, and remittances by immigrants to relatives abroad. These $130 billion of transfers are net U.S. outpayments (and therefore listed as a negative number in Table 24.1). They are listed as part of the current account because they can be thought of as the financial flows that accompany the exporting of goodwill and the importing of "thank you notes."

By adding all transactions in the current account, we obtain the **balance on current account** shown in item 10. In 2009 the United States had a current account deficit of $420 billion. This means that the U.S. current account transactions created outpayments from the United States greater than inpayments to the United States.

Capital and Financial Account

The bottom portion of the current account statement summarizes U.S. international asset transactions. It is called the **capital and financial account** and consists of two separate accounts: the *capital account* and the *financial account*.

Capital Account The capital account mainly measures debt forgiveness—which is an asset transaction because the person forgiving a debt essentially hands the IOU back to the borrower. It is a "net" account (one that can be either + or −). The $3 billion listed in line 11 tells us that in 2009 Americans forgave $3 billion more of debt owed to them by foreigners than foreigners forgave debt owed to them by Americans. The − sign indicates a debit; it is an "on-paper" outpayment (asset transfer) by the net amount of debt forgiven.

Financial Account The financial account summarizes international asset transactions having to do with international purchases and sales of real or financial assets. Line 12 lists the amount of foreign purchases of assets in the United States. It has a + sign because any purchase of an American-owned asset by a foreigner generates a flow of money toward the American who sells the asset. Line 13 lists U.S. purchases of assets abroad. These have a − sign because such purchases generate a flow of money from the Americans who buy foreign assets toward the foreigners who sell them those assets.

Items 11 and 12 combined yielded a $423 billion balance on the financial account for 2009 (line 14). In 2009 the United States "exported" $548 billion of ownership of its real and financial assets and "imported" $125 billion. Thought of differently, this surplus in the financial account brought in income of $423 billion to the United States. The **balance on the capital and financial account** (line 15) is $420 billion. It is the sum of the $3 billion deficit on the capital account and the $423 billion surplus on the financial account. Observe that this $420 billion surplus in the capital and financial account equals the $420 billion deficit in the current account. This is not an accident. The two numbers always equal—or "balance." That's why the statement is called the *balance* of payments. It has to balance. Let's see why.

Why the Balance?

The balance on the current account and the balance on the capital and financial account must always sum to zero because any deficit or surplus in the current account automatically creates an offsetting entry in the capital and financial account. People can only trade one of two things with each other: currently produced goods and services or preexisting assets. Therefore, if trading partners have an imbalance in their trade of currently produced goods and services, the only way to make up for that imbalance is with a net transfer of assets from one party to the other.

To see why this is true, suppose that John (an American) makes shoes and Henri (a Swiss citizen) makes watches and that the pair only trade with each other. Assume that their financial assets consist entirely of money, with each beginning the year with $1000 in his bank account. Suppose that this year John exports $300 of shoes to Henri and imports $500 of watches from Henri. John therefore ends the year with a $200 goods deficit with Henri.

John and Henri's goods transactions, however, also result in asset exchanges that cause a net transfer of assets from John to Henri equal in size to John's $200 goods deficit with Henri. This is true because Henri pays John $300 for his shoes while John pays Henri $500 for his watches. The *net* result of these opposite-direction asset movements is that $200 of John's initial assets of $1000 are transferred to Henri. This is unavoidable, because the $300 John receives from his exports pays for only the first $300 of his $500 of imports. The only way for John to pay for the remaining $200 of imports is for him to transfer $200 of his initial asset holdings to Henri. Consequently, John's assets decline by $200 from $1000 to $800, and Henri's assets rise from $1000 to $1200.

Consider how the transaction between John and Henri affects the U.S. balance-of-payments statement (Table 24.1), other things equal. John's $200 goods deficit with Henri shows up in the U.S. current account as a −$200 entry in the balance on goods account (line 3) and carries down to a −$200 entry in the balance on current account (line 10).

In the capital and financial account, this $200 is recorded as +$200 in the account labeled foreign purchases of assets in the United States (line 12). This +$200 then

carries down to the balance on capital and financial account (line 15). Think of it this way: Henri has in essence used $200 worth of watches to purchase $200 of John's initial $1000 holding of assets. The +$200 entry in line 12 (foreign purchases of assets in the United States) simply recognizes this fact. This +$200 exactly offsets the −$200 in the current account.

Thus, the balance of payments always balances. Any current account deficit or surplus in the top half of the statement automatically generates an offsetting international asset transfer that shows up in the capital and financial account in the bottom half of the statement. More specifically, current account deficits simultaneously generate transfers of assets to foreigners, while current account surpluses automatically generate transfers of assets from foreigners.

Official Reserves, Payments Deficits, and Payments Surpluses

Some of the foreign purchases of assets in the United States (line 12, Table 24.1) and the U.S. assets purchased abroad (line 13) are of so-called official reserves. **Official reserves** consist of foreign currencies, certain reserves held with the International Monetary Fund, and stocks of gold. These reserves are owned by governments or their central banks. For simplicity, we will assume for now that the entire stock of U.S. official reserves consists of foreign currency so we can speak of official reserves and foreign currency reserves interchangeably.

Although the balance of payments must always sum to zero, as in Table 24.1, in some years a net sale of official reserves by a nation's treasury or central bank occurs in the process of bringing the capital and financial account into balance with the current account. In such years, a **balance-of-payments deficit** is said to occur. This deficit is in a subset of the overall balance statement and *is not a deficit in the overall account*. Remember, the overall balance of payments is always in balance. But in this case the balancing of the overall account includes sales of official reserves to create an inflow of dollars to the United States. In selling foreign currency in the foreign exchange market, the treasury or central bank must draw down its stock of reserves. This drawdown is an indicator of a balance-of-payments deficit.

These net sales of official reserves in the foreign exchange market show up as a *plus* (+) item on the U.S. balance-of-payments statement, specifically as are foreign purchases of U.S. assets (line 12). They are a credit or an inflow of dollars to the United States, just as are John's proceeds from the sale of $200 of his assets to Henri in our previous example.

In other years, the capital and financial account balances the current account because of government purchases of official reserves from foreigners. The treasury or central bank engineers this balance by selling dollars to obtain foreign currency, and then adding the newly acquired foreign currency to its stock of official reserves. In these years, a **balance-of-payments surplus** is said to exist. This payments surplus therefore can be thought of as either net purchases of official reserves in the balance of payments or, alternatively, as the resulting increase in the stock of official reserves held by the government.

Net purchases of official reserves by the treasury or central bank appear on the U.S. balance sheet as U.S. purchases of foreign assets (line 13)—a *negative* (−) item. These purchases are a debit because they represent an outflow of dollars.

A balance-of-payments deficit is not necessarily bad, just as a balance-of-payments surplus is not necessarily good. Both simply happen. However, any nation's official reserves are limited. Persistent payments deficits must be financed by drawing down those reserves, which would ultimately deplete the reserves. That nation would have to adopt policies to correct its balance of payments. Such policies might require painful macroeconomic adjustments, trade barriers and similar restrictions, or a major depreciation of its currency. For this reason, nations strive for payments balance, at least over several-year periods.

> **WORKED PROBLEMS**
>
> **W 24.1**
>
> Balance of payments

QUICK REVIEW 24.1

- A nation's balance-of-payments statement summarizes all of the international financial transactions that take place between its residents and the residents of all foreign nations. It includes the current account balance and the capital and financial account balance.

- The current account balance is a nation's exports of goods and services less its imports of goods and services plus its net investment income and net transfers.

- The capital and financial account balance includes the net amount of the nation's debt forgiveness as well as the nation's sale of real and financial assets to people living abroad less its purchases of real and financial assets from foreigners.

- The current account balance and the capital and financial account balance always sum to zero because any current account imbalance automatically generates an offsetting international asset transfer.

- A balance-of-payments deficit exists when net sales of official reserves (mainly foreign currency) occur in the balance-of-payments statement; in contrast, a balance-of-payments surplus exists when net purchases of official reserves occur.

Flexible Exchange Rates

Both the size and the persistence of a nation's balance-of-payments deficits and surpluses and the adjustments it must make to correct those imbalances depend on the system of exchange rates being used. There are two pure types of exchange-rate systems:

- A **flexible- or floating-exchange-rate system** through which demand and supply determine exchange rates and in which no government intervention occurs.

- A **fixed-exchange-rate system** through which governments determine exchange rates and make necessary adjustments in their economies to maintain those rates.

We begin by looking at flexible exchange rates. Let's examine the rate, or price, at which U.S. dollars might be exchanged for British pounds. In **Figure 24.1 (Key Graph)** we show demand D_1 and supply S_1 of pounds in the currency market.

> **INTERACTIVE GRAPHS**
>
> **G 24.1**
>
> Flexible exchange rates

The *demand-for-pounds curve* is downsloping because all British goods and services will be cheaper to the United States if pounds become less expensive to the United States. That is, at lower dollar prices for pounds, the United States can obtain more pounds and therefore more British goods and services per dollar. To buy those cheaper British goods, U.S. consumers will increase the quantity of pounds they demand.

The *supply-of-pounds curve* is upsloping because the British will purchase more U.S. goods when the dollar price of pounds rises (that is, as the pound price of dollars falls). When the British buy more U.S. goods, they supply a greater quantity of pounds to the foreign exchange market. In other words, they must exchange pounds for dollars to purchase U.S. goods. So, when the dollar price of pounds rises, the quantity of pounds supplied goes up.

The intersection of the supply curve and the demand curve will determine the dollar price of pounds. Here, that price (exchange rate) is $2 for £1. At this exchange rate, the quantities of pounds supplied and demanded are equal; neither a shortage nor a surplus of pounds occurs.

Depreciation and Appreciation

An exchange rate determined by market forces can, and often does, change daily like stock and bond prices. When the dollar price of pounds *rises*, for example, from $2 = £1 to $3 = £1, the dollar has *depreciated* relative to the pound (and the pound has appreciated relative to the dollar). When a currency depreciates, more units of it (dollars)

key graph

FIGURE 24.1 The market for foreign currency (pounds). The intersection of the demand-for-pounds curve D_1 and the supply-of-pounds curve S_1 determines the equilibrium dollar price of pounds, here, $2. That means that the exchange rate is $2 = £1. Not shown, an increase in demand for pounds or a decrease in supply of pounds will increase the dollar price of pounds and thus cause the pound to appreciate. Also not shown, a decrease in demand for pounds or an increase in the supply of pounds will reduce the dollar price of pounds, meaning that the pound has depreciated.

QUICK QUIZ FOR FIGURE 24.1

1. Which of the following statements is true?
   a. The quantity of pounds demanded falls when the dollar appreciates.
   b. The quantity of pounds supplied declines as the dollar price of the pound rises.
   c. At the equilibrium exchange rate, the pound price of $1 is £$\frac{1}{2}$.
   d. The dollar appreciates if the demand for pounds increases.

2. At the price of $2 for £1 in this figure:
   a. the dollar-pound exchange rate is unstable.
   b. the quantity of pounds supplied equals the quantity demanded.
   c. the dollar price of £1 equals the pound price of $1.
   d. U.S. goods exports to Britain must equal U.S. goods imports from Britain.

3. Other things equal, a leftward shift of the demand curve in this figure:
   a. would depreciate the dollar.

   b. would create a shortage of pounds at the previous price of $2 for £1.
   c. might be caused by a major recession in the United States.
   d. might be caused by a significant rise of real interest rates in Britain.

4. Other things equal, a rightward shift of the supply curve in this figure would:
   a. depreciate the dollar and might be caused by a significant rise of real interest rates in Britain.
   b. depreciate the dollar and might be caused by a significant fall of real interest rates in Britain.
   c. appreciate the dollar and might be caused by a significant rise of real interest rates in the United States.
   d. appreciate the dollar and might be caused by a significant fall of interest rates in the United States.

Answers: 1. c; 2. b; 3. c; 4. c

---

are needed to buy a single unit of some other currency (a pound).

When the dollar price of pounds *falls*, for example, from $2 = £1 to $1 = £1, the dollar has *appreciated* relative to the pound. When a currency appreciates, fewer units of it (dollars) are needed to buy a single unit of some other currency (pounds).

In our U.S.-Britain illustrations, depreciation of the dollar means an appreciation of the pound, and vice versa. When the dollar price of a pound jumps from $2 = £1 to $3 = £1, the pound has appreciated relative to the dollar because it takes fewer pounds to buy $1. At $2 = £1, it took £$\frac{1}{2}$ to buy $1; at $3 = £1, it takes only £$\frac{1}{3}$ to buy $1.

Conversely, when the dollar appreciated relative to the pound, the pound depreciated relative to the dollar. More pounds were needed to buy a dollar.

In general, the relevant terminology and relationships between the U.S. dollar and another currency are as follows.

- Dollar price of foreign currency increases ≡ dollar depreciates relative to the foreign currency ≡ foreign currency price of dollar decreases ≡ foreign currency appreciates relative to the dollar.

- Dollar price of foreign currency decreases ≡ dollar appreciates relative to the foreign currency ≡ foreign currency price of dollar increases ≡ foreign currency depreciates relative to the dollar.

Determinants of Exchange Rates

What factors would cause a nation's currency to appreciate or depreciate in the market for foreign exchange? Here are three generalizations:

- If the demand for a nation's currency increases (other things equal), that currency will appreciate; if the demand declines, that currency will depreciate.
- If the supply of a nation's currency increases, that currency will depreciate; if the supply decreases, that currency will appreciate.
- If a nation's currency appreciates, some foreign currency depreciates relative to it.

With these generalizations in mind, let's examine the determinants of exchange rates—the factors that shift the demand or supply curve for a certain currency. As we do so, keep in mind that the other-things-equal assumption is always in force. Also note that we are discussing factors *that change the exchange rate*, not things that change *as a result of* a change in the exchange rate.

Changes in Tastes Any change in consumer tastes or preferences for the products of a foreign country may alter the demand for that nation's currency and change its exchange rate. If technological advances in U.S. wireless phones make them more attractive to British consumers and businesses, then the British will supply more pounds in the exchange market to purchase more U.S. wireless phones. The supply-of-pounds curve will shift to the right, causing the pound to depreciate and the dollar to appreciate.

In contrast, the U.S. demand-for-pounds curve will shift to the right if British woolen apparel becomes more fashionable in the United States. So the pound will appreciate and the dollar will depreciate.

Relative Income Changes A nation's currency is likely to depreciate if its growth of national income is more rapid than that of other countries. Here's why: A country's imports vary directly with its income level. As total income rises in the United States, people there buy both more domestic goods and more foreign goods. If the U.S. economy is expanding rapidly and the British economy is stagnant, U.S. imports of British goods, and therefore U.S. demands for pounds, will increase. The dollar price of pounds will rise, so the dollar will depreciate.

Relative Inflation Rate Changes Other things equal, changes in the relative rates of inflation of two nations change their relative price levels and alter the exchange rate between their currencies. The currency of the nation with the higher inflation rate—the more rapidly rising price level—tends to depreciate. Suppose, for example, that inflation is zero percent in Great Britain and 5 percent in the United States so that prices, on average, are rising by 5 percent per year in the United States while, on average, remaining unchanged in Great Britain. U.S. consumers will seek out more of the now relatively lower-priced British goods, increasing the demand for pounds. British consumers will purchase less of the now relatively higher-priced U.S. goods, reducing the supply of pounds. This combination of increased demand for pounds and reduced supply of pounds will cause the pound to appreciate and the dollar to depreciate.

According to the **purchasing-power-parity theory**, exchange rates should eventually adjust such that they equate the purchasing power of various currencies. If a certain market basket of identical products costs $10,000 in the United States and £5000 in Great Britain, the exchange rate should move to $2 = £1. That way, a dollar spent in the United States will buy exactly as much output as it would if it were first converted to pounds (at the $2 = £1 exchange rate) and used to buy output in Great Britain.

In terms of our example, 5 percent inflation in the United States will increase the price of the market basket from $10,000 to $10,500, while the zero percent inflation in Great Britain will leave the market basket priced at £5000. For purchasing power parity to hold, the exchange rate would have to move from $2 = £1 to $2.10 = £1. That means the dollar therefore would depreciate and the pound would appreciate. In practice, however, not all exchange rates move precisely to equate the purchasing power of various currencies and thereby achieve "purchasing power parity," even over long periods.

Relative Interest Rates Changes in relative interest rates between two countries may alter their exchange rate. Suppose that real interest rates rise in the United States but stay constant in Great Britain. British citizens will then find the United States a more attractive place in which to loan money directly or loan money indirectly by buying bonds. To make these loans, they will have to supply pounds in the foreign exchange market to obtain dollars. The increase in the supply of pounds results in depreciation of the pound and appreciation of the dollar.

Changes in Relative Expected Returns on Stocks, Real Estate, and Production Facilities International investing extends beyond buying foreign bonds. It includes international investments in stocks and real estate as well as foreign purchases of factories and production facilities. Other things equal, the extent of this foreign investment depends on relative expected returns. To make the investments, investors in one country must sell their currencies to purchase the foreign currencies needed for the foreign investments.

For instance, suppose that investing in England suddenly becomes more popular due to a more positive outlook regarding expected returns on stocks, real estate, and production facilities there. U.S. investors therefore will sell U.S. assets to buy more assets in England. The U.S. assets will be sold for dollars, which will then be brought to the foreign exchange market and exchanged for pounds, which will in turn be used to purchase British assets. The increased demand for pounds in the foreign exchange market will cause the pound to appreciate and therefore the dollar to depreciate relative to the pound.

Speculation Currency speculators are people who buy and sell currencies with an eye toward reselling or repurchasing them at a profit. Suppose speculators expect the U.S. economy to (1) grow more rapidly than the British economy and (2) experience more rapid inflation than Britain. These expectations translate into an anticipation that the pound will appreciate and the dollar will depreciate. Speculators who are holding dollars will therefore try to convert them into pounds. This effort will increase the demand for pounds and cause the dollar price of pounds to rise (that is, cause the dollar to depreciate). A self-fulfilling prophecy occurs: The pound appreciates and the dollar depreciates because speculators act on the belief that these changes will in fact take place. In this way, speculation can cause changes in exchange rates. (We discuss currency speculation in more detail in this chapter's Last Word.)

Table 24.2 has more illustrations of the determinants of exchange rates; the table is worth careful study.

Flexible Rates and the Balance of Payments

Flexible exchange rates have an important feature: They automatically adjust and eventually eliminate balance-of-payments deficits or surpluses. We can explain this idea through Figure 24.2, in which S_1 and D_1 are the supply and demand curves for pounds from Figure 24.1. The equilibrium exchange rate of $2 = £1 means that there is no balance-of-payments deficit or surplus between the United States and Britain. At that exchange rate, the quantity of pounds demanded by U.S. consumers to import British goods, buy British transportation and insurance services, and pay interest and dividends on British investments in the United States equals the amount of pounds supplied by the British in buying U.S. exports, purchasing services from the United States, and making interest and dividend payments on U.S. investments in Britain. The United States would have no need to either draw down or build up its official reserves to balance its payments.

Suppose tastes change and U.S. consumers buy more British automobiles; the U.S. inflation rate increases relative to Britain's; or interest rates fall in the United States compared to those in Britain. Any or all of these changes will increase the U.S. demand for British pounds, for example, from D_1 to D_2 in Figure 24.2.

If the exchange rate remains at the initial $2 = £1, a U.S. balance-of-payments deficit will occur in the amount of *ab*. At the $2 = £1 rate, U.S. consumers will demand the quantity of pounds shown by point *b*, but Britain will supply only the amount shown by *a*. There will be a shortage of pounds. But this shortage will not last because this is a

TABLE 24.2 Determinants of Exchange Rates: Factors That Change the Demand for or the Supply of a Particular Currency and Thus Alter the Exchange Rate

Determinant	Examples
Change in tastes	Japanese electronic equipment declines in popularity in the United States (Japanese yen depreciates; U.S. dollar appreciates).
	European tourists reduce visits to the United States (U.S. dollar depreciates; European euro appreciates).
Change in relative incomes	England encounters a recession, reducing its imports, while U.S. real output and real income surge, increasing U.S. imports (British pound appreciates; U.S. dollar depreciates).
Change in relative inflation rates	Switzerland experiences a 3% inflation rate compared to Canada's 10% rate (Swiss franc appreciates; Canadian dollar depreciates).
Change in relative real interest rates	The Federal Reserve drives up interest rates in the United States, while the Bank of England takes no such action (U.S. dollar appreciates; British pound depreciates).
Changes in relative expected returns on stocks, real estate, or production facilities	Corporate tax cuts in the United States raise expected after-tax investment returns in the United States relative to those in Europe (U.S. dollar appreciates; the euro depreciates).
Speculation	Currency traders believe South Korea will have much greater inflation than Taiwan (South Korean won depreciates; Taiwanese dollar appreciates).
	Currency traders think Norway's interest rates will plummet relative to Denmark's rates (Norway's krone depreciates; Denmark's krone appreciates).

FIGURE 24.2 Adjustments under flexible exchange rates and fixed exchange rates. Under flexible exchange rates, a shift in the demand for pounds from D_1 to D_2, other things equal, would cause a U.S. balance-of-payments deficit ab. That deficit would be corrected by a change in the exchange rate from $2 = £1$ to $3 = £1$. Under fixed exchange rates, the United States would cover the shortage of pounds ab by selling official reserves (here pounds), restricting trade, implementing exchange controls, or enacting a contractionary stabilization policy.

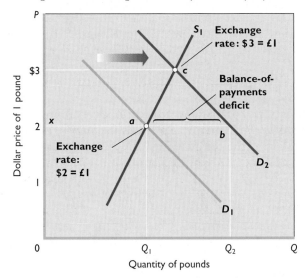

competitive foreign exchange market. Instead, the dollar price of pounds will rise (the dollar will depreciate) until the balance-of-payments deficit is eliminated. That occurs at the new equilibrium exchange rate of $3 = £1$, where the quantities of pounds demanded and supplied are again equal.

To explain why the increase in the dollar price of pounds—the dollar depreciation—eliminates the balance-of-payments deficit ab in Figure 24.2, we need to reemphasize that the exchange rate links all domestic (U.S.) prices with all foreign (British) prices. The dollar price of a foreign good is found by multiplying the foreign price by the exchange rate (in dollars per unit of the foreign currency). At an exchange rate of $2 = £1$, a British automobile priced at £15,000 will cost a U.S. consumer $30,000 (= 15,000 × $2).

A change in the exchange rate alters the prices of all British goods to U.S. consumers and all U.S. goods to British buyers. The shift in the exchange rate (here from $2 = £1$ to $3 = £1$) changes the relative attractiveness of U.S. imports and exports and restores equilibrium in the U.S. (and British) balance of payments. From the U.S. view, as the dollar price of pounds changes from $2 to $3, the British auto priced at £15,000, which formerly cost a U.S. consumer $30,000, now costs $45,000 (= 15,000 × $3). Other British goods will also cost U.S. consumers more, so that U.S. imports of British goods will decline.

From Britain's standpoint, the exchange rate (the pound price of dollars) has fallen (from $£\frac{1}{2}$ to $£\frac{1}{3}$ for $1). The international value of the pound has appreciated. The British previously got only $2 for £1; now they get $3 for £1. U.S. goods are therefore cheaper to the British, and U.S. exports to Britain will rise.

The two adjustments—a decrease in U.S. imports from Britain and an increase in U.S. exports to Britain—are just what are needed in terms of Figure 24.2 to decrease the quantity of pounds demanded from b to c, increase the quantity of pounds supplied from a to c, and thus correct the U.S. balance-of-payments deficit. These changes end when, at point c, the quantities of British pounds demanded and supplied are equal.

Disadvantages of Flexible Exchange Rates

Even though flexible exchange rates automatically work to eliminate payment imbalances, they may cause several significant problems. These are all related to the fact that flexible exchange rates are often volatile and can change by a large amount in just a few weeks or months. In addition, they often take substantial swings that can last several years or more. This can be seen in Figure 24.3, which plots the dollar-pound exchange rate from 1970 through 2009. (You can track other exchange rates, for example, the dollar-euro or dollar-yen rate, by going to the Federal Reserve Web site, **www.federalreserve.gov**, selecting Economic Research & Data, Statistical Releases and Historical Data, and finally, Exchange Rates and International Data.)

Uncertainty and Diminished Trade The risks and uncertainties associated with flexible exchange rates may discourage the flow of trade. Suppose a U.S. automobile dealer contracts to purchase 10 British cars for £150,000. At the current exchange rate of, say, $2 for £1, the U.S. importer expects to pay $300,000 for these automobiles. But if during the 3-month delivery period the rate of exchange shifts to $3 for £1, the £150,000 payment contracted by the U.S. importer will be $450,000.

That increase in the dollar price of pounds may thus turn the U.S. importer's anticipated profit into a substantial loss. Aware of the possibility of an adverse change in the exchange rate, the U.S. importer may not be willing to assume the risks involved. The U.S. firm may confine its operations to domestic automobiles, so international trade in this product will not occur.

The same thing can happen with investments. Assume that when the exchange rate is $3 to £1, a U.S. firm invests $30,000 (or £10,000) in a British enterprise. It

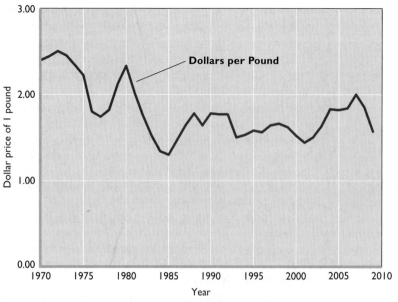

FIGURE 24.3 **The dollar-pound exchange rate, 1970–2009.** Before January 1971, the dollar-pound exchange rate was fixed at $2.40 = £1. Since that time, its value has been determined almost entirely by market forces, with only occasional government interventions. Under these mostly flexible conditions, the dollar-pound exchange rate has varied considerably. For instance, in 1981 it took $2.02 to buy a pound but by 1985 only $1.50 was needed to buy a pound. In contrast, between 2001 and 2007 the dollar price of a pound rose from $1.44 to $2.00, indicating that the dollar had depreciated relative to the pound. The dollar then sank back to $1.57 per British pound in 2009.

Source: Economic Report of the President, 2010, Table B-110. Earlier years from prior *Economic Reports.*

estimates a return of 10 percent; that is, it anticipates annual earnings of $3000 or £1000. Suppose these expectations prove correct in that the British firm earns £1000 in the first year on the £10,000 investment. But suppose that during the year, the value of the dollar appreciates to $2 = £1. The absolute return is now only $2000 (rather than $3000), and the rate of return falls from the anticipated 10 percent to only $6\frac{2}{3}$ percent (= $2000/$30,000). Investment is risky in any case. The added risk of changing exchange rates may persuade the U.S. investor not to venture overseas.[1]

Terms-of-Trade Changes A decline in the international value of its currency will worsen a nation's terms of trade. For example, an increase in the dollar price of a pound will mean that the United States must export more goods and services to finance a specific level of imports from Britain.

Instability Flexible exchange rates may destabilize the domestic economy because wide fluctuations stimulate and then depress industries producing exported goods. If the U.S. economy is operating at full employment and its currency depreciates, as in our illustration, the results will

be inflationary, for two reasons. (1) Foreign demand for U.S. goods may rise, increasing total spending and pulling up U.S. prices. Also, the prices of all U.S. imports will increase. (2) Conversely, appreciation of the dollar will lower U.S. exports and increase imports, possibly causing unemployment.

Flexible or floating exchange rates also may complicate the use of domestic stabilization policies in seeking full employment and price stability. This is especially true for nations whose exports and imports are large relative to their total domestic output.

Fixed Exchange Rates

To circumvent the disadvantages of flexible exchange rates, at times nations have fixed or "pegged" their exchange rates. For our analysis of fixed exchange rates, we assume that the United States and Britain agree to maintain a $2 = £1 exchange rate.

The problem is that such a government agreement cannot keep from changing the demand for and the supply of pounds. With the rate fixed, a shift in demand or supply will threaten the fixed-exchange-rate system, and government must intervene to ensure that the exchange rate is maintained.

In Figure 24.2, suppose the U.S. demand for pounds increases from D_1 to D_2 and a U.S. payment deficit *ab* arises. Now, the new equilibrium exchange rate ($3 = £1) is above the fixed exchange rate ($2 = £1). How can the

---

[1]You will see in this chapter's Last Word, however, that a trader can circumvent part of the risk of unfavorable exchange-rate fluctuations by "hedging" in the "futures market" or "forward market" for foreign exchange.

United States prevent the shortage of pounds from driving the exchange rate up to the new equilibrium level? How can it maintain the fixed exchange rate? The answer is by altering market demand or market supply or both so that they will intersect at the $2 = £1 rate. There are several ways to do this.

Use of Official Reserves

One way to maintain a fixed exchange rate is to engage in **currency interventions.** These are situations in which governments or their central banks manipulate an exchange rate through the use of official reserves. For instance, by selling some of its reserves of pounds, the U.S. government could increase the supply of pounds, shifting supply curve S_1 to the right so that it intersects D_2 at b in Figure 24.2, thereby maintaining the exchange rate at $2 = £1.

Notice that when the U.S. government sells some of its reserves of pounds, it is transferring assets to foreigners (since they gain ownership of the pounds). In terms of the balance-of-payments statement shown in Table 24.1, this transfer of assets enters positively on line (12), "Foreign purchases of assets in the United States." This positive entry is what offsets the balance-of-payments deficit caused by the fixed exchange rate and ensures that the U.S. balance of payments does in fact balance.

How do official reserves originate? Perhaps a balance-of-payments surplus occurred in the past. The U.S. government would have purchased that surplus. That is, at some earlier time, the U.S. government may have spent tax dollars to buy the surplus pounds that were threatening to reduce the exchange rate to below the $2 = £1 fixed rate. Those purchases would have bolstered the stock of U.S. official reserves of pounds.

Nations also have used gold as "international money" to obtain official reserves. In our example, the U.S. government could sell some of its gold to Britain to obtain pounds. It could then sell pounds for dollars. That would shift the supply-of-pounds curve to the right, and the $2 = £1 exchange rate could be maintained.

It is critical that the amount of reserves and gold be enough to accomplish the required increase in the supply of pounds. There is no problem if deficits and surpluses occur more or less randomly and are of similar size. Then, last year's balance-of-payments surplus with Britain will increase the U.S. reserve of pounds, and that reserve can be used to "finance" this year's deficit. But if the United States encounters persistent and sizable deficits for an extended period, it may exhaust its reserves, and thus be forced to abandon fixed exchange rates. Or, at the least, a nation whose reserves are inadequate must use less–appealing options to maintain exchange rates. Let's consider some of those options.

Trade Policies

To maintain fixed exchange rates, a nation can try to control the flow of trade and finance directly. The United States could try to maintain the $2 = £1 exchange rate in the face of a shortage of pounds by discouraging imports (thereby reducing the demand for pounds) and encouraging exports (thus increasing the supply of pounds). Imports could be reduced by means of new tariffs or import quotas; special taxes could be levied on the interest and dividends U.S. financial investors receive from foreign investments. Also, the U.S. government could subsidize certain U.S. exports to increase the supply of pounds.

The fundamental problem is that these policies reduce the volume of world trade and change its makeup from what is economically desirable. When nations impose tariffs, quotas, and the like, they lose some of the economic benefits of a free flow of world trade. That loss should not be underestimated: Trade barriers by one nation lead to retaliatory responses from other nations, multiplying the loss.

Exchange Controls and Rationing

Another option is to adopt exchange controls and rationing. Under **exchange controls** the U.S. government could handle the problem of a pound shortage by requiring that all pounds obtained by U.S. exporters be sold to the Federal government. Then the government would allocate or ration this short supply of pounds (represented by xa in Figure 24.2) among various U.S. importers, who demand the quantity xb. This policy would restrict the value of U.S. imports to the amount of foreign exchange earned by U.S. exports. Assuming balance in the capital and financial account, there would then be no balance-of-payments deficit. U.S. demand for British imports with the value ab would simply not be fulfilled.

There are major objections to exchange controls:

- **Distorted trade** Like *trade controls* (tariffs, quotas, and export subsidies), exchange controls would distort the pattern of international trade away from the pattern suggested by comparative advantage.
- **Favoritism** The process of rationing scarce foreign exchange might lead to government favoritism toward selected importers (big contributors to reelection campaigns, for example).

- **Restricted choice** Controls would limit freedom of consumer choice. The U.S. consumers who prefer Volkswagens might have to buy Chevrolets. The business opportunities for some U.S. importers might be impaired if the government were to limit imports.
- **Black markets** Enforcement problems are likely under exchange controls. U.S. importers might want foreign exchange badly enough to pay more than the $2 = £1 official rate, setting the stage for black-market dealings between importers and illegal sellers of foreign exchange.

Domestic Macroeconomic Adjustments

A final way to maintain a fixed exchange rate would be to use domestic stabilization policies (monetary policy and fiscal policy) to eliminate the shortage of foreign currency. Tax hikes, reductions in government spending, and a high-interest-rate policy would reduce total spending in the U.S. economy and, consequently, domestic income. Because the volume of imports varies directly with domestic income, demand for British goods, and therefore for pounds, would be restrained.

If these "contractionary" policies served to reduce the domestic price level relative to Britain's, U.S. buyers of consumer and capital goods would divert their demands from British goods to U.S. goods, reducing the demand for pounds. Moreover, the high-interest-rate policy would lift U.S. interest rates relative to those in Britain.

Lower prices on U.S. goods and higher U.S. interest rates would increase British imports of U.S. goods and would increase British financial investment in the United States. Both developments would increase the supply of pounds. The combination of a decrease in the demand for and an increase in the supply of pounds would reduce or eliminate the original U.S. balance-of-payments deficit. In Figure 24.2 the new supply and demand curves would intersect at some new equilibrium point on line *ab*, where the exchange rate remains at $2 = £1.

Maintaining fixed exchange rates by such means is hardly appealing. The "price" of exchange-rate stability for the United States would be a decline in output, employment, and price levels—in other words, a recession. Eliminating a balance-of-payments deficit and achieving domestic stability are both important national economic goals, but to sacrifice macroeconomic stability simply to balance international payments would be to let the tail wag the dog.

QUICK REVIEW 24.2

- In a system in which exchange rates are flexible (meaning that they are free to float), the rates are determined by the demand for and supply of individual national currencies in the foreign exchange market.
- Determinants of flexible exchange rates (factors that shift currency supply and demand curves) include changes in (a) tastes; (b) relative national incomes; (c) relative inflation rates; (d) real interest rates; (e) relative expected returns on stocks, real estate, and production facilities; and (f) speculation.
- Under a system of fixed exchange rates, nations set their exchange rates and then maintain them by buying or selling official reserves of currencies, establishing trade barriers, employing exchange controls, or incurring inflation or recession.

The Current Exchange Rate System: The Managed Float

Over the past 130 years, the world's nations have used three different exchange-rate systems. From 1879 to 1934, most nations used a gold standard, which implicitly created fixed exchange rates. From 1944 to 1971, most countries participated in the Bretton Woods system, which was a fixed-exchange-rate system indirectly tied to gold. And since 1971, most have used managed floating exchange rates, which mix mostly flexible exchange rates with occasional currency interventions. Naturally, our focus here is on the current exchange rate system. However, the history of the previous systems and why they broke down is highly fascinating. For that reason, we have included a discussion of these systems at the book's Web site (see Content Option for Instructors 2 [COI 2]).

The current international exchange-rate system (1971–present) is an "almost" flexible system called **managed floating exchange rates.** Exchange rates among major currencies are free to float to their equilibrium market levels, but nations occasionally use currency interventions in the foreign exchange market to stabilize or alter market exchange rates.

Normally, the major trading nations allow their exchange rates to float up or down to equilibrium levels based on supply and demand in the foreign exchange market. They recognize that changing economic conditions among nations require continuing changes in equilibrium exchange rates to avoid persistent payments deficits or surpluses. They rely on freely operating foreign exchange markets to accomplish the necessary adjustments. The result has been considerably more volatile exchange rates than those during the Bretton Woods era.

But nations also recognize that certain trends in the movement of equilibrium exchange rates may be at odds with national or international objectives. On occasion, nations therefore intervene in the foreign exchange market by buying or selling large amounts of specific currencies. This way, they can "manage" or stabilize exchange rates by influencing currency demand and supply.

The leaders of the *G8 nations* (Canada, France, Germany, Italy, Japan, Russia, United Kingdom, and United States) meet regularly to discuss economic issues and try to coordinate economic policies. At times they have collectively intervened to try to stabilize currencies. For example, in 2000 they sold dollars and bought euros in an effort to stabilize the falling value of the euro relative to the dollar. In the previous year the euro (€) had depreciated from €1 = $1.17 to €1 = $.87.

The current exchange-rate system is thus an "almost" flexible exchange-rate system. The "almost" refers mainly to the occasional currency interventions by governments; it also refers to the fact that the actual system is more complicated than described. While the major currencies such as dollars, euros, pounds, and yen fluctuate in response to changing supply and demand, some developing nations peg their currencies to the dollar and allow their currencies to fluctuate with it against other currencies. Also, some nations peg the value of their currencies to a "basket" or group of other currencies.

How well has the managed float worked? It has both proponents and critics.

In Support of the Managed Float

Proponents of the managed-float system argue that it has functioned far better than many experts anticipated. Skeptics had predicted that fluctuating exchange rates would reduce world trade and finance. But in real terms world trade under the managed float has grown tremendously over the past several decades. Moreover, as supporters are quick to point out, currency crises such as those in Mexico and southeast Asia in the last half of the 1990s were not the result of the floating-exchange-rate system itself. Rather, the abrupt currency devaluations and depreciations resulted from internal problems in those nations, in conjunction with the nations' tendency to peg their currencies to the dollar or to a basket of currencies. In some cases, flexible exchange rates would have made these adjustments far more gradual.

Proponents also point out that the managed float has weathered severe economic turbulence that might have caused a fixed-rate system to break down. Such events as extraordinary oil price increases in 1973–1974 and again in 1981–1983, inflationary recessions in several nations in the mid-1970s, major national recessions in the early 1980s, and large U.S. budget deficits in the 1980s and the first half of the 1990s all caused substantial imbalances in international trade and finance, as did the large U.S. budget deficits and soaring world oil prices that occurred in the middle of the first decade of the 2000s. The U.S. financial crisis and the severe recession of 2007–2009 greatly disrupted world trade. Flexible rates enabled the system to adjust to all these events, whereas the same events would have put unbearable pressures on a fixed-rate system.

Concerns with the Managed Float

There is still much sentiment in favor of greater exchange-rate stability. Those favoring more stable exchange rates see problems with the current system. They argue that the excessive volatility of exchange rates under the managed float threatens the prosperity of economies that rely heavily on exports. Several financial crises in individual nations (for example, Mexico, South Korea, Indonesia, Thailand, Russia, and Brazil) have resulted from abrupt changes in exchange rates. These crises have led to massive "bailouts" of those economies via loans from the International Monetary Fund (IMF). The IMF bailouts, in turn, may encourage nations to undertake risky and inappropriate economic policies since they know that, if need be, the IMF will come to the rescue. Moreover, some exchange-rate volatility has occurred even when underlying economic and financial conditions were relatively stable, suggesting that speculation plays too large a role in determining exchange rates.

Skeptics say the managed float is basically a "nonsystem" because the guidelines as to what each nation may or may not do with its exchange rates are not specific enough to keep the system working in the long run. Nations inevitably will be tempted to intervene in the foreign exchange market, not merely to smooth out short-term fluctuations in exchange rates but to prop up their currency if it is chronically weak or to manipulate the exchange rate to achieve domestic stabilization goals.

So what are we to conclude? Flexible exchange rates have not worked perfectly, but they have not failed miserably. Thus far they have survived, and no doubt have eased, several major shocks to the international trading system. Meanwhile, the "managed" part of the float has given nations some sense of control over their collective economic destinies. On balance, most economists favor continuation of the present system of "almost" flexible exchange rates.

Recent U.S. Trade Deficits

As shown in Figure 24.4a, the United States has experienced large and persistent trade deficits in recent years. These deficits rose rapidly between 2001 and 2006 before declining when consumers and businesses greatly curtailed their purchase of imports during the recession of 2007–2009. Even in 2009, however, the trade deficit on goods was still at $517 billion and the trade deficit on goods and services was $379 billion. The current account deficit (Figure 24.4b) reached a record high of $806 billion in 2006, and that amount was 6.0 percent of GDP. The current account deficit declined to $420 billion—2.9 percent of GDP—in the recession year 2009. Economists expect the trade deficits to expand, absolutely and relatively, toward prerecession levels when the economy recovers and U.S. income and imports again rise.

Causes of the Trade Deficits

The large U.S. trade deficits have several causes. First, the U.S. economy expanded more rapidly between 2001 and 2007 than the economies of several U.S. trading partners. The strong U.S. income growth that accompanied that economic growth enabled Americans to greatly increase their purchases of imported products. In contrast, Japan and some European nations suffered recession or experienced relatively slow income growth over that same period. So consumers in those countries increased their purchases of U.S. exports much less rapidly than Americans increased their purchases of foreign imports.

Another factor explaining the large trade deficits is the enormous U.S. trade imbalance with China. In 2007 the United States imported $257 billion more of goods and services than it exported to China. Even in the recession year 2009, the trade deficit with China was $220 billion.

FIGURE 24.4 U.S. trade deficits, 2001–2009. (a) The United States experienced large deficits in *goods* and in *goods and services* between 2001 and 2009. (b) The U.S. current account, generally reflecting the goods and services deficit, was also in substantial deficit. Although reduced significantly by the recession of 2007–2009, large trade deficits are expected to continue for many years to come.

(a)
Balance of trade

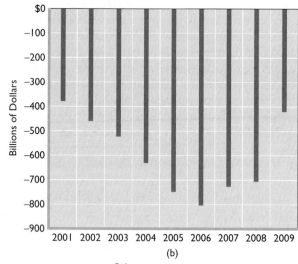

(b)
Balance on current account

Source: Bureau of Economic Analysis, **www.bea.gov**.

That deficit was double the combined deficits with Mexico ($43 billion), Germany ($37 billion), and Japan ($28 billion). The United States is China's largest export market, and although China has greatly increased its imports from the United States, its standard of living has not yet risen sufficiently for its households to afford large quantities of U.S. products. Adding to the problem, China's government has fixed the exchange rate of it currency, the yuan, to a basket of currencies that includes the U.S. dollar.

Therefore, China's large trade surpluses with the United States have not caused the yuan to appreciate much against the U.S. dollar. Greater appreciation of the yuan would have made Chinese goods more expensive in the United States and reduced U.S. imports from China. In China a stronger yuan would have reduced the dollar price of U.S. goods and increased Chinese purchases of U.S. exports. That combination—reduced U.S. imports from China and increased U.S. exports to China—would have reduced the large U.S. trade imbalance.

Another factor underlying the large U.S. trade deficits is a continuing trade deficit with oil-exporting nations. For example, in 2009 the United States had a $54 billion trade deficit with the OPEC countries.

A declining U.S. saving rate (= saving/total income) also contributed to the large U.S. trade deficits. Up until the recession of 2007–2009, the U.S. saving rate declined substantially, while its investment rate (= investment/total income) increased. The gap between U.S. investment and U.S. saving was filled by foreign purchases of U.S. real and financial assets, which created a large surplus on the U.S. capital and financial account. Because foreign savers were willing to finance a large part of U.S. investment, Americans were able to save less and consume more. Part of that added consumption spending was on imported goods.

Finally, many foreigners simply view U.S. assets favorably because of the relatively high risk-adjusted rates of return they provide. The purchase of those assets provides foreign currency to Americans that enables them to finance their strong appetite for imported goods. The capital account surpluses therefore may partially cause the high U.S. trade deficits, not just result from those high deficits. The point is that the causes of the high U.S. trade deficits are numerous and not so easy to disentangle.

Implications of U.S. Trade Deficits

The prerecession U.S. trade deficits were the largest ever run by a major industrial nation. Whether the large trade deficits should be of significant concern to the United States and the rest of the world is debatable. Most economists see both benefits and costs to trade deficits.

Increased Current Consumption At the time a trade deficit or a current account deficit is occurring, American consumers benefit. A trade deficit means that the United States is receiving more goods and services as imports from abroad than it is sending out as exports. Taken alone, a trade deficit allows the United States to consume outside its production possibilities curve. It augments the domestic standard of living. But here is a catch: The gain in present consumption may come at the expense of reduced future consumption. When and if the current account deficit

declines, Americans may have to consume less than before and perhaps even less than they produce.

Increased U.S. Indebtedness A trade deficit is considered unfavorable because it must be financed by borrowing from the rest of the world, selling off assets, or dipping into official reserves. Recall that current account deficits are financed by surpluses in the capital and financial accounts. Such surpluses require net inpayments of dollars to buy U.S. assets, including debt issued by Americans. Therefore, when U.S. exports are insufficient to finance U.S. imports, the United States increases both its debt to people abroad and the value of foreign claims against assets in the United States. Financing of the U.S. trade deficit has resulted in a larger foreign accumulation of claims against U.S. financial and real assets than the U.S. claim against foreign assets. In 2008, foreigners owned about $3.5 trillion more of U.S. assets (corporations, land, stocks, bonds, loan notes) than U.S. citizens and institutions owned in foreign assets.

If the United States wants to regain ownership of these domestic assets, at some future time it will have to export more than it imports. At that time, domestic consumption will be lower because the United States will need to send more of its output abroad than it receives as imports. Therefore, the current consumption gains delivered by U.S. current account deficits may mean permanent debt, permanent foreign ownership, or large sacrifices of future consumption.

We say "may mean" above because the foreign lending to U.S. firms and foreign investment in the United States increases the U.S. capital stock. U.S. production capacity therefore might increase more rapidly than otherwise because of a large surplus on the capital and financial account. Faster increases in production capacity and real GDP enhance the economy's ability to service foreign debt and buy back real capital, if that is desired.

Trade deficits therefore are a mixed blessing. The long-term impacts of the record-high U.S. trade deficits are largely unknown. That "unknown" worries some economists, who are concerned that foreigners will lose financial confidence in the United States. If that happens, they would restrict their lending to American households and businesses and also reduce their purchases of U.S. assets. Both actions would decrease the demand for U.S. dollars in the foreign exchange market and cause the U.S. dollar to depreciate. A sudden, large depreciation of the U.S. dollar might disrupt world trade and negatively affect economic growth worldwide. Other economists, however, downplay this scenario. Because any decline in the U.S. capital and financial account surplus is automatically met with a decline in the current account deficit, U.S. net exports would rise and the overall impact on the American economy would be slight.

Are Speculators a Negative or a Positive Influence in Currency Markets and International Trade?

Most people buy foreign currency to facilitate the purchase of goods, services, or assets from another country. A U.S. importer buys Japanese yen to purchase Japanese autos. A Hong Kong financial investor purchases Australian dollars to invest in the Australian stock market. But there is another group of participants in the currency market—speculators—that buys and sells foreign currencies in the hope of reselling or rebuying them later at a profit.

Contributing to Exchange-Rate Fluctuations Speculators were much in the news in late 1997 and 1998 when they were widely accused of driving down the values of the South Korean won, Thai baht, Malaysian ringgit, and Indonesian rupiah. The value of these currencies fell by as much as 50 percent within one month, and speculators undoubtedly contributed to the swiftness of those declines. The expectation of currency depreciation (or appreciation) can be self-fulfilling. If speculators, for example, expect the Indonesian rupiah to be devalued or to depreciate, they quickly sell rupiah and buy currencies that they think will increase in relative value. The sharp increase in the supply of rupiah indeed reduces its value; this reduction then may trigger further selling of rupiah in expectation of further declines in its value.

But changed economic realities, not speculation, are normally the underlying causes of changes in currency values. That was largely the case with the southeast Asian countries in which actual and threatened bankruptcies in the financial and manufacturing sectors undermined confidence in the strength of the currencies. Anticipating the eventual declines in currency values, speculators simply hastened those declines. That is, the declines in value probably would have occurred with or without speculators.

Moreover, on a daily basis, speculation clearly has positive effects in foreign exchange markets.

Smoothing Out Short-Term Fluctuations in Currency Prices When temporarily weak demand or strong supply reduces a currency's value, speculators quickly buy the currency, adding to its demand and strengthening its value. When temporarily strong demand or weak supply increases a currency's value, speculators sell the currency. That selling increases the supply of the currency and reduces its value. In this way speculators smooth out supply and demand, and thus exchange rates, over short time periods. This day-to-day exchange-rate stabilization aids international trade.

Absorbing Risk Speculators also absorb risk that others do not want to bear. Because of potential adverse changes in exchange rates, international transactions are riskier than

Summary

1. International financial transactions involve trade either in currently produced goods and services or in preexisting assets. Exports of goods, services, and assets create inflows of money, while imports cause outflows of money. If buyers and sellers use different currencies, then foreign exchange transactions take place so that the exporter can be paid in his or her own currency.

2. The balance of payments records all international trade and financial transactions taking place between a given nation and the rest of the world. The balance on goods and services (the trade balance) compares exports and imports of both goods and services. The current account balance includes not only goods and services transactions but also net investment income and net transfers.

3. The capital and financial account includes (a) the net amount of the nation's debt forgiveness and (b) the nation's sale of real and financial assets to people living abroad less its purchases of real and financial assets from foreigners.

4. The current account and the capital and financial account always sum to zero. A deficit in the current account is always offset by a surplus in the capital and financial account. Conversely, a surplus in the current account is always offset by a deficit in the capital and financial account.

5. Official reserves are owned by national governments and their central banks and consist of stocks of foreign currencies, certain reserves held with the International Monetary Fund, and stocks of gold.

Glossary

Note: Terms set in *italic* type are defined separately in this glossary.

ability-to-pay principle The idea that those who have greater *income* (or *wealth*) should pay a greater proportion of it as taxes than those who have less income (or wealth).

absolute advantage A situation in which a person or country can produce more of a particular product from a specific quantity of resources than some other person or country.

accounting profit The *total revenue* of a *firm* less its *explicit costs;* the profit (or net income) that appears on accounting statements and that is reported to the government for tax purposes.

acreage allotments program A pre-1996 government program that determined the total number of acres to be used in producing (reduced amounts of) various food and fiber products and allocated these acres among individual farmers. These farmers had to limit their plantings to the allotted number of acres to obtain *price supports* for their crops.

adverse selection problem A problem arising when information known to one party to a contract or agreement is not known to the other party, causing the latter to incur major costs. Example: Individuals who have the poorest health are most likely to buy health insurance.

advertising A seller's activities in communicating its message about its product to potential buyers.

AFL-CIO An acronym for the American Federation of Labor–Congress of Industrial Organizations; the largest federation of *labor unions* in the United States.

agency shop A place of employment where the employer may hire either *labor union* members or nonmembers but where those who do not join the union must either pay union dues or donate an equivalent amount of money to a charity.

aggregate A collection of specific economic units treated as if they were one. For example, all prices of individual goods and services are combined into a *price level*, or all units of output are aggregated into *gross domestic product*.

agribusiness The portion of the agricultural and food product industries that is dominated by large corporations.

Alcoa case A 1945 case in which the courts ruled that the possession of monopoly power, no matter how reasonably that power had been used, was a violation of the antitrust laws; temporarily overturned the *rule of reason* applied in the *U.S. Steel case*.

allocative efficiency The apportionment of resources among firms and industries to obtain the production of the products most wanted by society (consumers); the output of each product at which its *marginal cost* and *price* or *marginal benefit* are equal, and at which the sum of *consumer surplus* and *producer surplus* is maximized.

anchoring The tendency people have to unconsciously base, or "anchor," the valuation of an item they are currently thinking about on previously considered but logically irrelevant information.

antitrust laws Legislation (including the *Sherman Act* and *Clayton Act*) that prohibits anticompetitive business activities such as *price fixing*, bid rigging, monopolization, and *tying contracts*.

antitrust policy The use of the *antitrust laws* to promote *competition* and economic efficiency.

appreciation (of the dollar) An increase in the value of the dollar relative to the currency of another nation, so a dollar buys a larger amount of the foreign currency and thus of foreign goods.

asset Anything of monetary value owned by a firm or individual.

asymmetric information A situation where one party to a market transaction has much more information about a product or service than the other. The result may be an under- or overallocation of resources.

average fixed cost (AFC) A firm's total *fixed cost* divided by output (the quantity of product produced).

average product (AP) The total output produced per unit of a *resource* employed (*total product* divided by the quantity of that employed resource).

average revenue Total revenue from the sale of a product divided by the quantity of the product sold (demanded); equal to the price at which the product is sold when all units of the product are sold at the same price.

average tax rate Total tax paid divided by total *taxable income* or some other base (such as total income) against which to compare the amount of tax paid. Expressed as a percentage.

average total cost (ATC) A firm's *total cost* divided by output (the quantity of product produced); equal to *average fixed cost* plus *average variable cost*.

average variable cost (AVC) A firm's total *variable cost* divided by output (the quantity of product produced).

backflows The return of workers to the countries from which they originally emigrated.

balance of payments (See *international balance of payments*.)

balance-of-payments deficit The net amount of *official reserves* (mainly foreign currencies) that a nation's treasury or central bank must sell to achieve balance between that nation's *capital and financial account* and its *current account* (in its *balance of payments*).

balance-of-payments surplus The net amount of *official reserves* (mainly foreign currencies) that a nation's treasury or central bank must buy to achieve balance between that nation's *capital and financial account* and its *current account* (in its *balance of payments*).

balance on capital and financial account The sum of the *capital account balance* and the *financial account balance*.

balance on current account The exports of goods and services of a nation less its imports of goods and services plus its *net investment income* and *net transfers* in a year.

balance on goods and services The exports of goods and services of a nation less its imports of goods and services in a year.

bankrupt A legal situation in which an individual or *firm* finds that it cannot make timely interest payments on money it has borrowed. In such cases, a bankruptcy judge can order the individual or firm to liquidate (turn into cash) its assets in order to pay lenders at least some portion of the amount they are owed.

barrier to entry Anything that artificially prevents the entry of firms into an industry.

barter The exchange of one good or service for another good or service.

beaten paths Migration routes taken previously by family, relatives, friends, and other migrants.

behavioral economics The branch of economics that combines insights from economics, psychology, and neuroscience to give a better explanation of choice behavior than previous theories that incorrectly concluded that consumers were always rational, deliberate, and unemotional. Behavioral economics explains: *framing effects, anchoring, mental accounting,* the *endowment effect,* and how people are *loss averse.*

benefits-received principle The idea that those who receive the benefits of goods and services provided by government should pay the taxes required to finance them.

bilateral monopoly A market in which there is a single seller (*monopoly*) and a single buyer (*monopsony*).

bond A financial device through which a borrower (a firm or government) is obligated to pay the principal and interest on a loan at a specific date in the future.

brain drains The exit or *emigration* of highly educated, highly skilled workers from a country.

break-even output Any output at which a (competitive) firm's *total cost* and *total revenue* are equal; an output at which a firm has neither an *economic profit* nor an economic loss, at which it earns only a *normal profit.*

break-even point An output at which a firm makes a *normal profit* (*total revenue = total cost*) but not an *economic profit.*

British thermal unit (BTU) The amount of energy required to raise the temperature of 1 pound of water by 1 degree Fahrenheit.

budget constraint The limit that the size of a consumer's income (and the prices that must be paid for goods and services) imposes on the ability of that consumer to obtain goods and services.

budget line A line that shows the different combinations of two products a consumer can purchase with a specific money income, given the products' prices.

businesses Economic entities (*firms*) that purchase resources and provide goods and services to the economy.

business firm (See *firm.*)

cap-and-trade program A government strategy for reducing harmful emissions or discharges by placing a limit on their total amounts and then allowing firms to buy and sell the rights to emit or discharge specific amounts within the total limits.

capital Human-made resources (buildings, machinery, and equipment) used to produce goods and services; goods that do not directly satisfy human wants; also called capital goods.

capital and financial account The section of a nation's *international balance of payments* that records (1) debt forgiveness by and to foreigners and (2) foreign purchases of assets in the United States and U.S. purchases of assets abroad.

capital and financial account deficit A negative balance on its *capital and financial account* in a country's *international balance of payments.*

capital and financial account surplus A positive balance on its *capital and financial account* in a country's *international balance of payments.*

capital gain The gain realized when securities or properties are sold for a price greater than the price paid for them.

capital goods (See *capital.*)

capital-intensive goods Products that require relatively large amounts of *capital* to produce.

capitalism An economic system in which property resources are privately owned and markets and prices are used to direct and coordinate economic activities.

capital stock The total available *capital* in a nation.

cardinal utility Satisfaction (*utility*) that can be measured via cardinal numbers (1, 2, 3...), with all the mathematical properties of those numbers such as addition, subtraction, multiplication, and division being applicable.

cartel A formal agreement among firms (or countries) in an industry to set the price of a product and establish the outputs of the individual firms (or countries) or to divide the market for the product geographically.

causation A relationship in which the occurrence of one or more events brings about another event.

cease-and-desist order An order from a court or government agency to a corporation or individual to stop engaging in a specified practice.

ceiling price (See *price ceiling.*)

Celler-Kefauver Act The Federal law of 1950 that amended the *Clayton Act* by prohibiting the acquisition of the assets of one firm by another firm when the effect would be less competition.

central bank A bank whose chief function is the control of the nation's *money supply*; in the United States, the Federal Reserve System.

central economic planning Government determination of the objectives of the economy and how resources will be directed to attain those goals.

ceteris paribus **assumption** (See *other-things-equal assumption*.)

change in demand A movement of an entire *demand curve* or schedule such that the *quantity demanded* changes at every particular price; caused by a change in one or more of the *determinants of demand*.

change in quantity demanded A change in the *quantity demanded* along a fixed *demand curve* (or within a fixed demand schedule) as a result of a change in the product's price.

change in quantity supplied A change in the *quantity supplied* along a fixed *supply curve* (or within a fixed supply schedule) as a result of a change in the product's price.

change in supply A movement of an entire *supply curve* or schedule such that the *quantity supplied* changes at every particular price; caused by a change in one or more of the *determinants of supply*.

Change to Win A loose federation of American unions that includes the Service Workers and Teamsters and has a total membership of 6 million workers.

circular flow diagram An illustration showing the flow of resources from *households* to *firms* and of products from firms to households. These flows are accompanied by reverse flows of money from firms to households and from households to firms.

Clayton Act The Federal antitrust law of 1914 that strengthened the *Sherman Act* by making it illegal for firms to engage in certain specified practices.

climate-change problem The problem of rising world temperatures that most climate experts believe are caused at least in part by increased carbon dioxide and other greenhouse gases generated as by-products of human economic activities.

closed shop A place of employment where only workers who are already members of a labor union may be hired.

Coase theorem The idea, first stated by economist Ronald Coase, that some *externalities* can be resolved through private negotiations of the affected parties.

coincidence of wants A situation in which the good or service that one trader desires to obtain is the same as that which another trader desires to give up and an item that the second trader wishes to acquire is the same as that which the first trader desires to surrender.

COLA (See *cost-of-living adjustment*.)

collective action problem The idea that getting a group to pursue a common, collective goal gets harder the larger the group's size. Larger groups are more costly to organize and their members more difficult to motivate because the larger the group, the smaller each member's share of the benefits if the group succeeds.

collective bargaining The negotiation of labor contracts between *labor unions* and *firms* or government entities.

collective voice The function a *labor union* performs for its members as a group when it communicates their problems and grievances to management and presses management for a satisfactory resolution.

collusion A situation in which firms act together and in agreement (collude) to fix prices, divide a market, or otherwise restrict competition.

command system A method of organizing an economy in which property resources are publicly owned and government uses *central economic planning* to direct and coordinate economic activities; command economy; communism.

communism (See *command system*.)

comparative advantage A situation in which a person or country can produce a specific product at a lower *opportunity cost* than some other person or country; the basis for specialization and trade.

compensating differences Differences in the *wages* received by workers in different jobs to compensate for the nonmonetary differences between the jobs.

compensating wage differential (See *compensating differences*.)

compensation to employees *Wages* and salaries plus wage and salary supplements paid by employers to workers.

competition The presence in a market of independent buyers and sellers competing with one another along with the freedom of buyers and sellers to enter and leave the market.

competitive industry's short-run supply curve The horizontal summation of the short-run supply curves of the *firms* in a purely competitive industry (see *pure competition*); a curve that shows the total quantities offered for sale at various prices by the firms in an industry in the short run.

competitive labor market A resource market in which a large number of (noncolluding) employers demand a particular type of labor supplied by a large number of nonunion workers.

complementary goods Products and services that are used together. When the price of one falls, the demand for the other increases (and conversely).

complementary resources Productive inputs that are used jointly with other inputs in the production process; resources for which a decrease in the price of one leads to an increase in the demand for the other.

compound interest The accumulation of money that builds over time in an investment or interest-bearing account as new interest is earned on previous interest that is not withdrawn.

concentration ratio The percentage of the total sales of an industry made by the four (or some other number) largest sellers in the industry.

conflict diamonds Diamonds that are mined and sold by combatants in war zones in Africa as a way to provide the currency needed to finance their military activities.

conglomerate merger The merger of a *firm* in one *industry* with a firm in another industry (with a firm that is not a supplier, customer, or competitor).

conglomerates Firms that produce goods and services in two or more separate industries.

constant-cost industry   An industry in which expansion by the entry of new firms has no effect on the prices firms in the industry must pay for resources and thus no effect on production costs.

constant opportunity cost   An *opportunity cost* that remains the same for each additional unit as a consumer (or society) shifts purchases (production) from one product to another along a straight-line *budget line* (*production possibilities curve*).

constant returns to scale   Unchanging *average total cost* of producing a product as the firm expands the size of its plant (its output) in the *long run*.

consumer equilibrium   In marginal utility theory, the combination of goods purchased based on *marginal utility* (MU) and *price* (P) that maximizes *total utility*; the combination for goods X and Y at which $\mathrm{MU}_x/\mathrm{P}_x = \mathrm{MU}_y/\mathrm{P}_y$. In indifference curve analysis, the combination of goods purchased that maximize *total utility* by enabling the consumer to reach the highest *indifference curve*, given the consumer's *budget line* (or *budget constraint*).

consumer goods   Products and services that satisfy human wants directly.

consumer sovereignty   Determination by consumers of the types and quantities of goods and services that will be produced with the scarce resources of the economy; consumers' direction of production through their *dollar votes*.

consumer surplus   The difference between the maximum price a consumer is (or consumers are) willing to pay for an additional unit of a product and its market price; the triangular area below the demand curve and above the market price.

consumption of fixed capital   An estimate of the amount of *capital* worn out or used up (consumed) in producing the *gross domestic product*; also called depreciation.

copayment   The percentage of (say, health care) costs that an insured individual pays while the insurer pays the remainder.

copyright   A legal protection provided to developers and publishers of books, computer software, videos, and musical compositions against the copying of their works by others.

corporate income tax   A tax levied on the net income (accounting profit) of corporations.

corporation   A legal entity ("person") chartered by a state or the Federal government that is distinct and separate from the individuals who own it.

correlation   A systematic and dependable association between two sets of data (two kinds of events); does not necessarily indicate causation.

cost-benefit analysis   A comparison of the *marginal costs* of a government project or program with the *marginal benefits* to decide whether or not to employ resources in that project or program and to what extent.

cost-of-living adjustment (COLA)   An automatic increase in the incomes (wages) of workers when inflation occurs; guaranteed by a collective bargaining contract between firms and workers.

countercyclical payments (CCPs)   Cash *subsidies* paid to farmers when market prices for certain crops drop below targeted prices. Payments are based on previous production and are received regardless of the current crop grown.

craft union   A labor union that limits its membership to workers with a particular skill (craft).

creative destruction   The hypothesis that the creation of new products and production methods simultaneously destroys the market power of existing monopolies.

credible threat   In *game theory*, a statement of harmful intent by one party that the other party views as believable; often issued in conditional terms of "if you do this; we will do that."

cross elasticity of demand   The ratio of the percentage change in *quantity demanded* of one good to the percentage change in the price of some other good. A positive coefficient indicates the two products are *substitute goods*; a negative coefficient indicates they are *complementary goods*.

crowding model of occupational discrimination   A model of labor markets suggesting that *occupational discrimination* has kept many women and minorities out of high-paying occupations and forced them into a limited number of low-paying occupations.

currency appreciation   (See *exchange-rate appreciation*.)

currency depreciation   (See *exchange-rate depreciation*.)

currency intervention   A government's buying and selling of its own currency or foreign currencies to alter international exchange rates.

current account   The section in a nation's *international balance of payments* that records its exports and imports of goods and services, its net *investment income*, and its *net transfers*.

deadweight loss   (See *efficiency loss*.)

declining industry   An industry in which *economic profits* are negative (losses are incurred) and that will, therefore, decrease its output as firms leave it.

decreasing-cost industry   An industry in which expansion through the entry of firms lowers the prices that firms in the industry must pay for resources and therefore decreases their production costs.

deductible   The dollar sum of (for example, health care) costs that an insured individual must pay before the insurer begins to pay.

defaults   Situations in which borrowers stop making loan payments or do not pay back loans that they took out and are now due.

defensive medicine   The recommendation by physicians of more tests and procedures than are warranted medically or economically as a way of protecting themselves against later malpractice suits.

demand   A schedule showing the amounts of a good or service that buyers (or a buyer) wish to purchase at various prices during some time period.

demand curve   A curve illustrating *demand*.

demand schedule   (See *demand*.)

demand-side market failures Underallocations of resources that occur when private demand curves understate consumers' full willingness to pay for a good or service.

demographers Scientists who study the characteristics of human populations.

dependent variable A variable that changes as a consequence of a change in some other (independent) variable; the "effect" or outcome.

depreciation (of the dollar) A decrease in the value of the dollar relative to another currency, so a dollar buys a smaller amount of the foreign currency and therefore of foreign goods.

derived demand The demand for a resource that depends on the demand for the products it helps to produce.

determinants of demand Factors other than price that determine the quantities demanded of a good or service.

determinants of supply Factors other than price that determine the quantities supplied of a good or service.

developing countries Many countries of Africa, Asia, and Latin America that are characterized by lack of capital goods, use of nonadvanced technologies, low literacy rates, high unemployment, rapid population growth, and labor forces heavily committed to agriculture.

diagnosis-related group (DRG) system Payments to doctors and hospitals under *Medicare* based on which of hundreds of carefully detailed diagnostic categories best characterize the patient's condition and needs.

differentiated oligopoly An *oligopoly* in which firms produce a *differentiated product*.

differentiated product A product that differs physically or in some other way from the similar products produced by other firms; a product such that buyers are not indifferent to the seller when the price charged by all sellers is the same.

diffusion (Web chapter) The spread of an *innovation* through its widespread imitation.

dilemma of regulation The tradeoff faced by a *regulatory agency* in setting the maximum legal price a monopolist may charge: The *socially optimal price* is below *average total cost* (and either bankrupts the *firm* or requires that it be subsidized), while the higher, *fair-return price* does not produce *allocative efficiency*.

diminishing marginal returns (See *law of diminishing returns*.)

diminishing marginal utility (See *law of diminishing marginal utility*.)

direct foreign investment (See *foreign direct investment*.)

direct payments Cash subsidies paid to farmers based on past production levels; unaffected by current crop prices and current production.

direct relationship The relationship between two variables that change in the same direction, for example, product price and quantity supplied; positive relationship.

discrimination The practice of according individuals or groups inferior treatment in hiring, occupational access, education and training, promotion, wage rates, or working conditions even though they have the same abilities, education, skills, and work experience as other workers.

discrimination coefficient A measure of the cost or disutility of prejudice; the monetary amount an employer is willing to pay to hire a preferred worker rather than a nonpreferred worker.

diseconomies of scale Increases in the *average total cost* of producing a product as the *firm* expands the size of its *plant* (its output) in the *long run*.

dividends Payments by a corporation of all or part of its profit to its stockholders (the corporate owners).

division of labor The separation of the work required to produce a product into a number of different tasks that are performed by different workers; *specialization* of workers.

Doha Development Agenda The latest, uncompleted (as of mid-2010) sequence of trade negotiations by members of the *World Trade Organization;* named after Doha, Qatar, where the set of negotiations began. Also called the Doha Round.

dollar votes The "votes" that consumers and entrepreneurs cast for the production of consumer and capital goods, respectively, when they purchase those goods in product and resource markets.

domestic price The price of a good or service within a country, determined by domestic demand and supply.

dominant strategy In *game theory*, an option that is better than any other alternative option regardless of what the other firm does.

dumping The sale of a product in a foreign country at prices either below cost or below the prices commonly charged at home.

DuPont cellophane case The antitrust case brought against DuPont in which the U.S. Supreme Court ruled (in 1956) that while DuPont had a monopoly in the narrowly defined market for cellophane, it did not monopolize the more broadly defined market for flexible packaging materials. It was thus not guilty of violating the *Sherman Act*.

earmarks Narrow, specially designated spending authorizations placed in broad legislation by Senators and representatives for the purpose of providing benefits to firms and organizations within their constituencies without undergoing the usual evaluation process or competitive bidding.

earned-income tax credit (EITC) A refundable Federal tax credit for low-income working people designed to reduce poverty and encourage labor-force participation.

earnings The money income received by a worker; equal to the *wage* (rate) multiplied by the amount of time worked.

economic concentration A description or measure of the degree to which an industry is dominated by one or a handful of firms or is characterized by many firms. (See *concentration ratio*.)

economic cost A payment that must be made to obtain and retain the services of a *resource;* the income a firm must provide to a resource supplier to attract the resource away from an alternative use; equal to the quantity of other products that cannot be produced when resources are instead used to make a particular product.

economic efficiency   The use of the minimum necessary resources to obtain the socially optimal amounts of goods and services; entails both *productive efficiency* and *allocative efficiency*.

economic growth   (1) An outward shift in the *production possibilities curve* that results from an increase in resource supplies or quality or an improvement in *technology*; (2) an increase of real output (*gross domestic product*) or real output per capita.

economic immigrants   International migrants who have moved to a country from another to obtain economic gains such as better employment opportunities.

economic investment   (See *investment*.)

economic law   An *economic principle* that has been tested and retested and has stood the test of time.

economic model   A simplified picture of economic reality; an abstract generalization.

economic perspective   A viewpoint that envisions individuals and institutions making rational decisions by comparing the marginal benefits and marginal costs associated with their actions.

economic policy   A course of action intended to correct or avoid a problem.

economic principle   A widely accepted generalization about the economic behavior of individuals or institutions.

economic profit   The *total revenue* of a firm less its *economic costs* (which include both *explicit costs* and *implicit costs*); also called "pure profit" and "above-normal profit."

economic regulation   (See *industrial regulation* and *social regulation*.)

economic rent   The price paid for the use of land and other natural resources, the supply of which is fixed (*perfectly inelastic*).

economic resources   The *land*, *labor*, *capital*, and *entrepreneurial ability* that are used in the production of goods and services; productive agents; factors of production.

economics   The social science concerned with how individuals, institutions, and society make optimal (best) choices under conditions of scarcity.

economic system   A particular set of institutional arrangements and a coordinating mechanism for solving the economizing problem; a method of organizing an economy, of which the *market system* and the *command system* are the two general types.

economic theory   A statement of a cause-effect relationship; when accepted by all or nearly all economists, an *economic principle*.

economies of scale   Reductions in the *average total cost* of producing a product as the firm expands the size of plant (its output) in the *long run*; the economies of mass production.

economizing problem   The choices necessitated because society's economic wants for goods and services are unlimited but the resources available to satisfy these wants are limited (scarce).

efficiency gains from migration   Additions to output from *immigration* in the destination nation that exceed the loss of output from *emigration* from the origin nation.

efficiency loss   Reductions in combined consumer and producer surplus caused by an underallocation or overallocation of resources to the production of a good or service. Also called *deadweight loss*.

efficiency loss of a tax   The loss of net benefits to society because a tax reduces the production and consumption of a taxed good below the level of *allocative efficiency*. Also called the deadweight loss of the tax.

efficiency wage   A wage that minimizes wage costs per unit of output by encouraging greater effort or reducing turnover.

efficient allocation of resources   That allocation of an economy's resources among the production of different products that leads to the maximum satisfaction of consumers' wants, thus producing the socially optimal mix of output with society's scarce resources.

elastic demand   Product or resource demand whose *price elasticity* is greater than 1. This means the resulting change in *quantity demanded* is greater than the percentage change in *price*.

elasticity coefficient   The number obtained when the percentage change in *quantity demanded* (or supplied) is divided by the percentage change in the *price* of the commodity.

elasticity formula   (See *price elasticity of demand*.)

elasticity of resource demand   A measure of the responsiveness of firms to a change in the price of a particular *resource* they employ or use; the percentage change in the quantity of the resource demanded divided by the percentage change in its price.

elastic supply   Product or resource supply whose price elasticity is greater than 1. This means the resulting change in quantity supplied is greater than the percentage change in price.

emigration   The exit (outflow) of residents from a country to reside in foreign countries.

employer mandate   The requirement under the *Patient Protection and Affordable Care Act (PPACA)* of 2010 that firms with 50 or more employees pay for insurance policies for their employees or face a fine of $2000 per employee per year. Firms with fewer than 50 employees are exempt.

employment rate   The percentage of the *labor force* employed at any time.

empty threat   In *game theory*, a statement of harmful intent that is easily dismissed by the recipient because the threat is not viewed as being believable; compare to *credible threat*.

endowment effect   The tendency people have to place higher valuations on items they own than on identical items that they do not own. Perhaps caused by people being *loss averse*.

entitlement programs   Government programs such as *social insurance*, *Medicare*, and *Medicaid* that guarantee particular levels of transfer payments or noncash benefits to all who fit the programs' criteria.

entrepreneurial ability   The human resource that combines the other resources to produce a product, makes nonroutine decisions, innovates, and bears risks.

equality-efficiency trade-off   The decrease in *economic efficiency* that may accompany a decrease in *income inequality*; the accuracy. Insurance companies are willing to sell insurance against such losses.

insurance exchanges Government-regulated markets for health insurance in which individuals seeking to purchase health insurance to comply with the *personal mandate* of the *Patient Protection and Affordable Care Act (PPACA)* of 2010 will be able to comparison shop among insurance policies approved by regulators. Each state will have its own exchange.

interest The payment made for the use of money (of borrowed funds).

interest income Payments of income to those who supply the economy with *capital*.

interest rate The annual rate at which *interest* is paid; a percentage of the borrowed amount.

interest-rate-cost-of-funds curve (Web chapter) As it relates to research and development (*R&D*), a curve showing the *interest rate* the firm must pay to obtain any particular amount of funds to finance R&D.

interindustry competition The competition for sales between the products of one industry and the products of another industry.

interlocking directorate A situation where one or more members of the board of directors of a *corporation* are also on the board of directors of a competing corporation; illegal under the *Clayton Act*.

international value of the dollar The price that must be paid in foreign currency (money) to obtain one U.S. dollar.

invention (Web chapter) The first discovery of a product or process through the use of imagination, ingenious thinking, and experimentation and the first proof that it will work.

inverse relationship The relationship between two variables that change in opposite directions, for example, product price and quantity demanded; a negative relationship.

inverted-U theory of R&D (Web chapter) The idea that, other things equal, *R&D* expenditures as a percentage of sales rise with industry concentration, reach a peak at a four-firm *concentration ratio* of about 50 percent, and then fall as the ratio further increases.

investment Spending for the production and accumulation of *capital* and additions to inventories.

investment goods Same as *capital* or capital goods.

investment in human capital (See *human capital investment*.)

"invisible hand" The tendency of firms and resource suppliers that seek to further their own self-interests in competitive markets to also promote the interests of society.

kinked-demand curve The demand curve for a noncollusive oligopolist, which is based on the assumption that rivals will match a price decrease and will ignore a price increase.

labor People's physical and mental talents and efforts that are used to help produce goods and services.

labor force Persons 16 years of age and older who are not in institutions and who are employed or are unemployed and seeking work.

labor-force participation rate The percentage of the working-age population that is actually in the *labor force*.

labor-intensive goods Products requiring relatively large amounts of labor to produce.

labor productivity Total output divided by the quantity of labor employed to produce it; the *average product* of labor or output per hour of work.

labor union A group of workers organized to advance the interests of the group (to increase wages, shorten the hours worked, improve working conditions, and so on).

laissez-faire capitalism (See *capitalism*.)

land Natural resources ("free gifts of nature") used to produce goods and services.

land-intensive goods Products requiring relatively large amounts of *land* to produce.

law of demand The principle that, other things equal, an increase in a product's price will reduce the quantity of it demanded, and conversely for a decrease in price.

law of diminishing marginal utility The principle that as a consumer increases the consumption of a good or service, the *marginal utility* obtained from each additional unit of the good or service decreases.

law of diminishing returns The principle that as successive increments of a variable resource are added to a fixed resource, the *marginal product* of the variable resource will eventually decrease.

law of increasing opportunity costs The principle that as the production of a good increases, the *opportunity cost* of producing an additional unit rises.

law of supply The principle that, other things equal, an increase in the price of a product will increase the quantity of it supplied, and conversely for a price decrease.

learning by doing Achieving greater *productivity* and lower *average total cost* through gains in knowledge and skill that accompany repetition of a task; a source of *economies of scale*.

least-cost combination of resources The quantity of each resource a firm must employ in order to produce a particular output at the lowest total cost; the combination at which the ratio of the *marginal product* of a resource to its *marginal resource cost* (to its *price* if the resource is employed in a competitive market) is the same for the last dollar spent on each of the resources employed.

legal cartel theory of regulation The hypothesis that some industries seek regulation or want to maintain regulation so that they may form or maintain a legal *cartel*.

legal immigrant A person who lawfully enters a country for the purpose of residing there.

liability A debt with a monetary value; an amount owed by a firm or an individual.

loanable funds   *Money* available for lending and borrowing.

loanable funds theory of interest   The concept that the supply of and demand for *loanable funds* determine the equilibrium rate of interest.

lockout   An action by a firm that forbids workers to return to work until a new collective bargaining contract is signed; a means of imposing costs (lost wages) on union workers in a collective bargaining dispute.

logrolling   The trading of votes by legislators to secure favorable outcomes on decisions concerning the provision of *public goods* and *quasi-public goods*.

long run   (1) In *microeconomics*, a period of time long enough to enable producers of a product to change the quantities of all the resources they employ; period in which all resources and costs are variable and no resources or costs are fixed. (2) In *macroeconomics*, a period sufficiently long for *nominal wages* and other input prices to change in response to a change in a nation's *price level*.

long-run competitive equilibrium   The price at which firms in *pure competition* neither obtain *economic profit* nor suffer economic losses in the *long run* and in which the total quantity demanded and supplied are equal; a price equal to the *marginal cost* and the minimum long-run *average total cost* of producing the product.

long-run supply   In *microeconomics*, a schedule or curve showing the prices at which a purely competitive industry will make various quantities of the product available in the *long run*.

long-run supply curve   A schedule or curve showing the prices at which a purely competitive industry will make various quantities of the product available in the *long run*.

Lorenz curve   A curve showing the distribution of income in an economy. The cumulated percentage of families (income receivers) is measured along the horizontal axis and the cumulated percentage of income is measured along the vertical axis.

loss averse   In *prospect theory*, the property of people's preferences that the pain generated by losses feels substantially more intense than the pleasure generated by gains.

macroeconomics   The part of economics concerned with the economy as a whole; with such major aggregates as the household, business, and government sectors; and with measures of the total economy.

managed floating exchange rate   An *exchange rate* that is allowed to change (float) as a result of changes in currency supply and demand but at times is altered (managed) by governments via their buying and selling of particular currencies.

managerial prerogatives   The decisions that a firm's management has the sole right to make; often enumerated in the labor contract (work agreement) between a *labor union* and a *firm*.

marginal analysis   The comparison of marginal ("extra" or "additional") benefits and marginal costs, usually for decision making.

marginal benefit   The extra (additional) benefit of consuming 1 more unit of some good or service; the change in total benefit when 1 more unit is consumed.

marginal cost (MC)   The extra (additional) cost of producing 1 more unit of output; equal to the change in *total cost* divided by the change in output (and, in the short run, to the change in total *variable cost* divided by the change in output).

marginal cost–marginal benefit rule   As it applies to *cost-benefit analysis*, the tenet that a government project or program should be expanded to the point where the *marginal cost* and *marginal benefit* of additional expenditures are equal.

marginal product (MP)   The additional output produced when 1 additional unit of a resource is employed (the quantity of all other resources employed remaining constant); equal to the change in *total product* divided by the change in the quantity of a resource employed.

marginal productivity theory of income distribution   The contention that the distribution of income is equitable when each unit of each resource receives a money payment equal to its marginal contribution to the firm's revenue (its *marginal revenue product*).

marginal rate of substitution (MRS)   The rate at which a consumer is willing to substitute one good for another (from a given combination of goods) and remain equally satisfied (have the same *total utility*); equal to the slope of a consumer's *indifference curve* at each point on the curve.

marginal resource cost (MRC)   The amount the total cost of employing a *resource* increases when a firm employs 1 additional unit of the resource (the quantity of all other resources employed remaining constant); equal to the change in the *total cost* of the resource divided by the change in the quantity of the resource employed.

marginal revenue   The change in *total revenue* that results from the sale of 1 additional unit of a firm's product; equal to the change in total revenue divided by the change in the quantity of the product sold.

marginal-revenue–marginal-cost approach   A method of determining the total output where *economic profit* is a maximum (or losses are a minimum) by comparing the *marginal revenue* and the *marginal cost* of each additional unit of output.

marginal revenue product (MRP)   The change in a firm's *total revenue* when it employs 1 additional unit of a resource (the quantity of all other resources employed remaining constant); equal to the change in total revenue divided by the change in the quantity of the resource employed.

marginal revenue productivity   (See *marginal revenue product*.)

marginal tax rate   The tax rate paid on an additional dollar of income.

marginal utility   The extra *utility* a consumer obtains from the consumption of 1 additional unit of a good or service; equal to the change in total utility divided by the change in the quantity consumed.

market   Any institution or mechanism that brings together buyers (demanders) and sellers (suppliers) of a particular good or service.

market demand   (See *total demand*.)

market economy   An economy in which the private decisions of consumers, resource suppliers, and firms determine how resources are allocated; the *market system*.

market failure   The inability of a market to bring about the allocation of resources that best satisfies the wants of society; in particular, the overallocation or underallocation of resources to the production of a particular good or service because of *externalities* or informational problems or because markets do not provide desired *public goods*.

market for externality rights   A market in which firms can buy rights to discharge pollutants. The price of such rights is determined by the demand for the right to discharge pollutants and a *perfectly inelastic supply* of such rights (the latter determined by the quantity of discharge that the environment can assimilate).

market period   A period in which producers of a product are unable to change the quantity produced in response to a change in its price and in which there is a *perfectly inelastic supply*.

market system   All the product and resource markets of a *market economy* and the relationships among them; a method that allows the prices determined in those markets to allocate the economy's scarce resources and to communicate and coordinate the decisions made by consumers, firms, and resource suppliers.

marketing loan program   A Federal farm subsidy under which certain farmers can receive a loan (on a per-unit-of-output basis) from a government lender and then, depending on the price of the crop, either pay back the loan with interest or keep the loan proceeds while forfeiting their harvested crop to the lender.

median-voter model   The theory that under majority rule the median (middle) voter will be in the dominant position to determine the outcome of an election.

Medicaid   A Federal program that helps finance the medical expenses of individuals covered by the *Supplemental Security Income (SSI)* and *Temporary Assistance for Needy Families (TANF)* programs.

Medicare   A Federal program that is financed by *payroll taxes* and provides for (1) compulsory hospital insurance for senior citizens, (2) low-cost voluntary insurance to help older Americans pay physicians' fees, and (3) subsidized insurance to buy prescription drugs.

Medicare Part D   The portion of Medicare that enables enrollees to shop among private health insurance companies to buy highly subsidized insurance to help reduce the out-of-pocket expense of prescription drugs.

medium of exchange   Any item sellers generally accept and buyers generally use to pay for a good or service; *money;* a convenient means of exchanging goods and services without engaging in *barter*.

mental accounting   The tendency people have to create separate "mental boxes" (or "accounts") in which they deal with particular financial transactions in isolation rather than dealing with them as part of their overall decision-making process that considers how to best allocate their limited budgets using the *utility-maximizing rule*.

merger   The combination of two (or more) firms into a single firm.

microeconomics   The part of economics concerned with decision making by individual units such as a *household*, a *firm*, or an *industry* and with individual markets, specific goods and services, and product and resource prices.

Microsoft case   A 2002 antitrust case in which Microsoft was found guilty of violating the *Sherman Act* by engaging in a series of unlawful activities designed to maintain its monopoly in operating systems for personal computers; as a remedy the company was prohibited from engaging in a set of specific anticompetitive business practices.

midpoint formula   A method for calculating *price elasticity of demand* or *price elasticity of supply* that averages the two prices and two quantities as the reference points for computing percentages.

minimum efficient scale (MES)   The lowest level of output at which a firm can minimize long-run *average total cost*.

minimum wage   The lowest *wage* that employers may legally pay for an hour of work.

monetary policy   A central bank's changing of the *money supply* to influence interest rates and assist the economy in achieving price stability, full employment, and economic growth.

money   Any item that is generally acceptable to sellers in exchange for goods and services.

money capital   Money available to purchase *capital;* simply *money*, as defined by economists.

money income   (See *nominal income*.)

monopolistic competition   A market structure in which many firms sell a *differentiated product*, into which entry is relatively easy, in which the firm has some control over its product price, and in which there is considerable *nonprice competition*.

monopoly   A market structure in which there is only a single seller of a good, service, or resource. In antitrust law, a dominant firm that accounts for a very high percentage of total sales within a particular market.

monopsony   A market structure in which there is only a single buyer of a good, service, or resource.

moral hazard problem   The possibility that individuals or institutions will change their behavior as the result of a contract or agreement. Example: A bank whose deposits are insured against losses may make riskier loans and investments.

MR = MC rule   The principle that a firm will maximize its profit (or minimize its losses) by producing the output at which *marginal revenue* and *marginal cost* are equal, provided product price is equal to or greater than *average variable cost*.

MRP = MRC rule   The principle that to maximize profit (or minimize losses), a firm should employ the quantity of a resource at which its *marginal revenue product* (MRP) is equal to its *marginal resource cost* (MRC), the latter being the wage rate in a purely competitive labor market.

multinational corporations Firms that own production facilities in two or more countries and produce and sell their products globally.

mutual interdependence A situation in which a change in price strategy (or in some other strategy) by one firm will affect the sales and profits of another firm (or other firms). Any firm that makes such a change can expect the other rivals to react to the change.

Nash equilibrium In *game theory*, an outcome from which neither firm wants to deviate; the outcome that once achieved is stable and therefore lasting.

national health insurance (NHI) A program in which a nation's government provides a basic package of health care to all citizens at no direct charge or at a low cost-sharing level. Financing is out of general tax revenues.

National Labor Relations Act (NLRA) Act first passed as the Wagner Act of 1935; as amended, the basic labor-relations law in the United States; defines the legal rights of unions and management and identifies unfair union and management labor practices; established the *National Labor Relations Board*.

National Labor Relations Board (NLRB) The board established by the *National Labor Relations Act* of 1935 to investigate unfair labor practices, issue *cease-and-desist orders*, and conduct elections among employees to determine if they wish to be represented by a *labor union*.

natural monopoly An industry in which *economies of scale* are so great that a single firm can produce the product at a lower average total cost than would be possible if more than one firm produced the product.

negative externality A cost imposed without compensation on third parties by the production or consumption of sellers or buyers. Example: A manufacturer dumps toxic chemicals into a river, killing fish prized by sports fishers; an external cost or a spillover cost.

negative relationship (See *inverse relationship*.)

negative self-selection As it relates to international *migration*, the idea that those who choose to move to another country have poorer wage opportunities in the origin country than those with similar skills who choose not to *emigrate*.

negative-sum game In *game theory*, a game in which the gains (+) and losses (−) add up to some amount less than zero; one party's losses exceed the other party's gains.

net benefits The total benefits of some activity or policy less the total costs of that activity or policy.

net taxes The taxes collected by government less *government transfer payments*.

network effects Increases in the value of a product to each user, including existing users, as the total number of users rises.

net worth The total *assets* less the total *liabilities* of a firm or an individual; for a firm, the claims of the owners against the firm's total assets; for an individual, his or her wealth.

NLRB (See *National Labor Relations Board*.)

nominal interest rate The interest rate expressed in terms of annual amounts currently charged for interest and not adjusted for inflation.

nominal wage The amount of money received by a worker per unit of time (hour, day, etc.); money wage.

noncash transfer A *government transfer payment* in the form of goods and services rather than money, for example, food stamps, housing assistance, and job training; also called in-kind transfers.

noncollusive oligopoly An *oligopoly* in which the firms do not act together and in agreement to determine the price of the product and the output that each firm will produce.

noncompeting groups Collections of workers who do not compete with each other for employment because the skill and training of the workers in one group are substantially different from those of the workers in other groups.

nonexcludability The inability to keep nonpayers (free riders) from obtaining benefits from a certain good; a characteristic of a *public good*.

nonexhaustive expenditure An expenditure by government that does not result directly in the use of economic resources or the production of goods and services; see *government transfer payment*.

nonprice competition Competition based on distinguishing one's product by means of *product differentiation* and then *advertising* the distinguished product to consumers.

nonrenewable natural resource Things such as oil, natural gas, and metals, which are either in actual fixed supply or which renew so slowly as to be in virtual fixed supply when viewed from a human time perspective.

nonrivalry The idea that one person's benefit from a certain good does not reduce the benefit available to others; a characteristic of a *public good*.

nontariff barriers (NTBs) All barriers other than *protective tariffs* that nations erect to impede international trade, including *import quotas*, licensing requirements, unreasonable product-quality standards, unnecessary bureaucratic detail in customs procedures, and so on.

normal good A good or service whose consumption increases when income increases and falls when income decreases, price remaining constant.

normal profit The payment made by a firm to obtain and retain *entrepreneurial ability*; the minimum income entrepreneurial ability must receive to induce it to perform entrepreneurial functions for a firm.

normative economics The part of economics involving value judgments about what the economy should be like; focused on which economic goals and policies should be implemented; policy economics.

North American Free Trade Agreement (NAFTA) A 1993 agreement establishing, over a 15-year period, a free-trade zone composed of Canada, Mexico, and the United States.

occupation   A category of activities or tasks performed by a set of workers for pay, independent of employer or industry. Examples are managers, nurses, farmers, and cooks.

occupational licensing   The laws of state or local governments that require that a worker satisfy certain specified requirements and obtain a license from a licensing board before engaging in a particular occupation.

occupational segregation   The crowding of women or minorities into less desirable, lower-paying occupations.

official reserves   Foreign currencies owned by the central bank of a nation.

offshoring   The practice of shifting work previously done by American workers to workers located abroad.

oligopoly   A market structure in which a few firms sell either a *standardized* or *differentiated product*, into which entry is difficult, in which the firm has limited control over product price because of *mutual interdependence* (except when there is collusion among firms), and in which there is typically *nonprice competition*.

one-time game   In *game theory*, a game in which the parties select their optimal strategies in a single time period without regard to possible interaction in subsequent time periods.

OPEC   (See *Organization of Petroleum Exporting Countries*.)

open shop   A place of employment in which the employer may hire nonunion workers and the workers need not become members of a *labor union*.

opportunity cost   The amount of other products that must be forgone or sacrificed to produce a unit of a product.

opportunity-cost ratio   An equivalency showing the number of units of two products that can be produced with the same resources; the cost 1 corn $\equiv$ 3 olives shows that the resources required to produce 3 units of olives must be shifted to corn production to produce 1 unit of corn.

optimal amount of R&D   (Web chapter) The level of *R&D* at which the *marginal benefit* and *marginal cost* of R&D expenditures are equal.

optimal reduction of an externality   The reduction of a *negative externality* such as pollution to the level at which the *marginal benefit* and *marginal cost* of reduction are equal.

ordinal utility   Satisfaction that is measured by having consumers compare and rank products (or combinations of products) as to preference, without asking them to specify the absolute amounts of satisfaction provided by the products.

Organization of Petroleum Exporting Countries (OPEC)   A cartel of 12 oil-producing countries (Algeria, Angola, Ecuador, Iran, Iraq, Kuwait, Libya, Nigeria, Qatar, Saudi Arabia, Venezuela, and the United Arab Emirates) that attempts to control the quantity and price of crude oil exported by its members and that accounts for a large percentage of the world's export of oil.

other-things-equal assumption   The assumption that factors other than those being considered are held constant; *ceteris paribus* assumption.

output effect   The situation in which an increase in the price of one input will increase a firm's production costs and reduce its level of output, thus reducing the demand for other inputs; conversely for a decrease in the price of the input.

paradox of voting   A situation where paired-choice voting by majority rule fails to provide a consistent ranking of society's preferences for *public goods* or services.

parity concept   The idea that year after year the sale of a specific output of a farm product should enable a farmer to purchase a constant amount of nonagricultural goods and services.

parity ratio   The ratio of the price received by farmers from the sale of an agricultural commodity to the prices of other goods paid by them; usually expressed as a percentage; used as a rationale for *price supports*.

partnership   An unincorporated firm owned and operated by two or more persons.

patent   An exclusive right given to inventors to produce and sell a new product or machine for 20 years from the time of patent application.

Patient Protection and Affordable Care Act (PPACA)   A major health care law passed by the Federal government in 2010. Major provisions include an individual health insurance mandate, a ban on insurers refusing to accept patients with preexisting conditions, and Federal (rather than state) regulation of health insurance policies.

payroll tax   A tax levied on employers of labor equal to a percentage of all or part of the wages and salaries paid by them and on employees equal to a percentage of all or part of the wages and salaries received by them.

***P* = MC rule**   The principle that a purely competitive firm will maximize its profit or minimize its loss by producing that output at which the *price* of the product is equal to *marginal cost*, provided that price is equal to or greater than *average variable cost* in the short run and equal to or greater than *average total cost* in the long run.

per capita GDP   *Gross domestic product* (GDP) per person; the average GDP of a population.

per capita income   A nation's total income per person; the average income of a population.

perfectly elastic demand   Product or resource demand in which *quantity demanded* can be of any amount at a particular product *price*; graphs as a horizontal *demand curve*.

perfectly elastic supply   Product or resource supply in which *quantity supplied* can be of any amount at a particular product or resource *price*; graphs as a horizontal *supply curve*.

perfectly inelastic demand   Product or resource demand in which *price* can be of any amount at a particular quantity of the product or resource demanded; *quantity demanded* does not respond to a change in price; graphs as a vertical *demand curve*.

perfectly inelastic supply   Product or resource supply in which *price* can be of any amount at a particular quantity of the product or resource demanded; *quantity supplied* does not respond to a change in price; graphs as a vertical *supply curve*.

per se violations Collusive actions, such as attempts by firms to fix prices or divide a market, that are violations of the *antitrust laws,* even if the actions themselves are unsuccessful.

personal distribution of income The manner in which the economy's *personal* or *disposable income* is divided among different income classes or different households or families.

personal income tax A tax levied on the taxable income of individuals, households, and unincorporated firms.

personal mandate The requirement under the *Patient Protection and Affordable Care Act (PPACA)* of 2010 that all U.S. citizens and legal residents purchase health insurance unless they are already covered by employer-sponsored health insurance or government-sponsored health insurance (*Medicaid* or *Medicare*).

per-unit production cost The average production cost of a particular level of output; total input cost divided by units of output.

plant A physical establishment that performs one or more functions in the production, fabrication, and distribution of goods and services.

policy economics The formulation of courses of action to bring about desired economic outcomes or to prevent undesired occurrences.

political corruption The unlawful misdirection of governmental resources or actions that occurs when government officials abuse their entrusted powers for personal gain.

positive economics The analysis of facts or data to establish scientific generalizations about economic behavior.

positive externality A benefit obtained without compensation by third parties from the production or consumption of sellers or buyers. Example: A beekeeper benefits when a neighboring farmer plants clover. An *external benefit* or a spillover benefit.

positive sum game In *game theory,* a game in which the gains (+) and losses (−) add up to more than zero; one party's gains exceeds the other party's losses.

***post hoc, ergo propter hoc* fallacy** The false belief that when one event precedes another, the first event must have caused the second event.

potential competition The new competitors that may be induced to enter an industry if firms now in that industry are receiving large *economic profits.*

poverty A situation in which the basic needs of an individual or family exceed the means to satisfy them.

poverty rate The percentage of the population with incomes below the official poverty income levels that are established by the Federal government.

preferred provider organization (PPO) An arrangement in which doctors and hospitals agree to provide health care to insured individuals at rates negotiated with an insurer.

present value Today's value of some amount of money that is to be received sometime in the future.

price The amount of money needed to buy a particular good, service, or resource.

price ceiling A legally established maximum price for a good or service.

price discrimination The selling of a product to different buyers at different prices when the price differences are not justified by differences in cost.

price elasticity of demand The ratio of the percentage change in *quantity demanded* of a product or resource to the percentage change in its *price;* a measure of the responsiveness of buyers to a change in the price of a product or resource.

price elasticity of supply The ratio of the percentage change in *quantity supplied* of a product or resource to the percentage change in its *price;* a measure of the responsiveness of producers to a change in the price of a product or resource.

price fixing The conspiring by two or more firms to set the price of their products; an illegal practice under the *Sherman Act.*

price floor A legally determined minimum price above the *equilibrium price.*

price leadership An informal method that firms in an *oligopoly* may employ to set the price of their product: One firm (the leader) is the first to announce a change in price, and the other firms (the followers) soon announce identical or similar changes.

price-level stability A steadiness of the price level from one period to the next; zero or low annual inflation; also called "price stability."

price maker A seller (or buyer) of a product or resource that is able to affect the product or resource price by changing the amount it sells (or buys).

price support A minimum price that government allows sellers to receive for a good or service; a legally established or maintained minimum price.

price taker A seller (or buyer) that is unable to affect the price at which a product or resource sells by changing the amount it sells (or buys).

price war Successive and continued decreases in the prices charged by firms in an oligopolistic industry. Each firm lowers its price below rivals' prices, hoping to increase its sales and revenues at its rivals' expense.

principal-agent problem A conflict of interest that occurs when agents (workers or managers) pursue their own objectives to the detriment of the principals' (stockholders') goals.

principle of comparative advantage The proposition that an individual, region, or nation will benefit if it specializes in producing goods for which its own *opportunity costs* are lower than the opportunity costs of a trading partner, and then exchanging some of the products in which it specializes for other desired products produced by others.

private good A good or service that is individually consumed and that can be profitably provided by privately owned firms because they can exclude nonpayers from receiving the benefits.

private property The right of private persons and firms to obtain, own, control, employ, dispose of, and bequeath *land, capital,* and other property.

private sector   The *households* and business *firms* of the economy.

process innovation   (Web chapter) The development and use of new or improved production or distribution methods.

producer surplus   The difference between the actual price a producer receives (or producers receive) and the minimum acceptable price; the triangular area above the supply curve and below the market price.

product differentiation   A strategy in which one firm's product is distinguished from competing products by means of its design, related services, quality, location, or other attributes (except price).

product innovation   (Web chapter) The development and sale of a new or improved product (or service).

production possibilities curve   A curve showing the different combinations of two goods or services that can be produced in a *full-employment, full-production* economy where the available supplies of resources and technology are fixed.

productive efficiency   The production of a good in the least costly way; occurs when production takes place at the output at which *average total cost* is a minimum and *marginal product* per dollar's worth of input is the same for all inputs.

productivity   A measure of average output or real output per unit of input. For example, the productivity of labor is determined by dividing real output by hours of work.

productivity growth   The increase in *productivity* from one period to another.

product market   A market in which products are sold by *firms* and bought by *households*.

profit   The return to the resource *entrepreneurial ability* (see *normal profit*); *total revenue* minus *total cost* (see *economic profit*).

profit-maximizing combination of resources   The quantity of each resource a firm must employ to maximize its profit or minimize its loss; the combination in which the *marginal revenue product* of each resource is equal to its *marginal resource cost* (to its *price* if the resource is employed in a competitive market).

profit-sharing plan   A compensation device through which workers receive part of their pay in the form of a share of their employer's profit (if any).

progressive tax   A tax whose *average tax rate* increases as the taxpayer's income increases and decreases as the taxpayer's income decreases.

property tax   A tax on the value of property (*capital, land, stocks* and *bonds*, and other *assets*) owned by *firms* and *households*.

proportional tax   A tax whose *average tax rate* remains constant as the taxpayer's income increases or decreases.

proprietor's income   The net income of the owners of unincorporated firms (proprietorships and partnerships).

prospect theory   A *behavioral economics* theory of preferences having three main features: (1) people evaluate options on the basis of whether they generate gains or losses relative to the *status quo;* (2) gains are subject to diminishing marginal utility while losses are subject to diminishing marginal disutility; (3) people are *loss averse*.

protective tariff   A *tariff* designed to shield domestic producers of a good or service from the competition of foreign producers.

public assistance programs   Government programs that pay benefits to those who are unable to earn income (because of permanent disabilities or because they have very low income and dependent children); financed by general tax revenues and viewed as public charity (rather than earned rights).

public choice theory   The economic analysis of government decision making, politics, and elections.

public good   A good or service that is characterized by *nonrivalry* and *nonexcludability;* a good or service with these characteristics provided by government.

public interest theory of regulation   The presumption that the purpose of the regulation of an *industry* is to protect the public (consumers) from abuse of the power possessed by *natural monopolies*.

public sector   The part of the economy that contains all government entities; government.

public utility   A firm that produces an essential good or service, has obtained from a government the right to be the sole supplier of the good or service in the area, and is regulated by that government to prevent the abuse of its monopoly power.

purchasing power   The amount of goods and services that a monetary unit of income can buy.

purchasing power parity   The idea that exchange rates between nations equate the purchasing power of various currencies. Exchange rates between any two nations adjust to reflect the price level differences between the countries.

pure competition   A market structure in which a very large number of firms sells a *standardized product*, into which entry is very easy, in which the individual seller has no control over the product price, and in which there is no nonprice competition; a market characterized by a very large number of buyers and sellers.

purely competitive labor market   A *resource market* in which many firms compete with one another in hiring a specific kind of labor, numerous equally qualified workers supply that labor, and no one controls the market wage rate.

pure monopoly   A market structure in which one firm sells a unique product, into which entry is blocked, in which the single firm has considerable control over product price, and in which *nonprice competition* may or may not be found.

pure profit   (See *economic profit*.)

pure rate of interest   An essentially risk-free, long-term interest rate that is free of the influence of market imperfections.

quantity demanded   The amount of a good or service that buyers (or a buyer) are willing and able to purchase at a specific price during a specified period of time.

quantity supplied   The amount of a good or service that producers (or a producer) are willing and able to make available for sale at a specific price during a specified period of time.

quasi-public good A good or service to which excludability could apply but that has such a large *positive externality* that government sponsors its production to prevent an underallocation of resources.

R&D Research and development activities undertaken to bring about *technological advance*.

rate of exchange The price paid in one's own money to acquire 1 unit of a foreign currency; the rate at which the money of one nation is exchanged for the money of another nation.

rate of return (Web chapter) The gain in net revenue divided by the cost of an investment or an *R&D* expenditure; expressed as a percentage.

rational behavior Human behavior based on comparison of marginal costs and marginal benefits; behavior designed to maximize total utility.

real capital (See *capital*.)

real gross domestic product (GDP) *Gross domestic product* adjusted for inflation; gross domestic product in a year divided by the GDP *price index* for that year, the index expressed as a decimal.

real income The amount of goods and services that can be purchased with *nominal income* during some period of time; nominal income adjusted for inflation.

real interest rate The interest rate expressed in dollars of constant value (adjusted for *inflation*) and equal to the *nominal interest rate* less the expected rate of inflation.

real wage The amount of goods and services a worker can purchase with his or her *nominal wage*; the purchasing power of the nominal wage.

recession A period of declining real GDP, accompanied by lower real income and higher unemployment.

regressive tax A tax whose *average tax rate* decreases as the taxpayer's income increases and increases as the taxpayer's income decreases.

regulatory agency An agency, commission, or board established by the Federal government or a state government to control the prices charged and the services offered by a *natural monopoly*.

remittances Payments by *immigrants* to family members and others located in the origin countries of the immigrants.

rental income The payments (income) received by those who supply *land* to the economy.

renewable natural resources Things such as forests, water in reservoirs, and wildlife that are capable of growing back or building back up (renewing themselves) if they are harvested at moderate rates.

rent-seeking behavior The actions by persons, firms, or unions to gain special benefits from government at the taxpayers' or someone else's expense.

repeated game In *game theory*, a game which is played again sometime after the previous game ends.

replacement rate The birthrate necessary to offset deaths in a country and therefore to keep the size of its population constant (without relying on immigration). For most countries, the replacement rate is about 2.1 births per woman per lifetime.

resource A natural, human, or manufactured item that helps produce goods and services; a productive agent or factor of production.

resource market A market in which *households* sell and *firms* buy resources or the services of resources.

revenue tariff A *tariff* designed to produce income for the Federal government.

right-to-work law A state law (in 22 states) that makes it illegal to require that a worker join a *labor union* in order to retain his or her job; laws that make *union shops* and *agency shops* illegal.

risk The uncertainty as to the actual future returns of a particular *financial investment* or *economic investment*.

rivalry (1) The characteristic of a *private good*, the consumption of which by one party excludes other parties from obtaining the benefit; (2) the attempt by one firm to gain strategic advantage over another firm to enhance market share or profit.

rule of reason The rule stated and applied in the *U.S. Steel case* that only combinations and contracts unreasonably restraining trade are subject to actions under the antitrust laws and that size and possession of monopoly power are not illegal.

sales and excise taxes (See *sales tax; see excise tax*.)

sales tax A tax levied on the cost (at retail) of a broad group of products.

saving After-tax income not spent for consumer goods.

scarce resources The limited quantities of *land, capital, labor,* and *entrepreneurial ability* that are never sufficient to satisfy people's virtually unlimited economic wants.

scientific method The procedure for the systematic pursuit of knowledge involving the observation of facts and the formulation and testing of hypotheses to obtain theories, principles, and laws.

self-interest That which each firm, property owner, worker, and consumer believes is best for itself and seeks to obtain.

self-selection As it relates to international migration, the idea that those who choose to move tend to have greater motivation for economic gain or greater willingness to sacrifice current consumption for future consumption than those with similar skills who choose to remain at home.

seniority The length of time a worker has been employed absolutely or relative to other workers; may be used to determine which workers will be laid off when there is insufficient work for them all and who will be rehired when more work becomes available.

separation of ownership and control The fact that different groups of people own a *corporation* (the stockholders) and manage it (the directors and officers).

sequential game In *game theory*, a game in which the parties make their moves in turn, with one party making the first move, followed by the other party making the next move, and so on.

service An (intangible) act or use for which a consumer, firm, or government is willing to pay.

Credits

Note: Page numbers followed by n indicate notes.

Ability
  entrepreneurial, 10–11
  income inequality and, 414
  specialization and, 33
  wage differentials and, 279
Ability-to-pay principle, 344–345
Absolute advantage
  comparative advantage versus, 475
  defined, 475
Access to health care
  nature of problem, 434
  rising costs and, 434–435, 437
  spending and, 438
Acreage allotments, 401
Active antitrust perspective, 378
Adidas, 242
Adverse selection problem, 359–360
Advertising
  framing effects of, 127
  in monopolistic competition, 218
  in oligopoly, 234
  positive effects of, 234
  potential negative effects of, 234–235
Africa
  conflict diamonds and, 325
  elephant preservation, 325–326
African Americans
  African-American-White wage ratio, 425–426
  discrimination against, 424–426
  poverty among, 420
  unionization rate among, 287
Age
  in decision to migrate, 458
  immigration and, 458
Agency shop, 288
Aggregate, 6–7
Aggregate expenditures (AE) model,
  international trade and, 483–485
Aging population. *See also* Medicare; Social
    Security program
  health care costs and, 440
Agribusinesses, 397, 403
Agricultural Adjustment Act of 1933, 399
Agriculture, 391–407. *See also* Farm
    commodities
  criticisms of parity concept, 402
  criticisms of price-support system, 402–403
  economics of farm policy, 398–401
  ethanol market, 320, 401
  farm-household income, 397–398
  international trade and, 394, 397, 398, 400,
    403–405

  long run decline of industry, 395–397
  politics of farm policy, 403–405
  prices in, 381, 406
  recent farm policies, 405–406
  short run price and income instability,
    392–394
  subsidies for, 398–400, 401
  Sugar Program, 404–405
  in the U.S., 392, 395–406
Aid for Families with Dependent Children
    (AFDC), 423
AIDS epidemic, 437, 440
Airbus Industries, 242, 486
Aircraft, 158–159
Air pollution, 106, 110–111
  carbon dioxide emissions, 110–111, 320
  market for externality rights, 110–111
Akerlof, George, 360n
Alcoa case, 377
Allen, Paul, 307
Allocative efficiency, 58–59, 204, 442
  defined, 97, 188
  in monopolistic competition, 221–222
  in oligopoly, 235
Amazon.com, 190, 192, 233, 380
AMD, 378
American Airlines, 41
American Bar Association (ABA), 274
American Broadcasting Company, 379
American Federation of Labor and the
    Congress of Industrial Organizations
    (AFL-CIO), 287
American Medical Association (AMA), 274, 444
Americans with Disabilities Act of 1990, 384
Amtrak, 382
Anchoring
  credit card bills and, 127
  defined, 127
Anheuser-Busch InBev (A-B), 236–237
Annual percentage rate (APR), 307
Antidumping policy, 488–489
Antiques, price elasticity of supply and, 85–86
Antitrust policy, 88, 233, 374–388
  antitrust laws, 375–376, 378–381
  defined, 374
  enforcement issues, 378
  historical background of, 375
  interpretation issues, 376–378
AOL Time Warner, 387
Apple Computer, 123–124, 305
Appreciation
  defined, 504
  in exchange rates, 504
Archer Daniels Midland (ADM), 232, 381
Argyle, 212

Art
  price elasticity of supply and, 85–86
  price-fixing of, 381
  as public versus private good, 101
Asiana Airlines, 381
Asians
  immigration by, 458
  poverty among, 420
  unionization rate, 287
Asymmetric information, 357–371
  health care costs and, 439
  inadequate buyer information about sellers,
    358–359
  inadequate seller information about buyers,
    359–361
AT&T, 234, 378, 383, 386
Attainable combinations, 9
Australia
  land-intensive goods, 474
  as magnet country for immigration, 457
  population decline in, 314
Automated teller machines (ATMs), 261
Automobiles, lemon laws, 360
Average(s), in price elasticity of demand, 76
Average Crop Revenue Election (ACRE), 406
Average family wealth, 428
Average fixed cost (AFC)
  defined, 148–149
  shifts of cost curves, 151–152
Average product (AP)
  defined, 144
  law of diminishing returns and, 144, 147
Average revenue (AR), 165
Average tax rate, 340–341
Average total cost (ATC)
  defined, 149
  in long run, 153
  marginal cost and, 150–151
  in pure monopoly, 205, 209
  shifts of cost curves, 151–152
  size of firm and, 152
Average variable cost (AVC)
  defined, 149
  marginal cost and, 150–151
  shifts of cost curves, 151–152

Baby boomers, demographic changes and
    income inequality, 416
Backflows, 459, 461–462
Balance of payments (BOP)
  current account, 500–501
  deficits and surpluses, 502–503
  defined, 498
  flexible exchange rates and, 506–507
  U.S., 499–503

Balance-of-payments deficits, 502
Balance-of-payments surpluses, 503
Balance of trade, 500–501
Balance on current account, 501
Balance on goods and services, 500–501
Balance on the capital and financial account, 501–502
Bank(s), automated teller machines (ATMs) and, 261
Bankruptcy, personal, health care costs and, 437
Barnes & Noble, 380
Barriers to entry
    defined, 195
    economies of scale, 196, 205, 224
    licenses, 197
    in monopolistic competition, 218
    in oligopoly, 224
    ownership or control of essential resources, 197
    patents, 196–197, 206
    pricing, 195, 197
    in pure monopoly, 195–197
Barter, 33
Bastiat, Frédéric, 493, 493n
Bayer, 207
Beaten paths, 458
Beatles, 344
Beautiful Mind, A (film), 241n
Beer industry, oligopoly in, 236–237
Behavioral economics, 125–129
    anchoring and credit card bills, 127
    better consumer decisions and, 128–129
    framing effects and advertising, 127
    losses and shrinking packages, 126–127
    mental accounting and overpriced warranties, 128
Behavioralists, 377
Benefits-received principle, 344
Biases, in economic reasoning, 16
Bid rigging, 232
Bilateral monopoly, 275–276
    desirability of, 276
    indeterminate outcome of, 275–276
Birthrates, 313–314
Black markets
    exchange controls and, 510
    in human organs, 62–63
    price ceilings and, 62
Blacks. See African Americans
Blocked entry, in pure monopoly, 195
Blue Cross Blue Shield of Michigan, 380
Blue Moon, 237
Boeing, 158, 242, 379, 380, 486
Bonuses, 282
Borden, 232
Borders, 380
Borjas, George, 463n
Borrowing. See Credit; Loan(s)
Boudreaux, Donald, 42, 42n
BP, 207

Bradford, Scott C., 481n
Brain drain, 460–461
Brand names
    brand-name loyalty in oligopoly, 234–235
    product differentiation through, 217–218
    top global, 235
Brannock Device Company, 195
Break-even point, 167
Bretton Woods system, 510–511
Bribery, 368–369
British Airlines, 381
British thermal unit (BTU), 315–318
Brue, Stanley L., 454n
Bucks, Brian K., 428n
Budget constraint, consumer, 119–120, 133–134
Budget deficits, deficit spending, 339
Budget line
    characteristics of, 133–134
    consumer, 8–10, 134
    defined, 8, 133
Bureaucracy, inefficiency of, 368
Bureau of Economic Analysis (BEA), 501n
Burger King, 224
Burst.com, 387
Bush, George W., 387, 466
Business(es)
    in circular flow model, 41
    decisions of, 32
    defined, 41
    entrepreneurial ability and, 10–11
    legal forms of business. See Corporations; Partnerships; Sole proprietorships
    start-up. See Start-up firms
    types of, 41

Canada
    immigration from, 466
    North American Free Trade Agreement (NAFTA), 492
    supply and demand analysis for international trade, 483–485
    U.S. trade with, 473
Cancer, 445
Candlemakers, protectionism and, 493
Cap-and-trade program, 110–111
Capital. See also Capital goods; Investment
    defined, 10
    efficient, 155–156
    expansion due to immigration, 462
    interest and allocation of, 302
    as resource, 10
    role in wage determination, 267–268
Capital accumulation, in market systems, 37–38
Capital and financial account
    capital account, 501
    defined, 501
    financial account, 501–502

Capital goods. See also Capital
    defined, 11
    in market systems, 33
    in production possibilities model, 11
Capital-intensive goods, 474
Capitalism
    types of, 30
    in the United States, 30
Caps, health insurance, 447
Carbon dioxide emissions, 110–111, 320
Card, David, 463n
Cargill, 381, 392
Cargolux, 381
Cartels, 230–233
    legal cartel theory of regulation, 383
    oil industry, 231–232, 473, 513
    output in, 230–231
Cash, marginal utility and, 125
Causation, correlation versus, 17
Cease-and-desist orders, 376
Celler-Kefauver Act of 1950, 376, 381
Central banks. See Federal Reserve System
Ceteris paribus. See Other-things-equal assumption (ceteris paribus)
Chaloupka, Frank, 83n
Chamberlain, Andrew, 352, 352n
Change to Win, 287
Changing World Technologies, 320
Chase Manhattan, 379
Cheap foreign labor argument for trade protection, 489–490
Cheating
    incentives for, 227
    as obstacle to collusion, 232
Chemical Bank, 379
Chicago Board of Trade, as market, 48
Chief executive officers (CEOs), executive pay and, 283, 416
Children, poverty among, 420
Chi Mei Optoelectronics, 381
China
    cheap foreign labor argument for trade protection, 489–490
    command system in, 30, 39–40
    exports of, 512–513
    immigration from, 456
    international trade and, 473
    labor-intensive goods, 474
    U.S. trade with, 394
Choice. See also Decision-making process; Opportunity cost(s)
    consumer budget line and, 8–9, 10
    consumer choice, 119–120
    economic perspective and, 4
    exchange controls and, 510
    freedom of, in market systems, 31
    in market systems, 35–38
    opportunity costs and, 10
    present versus future, 16–18
Christie's, 381
Chunghwa Picture Tubes, 381

Circular flow diagram, 40–41
Circular flow model, 40–41
 government in, 337–338
 product market in, 41
 resource market in, 41
Cisco Systems, 157
Citizens Against Government Waste, 370
Civil Aeronautics Board (CAB), 383
Clayton Act of 1914, 376, 380
Clean Air Act of 1990, 106
Clinique, 224
Clinton, Bill, 386
Closed shop, 288
Coase, Ronald, 106
Coase theorem, 106
Coca-Cola, 88, 235, 242
Collective action problem, 366
Collective bargaining, 288–289
Collusion
 cartels and, 230–233
 covert forms of, 232
 defined, 227
 in game theory, 227
 monopolistic competition and, 217
 obstacles to, 232–233
 overt, 231–232
Command systems
 defined, 30
 demise of, 38–40
Commissions, 281–282, 282
Common Market. *See* European Union (EU)
Communications, in oligopoly, 233
Communications Workers, 287
Communism. *See* Command systems
Comparative advantage, 474–481
 absolute advantage versus, 475
 case for free trade, 481
 defined, 477
 gains from trade and, 478–480
 offshoring and, 437
 principle of comparative advantage,
  477–478
 specialization based on, 477–478
 terms of trade and, 478
 trade with increasing costs and, 481
 two isolated nations and, 475–477
Compensating differences
 defined, 279–280
 wage differentials and, 279–280, 464
Compensating wage differential, 279–280, 464
Competition
 discrimination and, 426
 health care prices and, 444
 imperfect, 164, 251–252
 import, 225–226
 market demand and, 50
 market failure in competitive markets, 93–99
 market models and, 164
 in market systems, 31–32, 36, 58–59
 monopolistic. *See* Monopolistic competition
 noncompeting groups, 279

 in oligopoly, 235
 pure. *See* Pure competition
Competitive bidding, 295
Complementary goods/resources, 462
 change in demand and, 52
 changes in prices of other resources,
  254–255
 cross elasticity of demand and, 88
 defined, 52
Compound interest, 300–301
ConAgra, 381
Concrete plants, 158
Conflict diamonds, 325
Conflict of interest, in principal-agent
  problem, 281–282
Conglomerate mergers, 379, 380
Connections, income inequality and, 415
Constant-cost industry
 defined, 182, 184
 long-run supply curve for, 184–185
Constant costs
 comparative advantage and, 476
 defined, 476
Constant returns to scale, 156
Consumer behavior, 116–130
 algebraic generalization, 121–122
 applications and extensions of, 123–125
 budget constraint, 119–120, 133–134
 consumer choice, 119–120
 demand curve, 119, 122–123, 137–138
 indifference curve analysis, 133–138
 law of diminishing marginal utility, 117–119
 numerical example, 120–121
 theory of, 119–122
 utility-maximizing rule, 120, 122–123
Consumer budget line, 8–10
 attainable/unattainable combinations, 9
 choice and, 8–9, 10
 income changes and, 10, 134
 indifference curve analysis, 133–134
 opportunity costs, 9–10
 sample, 8–9
 trade-offs, 9–10
Consumer choice, budget constraint and,
  119–120
Consumer demand, 50
Consumer equilibrium, 120
Consumer expectations, change in demand
  and, 52
Consumer goods
 defined, 11
 in production possibilities model, 11
Consumer Product Safety Commission
  (CPSC), 384, 385–386
Consumer Reports, 234, 361
Consumer sovereignty, 35
Consumer surplus, 188–189
 defined, 93
 in efficiently functioning markets, 93–95
Consumer tastes, in market systems.
  See Tastes

Consumption
 of health care services, 441, 443
 income distribution versus, 417
 nonrivalrous, 205
 personal consumption expenditures (C),
  314–317
 simultaneous, 205
Control of resources, as barrier to entry, 197
Coordination failures, in command systems,
  38–39
Copayments, 435, 446
Copyrights, 31
Corn, market for, 320, 401
Corn Belt, 401
Corn Products, 381
Corona, 237
Corporations
 in business population, 41
 defined, 41
 executive pay and, 283, 416
 income tax on, 86, 341, 345–346,
  350–351, 352
 multinational, 207
 principal-agent problem and, 281–282
 stockholders, 307–308
 taxation of, 341, 350–351, 352
Correlation, causation versus, 17
Corruption, 368–369
Cost, in pure monopoly, 204–206
Cost-benefit analysis. *See also* Marginal
  analysis; MB = MC rule; MR = MC rule
 concept of, 102–103
 decision to migrate, 457–458
 defined, 102
 for fast food, 5
 illustration, 103–104
 for immigration, 457–458, 467
 for public goods, 102–104
 of rent seeking, 367
Cost differences, as obstacle to collusion, 232
Cost minimization, resource pricing and, 249
Cost of health care, 434–447
 cause of rapid rise in, 439–445
 cost containment and, 445–447
 economic implications of rising costs, 437
 health care spending and, 435–436, 438
 increasing demand in, 439–441
 nature of problem, 434–435
 quality of care, 436–437
Council of Economic Advisers (CEA), 459
Countercyclical payments (CCPs), 406
Covert collusion, 232
Cox, W. Michael, 485
Craft unions, 274
Craig, Ben, 261n
Creative destruction, 37, 190–192, 378
Credible threats, 241–242
Credit. *See also* Loan(s)
 determining price of, 306–307
 interest rates and price of, 306–307
 usury laws and, 303

Credit cards, anchoring and credit card bills, 127
Crime, immigration and, 465
Crop revenue insurance, 396
Cross elasticity of demand, 87–88
  applications of, 88
  defined, 87
  income elasticity of demand compared with, 88
Crowding model, 426–429
  described, 426–427
  effects of crowding, 427
Crowe, Russell, 241n
Cuba, command system in, 30
Currency. *See also* Exchange rate(s); Money
  speculation in currency markets, 514–515
Currency interventions, 509
Current account, 500–501
  balance of trade on goods and services, 500–501
  balance on current account, 501
  defined, 500

Daily newspaper, 158
Deadweight losses, 98–99
Dean, 232
De Beers, 195, 212
Debt. *See* Credit; Loan(s); Public debt
Decision-making process. *See also* Choice
  behavioral economics and, 125–129
  marginal analysis in. *See* Marginal analysis
  sunk costs in, 158–159
  utility-maximizing rule, 120–121
Decreasing-cost industry
  defined, 185
  long-run supply curve for, 185–186
Deductibles, 435, 446
Defense Appropriation Act of 2008, 370
Defensive medicine, 440
Deferred compensation, stock options, 282, 283
Deficits, balance of payments, 502
Deficit spending, 339
Dell Computers, 157, 205, 305, 346
Dell Inc., 381
Del-Monte, 392
Demand, 48–53. *See also* Demand curve; Market demand
  bolstering agricultural, 401
  change in demand, 50–52, 52, 53, 59–60, 69–72, 294–295, 300
  change in quantity demanded, 53, 59–60
  change in supply and, 69–72
  cross elasticity of, 87–88
  defined, 48
  determinants of, 50
  for health care, 439–441
  income elasticity of, 88–89
  inelastic, 77–79, 392, 396–397
  lagging agricultural, 396
  law of demand, 49

for loanable funds, 298–299
marginal utility and, 119, 122–123
market demand, 50, 101, 252, 269
monopoly, 195, 197–200
as obstacle to collusion, 232
perfectly elastic, 77, 165
perfectly inelastic, 77
price elasticity of, 76–84, 200
for public goods and services, 101–102
in pure competition, 165–166
resource. *See* Demand for resources
short-run fluctuations in agricultural, 393–394
Demand curve
  consumer, 119, 122–123, 137–138
  defined, 49
  deriving, 122, 137–138
  kinked, 228–230
  labor, 278
  in monopolistic competition, 219
  price elasticity of demand along linear, 80–81
  in pure competition, 165–166
  in pure monopoly, 197–200
  utility maximization and, 122–123
Demand-enhancement model for unions, 273–274
Demand-for-pounds curve, 503
Demand for resources, 248–262
  determinants of, 253–256
  elasticity of, 256–257
  marginal productivity theory of income distribution, 260–262
  marginal productivity theory of resource demand, 249–253
  optimal combination of resources, 258–260
  resource pricing in, 249
Demand schedule, 48–49
  deriving, 122
Demand-side market failures, 93
Demographers, 313–314
Demographics
  fastest-growing occupations, 255–256
  health care costs and, 440
  income inequality over time and, 416
  population growth and, 313–315
  poverty rates of specific population groups, 420
  Social Security programs and, 341
Dentsply, 197
Dependent variable, 23
Depreciation. *See also* Inflation
  defined, 503
  in exchange rates, 502, 503
Deregulation, 383–384
Derived demand
  defined, 249
  resource demand as, 249
Determinants of demand, 50
Determinants of price elasticity of demand, 81–83

Determinants of supply, 54, 56
Deutsch, Larry, 237n
Developing countries, Sugar Program and, 404–405
Diagnosis-related group (DRG), 447
Diamonds
  conflict, 325
  diamond-water paradox, 124
  monopolies and, 212
Different costs
  comparative advantage and, 476
  defined, 476
Differentiated oligopoly, 224
Dilemma of regulation, 211
Diminished trade, flexible exchange rates and, 507–508
Diminishing marginal utility, 49, 117–119
Diminishing returns, 144–147
Direct payments, agricultural, 406
Direct relationships, 23
DirecTV, 380
Discrimination, 424–429
  competition and, 426
  costs of, 428
  defined, 424
  economic analysis of, 424–429
  income inequality and, 414, 424
  occupational segregation, 281, 426–429
  price, 207–209, 376, 380
  statistical, 426
  wage differentials and, 281
Discrimination coefficient, 424–425
Diseconomies of scale, 156
Distance, in decision to migrate, 457–458
Distorted trade, exchange controls and, 509
Diversification-for-stability argument for trade protection, 488
Diversity, of oligopolies, 228
Division of labor, in market systems, 33
Doctors. *See* Physicians
Doha Development Agenda, 405, 491
Doha Round, 404–405
"Dollar votes," 35
Domestic price, 482
Dominant firms, in oligopoly, 226
Dominant strategy, 241
Drops, health insurance, 447
Drugs. *See* Illegal drugs; Prescription drugs
Dumping
  defined, 488
  protection-against-dumping argument for trade protection, 488–489
DuPont, 197
DuPont cellophane case, 377–378

Earmarks, 366–367
Earned-income tax credit (EITC), 422, 423–424
Earnings opportunities, migration decision, 456–457
Easterlin, Richard, 126

Eastman Kodak, 380
eBay, 459
Echostar, 380
Eckstein, Otto, 369n
Economic(s)
    defined, 4
    macroeconomics, 6–7. *See also*
        Macroeconomics
    microeconomics, 6. *See also* Microeconomics
    normative, 7
    positive, 7
    purposeful simplifications in, 6
    scientific method and, 5–6
    theories of behavior and, 6
    of war, 14
Economic costs. *See also* Opportunity cost(s)
    defined, 141
Economic growth
    defined, 15
    environmental quality and, 330–331
    fastest-growing occupations, 255–256
    increases in resource supplies, 15–16
    production possibilities model and, 15–16
    technological advances, 16
Economic immigrants
    defined, 454
    economic effects of immigration, 456–458
Economic perspective
    choice in, 4
    defined, 4
    marginal analysis in, 5
    pitfalls in applying, 16–17
    purposeful behavior in, 4–5
    scarcity in, 4
Economic principle
    characteristics of, 6
    defined, 6
Economic (pure) profit, 142–143, 304–306
    defined, 142
    functions of, 307–308
    role of entrepreneur, 304
    sources of, 304–306
Economic rent, 294–297
Economic resources
    categories of, 10–11
    defined, 10
    increases in supplies, 15–16
    market systems and, 30–43
    scarce, 10
Economic systems
    command systems, 30, 38–40
    defined, 30
    market systems, 39–41. *See also* Market
        systems
Economies of scale, 153–156
    applications and illustrations, 157–159
    as barrier to entry, 196, 205, 224
    defined, 153–154
    efficient capital and, 155–156
    labor specialization and, 154
    managerial specialization and, 154–155

in oligopoly, 224
    other factors in, 156
    sources of, 157–159
Economist, The, 315, 315n, 417
Economizing problem
    defined, 7
    individuals', 7–11
    society's, 10–11
Education and training
    demand for highly skilled workers, 416, 455,
        456, 459
    income inequality and, 414
    law of diminishing returns, 144
    opportunity costs and, 9–10
    of physicians, 444
    property taxes and, 342
    skill transferability, 459
    specialty occupations of immigrants, 455,
        456, 459
    wage differentials and, 279, 416
Effective interest rate, 306–307
Efficiency
    allocative, 58–59, 97, 188, 204, 221–222,
        235, 442
    bureaucratic inefficiency, 368
    of energy use, 318–319
    equality-efficiency ratio, 419
    gains from entry, 191
    impact of immigration on, 459–460
    income equality versus, 417–419
    income inequality and, 418–419
    in industrial regulation, 382
    interest rates and, 303
    labor unions and, 290–291
    of majority voting, 362–363
    in market systems, 35–36, 38
    minimum efficient scale (MES), 156–157,
        396–397
    monopolistic competition and, 221–222
    oligopoly and, 235
    price and, 98–99
    productive, 58, 97, 187–188, 203–204, 221–
        222, 235
    pure competition and, 186–189
    pure monopoly and, 203–204, 205, 206
    Sugar Program, 405
    usury laws and, 303
    X-inefficiency, 205, 206, 258, 382
Efficiency gains from migration, 460
Efficiency losses
    of agricultural price supports, 400
    defined, 98
    of taxes, 349
Efficiency wages, 282
    pay for performance and, 281–282
Efficiently functioning markets, 93–99
    consumer surplus, 93–95
    deadweight losses, 98–99
    efficiency revisited, 96–98
    producer surplus, 95–96
Ehrlich, Paul, 314–315

Elastic demand, 77, 78–79
Elasticity, 75–90
Elasticity of product demand, 257
Elasticity of resource demand, 256–257
Electronic Benefit Transfer (EBT), 423
Elephant preservation, 325–326
Ellison, Lawrence J., 283
Elzinga, Kenneth, 237n
Employer mandate, for health-insurance
    coverage, 448
Employment effects
    of illegal immigrants, 464–465
    increased domestic employment argument
        for trade protection, 489
Empty threats, 241–242
Endowment effect
    defined, 129
    market transactions and, 129
Energy economics, 314–320
    efficient energy use, 318–319
    energy consumption measures, 315–317
    energy use in the U.S., 314–317
    gasoline market, 61–62, 71, 157, 358
    oil cartels, 231–232, 473, 513
    supply of cheap energy, 319–320
Enron, 384
Entitlement programs, 421–424
    public assistance, 422, 423–424, 463
    social insurance, 421–423
Entrepreneurs. *See also* Start-up firms
    corporate stockholders, 307–308
    economic (pure) profit and, 304–306
    entrepreneurial ability and, 10–11
    income shares and, 308
    profit rations entrepreneurship, 306
    profits and, 307–308
    technological advance and, 189–192
Environmental Performance Index (EPI), 331
Environmental Protection Agency (EPA), 384
Environmental quality
    economic growth and, 330–331
    farm policy and, 400
    fisheries management and, 327–329
    forest management and, 326–327
    pollution reduction and, 110–111, 320
    recycling and, 320
EOG Resources, 283
Equal Employment Opportunity Commission
    (EEOC), 384
Equality-efficiency trade-off, 419
Equilibrium GDP, international trade and,
    483–485
Equilibrium position
    defined, 136
    economic rent, 294–297
    equivalency at equilibrium, 136–137
    GDP. *See* Equilibrium GDP
    indifference map, 136–137
    for monopsony model, 272
    for purely competitive labor market,
        269–271

Equilibrium price level, 56–58
  in marginal-revenue-marginal-cost
    approach to profit maximization,
    175–176, 182–184
  world price, 483
Equilibrium quantity, 56–58
Equilibrium world price, 483
An Essay on the Principle of Population
    (Malthus), 313
Ethanol, market for, 320, 401
Ethics, health care costs and, 439, 440–441
Ethnicity. *See* African Americans; Hispanics
European Economic Community. *See*
    European Union (EU)
European Union (EU), 491–492
  monopolies and, 379
  U.S. trade with, 404
Euro Zone, 492
Excess capacity, in monopolistic
    competition, 222
Exchange controls
  criticisms of, 509–510
  defined, 509
Exchange rate(s)
  changes in supply and demand, 69–70
  depreciation, 502, 503
  exchange-rate risk, 514–515
  fixed, 503, 508–510
  flexible, 503, 506–508, 510–511
  managed float, 510–511
Excise taxes, 351, 352
  defined, 341, 352
  price elasticity of demand and, 83
Excludability, private versus public goods and,
    99, 100
Exclusive unionism, 274
Executive pay, 283, 416
Exit mechanism, 291
Expectations. *See* Consumer expectations;
    Producer expectations
Expenditures approach to GDP. *See also*
    Aggregate expenditures (AE) model
  government purchases, 338
  personal consumption expenditures,
    314–317
Explicit costs, 141, 304
Exports
  of China, 512–513
  equilibrium world price and, 483
  supply and demand analysis of, 482–483
Export subsidies, 486
Export supply curve
  Canada, 483–485
  defined, 483
  U.S., 482–483
Externalities, 104–109
  defined, 92, 104
  market-based approach to, 110–111
  market for externality rights, 110–111
  methods of dealing with, 108
  negative, 105, 108, 110–111, 349–350

optimal amount of externality reduction,
    108–109
  positive, 105–106, 439
Extraction costs, 322–324
Exxon, 379

Facebook, 205
Factors of production, 11
Fair Labor Standards Act of 1938, 276
Fair-return price, 210–211
Fallacy of composition, 16–17, 489
Farm commodities. *See also* Agriculture
  defined, 392
  economics of farm policy, 398–401
  farm-household income, 397–398
  price elasticity of demand and, 83
  price floors on wheat, 63–64
  prices of, 69
Fast food, cost-benefit perspective and, 5
Favoritism, exchange controls and, 509
Featherbedding, 289
Federal Communications Commission (FCC),
    197, 382
Federal Emergency Management Agency
    (FEMA), 370
Federal Energy Regulatory Commission
    (FERC), 382, 384
Federal government, 339–341. *See also*
    Public debt
  antitrust laws, 375–376, 378–381
  employment in, 342–343
  federal expenditures, 338, 339–340
  fiscal impact of immigration and, 465
  health care costs and, 437
  health-care legislation, 433, 434, 443,
    445–446, 447–450
  tax revenues, 340–341
Federal Insurance Contributions Act
    (FICA), 346
Federal Reserve System, 302, 428
  loanable funds theory of interest and, 300
  Survey of Consumer Finances, 428
Federal Trade Commission (FTC),
    375–376, 381
Federal Trade Commission Act of 1914,
    376, 381
Fee-for-service health care, 440
Fertility rate, 313–314
Financial economics, present value and, 301
Financial institutions. *See also* Bank(s)
  international financial transactions, 499
  loanable funds theory of interest and, 299
Financial services industry. *See* Financial
    institutions
First Data Corporation, 195
First-mover advantages, 243–244
Fisher, Irving, 301, 301n
Fisheries management, 327–329
  fishery, defined, 327
  fishery collapse, 327–328
  limits on catch sizes, 328–329

Fixed costs (FC)
  average, 148–149, 151–152
  defined, 147
  short-run production, 147
Fixed-exchange-rate systems
  defined, 503
  domestic macroeconomic adjustments and,
    508–510
  trade policies, 509
Fixed proportions, 254–255
Fixed resources, in production possibilities
    model, 11
Fixed technology, in production possibilities
    model, 11
Flexible-exchange-rate systems
  balance of payments and, 506–507
  current managed floating exchange rate
    system, 510–511
  defined, 503
  determinants of, 505–506
  disadvantages of, 507–508
Floating-exchange-rate systems
  current managed floating exchange rate
    system, 510–511
  defined, 503
  disadvantages of, 507–508
Food, Conservation, and Energy
    Act of 2008, 406
Food for Peace, 401
Food products, 392
Food-stamp program, 403, 423
Ford Motor, 41, 290
Foreign exchange market. *See* Exchange rate(s)
Forest management
  deforestation trend, 326
  optimal harvesting, 326–327
Four-firm concentration ratio, 218–219
Framing effects
  advertising and, 127
  defined, 127
France
  executive pay in, 283
  population decline in, 314
Frank, Robert, 126, 253
Fraud, insurance, 465
Freedom, in market systems, 38
Freedom of choice, in market systems, 31
Freedom of enterprise, in market systems, 31
Freedom to Farm Act of 1996, 405–406
Free entry and exit, pure competition and,
    165, 182–184, 191
Freeman, Richard, 463n
Free products and services, 4, 294–295
Free-rider problem, pay for performance and,
    100, 282
Free trade, case for, 481
Free-trade zones, 490–492
Frito-Lay, 127
Full employment
  immigration and, 462–463
  in production possibilities model, 11

Future and Its Enemies, The (Postrel), 42
Futures markets, commodities, 396
Future value, 301

G8 nations, 511
Gains from entry, 191
Gains from trade, 478–480
Game theory, 241–244
  collusion and, 227
  credible threats, 241–242
  defined, 226
  empty threats, 241–242
  first-mover advantages, 243–244
  incentives to cheat, 227
  mutual interdependence and, 227, 228
  oligopoly and, 226–227
  one-time game, 241
  preemption of entry, 243–244
  prisoner's dilemma, 226–227
  reciprocity strategies, 242–243
  repeated games, 242–243
Gasohol, 401
Gasoline market, 358
  changes in supply and demand, 71
  price ceilings in, 61–62
  price changes, 157
Gates, Bill, 8, 9, 307
Gateway, 387
General Agreement on Tariffs and Trade
    (GATT), 491
General Electric, 197, 234, 235
Generalizations
  defined, 6
  utility-maximizing rule, 121–122
General Mills, 233
General Motors (GM), 234, 242, 290,
    293, 308
Generic drugs, gains from entry, 191
Gentlemen's agreements, 232
Geographic immobility, wage differentials
    and, 280
Geographic specialization, 33
George, Henry, 296–297
Germany
  capital-intensive goods, 474
  executive pay in, 283
  exports of, 512
  international trade and, 473
Gifts, marginal utility and, 125
Gini ratio, 411, 412, 417
Global Corruption Barometer, 369
Globalization. *See also* Global perspective;
    International trade
  demand for labor, 267
Global perspective. *See also* Globalization;
    International trade
  agricultural labor force, 397
  agricultural subsidies, 398
  average income in selected nations, 8
  bribery in, 369
  carbon-dioxide emissions, 110–111

competition from foreign multinational
    corporations, 207
  deforestation, 326
  emigrant remittance, 462
  exports of goods and services as percentage
    of GDP, 474
  fertility rates, 313, 314
  foreign multinational corporations, 207
  health care spending, 436
  hourly wages of production workers, 267
  immigrants as percent of labor force, 457
  income inequality, 415
  Index of Economic Freedom, 32
  OPEC nations, daily oil production, 231
  shares of world exports, 473
  short-term nominal interest rates, 303
  tax burden, 339
  taxes on general consumption, 351
  top brand names, 235
  U.S. trade balances, 501
  wages of production workers, 267
  world's fisheries, 328
Gold, price elasticity of supply and, 86–87
Goods for the future, 16–18
Goods for the present, 16–18
Google, 41, 157, 190, 235, 459
Government. *See also* Federal government;
    Local government; Public debt; Public
    sector; State government
  apportioning tax burden, 344–346
  in circular flow model, 337–338
  cross elasticity of demand and, 88
  failure of. *See* Government failure
  federal. *See* Federal government
  fiscal impact of immigration and, 463, 465
  information failures and, 358–361, 439
  loanable funds theory of interest and,
    298–299
  local. *See* Local government
  in market systems, 34
  prices set by, 61–64
  public sector role of, 352–353
  redistribution role of, 352–353, 413–414
  role in economy, 34, 109–111
  state. *See* State government
Government Accountability Office (GAO), 370
Government failure, 361, 365–369
  bureaucratic inefficiency, 368
  corruption, 368–369
  cost-benefit analysis of vote seeking, 367
  defined, 365
  imperfect institutions, 369
  limited-choice, bundled-goods problem,
    367–368
  pork-barrel politics and, 366–367, 370
  public choice theory, 367–368
  special-interest effect, 366–367
Government intervention, direct controls,
    106–107
Government purchases (G), 338
  public debt and, 339

Government regulation
  antitrust policy and, 375
  competition as regulatory mechanism, 32
  price ceilings on gasoline, 61–62
  price floors on wheat, 63–64
  prices in regulated monopoly, 209–211
  rent controls, 62–63
  wage differentials and, 280–281
Graphical expression, 6, 22–26
  circular flow diagram, 40–41
  construction of graph, 22
  defined, 6
  demand curve, 48
  demand schedule, 48–49
  dependent variables, 23
  direct relationships, 23
  equation of linear relationship, 25
  graph, defined, 22
  independent variables, 23
  indifference curves, 133–138
  inverse relationships, 23
  law of diminishing marginal utility, 118
  law of diminishing returns and, 145–147
  of marginal cost (MC), 150
  of marginal revenue (MR), 166
  other things equal assumption, 23–24
  of price ceilings, 61–62
  of price discrimination, 209
  of price factors, 64
  slope of a line, 24–25
  slope of a nonlinear curve, 25–26
  subsidies for health care, 442
  supply curve, 53–54
  vertical intercept, 25
Great Depression, 14, 17
Great Recession of 2007-2009, 489
  fiscal policy during, 421–422
Greer, Douglas F., 237n
Grieco, Paul L. E., 481n
Grievance procedures, labor union, 288–289
Grogger, Jeffrey, 463n
Gross domestic product (GDP)
  equilibrium. *See* Equilibrium GDP
  health care spending in, 436
Growth. *See* Economic growth; Population
    growth
Guinness, 237

H1-B provisions, 455
Hand, Learned, 377
Hanson, Gordon H., 463n, 466n
Health care, 433–451. *See also* Physicians;
    Prescription drugs
  access to, 434–435, 437, 438
  black market for human organs, 62–63
  costs of, 434–447
  demand factors, 439–441
  gains from entry, 191
  health care industry, 434
  insurance for, 434–436, 439, 441–443,
    444–445

Health care—*Cont.*
  legislation for, 433, 434, 443, 445–446,
    447–450
  Medicaid, 423, 436, 437, 441, 449
  medical care and marginal utility, 125
  Medicare, 346, 421–422, 435, 437, 441,
    447, 449
  organ transplants, 62–63, 444
  poverty and, 423, 436, 437, 441, 449
  in Singapore, 448–449
  supply factors, 443–445
  vaccinations as positive externalities, 105–106
Health maintenance organizations (HMOs),
  446–447
Health savings accounts (HSAs), 446
Hedging, 396
Hedonism, 126
Heineken, 237
Heinz, 392
Herfindahl Index, 219, 226, 379–380
Heritage Foundation, 32n
Hershey's, 126
Hess, John, 283
Hess Petroleum, 283
Highly skilled workers, demand for, 416, 455,
  456, 459
Hispanics. *See also* Immigration
  discrimination against, 424–426
  poverty among, 420
  unionization rate, 287
Hitachi, 381
Holmes, Oliver Wendell, 344
Homogeneous oligopoly, 224
Honda, 290
Horizontal axis, 22
Horizontal mergers, 379
Hormel, 381
Hours of work, labor unions and, 288
Households
  in circular flow model, 41
  decisions of, 32
  loanable funds theory of interest and, 298–299
Howard, Ron, 241n
Hufbauer, Gary C., 481n
Hughes, 380
Hulu, 190
Human capital
  defined, 279
  immigration decision and, 456–457
  nature of, 279, 280
  wage differentials and, 279
Hunt, 392
Hynix Semiconductor, 381
Hypotheses, 5

IBM, 197, 235, 305, 377, 387
Icehouse, 237
Identity theft, immigration and, 465
Illegal drugs
  immigration and, 465
  legalization of, 83

Illegal immigrants
  debate concerning, 464–467
  decision to migrate, 456–458
  defined, 455
  employment effects of, 464–465
  origins of, 456
Immigration, 454–468
  decision to migrate, 456–458
  economic effects of, 458–461
  economic immigrants, 454, 456–458
  full employment and, 462–463
  illegal, 455–458, 464–467
  income inequality over time and, 416–417
  legal, 455–458, 466, 467
  legislation concerning, 466
  number of immigrants to the U.S.,
    455–456
  optimal, 467
  reform of, 466
Immigration Act of 1921, 466
Immigration Act of 1924, 466
Immigration Reform and Control
  Act of 1986, 466
Imperfect competition, 164, 251–252
Implicit costs, 141, 304
Import(s)
  equilibrium world price and, 483
  supply and demand analysis of, 483
Import competition
  defined, 225
  in oligopoly, 225–226
Import demand curve
  Canada, 483–485
  defined, 483
  U.S., 483
Import quotas, 404
  defined, 485
  economic impact of, 486–487
  net costs of, 487–488
Incentive functions, 295
Incentive pay plans
  defined, 281
  principal-agent problem in, 281–282
Incentives
  to cheat, 227
  income inequality and, 417–419
  in market systems, 38
  as problem in command systems, 39–40
Inclusive unionism, 274–275
Inco, 197
Income. *See also* Income distribution
  change in demand and, 51–52
  consumer budget line and, 10, 134
  exchange rates and, 505
  farm-household, 396, 397–398
  as flow, 414–415
  global perspective on, 8
  health care costs and, 439–440
  limited, of individuals, 7–8
  proportion of, and price elasticity of
    demand, 82

Income changes
  on budget line, 10, 134
  immigration and, 459
Income determination, resource pricing
  and, 249
Income distribution. *See also* Poverty; Transfer
    payments
  consumption versus, 417
  cost to society and individuals, 429
  entitlement programs in, 421–424, 463
  government role in, 352–353, 413–414
  immigration decision and, 456–457
  income inequality and, 410–430
  income redistribution, 349, 352–353
  income shares in the U.S., 308, 460–461
  marginal productivity theory of, 260–262
  by quintiles (fifths), 411–412
  taxation in, 349, 352–353, 413
  over time, 416–417
  in the U.S., 308, 411–414, 416–417,
    421–424, 428, 460–461
Income effect, 49, 122–123
Income elasticity of demand, 88–89
  cross elasticity of demand compared with, 88
  defined, 88
Income inequality, 410–430
  causes of, 414–415
  defined, 411
  distribution by quintiles (fifths), 411–412
  efficiency versus, 417–419
  Gini ratio, 411, 412, 417
  government redistribution and, 349,
    352–353, 413–414
  Lorenz curve, 411, 412, 413, 417
  marginal productivity theory of income
    distribution and, 260–262
  mobility and, 412–413, 456–463. *See also*
    Immigration
  time and, 412–413, 416–417
Income mobility, 412–413. *See also*
    Immigration
Income shares
  immigration and, 460–461
  in the U.S., 308, 460–461
Income tax
  corporate, 86, 341, 345–346, 350–351, 352
  personal, 340–341, 345, 350, 352
Income transfer, in pure monopoly, 204
Increasing-cost industry
  defined, 185
  long-run supply curve for, 185
Increasing opportunity costs, law of, 12–13
Independent action, monopolistic competition
    and, 217
Independent goods
  cross elasticity of demand and, 88
  defined, 52
Independent unions, 287
Independent variable, 23
Index of Economic Freedom, 32
India, immigration from, 456

Indifference curve analysis, 133–138
  consumer budget line, 133–134
  convex to origin, 135
  derivation of demand curve, 137–138
  downsloping, 134–135
  equilibrium at tangency, 136
  equivalency at equilibrium, 136–137
  indifference curves, defined, 134
  indifference map in, 135–137
Indifference maps
  equilibrium position, 136–137
  nature of, 135–136
  topographical maps and, 137
Individuals' economizing problem
  budget line and, 8–10
  limited income and, 7–8
  unlimited wants and, 8
Individual transferable quotas (ITQs), 329
Industrial regulation, 381–383
  defined, 374, 381
  legal cartel theory, 383
  natural monopoly, 381–382
  problems with, 382–383
  regulatory commissions, 382
  social regulation versus, 384
Industrial Revolution, 313
Industrial unions, 274–275
Industries
  decreasing-cost, 185–186
  long-run supply curve for constant-cost, 184
  with monopolistic competition, 218–219
  with oligopoly, 225–226, 236–237
Industry concentration
  Herfindahl Index and, 219, 226, 379–380
  in monopolistic competition, 218–219
  in oligopoly, 225–226
Inelastic demand, 77–79
  for agricultural products, 392, 396–397
Inelastic supply, of land, 294
Infant industry argument for trade
    protection, 488
Inferior goods
  defined, 52
  income elasticity of demand and, 88
Inferior options, utility-maximizing
    rule, 121
Infineon, 381
Infinite slopes, 24–25
Inflation, exchange rates and, 505
Inflexible prices. See Sticky (inflexible) prices
Information failures, 358–361
  asymmetric information, 358–361, 439
  inadequate buyer information about sellers,
    358–359
  inadequate seller information about buyers,
    359–361
  qualification, 361
Information technology
  economies of scale, 205
  start-up firms in, 459
Ingram Book group, 380

Innovation. See also Technology
  economic (pure) profit and, 304
  industrial regulation and, 382
  intellectual property and, 31, 191, 196–197
  technological advance and, 190
Insights, income elasticity of demand and, 88–89
Insurable risks, 304
Insurance
  crop revenue, 396
  health care, 434–436, 439, 441–443, 444–445
  information failure and, 439
  insurable/uninsurable risks, 304–305
  social, 421–423
  unemployment, 422–423
Insurance exchanges, 450
Insurance fraud, immigration and, 465
Intel, 157, 197, 235, 346, 459
Intellectual property, 31, 191
  as barrier to entry, 196–197
Interest, 297–303. See also Interest rate(s)
  characteristics of, 297–298
  compound, 300–301
  defined, 297
  loanable funds theory of, 298–299
  time-value of money and, 300–301
Interest groups
  farm policy and, 403
  logrolling and, 363, 403
  nature of, 363
Interest rate(s). See also Interest
  exchange rates and, 505
  loanable funds theory of interest, 298–299
  nominal, 302
  as percentage, 297
  price of credit and, 303, 306–307
  pure rate of interest, 298
  range of, 297–298
  real, 302
  role of, 302
  time-value of money and, 300–301
  usury laws, 303
Interest-rate risk, 297, 301
Interindustry competition, in oligopoly, 225
Interlocking directorates, 376
International asset transactions, 499
International Monetary Fund (IMF), 502, 511
International Nickel Company of Canada, 197
International trade, 472–495. See also Global
    perspective
  in aggregate expenditures (AE) model,
    483–485
  agriculture in, 394, 397, 398, 400, 403–405
  balance of payments, 499–503
  case for protection, 488–490
  comparative advantage in, 474–481
  economic basis for trade, 474
  equilibrium GDP and, 483–485
  exports. See entries beginning with "Export"
  fixed exchange rates, 508–510
  imports. See entries beginning with "Import"
  income inequality over time and, 416–417

international financial transactions, 499
  key facts, 473
  nature of, 499
  oligopoly in, 225–226
  production possibilities model and, 18
  supply and demand analysis of exports and
    imports, 482–485
  trade barriers, 485–488
  trade deficits, 473, 500, 512–513
  trade surpluses, 473, 500–501
  U.S. economy and, 394, 403–405, 473,
    474–481
  World Trade Organization (WTO) in,
    404–405, 491
Interstate Commerce Commission (ICC),
    382–383, 383
InterTrust, 387
Inverse relationships, 23
Investment, defined, 10
"Invisible hand," 38, 189, 295–296
iPods, 123–124, 190, 305
Irani, Ray, 283
Italy, population decline in, 314

Japan
  executive pay in, 283
  exports of, 512
  international trade and, 473
JBS, 392
Job information, lack of, and wage
    differentials, 280
Job protection, labor unions and, 288
Jobs, Steve, 305
John Deere, 249
Johnson & Johnson, 234

Kahneman, Daniel, 126
Katz, Lawrence, 463n
Kellogg's, 127, 233
Kennickell, Arthur B., 428n
Kentucky Fried Chicken (KFC), 379
Killarney's, 237
Kinked-demand curve, 229, 230
Kinked-demand theory, 228–230
Knowles, Beyoncé, 253, 410
Korean Air, 381
Krueger, Dirk, 417n

Labor. See also Labor market; Wage
    determination
  cheap foreign labor argument for trade
    protection, 489–490
  defined, 10, 267
  demand curve. See Labor demand curve
  market demand for, 269
  quality of, 268
  as resource, 10
  specialization of. See Specialization
  supply curve. See Labor supply curve
  unions. See Labor unions
  workplace safety, 360–361

Labor, Health and Human Services and Education Act (2008), 370
Labor demand curve
  changes in labor demand, 255
  declining occupations, 256
  fastest-growing occupations, 255–256
  in monopsony model, 272
  in purely competitive labor market, 269–271
  wage differentials and, 278
Labor force. *See* Unemployment
Labor-intensive goods, 474
Labor market. *See also* Labor; Labor demand curve; Labor supply curve
  agricultural, 397
  demand for highly skilled workers, 416, 455, 456, 459
  health care costs and, 437
  immigration and, 454–468
  offshoring of jobs, 437, 492–494
  specialization of, 154
Labor supply curve
  in monopsony model, 272
  in purely competitive labor market, 269–271
  wage differentials and, 278
Labor unions, 273–275, 287–291
  antitrust policy and, 375
  bilateral monopoly model, 275–276
  collective bargaining and, 288–290
  decline of unionism, 287–288, 416–417
  demand-enhancement model, 273–274
  economic effects of, 289–291
  exclusive/craft union model, 274
  inclusive/industrial union model, 274–275
  income inequality and, 416–417
  membership in, 287
  offsetting factors, 291
  wage determination, 273–275, 287–291
  wage differentials and, 280–281
  wage increases and unemployment, 275
Laissez-faire capitalism, 30, 378
Land
  defined, 10
  leasing agricultural, 396
  ownership of, 295–296
  quality of, 296
  as resource, 10
  single tax on, 296–297
Land-intensive goods, 474
Land rent
  alternative uses of land, 296
  determination of, 294
  inelastic supply of land, 294
  productivity differences and rent differences, 295
  rent-seeking behavior and, 367
  single-tax movement, 296–297
  as surplus payment, 295
Landrum-Griffin Act of 1959, 289
Language skills, in decision to migrate, 458
Large crop yields, price elasticity of demand and, 83

Latinos. *See* Hispanics
Law of demand, 49
Law of diminishing marginal utility, 117–119
  defined, 49, 117
  demand and, 119
  marginal utility, 117–119
  total utility, 117–119
  utility, defined, 117
  vending machines and, 117
Law of diminishing returns, 144–147
  application of, 144–147
  defined, 144
  graphical expression of, 145–147
  rationale for, 144–145
  tabular example of, 145
Law of increasing opportunity costs, 12–13
  economic rationale for, 13
  shape of curve, 13
Law of supply, 53
Learning by doing, 33, 156, 358
Leasing land, 396
Least-cost combination of resources
  defined, 258
  numerical illustration, 259–260
Least-cost production, 36
Legal cartel theory of regulation, 383
Legal immigrants
  decision to migrate, 456–458
  defined, 455
  family reunification and, 455–456
  origins of, 456
  quotas for, 455–456, 466, 467
  specialty occupations and, 455, 456, 459
Legal issues
  forms of business. *See* Corporations; Partnerships; Sole proprietorships
  immigration reform, 466
  legalization of drugs, price elasticity of demand and, 83
Legislation
  antitrust, 88, 233, 375–376, 375–381
  credit, 307
  farm policy, 405–406
  federal health care, 433, 434, 443, 445–446, 447–450
  immigration, 466
  labor market, 276
  negative externalities and, 92
Lemon laws, 360
Lenovo, 346
Lettuce, market for, 69
LG, 381
Licenses
  as barrier to entry, 197
  occupational licensing, 274, 358–359, 383
Lifestyle factors, health care costs and, 440
Limited-choice, bundled-goods problem, 367–368
Limited income, of individuals, 7–8
Limit pricing, in oligopoly, 233, 235
Linear relationship, equation of, 25

List, John, 129
Living standards, 313–314
Loaded terminology, in economic reasoning, 16
Loan(s). *See also* Credit
  demand for loanable funds, 298–299
  size of, and interest rates, 298
Loanable funds theory of interest, 298–299
  demand for loanable funds, 299
  extending the model, 299–300
  supply of loanable funds, 298–299
Local government
  employment in, 342–343
  finances in U.S., 342
  fiscal impact of immigration and, 465
Localized markets, 225
Location, product differentiation through, 217
Lockouts, 289
Logrolling, 363, 403
Long run
  decline of agriculture in, 395–397
  defined, 85, 143
  economies and diseconomies of scale and, 153–156
  price and output in monopolistic competition, 221
  price elasticity of supply and, 85
  production costs in, 152–157
  profit maximization in pure competition, 182–185
  pure competition in, 181–192
  real wages in, 268–269
  variable plant in, 143
Long-run supply curve
  for constant-cost industry, 184–185
  for decreasing-cost industry, 185–186
  defined, 184
  for increasing-cost industry, 185
L'Oreal, 224
Lorenz curve, 411, 412, 413, 417
Loss averse, 126
Loss-minimization, 171
Lotteries, income and payouts of, 342
Luck, income inequality and, 415
Luxuries
  necessities versus, 8, 82–83
  price elasticity of demand and, 82–83

Mach, Traci L., 428n
Macpherson, David A., 454n
Macroeconomics. *See also* Economic growth; Inflation; Unemployment
  defined, 6–7
  domestic macroeconomic adjustments, 510
  fixed-exchange rate systems and, 508–510
  microeconomics versus, 6–7
Magnet countries, 457
Majority voting, 362–365
  implications of, 363
  inefficient outcomes of, 362–363
  median-voter model, 364–365
  paradox of, 363–364

Major League Baseball
immigration and, 459
monopsony power of, 273
price discrimination and, 208
as pure monopolies, 195
Make-work rules, 289
Malthus, Thomas, 313, 314
Managed care, 446–447
Managed floating exchange rates, 510–511
criticisms of, 511
defined, 510
support for, 511
Management
labor unions and, 288
managerial specialization, 154–155
Marginal analysis. *See also* Cost-benefit
analysis; Marginal utility; MB = MC rule;
MR = MC rule; P = MC
in competitive markets, 59
defined, 5
economics of war and, 14
fast-food lines and, 5
optimal allocation and, 13–14, 59, 97–98
for public goods and services, 101,
102–104
in pure monopoly, 200–202, 209, 210
slopes and, 24
Marginal cost (MC)
average total cost (ATC) and, 150–151
average variable cost (AVC) and, 150–151
calculating, 149–150
defined, 149
graphical expression of, 150
law of supply and, 53
marginal decisions and, 150
marginal product and, 150, 258
marginal-revenue-marginal-cost approach
to profit maximization, 167–172
in pure monopoly, 204
short-run supply and, 173–176
Marginal-cost-marginal-benefit rule, 104
Marginal product (MP)
defined, 144, 250
law of diminishing returns and,
144, 147
marginal cost and, 150, 258
Marginal productivity theory
of income distribution, 260–262
of resource demand, 249–253
Marginal rate of substitution (MRS), 135
Marginal resource cost (MRC). *See also*
MRP = MRC rule
defined, 250
higher than wage rate, 271–272
Marginal revenue (MR)
defined, 165
differences in, 295
graphical expression of, 166
marginal-revenue-marginal-cost approach
to profit maximization, 167–172
in pure monopoly, 198–199, 204

Marginal revenue product (MRP), 249–251.
See also MRP = MRC rule
defined, 250
labor demand, 290–291
market demand for a resource, 252
productivity and, 249–250
product price and, 250
as resource demand schedule, 250–251
resource demand under imperfect product
market competition, 251–252
wage differentials and, 278–279
Marginal tax rate, 340–341
Marginal utility
algebraic generalizations, 121–122
applications and extensions, 123–125
defined, 117
demand and, 119, 122–123
law of diminishing marginal utility, 49,
117–119
numerical examples, 120–121
total utility and, 117–119
utility-maximizing rule, 120
Marginal utility per dollar, 120
Market(s). *See also* Demand; Market systems;
Supply
defined, 32, 48
in market systems. *See* Market systems
nature of, 48
role of, 48
Market demand, 50
for labor, 269
for private goods, 99
for a resource, 252
Market demand curve, in pure monopoly,
197–200
Market equilibrium, 56–61
changes in demand and, 59–60, 69–72
changes in supply and, 59–60, 69–72
complex cases, 59–60
efficient allocation, 58–59
equilibrium price, 56–58, 175–176,
182–184, 483
equilibrium quantity, 56–58
rationing function of prices, 58
Market failure, 92–112, 361
in competitive markets, 93–99
free-rider problem, 100, 282
government involvement and, 34, 109–111
information failure, 358–361, 439
nature of efficiently functioning markets,
93–99
Market for externality rights, 110–111
advantages of, 110–111
operation of market, 110–111
Market imperfections
imperfect competition, 164
marginal productivity theory of income
distribution and, 261–262
resource demand and, 251–252
wage differentials and, 280–281
Marketing loan program, 406

Market period
defined, 84–85
price elasticity of supply and, 84–85
Market power. *See also* Monopoly; Oligopoly
elasticity and, 86–87
income inequality and, 415
relevant market and, 377–378
Market segregation, 208
Market shares, monopolistic competition
and, 217
Market supply, 54
of labor, 269
Market systems, 30–43
bureaucratic inefficiency versus, 368
characteristics of, 30–34
circular flow model and, 40–41
competition in, 31–32, 36, 58–59
defined, 30
demise of command systems and, 38–40
efficiency in, 35–36, 38
fundamental questions of, 35–38
imperfect institutions in, 369
"invisible hand" and, 38, 189, 295–296
money in, 33–34
monopolistic competition. *See* Monopolistic
competition
oligopoly. *See* Oligopoly
overview of, 164
pure competition. *See* Pure competition
pure monopoly. *See* Pure monopoly
Marriott, 361
Martinez, Tracy, 224
Maturity, interest rates and, 297–298
Maximum willingness to pay, 93–94, 97–98
MB = MC rule. *See also* Cost-benefit analysis;
Marginal analysis
comparing MB and MC, 102
in competitive markets, 59
economics of war, 14
health care costs, 438
optimal allocation and, 13–14, 59, 97–98
for optimal immigration, 467
for optimal level of social regulation, 385
for optimal reduction of an externality, 109
for public goods, 101, 102–104
McCain, John, 370
McConnell, Campbell R., 454n
McDonald's, 35, 224, 235
McDonnell Douglas, 379, 380
Means tests, 423
Measurement units, slopes and, 24
Median family wealth, 428
Median-voter model, 364–365
Medicaid, 423, 436, 437, 441, 449
Medical care. *See* Health care
Medicare, 437
cost containment through, 447
described, 435
health care, 422, 435, 441, 449
payroll taxes, 341, 346, 350, 351
as social insurance, 421–422

Medium of exchange, money as, 33–34
Mental accounting
  defined, 128
  overpriced warranties and, 128
Mergers. *See also* Antitrust policy
  cross elasticity of demand and, 88
  guidelines for, 379–380
  in oligopoly, 225, 236–237
  types of, 379
Mexico
  cheap foreign labor argument for trade
    protection, 490
  comparative advantage, 475–477
  exports of, 512
  immigration from, 456, 458–463, 466
  land-intensive goods, 474
  North American Free Trade Agreement
    (NAFTA), 492
  opportunity-cost ratio, 476–477
Michelin, 207
Microeconomics
  defined, 6
  of government. *See* Public choice theory;
    Public goods and services; Taxation
  macroeconomics versus, 6–7
Micron, 381
Microporous, 380
Microsoft Corporation, 9, 42, 157, 194, 205,
    207, 235, 307
  antitrust case, 197, 377, 378–379, 386–387
Middle East, oil cartel, 231–232, 473, 513
Midpoint formula, 76
Military self-sufficiency argument for trade
    protection, 488
Miller Brewing Company, 236–237, 242
Minimum efficient scale (MES), 156–157,
    396–397
Minimum wage
  case against, 276–277
  case for, 277
  defined, 276
  evidence and conclusions, 277
Minus sign, in price elasticity of demand, 77
Misfortune, income inequality and, 415
Mobil, 379
Mobility. *See also* Immigration
  income inequality and, 412–413, 456–463
Mobil Travel Guide, 361
Molson Coors, 236–237
Monetary policy. *See* Federal Reserve System
Money. *See also* Currency; Interest
  defined, 34
  in market systems, 33–34
  as medium of exchange, 33–34
  resource pricing and, 249
  time-value of money and, 300–301
  value of, 297
Money supply. *See* Bank(s)
Monopolistic competition, 217–223
  characteristics of, 164, 217–218
  defined, 164, 217

efficiency and, 221–222
entry and exit, 218, 221
industries with, 218–219
price and output in, 219–221
product differentiation in, 217–218, 223
product variety and, 222–223
Monopolization, 375
Monopoly. *See also* Antitrust policy; Pure
    monopoly
  antitrust policy and, 375–381
  AT&T case, 378, 383
  diamonds and, 212
  industrial regulation in perpetuating,
    382–383
  Microsoft case, 197, 377, 378–379, 386–387
  monopoly behavior versus monopoly
    structure, 377
  natural, 157, 196, 207, 210, 375, 381–382
  near-monopolies, 195, 375
  regulated monopolies, 209–211
Monopoly demand, 197–200
  marginal revenue in, 198–199, 204
  monopolist as price maker, 195, 197, 199–200
  output and price determination, 200–203
  total-revenue test for price, 200
Monopoly power, 208
Monopsony, 271–273
  defined, 271
  equilibrium wage and employment, 272
  examples of, 273
  MRC higher than wage rate, 271–272
  upsloping labor supply to firm, 271–272
Moore, Kevin B., 428n
Moral hazard problem
  described, 359
  health care insurance and, 441
Moving costs, of immigrants, 457
MP3 players, 190, 305
MR = MC rule, 169–176
  antitrust policy and, 375
  defined, 169
  demand for resources and, 258–260
  in the long run, 181
  marginal cost and short-run supply, 173–176
  in pure monopoly, 200–202, 204, 209–210
  in the short run, 167–172
  still there motel and, 173
MRP = MRC rule. *See also* Marginal resource
    cost (MRC); Marginal revenue product
    (MRP)
  defined, 250
  in employing resources, 250
  for monopsony model, 271–272
  for purely competitive labor market, 269–271
Multilateral trade agreements, 490–492
Multinational corporations, 207
Murphy, Kevin, 438
Mutual interdependence
  complications of, 228
  defined, 224
  in game theory, 227, 228

noncollusive oligopoly and, 228–230
  in oligopoly, 224

Nash, John F., 241n
Nash equilibrium, 241–244
National, 392
National Basketball Association (NBA),
    monopsony power of, 273
National Committee for Health and Clinical
    Excellence, 443
National defense. *See also* Terrorist attacks of
    September 11, 2001
  economics of war, 14
  immigration and, 465–467
  imperfect institutions and, 369
  military self-sufficiency argument for trade
    protection and, 488
National Education Association (NEA), 274
National Football League (NFL), monopsony
    power of, 273
National Foundation for American Policy, 459n
National health insurance (NHI), 434
National income accounting. *See* Gross
    domestic product (GDP)
National Labor Relations Act (NLRA), 289
National Labor Relations Board (NLRB), 289
National Safety Council, 385
Native American Arts and Crafts, 224
Natural monopoly, 157, 196, 207, 210, 375,
    381–382
Natural resources, 312–332
  economics of, 321–329
  nonrenewable, 321, 322–325
  renewable, 321, 325–329
  resource supplies, 313–314
  role in wage determination, 268
Near-monopolies, 195, 375
NEC, 207
Necessities
  luxuries versus, 8, 82–83
  price elasticity of demand and, 82–83
Negative externalities, 105
  correcting for, 105, 106–108
  government intervention, 106–108
  market-based approach to, 110–111
  optimal amount of externality reduction,
    108–109
  of taxation, 107–108, 349–350
Negative self-selection, 463
Negative slope, 24
Negative-sum game, 241
Nestlé, 207
Net benefits, of natural resources, 321
Net costs
  of import quotas, 487–488
  of tariffs, 487–488
Net effect, 254
Net investment income, 501
Netscape Navigator, 197, 386
Network effects, 205
New York Stock Exchange, as market, 48

New York Times, 158
Nike, 242
90-10 ratio, 416
Nippon Cargo, 381
Nokia, 207, 235
Nominal interest rates, 302
Nominal wage, 267
Noncash transfers, 413
Noncollusive oligopoly, 228–230
Noncompeting groups
    defined, 279
    wage differentials and, 279
Nonprice competition
    defined, 218
    in monopolistic competition, 164, 218
    in pure monopoly, 195
Nonrenewable natural resources,
    322–325
    defined, 321
    incomplete property rights and excessive
        present use, 324–325
    present use versus future use of,
        322–324
Nonrivalrous consumption, 205
Nontariff barriers (NTB), 485–486
Nordhaus, William, 438
Normal goods
    defined, 51–52
    income elasticity of demand and, 88
Normal profit
    break-even point and, 167
    as a cost, 141–142
    defined, 142
    in monopolistic competition, 221
    in profit rations entrepreneurship, 306
    technological advance and, 189–190
Normative economics, 7
North American Free Trade Agreement
    (NAFTA), 492
North Korea, command system in, 30, 39
Norwegian American Foundation, 370
Novell, 387
Number of buyers, change in demand and,
    51, 52
Number of sellers
    change in supply and, 55–56
    monopolistic competition and, 217
    as obstacle to collusion, 232
    in pure competition, 164

Obama, Barack, 433, 447
Occidental Petroleum, 283
Occupation(s). *See also* Education and
    training
    demand for highly skilled workers, 416, 455,
        456, 459
    occupational licensing, 274, 358–359, 383
    specialty occupations of immigrants, 455,
        456, 459
Occupational Safety and Health
    Administration (OSHA), 384

Occupational segregation, 281
    crowding model, 426–429
    defined, 426
    economics of, 427
    eliminating, 427–429
Office Depot, 380
Office of Immigration Statistics, 455n, 456n
Official reserves, 502, 509
Offshoring, 437, 492–494
Oil industry
    cartels in, 231–232, 473, 513
    daily production, 231
    supply of cheap energy, 319–320
Oligopoly, 223–237
    advertising and, 234
    antitrust policy and, 376
    cartels and, 230–233
    characteristics of, 164, 223–225, 226–227
    defined, 164, 223
    efficiency and, 235
    game theory and, 226–227
    industries with, 225–226, 236–237
    kinked-demand theory and, 228–230
    mergers and, 225, 236–237
    noncollusive, 228–230
    price leadership model, 233
Olympics, preset ticket prices, 72–73
One-time game, 241
Open shop, 288
Opportunity cost(s). *See also* Economic costs
    budget line, 9–10
    choice and, 10
    defined, 4
    economic (pure) profit and, 142–143
    explicit, 141, 304
    implicit, 141, 304
    law of increasing, 12–13
    long run, 143
    in marginal-revenue–marginal-cost
        approach to profit, 182–184
    normal profit as cost, 142
    short run, 143
    in theory of consumer behavior, 124–125
Opportunity-cost ratio, 476–477
Oprah Winfrey Show, 9
Optimal allocation, in marginal analysis,
    13–14, 59, 97–98
Optimal immigration, 467
Optimal level of social regulation, 385
Optimal reduction of an externality, 109
Oracle, 283
Organisation for Economic Cooperation and
    Development (OECD), 339n, 351n,
    436n, 457n
Organization of Petroleum Exporting
    Countries (OPEC), 231–232, 473, 513
Organ transplants, 62–63, 444
Other-things-equal assumption (*ceteris paribus*)
    defined, 6
    in graphical expression, 23–24
Ottaviano, Gianmarco, 463n

Output. *See also* Total output
    in cartels, 230–231
    coordination problem in command systems,
        38–39
    impact of immigration on, 459–460
    in market systems, 36–37
    in monopolistic competition, 219–221
    in oligopoly, 226–237
    in pure monopoly, 200–203, 204
    short-run fluctuations in agricultural,
        392–393
Output effect, 254
Outsourcing
    health care costs and, 437
    offshoring, 437, 492–494
Overt collusion, 231–232
Ownership of resources, as barrier to entry, 197

Packaging
    product differentiation through, 217–218
    size reductions, 126–127
Papa, Mark, 283
Paradox of voting, 363–364
    outcomes and, 364
    preferences, 363–364
Parity concept
    criticisms of, 402
    defined, 399
    purchasing power parity, 505
Parity ratio, 399
Partnerships
    in business population, 41
    defined, 41
Part-time workers, health care costs and, 437
P = ATC
    dilemma of regulation and, 211
    as fair-return price, 210–211
    in monopolistic competition, 221
    in oligopoly, 235
Patents, 31, 191
    as barrier to entry, 196–197, 206
Patient Protection and Affordable Care Act
    (PPACA), 433, 434, 443, 445–446
    alternatives, 450
    major provisions, 447–450
    objections, 450
Pay for performance, 281–282
    free-rider problem and, 100, 282
    negative side effects of, 282
    principal-agent problem, 281–282
Payoff matrix, 226–227
Payroll taxes, 341, 346, 350, 351
PepsiCo, 88, 242, 379
Percentages
    interest rates as, 297
    in price elasticity of demand, 76–77
Perfectly elastic demand, 77, 165
Perfectly inelastic demand, 77
Perfectly inelastic supply, 294
Peri, Giovanni, 463n
Perri, Fabrizio, 417n

Per se violations, 380
Personal consumption expenditures (C), 314–317
Personal income tax, 340–341, 345, 350, 352
Personal mandate, for health-insurance coverage, 448
Per-unit costs, 148–149
Pet, 232
Pfizer, 159, 197
Philip Morris Company, 237
Philippines, immigration from, 456
Physicians. *See also* Health care
 demand for health care and, 440
 supply of health care and, 444
Physician's Health Plan of Michigan, 380
Picasso, Pablo, 280
Piece rates, 281, 282
Pixar Animation Studios, 305
Pizza Hut, 379
Plant capacity
 in long run, 143
 in short run, 143
P = MC
 antitrust policy and, 375
 dilemma of regulation and, 211
 monopolistic competition and, 221
 in oligopoly, 235
 as socially optimal price, 210
Policy issues. *See also* Government
 pure monopoly and, 206–207
 resource pricing and, 249
Political action committees (PACs), 403
Political issues
 in farm policy, 403–405
 minimum wage, 276–277
 special interests, 363, 403
Pollack, Andrew, 445n
Pollution, air, 106, 110–111, 320
Polypore, 380
Population Bomb, The (Ehrlich), 314–315
Population growth
 birthrates and, 313–314
 resource consumption per person, 314–317
 single tax on land and, 296–297
 trends in, 313–314
Pork-barrel politics, 366–367, 370
Positive economics, 7
Positive externalities, 105–106
 defined, 105
 health care costs and, 439
Positive-sum game, 241
Post, 233
Post hoc fallacy, in economic reasoning, 17
Postrel, Virginia, 42
Poverty, 419–424
 defined, 419
 entitlement programs and, 421–424, 463
 health care and, 423, 436, 437, 441, 449
 health-insurance coverage and, 448–450
 incidence of, 420
 income inequality and, 410–430

measurement of, 420–421
 trends in, 420–421, 428
Poverty rate, 419–421
Prante, Gerald, 352, 352n
Preemption of entry, 243–244
Preexisting conditions, health insurance coverage for, 447
Preferences
 consumer, 119
 income inequality and, 414
 limited-choice, bundled-goods problem, 367–368
 paradox of voting and, 363–364
Preferred provider organizations (PPOs), 446
Prescription drugs, generic drugs, gains from entry, 191
Present value
 calculating, 321–322
 compound interest, 300–301
 defined, 321
 in natural resource economics, 321–322
Preset prices, 72–73
Price(s). *See also* Equilibrium price level; Inflation; MR = MC rule; Price elasticity of demand; Price elasticity of supply
 agricultural, 381, 406
 in cartels, 230–231
 ceilings on, 61–63
 change in demand and, 50–52, 53, 59–60, 69–72
 change in prices of other resources, 254–255
 change in supply and, 54–56, 59–60, 69–72
 consumer choice and, 119–120
 control over, 218
 efficiency and, 98–99
 equilibrium price, 56–58, 175–176, 182–184, 483
 equilibrium world price, 483
 floors on, 63–64
 government-set, 61–64
 immigration and, 465
 inflexible, 230
 law of demand and, 49
 in marginal-revenue-marginal-cost approach to profit maximization, 176
 marginal revenue versus, 198–199
 in market systems, 32, 36–37
 in monopolistic competition, 219–221
 in oligopoly, 224, 228–229
 preset, 72–73
 product differentiation through, 217–218
 in pure monopoly, 195, 197, 198–200, 202, 207–209
 rationing function of, 58
 in regulated monopoly, 209–211
 of related goods, 52
 relative, 49
 resource, 54–55, 56
 scalping and, 58

sticky, 230
 in supply and demand analysis of exports and imports, 482–485
Price ceilings, 61–63, 303
 black markets and, 62–63
 graphical analysis, 61–62
 rationing and, 58, 62
Price changes
 on budget line, 134
 health care costs and, 439
 in oligopoly, 228–229
Price discrimination, 207–209, 376, 380
 conditions for, 208
 defined, 207
 examples of, 208
 graphical analysis, 209
Price effects, of illegal immigration, 465
Price elasticity of demand, 76–84
 applications of, 83
 defined, 76
 determinants of, 81–83
 formula for, 76–77
 interpretation of elasticity, 77
 total-revenue test, 77–81, 200
Price elasticity of supply, 84–87
 applications of, 85–87
 defined, 84
 long run, 85
 market period, 84–85
 short run, 85
Price-fixing, 380
Price floors, 63–64
 additional consequences of, 64
 defined, 63
 effect of, 63–64
 graphical analysis, 64
Price leadership
 defined, 233
 in oligopoly, 233
Price makers, in pure monopoly, 195, 197, 199–200
Price supports
 criticisms of, 402–403
 defined, 399
 economics of agricultural, 399–400, 404–405
Price takers, pure competition and, 165, 195
Price wars, 230, 233
Pricing, resource, 249
Pricing power
 as barrier to entry, 195, 197
 elasticity and, 86–87
 in pure monopoly, 195, 197, 198–200, 202
Principal-agent problem
 defined, 365
 pay for performance and, 281–282
 representative democracy and, 365–367
Principle of comparative advantage, 477–478. *See also* Comparative advantage
Prisoner's dilemma, 226–227
Private bargaining, 106

Private goods and services
  characteristics of, 99–100
  demand for, 99
  preferences through majority voting, 363
  private goods, defined, 99
Private property
  land ownership, 295–296
  in market systems, 30–31, 42
Procter & Gamble, 127, 234
Producer expectations, change in
    supply and, 55
Producer surplus, 188–189, 400–401
  defined, 95
  in efficiently functioning markets, 95–96
Product attributes, in monopolistic
    competition, 217
Product demand, elasticity of, 257
Product development. *See* Research and
    development (R&D)
Product differentiation
  defined, 217
  in monopolistic competition, 217–218, 223
  in oligopoly, 224
Production, exchange rates and, 505–506
Production costs, 140–160
  applications and illustrations, 157–159
  economic, 142–143
  least-cost, 36
  long-run, 152–157
  in market systems, 35–36
  short-run, 144–152, 175
  sunk costs in decision making, 158–159
Production possibilities curve, 11–14
  defined, 11–12
  law of increasing opportunity costs, 12–13
  sample, 12
Production possibilities model, 11–18
  assumptions of, 11
  economic growth and, 15–16
  economics of war and, 14
  future and, 16–18
  international trade and, 18
  law of increasing opportunity costs, 12–13
  optimal allocation and, 13–14
  production possibilities curve, 11–14
  production possibilities table, 11
  unemployment and, 14–15
Production possibilities table, 11
Productive efficiency, 203–204, 221–222
  defined, 58, 97, 187–188
  in oligopoly, 235
Productivity. *See also* Economies of scale
  changes in, 253–254
  general level of wages and, 267–268
  health care prices and, 444
  labor unions and, 289–291
  marginal revenue product (MRP) and,
    249–250
  real wages and, 268
  rent differences and, 295
  resource demand derived from, 253–254

Product markets, 249
  changes in product demand, 253
  in circular flow model, 41
  resource demand derived from, 253
Product variety
  benefits of, 223
  in monopolistic competition, 222–223
Professional organizations
  craft union model for, 274
  occupational licensing, 274, 358–359
Professional sports teams
  Major League Baseball, 195, 208, 273, 459
  monopsony power of, 273
  price discrimination and, 208
  as pure monopolies, 195, 208
Profit
  discrimination and, 426
  economic (pure), 143, 304–306
  in monopolistic competition, 221
  normal profit, 141, 142
  resource allocation and, 307–308
  start-up firms and, 459
Profit maximization
  in long run, 182–185
  marginal-revenue-marginal-cost approach,
    167–172
  in monopolistic competition, 219–221
  for nonrenewable natural resources,
    322–324
  numerical illustration, 259–260
  profit-maximizing combination of
    resources, 258–260, 260
  in pure competition, 166–176, 182–185
  in pure monopoly, 200–203
  in short run, 166–176
  total-revenue-total cost approach, 166–167
Profit-sharing plans, 282
Progress, in market systems, 37
Progress and Poverty (George), 296–297
Progressive taxes, 340, 341, 345, 353–354
Property rights
  excessive present use of natural resources
    and, 324–325
  fisheries management and, 327–329
  forest management and, 326–327
  in market systems, 30–31
Property taxes, 342, 346, 351, 352
Proportional taxes, 345
Proprietary income, 337
Prospect theory, 125–129
  anchoring and credit card bills, 127
  better consumer decisions and, 128–129
  endowment effect and market
    transactions, 129
  framing effects and advertising, 127
  losses and shrinking packages, 126–127
  mental accounting and overpriced
    warranties, 128
Protection-against-dumping argument for
    trade protection, 488–489
Protectionism, proponents of, 493

Protective tariffs, 485
Public assistance programs, 422, 423–424, 463
Public choice theory, 361–365
  defined, 361
  farm policy and, 403
  government failure and, 367–368
  majority voting in, 362–365
Public debt, government purchases and, 339
Public finance, 337
Public goods and services, 99–104
  characteristics of, 100–101
  cost-benefit analysis for, 102–104
  demand for, 101–102
  externalities and, 104–109
  free-rider problem and, 100, 282
  information failures, 358–361
  marginal analysis, 101, 102–104
  optimal quantity of, 101
  preferences through majority voting, 363
  private goods and services versus, 99–100
  private goods versus, 100
  public goods, defined, 100
Public interest theory of regulation, 382
Public ownership, of natural monopoly, 382
Public regulation, of natural monopoly,
    381–382
Public sector. *See also* Government
  circular flow model and, 337–338
  defined, 336
  government finance and, 338–339
  government purchases, 338
  income redistribution and, 349, 352–353,
    413–414, 421–424
  quasi-public goods and, 104
  resource reallocation and, 104
Public utilities
  deregulation of, 383–384
  as natural monopoly, 381–382
  price discrimination in, 208
  as regulated monopolies, 209–211
Purchasing power parity, 505
Pure capitalism, 30
Pure competition, 163–192
  antitrust law and, 375
  characteristics of, 164–165
  defined, 164
  demand in, 165–166
  efficiency and, 186–189
  free entry and exit in, 165, 182–184, 191
  "invisible hand" and, 38, 189, 295–296
  in long run, 181–192
  loss-minimizing case, 171
  marginal cost and short-run supply,
    173–176
  as market model, 164
  occurrence of, 164–165
  price takers in, 165, 195
  profit maximization in long run, 182–185
  profit maximization in short run, 166–176
  purely competitive labor market, 269–271
  pure monopoly versus, 195, 202

Pure competition—*Cont.*
    resource demand and, 251–252
    in short run, 163–179
    shutdown case, 171, 172, 177
Pure monopoly, 194–213
    barriers to entry, 195–197
    characteristics of, 164, 195–197
    defined, 164, 195
    economic effects of, 203–207
    examples of, 195
    marginal analysis, 200–202, 204, 209, 210
    monopoly demand, 197–200
    objectives of study of, 195
    output and price determination,
        200–203, 204
    price discrimination, 207–209
    pricing power in, 195, 197, 198–200, 202
    pure competition versus, 195, 202
    regulated monopoly, 209–211
Pure profit. *See* Economic (pure) profit
Pure rate of interest, 298
Purposeful behavior, 4–5
Putin, Vladimir, 314
Pyramid, 237

Qualification
    information failures, 361
    taxation, 350
Quality
    of health care, 436–437
    of labor, role in wage determination, 268
    of land, 296
    of resources, productivity changes and, 254
Quantity
    change in productivity and, 253
    change in quantity demanded, 53, 59–60
    change in quantity supplied, 56, 59–60
    equilibrium, 56–58
Quasi-public goods, 104
Quotas
    in fisheries management, 329
    immigration, 455–456, 466, 467
    import, 404, 485–488
    individual transferable quotas (ITQs), 329
    for legal immigrants, 455–456, 466, 467

Rate regulation, 209–211
Rates of return, technological advance
    and, 190
Rational behavior
    consumer, 119
    defined, 119
Rational self-interest, purposeful behavior
    and, 4–5
Rationing
    prices and, 58, 62
    usury laws and, 303
Real estate, exchange rates and, 505–506
Real GDP. *See* Gross domestic product (GDP)
Real interest rates, defined, 302
RealNetworks, 387

Real wages
    defined, 267
    long-run trend of, 268–269
    productivity and, 268
Recession. *See also* Great Recession of
    2007–2009
    as obstacle to collusion, 232
Reciprocity strategies, 242–243
Recycling, 320, 352–353
Red Dog, 237
Redistribution of income, 349, 352–353
Red Wolf, 237
Regressive taxes, 345, 354
Regulation. *See* Government regulation
Relative interest rates, exchange rates
    and, 505
Relative price, 49
Remedies, for monopoly, 378
Remittances, 461–462
Renewable natural resources, 325–329
    defined, 321
    fisheries management, 327–329
    forest management, 326–327
Rent
    economic, 294–297
    land, 294–297, 367
Rent controls, 62–63
Rent-seeking behavior, 205–206, 367,
    400, 403
Repeated games, 242–243
Replacement rate, 313–314
Representative democracy, principal-agent
    problem in, 365–367
Resale, lack of, in pure monopoly, 208
Research and development (R&D)
    as barrier to entry, 197, 206
    gains from entry, 191
    interest and, 302
    oligopoly and, 234
Residual claimants, 304
Resource allocation. *See also* Resource
    markets
    demand in. *See* Demand for resources
    global, 405
    marginal productivity theory of income
        distribution and, 260–262
    profit and, 307–308
    resource pricing and, 249
    supply of energy in. *See* Energy economics
Resource markets. *See also* Demand for
    resources; Interest; Natural resources;
    Profit; Rent; Supply of resources; Wage
    determination
    in circular flow model, 41
    immigration and, 462
    MRP = MRC rule and, 250
    public sector role in reallocation, 104
    resource demand as derived demand, 249
    resource prices and, 54–55, 56, 249
Restraints of trade, 375–376
Revenue tariffs, 485

Ricardo, David, 475
Right-to-work laws, 288
Risk. *See also* Uncertainty
    of agricultural operations, 396, 398
    economic (pure) profit and, 304–306
    exchange-rate, 514–515
    income inequality and, 414
    interest-rate, 297, 301
    types of, 304
    uninsurable, 304–305
Rivalry
    private goods and, 99
    private versus public goods and, 100
Rock and Roll Hall of Fame (Cleveland), 370
Rodriguez, Alex, 9
Royal Dutch/Shell, 207
Royal Philips, 207
Royalties, 281–282
Rule of reason, 377, 378, 380
Russia
    command system in, 30, 39
    immigration from, 458
    population decline in, 314
    U.S. trade with, 394

SABMiller, 236–237
Saffer, Henry, 83n
Sales taxes, 341, 345, 351, 352
Salmon, market for, 70–71
Samsung, 381
Samuel Adams, 237
Scale
    constant returns to, 156
    diseconomies of, 156
    economies of, 153–156, 157–159
    minimum efficient, 156–157
Scalping, 58
Scarcity
    economic perspective and, 4
    economic resources and, 10
    marginal analysis and, 5
Schumpeter, Joseph, 190, 190n
Scientific method
    defined, 5–6
    elements of, 5–6
Sears, 234
Self-interest, in market systems, 31–32, 38
Self-selection
    defined, 459
    immigration and, 459, 463
    negative, 463
Self-sufficiency output mix, 477
Seniority, labor unions and, 288
September 11, 2001 terrorist attacks, 14
Sequential game, 243
Services
    private. *See* Private goods and services
    product differentiation through, 217
    public. *See* Public goods and services
Service Workers, 287
Sharp, 381

Sherman Act of 1890, 375–376, 377, 378, 381, 386
Shortage, defined, 57–58
Short run
  agricultural price and income instability in, 392–394
  defined, 85, 143
  fixed plant in, 143
  law of diminishing returns and, 144–147
  price and output in monopolistic competition, 219–221
  price elasticity of supply and, 85
  production costs in, 144–152, 175
  production relationships in, 144–147
  profit maximization in pure competition, 166–176
  pure competition in, 163–179
Short-run supply curve, 175
Shutdown, 171, 172, 177
Simultaneous consumption, 205
Simultaneous game, 241
Singapore, health care in, 448–449
Single seller, in pure monopoly, 195
Single-tax movement, 296–297
Size of firm, long-run production costs and, 152
Skill transferability, 459
Slope of a nonlinear curve, 25–26
Slope of a straight line, 24–25
  infinite, 24–25
  marginal analysis and, 24
  measurement units and, 24
  negative, 24
  zero, 24–25
Small business. *See* Entrepreneurs; Start-up firms
Smith, Adam, 38, 124, 295–296, 475, 475n
Smoot-Hawley Tariff Act of 1930, 489
Snyder's of Hanover, 380
Social insurance programs, 421–423
Socialism. *See* Command systems
Socially optimal price
  dilemma of regulation and, 211
  formula for, 210
Social regulation, 384–388
  characteristics of, 384–385
  criticisms of, 385–386
  defined, 374, 384
  industrial regulation versus, 384
  optimal level of, 385–386
  regulatory commissions, 384
  support for, 385
Social Security program, 314
  financing, 341, 346
  payroll taxes, 350, 351
  as social insurance, 421–422
Society, economizing problem of, 10–11
Sole proprietorships
  in business population, 41
  defined, 41
Sony, 207

Sotheby's, 381
South Korea
  executive pay in, 283
  international trade, 474
  market system in, 39
Soviet Union, former. *See also* Russia
  command system in, 30, 39–40
Special interests
  farm policy and, 403
  nature of interest groups, 363
  political logrolling and, 363, 403
  rent seeking and, 367
  special-interest effect, 366–367
Specialization
  comparative advantage and, 477–478
  defined, 33
  division of labor and, 33
  gains from, 492–494
  geographic, 33
  international trade, 475
  labor, 154
  managerial, 154–155
  in market systems, 33
  occupations of immigrants and, 455, 456, 459
  offshoring and, 492–494
Specific excise tax, 351
Speculation
  in currency markets, 514–515
  in determination of exchange rates, 506
Sprint, 380
Stability, flexible exchange rates and, 508
Standardization, in pure competition, 164–165
Standard Oil, 207
Standard Oil case, 377
Staples, 380
Starbucks, 157, 190
Start-up firms. *See also* Entrepreneurs
  entrepreneurial ability and, 10–11
  immigrants as founders of, 459
  information technology, 459
  life expectancy, 190
  successful, 157
  technological advance and, 189–192
State government
  employment in, 342–343
  finances in U.S., 341–342
  fiscal impact of immigration and, 465
  health care costs and, 437
State taxes, 341–342
Statistical discrimination, 426
Status quo, 125
Sticky (inflexible) prices, in oligopoly, 230
Stock exchanges, 48
Stock market crash of 1929, 17
Stock options, 282, 283
Stocks, exchange rates and, 505–506
Strategic behavior, in oligopoly, 224
Street entertainers, 100
Strikes, 289–290
Structuralists, 377

Subsidies
  agricultural, 398–400, 401
  change in supply and, 55, 56
  for consumers, 107
  in correcting for positive externalities, 107–108
  criticisms of, 402–403
  export, 486
  as government intervention, 107–108
  government provision, 107–108
  for suppliers, 107, 398, 399–400
  tax subsidies for health care, 441–442
Substitute goods
  ATMs, 261
  change in demand and, 52
  change in supply and, 55, 56
  cross elasticity of demand and, 87–88
  defined, 52
  ease of resource substitutability, 257
  lack of, in pure monopoly, 195
  marginal rate of substitution (MRS), 135
  prices of, 52
  substitutability and price elasticity of demand, 81–82
Substitute resources, 462
  changes in prices of other resources, 254–255
Substitution effect, 49, 122–123, 254
Sugar Program, 404–405
Sunk costs, in decision making, 158–159
Sun Microsystems, 386, 387, 459
Sunstein, Cass, 128n
Superstars, 253, 416
Supplemental Nutrition Assistance Program (SNAP), 422, 423
Supplemental Security Income (SSI), 422, 423, 436, 463
Supply, 53–56. *See also* Market supply
  change in demand and, 69–72
  change in quantity supplied, 56, 59–60
  change in supply, 54–56, 59–60, 69–72, 175, 299
  defined, 53
  determinants of, 54, 56
  inelastic, 294
  law of supply, 53
  of loanable funds, 298–299
  market supply, 54
  price elasticity of, 84–87
  resource. *See* Supply of resources
  restricting agricultural, 401
  short-run, 173–176
  supply curve, 53–54
Supply curve, 53–54
  labor, 269–271, 278
  lack of, in pure monopoly, 201–202
Supply factors, health care, 443–445
Supply-of-pounds curve, 503
Supply of resources
  energy economics, 314–317
  environmental quality and, 330–331

Supply of resources—*Cont.*
  increase in, 15–16
  natural resource economics, 321–329
  population growth and, 313–314
  resource consumption per person, 314–317
Supply schedule, 53
Supply-side market failures, 93
Surplus
  balance of payments, 503
  defined, 57
  producer, 400–401
  reduction of agricultural, 400–401
Surplus payment, land rent as, 295
Sushi, market for, 71–72
Switzerland, as magnet country for
    immigration, 457

TAC (total allowable catch), 329
Taco Bell, 119, 379
Taft-Hartley Act of 1947, 289
Target, 233, 242
Tariffs
  defined, 485
  direct effects, 486–487
  economic impact of, 486–487
  indirect effects, 487
  net costs of, 487–488
Taste-for-discrimination model,
    discrimination coefficient, 424–425
Tastes
  blindfold taste tests of beer, 236
  change in demand and, 51, 52
  in determination of exchange rates, 505
  in market systems, 37
Taxable income, 340
Taxation
  apportioning tax burden, 344–346
  changes in supply and, 55, 56
  corporate, 341, 350–351, 352
  earned-income tax credit (EITC), 422,
    423–424
  efficiency loss of tax, 349
  elasticity of tax incidence, 347–348
  excise, 83, 341, 351, 352
  federal tax revenues, 340–341, 348–349
  as government intervention, 107
  health-insurance coverage and, 450
  incidence of U.S. taxes, 350–351
  income distribution and, 349, 352–353, 413
  interest rates and, 298
  marginal tax rate, 340–341
  negative externalities and, 107–108, 349–350
  payroll, 341, 346, 351, 352
  personal, 340–341, 345, 350, 352
  progressive, 340, 341, 345, 353–354
  property, 342, 346, 351, 352
  proportional, 345
  regressive, 345, 354
  sales taxes, 341, 345, 351, 352
  single tax on land, 296–297
  specific taxes, 107, 351, 352

state taxes, 341–342
Tax Freedom Day (U.S.), 338
tax structure in U.S., 353–354
value-added, 346
Tax Freedom Day (U.S.), 338
Tax incidence
  defined, 347
  division of burden, 347
  elasticity and, 347–348
  probable, 352
  in the U.S., 350–351
Tax subsidy
  defined, 441
  health care, 441–442
Teamsters Union, 287
Technology. *See also* Innovation
  advances in, 16, 37, 189–192, 205, 206, 235,
    254, 268, 395–396, 444–445
  agricultural supply increases and, 395–396
  changes in supply and, 55, 56
  competition and, 189–192
  economic growth and, 16
  health care prices and, 444–445
  industrial regulation in perpetuating
    monopoly, 382–383
  in market systems, 33, 37
  oligopoly and, 235
  productivity changes and, 254
  pure monopoly and, 205, 206
  role in wage determination, 268
Temporary Assistance for Needy Families
    (TANF), 359, 422, 423, 436
Temporary workers, health care costs and, 437
Tennessee Valley Authority (TVA), 382
Terms of trade
  comparative advantage and, 478
  defined, 478
  flexible exchange rates and, 508
Terrorist attacks of September 11, 2001, 14
Thaler, Richard, 128n
Third-party payments, health care, 439
Ticket scalping, 58
Time
  ease of resource substitutability, 257
  income distribution over, 416–417
  income inequality and, 412–413, 416–417
  marginal utility and, 124–125
  price elasticity of demand and, 83
  price elasticity of supply and, 85
  specialization and, 33
  in theory of consumer behavior, 124–125
Time-value of money
  compound interest, 300–301
  future value, 301
  present value, 300–301, 321–322
Time Warner Communications, 234, 379, 383
Tobacco subsidies, 402–403
Topel, Robert, 438
Topographical maps, indifference maps
    and, 137
Total allowable catch (TAC), 329

Total cost (TC)
  average total cost (ATC), 149
  defined, 148
  graphical expression of, 168
  in market systems, 35
  ratio of resource cost to, 257
  short-run production, 148
Total fertility rate, 313–314
Total output. *See also* Gross domestic product
    (GDP); Output
  interest and, 302
Total product (TP)
  defined, 144
  law of diminishing returns and, 144, 147
Total revenue (TR)
  defined, 77, 165
  graphical expression of, 166, 168
  in market systems, 35
  price elasticity and, 81
  total-revenue test for price elasticity,
    77–81, 200
Total-revenue–total-cost approach, 166–167
Total utility
  defined, 117
  income equality in maximizing, 417–418
  marginal utility and, 117–119
Toyota, 207, 235, 242, 290
Trade Adjustment Assistance Act of
    2002, 492
Trade barriers
  net costs of, 487–488
  types of, 485–488. *See also* Import quotas;
    Tariffs
Trade barrier wars, 489
Trade deficits
  causes of, 512–513
  defined, 473, 500
  implications of, 513
  increased current consumption, 513
  increased U.S. indebtedness, 513
  of the U.S., 512–513
Trademarks, 31
Trade-offs, budget line, 9–10
Trade surplus, 473, 500–501
Trading possibilities line, 478–479
Training. *See* Education and training
Transfer payments. *See also* Income
    distribution
  in government finance, 338
  income transfer in pure monopoly, 204
  noncash transfers, 413
Treble damages, 376
Trump, Donald, 7
Trusts, defined, 375
Truth in Lending Act of 1968, 307
Tying contracts, 376, 380–381
Tyson, 392

UCAR International, 381
Ultra Petroleum, 283
Unattainable combinations, 9

Uncertainty. *See also* Risk
  flexible exchange rates and, 507–508
Underground economy. *See* Black markets
Unemployment
  immigration and, 462–463
  income inequality and, 415
  minimum wage and, 276–277
  in production possibilities model, 14–15
  union wage increases and, 275
Unemployment compensation, 422–423
Unemployment insurance, 422–423
Unilever, 207, 234
Uninsurable risks
  profit as compensation for, 305
  sources of, 304–305
Unionization rate, 287
Unions. *See* Labor unions
Union shop, 288
United Autoworkers, 287
U.S. Bureau of Labor Statistics, 255–256
U.S. Census Bureau, 412, 456
U.S. Department of Agriculture (USDA),
    395–396, 401
U.S. Department of Commerce, 405, 499, 500n
United States dollar. *See* Exchange rate(s)
United States economy. *See also* Federal
    government
  agriculture in, 392, 395–406
  balance of payments, 499–503
  capital-intensive goods, 474
  capitalism in, 30
  circular flow model and, 337–338
  comparative advantage, 475–477
  covert collusion in, 232
  economics of war and, 14
  energy economics in, 314–317
  Environmental Performance Index (EPI), 331
  executive pay in, 283, 416
  export supply, 482–483
  fastest-growing occupations, 256
  federal finances in, 339–341
  fisheries management in, 327–329
  forest management in, 326–327
  gasoline market in, 61–62, 71, 358
  general level of wages in, 267–268
  Great Depression and, 14, 17
  Great Recession of 2007-2009. *See* Great
    Recession of 2007-2009
  health care in, 346, 433–451
  highest-paid CEOs, 283
  immigration and, 454–468
  impact of taxes and transfer payments in, 413
  import demand, 483
  imports of, 394
  income distribution in, 308, 411–414,
    416–417, 421–424, 428, 460–461
  income shares in, 308, 460–461
  international trade and, 394, 403–405, 473,
    474–481. *See also* International trade
  labor unions in, 273–275, 287–291
  local finances in, 342–343

  as magnet for immigration, 457, 460–461
  minimum wage, 276–277
  monopsony in, 273
  multilateral trade agreements, 490–492
  North American Free Trade Agreement
    (NAFTA), 492
  offshoring of jobs and, 492–494
  opportunity-cost ratio, 476
  poverty measures in, 419–421
  rapidly-declining populations, 256
  specialization and, 492–494
  state finances in, 341–342
  supply and demand analysis for
    international trade, 482–485
  taxes in, 350–354
  terrorist attacks of September 11, 2001, 14
  trade adjustment assistance, 492
  trade deficits, 512–513
  water use in, 316, 317
  wealth distribution in, 414–415, 428
U.S. Environmental Protection Agency
    (EPA), 384
U.S. Federal Communications Commission
    (FCC), 197, 382
U.S. Federal Trade Commission (FTC),
    375–376, 381
U.S. Food and Drug Administration (FDA),
    191, 384, 387
U.S. Justice Department, 242, 375–376, 376,
    381, 386–387
U.S. Postal Service, 190, 192, 206, 382
U.S. Steel case, 377, 381
U.S. Supreme Court, antitrust policy and, 377
United Steelworkers, 287
Unit elasticity of demand, 77, 80
University of Nebraska Medical Center, 370
Unrelated goods, 52
Uruguay Round, 491
User cost
  of extraction, 322
  in present use versus future use, 322–324
Usury laws, 303
Utility
  defined, 4, 117
  law of diminishing marginal utility, 117–119
  marginal utility. *See* Marginal utility
  total utility, 117–119, 417–418
  utility-maximizing rule, 120–125
Utility-maximizing rule, 120–125
  algebraic generalization, 121–122
  defined, 120
  demand curve and, 122–123
  numerical example, 120–121
Utz Quality Foods, 380

Vaccination, as positive externality, 105–106
Value-added tax (VAT), 346
Variable costs (VC)
  average (AVC), 149
  defined, 147
  short-run production, 147–148

Variables
  dependent, 23
  independent, 23
Variety
  behavioral economics and, 125–126
  benefits of, 223
  in monopolistic competition, 222–223
Verizon, 234
Verson stamping machine, 157–158
Vertical axis, 22
Vertical intercept, 25
Vertical mergers, 379, 380
Voice mechanism, 291
Voluntary export restriction (VER), 486
Voting. *See* Majority voting

Wage(s). *See also* Wage determination
  defined, 267
  efficiency, 282
  general level of, 267–269
  real, 268
  unemployment and union wage
    increases, 275
Wage determination, 266–284
  average wage of selected occupations, 277
  bilateral monopoly model of, 275–276
  CEO pay, 283, 416
  definitions, 267
  education and, 279, 416
  general level of wages, 267–269
  global perspective on wages of production
    workers, 267–269
  immigration and, 459–460, 464–467
  labor unions and, 273–275, 287–291
  minimum-wage controversy in, 276–277
  monopsony model of, 271–273
  pay for performance, 100, 281–282
  prejudice and market African-American-
    White wage ratio, 425–426
  productivity and, 267–268
  in purely competitive labor market,
    269–271
  wage differentials, 277–281
Wage differentials, 277–281
  defined, 277
  education and, 279, 416
  marginal revenue productivity,
    278–279
  market imperfections, 280–281
  noncompeting groups, 279
Wage effects, of illegal immigration, 465
Wage growth, health care costs and, 437
Wage rates
  defined, 267
  impact of immigration on, 459–460, 465
  labor unions and, 275, 280–281, 288
Walmart, 41, 190, 233, 242, 293, 308
Walt Disney Company, 234, 235, 379
War. *See also* National defense
  economics of, 14
  price wars, 230, 233

Warranties, 361
  overpriced, mental accounting and, 128
Water, use of, 316, 317
Watford, Michael, 283
Wealth, unequal distribution of, 414–415, 428
Wealth of Nations, The (Smith), 38
Wendy's, 361
Western Union, 195
Wham-O, 195
Wheat, price floors on, 63–64
Wheeler-Lea Act of 1938, 376
Whites
  African-American-White wage ratio,
    425–426
  poverty among, 420
  unionization rate, 287

Whole Foods Markets, 449
Winfrey, Oprah, 9, 410
Winner-take-all markets, 253
Women
  crowding model and, 427
  poverty among, 420
  unions and, 287
Woods, Tiger, 410
Workplace safety, 360–361
Work rules, 289
World Bank, 462n
WorldCom, 380
World Health Organization (WHO), 448
World price, 482
World Trade Organization (WTO),
    404–405, 491

Xerox, 197
X-inefficiency, 205, 206, 258, 382

Yahoo!, 459
Yale University, Environmental Performance
    Index (EPI), 330–331
YouTube, 190
Yum! Brands, 379

Zero slopes, 24–25
Zero-sum game, 241
Z visas, 466

Relevant economic statistics, selected years, 1987–2009

	1987	1988	1989	1990	1991	1992	1993	1994	1995	1996
1 Sales by manufacturers (billions of dollars)*	2378.2	2596.2	2745.1	2810.7	2761.1	2890.2	3015.1	3255.8	3528.3	3757.6
2 Profits by manufacturers (billions of dollars)*	173.0	215.3	187.6	158.1	98.7	31.4	117.9	243.5	274.5	306.6
3 After-tax manufacturing profits per dollar of sales (cents)*	4.9	5.9	4.9	3.9	2.4	0.8	2.8	5.4	5.6	6.0
4 Index of business sector productivity (1992 = 100)	90.3	91.6	92.6	94.5	96.0	100.0	110.5	101.4	101.5	104.4
5 Annual change in business sector productivity (%)	0.3	1.5	1.0	2.1	1.5	4.2	0.5	0.9	0.0	2.9
6 Nonagricultural employees in goods-producing industries (millions)	23.5	23.9	24.0	23.7	22.6	22.1	22.2	22.8	23.2	23.4
7 Nonagricultural employees in service-providing industries (millions)	78.6	81.4	84.0	85.8	85.8	86.6	88.6	88.6	94.1	96.3
8 Compensation of employees (billions of dollars)	2735.6	2954.2	3131.3	3326.2	3438.4	3647.2	3790.6	3980.9	4178.8	4387.7
9 Average weekly hours in manufacturing industries**	40.9	41.0	40.9	40.5	40.4	40.7	41.1	41.7	41.3	41.3
10 Average hourly earnings in private nonagricultural industries (dollars)	9.14	9.44	9.80	10.20	10.52	10.77	11.05	11.34	11.65	12.04
11 Average weekly earnings in private nonagricultural industries (dollars)	317.16	326.62	338.10	349.75	358.51	368.25	378.91	391.22	400.07	413.28
12 Federal minimum wage rate (dollars per hour)	3.35	3.35	3.35	3.80	4.25	4.25	4.25	4.25	4.25	4.25
13 Prime interest rate (%)	9.31	9.32	10.87	10.01	8.46	6.25	6.00	7.15	8.83	8.27
14 Ten-year Treasury bond interest rate (%)	8.39	8.85	8.49	8.55	7.86	7.01	5.87	7.09	6.57	6.44
15 Net farm income (billions of dollars)	38.0	39.6	46.5	46.3	40.2	50.2	46.7	52.6	39.8	58.9
16 Index of prices received by farmers (1990–1992 = 100)	89	99	104	104	100	98	101	100	102	112
17 Index of prices paid by farmers (1990–1992 = 100)	87	91	96	99	100	101	104	106	108	115
18 Persons below poverty level (millions)	32.2	31.7	31.5	33.6	35.7	38.0	39.3	38.1	36.4	36.5
19 Poverty rate (% of population)	13.4	13.0	12.8	13.5	14.2	14.8	15.1	14.5	13.8	13.7
20 U.S. goods exports (billions of dollars)	250.2	320.2	360.0	387.4	414.1	439.6	456.9	502.9	575.2	612.1
21 U.S. goods imports (billions of dollars)	409.8	447.2	477.7	498.4	491.0	536.5	589.4	668.7	749.4	803.1
22 U.S. Population (millions)	242.8	245.0	247.3	250.1	253.5	256.9	260.3	263.4	266.6	269.7
23 Legal immigration (thousands)	599.9	641.3	1090.2	1535.9	1826.6	973.4	903.9	804.0	720.2	915.6
24 Industry R&D expenditures (billions of dollars)	90.2	94.9	99.9	107.4	114.7	116.7	115.4	117.4	129.8	142.4
25 Price of crude oil (U.S. average, dollars per barrel)	15.40	12.58	15.86	20.03	16.54	15.99	14.25	13.92	14.62	18.46

*Revised definition for this series beginning in 1973.

**Includes overtime.

***Data for 2009 and the immediate prior years are subject to change because of subsequent government data revisions.